The Essential Writings

John D. Caputo, *series editor*

PERSPECTIVES IN
CONTINENTAL
PHILOSOPHY

JEAN-LUC MARION

The Essential Writings

EDITED BY KEVIN HART

FORDHAM UNIVERSITY PRESS
New York ■ 2013

Fordham University Press has no responsibility for the persistence or accuracy of URLs for external or third-party Internet websites referred to in this publication and does not guarantee that any content on such websites is, or will remain, accurate or appropriate.

Fordham University Press also publishes its books in a variety of electronic formats. Some content that appears in print may not be available in electronic books.

Library of Congress Cataloging-in-Publication Data

Marion, Jean-Luc, 1946–
    The Essential writings / Jean-Luc Marion ; edited by Kevin Hart. — First edition
        pages cm. — (Perspectives in Continental Philosophy)
    Summary: "The Essential Writings is an anthology of Marion's diverse writings in the history of philosophy, Christian theology, and phenomenology. The general introduction provides students with sufficient background for them to tackle the work of this important contemporary philosopher without first having to take preliminary courses on Husserl and Heidegger" — Provided by publisher.
    Includes bibliographical references and index.
    ISBN 978-0-8232-5105-6 (hardback) — ISBN 978-0-8232-5106-3 (paper)
    1. Philosophy, Modern—20th century.   I. Hart, Kevin, 1954–   II. Title.
    B2430.M281H37 2013
    194—dc23

                                                                2013006700

Printed in the United States of America

15 14 13   5 4 3 2 1

First edition

To David Tracy

Contents

Acknowledgments

My thanks to Jeff Kosky for answering questions about translations of Jean-Luc Marion's texts, and to Claire Lyu for her critical reading of my introductions. Thanks to Jessie Wright for assistance in scanning texts by Marion. It is always a pleasure to work with Fordham University Press: I am thankful to Helen Tartar for her enthusiasm for this project, to Tom Lay for guiding the book through the Press, and to Gregory McNamee for his meticulous copy editing of the text. My greatest debt is of course to Jean-Luc Marion, for answering all manner of questions about his work and for the intellectual exchange and friendship that form the ground of the enterprise.

The Essential Writings

Introduction

KEVIN HART

Jean-Luc Marion (b. 1946) commands our attention for three interrelated reasons: for his historical work on René Descartes, for his essays on the borderlines of philosophy and theology, and for his reformulation of phenomenology in terms of what he calls "saturated phenomena."[1] That Marion developed his understanding of saturated phenomena by way of an historical study, *Réduction et donation: Recherches sur Husserl, Heidegger et la phénoménologie* (1989), brings him into focus as a historian of philosophy for a second time, although what he has done with that idea has made him into a creative philosopher in his own right. Before he came upon the idea, however, he was attentive to the "blank theology" in Descartes—blank because Descartes declined to fill in the place where a theology should be in his thought—and to the subtle ways in which idolatry can creep into our thinking about God by way of metaphysics.[2] That a historian of the preeminent French philosopher, the seventeenth-century author of the arresting claim that everyone knows, *cogito, ergo sum*, should also become a historian of Edmund Husserl and Martin Heidegger, the two major German phenomenologists of the early twentieth century, is not an accident.[3] For one can easily make a case that Descartes is himself the father of phenomenology, a negligent father perhaps, since he seems to have introduced it and then forgotten it, but the father nonetheless.[4]

Phenomenology has led a vibrant life since Descartes, and one index of its vitality is how often and how successfully it has reimagined itself from unforeseen points. "There is no such thing as *the one* phenomenology," Heidegger declared in a lecture given in Marburg in 1928, adding, "and if there could be such a thing it would never become anything like a philosophical technique."[5] Why the insistence on plurality? Because, Heidegger tells us, "implicit in the essential nature of all genuine method as a path toward the disclosure of objects is the tendency to order itself always toward that which it itself discloses." In saying this, Heidegger was distinguishing his philosophy partly from Husserl's and partly from others in the new field that had been formed, Max Scheler's being the best known among them. It was Scheler who had already made clear some fourteen years earlier that, in his judgment, phenomenology could never properly be regarded as a coherent school since its insights turned on disparate individual experiences and not, as Husserl advocated, a single rigorous method.[6] The dividing of phenomenology was not simply a matter of diverse experiences, though. Phenomenology itself fractured into competing groups.

First there was the "Munich Circle" (Johannes Daubert, Moritz Geiger, Adolph Reinarch, and others), whose members were originally drawn to Husserl's *Logische Untersuchungen* (1900–1901), and who clung to the metaphysical realism they saw there when Husserl turned towards what they believed to be transcendental idealism in *Ideen* I (1913).[7] And then there was the Göttingen Philosophical Circle (Hedwig Conrad-Martius, Roman Ingarden, Max Scheler, Edith Stein, among others, including some who came from Munich, giving rise to the idea of an "invasion" of Göttingen from Munich) who, again, held to a realist interpretation of phenomenology.[8] It seems likely that both groups took the Husserl of *Ideen* I to treat consciousness as necessary to reality whereas Husserl himself took it to be only sufficient.[9] In any case, the field was not solely always populated by Husserl, his students and his admirers: Alexander Pfänder's *Phänomenologie des Wollens* (1900) came out the same year that Husserl published his sustained refutation of psychologism in the first volume of *Logische Untersuchungen* (1900) and a year before the second volume with its investigations into expression and meaning, pure grammar, the relations of parts and wholes, intentional experiences, and so on.[10] Phenomenology for Pfänder was first a descriptive psychology, one that distanced itself from the empirical psychology of his teacher, Theodor Lipps, but before long Pfänder would come under the influence of Husserl.[11]

Why could phenomenology never become a matter of technique? Because it is "genuine questioning" (328), Heidegger thought: genuine in that questions arise from encounters with phenomena and not from a preestablished program or *Weltanschauung*, worldview.[12] Of course, phenomenology has its own procedures, and Husserl in particular places a heavy emphasis on method; but a phenomenology that has become merely a routine, a way of calmly fitting phenomena into its own predetermined schema, would be self-contradictory. Over the decades Heidegger would develop his distaste of technique into a full-scale critique of technology, and would convict technology as a final and tenacious harbinger of metaphysics.[13] Less well known is that Husserl also had set his jaw against mere technique. As early as 1891, in a review of the first volume of Ernst Schröder's *Vorlesungen über die Algebra der Logik: Exakte Logik* (1890), he reflected sourly, "One can be an outstanding technician in logic while being a very mediocre philosopher of logic."[14] He cites George Boole as an example. The complaint against the creator of Boolean logic was not an isolated observation in a review, or a fear of abstraction, but rather an early sign of his objection that symbolic logic can be used—and frequently is—without philosophical understanding.[15] Had Husserl lived to see how Boolean logic would become the basis of computer science, he would have been all the more dismayed.

Later, just a few years after Heidegger's 1928 Marburg lecture, Husserl linked "technique" and "crisis." In *Die Krisis der europäischen Wissenshaften*, left unfinished at the time of Husserl's death in 1938, we hear the following complaint about mathematics, the subject to which he devoted his youth and early manhood: "Like arithmetic itself, in technically developing its methodology it is drawn into a process of transformation, through which it becomes a sort of technique; that is, it becomes a mere art of achieving, through a calculating technique according to technical rules, results the genuine sense of whose truth can be attained only by concretely intuitive thinking actually directed at the subject matter itself."[16] In an essay related to the *Krisis*, "Der Ursprung der Geometrie" (1936), Husserl reiterated this regrettable situation. We have lost "original truth-meaning," even in mathematics; truths are "sedimented" and have become mere "working materials," and so scientists have become progressively distanced from a tradition "which involved original self-evidence at its actual first beginning."[17] Our response should be, Husserl says, to engage in *Rückfrage*, questioning back through the various sediments of learning in order to reactivate the original impulses of truth and once more demand original self-evidence for truth. This is phenomenology as Husserl conceived it, and if followed in line with his lights it would overcome the crisis that he thought European science was currently undergoing.

After Heidegger's 1928 lecture in Marburg phenomenology was to accommodate other stances, some of which would limit it, some of which would live at its limits, and others of which would reverse it or transmute it in one way or another. All would look back for inspiration to Husserl and Heidegger. So one finds, for example, the intentional analysis of Emmanuel Levinas that is focused on phenomena as distinct from his discussions of what he calls the enigma of the human, Maurice Merleau-Ponty's phenomenology of perception that recognizes the reduction as partial at best, and Jean-Yves Lacoste's phenomenology of liturgy, which identifies aspects of human being that phenomenology cannot explore satisfactorily.[18] At the boundary of what Husserl proposed, one finds Jean-Paul Sartre's existentialism and, at another point, Jacques Derrida's deconstruction, which, he said, can be experienced only if one traverses transcendental phenomenology.[19] Eugen Fink attempts to save Husserl's reduction from the fatal charge of circularity by further developing the master's meontology of the transcendental subject.[20] Decades later, Nicolas Abraham proposes a "transphenomenology" with a view to reinvigorate psychoanalysis in the 1960s, and Daniel Dennett advocates in the 1990s a "heterophenomenology" that attends to other persons in preference to one's self, adding other available evidence to what this phenomenology can provide in order to come up with a subjective and objective estimation of the person's beliefs about the world.[21] Somewhere to the side of these figures, Michel Henry reverses everything inherited from Husserl and Heidegger by arguing for a nonintentional phenomenology that he takes to be prior to its intentional counterpart.[22]

Not only has phenomenology been able to reinvent itself, even at the cost of rejecting or devaluing what outsiders and some insiders may regard as one or more of its essential elements (reduction, intentionality, and transcendental consciousness, for instance) but also it has been remarkably successful at fertilizing related movements and sometimes has been invigorated by partially inhabiting them. Existentialism and hermeneutics, deconstruction, psychoanalysis and theology, not to mention sectors of analytic philosophy, have all been influenced to a greater or lesser extent by phenomenology. In turn, phenomenology has learned from these disciplines and from the arts, both in general and in particular. Like analytic philosophy, it has spread across the world—one can encounter it anywhere from Iceland to Japan, either direction one travels to get there—and has engaged with every area of philosophy, from aesthetics to cognitive science.[23] It has generated insider battles between those who place a strong emphasis upon the transcendental in phenomenology and those who wish to naturalize its insights, between those who retain or augment the reduction and those who drop it, between those who affirm a "theological turn" and others who decry it, between those on the West Coast of the United States for whom Frege looms large and those on the East Coast who read Frege through Husserl.[24] Unlike analytic philosophy, however, phenomenology can deem itself to be without limits in the sense of not being constrained by philosophy. That it arose as a movement within modern philosophy, with Descartes (or, more surely, with Hegel or, more surely still, with Husserl), no one will deny; but that it is at heart restricted to academic philosophy few seasoned phenomenologists will readily concede. Not without reason might one take Francis Ponge, Paul Cézanne, or Paul Klee to be a philosophically untutored yet exacting phenomenologist.[25] The aesthetic gaze, Husserl intimated more than once, is close to the phenomenological gaze, and the artist supplies grounds that are appropriate to the artwork though not the essay in philosophy.[26] Also, for Henry, Christianity is already phenomenological in structure.[27] And so a question must be posed: Is there anything to prevent us definitively from seeing phenomenology namelessly at work anywhere or everywhere? At times the word seems to be written on elastic.

Inevitably, then, there are those who seek to purify phenomenology, to keep it faithful to its original inspiration. We might be tempted to regard Jean-Luc Marion as one of these people.[28] It is certainly possible to see him returning us to the early Husserl, author of the *Logische Untersuchungen* (1900–1901) and *Die Idee der Phänomenologie* (1907), and to some of those whose research influenced him, especially Bernard Bolzano, Alexius Meinong, and Kasimierz Twardowski, who all worked on the theory of the object.[29] In particular, Marion asks us to look closely at the all-important "principle of all principles" in *Ideen* I §24—"*everything originarily . . . offered to us in intuition is to be accepted simply as what it is presented as being, but also only within the limits in which it is presented there*"—and not to contest its authority, or to interpret it less than stringently, as he believes Husserl did under the pressure of Cartesian assumptions.[30] There is a sense therefore in which Marion seeks a phenomenology that is purer than Husserl's. We see this in his affirmation of the "third reduction," a more thorough reduction, he believes, than those practiced by Husserl and Heidegger, one that yields "the pure form of the call."[31] We see it in *Étant donné: Essai d'une phénoménologie de la donation* (1997) when we find Marion disengaging phenomenology and hermeneutics at their undermost level of contact as determined by Heidegger, that of fore-having (*Vorhabe*), fore-conception (*Vorgriff*) and fore-sight (*Vorsicht*), and reattaching hermeneutics to phenomenology only once the phenomenon has been received.[32] We also detect this tendency when we find Marion extending the scope of phenomenology so that it includes not just objects and being but givenness, and pointing us to the Husserl of *Die Idee der Phänomenologie* as his warrant for doing so. To describe pure givenness, *Gegebenheit* or *donation*, as the basic structure of phenomenality would be the most thoroughgoing assignment for any phenomenologist, if not the most difficult: an equivocal honor usually reserved for the phenomenology of time. Yet Marion does not bring us back to phenomenology as a rigorous method, as Husserl and Heidegger believed it to be in their different ways, but commends his practice as a "counter-method."[33] He does not argue for transcendental subjectivity; instead, he urges us to accept the human being as *l'adonné*, the gifted one (or the devoted one) who receives selfhood from what is given, not who restricts the given by constituting it by way of intentionality, which is a structure of transcendental consciousness.

In fact, far from being a formalist or a traditionalist, Marion is criticized by self-appointed guardians of phenomenology for exceeding its proper limits. Dominique Janicaud is only the most vocal of those who have charged Marion, among others, with the illegal importation of theological themes into what Heidegger determined as the properly atheistic method of phenomenology.[34] Something has changed for the worse, he fears. Phenomenology that once affirmed that everything visible relies on the flesh of the world now looks beyond corporeality and claims that, "the very concept of Revelation [*le concept même de Révélation*] belongs by right to phenomenality."[35] Thus Janicaud charges the new French phenomenologists with introducing God into the secular world of philosophy, either by way of transcendence (Levinas, Marion) or by way of radical immanence (Henry).[36] We have heard this sort of charge before, when Heidegger castigated Scheler for giving "the impression that phenomenology is something 'for becoming Catholic.'"[37] Scarcely a purist, Marion might be seen as someone who has sought to introduce what seems alien to phenomenology, the divine, to saturate the horizon of intentionality, and to develop the reduction in an unexpected direction. He does not even return to the principle of all principles in a conservative spirit, for he contends that it is unsatisfactory as stated. The emphasis on intuition can easily be taken to bespeak a reliance on intentionality, which was precisely Husserl's error, he believes. Besides, Marion wishes to establish that givenness precedes intuition. A better principle, he thinks, would be "*Autant de réduction, autant de donation*" [So much reduction, so much givenness], a statement that he takes to peg "first philosophy," albeit by way of stating what is in effect the "last principle" of philosophy, the one that comes after Husserl's attempts to formulate a ground of phenomenology: "So much appearing, so much reduction," "back to the things themselves," and the principle of all principles.[38]

Before we can place Marion's achievement with any exactness, though, we need to go back and retrace phenomenology less as a modern movement with great flexibility than as a way of thinking inherited from the ancient world and gradually focused by modern philosophy with respect to particular issues (constitution, intuition and intentionality, among others). And we need to begin by seeking to understand what "phenomenon" means and why the study of phenomena is so important.

From Phenomenon to Phenomenology

The word "phenomenology" comes from the Greek noun φαινόμενον (pl. φαινόμενα), which itself derives from the verb φαίνεσθαι, "to show itself," so τὰ φαινόμενα are those things that show themselves. Yet phenomena do not always display themselves at first or fully or in all the ways in which they can appear; they need to be brought into view and to show us how we may properly approach them. For the Greeks, a phenomenon can also show itself in a misleading way, not from itself, and so we inherit an ambiguity in the concept, though not in the word, "phenomenon." When we talk of an appearance we may have in mind an illusion or a semblance of something real. Not so in phenomenology. For Husserl, it is the gentle art of passing from "the natural attitude" [*die natürliche Einstellung*] to the transcendental sphere. The natural attitude is the uncritical belief that the world and everything in it is factually given to us irrespective of consciousness; and when we begin to philosophize, to think transcendentally, the naïveté of this assumption is quickly called into question.[39] More generally, we might say that phenomenology is the art of nudging phenomena so that they manifest themselves to us as they are, which means recognizing them in their proper region of being (how they give themselves to us). Phenomena are not apparent, and paradoxically, as Heidegger clearly saw, phenomenology is at heart devoted to the unapparent.[40] When doing phenomenology in English nowadays we usually speak of appearings and not appearances in order to prevent misunderstanding. (Appearances are still spoken of when discussing the Kantian philosophy, however.) In modern phenomenology, there is no suggestion that a reality hides behind or above a phenomenon. It is the appearing that is taken as properly basic.

This was not always so in philosophy. As one would expect, for the Greeks in general a phenomenon was an event or an object that could be observed. Yet Plato looked at phenomena around him, and contrasted them with the ideas that could be grasped by the mind. Some of what he called "ideas" or "forms" we would call "universals" while what he called "phenomena" we would call "particulars." My fountain pen and my stone paperweight are both black: the pen and the paperweight are particulars, and the blackness they share is a universal. For Plato, phenomena are imitations of the intelligible ideas, and as he argues in *The Republic* VII 517b the aim of philosophy is to pass from phenomena to the ideas, leaving "the region revealed through sight" [τὴν μὲν δι' ὄψεως φαινομένην ἕδραν] in order to ascend to the "intelligible region" [νοητὸν τόπον].[41] Aristotle rejected his master's teaching that these forms, exterior to phenomena, are the proper objects of knowledge, and argued instead that intelligibility was to be found by familiarity with phenomena, but not the single experience of them. In the *Posterior Analytics* 88a he tells us "it is from the repetition of particular experiences that we obtain our view of the universal."[42] Yet it is in ancient astronomy as much as philosophy that we find a salutary lesson about how the Greeks considered phenomena. In seeking to explain the motions of the planets and stars some astronomers proposed theories to which some heavenly motions did not fit. In response, there was a call "to save the phenomena," an expression one finds neither in Plato nor in Aristotle.[43] Ptolemy in book XIII of his *Almagest* proposes that we should come up with simple hypotheses that explain heavenly motions for in doing so "each of the phenomena is duly saved by the hypothesis."[44] And Proclus in his *Hypotyposis*, based on Ptolemy, also speaks of the need "to save the phenomena" [σώζειν τὰ φαινόμενα].[45] The reliance of a theory on all observable phenomena may well go back to Plato himself. In his commentary on Aristotle's *De caelo* Simplicius records the story told by Sosigenes that Plato asked astronomers, "On what hypotheses of uniform and ordered motions could the phenomena concerning the motion of the planets be preserved?"[46] To save the phenomena was for theory to render phenomena intelligible.

The Greek word "phenomenon" finally meets up with its companion Greek word "logos" only in the eighteenth century. It was Johann Heinrich Lambert who, in the second volume of his *Neues Organon* (1764), proposed a theory of appearance, in the sense of illusion, which he called phenomenology.[47] In a letter to Lambert of September 2, 1770, Immanuel Kant shifts the meaning of the word: "A quite special, though purely negative science, general phenomenology (*phaenomologica* [*sic*] *generalis*), seems to me to be presupposed by metaphysics. In it the principles of sensibility, their validity and their limitations, would be determined, so that these principles could not be confusedly applied to objects of pure reason, as has heretofore almost always happened."[48] Some years later, in 1781, this insight would be fully developed in his *Kritik der reinen Vernunft*, where it is argued that our cognitive faculties shape the intuitions that come to us, so that we grasp things in terms of cause and effect, for example. All that we can know, Kant argues, are what show themselves by way of the categories of the understanding. These phenomena, as he calls them, may not be all that is real but we cannot have theoretical knowledge of anything in the noumenal world.

Now Kant's account of phenomena or appearances is subject to differing interpretations. Some take him to argue that appearances are merely representations of noumena, which pushes him into skeptical idealism. Others maintain that when Kant speaks of appearances as representations he is thinking in a transcendental register, and therefore concerned with the condition of possibility for knowing objects and not the objects themselves. On this interpretation, we cannot know with any theoretical certainty if appearances are aspects of noumena, but it is possible that they may be so.[49] (Either way one reads Kant, though, phenomena for Husserl are quite different: for him, there is nothing beyond the phenomenon.) Later, in 1786, in his *Metaphysische Anfangsgründe der Naturwissenshaft*, Kant spoke more directly of phenomenology as the modal aspects of motion and rest, that is, the possibility, actuality and necessity of motion and lack of motion.[50] And there the word may well have come to rest itself were it not that Hegel took it up and put it at the very beginning of the title of his brilliant and passionate early work *Phänomenologie des Geistes* (1807).

Let us see what "phenomenology" means for Hegel. He uses the word only when speaking of *Geist*, usually (and roughly) translated as "mind" or "spirit," and he uses "phenomenon," preferring the German *Erscheinung* [appearance] in lieu of *Phänomen*, at key moments. Here he is in the midst of considering how philosophy, considered as a strict science, begins to appear against the ground of other knowledge:

> But science, in the very fact that it comes on the scene, is itself a phenomenon [*Erscheinung*]; its 'coming on the scene' is not yet *itself* carried out in all the length and breadth of its truth. In this regard, it is a matter of indifference whether we consider that it (science) is the phenomenon [*Erscheinung*] because it makes its appearance alongside another kind of knowledge, or call that other untrue knowledge its process of appearing [*ihr Erscheinen zu nennen*]. Science, however, must liberate itself from this phenomenality [*Scheine*], and it can only do so by turning against it.[51]

Rigorous philosophical knowledge must be distinguished from the path that led to such knowledge, its process of appearing, which is inevitably pre-philosophical. How can one draw such a distinction? Only by undertaking "the exposition of knowledge as a phenomenon" [*die Darstellung des erscheinenden Wissens*], Hegel tells us.[52] The phenomenology of spirit will therefore be the demonstration of how consciousness experiences the unfolding of what gives itself to it, and it will overcome the problem of there being a path to philosophy by showing that consciousness, in its dialectical progress to self-consciousness, reason, and finally spirit, progressively absolves itself of any reliance on this path. Finally, philosophy is able to manifest itself as "absolute knowing," unconditioned by its mode of appearing. The history of philosophy, for Hegel, is a development of "thinking reason" through "a series of appearances"; it follows an "inner necessity" and so has an end: the presentation of the Idea in and for itself.[53]

Husserl observed in conversation with Dorion Cairns and Eugen Fink in October 1931 that he had never read Hegel (and yet the very next month, Cairns reports of the master that "he recognizes Hegel as a forerunner and a genius").[54] Certainly Husserl did not endorse "the dialectic in the constitution of reality as ground for supposing a new formal logic" (52). He had published his *Formale und transzendentale Logik* two years before, and had shown how the truths of logic are constituted, made present, by quite other means. Yet when Fink says to Cairns, "Phenomenology is the coming to self-awareness of the ego and its own activities" (14) we hear Husserl and also something of Hegel, perhaps because Fink read Hegel very closely. Nonetheless, we can erase the Hegelian aura completely from Fink's definition and use it to approach what Husserl understood by phenomenology. It is a philosophy of wakefulness. It invites us to see that human consciousness is transcendent, directed towards the world, or—in Husserl's borrowing from Franz Brentano, a formulation that was to prove highly influential—consciousness has an intentional structure; it is always consciousness of something other than itself, and it prompts us to discover how we can exfoliate our experience of the world, including our recollections of our dealings in it, in concord with our various intentional engagements with it.[55] For Husserl, a phenomenon must always be able to be experienced, although "experience" is not used here in any of the usual ways. "Experience," for Husserl, is not the living through of particular events external to consciousness but "the relevant acts of perceiving, judging etc, with their variable sense-material, their interpretative content, their assertive character, etc."[56] So experience, for phenomenology, is given to us by way of diverse intentional acts; we live through them but they do not appear to us as objectified events.

Let us assume that a human being can be rightly regarded as a phenomenon: a claim that is hotly debated these days, as we shall see. I can read a letter or an email from Robert in which he is presented to me only by way of writing; here his being is given to me without being, for I cannot see him, shake his hand, or talk with him. I can look at his photograph, and only an aspect of him—indeed, a temporal profile of an aspect—is given to me pictorially. I have his resemblance but not his identity. I can imagine being with him, in which case his being as given to me is restrained or distorted by the play of "as if." I can anticipate spending time with him again: his being is given to me without any concrete realization of that being, and all I have are thin or rich ideas of what our time together will be like, some or all of which may be unrealized. I can remember occasions with him, and again I am restricted to aspects and profiles of his being. And naturally

I can perceive him in face-to-face contact, have a fulfilled (or even fulfilling) intention, and enjoy my time with him as completely as life allows.[57] Because it is earthly life, even when face-to-face my intention to see Robert will be both fulfilled and unfulfilled; there are always going to be absences as well as presences, even in the one perceptual act.

Phenomenology is therefore the study of the different ways in which phenomena are absent from us as well as present to us; it allows us to stand aside from our selves, as it were, and reflect on our various relations with phenomena—anticipating, remembering, imagining, desiring, perceiving, and so on—and so to see how they are concretely embedded on our intentional horizons, whether those intentionalities are unfulfilled, partly fulfilled, fulfilled, or fulfilling. Its guiding question is not "What?" or "Why?" but "How?" Its mode of proceeding is not to abstract from a situation until one can find an appropriate formula for it but to offer precise description of what is before one. Phenomenology is difficult to practice, and at the same time immensely satisfying, because we put aside received belief in apparently natural categories and schemas, and look for ourselves at what is given to us. Yet it is not solely subjective: the subjectivity in question is not empirical, it answers to a noematic structure, one that is available to an inter-subjective community. And it is difficult because we are enjoined not to linger at the level of description but to seek to uncover how what we describe has been constituted, made present, by way of our intentional rapport with it.[58] As I said a little earlier, we must nudge phenomena by passing to the transcendental attitude in order to see how they manifest themselves to us.

A phenomenon has a genitive and a dative aspect: a manifestation is always *of* something and always *to* someone. With Robert I have a complex temporal phenomenon (if he *is* one), but not all phenomena are the same. There is a vast difference between the number one and one friend, for example, not only in themselves but also more importantly in how they give themselves to consciousness. The number gives itself wholly to me by way of understanding; nothing is left of it once I have grasped its meaning. My friend is different: he remains a mystery to me no matter how well I think I know him. This is not because there is some elusive spiritual dimension to him that, for Kantian reasons, I cannot apprehend. Not at all: it is because my friend has many aspects that I cannot grasp (Robert as husband, father, son, brother), and many temporal profiles I have not seen (Robert as child, adolescent, young adult), because I cannot fathom all that he thinks and feels. My lived body orients my entire relation with him, by being here or there, in Charlottesville or Sydney, absent or present to him; it is not just so much *res extensa*, an objective body taking up space, but something that is not even visible, that enables me to experience everything in the world. I feel the pressure of a hand shaking mine; I see a smile beginning to emerge on his face. I hear sentences spoken to me (and take in their tone, their timbre, their rhythm) not as so much raw data that I receive but as a lived event. I am not solely a transcendental subject, as Kant proposed, but as Husserl and others maintain—Merleau-Ponty and Henry above all—an animated body, *Leib* not *Körper*, that encounters the world through touch, sight, smell, taste and hearing, not only through the intellect.[59] My pre-predicative experience is as important as my judgments about it, perhaps more so. To be sure, I apprehend Robert as a whole each time I am with him, and all the aspects of him that I do not see are cointended, as

Husserl would say. And it may be that Robert has a soul that will survive his death, but phenomenology devotes little time to this, even though for Husserl transcendental subjectivity is not subject to death.[60] What I can know of Robert's soul, if I must talk in this way, is that it is a moment of his body and requires that body in order to function. There is enough in Robert that is manifest to me, and that I cannot master, without me having to add further items.

There is a difference between the number one and one friend, then; and of course neither is like the phenomenon of friendship, which also gives itself to me in all manner of ways, requiring me to bring it into the light of understanding by posing appropriate questions about it as they press themselves upon me through my experience. Does friendship presume a numerical cap? (I cannot have hundreds of friends, as some people say they have on Facebook, and still be talking in a meaningful way of *friends*. Nor can I not make another friend because I already have a particular number of them.) We usually know when a friendship ends, but can we know when it has begun? Does friendship presume symmetrical relations or asymmetrical ones? In what way or ways does friendship differ from love? How can one tell a friend from a flatterer?[61] When Husserl inaugurated modern phenomenology he gave a rallying cry, "we must go back to the 'things themselves'" [*Sachen selbst' zurückgehen*].[62] This is not a call to limit the range of phenomena to natural objects but rather to stop philosophizing in consonance with the usual rubrics and get down to business and examine matters as we directly encounter them. Heidegger has some apt words here:

> The principle is that we should inquire into and work upon the objects of philosophy just the way they show up. Thus, the tendency to press on to the real issues themselves, to free them from presuppositions, overlays from the tradition, and hasty questions laden with presumptions. This is the proper thrust of phenomenology: to get to the real issues themselves. A "phenomenon" simply means a given object of philosophical research insofar as it is apprehended with the intention of understanding it as it is.[63]

Phenomenology is therefore the study of phenomena understood broadly, numbers and texts, physical objects and events, problems and values, feelings and ideas, the apparent and the nonapparent, the body, the ego and its intentional relations, and so on. We have not yet reached a fine and exact appreciation of "phenomenon," as Husserl uses the word, but we have already come to see that phenomenology seeks to wake us up and see everything freshly. In an important sense, though one that is not to be abused, it is the poetry of philosophy.

Phenomenology: A Closer Look

In order to grasp Marion's inflection of phenomenology, even to be able to read a page of *Étant donné* or *De surcroît: Études sur les phénomènes saturés* we need to have a closer knowledge of Husserl and Heidegger. We have not yet come even to a basic comprehension of what Husserl proposes and a sense of what he inherited from nineteenth-century philosophy. Earlier we jumped from Kant to Hegel and then from Hegel to Husserl, each time using the word "phenomenon" as a springboard. If we look back over the terrain, we will notice a couple of sharp changes. Kant's Copernican revolution in philosophy consists of severely changing how we figure the acquisition of knowledge. To know is no longer to have established a correspondence between our minds and the universe but to have made an accommodation of the universe to the structure of our minds. All the understanding can do a priori, Kant says in the *Kritik der reinen Vernunft*, is "to anticipate the form of a possible experience in general."[64] Accordingly, "the proud name of an Ontology that presumptuously claims to supply, in systematic doctrinal form, synthetic *a priori* knowledge of things in general (for instance, the principle of causality) must, therefore, give place to the modest title of a mere Analytic of pure understanding" (A 247). With Hegel, and in various philosophical currents outside idealism, most notably in Bolzano and Meinong, the emphasis shifted from knowing to being, or more particularly to the relations between them.

At the same time, there was a transformation from regarding understanding as a function of established mental categories to figuring it as a matter of being aware of what the world presents to it. Husserl regarded Brentano's doctrine of intentionality as pivotal in this respect. For all of the change from knowing to being that was in the air, Husserl was deeply concerned with the theory of knowledge, and his phenomenology persists as a philosophy of consciousness: not an experiential psychology, which remains a worldly affair, but a philosophy, which seeks to rise above the world.[65] For Husserl, "all ontologies become subject to reduction," for otherwise they would exist within the natural attitude.[66] This is not to say that there can be no formal ontology; on the contrary, one of the achievements of the *Logische Untersuchungen* is the development of the study of relations, parts and whole, and so forth, as distinct from formal apophantic logic that is concerned with meaning. Formal ontology explains how the syntax of the mind works without having to posit an inner theater of consciousness and to deal with the knotty epistemological problems that this generates. Yet it was Husserl's student, Heidegger, who closed the door on epistemology, more than a little loudly, in his *Kant und das Problem der Metaphysik* (1929). For Heidegger, Kant's first *Kritik* is in fact a "laying of the ground for metaphysics and thus of placing the problem of metaphysics before us as a fundamental ontology."[67]

Awareness: this is a key word for Husserl. In German, the word is *Anschauung* or *Intuition*, and when either gets translated into English as "intuition" we should not hear or overhear anything like a sixth sense. It is awareness, understood as broadly as possible. I have already evoked the "principle of all principles," which Husserl regarded as primordial: we are to accept everything originarily given to us in intuition, each and every *originär gebende Anschauung*. "One must have the courage to accept what is really to be seen in the phenomenon precisely as it presents itself rather than interpreting it away, and *honestly* to describe it."[68] *In the phenomenon*, note: Husserl is not making a point about empirical observation. But how do we pass from an event or an object to a phenomenon? By a conversion of the gaze will be Husserl's answer, and one that he tries to make ever clearer and finer in the years from 1907 until his death in 1938. We are characteristically living in the natural attitude, in which, as already indicated, we are led to believe that events and objects are "out there," existing entirely independently of our consciousnesses and appearing to us as such. The natural attitude has its uses, Husserl thinks, but it is naïve because those who think within it pay no attention to how human subjectivity constitutes events and objects, renders them present, and we attain a philosophical stance only when we perform the ἐποχή, the setting aside of everything in the world, including the pregiven world itself, so that we are unconcerned whether reality is external or internal, indeed whether anything exists at all, focusing only on our experience of what is intended. At first, this may seem to resemble Cartesian doubt; but Husserl is not proposing to doubt existence in order to find bedrock, the *cogito*, he is wishing only to disconnect our consciousness from the world so as to engage in radical philosophical reflection.[69] There is no "modalization"—change of belief from affirmation to doubt, say—in accomplishing the ἐποχή; there is only a suspension of judgment about the world and the modes of explanation that are characteristic in it and about it.

Before evoking what happens after the ἐποχή, in the conversion of the gaze, a word needs to be said about the different directions in which ἐποχή can proceed, and a word too about a reduction that can take place within the natural attitude and that leaves one there. First, let us consider the ambiguity of bracketing. One can suspend all theses about a transcendent entity—anything outside consciousness—including the existential thesis. Whether something exists outside me or inside me is no longer of any interest; it has been disconnected from the world and its modes of explanation. It is in this sense that the highest art is deeply phenomenological in impulse. Eugenio Montale's piercing lyric "L'anguilla" yields nonthetic experience of eels; it suspends reference to a particular eel or to the details of the Anguilliformes in order to let us grasp experientially the being of an eel. Consider the opening lines of the poem, given in English translation:

The eel, the siren
of freezing waters, abandoning the Baltic
for our warm seas,
our estuaries and rivers, ascending
deeply against the water's force
from branch to branch, and then
from stream to stream, threading
ever inwards, ever deeper into the heart
of the rock, thrashing
through mud until one day
a light shot from the chestnut trees
catches its sparkle in pools of dead water.[70]

In reading the original poem in *La Bufera e altro* (1956), we can *think* and *feel* the movements of an eel as given to us in quicksilver Italian with a precision that cannot be achieved in the slower technical language of zoology that labors in the natural attitude. Yet the ἐποχή also moves in another direction, for one can suspend the ego as it is undergoing a "lived-process," and thereby "find psychic states and psychic subject and psyche."[71] The reduction is carried out in both exercises of bracketing, although it is more difficult to achieve when directed toward the ego.

In phenomenology we talk often about reduction, and Marion's philosophy turns ineluctably around this idea, as we shall see. Most often we talk of the *phenomenological* reduction (because it allows us to grasp an entity as phenomenon) or the *transcendental* reduction (because it involves a shift to the transcendental attitude). There are many reductions that Husserl distinguished, some of which are executed after we have passed from the natural attitude.[72] Yet there is one that can be undertaken within the natural attitude. Scientists do it all the time, and so do most of us. Here is an example. I am asked by my dean to consider taking on an additional responsibility in the College of Arts and Sciences. Before I agree, I turn the proposal over in my mind, looking at it this way and that way, seeing if I could possibly do the job. Perhaps I would have time to do it if I withdrew from a couple of speaking engagements, or condensed a graduate seminar to six weeks. (But no: I have already bought air tickets to the conferences; the material to be taught is too difficult to compress into half a semester of double-length seminars.) Perhaps it would work if I assigned some of my duties as chairman to another member of the department. (Again, no: only I know the full background to some of the problems that need to be addressed over the coming year.) Perhaps I could take on the extra load on the weekends. (My family would complain; besides, I need to see people on the ground as part of the undertaking.) Perhaps I could seek administrative help in order to carry out the charge. (No point: there is too much confidentiality involved.) Perhaps the job has been misconceived and is really far simpler than has been presented to me. (Reflection tells me that in fact it is more ramified than what I was told.) In the end, by a process that Husserl calls "imaginative variation," I will have come to the essence of the responsibility itself and whether I can take it on, and will see that I cannot. I will have effectuated an eidetic reduction, been led back to the εἶδος of the particular commission and be able to judge my capacity to do it, and so will be able to make an appropriate decision based on the essence of the task.

The eidetic reduction is entirely different from the phenomenological or transcendental reduction. With this latter reduction the ἐποχή serves as a preparation for the more thoroughgoing act of leading one back to the transcendental aspect of consciousness.[73] By abstaining from the usual forms of explanation of events that we use in the natural attitude, by surely setting them aside when considering the ego, we can adopt the transcendental attitude. In the Kantian language that Husserl uses, we pass from transcendence (everything outside pure consciousness) to the transcendental (conditions of possibility) or, as Husserl likes to say, we proceed from empirical consciousness to the realm of pure immanence. We are led back to the aspect of consciousness that is structured by intentionality. Husserl calls this passage the phenomenological or transcendental reduction. "Given in and through this liberation," he says, "is the discovery of the universal, absolutely self-enclosed and absolutely self-sufficient correlation between the world itself and world-consciousness."[74] This means, as he goes on to say, that having made the reduction one can see "the absolute correlation between beings of every sort and every meaning, on the one hand, and absolute subjectivity, as constituting meaning and ontic validity in this broadest manner, on the other hand" (151–152).

In moving from the natural to the transcendental attitude, we stand, as it were, *"above"* one's "natural being" and *"above* the natural world" (152) without losing either because their existence is not doubted or denied. From this vantage point we see that the things and events we experience are constituted by our nonempirical, unconditioned subjectivity.

(Fink speaks with feeling and reason of the "awful tremor" of passing through the reduction, of denaturalizing the world, realizing that its significance is constituted.[75]) What we now see is the world and everything we encounter in it *as phenomenon*. Once we have passed to the transcendental attitude, Husserl says, we see with astonishment that in the realm of immanence each and every phenomenon has two poles: the appearing and what appears. This discovery was announced in *Die Idee der Phänomenologie* (1907), although it was not until *Ideen* I (1913) that Husserl described this dyadic structure in terms of noesis and noema.[76] My intentional acts constitute phenomena—render them present—and therefore have correlates. We speak of a noetic act, which is real (*reel*, in Husserl's terminology) and a noema, which Husserl says is *irreel* because it is constituted and not given directly in experience. Husserl does not doubt that there is sensuous content in many phenomena, yet this hyletic data, as he calls it, is contained in and shaped by noesis. The noema that results is no more than the object or event as actively meant by intentional consciousness; it is not a quasi-entity of any sort that mediates my consciousness and the world.

The transcendental reduction not only yields us phenomena, immanent essences, but also, and more importantly, signals how they are constituted and how they are charged with particular meanings each time they appear on an intentional horizon. I can contemplate how my particular intentional relations, from anticipation to recollection, have caught phenomena in their web, as it were, and marked them accordingly. This is particularly true of objectifying acts in which an object is merely referred to with nothing following from the reference. "Contemplation" suggests being passive with respect to phenomena, and there is certainly an element of reflective enjoyment in the gaze.[77] Nonetheless, for Husserl phenomenology is systematic philosophy, and it can be systematic only in the transcendental attitude. Unlike Kant in the *Kritik der reinen Vernunft* there can be no transcendental deduction of the pure concepts of the understanding; everything that matters in phenomenology must be in consciousness or given to consciousness and hence patiently tracked and captured by intentional analysis.[78] This is true of "value-Objects," the things that compose the world in which we live and move, and also of "nature-Objects," which are the concern of the positive sciences.[79] As one might expect, Husserl wishes to show us how to unpack the full intentional meaning of our ordinary experiences; also, though, he wants to uncover the phenomenological bases of the sciences, including logic and mathematics. *Ideen* begins by introducing a pure phenomenology and, by the third volume, is seeking the foundations of the positive sciences. Husserl's first book was *Philosophie der Arithmetik* (1891), one of the last he saw through the press was *Formale und transzendentale Logik* (1929), while *Erfahrung und Urteil: Untersuchungen zur Genealogie der Logik* (1948) was published posthumously. Only if we lead the sciences back to their origin in intuition, he thought, can we prevent them from stagnating as mere techniques of research, a theme I have already touched on.

It should be pointed out in passing that Husserl's investigations into the ground of modern science sometimes led him to conclusions apparently at odds with how we usually think about the universe. His regular way of working was to write for his own benefit on one or another problem until such a time as he felt the need to compose a book. These manuscripts, written in a style of shorthand known as *Gabelsbergerschrift*, bear on all aspects of phenomenology, were unrevised and not intended for publication. In one of the better known, written in 1934 and later nicknamed "The Earth Does Not Move," Husserl contests the right of the Copernican model of the Earth's position in space to subordinate in all respects the premodern idea of the earth as primary ground of experience. Needless to say, Husserl is not defending the Ptolemaic view of the universe. He includes himself when he speaks in the manuscript of "We Copernicans, we moderns."[80] Rather, he is resisting the manner in which modern astrophysics seeks to homogenize all space, including our primordial sense of the earth as *Erdboden*, "earth-ground." The earth cannot be regarded indifferently as one "star" among others in the universe because the earth is constitutive of our experience of space and motion. Even were there a "flying-machine" on which people are born, live and die—we might think of the starship *Enterprise* in *Star Trek: The Next Generation*—it could not function as a ground. "Must I not conceptually transfer to the flying-machine in constitutive validity (according to the form) what in general endows the earth with the sense of my ground, as the ground of my flesh?" (125). There is an original sense of "earth-ground" that is pregiven to us, even in the space age, and that is essential even when we accept, as we must, a Copernican view of the universe. Captain Jean-Luc Picard has his earth-ground on Earth; Commander Worf has his on the Klingon home world, and so on. Considered phenomenologically, "the earth does not move" (118, 122); it is the ground against which we experience everything in space and time. This is "saving the phenomena" in a different way than the ancient Greeks understood the expression.

Given that phenomenology is a philosophy of subjectivity for Husserl, it would follow that he will encounter paradoxes when it comes to talking about the universe before there was any such subjectivity. Because of geological research and the fossil record, we can readily conceive of life before humans, before mammals, and even before the dinosaurs. Without subjectivity on Earth, however, there would be no constituted phenomena. Now Husserl does not want to make the absurd suggestion that the world comes into existence only with the emergence of human beings—the view that consciousness is necessary to reality—nor does he wish to endorse Bishop Berkeley's thesis *esse est percipi*, to be is to be perceived, in order to claim that when human beings are not attending to the world God is.[81] Nonetheless, he maintains that, "*Nature, as mere nature, contains no values.*"[82] A Protoceratops walking in what we now call China in the Cretaceous Period may have seen many a sight we would call beautiful or sublime if we could visit it in a time machine; but, for Husserl, the dinosaur witnessed nothing of the sort, for neither beauty nor the sublime is an objective property belonging to natural formations. Natural formations must be constituted as phenomena in order to be hailed as beautiful or sublime, and only those beings with subjectivity can engage in constitution. Presumably, human beings first brought about the reduction in Altamira, Kakadu, Lascaux, and other prehistoric sites. Can a dolphin, an ape, or a cat perform the reduction, even to some extent? Husserl shows no interest in the question, and we can only speculate. As we shall see, Heidegger thinks that only human beings can perform reduction.

Not only was phenomenology interested in grounding the sciences but also Husserl saw it as a science in itself: the true, foundational science on which all others depend. Because phenomena are examined immanently, their truth should become self-evident.

(This is the meaning of *Evidenz*.) And yet this examination of phenomena, this seeing of essences, demands of its votaries tremendous concentration. Often, and to the horror of his younger collaborators, Husserl would sigh that he had not yet found any insights of which he was certain. He was, he liked to say, a perpetual beginner in a philosophy of infinite tasks. Because of the sheer difficulty of doing phenomenology, he always affirmed that it was a discipline to be pursued by a philosophical community for generation after generation. That the good phenomenologist (that is, the highly trained and scrupulously honest one) would not come up with aberrant descriptions of phenomena by dint of his or her individuality is to be guaranteed by the transcendental community at the base of individual subjectivity. Yet the phenomenology of inter-subjectivity, the topic of three thick volumes in the *Husserliana*, is one of the most vexed parts of the corpus. Scheler, remember, despaired of phenomenology ever achieving a fixed method because of the different experiences of its practitioners. That Husserl had sufficient difficulty in constituting the sense of another ego in the fifth of the *Cartesianische Meditationen* is an index of the challenge of disclosing a layer of inter-subjectivity at the base of individual subjects.

Descartes

There is a great deal more to say about Husserlian phenomenology: I have said nothing about the phenomenology of logic and mathematics, about active and passive syntheses, about the phenomenology of time, about genetic and generative phenomenology, and much more.[83] So far at least these things are not essential for a first encounter with Marion's thought. For many American readers of Marion it might seem peculiar to have spent so much time on Husserl, for the Marion who came to light in the United States was the author of a book translated as *God Without Being* (1991), a follower of Heidegger who was intent on criticizing the philosopher from the perspective of Christian faith. Only thereafter, in the writings that would lead up to the discovery and exploration of saturated phenomena, did Marion come closer to Husserl in some respects than Heidegger. Some of what Marion draws on from Heidegger's phenomenology will be indicated over the coming pages, especially Heidegger's rethinking of the reduction, but before then I want to discuss Marion's relationship with Descartes. Again, it would seem odd to someone who read Marion's publications in their historical order to talk about Husserl or Heidegger before Descartes. For Marion emerged in France as a historian of Descartes, and only later as a phenomenologist whose relations with Husserl and Heidegger need to be documented and explored. As a young man, he studied with Ferdinand Alquié, scholar of Descartes and Kant (and, as a spicy side dish, surrealism) who advised both his Doctorat du troisième cycle and Doctorat d'État, each of which was centered on Descartes; and today he serves as Director of the Centre d'études cartésiennes. Yet there is an advantage in approaching Marion by way of Husserl and Heidegger, for his most provocative work has been in revising phenomenology. At the same time, it would be a mistake, one that would skew our estimation of his contribution to philosophy, were we not to take account of his scholarly and interpretive work on Descartes. It touches all he does.[84]

The following little story will show us why. On April 15, 1630, Descartes wrote to Father Marin Mersenne about the latter's view that there are mathematical truths that exist independently of God. The philosopher's objection to the eminent mathematician illuminates much of what Marion values in Descartes. For what is at issue for Descartes is, as he says in his letter, "That the mathematical truths you call eternal have been established by God and depend entirely on him, just as much as all the rest of his creatures. It is in fact to speak of God as a Jupiter or Saturn, and to subject him to the Styx and the Fates, to say that those truths are independent of him. Do not hesitate, I tell you, to avow and to proclaim everywhere, that it is God who has established the laws of nature, as a King establishes laws in his Kingdom."[85] And yet, for all this show of protestation, Descartes did not propose, let alone develop, a theology. As noted earlier, he merely left a space for it in his work. And so in *Sur la théologie blanche de Descartes* (1981), Marion speaks of Descartes's *blanche théologie*, his blank or white theology. Had Descartes written on this blank page he would surely have given us a theology in which God is sovereign and infinite, unable to be grasped by way of concepts, a theology that is sharply opposed to all idolatry, including conceptual idolatry: the view that we can understand God by way of concepts. Descartes's theology would therefore not be framed in the language of metaphysics, as he inherited it from Francisco Suárez, the preeminent Jesuit philosopher, whose *Disputationes Metaphysicae* (1597) strongly marked the teaching of philosophy at the Collège Henri IV de La Flèche where Descartes studied as a boy. Suárez argues that mathematical truths are true not because God thinks of them but because they are true, and Mersenne, who also studied at La Flèche, follows him in this.[86] More generally, Suárez restricts the sense of analogy at issue when talking of God to an analogy of attribution, thereby excluding analogy of proportionality as proposed by Aquinas in *De Veritate* q. 2 art. 11 and by Cardinal Cajetan in his commentary on Aquinas's *De Ente et essentia*, q. 2.[87]

If Descartes leaves us a "blank theology," he also bequeaths us a "gray ontology." Marion's first book is entitled *Sur l'ontologie grise de Descartes* (1975), and it seeks to show that in the *Regulae ad directionem ingenii* (1684) Descartes attempts to change the very ground of intelligibility. No longer is it the being of God but the mind of human beings. On Descartes's understanding, human beings can in principle master all that is by casting a gaze upon the universe; we can translate being into so many objects of knowledge: a knowledge that must meet very high standards of clarity and rigor. Descartes's overriding concern is epistemology, theory of knowledge, not ontology; all that he gives us in that way is a "gray ontology," one that is hidden by the overt drive to know. In his first two books, then, Marion is able to identify in Descartes both an implicit liberation of God from the sticky net of metaphysics and a commitment to the metaphysics of the human subject. His own work as a historian of philosophy (though one always on the path to original philosophy) will be to develop a theology that Descartes declined to elaborate, and to criticize the metaphysics of the subject that is introduced by Descartes and that raises human being to the status of God. The words that Marion chooses to conclude *Sur le prisme métaphysique de Descartes* (1986) are well worth quoting: "Descartes remains one of our closest contemporaries. To the reasons that our forerunners have already given for this, we will add two: Descartes teaches us what is at stake in the onto-theo-logical constitution of all metaphysics, and Descartes recognizes limits to onto-theo-logical constitution to the point of exposing it to its eventual destitution."[88] But what is the "onto-theo-logical" constitution of metaphysics? What is the stake at issue? And what is this destitution?

Let us begin with the middle question. The stake at issue is the nature of God: to protect his aseity and transcendence, on the one hand, and to multiply critiques of idolatry, on the other. So it is no surprise to find that Marion avows God's infinity. To be sure, this demand derives from Descartes who writes of *Deus infinitus* and *substantia infinita*, but it does not come solely from him.[89] Aquinas developed the idea in the *Summa Theologiae* 1a q. 7, and a very similar view was proposed and defended by Duns Scotus in his Oxford commentary on Peter Lombard's *Sententiae*. Far earlier, and far more importantly because it forms the intellectual basis for the doctrine of the Trinity and establishes a major line in Christian spirituality, it was developed by Gregory of Nyssa in his *Contra Eunomium* and his homilies on the Canticle, among other places.[90] We always need to remember that Marion as historian is attentive to theological as well as philosophical pedigrees of ideas, and that he reads the Greek and Latin Fathers not just out of doctrinal interest but because they have made profoundly important contributions to philosophy. The divine infinity means that there can be no common bond between God and what is created: it is interesting that Marion, unlike Levinas, does not take up Descartes's idea of the infinite being prior to the finite in human beings.[91] Not that Marion denies the *imago dei*; rather, his emphasis is on the aseity and transcendence of the divine. The wholly transcendent God is not to be made subject to human cognition regarded as able to grasp anything and everything in principle by way of clear and distinct ideas, the certainty of which is underwritten by the discovery of the *cogito* as *fundamentum certum et inconcussum*.

Infinity, for Marion, falls outside the purview of metaphysical concepts, at least when it is used as one of the divine names. We cannot think the being of beings by way of infinity, and we cannot determine any science of beings by reference to infinity. To see how significant this claim is, we need to return to the first question. What is the "onto-theo-logical" constitution of metaphysics? The word "metaphysics" is variously used in the western tradition. We speak of *metaphysica generalis*, which is the science of being as such, that is, Aristotle's ὄν ἧ ὄν and Suárez's *ens inquantum ens*, and we also speak of *metaphysica specialis*, which is the science of one sort of being (the soul, freedom or God): Kant's metaphysics of morals is an example.[92] Marion takes his cue from Heidegger's diagnosis of metaphysics as having an onto-theio-logical structure. Observe the more precise spelling of the word. "The essential constitution of metaphysics," Heidegger says, "is based on the unity of beings as such in the universal and that which is highest," that is, the generality of ὄντος and the elevation of the θεῖον.[93] Metaphysics is therefore that discourse which gathers together all beings and refers them to the highest ground. Notice that the proper word here, taken from Aristotle, is θεῖον and not ὁ θεὸς, which we find in the New Testament. Metaphysics has an onto-*theio*-logical structure because of the nature of philosophy, not because of a convergence of Greek philosophy and the Christian concept of God. Heidegger finds metaphysics in this sense (and in all manner of variations) in philosophy from Plato to Nietzsche. Husserl succumbs to it when he becomes committed to transcendental idealism, and Heidegger is the first to identify it, to signal that it is to be overcome, and then to admit that it must be left to peter out.

Only God is infinite, Descartes avers, and this infinity cannot be constituted onto-theo-logically, Marion adds. Marion's Descartes is not Heidegger's or Husserl's or Hegel's. He is the philosopher who designates the limits of metaphysics, and he does so twice: by showing that metaphysics cannot exhaustively describe the ego, and by indicating that God cannot be trammeled by metaphysics, either.[94] The ego, for Descartes, is determined not by thinking itself, as it is by Malebranche and Spinoza, Kant and Hegel, even Nietzsche, but (Marion argues) by a relation with another, God;[95] and God is characterized most surely by the trait of infinity, which escapes metaphysics as Descartes construes it. Blaise Pascal, Descartes's great contemporary, also thinks of God as infinite, though unlike Descartes he does not distinguish sharply between the infinite and the indefinite. Space, Descartes tells us, is indefinite; yet Pascal speaks in the *Pensées* of the "infinite immensity of spaces," of "infinite . . . numbers" and "infinite speed."[96] Another, more salient, difference between the two is that, for Marion, Pascal regards metaphysics as merely an order of concepts, one with its own rigor, to be sure, and higher than the order of the flesh, but one that is lower than the order of charity or *caritas*. This highest order has no interest in criticizing or refuting metaphysics; it has its own logic, that of charity, which it follows without deviation. In short, charity does not need to engage metaphysics; its very existence and persistence shows that metaphysics, though it follows method step by step, is destitute of charity.[97]

Now Heidegger attests two ways of dealing with metaphysics: it can be overcome, which he came to think could not be achieved without falling back into metaphysics, or we can twist ourselves away from it by asking new questions, adopting a new style and syntax (as in some writings of the 1930s, most notably the *Beiträge zur Philosophie* and *Besinnung*) and by directing our thought to poetry. There is *Überwindung*, then, and *Verwindung*: the first embraced by Heidegger and then given up for the second, and the second variously endorsed and finessed by Derrida, Rorty, and Vattimo. *Verwindung* for Derrida occurs by way of close reading, for Rorty through irony, and for Vattimo through hermeneutics.[98] All respond to metaphysics considered historically (ultimately agreeing with Hegel's hypothesis that the history of philosophy is itself philosophical). To these two ways of freeing ourselves from metaphysics Marion adds a third, charity, which he points out does not rely on any historical thesis:

> Pascal does not refute Descartes's redoubled onto-theo-logy; he simply sees it. But he *sees* it from the point of view of a more powerful order, charity, which, simply by considering metaphysics as an inferior order, judges it and leaves it destitute. Metaphysics undergoes neither refutation nor recuperation, nor even delimitation: it appears as such—vain in the gaze of charity. The metaphysics left destitute still remains, but in its order and its place, which from now on has lost primacy.[99]

Only when we read Marion on Descartes can we grasp why he is at heart a philosopher of love, both divine and human.

Theology

The Marion who first appeared in the English-speaking world seemed to be a Catholic theologian strongly influenced by Heidegger rather than, as now, a philosopher concerned with a certain sort of phenomena he calls "saturated." The two individuals are not distinct, of course—as recently as 2010 Marion published a collection of "confessional" pieces, *Le croire pour le voir*—but we need to understand the Marion whose reputation was established in the United States through a book translated as *God Without Being* (1991) and introduced by Chicago theologian David Tracy. The book had been published in French as *Dieu sans l'être: Hors-texte* in 1982. A version of its second chapter had appeared in the important collection *Heidegger et la question de Dieu* in 1980, and it had been preceded by Marion's own *L'idol et la distance* (1977), which was rendered into English much later, in 2001, and by his contributions to the Catholic journal *Résurrection* in the late 1960s and early 1970s.[100] In France, the Marion of *Dieu sans l'être* was mainly known as a scholar of Descartes—*Sur l'ontologie grise de Descartes* (1975), *Sur la théologie blanche de Descartes* (1981)—with a firm orientation to theological questions. *L'idol et la distance* had offered not just an alternative to the "death of God"; it had argued that the God of metaphysics was no God at all, and had forcibly put before us the thought of a difference between God and the world, not a difference between beings and being, or—in another register—*la différance* of deconstruction.

Without doubt, the author of *Dieu sans l'être* was cutting across the Maurice Blanchot of *L'entretien infini* (1969), the Roland Barthes of *Le plaisir du texte* (1973), and the Derrida of *Glas* (1974); and the author of *God without Being* was received in a North American context that had been dominated by a concern with *le texte* for almost fifteen years, even though the influence of the Yale School had subsided after 1987 with the controversy over Paul de Man's wartime writings for the Belgium paper *Le Soir* in the period 1939–43.[101] If French ears heard Marion telling them in his title in Heideggerian tones that God is without being, they also heard him saying that his interest is in the God who does not have to be God, the divinity that (as Pascal would have approved) does not have to serve as the ground of any philosophical or theological system. Also, though, they heard him distinguishing himself from Derrida, for Marion was interested in God without letters (*lettres = l'être*) or, as the title went on to say, "*Hors-texte*," "outside the text." For a generation that had learned from Derrida, "*There is nothing outside of the text* [there is no outside-text; *il n'y a pas de hors-texte*]," the very title of Marion's book was a provocation.[102] God, Marion says, is outside the text and yet without being. What could this mean?

It does *not* mean that God does not exist: Marion is very clear on that point. It means, as we might expect from his work on Descartes, that metaphysics, regarded as discourse on being as a whole and as the highest being, is unable satisfactorily to describe the God who reveals himself in and through Jesus of Nazareth. It also means that Heidegger's determination of the ontico-ontological difference, between beings and being, is also unable to help us approach God. There are in fact two modes of idolatry, Marion points out, one that figures God by way of onto-theio-logy, fashioning him as the *ens summum*, the highest being; and another, favored by theologians impressed by Heidegger, in which

Sein, being considered beyond the limits of metaphysics, is thought before God or as God.[103] Marion's case is at heart based on the proper order of the divine names. Is the first divine name *bonum*, as it is for Pseudo-Dionysius the Areopagite and those who follow him? Or is it *Qui est*, as Thomas Aquinas maintains in *Summa Theologiae* 1a q. 13 art. 11?[104] In *Dieu sans l'être* Marion urges us to recognize God as the One who determines himself with respect to us as love, ἀγάπη, first and foremost. Does Aquinas's conception of God also fall victim to metaphysics? He defines the deity as *ipsum esse subsistens omnibus modis indeterminatum*, and Marion calls to mind that this conception of *esse* "immeasurably surpasses the *ens commune* of creatures" and so God's transcendence of creation, his "distance" as Marion calls it in fidelity to Hans Urs von Balthasar, is preserved.[105] Nonetheless, the Aquinas who comes into view in *Dieu sans l'être* does not figure God as love.

There are two broad ways of doing theology, Marion thinks: theo*logy*, which begins from human thought and speech about God, and ultimately reduces the deity to the bounds of human concepts and language, and *theo*logy, which responds to the revelation of God. No matter how well it is deployed, theo*logy* remains idolatrous, while *theo*logy responds to the icon of the living God, the Jesus who dies for us on the cross, who stands above all being and nonbeing and cannot be caught within metaphysics as onto-theio-logy. For these reasons, Marion writes "God" as crossed out ("G⊗d"), in the same way that Heidegger writes "Being" as crossed out in order to suspend any metaphysical implications that the word may have for his readers.[106] Or, rather, not quite in the same way, since Marion's G⊗d, who is love, ἀγάπη, is the deity who is revealed to us in and through the crucifixion of Jesus of Nazareth. This is the G⊗d of *theo*logy; and theologians will recognize that in thinking this way Marion draws close to modern theologians Karl Barth and Hans Urs von Balthasar in preference to Paul Tillich and Karl Rahner. The latter two are correlational theologians, that is, Christian thinkers concerned to give Christian answers to questions that arise in secular culture, while the former two are noncorrelational, attesting that God's Word breaks into the world. Correlational theologians prize the metaphor of *dialogue* with the world; noncorrelational theologians prefer *proclamation* to the world. Marion does not speak of proclamation; instead, he thinks of God giving himself, coming to us as pure gift in excess of all talk of being and beings.

Throughout *Dieu sans l'être*, Marion draws on the distinction, beloved of John of Damascus and Theodore the Studite, between an idol and an icon, although he seeks to rephrase each in phenomenological rather than dogmatic terms.[107] Readers of *L'idol et la distance* (1977) were already familiar with this approach, and with the deep theological desire to protect God's transcendence or distance from the world. "The idol does not indicate, any more than the icon, a particular being or even class of beings," he writes in *Dieu sans l'être*. "Icon and idol indicate a *manner* of being for beings, or at least for some of them."[108] A gaze can always comprehend an idol and so, because it is always in quest of the visible, it never reaches God at all. Yet an idol is not without power; it marks the coming of the divine if only to the extent that it can be supported by human vision. This is what makes it an *idol*, not a piece of sculpture or the deity. By contrast, the icon is indexed to the invisible; it presents it, though always *as invisible*. We do not really behold

Jesus in an icon, after all, but we become subject to his invisible gaze when we kneel before him as painted in an icon. Notice that Marion's distinction is between two incompatible modes of being. No countenance is given to the approach to God made familiar by the Victorines, especially Richard of St Victor, whose theological method is nicely captured by the expression *per visibilia ad invisibilia*.[109] We do not ascend from the visible to the invisible in the sense of progressing, by grace and spiritual discipline, from the one to the other; instead, we are converted from one way of thinking (dominated by metaphysics) to another (nourished by love).

Dieu sans l'être may seem to be a philosophical engagement with theological issues and method, one that is unusual in that it puts itself at the service of noncorrelational theology, for most philosophers are drawn to correlational theology. It would be more accurate, though, to see it as a phenomenological engagement with the question of how God gives himself to the world. For phenomenology is not restricted to philosophical questions, even though it was spawned by philosophers; it looks to the things themselves, and here the crucial matter is how we think of God: as the highest being or as the loving deity who gives himself freely to us. As phenomenologist, Marion must therefore perform a reduction; and here we run up against a problem, for Husserl is very plain that, while the reduction seeks to render transcendence immanent to consciousness, God's mode of transcendence forever escapes reduction.[110] Husserl worked with a conception of God as early as 1908—"the divine All-Consciousness"—and, in his last maturity, believed that "ethical-religious questions are the last questions of phenomenological constitution," but his remarks on this idea of God are sketchy at best, and we cannot propose a definite convergence between this deity and the God of Jesus.[111] Yet, beginning with Heidegger, phenomenologists have sought to develop the reduction, and Marion is no exception.[112] Heidegger argues that a *Grundstimmung*, a fundamental mood or attunement, can be awakened and it will jolt one so that things are rendered unfamiliar. Husserl had worked on mood as a synthetic unity of feelings but not specifically with respect to reduction, which he would have regarded as overly anthropological. For Heidegger, though, mood can serve as ἐποχή and prompts reduction. He considers several: fright (*Erschrecken*), restraint (*Verhaltenheit*), foreboding (*Ahnung*), and even timidity (*Scheu*). Yet he proposes two fundamental moods that are especially appropriate for our times: *Angst* ("anxiety" or, better, "dread") and *Langeweile* (the sense of time not passing or "deep boredom").

The former is the more familiar to students of European philosophy, since it is analyzed in a few coruscating pages of Heidegger's inaugural lecture at Freiburg im Breisgau, "Was ist Metaphysik?" (1929). Heidegger argues there that *Angst* is not felt in the face of this or that threat but has no proper object. One feels uncanny, one loses one's hold on things, and, as he says, "Anxiety makes manifest the nothing."[113] In his lectures of 1929–30, *Die Grundbegriffe der Metaphysik: Welt—Endlichkeit—Einsamkeit*, Heidegger underscores that there are several fundamental attunements, each of which "belongs to the being of man," and dilates on the one he regards as peculiarly suited to the modern age.[114] This is deep boredom; it exposes us to the world as such and to our involvement with everything in it. In particular, it awakens us to the phenomena of world, individuation, and finitude. Only human beings have this fundamental attunement, Heidegger thinks, for animals are "poor in world" (§45) and so cannot accomplish reduction, which, for Heidegger, is to switch our attention from beings to being.[115] Without fundamental attunements, there can be no philosophizing; the thinker needs to be detached from the familiar in order to think. Marion agrees, and regards deep boredom as precipitating reduction. Yet it is not a reduction that leads us to being without beings; it is a reduction that brings us to the primary mode of phenomenality, namely givenness, which he takes to be *not* that which is given in constitution.[116] I shall say a few words about this "third reduction," as Marion calls it, in the next section. Now, though, we might ask questions more appropriate to the Marion of *Dieu sans l'être*. What of the Christian? Is there a fundamental attunement that prompts the Christian to listen for the Word of God?

These are questions that animate Marion in *Dieu sans l'être*. Like Heidegger, he distinguishes deep boredom from dread; unlike Heidegger, he assigns a biblical signature to this boredom.[117] "Boredom, in disengaging itself from ontological difference, undoes being from its very beingness, abolishes the very name of being," he tells us (120). He moves immediately from existential boredom to vanity, citing Ecclesiastes 1: 2 ("Vanity of vanities, saith the Preacher, vanity of vanities; all *is* vanity," KJV). "The gaze of boredom," he continues, "exceeds the world only by taking it into view from another pole—G⊗d; vanity strikes the world as soon as the world finds itself taken into view—envisaged—by another gaze than its own, under the gaze, impracticable to man, of G⊗d" (128–29). Right away we recall Pascal in the *Pensées*—"without the hunger for spiritual things, we would get bored [with eating and sleeping]"—and remember that, in his higher self, Marion is often more Pascalian than Cartesian in the area of religion.[118] The crucial difference is not between beings and being but between love and being. "Only love does not have to be," Marion says (138), a theme deepened in *Le phénomène érotique* (2003) and by which he means it cannot be encapsulated by onto-theio-logy or even indicated by "being" considered nonmetaphysically. We need another vocabulary to think of love: that of the gift.

Saturated Phenomena

"To give pure giving to be thought—that, in retrospect it seems to me, is what is at stake in *God without Being*. It is also the task of my future work" (xxv). Thus Marion concludes the preface to the English translation of *Dieu sans l'être* in January 1991. By that time he had already written *Réduction et donation* (1989), which outlines the third reduction, and his next major work was to be *Étant donné* (1997). It is in the passage from the one to the other that Marion changes from being a historian of philosophy to being an original philosopher in his own right (without, however, giving up the history of philosophy). It is in *Étant donné* that Marion proposes his theory of an ensemble of phenomena that are "saturated" with intuition instead of being shaped by intentionality.[119] If Husserl's reduction yields phenomena as present objectivities, as correlatives to noetic acts, and Heidegger's allows us to pass from beings to being, then Marion's "third reduction" requires us to go further and to receive givenness. Over the history of modern phenomenology the focus shifts from knowing a phenomenon to identifying its phenomenality, that is, the way in which it concretely gives itself to us, and, from there, to recognizing givenness as the immanent structure of phenomenality. Needless to say, this structure of givenness varies from phenomenon to phenomenon, and turns on how something is received. What a physical object gives is not the same as what is given by a number or a painting or a story or divine revelation.

In *Réduction et donation*, Marion critically examines both Husserl's and Heidegger's sense of "reduction." The "principle of all principles" of *Ideen* I plainly tells us that *"everything originarily . . . offered to us in intuition is to be accepted simply as what it is presented as being, but also only within the limits in which it is presented there."* And there is considerable evidence that Husserl wished to prize originary givenness: "Absolute givenness is an ultimate," he writes in 1907.[120] Nevertheless, Marion points out, Husserl compromises this principle by indexing phenomenality to intentional consciousness. This occurs, Marion thinks, by dint of an ambiguity in the word "phenomenon" as Husserl uses it, one that is rooted in the *Logische Untersuchungen* (1900) and *Die Idee der Phänomenologie* (1907). To cite the latter: "The word 'phenomenon' is ambiguous in virtue of the essential correlation between *appearance and that which appears*."[121] The word "phenomenon," Marion says, "does not apply first, nor only, to the object that appears, but indeed to the lived experience in which and according to which it appears. . . . Even and especially if one takes intentionality into account, *Erscheinung* [phenomenon] is approached on the basis of the immanence of *Erlebnis* [lived experience]—and therefore, inevitably, never on the basis of the appearing of the object itself, which is by definition conditioned" (53). So it is consciousness that, for Husserl, "radically determines phenomenality by imposing upon it the actuality of presence, the absoluteness of intuition, and the test of lived experience" (54). Marion does not cite Husserl's Amsterdam Lectures (1928), although they would serve his purpose. "In a way, and perhaps stretching the point a little, one can say of every mental process that in it something is appearing to the particular 'I' insofar as the 'I' is somehow conscious of it. Accordingly, phenomenality, as a characteristic that specifically belongs to appearing and to the thing that appears, would, if understood in this broadened sense of the term, be the fundamental characteristic of the mental."[122] Although he admits that phenomenality belongs in part to the phenomenon, what interests Husserl is that it is a mark of the mental, of the transcendental gaze upon the world. And this is why, for Marion, Husserl's phenomenon is no more than a "flat phenomenon."[123]

Marion's project is to restore phenomenality fully to the phenomenon.[124] It has two stages. First, he identifies and rejects the various attempts proposed by Leibniz, Kant and Husserl to restrict it.[125] Leibniz proposes the principle of sufficient reason for phenomena to appear, to which Marion responds with a principle of *in*sufficient reason: it is the phenomenon, not consciousness, that determines appearing.[126] Kant's definition of the possible in the first *Kritik* as transcendental condition for appearing similarly limits phenomena in advance, as does Husserl's structure of intentional consciousness. Second, Marion seeks to reduce the phenomenon beyond objectness (Husserl) and being (Heidegger) to givenness. All in all, we might understand his project as a long delayed and sympathetic response to Daubert and others who objected to Husserl's doctrine of the noema and what they took to be transcendental idealism. The proper reaction to Husserl is not to keep affirming Platonic realism, Marion thinks, but to free the phenomenon from transcendental consciousness. This means several things.

First, as Marion says, one must affirm a variation of the phenomenological *dictum*: not "So much appearance, so much indicating of being" [*wie viel Sein, so viel Hindeutung aufs Seyn*] (Herbart), or "So much appearance, so much Being—which is only covered up and falsified thereby" [*Soviel Schein, soviel (durch ihn nur verdecktes, verfälschtes) Sein*] (Husserl), or "so much seeming, so much being" [*soviel Schein—soviel Sein*] (Heidegger) but instead "So much reduction, so much givenness" [*Autant de réduction, autant de donation*].[127] Reduction leads us not to transcendental consciousness, not to a deep self that is distinguishable from the empirical self, but to the phenomenality of the phenomenon. It saves us from what Marion sees as the philosophical schizophrenia—a division between empirical and transcendental consciousness—that one finds in Husserl.[128]

Second, the domain of phenomenality is extended across the board: unrestricted now by the present objectiveness of the noema, or even by nonobjectified being, it makes available in principle an entire host of new phenomena for study, specifically what Marion calls "saturated phenomena." Phenomena give themselves before they show themselves: another aspect of the truth that phenomenology begins from the unapparent.[129] (Note, though, that not all phenomena actually show themselves; not all givenness is phenomenalized. Kant's and Husserl's versions of the transcendental "I," for example, are never phenomenalized.)

Third, if phenomenology is oriented to what gives itself and what is received, rather than to the constitutive powers of transcendental consciousness, Marion must deny that there is a deep self of any sort, certainly nothing that can be called an "I." There never has been a transcendental consciousness in human beings, let alone a self-grounding *cogito*, as many readers of Descartes have believed in. Above all, we should talk not talk of what modern philosophy calls "the subject": human being determined on the a priori ground of consciousness, whether "self-consciousness" or "transcendental consciousness" or the Freudian triad of ego, id, and super-ego. Instead, we should talk of *l'interloqué* or, better, *l'adonné*, the gifted one, the one who receives phenomena and builds selfhood from them, the devoted one whose being is thoroughly a posteriori and who has no a priori horizon but one that is saturated by givenness.[130]

Phenomena are "saturated," Marion proposes, whenever there is an excess of intuition over intention; and this means that not all phenomena are saturated. There are phenomena that are weak in intuition. The phenomenality of the number three, for instance, is entirely consumed by its meaning. And there are "common law" phenomena, such as objects in a physics lab, the phenomenality of which is fully accounted for by their present objectivity with respect to consciousness. What fascinates Marion, however, are those phenomena that exceed or overflow our intentional horizons, paradoxes that cannot be anticipated or captured by our concepts. It is Kant, not Descartes, who provides Marion with the ground against which he cuts his figure. For Marion turns to the table of categories in the *Kritik der reinen Vernunft* in order to determine the different sorts of saturation. Kant identifies the four sorts of judgment that human understanding makes, and then posits the concepts of the understanding, otherwise known as the categories, as the ways in which intuitions are adapted by judgments and which unify them. Aristotle also wrote of categories, but strictly speaking his treatise relates to entities and Kant's to phenomena. Unease with Aristotle's tenfold division—substance, quantity, quality, relation, place, time, posture, state, action, affection—characterized much Neoplatonist discussion and lasted far into the Middle Ages.[131] Could the categories be simplified? (In *Enneads* VI: 1–3 Plotinus accepted only the first four categories.) Had Aristotle clarified the categories in his more mature works? (In his commentary on the *Categories* Ammonius appeals to the *Metaphysics*.) Was there a principle that would make the categories cohere?

Kant's answer to this final question was that Aristotle's *Categories* contained no principle at all and was no more than a "rhapsody."[132] Yet the list could be revised—in essence, condensed—and then the completeness of the categories justified by transcendental means. A principle was needed. The act of judging provided Kant with what he wanted, for judgment unifies a manifold, and logic indicates the limited number of ways in which manifolds can be unified. Judgment occurs in the faculty of the understanding, and the understanding is entirely populated by such acts. "Now among the manifold concepts which form the highly complicated web of human knowledge," Kant writes in the first *Kritik*, "there are some which are marked out for pure *a priori* employment, in complete independence of all experience; and their right to be so employed always demands a deduction" (B 117). Then we are given a long, complicated transcendental deduction. We should not think of "deduction," as used here, as a logical procedure but as a legal action. What we have in the first *Kritik* is a quasi-legal argument as to the warrant of the categories, an action in which reason itself is brought to trial. Kant concludes that the categories shape the ways in which intuitions give themselves to the understanding. No phenomena, Kant argues, abide outside the categories; and the categories exhaust the powers of the understanding. There are four categories—Quantity, Quality, Relation, and Modality—and three subsets of each.[133]

It may be wondered on what ground Marion can accept Kant's categories and the principles of pure understanding.[134] Not everyone who has inherited from the tradition of the critical philosophy (and all phenomenologists have, albeit sometimes in the mode of rejecting one or another piece of the architecture) has done so. Fichte objected in the *Wissenschaftslehre* (1794) that Kant had "by no means *established*" the categories, maintaining that the transcendental deduction was no more than merely a disguised affirmation of their existence.[135] Schelling agreed, denying that judgment actually serves as a basic principle that "would guarantee the completeness and correctness" of the list of categories.[136] Hegel regarded Kant's way of determining the categories to be "an outrage of scientific thinking."[137] Husserl had many reservations about the Kantian transcendental ego.[138] And Heidegger argued that Kant did not place the categories in the right part of his architectonic: they belong neither to the Transcendental Aesthetic nor to the Transcendental Logic but are rooted in the pure time-related syntheses, that is, in the self-affection of time.[139] Marion, however, sets off "by following the lead of the categories of the understanding defined by Kant," and thereby tacitly endorses the idea of an understanding that is held together by transcendental apperception and is structured in a particular manner. Now where the categories adequately combine intuition and concept, Marion's saturated phenomena are characterized by an overflow of intuition.

Saturated phenomena involve not simply an adaptation of Kant's table but an inversion of each category. Should we regard this situation as a deconstruction of the Kantian categories—that is, a provisional inhabiting of them only to reverse and displace them—or as admitting that Kant got something fundamentally right about the nature of the subject? If the former, we are dealing with a very peculiar version of deconstruction, to which I shall return, and if the latter, it will be impossible to reconcile Marion's vision of *l'adonné* (always the "me" rather than the "I") with the a priori concepts that abide deep in the Kantian subject, and especially his questioning of "the transcendental sense of the I."[140] I leave the problem for a while in order to focus on saturation.

Saturation occurs in various ways: (1) With respect to quantity, an *event is invisable*; it cannot be aimed at. No one could foresee how the battle of Waterloo would play itself out, for example. (2) With respect to quality, an *idol* is unbearable; it dazzles us, and we must look away. Think of looking at a late Turner canvas, "The Burning of the Houses of Parliament" (1834–35), for instance. Or, turning to nature, recall Felice's remark about the tulips to Marguerite in Balzac's *La recherche de l'absolu* (1834), "Mademoiselle, these flowers are beautiful, but to love them we must perhaps have a taste of them, and know how to understand their beauties. They dazzle me [*m'éblouissent*]." To which Marguerite replies, "Yes, you are right, those colors are dazzling; they give pain [*Vous avez raison, ces couleurs papillotent et font mal*]."[141] (3) With respect to relation, the *flesh* is absolute: it has no noetic formation and thus foregoes the horizon of objectness entirely. When I touch myself, pure auto-affection occurs. And (4) with respect to modality, an *icon* is irregardable; we cannot gaze upon it. Another's face cannot be objectified, for instance. (Here, the reference to "other" denotes the ethical transcendence of the other person for Marion as for Levinas.) *Étant donné* sketches these four sorts of saturation, noting that some of them have been registered earlier in the history of philosophy: Descartes's infinity, Kant's sublime, and Husserl's internal consciousness of time all prefigure one or another aspect of the theory of saturated phenomena (219–220). This introduction is not the place to detail the richness and speculative brilliance of Marion's sketch of saturated phenomena: specific examples are explored in *De surcroît* (2001). *Étant donné* is primarily a work of phenomenological theory. Although it considers some examples—including memorable readings of a genre painting ("a rustic house, a servant at the window, two animals and a man outside beside the table") and of Caravaggio's "The Calling of Saint Matthew" (1599–1600)—it is mainly focused on reworking the idea of phenomenology according to the primacy of the "self" of the phenomenon.[142]

Five caveats will help orient a first reading of these intriguing phenomena. First, in case one assumes that we are dealing with extraordinary appearings, Marion underlines that saturation is banal: it occurs all the time, in perfectly ordinary situations.[143] We should not think of the excess of intuition always resulting in elation or a privileged moment, for it can be disappointing or frustrating. After all, we cannot grasp what is happening by way of concepts. (Nor indeed can we always distinguish degrees of excess.) Second, this phenomenology does not take place in the figure of experience but in terms of counter-experience.[144] Saturated phenomena run against the conditions of possibility for weak or common law phenomena. I do not experience a saturated phenomenon as an object; on the contrary, I find myself overwhelmed by an excess of intuition that makes me look away. (In this sense Marion is at the antipodes of classical phenomenology.) I have no concepts that can be adequate to what gives itself to me. Third, I do not constitute a saturated phenomenon: I receive it. Fourth, it will be noted that the Marion of *Étant donné* (and perhaps earlier, of *La croisée du visible* (1991)) rehabilitates the idol from its sharp contrast with the icon in *Dieu sans l'être*: we are talking now of idols in a broader sense than is usually done in religion. And finally, the theory of saturated phenomena allows Marion to propose a theory of divine revelation. It is saturation to the second degree.[145]

A Little More Theology (and a Touch of Atheism)

Revelation has come under sharp critique in modernity. One thinks first of all of Fichte's *Versuch einer Kritik aller Offenbargung* (1793) and Kant's *Die Religion innerhalb der Grenzen der blossen Vernunft* (1794), each of which sought to bring revelation under the aegis of ethics. Yet we think too of Karl Barth's riposte to this challenge, his insistence on the self-revelation of God: itself a modern notion, relying in part on a Cartesian notion of selfhood. If, as David Tracy urges us to accept, Marion is a noncorrelational theologian in *Dieu sans l'être*, we would expect him to side with Barth or von Balthasar rather than with Fichte and Kant. Yet things are not quite so straightforward with the Marion of *Étant donné* and beyond. I quote from a discussion. "I suggest that revelation—of course, for me, the revelation of Christ, but also any kind of revelation, if there are other claims to revelation—can acquire phenomenological status and match other kinds of phenomena. In that precise sense, the distinction between the field of philosophy and the field of theology, the 'limits' between them in the meanings of Kant and Fichte, could be bridged to some extent."[146] Marion therefore seeks to bridge the abyss between the Enlightenment and Barth's theology of revelation from the side of Fichte and Kant. Revelation is a phenomenon; and yet a Barthian would object that revelation partly reveals and partly re-veils God, and that this concealment is more primitive than our not being able to view an aspect of a phenomenon.[147] The very holiness of revelation requires concealment, for otherwise it would not be the revelation of *God*, who must always be acknowledged, as Augustine says, as *deus semper maior*.[148] If divine revelation is a phenomenon, it is a peculiar sort. Marion would agree: unlike even saturated phenomena it has four features. It is an event that cannot be foreseen; it is an idol in that it dazzles us; it is absolute insofar as it must "appeal to our senses"; and it is an icon, for it features the otherness of the divine who is the Other par excellence.[149]

Many theologians would have no difficulty in agreeing with Marion that a positive revelation cannot be foreseen by natural means, though there is room to debate the role of prophesy with respect to the Christian revelation. That revelation is iconic would be widely agreed as well, though perhaps more surely by Catholic and Orthodox than by evangelical Christians or any others who rely on verbal revelation. Whether it must dazzle us is a question that calls for discussion, not least of all for anyone who accepts the sharp distinction between the icon and the idol as delineated in *Dieu sans l'être*. We think of the transfigured Christ as dazzling ("and his face did shine as the sun, and his raiment was white as the light," Matt. 17: 2, KJV), yet the resurrected Christ does not always dazzle those to whom he appears. Think of the story of the disciples on the road to

Emmaus who at first do not recognize the risen Christ and see him as entirely ordinary (because "their eyes were holden," Luke 24: 16, KJV). More debate is likely to turn on the view that a revelation must "appeal to our senses." To be sure, we recall Scripture, "That which was from the beginning, which we have heard, which we have seen with our eyes, which we have looked upon, and our hands have handled, of the Word of life" (I John 1: 1, KJV). Such is John's testimony regarding Jesus of Nazareth, a confession that informs sacramental theology; and if we think of revelation also coming through the reading of Scripture and preaching about it we must also admit that there is an appeal to the senses. Yet this appeal is not without a horizon, for we have an intentional rapport with Scripture when reading it, and with a homily when hearing it unfold. In addition, many theologians would object that revelation should not be treated as an eidetic possibility.[150] It is an existential reality in which one finds oneself confronted by God. Marion might respond by observing that, as we all know, devout Christians regard the revelations of other religions as possibilities rather than realities. To which a Christian theologian might reply: The living God would certainly saturate a horizon, but could a *possibility* do the same?

Also, there is a distinction between general and special revelation that needs to be respected. Consider Teresa of Ávila's testimony in her autobiography about seeing Christ: "All the time Jesus Christ seemed to be at my side, but as this was not an imaginary vision I could not see in what form. But I most clearly felt He was all the time on my right, and was a witness of everything that I was doing." She reflects on her experience: "For if I say that I do not see Him with the eyes of the body or the eyes of the soul, because this is no imaginary vision, how then can I know and affirm that he is beside me with greater certainty than if I saw Him?" A little later she adds, "He appears to the soul by a knowledge brighter than the sun. I do not mean that any sun is seen, or any brightness, but there is a light which, though unseen, illumines the understanding so that the soul may enjoy this great blessing, which brings very great blessings with it."[151] This account does not appeal to the senses, unless one includes Origen's "spiritual senses," although Marion's hypothesis of saturated phenomena helps us to grasp some of what Teresa is recounting.[152] One may well propose that God reveals himself to us *modus sine modo*, in a way without a way, not in terms of the senses but quite otherwise. Such seems to be what Teresa has in mind, and a more careful writer such as Bernard of Clairvaux adds support to this view.[153]

These are not the only questions that trouble theologians when they read Marion. The rejection of the transcendental subject and its replacement by *l'adonné* is of more philosophical than theological interest, although it remains to be seen how well *l'adonné* can support a fully articulated moral theory. To date, Marion has shown little interest in moral issues as distinct from engaging Levinas on the question of ethics as first philosophy. To be sure, he has a developed theory of love; but can an appeal to love satisfy all questions in moral theology? The theologian knows that the "I" is not the same as the soul, and therefore looks with interest, not dismay, at Marion's criticisms of the transcendental "I" and its replacement with the "me" of *l'adonné*. At the same time, however, one wishes to see Marion elaborate a theory of the soul. If Christ saves us, what is it that Marion thinks is saved? To which can be added a related question: How can *l'adonné* be converted? At the moment, Marion does not have a theory of action, a philosophy of the human will, which would be able to answer the question satisfactorily. It remains to be seen whether his adoption of remonstration from Augustine's *Confessions* can serve as a platform from which to answer these questions.[154]

Philosophers are not required to supply theological anthropologies. That is a task for theologians. Yet some phenomenologies lend themselves more surely to theological themes than others. For example, Fink's account of the reduction, in which the person performing it unhumanizes himself or herself, might be interpreted by way of κένωσις.[155] (Yet it might also be read by way of Gnosticism.[156]) When reading Marion, and being aware that he is a practicing Catholic, we might ask ourselves whether his account of *l'adonné* can square with any theological anthropology. No notice is taken by Marion of any evil that *l'adonné* performs or is subject to. As a philosopher, he may have nothing to say about sin, original or actual, yet as a Catholic intellectual he is bound to have considered views on both. A Christian phenomenologist of the older school might argue that intentionality is skewed by concupiscence: one looks only to partial goods or is oriented towards disordered goods unless divine grace comes to one's aid. Could one also argue that *l'adonné*'s ability to receive phenomena is in some way restricted or skewed by concupiscence? To date, Marion has not indicated his views on the question or any possible answers to it.

Finally, there is the objection of the atheist to saturated phenomena. Jocelyn Benoist asks Marion in a talk on the so-called "theological turn" in phenomenology, "What will you say to me if I say to you that where you see God, I see nothing?"[157] Or, rather than nothing, Benoist adds, "another thing," for example, "the infinite forest of sensible life, or the metamorphoses of the divine in our daily affair of being loved, rather than the monotheistic idol (a concept that seems to me to be quite metaphysical even so)?" Marion responds by pointing out that to describe this "infinite forest" one needs to have recourse to saturated phenomena, and that being loved also calls for the sort of treatment that Marion explores in *Le phénomène érotique* (2003). Perhaps the objection can be rephrased without reference to God, the infinite, or even love: "What will you say to me if I say to you what where you see saturation, I see merely an ordinary phenomenon (and I take 'phenomenon' more broadly than 'present object')?" For example, where Marion is confronted by otherness when looking at another's face, another person might say that he sees a human face. To be sure, this objector might admit that the other person is unique in terms of personality and genetic composition but may point out that he or she is unique only in relation to *Homo sapiens* as a species. In the end, Marion will have little alternative but to suggest, as phenomenologists often do, that the objector is not looking hard enough and responding justly enough to the phenomenon. One must know how to look at the face and be deflected from it, he might say, and to do so following the way in which it gives itself. How can one not acknowledge the counterintentionality of the face? Arguments between phenomenologists have a way of ending with one of them saying, "Look again!" The same expression, of course, often keeps arguments going.

Marion "in Context"

The proper context in which to situate Marion is very broad indeed. His work asks to be placed with respect to both modern western philosophy and Christian theology from its beginnings with the Apostolic and Church Fathers. Gregory of Nyssa, Pseudo-Dionysius, and Maximus the Confessor are not simply references for Marion; they are the textual sites for phenomenological investigations of manifestation and obscurity.[158] Within the narrower frame of the most pressing modern contexts, one must pay special attention to Husserl and Heidegger, and, more narrowly still, one must look to the French philosophers whose works have shaped Marion's, either through his agreements with them or through his quarrels with them. Sometimes Marion is a magpie in that he borrows large parts of another's thought on the ground that he has no objections to it and that it fits with his theory. His hermeneutics, for example, is largely taken from Paul Ricoeur, with the proviso, as we have seen, that interpretation begins, for him, only once *l'adonné* has received a phenomenon.[159] Largely but not exclusively: for in *Au lieu de soi: L'approche de Saint Augustin* (2008) Marion uses the theory of saturated phenomena as a hermeneutic in reading the *Confessions*. To give a finer sense of Marion's immediate context I shall situate him briefly with respect to three major French philosophers who have been his seniors—Michel Henry, Emmanuel Levinas, and Jacques Derrida—all the time knowing that each relationship could easily become the subject of a book.[160] It would be extremely interesting to involve Marion in a discussion with analytic philosophers, beginning with the Wilfred Sellars who tells us that "the given" is a myth, and continuing with Robert Brandom and John McDowell.[161] Yet this is a discussion still to take place in earnest, and a context still to form with clear lines of debate.

Michel Henry

Michel Henry (1922–2002) is best known for his contestation of all forms of ecstatic phenomenology, that is, all philosophies of disclosure that affirm the primacy of intentionality. On his view, as copiously elaborated in *L'essence de la manifestation* (1963), "Transcendence rests upon immanence."[162] All intentionality, all manifestation in the world, is rooted in a prior nonintentional subjectivity; and the labor of Husserl and Heidegger, for all its force and brilliance, fails to acknowledge this priority and to explore nonintentional life. This failure allows Henry to call their philosophies examples of "ontological monism," the view that there is one, and only one, ontology, that of the world.[163] Accordingly, classical phenomenology examines a mode of manifestation in which being is as much hidden as it is revealed.[164] First and foremost, Henry thinks, we should attend to the invisible yet deeply felt life of consciousness, which is itself parousia or full presence, that abides in solitude and darkness, without image and without world. This requires us to inspect the auto-affectivity of life with its poles of suffering (passivity) and joy (active receptivity), which Henry regards as the most basic mode of phenomenality.[165]

Marion has never agreed with Henry that the essence of manifestation is the pure immanence of life or, to say the same thing another way, that "the creator of phenomenality, is consciousness itself."[166] For him, as we know, givenness is the "self" of the phenomenon, the immanent structure of phenomenality. And yet Henry's rejection of the primacy of intentionality presses on Marion's mature thought: he too does not accept that fulfilling intuition determines all the modes of phenomenality, only those that Husserl and Heidegger analyze. The domain of phenomenality is larger than has been imagined, larger than the realm of objects and even being. Also, Marion's account of the third type of saturation, the flesh, is deeply indebted to Henry. Before I say a word or two about that connection, however, something needs to be said about what Marion admires about Henry's explication of Descartes. For Henry, the *cogito* needs to be disengaged from Kant's misunderstanding of it as meaning not "I think" but "I represent to myself that I think," for it is this interpretation that directs Husserl and Heidegger in their reading of the father of modern philosophy.[167] It must mean, as Henry thinks it did for Descartes, "that which appears to itself immediately in everything that appears, or rather in pure appearing (what Descartes calls thought)," and what Henry calls *cogitatio*, soul or life, to distinguish it from the Kantian and Heideggerian sense of the *cogito* as an objective reality.[168] The *res cogitans* has its origin in a primal act of feeling, not thinking. This feeling is immanent and invisible; it is an example of what Henry—here indebted to Maine de Biran—calls flesh, not biological tissue such as skin, fat and muscle but inner, subjective life as distinct from the physical body that can be weighed on a pair of scales. As Henry states, *"From an ontological point of view, there is . . . no difference between 'flesh' and 'spirit.'"*[169] Thus understood, the flesh is nonintentional, without horizon, and therefore absolute. It is an inversion of the Kantian category of relation.

Henry's declaration that transcendence relies on immanence turns on a demonstration that the act of sensing something is preceded by a self-reception before any self-affection produced by time.[170] This is the basis of his deep disagreement with Heidegger, for whom Dasein is temporalized at the undermost level of its being. From this ground, Henry develops a range of novel analyses of art, Christ and Marx, along with criticisms of our modern technological culture as essentially barbaric. Always they differ from anything one has previously read on the subject, and always they are the same as Henry's enstatic phenomenology. Marion bypasses Henry's rethinking of Marxism as a philosophy of life; unlike so many French philosophers of the generation before him—Althusser, Balibar, Derrida, Garaudy, Lefebvre, Sartre—he shows no intellectual affinity with Marxism. And Marion's approach to Christian revelation as fourfold saturation differs markedly from Henry's stress on God as Life, and the purported almost perfect continuity between the Gospel of John and his own nonintentional phenomenology.[171] Yet Marion is obliged to Henry for encouraging him to write on the visual arts, which he does with compelling insight not only in *La croisée du visible* but also from time to time in his more theoretical writings. If Henry's theme in the arts is seeing the invisible—that is, passing from what we see in a painting to the seeing itself—then Marion's is how the invisible crosses the visible.[172]

Emmanuel Levinas

Emmanuel Levinas (1906–95) studied with Husserl and Heidegger in Freiburg im Breisgau, and introduced phenomenology to France with his *Théorie d'intuition dans la phénoménologie de Husserl* (1930). In that treatise Levinas found himself disagreeing with Husserl about the methodological need for the transcendental reduction, which he believed yielded only "a purely contemplative and theoretical sight which considers life but is distinct from it."[173] He observed that a reduction to a transcendental ego is only a first step in phenomenology, for "We must also discover 'others' and the intersubjective world" (150), and he ended his study by anticipating the publication of Husserl's work on an "intersubjective reduction" (151). Over the course of his own writing, Levinas set aside all forms of reduction yet persisted with intentional analysis: the discovery of unacknowledged horizons that give unsuspected meaning to our thoughts.[174] Phenomenology touches one of its limits with reduction, which Levinas believed to reintroduce theory into a discourse that otherwise declared itself to be on the side of the concrete, and touches another limit when it considers human beings. The human, he argued, is an enigma, not a phenomenon. To return to my earlier example, no matter how hard I try to do so, I cannot grasp my friend Robert in my gaze and make him an object within my intentional horizon.[175] Unlike objects, human beings resist becoming completely visible. The other person, Levinas proposes, transcends me: "this height is no longer the heavens but the Invisible."[176] This transcendence, Levinas urges, is not to be figured as negative but is rigorously expressed by infinity.

"Infinity" here does not bespeak an affirmation of the infinite God of Gregory of Nyssa or Thomas Aquinas. Levinas's reference is to Descartes: not to his belief in the infinity of God but to the proposal in the third Meditation that "in some way I have in me the notion of the infinite earlier than the finite."[177] (Levinas insists that the claim of infinity takes place before any choice for or against God has been made.[178]) The other person is exterior to me, above me, and this is what the infinity within me bespeaks. This other person is not divine—agreed; and yet the trace of divinity passes through another person when I go to help him or her. In a novel that Levinas thoroughly admired, Vasily Grossman's *Life and Fate* (1980), the narrator evokes "the kindness of an old woman carrying a piece of bread to a prisoner, the kindness of a soldier allowing a wounded enemy to drink from his water-flask, the kindness of youth towards age, the kindness of a peasant hiding an old Jew in his loft."[179] In performing acts such as these—acts that are ordinary yet extraordinary—one moves, Levinas thinks, in the trace of infinite goodness that exceeds all being, and all totalities that seek to gather beings into a unity. It is in encountering the other person and recognizing the claim that he or she has on me, a claim that has never been forged in any present moment—past, present, or to come— but that immemorially impinges on me without respite, that I overcome what he calls the *il y a* ("there is"). Where Heidegger wrote of *Angst* in *Sein und Zeit* as Dasein's fundamental attunement, its projection into nothingness, Levinas identified a contrary experience: the sense of the sheer excess of being that we cannot shake off. We are plagued by the anonymous return of being, even in states of *ennui* and dread; it is the dreary experience of insomnia where the night has weight and when one's "I" is no longer personal but something that merely drags itself through time.[180] This *il y a* is neither subjective nor objective; it is neutral, an excluded middle. As we have seen, Marion speaks of boredom rather than the *il y a*; and where Levinas proposes ethics as the way of escaping the torment of being, Marion points us to charity as the way of avoiding the inevitable self-realization "I am, therefore I am lacking."[181] Levinas had long been chary of speaking of love, fearing the Romantic connotation of fusion, and it was perhaps Marion who helped to convince him, in his last writings, to use the word and the concept in another manner.[182]

Despite Marion's immense respect for Levinas, his conviction that he was "the greatest of French philosophers since Bergson," and his broad agreement with the general cast of his ethics, he disagrees with him on several points.[183] We are always and already obliged to the other person, Levinas avers, while Marion counters by saying, "The injunction of obligation toward the other (*autrui*) leads, in reality, to the neutralization of the other as such."[184] Levinas affirms that ethics is first philosophy, and adopts a highly critical view of art, accepting only that sort of art that embodies a self-criticism of its will to perfection.[185] At root, he remains in the wake of Jena Romanticism and the various notions of the avant-garde that it spawned.[186] Marion, however, highly values art, and does not contrast it to ethics. Levinas seeks to explain and value the word "God" but outside the phenomenality of revelation: the word finally *means* a responsibility for the other person without the expectation of symmetrical return.[187] Unlike Kant, ethics is not subject to universalization; it is not a law but the conviction of being a hostage of the other person. To be sure, as soon as there are three (and in society there always are) one is obliged to distribute one's time and concern, but the burden of responsibility for the other person prevents distributive justice from closing in on itself and becoming a system, a politics of the Good in preference to many small acts of individual goodness. Finally, as we know, Marion seeks to grasp revelation as saturation to the second degree. Where Levinas underlines the importance of an original alterity, the other person who is elevated above me, Marion discerns an original alterity at the heart of the *cogito*, namely God.

Jacques Derrida

Marion begins *Dieu sans l'être* by distancing himself from his older contemporaries. Georges Bataille had celebrated transgression, Barthes had written of the "pleasure of the text," and Derrida had testified time and again to his love of "slow reading," which, as Nietzsche put it, is "a goldsmith's art and connoisseurship of the word which has nothing but delicate, cautious work to do and achieves nothing if it does not do it *lento*."[188] Marion starts his book by resonating with these thoughts, though at another octave: "One must admit that theology, of all writing, certainly causes the greatest pleasure," he says. "Precisely not the pleasure of the text [*le plaisir du texte*], but the pleasure—unless it have to do with a joy—of transgressing it: from words to the Word, from the Word to words" (1). In doing *theo*logy one passes from what one reads (Scripture) to the one in whom one believes (Christ, the Eternal Word) and back again in a never-ending dialectic, one that Anselm summed up as *fides quaerens intellectum*, faith in quest of understanding. Yet Marion had attended Derrida's lectures, and much of his work involves either a direct or oblique engagement with him.

Derrida's writing falls under the rubric of deconstruction, which is his inflection of two German words, both used by Heidegger—*Destruktion* and *Abbau*—which mean destructuring or unbuilding an edifice so that its mode of construction can be inspected.[189] One can read a text slowly in order to see how it is put together, in what ways it covertly adheres to metaphysical assumptions or seeks to free itself from them. Deconstruction, however, came to be less technical than this gloss suggests; it became an affirmation of what Derrida called *la différance*, the quasi-transcendental play of signification. There are, it turned out, many ways in which text and meaning fail to coincide perfectly, many ways in which otherness is irreducible to sameness. In reading after reading of philosophical, literary and other texts Derrida would show how even the most self-contained of writings is exceeded by *la différance* and the other nicknames he gave to it, including *khōra, pharmakon*, and *le supplément*. Now in the preface to the English edition of *Dieu sans l'être* Marion refers to the destitution of metaphysics, which I have already noted as "an ahistorical 'deconstruction' of the history of metaphysics. At least it claims to outline this 'deconstruction' within the framework of a phenomenology that is pushed to its utmost possibilities" (xxii). And Marion refers us to Derrida's remarks on *Dieu sans l'être* in *Psyché* (1987).[190] Since Derrida comments on the French edition of the work, no mention is made of Marion's use of the word "deconstruction." Derrida is well known for saying, "There is no *one* deconstruction. There are only singular movements, more or less idiomatic styles, strategies, effects of deconstruction that are heterogeneous from one place to another, from one (historical, national, cultural, linguistic, even 'individual') situation to another."[191] Yet when Derrida hears Marion talking of deconstruction at Villanova University in 1997 he registers disapproval. Marion says that with the transfiguration of Christ "there was an excess of intuition over the concept or the signification. So, we have deconstruction in that sense." To which Derrida replies, "If deconstruction . . . is interested in the excess I was mentioning a moment ago, in some excess, it is not an excess of intuition, of phenomenality, of fullness, of more than fullness. The excess, the structure, in which I am interested, is not an excess of intuition."[192]

There is no one deconstruction for Derrida because the word "deconstruction" itself can be inscribed in different textual chains and so take on unexpected significations and suggest new strategies of reading and acting, but it will always serve in the interest, as it were, of difference and spacing, and not donating intuition. Certainly Marion does not think that he and Derrida are close in terms of philosophical approach, even when he uses the word "deconstruction." Listen to *Étant donné*: "Deconstruction," he writes (with Derrida in mind), "which only considers sensible intuition (for categorial [*catégoriale*] intuition) perhaps still resists it), does not broach givenness, which would secure for it any and all pertinence in phenomenology. Deconstruction therefore remains a mode of givenness—to be quite exact that of givenness deferred" (55; trans. slightly modified). That is, the stream of noetic modifications never results in a determinate correlate with a single thetic characteristic. For Marion, Derrida is fixated on the primacy and fullness of intuition in Husserl, whereas the right angle of critique with respect to Husserl is to overcome a reliance on intuition because this is precisely what always recurs to intentionality and hence transcendental consciousness. Phenomenality is properly identified and acknowledged—one might say "freed"—only when it is not determined by transcendental consciousness.

Earlier I observed that in his inversion of the Kantian table of categories Marion is either enacting a peculiar sort of deconstruction or is affirming, albeit tacitly, that Kant is somehow right about the structure of the human subject. Neither would suit his purposes. We may put the word "deconstruction" to one side. When Marion uses it to describe what he does, he uses it in a sense so much at variance with Derrida's as to bring about confusion. We may also doubt that Marion, who urges us to jettison the subject in favor of *l'adonné*, does not subscribe to Kantian metaphysics in general or the Kantian subject in particular. What Marion intends to do with the table of categories is to perform a reduction on them; he wishes to lead them back from a metaphysical account of subjectivity to a nonmetaphysical account: not by way of the transcendental "I" but by testing the limits of the categories and seeing what happens if one puts pressure on them by examining phenomena that are strong in intuition rather than weak in intuition. How Marion uses the notion of reduction, and whether his uses of it are always justified, would merit a long essay in itself. Rather than embark on such a project, I shall restrict myself to the main engagements between Derrida and Marion. There are two: a difference over apophatic theology, and a disagreement over the nature of the gift.

In "Comment ne pas parler: *Dénégations*" (1986) Derrida sought to distinguish deconstruction from what he called "negative theology," and he did so in response to claims that deconstruction is itself a displaced negative theology. He had earlier reflected in "Différance"(1968) that in order to evoke *la différance* he would "often have to take recourse" to linguistic forms that "resemble those of negative theology, occasionally even to the point of being indistinguishable from negative theology," while nonetheless insisting that *la différance* is "not theological, not even in the order of the most negative of negative theologies, which are always concerned with disengaging a superessentiality beyond the finite categories of essence and existence, that is, of presence, and always hastening to recall that God is refused the predicate of existence, only in order to acknowledge his superior, inconceivable, and ineffable mode of being."[193] Now it is conventional in theology, especially the theology that looks back to the Greek Fathers, to distinguish kataphatic from apophatic theology, that is, a theology that begins with divine revelation and traces how it is received and a theology that attempts to approach God from beneath, as it were, and progressively takes away speech about God the closer it comes to the divine. These two theological approaches are sometimes referred to, somewhat misleadingly, as positive (or affirmative) and negative theology. Derrida's long essay examines passages from Plato, Pseudo-Dionysius the Areopagite, and Heidegger. Among other things, the essay argues that deconstruction is not a negative theology, and that Christian discourse on the ineffable deity never really addresses the Other; it is always deflected towards a prior determination of absolute alterity (such as he believes *la différance* to be), namely God as triune. There is no pure experience of prayer, then, only experiences in which prayer supplements itself with quotations, and invariably submits to writing and the *différance* that is associated with it in all its forms. Those who say that the Christian God escapes what Derrida calls "the metaphysics of presence" are mistaken. Even when regarded as "beyond being," the Christian God is a "superessentiality," and negative theology remains caught up in metaphysical assumptions and is therefore subject to deconstruction.

Marion responds to Derrida in an essay first delivered in English at Villanova University, with Derrida in the audience, in 1997, and now contained in *De surcroît*. In this essay, entitled "Au nom ou comment le taire," he argues there that Derrida is mistaken to think of theology as having just two threads, kataphatic and apophatic, for there is a third thread that Pseudo-Dionysius identifies: no longer an affirmation or a denial but a reference to God who is beyond all naming. The God beyond being cannot be touched by metaphysics, Marion urges, and certainly escapes what Derrida calls "the metaphysics of presence."[194] None of the divine names gives us the divine essence, and all we can have is a "*pragmatic theology of absence*."[195] We can name any created thing but the name of the triune God "surpasses all signification" (156) and therefore cannot be incorporated in any ontic or ontological horizon. Nonetheless, we may speak of the phenomenality of God, which is received as an intuition of the terror of the divine incomprehensibility. "*It is* a fearful thing to all into the hands of the living God" (Heb. 10: 31, KJV). Far from "negative theology" having the form of onto-theio-logy, as Derrida maintains, it gives us a name above all names in which we may dwell "without saying it, but by letting it say, name, and call us" (162).[196] Once again, we find Marion re-thinking and re-launching elements of patristic Greek theology in a radical phenomenology.

Does this mean that Marion is proposing theology in the guise of philosophy? The question comes up time and again, in part because of Marion's attempt to think revelation as saturation to the second degree. It also rises in terms of Marion's theory of the gift, which is worked out by way of criticism of Derrida's deconstruction of giving in *Donner le temps* (1991). There Derrida contests Marcel Mauss's hypothesis in his *Essai sur le don* (1923) that gifts are exchanged, arguing that, if there is such a thing as a gift, it cannot be exchanged (which would simply annul the gift as gift) but must be given so that it cannot be returned, not even by way of an expression of gratitude or ingratitude. The gift does not appear, then; it is never lodged in any present moment, since it cannot be anticipated, recognized, or returned. And so, if there is such a thing as a gift, it falls outside phenomenology.[197] Marion had been thinking of gift giving for many years before Derrida's remarkable study.[198] No surprise then that he takes on Derrida's claim in the second book of *Étant donné*. Sympathetic in some respects to what Derrida argues, Marion nonetheless proposes that if we reduce the gift fully, freeing it from the metaphysics of cause and effect, we can reach a more profound level of gift giving.

What seems to be beyond phenomenology is in fact open to phenomenological exploration, if phenomenology is released from its metaphysical commitments. We can bracket the giver, the givee, and the gift itself. When I give to a charity to help the sick and poor in Africa, for example, I have no idea to whom I am actually giving my money: nothing in fact returns to me. The one to whom I have in fact given without knowing it cannot respond with gratitude or ingratitude, since my gift is bundled up with other donations and has no name associated with it. (Things are plainly different when one sponsors a child through World Vision and receives a photograph of a child.) And the gift itself can be reduced; strictly speaking, it is not an object that is transferred from one person to another. Released from metaphysical assumptions about all three aspects of gift giving, the gift is rightly seen in the light of givenness rather than economy. The gift relies on no reasons outside itself; it has no sufficient reason, no conditions of possibility—whether metaphysical (Aristotle) or transcendental (Kant)—and no consciousness. Its reason is entirely immanent, or, if you wish, is supplied by givenness as the structure of the gift's phenomenality. Forgiveness and sacrifice, for example—concepts examined in *Certitudes négatives* (2010)—transcend all economic exchange, as Derrida argues, and look to no authority other than the very acts in which they are given.[199]

Derrida will remain suspicious that at heart Marion is doing theology when developing his phenomenology of the gift. "My hypothesis," Derrida says to Marion in a public debate at Villanova, "concerns the fact that you use or credit the word *Gegebenheit* with gift, with the meaning of gift, and this has to do with—I will not call this theological or religious—the deepest ambition of your thought. For you, everything that is given in the phenomenological sense, *gegeben, donné, Gegebenheit*, everything that is given to us in perception, in memory, in a phenomenological perception, is finally a gift to a finite creature, and it is finally a gift of God."[200] (What's odd here is that the expression "gift of God" is nothing if not "theological or religious.") It is precisely this implication that everything is finally a divine gift that Marion rejects. "I am not trying to reduce every phenomenon to a gift and then to say, after that, since this is a gift, and given to a finite mind, then there is perhaps a giver behind it all." As noted, Marion brackets the giver, whether it is you, or I, or God the Father. "My project," he continues, "attempts, on the contrary, to reduce the gift to givenness, and to establish the phenomenon as given" (70).

Conclusion

"Givenness": such is Marion's *maître mot*. Under its shelter we can find everything that he wishes to tell us, at least since *Réduction et donation* and up to *Certitudes négatives* (2010) and *The Reason of the Gift* (2011). He proposes that we pass from thinking of the possible to being receptive to the impossible, to entering into a world of paradoxes, saturated phenomena, that is exactly the world in which we live. An introduction can only lead a reader into his work and not take him or her to its very limits.[201] Marion is still a bird in flight, and while we may think that we can tell where he is headed—deeper reflection on the divine, perhaps with a more intimate rapport with Scripture, further work on Descartes, and on the visual arts—we can have at best only anticipations that may be disappointed. Marion's writing is itself a phenomenon, an *event*, in all senses of the word: what is to come cannot be anticipated by anyone, yet we may well be assured that we shall be discussing what he has already given us for many years to come.

PART I

Metaphysics and Its Idols

The Idol and Distance was Jean-Luc Marion's first extended foray into the phenomenology of religion. It appeared in France in 1977 and was belatedly translated into English in 2001. His second book in the phenomenology of religion, *God Without Being*, was published in France in 1982, appearing in English translation, with a foreword by the American Catholic theologian David Tracy, in 1991. For Anglophone readers at least, *God Without Being* introduced Marion to the English-speaking world, and in doing so it set the vanishing points of his reception here, which are still in place today, even though they are gradually being adjusted by the impact of his later thought centered on the "saturated phenomenon."

In *God Without Being*, Marion appears as a Catholic Heideggerian, a philosopher by training, though one with a very strong theological bent. His expertise in the history of philosophy is everywhere apparent, as is his familiarity with the thought of his radical older contemporary, Jacques Derrida.[1] Like Heidegger, Marion wishes to disengage the thought of God from that of being. Heidegger had observed in a discussion with students at the University of Zurich in 1952 that were he to write a theology the word "being" would not figure in it, and he also insisted that Christian faith had no use for being.[2] Metaphysics is produced, Heidegger argues, in and through the forgetting of being by dint of undue attention to beings. The ontological difference between being and beings allows one to construe God as a being, albeit the highest being or the first being. In Marion's terms, this is conceptual idolatry. Yet it is not the only form of idolatry to be generated by philosophy. For Marion detects a more subtle form of idolatry in Heidegger's own thought. In releasing being from beings, Heidegger nonetheless continues to think God from the basis of being. By rights, Marion believes, God should be first; and yet in Heidegger's later thought being, or the question of being, is given priority with respect to the question of God. This tendency is heavily marked in some of Heidegger's French followers, Marion argues. In their defenses of Heidegger, Jean Beaufret and François Fédier only further entrench the idolatry that Marion detects.

The young Marion is fluent not only in the language of phenomenology but also in the language of the Church Fathers, especially the Greek Fathers. He adopts the distinction between idol and icon, as elaborated by St John of Damascus, St Theodore the Studite, and others, and seeks to treat it phenomenologically.[3] One important influence on Marion, early and late, is the work of Pseudo-Dionysius the Areopagite, for whom the first of the divine names is the good.[4] When we think today of the first divine name as being, it is because of the immense authority of St Thomas Aquinas; and Marion objects to this rerouting of the tradition. To be sure, as Marion admits, Aquinas "does not chain God either to Being or to metaphysics" when he thinks of God as *esse* (more strictly as *ipsum esse subsistens omnibus modis indeterminatum*).[5] For *esse* is not the same as *ens commune*; it does not derive from a prior notion of being but is rather the absolutely singular mode of being that is unique to God's essence. The question will be taken up in more detail by Marion in "St Thomas Aquinas and Onto-Theology," also included in this collection.[6] For Marion, God gives himself to us outside the horizon of being—created being, or common being—as ἀγάπη, divine love.

Naturally, the earlier book, *The Idol and Distance*, should be read before *God Without Being*. Here one finds five rich contexts for the later book: the "God" who comes into view through the lens of onto-theio-logy; Nietzsche's proclamation of the twilight of the idols; Hölderlin's insistence on the withdrawal of the divine from the world; Pseudo-Dionysius's account of praise; and a study of the distance that the Father requires in order to remain hidden. When Nietzsche had a madman declare that God is dead in *The Gay Science* (1887), Marion argues, he was responding to the collapse of God as a metaphysical concept and as a moral exemplar, that is, as an idol.[7] When Hölderlin spoke of the "default of God," however, he saw that the turn away from God in the Enlightenment is coordinate with God's withdrawal from the world. More profoundly still, Marion holds, Christian theology has recognized that God presents himself to us only in the mode of withdrawal. "The one who would like an evidence of God other than this manifest withdrawal undoubtedly does not know what he asks for."[8] God the Father remains hidden; he withdraws from the space of manifestation precisely in order to reveal the Son and to enable a relation with the Christ and, though Christ, with himself. It is precisely this "paternal distance" that metaphysics occludes.

Is Marion guilty of confusing philosophical and theological procedures? Does he put phenomenology at the service of Christian dogma? Dominique Janicaud has convicted Marion on both counts.[9] Yet Marion answers both questions in the negative: "Between phenomenology and theology, the border passes between revelation as possibility and Revelation as historicity. There can be no danger of confusion between these domains."[10] Marion is not thereby disposed to rule a line under the history of "Christian philosophy." In an essay on the debate around this notion, conducted in France in the 1930s, he admits that "the term . . . may turn out to be more of a handicap than an opportunity" yet he finally suggests, "that the concept of 'Christian philosophy' today may be neither obsolete nor contradictory—nor without a future."[11]

K.H.

The Marches of Metaphysics

Remain the celestial, the one killed . . .

—René Char

§1. The Idol

It remains, then, to question. To question a statement before debating its validity, before invalidating or affirming it. More than deciding whether or not "God is dead," I will ask, perhaps with greater reason and profit, under what conditions the statement "God is dead" becomes, or remains, thinkable. If what one names "God" passes into the emptiness of a death at a given point in the history of thought, let us say, to be simple, when a "madman" proclaims it to a public who hears nothing (and laughs), in the second half of a century that is numbered the nineteenth since the life, death, and (for some) resurrection of Jesus, the Christ, then that "God," from the very first, was not one. For a "God" who can die harbors already, even when he is not yet dying, such a weakness that from the outset he falls short of the idea that we cannot not form of a "God." And is it not the least of courtesies that he should satisfy a propaedeutic concept, even if it is only our own? A "God" who decides to die dies from the beginning, since he undoubtedly needs a beginning—which means that the "death of God" sets forth a contradiction: that which dies does not have any right to claim, even when it is alive, to be "God." What is it that dies in the "death of God" if not that which could not in any case merit the name of "God"? And therefore the "death of God" expresses, beyond the death of "God," the death of that which announces it: the death of the "death of God" itself. The contradiction of the terms of the proposition comes to completion in the self-erasure of the proposition: it renders null and void that which it states by annulling the object of the statement. Nevertheless, the statement still has meaning and pertinence, and we are

41

not done meditating on it. Might not the argumentation that here denounces a sophism be itself, par excellence, sophistic, avoiding the true and fundamental question with a formal remark? Let us start again then. In order to establish an atheism in the modern sense of the term, that is, a doctrine that denies existence to any "supreme Being" (or the like), one requires a demonstration, and a rigorous one. One requires, therefore, a conceptual thinking that is compelling. And thus a concept of "God" is necessary here, a concept that would enter into the demonstration to provide the ultimate point on which it rests. It does not matter whether that concept is negative or positive, whether it issues from this or that cultural sphere, provided that it ensure a rigorous—that is, a defined—object for the demonstration. In its conclusion of exclusion, that demonstration is worth as much as the concept of "God" that sustains it. The reasoning of a conceptual atheism, which is the only compelling one, proceeds hypothetically: if "God" is x, while x is y (contradictory, illusory, dangerous, unhealthy, alienating, etc.), then "God" is y; therefore, if y suffices to disqualify that which it connotes (and we admit this), "God is dead." This calls for two remarks. First, that atheism, conceptual of course, is only ever valid as far as the concept of "God" that it mobilizes extends. For the demonstration that refutes "God" demands from him one last service: to furnish the object that supports and nourishes the refutation. If, then, "God" covers a particular semantic terrain, the refutation will not eliminate God absolutely but only the meaning of God that its initial "God" offers to be disputed. In order to refute the Absolute absolutely, it would be necessary, as it would be, moreover, to demonstrate a nonexistence in general, to enumerate exhaustively all the possible concepts of "God," in order to rely on them to the point of rejecting them all. Conceptual atheism becomes rigorous only by remaining regional. Thus can it ceaselessly reproduce itself and find new faces for itself. Thus can it progress without ever extinguishing, even for the one who practices it, even the hint of a question of God, as a question of the indeterminate itself—let us say, of the Ab-solute. Thus, finally, can the "believer" practice conceptual atheism just as well as the unbeliever: as a rigorous atheist with respect to a particular idea of God, the one who pronounces that atheism does not claim to decide on the Ab-solute. Atheism remains demonstrative by recognizing itself to be circumscribed. It is an atheism that is indefinitely duplicated because rigorously finite.

Next, one notices the unevenness of conceptual atheism, or rather the metamorphosis of the concept that sustains it. Before the demonstration, the concept "God" neither permits nor mobilizes a refutation unless it attains, in one way or another, God, whether the true God or the supposedly such. It is necessary that the concept merit the attention of a polemic—in a word, that "God" be God. But at its end, the completed demonstration takes away from the initial concept of "God" any usefulness ("God is dead"); consequently, the final disqualification springs back retroactively upon the original point on which it rests; if one has demonstrated that "God" does not hold, in what way has one touched God? In fact, in order to conclude, the reasoning must destroy the point on which it rests; but then it concludes nothing, unless that the initial point of support in fact ensured no support at all for the demonstration. The rigor of the conclusion is paid for by the rigor of the condition: "God" is dead only if "God" can die, that is, if in the first place it was not a question, in the demonstration, of God. This reasoning highlights the contradiction of its object only by showing the emptiness of its success: only the shadow of God, "God," remains prey to it. The prey rewards it only with a skin. The demonstration locates, enumerates, and authenticates shadows, which in return disqualifies it: the more the demonstration triumphs over so many indefinitely pursued "Gods," the more it betrays the emptiness of the self-critical procedure that both qualifies and disqualifies it. Conceptual atheism remains rigorous only by remaining not only regional but irrelevant. The collapse through self-critique projects it, moreover, into the repetition of the critique. The path of regional critiques ensues, quite logically, from the unavoidable self-critique that concludes each of them. Atheism progresses with each of the concepts of "God" that its self-falsification aims at, invests, and rejects. Progress belongs to conceptual atheism as intimately as suicidal humility characterizes it. Hence its indispensable theological function, as we shall see, and the respect that it is suitable to show it.

But there remains, or there appears, an objection. Why suppose there to be a contradiction in the sentence "God is dead"? Further, why would the contradiction not be the sign of another rigor, that of the tautological and abstract identity "God is God?" Answer: there is no answer; the objection holds completely. But precisely, it holds only on certain conditions, among which are the following: that one renounce conceptual atheism in order to think death and contradiction on the basis of "God," that is, that one renounce the defined security of the quotation marks: that instead of forming a concept-object of "God," upon which to operate a refutation without any risk other than suicidal, one admit that God, by undefinable definition, remains problematic enough that no concept, not even those of death, contradiction, and "God," is sufficient to reform him as incapable of supporting or reinvesting them. In this case God becomes the center of a discourse that orders itself in relation to him, and that understands itself, modifies itself, even overcomes itself, so as to put itself in a position to overcome this last atheistic presupposition: that "God" is defined as one who does not resist death: Would it not be the case that conceptual atheism becomes rigorously conclusive only by ceasing to operate on "God" in order to begin asking itself about God? Would it not manage to do this only by undertaking to confront openly, without the ghostly and finite intermediaries that it domesticates so easily, God as a question? Perhaps. And all the more so insofar as those who meditated on the "death of God" most decisively—Hegel, Hölderlin, Nietzsche, Heidegger, and a few others (among whom Feuerbach is not)—read in that pronouncement something completely other than a refutation of (the existence of) God. They recognized in it the paradoxical but radical manifestation of the divine. We will be able to follow them "from afar" (Luke 22:54) only on condition, first, that we not confuse the death of "God" with the question of God, or more exactly, the "death of God" with the "twilight of the idols."

From God (*Gott*) to the idol (*Götze*), barely one letter is substituted: the last one. The gap that it manifests should become questionable for us: *z/x*, so to speak. Why the idol here? In order to perceive it, and to specify that upon which a crepuscular light today falls, it is necessary to outline the function, or rather the functioning, of the idol. This presupposes to begin with a certain reservation concerning not the idol but indeed the overly easy critique that one commonly gives of it. The idol does not personify the god, and consequently it does not deceive the worshipper who does not see the god in person in it. Quite to the contrary, the worshipper knows himself to be the artisan who has worked with metal, wood, or stones to the point of offering the god an image to be seen (εἴδωλων) so that the god should consent to take on a face in it. The divine does not produce the idol and does not show up as an idol. The worshipper is perfectly aware that the god does not coincide with the idol. What, then, does the worshipper worship in the idol? The face that the god, or rather the divine, wants to find in it. More exactly, perhaps, what man, in the city or community, experiences as divine, as the divinity that precedes any face and any image. Man becomes religious by preparing a face for the divine: he takes it upon himself to fashion the face, and then to ask the divine to invest it, as radically as possible, so as to become his god. Who can decide on the authenticity of the divine that is thus envisaged in the idol? Who can disqualify the form wherein humanity archaically outlines its silhouette in order, like the χοῦρος, to give to the divine the principal form of Apollo? Who can deny that the chosen divinity remains in what is delimited by the columns, pediments, and spacings of a Doric temple? Iconoclastic crudeness sometimes overturns idols because it does not understand them, or more, does not see them, is it necessary, however, to receive the idol as a correct face of the divinity? Without any doubt, but on condition that the nature of such a divinity be evaluated. It falls to man to experience and establish it. In the idol the human experience of the divine precedes the face that that divinity assumes in it. We experience ourselves at our best in the divine. We fashion a face in order to ask the divine to open up in it, to look at us in it, to smile and to threaten. The idol must fix the distant and diffuse divinity and assure us of its presence, of its power, of its availability. Just as our experience precedes the face of the divine, so our vital interest proceeds from it: the idol fixes the divine for us permanently, for a commerce where the human hems in the divine from all angles. What is peculiar to the idol, therefore, has to do with this: the divine is fixed in it on the basis of the experience of the divine that is had by man, who, by relying on the idol's mediation, attempts to attract the benevolence and the protection of what appears in it as a god. The idol presupposes neither the trickery of the priest nor the stupidity of the crowd (as certain biblical authors repeatedly agree, as well as do, beyond the Fathers, including Augustine, Bayle, Fontenelle, and Voltaire). It is characterized solely by the subjection of the divine to the human conditions for experience of the divine, concerning which nothing proves that it is not authentic. The human experience of the divine precedes the idolatrous face. The idolatrous face elaborated by man precedes its investiture by the god. In the idol the divine undoubtedly assumes the actual face of a god. But that god takes its form from the features that we have fashioned for it, in conformity with what we actually experience concerning the divine. In the cases of life and death, of peace and war, of love and drunkenness, of spirit and beauty, we indisputably experience the irrepressible and panic capital of the divine, and we decipher or divine therein faces that we model in order that we might fix so many gods in them. These gods, therefore, conform first to us, or, less summarily, to the modalities of our multiform perception of the divine. The idol reflects back to us, in the face of a god, our own experience of the divine. The idol does not resemble us, but it resembles the divinity that we experience, and it gathers it in a god in order that we might see it. The idol does not deceive; it apprehends the divinity. It apprehends the divinity, and, even when it terrorizes, it reassures by identifying the divinity in the face of a god. Hence its prodigious political effectiveness: it renders close, protective, and faithfully sworn the god who, identifying himself with the city, maintains an identity for it. This is indeed why politics always gives rise to idols, even after paganism; "Big Brother," the "Great Helmsman," the *Führer*, or the "Man we love best" must be divinized: made into gods, they conjure the divine or, more vulgarly, destiny. Idolatry gives the cult of personality its true dignity—that of a familiar, tamed (and therefore undangerously terroristic) figure of the divine. Idolatrous temptation for ancient Israel always depended on political necessities. Conversely, it is to politics first that our time owes the fact that we are not lacking for new idols.

The idol therefore delivers us the divine, wherefore it neither deceives nor disappoints. It delivers the divine to us to the point of enslaving it to us, just as much as it enslaves us to it. The contract that the idol draws up subsidizes the absence of the gods. It is to that very familiarity that one must attribute the disappearance of the sacred and of polytheism, which the late seventeenth century definitively censures: twilight of the divine. Perhaps more surely than any rationalist and/or Christian critique, an overabundant and polymorphous deification annihilated the play of the idol, of the divine, and of the gods. In fact, what the idol works to reabsorb is, precisely, the distance and the withdrawal of the divine: but by establishing such an availability of the divine within the fixed, if not frozen, face of the god, does one not deceitfully but radically eliminate the lofty irruption and the undeniable alterity that properly attest the divine? Subsidizing the absence of the divine, the idol makes the divine available, secures it, and in the end distorts it. Its culmination mortally finishes the divine. The idol attempts to bring us close to the divine and to appropriate it to us: because he fears atheism (in the original sense: being deserted by the gods),[1] the worshipper puts his hand on the divine in the form of a god; but that handling loses what it seizes: there remains to it but an amulet that is too well known, too manipulable, too secure. Everything is set up to allow a Feuerbachian reappropriation of the divine: since, like a mirror, the god reflects back to me my experience of the divine, why not reappropriate for myself what I attribute to the reflection of my own activity? The inversion of the attribution of attributes (a reversed exchange of properties) presupposes that the latter are taken in the same way for both the god and the worshiper. Such a univocity presupposes in its turn that no distance keeps the idol outside of my reach. I attribute to myself the properties of the divine only if properties can be common both to me and to the divine—that is, only if the divine always already belongs to my sphere, as an idol that is close and, for that very reason, vain. Considering the divine as "prey to be captured" (Paul, Philippians 2:6), the idol lacks the distance that identifies and authenticates the divine as such—as what does not belong to us but befalls us. To the idol, by counterpoint, answers the icon. Whose face does the icon offer? "Icon of the invisible God" (Colossians 1:15), says Saint Paul of Christ. It is the figure not of a God who in that figure would lose its invisibility in order to become known to us to the point of familiarity, but of a Father who radiates with a definitive and irreducible transcendence all the more insofar as he unreservedly gives that transcendence to be seen in his Son. The depth of the visible face of the Son delivers to the gaze the invisibility of the Father as such. The icon manifests neither the human face nor the divine nature that no one could envisage but, as the theologians of the icon said, the relation of the one to the other in the hypostasis, the person.[2] The icon conceals and reveals that upon which it rests: the separation in it between the divine and its face. Visibility of the invisible, a visibility where the invisible gives itself to be seen as such, the icon reinforces the one through the other. The separation that joins them in their very irreducibility finally constitutes the ground of the icon. *Distance*, which it is above all no longer a question of abolishing, but of recognizing, becomes the motif of vision, in the double sense of motif: a motivation and a figurative theme. The topology of the mirror, where the idol reflected back to us the authentic but closed image of *our* experience of the divine, is replaced by the typology of the prism: a multiplicity of colors breaks down, or rather orchestrates, that which a prism multiplies according to our power to see—light called white (which it is not) since it remains invisible at the very moment that it renders all things visible. We should remark that in the art of the icon, the codified colors (gold, red, blue, yellow, etc.) do not resemble any "thing" that is supposed to be intrinsically colored thus; their significance is affirmed within a purely semiotic (in this case liturgical) field, where they announce eternity, divinity, glory, humanity, etc. The colors serve in no way as signs of visible things that one would have to give to be seen, because they already are so (to reproduce). They signal from the visible to the irreducible invisibility that it is a question of producing, of making advance into the visible inasmuch as invisible. The icon properly manifests the nuptial distance that weds, without confusing, the visible and the invisible—that is, the human and the divine. The idol tries to abolish that distance through the availability of the god who is placed permanently within the fixity of a face. The icon preserves and highlights that distance in the invisible depth of an insurpassable and open figure. For the point of view of desire, and therefore of the idolatrous object, as opposed to a god whose insistence one both fears and hopes for at the same time, a god that makes itself a little too pressing and that one can thus lead in one's own way, the icon substitutes a sort of negative theophany: the figure remains authentically insurpassable (norm, self-reference) only in that it opens in its depths upon an invisibility whose distance it does not abolish but reveals.

Hence a question: can the dialectic of atheism, and of the concept that supports but disqualifies it, have any decisive relation with the idol? As idol, the concept arranges a presence of the divine without distance, in a god who reflects back to us our experience or thought, with enough familiarity that we always master its play. It is always a question of keeping the foreignness of the divine out of play through the idolatrous filter of the concept or through the facelike conception of an idol. It is just such a function of the concept of "God" that we must now clarify. From there another question could arise: could not the concept function, also and first, as icon, in the sense that, just as the icon offers the figure of the invisible, "words are not the translation of something else that was there before them"[3] (L. Wittgenstein) but the very pronouncement of what remains at the same time forever ineffable?

§2. The "God" of Onto-Theology

Thus, one could interpret the concept, or rather concepts, of "God" as idols, or rather as agents of what the idol, for its part, also brings about—the making available of the divine in a face, which one names the god. Therefore, the philosopher or, better, the metaphysician names the divine: he fixes it as ἰδεα τοῦ ἀγάθου (Plato), as νοήσεως νόησις (Aristotle), as the One (Plotinus). He introduces between the divine, or later the God of Jesus Christ, and naming a simple, banal—and formidable—equals sign; he will speak, like Kant, for example, of the "existence of a moral founder of the world, *that is to say* of God."[4] There is no difficulty in the fact that such a concept might be established by the philosopher as playing the role of a foundation or of a principle of the divine; or, if there is a difficulty, it concerns only the philosopher and his own effort at thinking. That at the end of the demonstration, once the divine has been rigorously identified in a particular concept (once the "proof for the existence of God" has been completed, as one says, or used to say), the philosopher should surreptitiously identify, as if obviously and easily, *this* concept of the divine with something or someone indicated by *God*—this would find confirmation only if God himself confirmed the identification, in short, the question of the existence of God is posed less before the proof than at its end, when it is no longer a question simply of establishing that some concept can be called *God*, nor even that a certain being puts that name into operation, but more radically that that concept or that being coincides with God himself. Thus the five ways that Saint Thomas traces out do not lead absolutely to God; the first leads to the first mover and, once the demonstration has ended, must add innocently, in passing, "and everyone understands this to be God"; the second leads to the first efficient cause, of which it is still necessary to specify that "everyone names it God"; the third leads to the cause of a necessity, which it is still necessary to identify as "what everyone says to be God"; the fourth recognizes a cause of perfection but must also admit that "we say that it is God"; the fifth, finally, indeed locates a final end but must also underline that "we say that it is God."[5] Question: who states the equivalence between the ultimate term at which the demonstration—and therefore rational discourse—ends and the God whom "all" recognize? "All," no doubt, but by what right? Who are these "all," and why can they establish an equivalence that neither the theologian nor the philosopher grounds, but upon which they ground themselves? Upon what foundation does the discourse here rest so as to assimilate to a God outside of all discourse the concepts of first, unmoved mover, efficient cause, necessity, perfection, and end? One might respond, perhaps, that with Thomas Aquinas the saint also speaks, that the religious man mobilizes authorities that are other than conceptual, that the philosopher finally appeals to theology (and here, precisely, to the doctrine of divine names that Question XIII will examine). These correct remarks support the Thomistic procedure only by rendering it even more questionable: one therefore needs an authority external to the proof in order that the proof become a "way" that leads to the referent that remains outside of all discourse and properly other (divine). The conceptual discourse admits that it does not produce that authority, since it reaches its ultimate result only through the ungrounded parenthetical phrase of a "that is to say" that is all the less evident insofar as is given as such. When other recourses disappear (such as the *sensus Ecclesiae*, theology as such, holiness), when the consensus of "all" is replaced by the idiomatic phrase "by this I mean . . ." who will still be able to guarantee the well-foundedness of the equivalence between a probing discourse and its beyond? When Malebranche posits that "By divinity we mean infinity,

Being without restriction, infinitely perfect Being,"[6] he hardly says more, and perhaps even less, than Descartes—"By the name of God, I mean a certain infinite, independent, supremely intelligent, supremely powerful substance"[7]—and than Spinoza—"By God, I mean an absolutely infinite being, that is, a substance made up of infinite attributes."[8] The coincidence of a consensus is now replaced by a perhaps simply nominal definition that attempts to hem in the irreducible Other with a verbal infinity. Properly speaking, what affinity remains between the already supreme being and the phantom-like silhouette that is woven by infinities that are redoubled infinitely in a perhaps meaningless inflation? The closer the concept comes that holds the place of the divine, the more its claim to take its place becomes suspect. When, crowning this labor, Hegel finally states what thought had been aiming at since the ruin of the theories of analogy, and postulates that revealed religion is identical with manifest religion, because "the divine nature is the same (*dasselbe*) as human nature, and that very unity is what needs to be taken into view,"[9] he perhaps indicates the supreme proximity of the divine only by carrying to its highest point the suspicion that the divine, here, coincided with the human only inasmuch as it was never distinguished from it, and never offered anything other than its image reflected by infinity. Feuerbach will do nothing other than formulate this suspicion. The irreducible gap between the final concept anti the first approach of God never shone forth as much as with the identification of "God" with the discourse of proof. It does not suffice arbitrarily to baptize that last concept, at the price of a play on words (*Geist*, for example), or a falsely evident equivalence ("that is"), in order for thought to reach, in addition to its proof, what that proof aims at—the divine, or even God himself. Everything happens as if thought led easily, rigorously, and demonstratively to a final concept so as to grasp in it that which takes the place of God: a conceptual Tantalus. The proximity of the idol masks and marks the flight of the divine, and of the separation that authenticates it. By excessively appropriating "God" to itself through proof, thought separates itself from separation, misses distance, and finds itself one morning surrounded by idols, by concepts, and by proofs, but abandoned by the divine—atheistic. Hence, in this sense, the radically atheistic pronouncement of metaphysics, that of Leibniz: "Thus it is necessary that sufficient Reason, which has no need of another Reason, be outside this succession of contingent things, and be found in a substance, which is a cause, or which is a necessary Being, carrying within itself the reason for its existence; otherwise one would not yet have a sufficient reason in which one might finish. And it is this final reason for things that is called God."[10] In what way can sufficient reason, as final reason (*ultima ratio*) made substance, in a word, as the hypostasis of the principle of reason, that is, of the principle of our comprehension of all beings, claim, as little as that might be, to identify itself with God? If it does claim to do this, in what way does that claim avoid interposing an idolatrous face between the divine separation and the human gaze? If it does claim to do so, as it seems to, in the name of what rigor does it produce such a conceptual idol?

It would be necessary to think here, as much as a summary thought can claim to, of what Heidegger renders comprehensible under the title of the onto-theological constitution of metaphysics. Where until now I have written "philosopher," it was in fact necessary to understand "thinker of metaphysics." The production of a concept that makes a claim to equivalence with God indeed pertains to metaphysics. For the question of knowing how God enters into philosophy is decided, in the sense that Heidegger proceeds, only on the basis of philosophy itself, on condition, however, that we understand philosophy in its essence, namely, in its historial face as metaphysics. Metaphysics thinks Being, but in its own way. It does not cease to think it, but only on the basis of the beings that Being sets forth or in which Being puts itself into play.[11] Thus Being, which coincides with no being (ontological difference), nevertheless gives itself to be thought only in the case of a being. Indeed, being declines in a substantive manner a neuter participle (ὄν) that is governed, if one is vigilant to it, by the verbality that thus undertakes to be, that is, to let be. The same ὄν wavers between a being (a "thing") and an undertaking to be, only in that first and more fundamentally ὄν conjoins, composes, and unfolds these two operations, or, if one will, these two interpretations, as one and the same. What Heidegger thus designates as unfolding, refolding, and fold, metaphysics ends up understanding in its own way, which means not understanding it as such; thus, it privileges beings in their Being, more than Being, which no being reifies and which, nevertheless, promotes each being. Metaphysics deploys this privilege of beings in and over their Being in two ways. First, by thinking, in the mode of the question that opens Book Z of Aristotle's *Metaphysics*, ὄν as οὐσία, essence, or, if one will, even substance,[12] but especially the privilege of presence over the other temporalizations of time (which "past" and "future" no longer give, since they are ordered on the basis of the present). This privilege delivers Being in presence, and in the beings that spring from it, but it also annuls Being in it. Thus, since a being, inasmuch as present, presents the achievement of Being, Being manifests itself all the more (verbally) insofar as a being presently (substantially) remains the place of presence. Hence, second, the movement to the supreme being. The supreme being in its turn delivers the most present figure of presence, which alone permits each—non-supreme-being to remain already. The supreme being in this sense, exemplarily, grounds each being in its Being, since Being plays fully in it as presence. But conversely, that supreme being itself finds its ground only in the present beingness in which Being is bound up and expressed. If Being did not announce itself in presence, the supreme being would exercise no foundational decision concerning other beings. This reciprocal play between the Being of beings in general (ontology, general metaphysics) and the supreme being (special metaphysics, theology) does not define the onto-theological constitution of metaphysics but results from it and, in a sense, marks its profound conciliation (*Austrag*, as Heidegger says): "The onto-theological constitution of metaphysics proceeds from the superior power of Difference, which holds separated one from another, and related one to another (*aus- und zueinanderhält*), Being as ground and beings as what is rationally grounded and grounding (*als gegründet-begründendes*)."[13] The reciprocity of beings in their Being and of the supreme being is constituted in their relation of mutual grounding. The supreme being gives the reason for beings in their Being, but thereby shows Being at work, including and first in itself. In this play—engendered characteristically by metaphysics—the supreme being is called upon only to ensure the foundation; making the theology of onto-theology culminate on this point, Leibniz will say in order to "give reason" in "carrying the reason for its existence within itself." It can give the reason for beings in an absolutely satisfactory (sufficient) manner only by giving the reason for itself by itself. Thereby, it does not so much attain ontic independence as manifest its radical dependence with regard to onto-theology, which gives rise to and finds in it the *ultima ratio* that it needs in order to give the reason for (in the sense that one gives up one's arms) other beings infinitely multiplied by their finitude. Thus, "The Being of beings, in the sense of ground, can be represented fundamentally only as *causa sui*. But that is to name the metaphysical concept of God. Metaphysics must think far ahead in the direction of God, because Being is the business of thought, but Being taken in the multiple ways of foundation: as λόγος, as ὑποχείμενον, as substance, as subject." "Conciliation puts Being forward to us and confers it upon us as the ground that brings and presents, a ground that itself needs a rational grounding (*Begründung*) appropriate to it on the basis of what it itself rationally grounds, that is, on the basis of a causation (*Verursachung*) by the most primordial thing (*ursprünglichste Sache*). Which is the cause (*Ursache*) as *causa sui*. Thus sounds, in the measure of that which is in question, the name that God has in philosophy."[14] Descartes's thinking, which is the first to think God as *causa sui* on the basis of the exuberance of his power, finds in Leibniz its authentic metaphysical status. The supreme being, provoked by the onto-theological constitution of metaphysics, completes its grounding-in-reason, which is its sole raison d'être (the supreme being), only by becoming an absolute ground, a ground that grounds itself. Metaphysics does not attain and does not conceive the divine, the gods, and still less God, for themselves, but it meets them as if by accident, along the detour (sometimes experienced brutally by the two parties) of a process that goes from the ἀκρότατον ὄν to the *causa sui*—which means that "the theological character of ontology does not have to do with the fact that Greek metaphysics was later taken up and transformed by the ecclesial theology of Christianity. It has much rather to do with the manner in which being, from the beginning, is un-concealed (*entborgen*) as being"; "God can enter into philosophy only in the measure that the latter, of itself and in conformity with its essence, demands that, and specifies how, God enters into it."[15] The supreme being of metaphysics, which culminates in the figure of the *causa sui*, depends fundamentally on the very essence of metaphysics and, finally, on nothing other. Moreover, this is why the supreme being, and with it an onto-theological constitution, remains the same where God, as Christian, disappears. One could show this easily for Feuerbach (M. Stirner did it, in the case of B. Bauer); one has already tried to show it for Marx; as for Nietzsche, Heidegger himself indicated it in a central manner (§§4–6). This, moreover, is why Plato, Aristotle, and Plotinus did not await Christianity in order to put the onto-theological constitution into operation. The supreme being, whatever it may be, belongs to metaphysics and finds in it alone its rigor, its scope, and its limits.

Hence a directive for thought that is absolutely decisive for my argument. The *causa sui* is theologically valid only in onto-theology, where it masters the divine function and uses it at the very moment that it reveres it. The characteristics of the idol are equally suitable for a "God" who serves as ground, but himself receives a ground; a God who expresses supremely the Being of beings in general and, in this sense, reflects back to them a faithful image of that whereby they are and of that which they are supremely; a God who remains distant from common ontology only within a Conciliation (*Austrag*) that preserves a fundamental familiarity. Produced by and for onto-theology, this "God" is ordained by it like the idol by the city (unless the political game of the idol refers back, conversely, to onto-theology)—with this slight difference that the idol here remains conceptual: not only does it not refer back, like the icon, to the invisible, but it does not even any longer offer any face where the divine looks at us and gives itself to be stared at: "To this God man cannot pray or offer anything, nor can he fall before him in respect, nor play music or dance. Consistent with this, atheistic thought [*gott-lose* in the Pauline sense], which must abandon the God of the philosophers, God as *causa sui*, is perhaps closer to the divine God. Which means only this: the latter is more freely open than onto-theology would like to believe."[16] It would perhaps be necessary to admit that another path remains open—that which would attempt to envisage, as concerns the divine, another figure than the onto-theological "God." And it would perhaps be necessary to admit therefore that the death of such a "God" does not close that other path or affect the possibility of keeping oneself open for the divine *Wesen* (as Heidegger says, we shall see, in the case of Nietzsche, in § 4). How should we proceed in order to reach that opening? It would be a little too visibly facile to oppose a "true" God to the "God" of onto-theology since, in fact, for us, the one and the other are historially imbricated. Perhaps it would be necessary first to keep silent: "Whoever has any experience of theology taken in its developed completion, whether it be the theology of Christian faith or, just as well, that of philosophy, prefers today to keep silent, as soon as he approaches the domain of the thought of God."[17] But in order to keep silent, it is not enough no longer to be able to say anything, nor even no longer to speak at all. To keep silent is first to reach the site where the speech that states and discourses is no longer acceptable. Onto-theology, precisely, does not allow us to reach that site, since it does not cease, even and especially in the time of triumphant atheism, to force-feed us with ever more supreme beings (and grammar must then suffer much worse than the reduplication of the superlative). When it is a question of God, one must deserve even one's silence. That is why Heidegger elaborates elsewhere what he here calls "keeping silent." He elaborates it in relation to Saint Paul and Paul's effort to designate another discourse (and therefore a silence) than that of the Greeks, and therefore of philosophy. It is

> this uncovering of beings that first made it possible for Christian theology to grab hold of Greek philosophy—to its profit or to its loss is up to the theologians to decide—on the basis of the experience of Christianness (*des Christlichen*), inasmuch as they meditate on what is written in Saint Paul's first letter to the Corinthians: οὐχὶ ἐμώρασεν ὁ θεὸς τὴν σοφίαν τοῦ κόσμου, Has not God convicted the wisdom of the world of folly? (I Corinthians 1:20). Now, the σοφία τοῦ κόσμου is that which, according to 1:22, the ἕλληνες ζητοῦσιν, what the Greeks seek. Aristotle very explicitly calls the πρώτη ʾλοσοφία (philosophy properly speaking) ζητουμένη—sought after. Will Christian theology decide yet again to take seriously the word of the Apostle, and, consistently with this, to take seriously that philosophy is folly?[18]

To take seriously that philosophy is a folly means, for us, first (although not exclusively) taking seriously that the "God" of onto-theology is rigorously equivalent to an idol, that which is presented by the Being of beings thought metaphysically; and therefore it means that the seriousness of God cannot begin to appear and grab hold of us unless, through a radical reversal, we claim to advance outside of onto-theology. One should give us credit for being fully aware that this undertaking is a folly and a danger, pretension, and vanity. It is not a question, as with everyone, of "overcoming metaphysics," but of at least posing the question correctly: does the onto-theological idol, triumphant, or ruined (it does not matter here), close all access to the icon of God as "icon of the *invisible* God"? According to a well-grounded appearance, Heidegger does not here indicate how to accomplish the step back outside of the idol toward the icon. The text from the apostle Paul, which he cites against a theology that is too accommodating toward onto-theological σοφία, says, however, one word more: to the folly that one must take seriously there corresponds a λόγος that is foreign to onto-theologic, the λόγος τοῦ σταροῦ (1:18), that of the cross—of the cross where the Word was crucified. On the cross the Word kept silent, but in that way another paradoxical light manifested itself, an *other* discourse. Perhaps it would be necessary to attempt with this discourse to take onto-theology up again from the place where we are. We undoubtedly cannot get out of it, as if one could pass through the idolatrous mirror, nor can we recede back toward a conceptual state of nature that no history would have marked irremediably. There remains, therefore, only one path: to travel through onto-theology itself all along its limits—its marches. The marches do not only delimit a territory, like borders. They defend it, like a glacis, a line of fortifications. They also surround it, an already foreign territory, exposed to danger, half unknown. To take onto-theology tangentially, from the angle of its lines of defense, and thus to expose oneself to what already no longer belongs to it: this will be our way of entering conceptually into the seriousness of a folly, of the folly that aims at the icon and rejects the idol.

§3. Discourse to the Athenians

To recognize onto-theology as having marches presupposes to begin with—this will be our first presupposition—that onto-theology is admitted as the constitution of metaphysics. In fact, it could perfectly well not be. But this first assumption is not enough. Several indications of exteriority can be envisaged that pass beyond onto-theology. First, the "overcomings" that, in effect, rid themselves (or so they think) of the very terms of the question; I shall attempt not to founder in any such triviality. Next, the properly philosophical meditation on the metaphysical primacy of presence in temporalization, and therefore also of the onto-theological constitution; that meditation, which Heidegger pursued from *Sein und Zeit* all the way to *Zeit und Sein*, remains within the field of philosophy, or it seems to. I shall come back to this below (§ 17). There remains a final way of proceeding, which questions onto-theology not starting from its interior limit but, as they say, starting from the outside edge of the limit, that which opens immediately upon the foreign: with a view to a non-onto-theological theology. Let us clarify the ultimate presupposition: must one exclude that the λόγος τοῦ σταροῦ, still functions as a λόγος even though, or because it pertains to the Cross, whose folly convicts the wisdom that the Greeks seek of folly? Can this logic be approached by a discourse and offer the support for it? Does this discourse put into play a fundamental position other than onto-theology and the idol of "God" as supreme being? I will try to see how, in fact, other constellations rise in other skies: thus distance, the Father, withdrawal, filial abandon, the traverse of distance. It goes without saying that this elucidation cannot be sketched out polemically. Whoever claims to jump outside of onto-theology in one leap is exposed to the danger of repeating it, by a slight, naively critical inversion. Distance shall become inchoatively intelligible to us only if we discover it starting from onto-theology itself and from its most identifiable state. Distance plays within onto-theology from the beginning, like air, water, and time make the best-tuned woodwinds play: in order to make them explode and/or adapt themselves to daily use. It is therefore necessary to take onto-theology obliquely, not head-on: because no thought can or wants to absorb it, distance remains present to onto-theology, concealed, superimposed. Any metaphysician, if he is among the greatest, maintains, within onto-theology, an oblique relation to it. Distance works him as unbeknownst to him. I shall not be ridiculous enough to "critique" Nietzsche (a ridiculousness almost as great as the claim to "explain" him) on the basis, for example, of the theology revealed by the New Testament. I shall attempt—which appears to me infinitely more risky, decisive, and respectful—to take Nietzsche into view starting from distance. It will therefore be a question, for anyone who admits, like I do, the insurpassable primacy of Christian revelation, to take Nietzsche, the last metaphysician, into view starting from distance, in order no longer to find a Nietzschean position of Christianity, but, following Heidegger's injunction, in order to assign onto-theology to a position of "folly" starting from Christ and Christianity, as the "folly/discourse of the Cross." Can one take onto-theology into view starting from what, in Christianity, might escape it? Once again, it is not a question of critique, nor of recuperation, nor of an inversion of the terms of our reading. It is not a matter of questioning Christianity starting from onto-theology, but of sketching out a perspective on onto-theology—in its Nietzschean culmination—starting from the Christianity made manifest by the apocalypse of Christ. Nietzsche deserves more and, ironically, expected more from his readers than a hagiography that is steeped in piety or packed with polemic and that undoubtedly obscures profoundly the true stakes of what he had to say. Just as one (Heidegger) uncovered a relation between Nietzsche and metaphysics that is more decisive and intimate than the simple critique of "Platonism," so it remains (because of Heidegger's work) to glimpse that his relation to the question of the divine and of Christ is more decisive and intimate than a banal declaration of "atheism." Far from blunting onto-theology and the height to which he carries it, to read Nietzsche starting from Christianity—its march—would perhaps be one of the least unworthy homages.

By way of the Nietzschean threshold, I shall enter into commerce with other border territories of onto-theology: Hölderlin and Denys the Areopagite. This calls for three remarks. This choice reflects an inexcusable, irremediable, but undoubtedly unavoidable arbitrariness. I shall therefore not remedy that arbitrariness by adding some motif to the sequence: the same question seemed to me to traverse these figures—that which is formulated here, according to the naming that I brought it, by *distance*: a distance outside of onto-theology for Nietzsche, a filially received distance of the presence of a God who is paternally in withdrawal for Hölderlin, and a distance traversed liturgically toward the Requisite by the discourse of praise of requestants for Denys. In all of these cases, the indisputably apparent absence of the divine becomes the very center of a questioning concerning its manifestation. Each in his own way, they all recognize that absence, or that withdrawal, as the task of thinking that properly falls to them. My undertaking therefore aims at nothing other than to allow them to speak symphonically, without summoning them in a police-like fashion to a question that would remain foreign to them. Or rather, the distance of God was born for me as from their successive, diverse, unexpected—and harmonically fortuitous— insistences. It is they who summoned my attention and gave rise to the unique question that now, apparently, summons them. My path shall often seem arbitrary. The cavalier alacrity of certain "interpretations" (the quotation marks indicating, by understatement, the mistranslations or the misinterpretations) shall seem violent, and even not very serious or objective, to the specialists of Nietzsche, Hölderlin, and Denys. One might even be surprised by the little attention paid to the very important secondary literature dedicated to these authors. To this there are several responses. Having myself the role, elsewhere and sometimes here, of the specialist, I share in advance certain indignations, and I can only accept them, since elsewhere I permit myself similar ones. That said, one must not confuse the silences that a fragmentary essay can or must allow itself with the massive ignorances that I have attempted to sweep away, and that others have helped me to make up for. One must also ask whether objectivity would be in place here: the very particular and precise point of view that guides me here—distance—often takes the finest and most exhaustive studies by surprise; above all, the thinkers gathered here could not be taken as the objects of a technical examination since they obviously command the questioning to which they gave rise. Perhaps the most direct possible approach to them—I do not mean the most naive—alone allows me not to lower them to the level of a text to be explicated or of a thesis to be decided. It is a matter here of nothing other than following as clearly as possible what Nietzsche, Hölderlin, and Denys can still give us to think with regard to distance.[19] My means had to comply with that urgency and that authority. This is the only excuse for their weaknesses. Finally, and conversely, why have I chosen these texts and not others? And moreover why texts? It is not so much a matter of explicating authors as it is of asking them to explicate the situation in which we find ourselves. All are in tune (like the strings of an instrument: in order to allow different sounds but with regulated differences) in helping us to think the idea that the "death of God" far from implying the disqualification of the question of God or of the divine, urgently restores the question of their panic, immediate and open confrontation. The disappearance of the onto-theological idol provokes, in concert, the frenetic search for a *corps à corps*, which one hopes to be sometimes nuptial, with the divine, in the disinherited madness of a sadistic insignificance. The unavoidable and mutely urgent task then becomes to learn that only separation can define approach, and withdrawal advent. What we here name distance attempts to apply itself to this. It therefore is not a matter, for me, of explicating authors, but of allowing them to instruct us about distance. The rupture of texts shall therefore be the sign of a doubly suitable incompleteness. This is so, first, because the arbitrariness of our choices and the insufficiency of our readings reflect, and issue from, the urgency of our task: "Some days, one should not be afraid of calling things impossible to describe" (R. Char).[20] I believed that those days had come. Next, this is so because distance presupposes the insufficiency of discourse: an ideological framework, a merely coherent group of theses, even a program of studies would definitively close access to distance, since distance implies withdrawal as a mode of advent, and it requires nonful-fillment as a decency with respect to discourse; would this not be the most elementary propriety, as well as the greatest audacity?

Hence the discourse to the Athenians. My own discourse does not in fact remain soli-tary, unheard of, or even original (originality, so recent an invention, claims to attest an author, while it relieves itself of an origin): it reproduces, I mean to say, it must try to rediscover, if it wants only to remain, the theological situation, the tactical disposition, and the crucial reversal of the discourse that the apostle Paul held on the Areopagus before the Athenians (Acts of the Apostles 17:16–34). First, the theological situation: Paul enters into a city (and therefore into a politics) that he (and he alone) sees to be "devoted to idols" (17:17). What idols? The discourse will later speak of idols "of gold, silver, stone, sculpture of art and of the human conception" (17:29)—thus, idols in the monumental sense of the term. But curiously, the mention of general idolatry is followed first by the enumeration of "those who find themselves passing by" (17:17), that is, beside the Jews and pagan worshippers, "some Epicurian and Stoic philosophers" (17:18). Everything happens as if the philosophers also came under the jurisdiction of idolatry—only having purified it, that is, having conceptualized it. Their "God" receives—as a supreme honor, but also as the price of its idolatrous compromise—a definition. The fact that here the "atheism" of the Epicurians is assimilated with the logical and physical "God" of the Sto-ics further confirms the conceptual idolatry. The Epicurians would benefit, in this sense, from a favorable prejudice—theologically speaking. Visible idolatry is no more refuted by substituting one image for another, than conceptual idolatry collapses before another concept of "God." It is effaced only before the absence of a concept, an absence that is definitive and that initiates another approach to God as the "unknown God" (1.7:23). Using the "unknown god" whose idol appeared among the mass of others—of the known gods, Paul does not undertake to reveal their until-then concealed identity. For if he declares that "I announce to you the one whom you worship without knowing him" and if he indeed announces the "God who made the world, and all that is in it" (17:24), this latter retrocedes not only from the world, but also from the understanding that measures the world and is finally; measured by the world: the Ab-solute. He is the Unthinkable, insofar as He reveals the distance of Goodness in the encounter of cre-ation, as Denys will say (§§ 13–14). The relation to God escapes the conceptualization in which we comprehend idols, in order to comprehend us, as incomprehensible. Hence the tactical disposition that one would have to be able to borrow from Paul. The incom-prehensible comprehends us because "In Him we live, we move, and we are": the Being of beings itself, like (Nietzschean?) "life" or (dialectical?) movement, which also name it in their own way, results from the incomprehensible; far from our attaining it, it comes to us, as one of the gifts of the Unthinkable. This means that the idols no longer mediate our relation to the "God," but we ourselves are immediately summoned to mediate the deformed relation of the idols to God. The place of the debate is displaced: naked, with unveiled face before the faceless God, we no longer look at him in an idolatrously pri-vileged face, but He first looks at us and looks after us under his invisible look. The invis-ible look of God summons us to see his very invisibility. In this sense "we are God's offspring" (17:29). The resemblance henceforth becomes the exposed place that mobilizes us for a mutual look: could God not annihilate us, in favor of an idol of man, as we missed him in the case of those idols that we indefinitely rejected? The confrontation with the "living" God, a terrible thing except for the one who happily ignores it, follows the collapse of the idols. "Who shall be able to stand it?" The *dies irae* terrorizes, first and fundamentally, because he uncovers to us the invisible face that looks at us and that no one can envisage. Thus Paul evokes the only imaginable face of the invisible, the risen Christ (17:31–32), "icon of the invisible God." It is at this precise moment—the essential moment—that the crowd draws aside and laughs (as it also laughs when the Nietzschean madman announces the inaudible and unheard of, that "God is dead"; see § 4). The tactics fail here, as do all tactics, rhetorics, or pragmatics as soon as it is a question of the essential. In the first letter to the Corinthians, Paul will replace the impossibility of making the invisible seen with the crucial reversal. That crucial reversal consists in beginning with the λόγος of the Cross, against the wisdom of the world, with the "folly of the kerygma" that "scandalizes," with the "crucified Christ" (see §2). Hence the direct passage to the icon, which the collapse of the idols does not suffice to receive or even to glimpse. Hence the direct contemplation of the "paradox of this face,"[21] of the envisigeable face of the Invisible, a paradox in the sense that "glory," and to begin with the "glory of God," gives itself to be seen at an angle, sideways, askew—in a word inverted (παρά–δόξον). For us, this means first that the journey through the idols, their collapse and the unthinkable that they deliver from another "great closing," could be completed only in the iconic face of Christ. It means, next, that the attention that will perhaps be paid to the beginning of my essay would then have to undergo, as the discourse to the Athenians requires, ironic or disdainful resistance when and each time that, paradoxically, the Christ will arise therein as the figure of revelation and as the only norm. The correctness of my argument will be verified, in a sense, only by its failure—provided that this be theological and not literary. Failure speaks, in its own way, as an adman and therefore with little importance, the crucial logic, or rather it inscribes discourse in that logic. But in this status failure remains as provisional as it is serious: for some nevertheless listened to Paul. Among them was a certain Denys, called the Areopagite, the very one whom the tradition wants to recognize, despite the gap of several centuries, in the author of the Dionysian corpus, and in whom that author wants one to recognize him.

Hence nothing could be more rigorous than to complete, with a reading of Denys, a text that the recollection of the discourse to the Athenians inaugurates—the one issues, as certainly as paradoxically, from the other. Thus I write for Denys, and those like him.

Double Idolatry

In homage to Maurice Clavel

1. The Function of the Idol

One would have to begin, of course, with a dialogue with Nietzsche, and with the mad-man of *Fröhliche Wissenschaft*, hence first by a more essential concept of the idol. This more essential concept of the idol, in fact, must be developed in such a way that it may rightly accommodate the intellectual representation of the divine and offer the framework of an interpretation, or better, of a reinterpretation, of the "death of God" One therefore must trace, at least in outline, the contours of a figure of the idol—figure the figure, sche-matize the schema. This redoubling, which comes quite naturally and as if inevitably to the pen, betrays in advance the fact that the idol summons the ambivalence of its domains of application, perceptible and intelligible, or rather "aesthetic" and conceptual.

Does figuring the idolatrous figure imply returning to it the caricature with which one so often reproached it for imposing on the divine? But the idol has nothing caricatu-ral, deceitful, or illusory about it. It shows only what it sees; that *eidōlon* remains directly invested by and tied to **eidō*, does not simply indicate to us a neutral or insignificant etymological fact, but exactly reflects a founding paradox. The idol shows what it sees. It shows that which, indeed, occupies the field of the visible, with neither deceit nor illu-sion, but which indissolubly invests it only on the basis of vision itself. The idol supplies vision with the image of what it sees. The idol produces (itself) in actuality (as) that at which vision intentionally aims. It freezes in a figure that which vision aims at in a glance. Thus does the mirror close the horizon, in order to offer sight the only object at which sight aims, namely, the face of its very aim: the gaze gazing at itself gazing, at the risk of seeing no more than its own face, without perceiving in it the gaze that gazes. Except, for the idol, no mirror precedes the gaze, nor, as if accidentally, encloses its space of vision;

to be reflected, and upon itself alone, idolatrous vision mobilizes no other instance than itself. In the future of its aim, at a certain point that nothing could foresee, the aim no longer aims beyond, but rebounds upon a mirror—which otherwise never would have appeared—toward itself; this invisible mirror is called the idol. It is not invisible in that one cannot see it, since to the contrary one sees nothing but it; it is invisible because it masks the end of the aim; starting with the idol, the aim no longer progresses, but, no longer aiming, returns upon itself, reflects itself, and by this reflex, abandons as unbearable to live—not visible because neither aimed at nor *visable*—the invisible.

The invisible mirror therefore does not produce the reflexive return of the aim upon itself, it results from it: it only offers, so to speak, the trace of the bounce, the imprint of the absorption of the aim, then of its takeoff, in return, upon itself. This wooden board, the idol, has the quasi value of a springboard for vision that, having advanced so far, returns from it toward itself. As the sediment in a wine indicates maturation and the fact that no further change is possible, so the idol constitutes only a sedimentation of the aim of the invisible and of the divine, hence what remains once the aim is stopped by its reflection. In the idol, as a statue or painting, the aim settles. The inversion of the aim determines the point of invisibility, and the reflection gives rise to the mirror. The invisible mirror is not so much the unseen cause of the reversal of vision as it is this reversal of vision that fixes, on a limit, the invisible. Thus, the idol only freezes itself in the firmness of a figure starting from the instance of a reversal. The figure results from the reversal upon/before the invisible, and not the inverse. The idol therefore appears as a reflection on the individual: an aim toward the *visable* that, at a certain point of the aim, is inflected upon itself, is reflected upon itself in order to characterize as invisible that at which it no longer can aim. The invisible is defined by the reflection whose defection abandons the visible as not *visable*, hence not visible—in short, invisible.

So the idol all the more masks the invisible when it is marked with visibility. The more it misses, by default, the invisible, the more it can be remarked as visible. The statue of one of these *kouroï* that, even in a room of the National Museum of Athens, still overcome us with their powerful and well-balanced splendor, indeed bears the sign of the divine. No one has the authority to deny that the divine marked the sacred sites, temples, and statues. Above all, no one has the power to do so. The fact is that the idol registers, as a low-water mark signals a rise in the water level, a certain advance of the aim at the divine, to the point of a certain reflection and defection. The testimony of the idols indeed may have lost its pertinence for us: but it is not thereby disqualified as such, namely, as divine, but simply struck with insignificance. For if the idols forged by the Greeks no longer show us the divine, the fault (if fault need be indicated) comes back neither to the divine nor to the Greeks. Simply, among us there are no longer any Greeks for whom alone these stone figures could indicate by their invisible mirror a reflection upon the invisible, whose visible low-water mark well corresponds to that particular experience of the divine attained only by the Greeks. The idols of the Greeks betray, silently and incomprehensibly, an absolutely actual experience of the divine, but an experience that was realized only for them. What renders the Delphic Oracle mute stems, not from any fraud finally exposed (Fontenelle), hut from the disappearance of the Greeks. The idol always marks a true and genuine experience of the divine, but for this very reason announces its limit: as an experience of the divine, starting in this way with the one who aims at it, in view of the reflex in which, through the idolatrous figure, this aim masks and marks its defection with regard to the invisible, the idol always must be read on the basis of the one whose experience of the divine takes shape there. In the idol, the divine indeed has a presence, and it indeed offers itself to an experience, but only starting from an aim and its limits. In a word, the divine is figured in the idol only indirectly, reflected according to the experience of it that is fixed by the human authority—the divine, actually experienced, is figured, however, only in the measure of the human authority that puts itself, as much as it can, to the test. In the idol, the divine function of *Dasein* is thus betrayed and calibrated. Which means that the idol never reaches the divine as such, and that, for this very reason, it never deceives, deludes, or misses the divine. As a divine function of *Dasein*, it offers the index of an always-real experience of *Dasein*. Only foolishness could doubt that the idol reflects the divine, and that in a way it may yet incite us to evoke for ourselves the experience of which it remains the sediment. But for this validity and this innocence, the idol pays the price of its limitation: it is an experience of the divine in the measure of a state of *Dasein*. What renders the idol problematic does not stem from a failure (e.g., that it offers only an "illusion") but, on the contrary, from the conditions of its validity—its radical immanence to the one who experiences it, and experiences it, rightly so, as impassable. To each epoch corresponds a figure of the divine that is fixed, each time, in an idol. In fact, it is not by chance that Bossuet risks the term *epoch* in a universal history that, from one end to the other, meditates on the succession of idols,[1] Only the genuineness of the idol, as a limited and hence real (real because limited) way of taking the divine into view, allows one to conceive the fraternity that Hölderlin recognizes between Heracles, Dionysus, and Christ.[2] The idol indeed testifies to the divine, from the point of view of the aim that produces it as its reflection. Each time, therefore, the idol testifies to the divine, but each time the divine thought starting from its aim, limited to a variable scope by *Dasein*. Therefore, the idol always culminates in a "self-idolatry" to speak like Baudelaire.[3] The idol: less a false or untrue image of the divine than a real, limited, and indefinitely variable function of *Dasein* considered in its aiming at the divine. The idol: the image of the divine that *Dasein* forms, hence that much less God than, in a more real way, a figure of the divine. Form an image of the divine? Usage instead says: "form an idea of . . ." Could this be because, preeminently, the idea would constitute the culmination of the idol?

2. The Ambivalence of the Conceptual Idol

The concept, when it knows the divine in its hold, and hence names "God," defines it. It defines it, and therefore also measures it to the dimension of its hold. Thus the concept on its part can take up again the essential characteristics of the "aesthetic" idol:[4] because it apprehends the divine on the basis of *Dasein*, it measures the divine as a function of it; the limits of the divine experience of *Dasein* provoke a reflection that turns it away from aiming at, and beyond, the invisible, and allows it to freeze the divine in a concept, an invisible mirror. Notably, the "death of God" presupposes a determination of God that formulates him in a precise concept; it implies then, at first, a grasp of the divine that is limited and for that reason intelligible. One therefore must add quotation marks to what is thus named God—"God"—that indicate less a suspicion than a delimitation: the "death of God" presupposes a concept equivalent to that which it apprehends under the name of "God." It is on the basis of this concept that the critique exerts its polemic: if "God" includes alienation in its concept (Feuerbach, Stirner, Marx), or a nimble figure of the will to power (Nietzsche), then it will—to the point of absolute disappearance—undergo the consequences of this concept. Which implies, obviously, the equivalence of God to a concept in general. For only this equivalence renders "God" operative as a concept. Which means that an atheism (conceptual, naturally, and not every atheism—even though the tie between conceptual atheism and sociological atheism may he of consequence) is worth only as much as the concept that contains it. And, as this concept of "God" accedes to the precision that will render it operative only by remaining limited, one must say that a conceptual atheism can assure its rigor, demonstrativeness, and pertinence only because of its regionalism; not *in spite of* it, but indeed *because of* it: regionalism indicates that for the term, by definition undefined, of *God*, the concept substitutes some precise definition, "God," over which, through the determining definition, understanding will exercise its logic. Thus the conceptual atheisms imply the substitution for *God* of a given regional concept—called "God"; therefore they bear only on concepts each time fostering this "God" that they announce. The "so-called gods" (René Char) substitute for *God* the "gods" that, conceptually we are limited to expressing. This "God," that a concept suffices to express, nevertheless has nothing illusory about it. It dearly exposes what *Dasein*, at the moment of a particular epoch, experiences of the divine and approves as the definition of its "God." Only such an experience of the divine is not founded so much in God as in man: and, as L. Feuerbach says exactly "man is the original of his idol"[5]—man remains the original locus of his idolatrous concept of the divine, because the concept marks the extreme advance, then the reflected return, of a thought that renounces venturing beyond itself, into the aim of the invisible.

It now becomes possible to ask what concept rigorous because regional—offers the "death of God" its idolatrous support. To this question, Nietzsche himself, explicitly and in advance, responds: "Does morality make impossible this pantheistic affirmation of all things too? At bottom [*im Grunde*], it is only the moral god that has been overcome. Does it make sense to conceive a 'god beyond good and evil'?"[6] Only the "moral God" can die or even be discovered as already dead; for he alone, as "*moral* God," is amenable to the logic of value: he himself operates and is comprehensible only in the system of values of morality as counternature; thus does he find himself directly hit the moment that, with nihilism, "the highest values are devalued." Nihilism would have no hold over "God" if, as "moral God," he were not exhausted in the moral domain, itself taken as the ultimate figure of "Platonism?' Recognizing, according to the very letter of the Nietzschean text, that only the "moral God" dies, does not amount to dulling the radicality of his argument, but, on the contrary, to disengaging its condition of possibility This condition of possibility presupposes, obviously, the equivalence between God and an idol (the regional concept), here the "moral God." Hence a double question. (*a*) What scope are we to acknowledge in this idol? (*b*) What origin are we to attribute to it?

We can fix its scope, provisionally by reference to what it does not exclude: the "death of God" as "moral God" leaves intact, even more opens and provokes, the coming of the new gods," whose affirmative function upholds this world, which becomes the only world. Thus even within the Nietzschean argument, the death of God is valid only as far as the idol that renders it thinkable aims, since, beyond this *Götzendämmerung* there is another dawn of the divine. As for the status of this new rising of the divine, only later can we conduct an examination of it. As to the origin of this idol, it is easily located. Feuerbach, in construing the whole of philosophy of religion as an idolatry—not in order to denounce its bankruptcy, but indeed to consecrate in it a finally legitimate appropriation—remarks that in it idolatry deploys all of its rigor in thinking "God" as moral: "Of all the attributes which the understanding assigns to God, that which in religion, and especially the Christian religion, has the pre-eminence, is moral perfection. But God as a morally perfect being is nothing else than the realized idea, the fulfilled law of morality . . . The moral God requires man to be as he himself is"[7] But, here as often, Feuerbach is hardly valid except as a relay in the direction of Kant, who explicitly thinks of God as "a moral author of the world."[8] To show that this equivalence acts as an idol, in the strict sense that we defined it, does not present, at least in one sense, any difficulty. The apprehension of "God" as moral author of the world implies an actual experience of God (who would risk doubting the religious authenticity of Kant's practical philosophy?) but founded on a finite determination of "God" (from the sole practical point of view), starting not from the nature—if there is one—of God, but indeed from human *Dasein*'s experience of it. This last characteristic Kant explicitly introduces: "This idea of a moral Governor of the world is a task presented to our practical reason. It concerns us not so much to know what God is in Himself (in His nature) as what He is for us as moral beings";[9] thus indeed it is uniquely for us, without regard for his own nature, that "God" can he expressed "as moral essence," "moral being." Even more than Kant, Fichte brutally formulates the idolatrous reduction of the "moral God": "This living and effective moral order is identical with God. We do not and cannot grasp any other God."[10] Thus, either Nietzsche has nothing precise in view, and his argument regresses from conceptual rigor to foundering in a pathos one might call "poetic," to spare it any more ambiguous qualifiers, or else he denounces as a crepuscular idol the Kantian (and thereby "Platonic") identification of God with the "moral God." Such an identification calls for two criticisms.

One is developed by Nietzsche's whole argument—namely, that this idea is equivalent to an idol: *Götzendämmerung*, so that, if, as according to Schelling's statement, "God is something much more real than a simple moral order of the world,"[11] then the crepuscular idol releases, by its disappearance, the space of an advent of the divine other than the moral figure. Because by its idolatrous disposition it holds a strictly regional validity, conceptual atheism is even more valid here as a liberation of the divine. The true question, concerning Nietzsche, does not concern his so-called (and vulgar) atheism; it asks if the liberation of the divine, which it attempts, accedes to a true liberation or fails along the way.

However, another infinitely more radical critique arises here—it no longer asks simply whether conceptual atheism, since it has rigor only in remaining regional, must necessarily be recognized as idolatrous, hence to be rejected; it wonders whether idolatry does not affect as much, or more, the conceptual discourse that pretends to accede positively to God. In the end Kant and Nietzsche equally admit the equivalence of God with the "moral God," so that the same idolatry affects the thinker of the categorical imperative as much as the thinker of the "death of God," Hence the suspicion that idolatry before characterizing conceptual atheism, affects the apologetic attempts that claim to prove, as one used to say, the existence of God. Every proof, in fact, demonstrative as it may appear, can lead only to the concept; it remains for it then to go beyond itself, so to speak, and to identify this concept with God himself. Saint Thomas implements such an identification by an "id quod omnes nominunt," repeated at the end of each of his *viae* (*Summa theologica* Ia,q.2,a.3), as Aristotle concluded the demonstration of *Metaphysics* (A:7) by *touto gar ho theos* "for this is the god" (1:072b29–30.), and as, above all, Leibniz ended at the principle of reason asking, "See at present if that which we have just discovered must not he called God."[12] Proof uses positively what conceptual atheism uses negatively: in both cases, equivalence to a concept transforms God into "God," into one of the infinitely repeatable "so-called gods." In both cases, human discourse determines God. The opposition of the determinations, the one demonstrating, the other denying, does not distinguish them as much as their common presupposition identifies them: that the human *Dasein* might, conceptually, reach God, hence might construct conceptually something that it would take upon itself to name "God," either to admit or dismiss. The idol works universally, as much for denegation as for proof.

3. Metaphysics and the Idol

The first idolatry can be established rigorously starting from metaphysics to the extent that its essence depends on ontological difference, though "unthought as such" (Heidegger). The result that we have just obtained raises, by its very radicality a question that is delicate because universal. We went from idolatry to conceptual atheism in order to bring to light the idolatrous presupposition of every conceptual discourse on God, even the positive. But in showing too much we no longer show anything: in extending the suspicion of idolatry to every conceptual enterprise concerning the divine, do we not run the risk of disqualifying this very suspicion? The localization of idolatry can assure its claims only by limiting itself, that is, by marking off precisely the field of its application. To suppose that such a field could be defined without contradiction implies a universal characteristic of metaphysical thought as such, or even a characteristic of thought that makes it appear as universally metaphysical. Heidegger was able to bring this characteristic to light as ontological difference. We admit therefore, without arguing or even explaining it here, the radical anteriority of ontological difference as that through and as which the *Geschick* of Being deploys beings, in a retreat that nevertheless saves a withdrawn proximity. We also admit that ontological difference is operative in metaphysical thought only in the forgetful figure of a thought of Being (thought summoned to and by Being) that, each time, keeps ontological difference unthought as such: "The thinking of metaphysics remains involved in the difference which as such is unthought."[13] Thus Being never finds itself thought as such, but always and only as the unthought of being [*das Seiendes*] and its condition of possibility. Such that the thought of Being is obscured even in the question "*ti to on?*" where the *on hē on* indicates more the beingness of beings (*Seiendheit, ousia, essentia*) than Being as such. Beingness thus transforms the question of Being as well into a question of the *ens supremum*, itself understood and posited starting from the requirement, decisive for being, of the foundation. In this way, the two questions lead the interrogation concerning Being back to the assurance of the foundation: "The onto-theological constitution of metaphysics stems from the prevalence of that difference which keeps Being as the ground, and beings as what is grounded and what gives account, apart from and related to each other."[14] The divine appears thus only in ontological difference unthought as such, hence also in the figure of the founding funds required for the securing of beings, funds having to be placed in security, hence to found. Onto-theo-logy disengages, of itself, a function and hence a site for every intervention of the divine that would be constituted as metaphysical: the theological pole of metaphysics determines, as early as the setting into operation of the Greek beginning, a site for what one later will name "God." Such that "God can come into philosophy only insofar as philosophy of its own accord and by its own nature, requires and determines that and how God enters into it."[15]

The advent of something like "God" in philosophy therefore arises less from God himself than from metaphysics, as destinal figure of the thought of Being. "God" is determined starting from and to the profit of that of which metaphysics is capable, that which it can admit and support. This anterior instance, which determines the experience of the divine starting from a supposedly unavoidable condition, marks a primary characteristic of idolatry. Nevertheless, it does not yet suffice to interpret the theological discourse of onto-theology as an idolatry For it is suitable also to determine the scope, limited but positive, of the concept that idolatry sets in equivalence with "God." In order to do so, we will admit with Heidegger, but also as a historian of philosophy that this concept finds a complete formulation, in modernity (Descartes, Spinoza, Leibniz, but also Hegel), with the *causa sui*: "The Being of beings is represented fundamentally, in the sense of the ground, only as *causa sui*. This is the metaphysical concept of God . . . The cause [*Ur-Sache*] as *causa sui*. This is the right name for the god of philosophy."[16] In thinking "God" as *causa sui*, metaphysics gives itself a concept of "God" that at once marks the indisputable experience of him and his equally incontestable limitation; by thinking "God" as an efficiency so absolutely and universally foundational that it can be conceived only starting from the foundation, and hence finally as the withdrawal of the foundation into itself, metaphysics indeed constructs for itself an apprehension of the transcendence of God, but under the figure simply of efficiency of the cause, and of the foundation. Such an apprehension can claim legitimacy only on condition of also recognizing its limit. Heidegger draws out this limit very exactly: "Man can neither pray nor sacrifice to this God. Before the *causa sui*, man can neither fall to his knees in awe nor can he play music and dance before this god."

"The god-less thinking which must abandon the God of philosophy God as *causa sui*, is thus perhaps closer to the divine God. Here this means only: god-less thinking is more open to Him than ontotheologic would like to admit."[17] The *causa sui* offers only an idol of "God" so limited that it can neither aspire to worship and adoration nor even tolerate them without immediately betraying its insufficiency. The *causa sui* says so little about the "divine God" that to assimilate it with the latter, even with the apologetic intention of furnishing a supposed proof, amounts to speaking crudely even in blasphemy: "a God who must permit his existence to be proved in the first place is ultimately a very ungodly God. The best such proofs of existence can yield is blasphemy."[18] Blasphemy, here, barely constitutes the obverse of an idolatry of which conceptual atheism would present the reverse. In both cases, God is second to "God," that is, to a concept that is limited—to the cause as foundation—and, at this cost only operative at the heart of metaphysics. Idolatry attempts to speak the good side of that of which *blasphemy* speaks the *bad*; of that which blasphemy speaks *bad*ly idolatry imagines itself to speak well. Each fails to see that they speak the same name; well or badly hardly matters, since the whole question consists in deciding whether a proper name can appropriate God in a "God"; the unconscious blasphemy of idolatry thus can be denounced authentically only by also unveiling the thoughtless idolatry of blasphemy. Only on the basis of a concept will "God" be, equally, refuted or proved, hence also considered as a conceptual idol, homogeneous with the conceptual terrain in general.

What have we gained so far? Have we not simply come back to our point of departure, the suspicion of idolatry applied to the concept? We have come back to it, but with a determination that characterizes it in a decisive manner: the conceptual idol has a site, metaphysics; a function, the theology in onto-theology; and a definition, *causa sui*. Conceptual idolatry does not remain a universally vague suspicion but inscribes itself in the global strategy of thought taken in its metaphysical figure. Nothing less than the destiny of Being—or, better, Being as destiny—mobilizes conceptual idolatry and assures it a precise function. We therefore end up, in a reading of Heidegger, inverting word for word the imprudent and hasty formula of Sartre, speaking of "the *Ens causa sui* which the religions name God."[19] Now, only metaphysics is willing and able to name the *Ens causa sui* by the name of God, because to begin with only metaphysics thinks and names the *causa sui*. On the contrary, "the religions," or, to remain precise, the Christian religion, does not think God starting from the *causa sui*, because it does not think God starting from the cause, or within the theoretical space defined by metaphysics, or even starting from the concept, but indeed starting from God alone, grasped to the extent that he inaugurates by himself the knowledge in which he yields himself—reveals himself. Bossuet says some very wise things; under the deliberately nonelaborated triviality of his remarks he states that "our God . . . is infinitely above that first Cause and prime mover known by philosophers, though they did not worship it."[20] To reach a nonidolatrous thought of God, which alone releases "God" from his quotation marks by disengaging his apprehension from the conditions posed by onto-theo-logy one would have to manage to think God outside of metaphysics insofar as metaphysics infallibly leads, by way of blasphemy (proof), to the twilight of the idols (conceptual atheism). Here again, but in the name of something like God and no longer of something like Being, the step back out of metaphysics seems an urgent task, although not a noisy one. But in view of what, this step back? Does the overcoming of idolatry summon us to retrocede out of metaphysics, in the sense that *Sein und Zeit* attempts a step back toward Being as such by the meditation of its essential temporality? Does retroceding from metaphysics, supposing already that in doing so there arrives the thought devoted to Being as Being, suffice to free God from idolatry—for does idolatry come to completion with the *causa sui*, or, on the contrary, does the idolatry of the *causa sui* not refer, as an indication only, to another idolatry more discrete, more pressing, and therefore all the more threatening?

4. The Screen of Being

Thus far, in what way have we advanced? Have we not simply taken up the Heideggerian meditation on the figure that the divine assumes in the onto-theo-logy of metaphysics, to identify it, with some violence, with our own problematic of the idol? Does not this perhaps forced identification simply offer a new case of a deplorable but persistent mania—that of taking up within a theological discourse, in spite of them, the moments of the Heideggerian discourse, in a game where one and the other party lose infinitely more than they gain? Precisely we must now indicate how the problematic of idolatry, far from falling here into disuse, finds the true terrain of a radical discussion when it encounters the attempt of a thought of Being as Being.

However, before outlining this paradox, and in order better to take it into view, let us look back to Nietzsche. The "death of God," as death of the "moral god," confirms the twilight of an idol; but, just because it has to do with an idol, the collapse entails, even more essentially than a ruin, the clearing of a new space, free for an eventual apprehension, other than idolatrous, of God. This is why Nietzsche announces "new gods" as an authentic possibility that their ardent expectation renders foreseeable. But these new gods can never be rendered visible unless their apprehension is submitted to the will to power, which controls the horizon of all beings, as the beingness of beings—"*höchste Macht—das genügt!*" Freed from moral idolatry, the gods nevertheless remain subject to other instances, to another unique instance of which they are the function, the will to power; for they constitute, purely and simply, states and figures of it. The new gods depend on "the religious, that is to say god-forming [*gottbildende*] instinct."[21] Thus, one idolatrous apprehension succeeds another: the manifestation of the divine only passes from one (moral) condition to another (*Wille zur Macht*), without the divine's ever being freed as such. Just as we were able to venture that Nietzsche, because he carries metaphysics to completion, constitutes its last moment, so must we suggest that Nietzsche renders the twilight of the idols crucial only by himself consummating a new (final?) development of the idolatrous process. The will to power forges "gods" at every instant: there is nothing, in the modern sense, more banal than a "god"; we never stop seeing ourselves, to the point of obsessional disgust, surrounded by them: each instant not only furnishes them but even demands and produces them. For, to a universal domination of the will to power that gives the seal of the eternal to becoming, there must correspond, according to the rigor of onto-theo-logy, the triumphant brilliance of a unified figure of the divine, hence of the maximum become actual of a state and of a figure of the will to power. The barbarous surging forward of terrible and trivial "idols" (for we very rightly name them "idols"), of which our nihilistic age ceaselessly increases the consumption, marks the exasperation of idolatry and not, to be sure, the survival of some natural—then delinquent—desire to see God.

It does not suffice to go beyond an idol in order to withdraw oneself from idolatry. Such a reduplication of idolatry, which even Nietzsche cannot avoid, we can suspect in Heidegger in a way even more vast and hence more dangerous than in Nietzschean expectation. For Nietzsche the "death of God" opens in nihilism, and it is through endured nihilism that the will to power accedes to a figurative production of new gods. The essence of technology, culminating in Enframing (*Gestell*), completes nihilism, but in such a way that nihilism opens to the possibility of a salvation. In fact, by carrying the interpretation of the Being of beings as present and presence (*Anwesenheit*) to its insurmountable end, hence by declaring the privilege of beings over their beingness and also by forgetting that, in ontological difference, what does not cease to be forgotten is precisely Being, Enframing carries ontological difference to its height, manifesting it all the more clearly that it does not think it as such. Where danger increases, salvation increases also. Enframing poses ontological difference as a problem by the fact that, with a massive and equal force, it both produces and fails to recognize it, Thus, as and because nihilism does not cease to aim at the advent of "new gods," and in a sense provokes that advent, so "with the end of philosophy, thinking is not also at its end, but in transition to another beginning."[22] The other beginning attempts to think ontological difference as such, hence to think being as Being. To this "other beginning" Heidegger designates a precise function and stake, in opposition to ontological difference, and does not burden it with any problematic character, future or fantastic. The "new beginning," which is compelled to think Being as such and hence accomplishes a step back from philosophy; is realized in *Sein und Zeit* or at least in its aim. The "new beginning," just like the "new gods," belongs to no future, since it can only open a future without prospect that the repeated pretension of the present does not immediately govern. In short, it is carried out before us and, one must hope, with us. And thus, the "new beginning" that breaks with unthought ontological difference, hence with the *causa sui* of onto-theo-logy, undertakes to conceive the "divine god": or at least does not close itself to this possibility or, better, opens it. We therefore conclude that the "new beginning," in charge of Being as Being, attempts to approach the god qua god. Hence the decisive declaration, which with its harmonics we must now hear: "Only from the truth of Being can the essence of the holy be thought. Only from the essence of the holy is the essence of divinity to be thought. Only in the light of the essence of divinity can it be thought or said what the word 'God' is to signify . . . Being."

"In such nearness, if at all, a decision may be made as to whether and how God and the gods withhold their presence and the night remains, whether and how the day of the holy dawns, whether and how in the upsurgence of the holy an epiphany of God and the gods can begin anew [*neu beginnen*]. But the holy, which alone is the essential sphere of divinity, which in turn alone affords a dimension for the gods and God, comes to radiate only when Being itself beforehand and after extensive preparation has been illuminated and is experienced in its truth."[23] Each of these texts obeys a strictly regulated superposition of conditions that imply each other and interweave with one another. Thus does Being determine beings by the clearing of its retreat; the advance of beings, which Being (*das Heile*) maintains intact, crowns in its turn the most protected among them by the glory of the holy (*das Heilige*); yet only the brilliance of the holy can assure the opening of something like a divine being (*das Gottliche*); and only the virtue of the divine can charter and support the weight of beings, at this point notable because one must recognize on their countenances the face of the gods (*die Götter*). Finally only the tribe of the gods can yield and guarantee a sufficiently divine abode so that someone like the God of Christianity or another (only the claim to unicity being in question here) can have the leisure to render itself manifest. These interwoven conditions all gather together in the play of that which elsewhere (in his strange lecture *The Thing*) Heidegger names the Fourfold or the Square (*Geviert*), of which the four instances, Earth and Sky, mortals and the divinities, buttress one another, hence confirm and repel one another, in an immobile and trembling tension where each owes its advent only to the combat with the others, and where their mutual struggles owe the harmonious equilibrium of their (dis) entanglement(s) only to Being, which convokes, mobilizes and maintains them. The gods need only play their part here, in a Fourfold; as one barely can say that God suffices to maintain the role of the gods, even less could one envisage him withdrawn from the Fourfold; neither withdrawn nor, of course, initiator or master.[24]

To the thought that is attached to thinking Being as Being, outside of metaphysics, in the definite confrontation with ontological difference meditated as such, the question of "the existence of God" inevitably will appear misplaced, hasty and imprecise. Imprecise, for what does it mean *to exist*, and is this term suitable to something like "God"? Hasty, since before coming to "God," even as a hypothesis, one must pass through the dazzling but trying multiplicity of the gods, then through the miraculous simplicity of the divine and of the holy, in order finally to end at the very question of Being. The "marvel of all marvels" consists no more in the existence of "God" than in the existence of any other being, or even in what "existence" (metaphysically) means, but in the fact, more simple and therefore more difficult to think, *that* what-is *is*.[25] What is essential in the question of "the existence of God" stems less from "God" than from existence itself, therefore from Being. Thus, in the end, this question appears misplaced—at once unsuitable and dislodged from its proper site: the truth on "God" could never come but from where truth itself issues, namely from Being as such, from its constellation and from its opening. The question of God must admit a preliminary, if only in the form of a preliminary question. In the beginning and in principle, there advenes neither God, nor a god, nor the *logos*, but the advent itself—Being, with an anteriority all the less shared in that it decides all the rest, since according to and starting from it there literally remain only beings, and nothing other than beings and the nothing. The very question of the ontic priority of "God" can be posed only at the heart of this advent. But what is more decisive, in the order of thought, than, precisely, the order of questions that provoke it?

We therefore posit that here again, a second time, and beyond the idolatry proper to metaphysics, there functions *another* idolatry, proper to the thought of Being as such. This affirmation, as blunt as it may seem, derives nevertheless directly from the indisputable and essential anteriority of the ontological question over the so-called ontic question of "God." This anteriority suffices to establish idolatry. We furnish nevertheless two confirmations, which permit us to connect two of the moments of the idol to two of Heidegger's decisions. (*a*) The idol determines the "god" on the basis of the aim, hence of an anterior gaze. But in the texts examined above, the dependence of "God" on the gods, then on divinity on the holy, and finally on Being, does not seem to have its origin in an ontically identifiable gaze; thus Heidegger would not satisfy one of the conditions of the idol. In fact, one should not forget, in reading the texts subsequent to the "turn," the (in fact *definitive*) accomplishment of earlier texts having to do with the analytic of *Dasein* and the fundamental essence of phenomenology. To say Being/*Sein* quite simply would not be possible if man were not able to attain his dignity of *Dasein*; *Dasein* here indicates what is peculiar to the human being, which consists in the fact that, in this being, not only its Being is an issue (as *Sein und Zeit* repeats in 1927), but more essentially, as Heidegger says in 1928, Being itself and its comprehension: "Human *Dasein* is a being with the kind of being [*Seinsart*] to which it belongs essentially to understand something like Being [*dergleichen wie Sein zu verstehen*]."[26]

The later isolated anteriority of *Sein* is secured concretely by *Dasein* over itself; phenomenologically the anteriority of Being can be developed and justified only by the anteriority of the analytic of *Dasein*. Therefore, one must admit the absolute phenomenological anteriority of *Dasein*, as comprehension of Being, over all beings and over every regional ontic investigation. Heidegger characterized this privileged situation of *Dasein* when he spoke of its "peculiar neutrality."[27]

Related to a religious law, or to the ontic existence of "God," the phenomenological privilege of *Dasein* lays itself open to "the semblance of an extremely individualistic, radical atheism, *Schein eines extrem individualistischen, radikalen Atheismus.*" Doubtless it is a question only of appearance, if one bears in mind an existential option: certainly Heidegger himself does not belong among those whom he later will name the "public scoundrels!" Still, taken in its phenomenological definition, hence as *Kategorienforschung*, "philosophical research is and remains an atheism";[28] atheism here indicates less a negation than a suspension. But such a suspension—phenomenologically inevitable— implies theologically an instance anterior to "God," hence that point from which idolatry could dawn. No doubt "the ontological interpretation of *Dasein* as Being-in-the-world tells neither for nor against the possible existence of God [*ein mögliches Sein zu Gott entschieden*],"[29] but the very possibility of this indecision implies a suspension. This suspension in turn implies, from an anterior because exterior point of view, an aim that suspends every ontic position; *Dasein* exerts this aim, and no term could appear unless aimed at and seen by it. *Dasein* precedes the question of "God" in the very way that Being determines in advance, according to the gods, the divine, the holy, "God," his life and his death. "God," aimed at like every other being by *Dasein* in the mode of a placement in parentheses, submits to the first condition of possibility of an idolatry.

The idol is constituted by the thrust of an aim anterior to any possible spectacle, but also by a first visible, where, settling, it attains, without seeing, its invisible mirror, low-water mark of its rise. Does one find in the Heideggerian text a thesis that confuses the first visible with the invisible mirror? The thought that thinks Being as such cannot and must not apprehend anything but beings, which offer the path, or rather the field of a meditation, of Being. Any access to something like "God," precisely because of the aim of Being as such, will have to determine him in advance as a being. The precomprehension of "God" as being is self-evident to the point of exhausting in advance "God" as a question. Heidegger often repeats that the believer, because of his certainty of faith, can well conceive the philosophical question of Being but can never commit himself to it, held back as he remains by his certainty The remark can at the least be reversed: assured of the precomprehension of every possible "God" as being and of his determination by the anterior instance of Being, Heidegger can well conceive and formulate the question of God (without quotation marks) but can never seriously commit himself to it. Precisely because in advance and definitively, "God," whatever his future figure may be, strictly *will be*: "The Gods only signal simply because they are"; "God is a being who, by his essence, cannot not be"; "that being which can never not be. Thought 'theologically,' this being is called 'God'"; "And the gods likewise: to the degree that they are, and however they are, they too all stand *under 'Being.'*"[30] In short, "God" first becomes visible as being only because he thus fills—at least in one sense—and reflexively refers (invisible mirror) to itself an aim that bears first and decidedly on Being. In other words, the proposition "God is a being" itself appears as an idol, because it only returns the aim that, in advance, decides that every possible "God," present or absent, in one way or another, has to be. Which is formulated strictly by the sequence: "For the god also is—if he is—a being and stands as a being within Being and its coming to presence, which brings itself disclosingly to pass out of the worlding of the world [*auch der Gott ist, wenn er ist, ein Seiender*]."[31]

But is it self-evident that God should have to be, hence to be as a being (supreme, plural—however one wants) in order to give himself as God? How is it that Being finds itself admitted without question as the temple already opened (or closed) to every theophany, past or to come? And could one not even suspect, on the other hand, that, by the definition and axiom of the thought of Being as such, the temple of Being could in no way assist, call for, admit, or promise whatever may be concerning what one must not even *name*—God? And if this suspicion need not be confirmed, at least one can raise it legitimately, and one has to be amazed that it does not amaze more both the believers and the readers of Heidegger. Undoubtedly, if "God" is, he is a being; but does God have to be?

In order not to have to avoid this question, and because it appears to us incontestable that the texts of Heidegger do avoid it, we would say that in this precise sense, one must speak of a second idolatry. That it bears on the "more divine god"[32] does not invalidate but confirms this idolatry: for what "God" thus allows that an aim should decide his greater or lesser divinity, if not that "God" which results from a gaze that is both pious and blasphemous? What assurance would permit the introduction of a more legitimate equivalence between God and Being (where he still would play the role of a being) than the one obtaining between God and the *causa sui* "God" of metaphysics? Or again, does not the search for the "more divine god" oblige one, more than to go beyond onto-theology, to go beyond ontological difference as well, in short no longer to attempt to think God in view of a being, because one will have renounced, to begin with, thinking him on the basis of Being? To think God without any conditions, not even that of Being, hence to think God without pretending to inscribe him or to describe him as a being.

But what indeed can permit and promise the attempt at a thinking of God without and outside of ontological difference?—The danger that this critical demand may in fact render thought on the whole immediately impossible cannot be minimized. Indeed, to think outside of ontological difference eventually condemns one to be no longer able to think at all. But precisely, to be no longer able to think, when it is a question of God, indicates neither absurdity nor impropriety, as soon as God himself, in order to be thought, must be thought as "id quo majus cogitari nequit," in other words, as that which surpasses, detours, and distracts all thought, even nonrepresentational. By definition and decision, God, if he must be thought, can meet no theoretical space to his measure [*mesure*], because his measure exerts itself in our eyes as an excessiveness [*démesure*]. Ontological difference itself, and hence also Being, become too limited (even if they are universal, or better: because they make us a universe, because in them the world "worlds") to pretend to offer the dimension, still less the "divine abode" where God would become thinkable. Biblical revelation seems, in its own way, to give a confirmation of this, or at least an indication, when it mentions, in the same name, what one *can* (but not must) comprehend as *Sum qui sum*, hence God as Being, and what one *must*, at the same time, understand as a denegation of all identity—"I am the one that I want to be." Being says nothing about God that God cannot immediately reject. Being, even and especially in Exod. 3:14, says nothing about God, or says nothing determining about him. One therefore must recognize that the impossibility, or at least the extreme difficulty, of thinking outside of ontological difference could, in some way, directly suit the impossibility—indisputable and definitive—of thinking God as such. Ontological difference, *almost* indispensable to all thought, presents itself thus as a *negative* propaedeutic of the unthinkable thought of God. It is the ultimate idol, the most dangerous but also the most educational and, in its way, profitable, since it offers itself as an obstacle that, beaten down and trampled, becomes an ultimate scaffolding—*scabellum pedibus tuis*—without entering into the unthinkable, the indispensable unthinkable. For the unthinkable here has no provisional or negative acceptation: indispensable, indeed, the unthinkable offers the only appraised face of the one of whom it is question of thinking. Concerning God, let us admit clearly that we can think him only under the figure of the unthinkable, but of an unthinkable that exceeds as much what we cannot think as what we can; for that which I may not think is still the concern of *my* thought, and hence to *me* remains thinkable. On the contrary, the unthinkable taken as such is the concern of God himself, and characterizes him as the *aura* of his advent, the glory of his insistence, the brilliance of his retreat. The unthinkable determines God by the seal of his definitive indeterminateness for a created and finite thought. The unthinkable masks the gap, a fault ever open, between God and the idol or, better, between God and the pretension of all possible idolatry The unthinkable forces us to substitute the idolatrous quotation marks around "God" with the very God that no mark of knowledge can demarcate; and, in order to say it, let us cross out G⊗d, with a cross, provisionally of St. Andrew, which demonstrates the limit of the temptation, conscious or naive, to blaspheme the unthinkable in an idol. The cross does not indicate that G⊗d would have to disappear as a concept, or intervene only in the capacity of a hypothesis in the process of validation, but that the unthinkable enters into the field of our thought only by rendering itself unthinkable there by excess, that is, by criticizing our thought. To cross out G⊗d, in fact, indicates and recalls that G⊗d crosses out our thought because he saturates it; better, he enters into our thought only in obliging it to criticize itself. The crossing out of G⊗d we trace on his written name only because, first, He brings it to hear on our thought, as his unthinkableness. We cross out the name of G⊗d only in order to show ourselves that his unthinkableness saturates our thought—right from the beginning, and forever.

To think G⊗d, therefore, outside of ontological difference, outside the question of Being, as well, risks the unthinkable, indispensable, but impassable. What name, what concept, and what sign nevertheless yet remain feasible? A single one, no doubt, love, or as we would like to say, as Saint John proposes—"God [is] *agapē*" (1 John 4:8). Why love? Because this term, which Heidegger (like, moreover, all of metaphysics, although in a different way) maintains in a derived and secondary state, still remains, paradoxically, unthought enough to free, some day at least, the thought of G⊗d from the second idolatry. This task, immense and, in a sense, still untouched, requires working love conceptually (and hence, in return, working the concept through love), to the point that its full speculative power can be deployed. We could not undertake here, even in outline, to indicate its features. May it suffice to indicate two decisive traits of love, and their speculative promise.

(a) Love does not suffer from the unthinkable or from the absence of conditions, but is reinforced by them. For what is peculiar to love consists in the fact that it gives itself. Now, to give itself, the gift does not require that an interlocutor receive it, or that an abode accommodate it, or that a condition assure it or confirm it. This means, first, that as love, God can at once transgress idolatrous constraints; for idolatry—especially the second—is exercised by the conditions of possibility (Being, if "God" is a being, the "divine abode," if "God" depends on the divine, etc.) which alone arrange for God a place worthy of him, and thus, if the conditions of that worthiness cannot be brought together, close his domain to his heirs, and hence assign him to marginality. If, on the contrary, God is not because he does not have to he, but loves, then, by definition, no condition can continue to restrict his initiative, amplitude, and ecstasy. Love loves without condition, simply because it loves; he thus loves without limit or restriction. No refusal rebuffs or limits that which, in order to give itself, does not await the least welcome or require the least consideration. Which means, moreover, that as interlocutor of love, man does not first have to pretend to arrange a "divine abode" for it—supposing that this very pretension may be sustained—but purely and simply to accept it; to accept it or, more modestly, not to steal away from it. Thus, even the inevitable impotence of man to correspond to the destiny that love gratuitously imposes upon him is not enough to disqualify its initiative or its accomplishment. For, in order to accomplish the response to love, it is necessary and sufficient to will it, since will alone can refuse or receive so that man cannot impose any condition, *even negative*, on the initiative of G⊗d. Thus no aim can any longer decide idolatrously on the possibility or impossibility of access to and from "God."

(b) There is more: to think G⊗d as *agapē* equally prohibits ever fixing the aim in a first visible and freezing it on an invisible mirror. Why? Because, as opposed to the concept that, by the very definition of apprehension, gathers what it comprehends, and, because of this, almost inevitably comes to completion in an idol, love (even and especially if it ends up causing thought, giving rise—by its excess—to thought) does not pretend to comprehend, since it does not mean at all to take; it postulates its own giving, giving where the giver strictly coincides with the gift, without any restriction, reservation, or mastery. Thus love gives itself only in abandoning itself, ceaselessly transgressing the limits of its own gift, so as to be transplanted outside of itself. The consequence is that this transference of love outside of itself, without end or limit, at once prohibits fixation on a response, a representation, an idol. It belongs to the essence of love—*diffusivum sui*—to submerge, like a ground swell the wall of a jetty, every demarcation, representational or existential, of its flux: love excludes the idol or, better, includes it by subverting it. It can even be defined as the movement of a giving that, to advance without condition, imposes on itself a self-critique without end or reserve. For love holds nothing back, neither itself nor its representation. The transcendence of love signifies first that it transcends itself in a critical movement where nothing—not even Nothingness/Nothing—can contain the excess of an absolute giving—absolute, that is, the defeat of all that is not exercised in that very abandon.

The second idolatry therefore can be surpassed only in letting God be thought starting from his sole and pure demand. Such a demand goes beyond the limit of a concept—even that of metaphysics in its onto-theo-logy—but also the limit of every condition whatsoever—even that of Being conceived in ontological difference. God can give himself to be thought without idolatry only starting from himself alone: to give himself to be thought as love, hence as gift; to give himself to be thought as a thought of the gift. Or better, as a gift for thought, as a gift that gives itself to he thought. But a gift, which gives itself forever, can be thought only by a thought that gives itself to the gift to be thought. Only a thought that gives itself can devote itself to a gift for thought. But, for thought, what is it to give itself, if not to love?

5. Note on the Divine and Related Subjects

The first version of the present text appeared in 1980 in a collection dedicated entirely to Heidegger and the question of God, *Heidegger et la question de Dieu* (Paris: Grasset, 1980). That collection took up the proceedings of a private colloquium, organized a few months before by the Irish College in Paris, where my text had been discussed. J. Beaufret and F. Fédier were kind enough to react to my theses and to offer those valuable remarks in the printing of the same volume. I would like to offer here a few points in response to their respective statements.

"All the same one would have to learn to read otherwise than in the bind of someone who is at a complete loss"[33] this passage from the *Letter on Humanism*" ("Heidegger et la theologie," p. 30) which I analyzed above (pp. 39 ff.) and which poses as preliminary to any manifestation of "God" that of the "gods," of the divine, of the holy, of the safe, and finally of Being. Playing, on that occasion, the role of the "someone," I would like to speak about the "loss." To begin, let us clear up a misunderstanding: if "monotheism is the point of view of those who declare false what would inspire in others the highest veneration" (J. Beaufret, p. 34), then I am not "monotheistic"; or rather, my personal attempt to *accede* to monotheism does not imply any declaration of falsification with regard to other venerations, since the theory of the idol that I outline has precisely no other consequence than to give legitimacy to other venerations and for that very reason to explain their multiplicity, hence to limit their dignity. For one can ground the legitimacy of multiple "venerations." only by a doctrine that limits them; one will have the generosity to grant me that, as to grant me that the reading of Hölderlin does not remain totally foreign to me. I wonder moreover how one can defend the reduction of the divine without presenting a doctrine of the idol—my own or, if it may be found, a better one. After this pointless reproach, let us get to the essential. Beaufret underlines that Heidegger simply wants to allow this to be thought: "Even more sacred than every God is consequently the world" (p. 33); consequent to what? "Quite simply" consequent to this: "The Deity without belonging to the holy, is no longer even the Deity but a vain pretension of a being, reputed to be All-Powerful, to usurp the center of that of which he represents only one region" (p. 31). In this authoritative exegesis of the contested passage of the *Letter*, I would like to raise two points. (*a*) "a being, reputed to be All-Powerful": the commentator takes up again, without questioning it, Heidegger's assumption: every "God" by precomprehension, is defined as a being, and, if one holds to the discourse of metaphysics, a being characterized by omnipotence. These two assumptions I indeed had mentioned in the initial text. I simply ask: just as the metaphysical determination of "God" as all-powerful is not self-evident (Heidegger himself having allowed us to glimpse this), must one admit that the determination of "God" as "a being" is itself self-evident? How is it that this question arouses no other response than the implicit accusation of misinterpretation or the assurance of its banality?

In fact, there is nothing banal about it, in view of its immediate result, to which the authoritative commentary holds, moreover correctly above all. This result posits (*b*) that once "God" is defined as a "being," his pretension to fix himself as an absolute center becomes a usurpation. "God," playing the character of a "being," usurps the center of the "world; a center that returns to the *Geviert*; which alone makes a world. I had not brought up anything else, in order to found the diagnostic of idolatry; and hence Beaufret concedes my point of departure. I ask for nothing more. Or rather I do, on this basis: is it self-evident that "God," or rather G⊗d, should *be*, should have to be, should have to be like one of the "regions" of that of which the *Geviert* alone assures the conjunctions? Do these questions have any foundation with relation to the text of the Letter? The exegete at least confirms that they indeed have a basis in it. But then why take them to be inaudible, and degrade them to the realm of gain and loss?[34]

Coming back, in a brief and beautiful text entitled "Heidegger et Dieu," on the same passage from the *Letter*, Fédier remarks inversely that "Heidegger does not at all pretend to submit God to Being. He contents himself with soberly signaling that each time it is a question of thinking God, one will have first to think Being" (p. 44). In fact the distinction is right in a way, since Heidegger invokes only a precedence (*erst, zuvor*, etc.) of Being over "God." We concede this voluntarily, although subject to examination of still unpublished texts. Once this is admitted, is the diagnostic of idolatry put into question? The simple fact that, according to Fédier himself, "God," in order to reveal himself, hence in order to give himself, must satisfy preliminary conditions, and even preliminaries of thought, far from invalidating, rather confirms this diagnostic. The declaration of reassuring intentions that follows—"In *this* limited sense, the god depends on Being. The Greeks said: 'even the gods obey Necessity.' In this limited sense, the thought of Being is higher than the thought of God" (p. 45)—reconciles nothing. For beside the fact that Greek thought concerning the gods does not constitute an absolute reference by itself, and especially beside the fact that it is not a question of thought as preliminary (an anterior aim), but rather of envisaging the hypothesis of an unthinkableness that goes beyond all thought, "*this* limited sense" was defined a few lines above: "All that is in the world, and even that which comes into it, like the god, is lit up by the light of Being." This sequence would merit word-for-word examination. I ask, among other things: (1) On what rests the definition and legitimacy of "All"? (2) In what sense can one think "to come" into the world, and do all the "gods" come into it in the same sense as the Johannine *erkhomenos*? (3) Does that which Being projects in matters of light illuminate with glory the "gods" as such, or, on the contrary, does it not sometimes obfuscate precisely that by which it/they reveal(s) itself/themselves as "God," or G⊗d? In short, does the light of Being glorify the G⊗d who, according to the Apostle Paul, only reveals himself as a folly? In illuminating this being, a Jew on the cross, does the light of Being permit one to recognize more than an ignominious death? And if not, can one still affirm that Being accommodates all the gods as such by the simple fact that it allows them to be seen as beings? We simply ask, is the "light of Being" qualified to accommodate every revelation?

If we renounce the untenable positions of Beaufret and Fédier—which consist in minimizing the idolatrous violence of the text of the *Letter*, at the risk of rendering their respective commentaries even *more* indisputably idolatrous—are we condemned to a "condemnation" of Heidegger, with the odiousness and ridiculousness of such a pretension? Not at all. We rediscover the pure and simple way in which Heidegger understood his own text. In fact, we have the good fortune that our question concerning *this* text of the *Letter* was posed to Heidegger, during a session of the Evangelical Academy of Hofgeismar, in December 1953. And Heidegger responded: "With respect to the text referred to from the 'Letter on Humanism,' what is being discussed there is the God of the poet, not the revealed God. There is mentioned merely what philosophical thinking is capable of on its own. Whether this may also be of significance for theology cannot be said because there is for us no third case by which it could be decided."[35] I cannot but fully subscribe to this position, which admits—against the zeal of the exegetes—the irreducible heteronomy, with regard to "God," of that which thought (philosophical or poetic?) can do on the one hand, and that which revelation gives. Revelation (I say, icon) can neither be confused with nor subjected to the philosophical thought of "God" as being (I say, idol). Heidegger says it, and confirms me in a word, there where I wandered about with neither grace nor progress. The G⊗d who reveals himself has nothing in common (at least in principle, and provided that he not condescend to it) with the "God" of the philosophers, of the learned, and, eventually of the poet.

May the exegetes allow me to rely against or without them, on Heidegger's statement. For, if it surprises one to be at a total loss,[36] some can find themselves "ashamed like a fox taken by a hen," to leave the last word, all the same, to the poet.[37]

PART II

Saturation, Gift, and Icon

Marion began his academic career as a historian of early modern philosophy, and he remains a historian of philosophy even when writing original philosophy. He is widely admired as a scholar of Descartes and still produces important work on the philosopher. Concerned as a historian with the constitution of metaphysics, he found himself having to approach metaphysics from a place that was itself nonmetaphysical or at least seeking to be neutral with respect to metaphysics: phenomenology.[1] So it was no accident that, beginning in the 1980s, he started to become interested in the history of phenomenology. The French original of "The Breakthrough and the Broadening" appeared in *Philosophie* in 1984 and became the opening chapter of *Réduction et donation* (1989). With hindsight, we can see here the beginning of a change in Marion's work: the historian of philosophy was on his way to become an original philosopher himself. We can also see that this path is not straightforward. Nor has it reached an end.

Philosophizing started for Marion when he hit upon the idea of the saturated phenomenon, and almost all of his original work in philosophy since that discovery has been devoted to explicating and exploring new facets of saturated phenomena (or, as he sometimes says, paradoxes).[2] The idea of phenomena saturated with intuition could be thought only by way of a patient re-reading of phenomenology from the very beginning, that is, from the *Logical Investigations* (1900–1901) and *The Idea of Phenomenology* (1907). The breakthrough of the *Logical Investigations* is Husserl's insight that everything that is constituted as a phenomenon must be led back to its ground in intuition. The broadening of phenomenology is the recognition that intuition is offered as a mode of givenness (*Gegebenheit*). For it is givenness that is anterior to everything in the repertoire of phenomenology—intentionality, intuition, constitution, noesis and noema, and all the rest—and the questions that animate Marion at this stage of his work are whether the reduction can lead us to givenness, and whether the thought of givenness points us to the question of being.

"So much appearance, so much being": such is the shared fundamental thesis of phenomenology for Husserl and Heidegger, although Marion's statement of it has a more Heideggerian ring than a Husserlian one. Certainly for both of them appearing is prior to the distinction between illusion and reality. Yet this thesis presumes that appearing gives itself in one or another region of being. To recognize and delineate *how* the phenomenon gives itself is the task of reduction. Accordingly, Marion formulates his basic position, in contradistinction to Husserl and Heidegger, as "So much reduction, so much givenness."[3] With this move he introduces a new narrative into the history of phenomenology. The first reduction is Husserl's, and turns on what can be presented objectively to consciousness; the second reduction is Heidegger's, and is centered on being; and the third reduction is Marion's: It focuses on givenness. Strictly speaking, the prompt to the third reduction precedes being since it is prior to all ontology. It is the pure form of the call, beyond any and all interest in being or beings, and made evident in deep boredom. Marion reaches this conclusion by way of a subtle reading of Heidegger on the fundamental attunements of *Angst* and *Langeweile*, dread and deep boredom.[4] *Angst* exposes *Dasein* to the nothing, Heidegger says, and eventually concludes that being calls us from the heart of this nothing. Marion, however (with a nod to Pascal), argues that deep boredom, in its indifference to being and beings, releases us from the call of being and exposes us to something prior to being: the pure call.[5] He gives as examples the calls of God in the Jewish and Christian traditions, and the call of the Other, as evoked by Emmanuel Levinas.[6] But Marion is pressing neither religion nor ethics into the service of phenomenology. The call is strictly unconditioned and relies on no authority; it leads us back not to a subject with an intentional horizon, or to *Dasein*, but to the one who receives the call, which Marion calls first *l'interloqué* and then *l'adonné*.[7]

On Marion's reading, Husserl interprets the phenomenality of the phenomenon as givenness, certainly in the *Logical Investigations* and all the more surely in *The Idea of Phenomenology*, and he takes this givenness to be present to consciousness. By means of reduction, the passage from transcendence to the immanence of consciousness, one can become certain of this presence. For Husserl, then, all constitutive acts are grounded in representation; even acts of desire and the will ultimately rely on the power of representation.[8] Epistemology is granted high prestige here, and this is precisely the point at which Levinas focuses his critique of Husserl. Marion has learned deeply from this analysis, and he regards Levinas as the greatest of French phenomenologists.[9] Far from endorsing the importance of consciousness, and so developing yet another variation of the philosophy of the subject, Marion attends to *l'adonné*, the gifted one, who receives givenness and who is prior to *Dasein* and the subject, and hence anterior to representation and being. Before we can get to Marion's discussion of *l'adonné*, though, we must pass through his account of the given. This takes up the two central books of *Being Given*. Offered here is his "Sketch of the Saturated Phenomenon," which is a more careful and refined version of an earlier essay, "The Saturated Phenomenon," Marion's first attempt to present himself as an original thinker.[10] In both studies, he analyzes four ways in which phenomena can be saturated with intuition, and these four ways are indexed to Kant's table of categories: quantity, quality, relation, and modality.[11] The event overflows quantity; the idol, quality; the flesh, relation; and the icon, modality. The event is unforeseeable, the idol dazzles us, the flesh is absolute, and the face cannot be objectified. It will be noted that the idol, subject to severe strictures in *The Idol and Distance* and *God Without Being*, is rehabilitated in *Being Given*.

The broadening of phenomenology accomplished by Marion allows for a new approach to the phenomenology of revelation, as we shall see in the fourth section of this collection. Yet it would be a mistake to limit saturated phenomena to extraordinary events. For saturation occurs everywhere: it is "banal," Marion tells us. We do not live simply in a world of experience but also in a world of "counter-experience" in which we are dazzled by a phenomenon or disappointed by our inability to master one. Everyday life is taken up by the many ways in which one seeks to deal with the excess that overflows one's gaze. The theory of saturated phenomena allows us to see an entire range of manifestations that have always been there but have not been noticed or, if they have, mainly by visual artists and poets and not by philosophers. Fred Williams brings the Lal-Lal Falls into sight; David Campbell allows us to see the Monaro as never before.

In the second book of *Being Given*, Marion develops a thorough account of the gift. It is clear that he does so in large part to distinguish his sense of the gift from Jacques Derrida's. For Derrida, a gift, if there is such a thing, cannot be given, for it will always fall back into a circuit of exchange.[12] Gifts would never appear, never be phenomena, and never be present. Rather than include Marion's response to Derrida's theory of the gift, I have chosen one of his later essays, "The Reason of the Gift," which recapitulates the argument of *Being Given*—including the triple bracketing of the gift: a gift without a giver, a gift without a givee, and a gift without exchange value—while also offering further reflections. Before Marion, it was thought that the questions of the gift and givenness did not have a common root. It is Marion's claim to have found that root. Readers of *Being Given* find themselves in a dense text of phenomenological theory, and may well miss the concrete examples that make phenomenology so rewarding. In "The Reason of the Gift," however, one finds a fascinating analysis of the phenomenon of fatherhood, an unusual phenomenon in that it gives itself only insofar as it gives. The same would be true, or even truer, of motherhood.

Of the four modes of saturation, the one presented here in a detailed analysis is the icon. "The Icon or the Endless Hermeneutic" is from *In Excess*, the book that follows *Being Given* and that examines more concretely the four modes of saturation. The icon has already appeared in Marion's earlier, more theological work, though in his later writing there is an engagement with Levinas that enriches the discussion and gives it a particular inflection that adds to the concerns of this section. "The face," he says, "saturated phenomenon according to modality," does something remarkable. It "accomplishes the phenomenological operation of the call more, perhaps, than any other phenomenon (saturated or not)," and with this claim Marion seeks to dislodge Levinas's main thesis: "its call must be defined not only as the other person of ethics (Levinas), but more radically as the icon."

K.H.

The Breakthrough and the Broadening

1. Two Interpretations and a Broadening

"A breakthrough work, *ein Werk des Durchbruchs*"—it is with these words that Husserl salutes the *Logical Investigations* thirteen years after their first edition of 1900–1901. This turn of phrase barely conceals a depreciation under the praise. In the same year, Husserl publishes the first volume of the *Ideen*, and if he still salutes the *Investigations*, he does so in the way that a traveler salutes, from a boat that withdraws, the land forever left behind. In 1913 the breakthrough fades before that which it rendered possible; Husserl confirms this straightaway: "a break-through work and, just as well, less an end than a beginning."[1] Hence the paradox that does not cease to dominate the interpretation of the *Logical Investigations*: the breakthrough is recognized only in order to serve immediately as a beginning for the later phenomenology; whether this shift appears as a questionable deviation (as it is for Ingarden and his disciples[2]) or the only correct path (as for Husserl himself) matters little since in both cases the breakthrough of 1900–1901 can be understood only in relation to what it does not yet state. Now, even supposing that the whole theoretical achievement of the breakthrough of 1900–1901 can be found again, in its entirety, in the later texts (which remains to be proved, as Sartre, among others, has shown), one must in any case admit that it was won without the array of the later phenomenological orthodoxy. And therefore, if there is a breakthrough, we should be able to read it solely according to the discourse of the *Investigations*. This work does not consist first in identifying the theses and the authors that they critique in the measure of their advance; some excellent studies[3] have shown that Husserl's adversaries remain largely unaware of the metaphysical situation that determines them, so that we cannot expect more of them than a doxographical identification of the first theoretical decisions of the *Investigations*. The breakthrough can receive its properly metaphysical dignity only from an interpretation that is itself awake to the essence of metaphysics. Thus, it has found only two problematics powerful enough to put us on the trail of their metaphysical situation. But these two problematics, following two opposite directions, radicalize the breakthrough to the point of abolishing what is at stake in a real effort to situate it. In one case—Heidegger—Husserl reaches in the *Investigations*, and especially in the Sixth, the categorial intuition of Being; he therefore extracts himself from the Neo-Kantian dissimulation of the ending metaphysics, in order to open himself to a givenness of Being: "In order even to lay out the question of the meaning of Being, it was necessary that Being be *given*, so that one be able to ask after its meaning. Husserl's tour de force consisted precisely in bringing Being to presence, making it phenomenally present in the category. Through this tour de force," Heidegger adds, "I finally had a ground: 'Being' is not a simple concept, a pure abstraction obtained thanks to a deductive operation."[4] To be sure, Husserl does not really unfold the question of the meaning of Being (*Sinn des Seins*); it nonetheless remains that, once accomplished, the breakthrough does allow one to pose the question of Being, as it were, already beyond metaphysics: Hence the direct filiation, which Heidegger never explicitly formulates but ceaselessly suggests, between, on the one hand, the *Logical Investigations*, which lead to the categorial intuition that gives Being, and, on the other hand, *Sein und Zeit*, which constructs the question of Being starting from the analytic of *Dasein*. According to this topic, the breakthrough of 1900–1901 anticipates the destruction of ontology and thus accomplishes the end of metaphysics. The breakthrough breaks beyond metaphysics.

The other approach—which we owe to J. Derrida, who thus acquired a definitive phenomenological merit—inverts this perspective entirely. The breakthrough of the *Investigations* certainly does consist in freeing up signification (*Bedeutung, meinen*) in its a priori ideality. But far from drawing the consequences of this—namely, that signification signifies by itself, without in any way having to go back to an intuitive presencing—Husserl would have ceaselessly led signification back to a fulfilling intuition, which secures it in evident presence. Thus phenomenology would perpetuate, even against its intention—against the intentionality of signification—the primacy of presence, and it would founder in a final "adventure of the metaphysics of presence"; in short, "the adherence of phenomenology to classical ontology"[5] would be betrayed by its recourse to intuition to secure presence for signification, but above all by the unquestioned primacy of presence itself in and over signification. To overcome metaphysics as a "metaphysics of presence" would require that one overcome phenomenology, by playing against it one of its potentialities that had been censured as early as the First Investigation—by playing the indication (*Anzeichen*), the sign foreign to all presence, against the sign that is endowed with a signification that awaits its intuitive fulfillment. Within this topic, according to the development that leads it to the "principle of principles" of 1913, the breakthrough of 1900–1901 restores metaphysics by extending the ontological primacy of presence. The breakthrough does not pass beyond metaphysics but rather leads back to it.

The conflict of these two interpretations orients the *Logical Investigations* in two opposite directions. Either, reading them on the basis of the Sixth and final investigation, one can retain the categorial givenness of Being, and it then becomes possible to pass on to ontological difference by carrying out the "destruction of the history of ontology." Or else, reading them on the basis of the First Investigation, one retains the primacy of presence which is all the more clear insofar as the intentionality of the a priori allows one to contest it; then it becomes necessary to move on to *différance*, in order to work at deconstructions without end or beginning. This conflict, which is in fact unavoidable, gives rise to two main difficulties among many. (1) In Husserl's own eyes, and putting aside the continuation of the *Ideen*, in what did the breakthrough of the *Logical Investigations* consist? Does the consciously Husserlian motive for the breakthrough, if there is one, concern—either directly or indirectly—metaphysics as eventually thematized by the primacy of presence? (2) Heidegger retains from the Sixth Investigation the categorial *givenness* of Being; Derrida stigmatizes in the First Investigation the presentifying *intuition*. Supposing that it is founded in the texts, would this distinction not offer a conceptual range sufficient enough that the two readings, instead of being in confrontation, might be arranged more subtly? In short, if it is a matter of defining metaphysics in order to put it in question, is the characteristic of givenness equivalent to the characteristic of presence through intuition? It is at some peril that we must now risk an examination of these questions.

If Husserl does not understand the *Investigations* as a "breakthrough work" until 1913, he very consciously recognizes as early as 1900 the "difficulties of pure phenomenological analysis," and he indicates the reason for this: "The source of all such difficulties lies in the unnatural direction of intuition and thought which phenomenological analysis requires," or again in "an anti-natural *habitus* of reflection."[6] Such a *habitus* requires that one not take objects as actual but rather the acts that underlie them. The "things in question" are not those that we would naturally be inclined to consider actual, but rather those that we overlook—the acts. In order to substitute for things (*Dinge*), which are perhaps only words, the corresponding actuality, in order to return each time to the thing in question (*Sache*), one must lead reflection back toward its own acts, and therefore lead conceptions back toward the intuition that corresponds to them (or not): "Logical concepts . . . must have their origin in intuition." To return to the things in question implies turning thought toward intuition, in return: "We must go back to 'the things themselves' [*auf die 'Sachen selbst' zurückgehen*]. We desire to render self-evident in fully developed intuitions [*vollentwickelten Anschauungen*] that what is here given in actually performed abstractions is what the word-meanings in our expression of the law truly and actually stand for."[7] The return to the thing at stake demands that thought lead its words to their intuition. The verification of statements presupposes their repetition on the basis of the actually performed intuition, and therefore on the basis of acts: "It is purely on the basis of internal intuition [*Innenschau*] and of the analysis of the intuited [*Geschauten*], and in an intuitive [*intuitiven*] reascent to general necessities, that affirmations will be gained as affirmations of essences. These are not essential necessities that are only supposed or claimed, but rather the necessity and the unconditioned universality of their validity will come to be intuited itself [*selbst zum Geschauten*]."[8] Such a return to the things themselves as a leading-back [*reconduction*] to intuition has force only if it is a matter of thus bringing to its eventual evidence what, according to the natural orientation of thought, precisely does *not* offer any intuition. Moreover, Husserl admits the phenomenological difficulty only because he demands intuition in logic—what he does not hesitate to name "the intuitive fulfillment [*Vollzug*] of our abstraction."[9] The rule of the return to intuition, and therefore of the reversal of the natural direction, is thus developed "in general. Each thought, or at least each consistent thought, can no doubt become intuitive."[10] In the preface essay to the *Investigations*, itself also written in 1913 (and published by E. Fink in 1939), Husserl can explain the breakthrough by the unqualified return to intuition: "my method is strictly 'intuitive' [*intuitiv*], that is to say radically intuitive [*anschauliche*] in the broadened sense that I give to this term [*in meinem erweiterten Sinne*], and . . . it is precisely this that constitutes the very profound difference that separates my rationalism and my idealism from those that have preceded them and from all the scholastic ontologies."[11] One must speak of a "breakthrough" because one must lead every thought back to its intuitive actualization (its acts). This later self-interpretation does not deviate from the initial intention, since as early as 1901 Husserl claimed in a self-presentation "to have discovered a corner-stone [*ein Grund- und Eckstein*] for all phenomenology and for any future theory of knowledge" in what he already named "a fundamental broadening, until now not accomplished [*fundamentale und bisher nicht vollzogene Erweiterung*], of the concepts of perception and of intuition."[12] We therefore conclude: the breakthrough . . . of the *Investigations* has to do with the elevation of intuition, as the worker of evidence, to the level of an "adequate phenomenological justification" of all statements, that is, to the absolutely "decisive [*massgebend*]" role of the "descriptive character of phenomena, as experienced by us."[13] The overture and the finale match: the phenomenological breakthrough is accomplished by leading back to intuition everything that claims to be constituted as a phenomenon. This result gives rise to two confirmations.

First, it appears difficult to maintain that the "principle of principles" formulated in the *Ideen* of 1913 would orient the phenomenological enterprise in a new direction, or even contradict the original injunction of the "return to the things themselves." The preface that remained unpublished (written in 1913, to be sure, but for the *Investigations*) in fact does not hesitate to recognize that they "radically profess the principle of all principles," namely the "right of what is seen clearly, which precisely, as such, is what is 'originary,' what is before any theory, what gives the ultimate norm." This de jure principle is carried out when, "following the evidence of experience and ultimately of originarily giving perception in its harmonious progression, we speak straightforwardly about things that are," for "then precisely we accept what is immediately given to us as something that is and we question it concerning its properties and its laws." This principle contradicts the "return to the things themselves" all the less insofar as it explicitly includes it: "This intuitive method, appealing as it does to the things themselves here in question, that is, to the knowledge 'itself' (precisely in its direct, intuitive givenness), is what the second volume of these *Logical Investigations* employs, which, in my opinion then, was not written for nothing [*nicht umsonst*]."[14] For Husserl at least, the "principle of principles" does not limit the "return to the things themselves," but rather constitutes its accomplishment and truth: to return objects to acts implies that "the originarily giving intuition is a source of right for cognition."[15]

Couldn't one nevertheless object to this conciliation of the two principles that it appeared precisely in 1913, in a rereading of the *Investigations* that was contemporaneous with the turn taken in the *Ideen*? This objection loses a great deal if one notes that several texts from the *Investigations* themselves anticipate the "principle of principles." Let us cite two. First, this extreme argument from the Sixth Investigation: "If the peculiar character of intentional, experiences is contested, if one does not want [*will*] to admit what for us is most certain [*was uns als das Allersicherstegilt*], that being-an-object consists phenomenologically in certain acts in which something appears, or is thought as our object, it will not be intelligible how being-an-object can itself be objective to us."[16] What is most certain, what Descartes named the *inconcussum quid*, and which alone renders possible the Being of the object as object, has to do with this: the object consists only in certain acts, acts whose primacy stems from their ability to allow the given to appear as an intentional lived experience. Whoever refuses here the "legitimate source" of any appearance, namely lived experiences, cannot be refuted since lie excludes himself from the terrain of givenness, where alone an argument becomes possible. If the conditions of possibility of the Being-object, namely intuition in its lived experiences, are rejected, then the eventual objects of experience are also rejected, But another text immediately presents itself, a text that closes the introduction to the second volume of the *Investigations* under the unambiguous title of "principle of the absence of presuppositions [*Prinzip der Voraussetzunglosigkeit*]." It demands that one ensure the return to the things themselves by means of respect for the sole authority of intuition: "If such a 'thinking over' of the meaning of knowledge is itself to yield, not mere opinion, but the evident [*einsichtig*] knowledge it strictly demands, it must be a pure intuition of essences, exemplarily performed on an actual *given* basis of experiences of thinking and knowing." Intuition itself cannot be understood as a last presupposition, since it is neither presupposed, nor posited, nor given, but originarily giving. Intuition sees what theories presuppose of their objects; as intuition gives, with neither reason nor condition, it precedes the theories of the given, in the capacity of a "theory of all theories,"[17] perhaps in the sense that, according to Aristotle, the impossibility of securing science solely by the repetition of science (οὐδ' ἐπιστήμης ἐπιστήμη) requires admitting the *nous* within the principle of principles (νοῦς ἂν εἴη τῶν ἀρχῶν). It remains the case that in order to take on such a function, intuition must free itself from the limits that theory commonly imposes on it.

Hence the second confirmation of the breakthrough: what Husserl thematizes as an intuitive return to the things themselves requires "a new notion of intuition" that is freed from "the usual notion of sensuous intuition."[18] Intuition becomes the principial recourse of every concept only by being the first to undergo the phenomenological reform, in this case by submitting itself to a "fundamental broadening," by becoming "intuitive in the broadened sense that [Husserl] gives to this term."[19] One could not deny that the phenomenological redeployment of intuition, although announced as early as the Second Investigation, is not accomplished until the Sixth Investigation; as early as its introduction, it announces "an *unavoidable broadening* [*Erweiterung*] *of the originally sense-turned concepts of intuition and perception,* which permits us to speak of *categorial*, and, in particular, of *universal intuition*."[20] In fact, as if the essential decision that makes the breakthrough actual did not cease to delay its true accomplishment, the Sixth investigation will fulfill the promises of the prefaces of the First and the Second Investigations only in the second part; the first part still hesitates, as it were, to enter into the ultimate debate: "In our next chapter, which deals generally with categorial forms we shall show the need to widen [*Erweiterung*] the concepts of perception and other sorts of intuition." In fact, one will have to wait until §45, explicitly entitled "Broadening of the Concept of Intuition [*Erweiterung des Begriffes Anschauung*]," for Husserl to dare to admit before the categorial object that "we cannot manage without these words, whose broadened sense [*erweiterter Sinn*] is of course evident"—the words, unavoidably, of "'intuition,' or . . . 'perception' and 'object.'"[21] If one recognizes the guiding thread of intuition, then the direct unity of the First Investigation with the Sixth becomes clear. The First Investigation (and its prefaces) posits as the principle of principles the universal and intuitive return to the things themselves. In order to exercise the right of the concrete, intuition itself must become fit for its principial phenomenological function, in a final and most difficult effort which mobilizes the whole of the Sixth Investigation: to render even the domain of the categories intuitively given. The First Investigation "therefore has only a preparatory character [*vorbereitenden Charakter*]," since it does not yet have at its disposal the concept of intuition that it claims to put into operation; on the contrary, the Sixth Investigation, "the cornerstone of all phenomenology," must be recognized as "the most extended, in fact the most mature, and also the richest in its results, of the entire book [*aufgereifteste und wohl auch ergebnisvollste*]."[22] Should we be surprised that the path of the *Investigations* proceeds in the reverse of an analytic order, and that the point of departure already implies results that are still to come? We can certainly be surprised by this, but on the condition that we admit that Husserl had warned that phenomenology cannot not advance in this way: "we must, in our exposition, make use of all the concepts we are trying to clarify. This coincides with a certain wholly irremovable defect which affects the systematic course of our basic phenomenological and epistemological investigations . . . We search, as it were, in a zig-zag fashion, a metaphor all the more apt since the close interdependence of our various epistemological concepts leads us back [*zurückkehren*] again and again to our original analyses, where the new confirms the old, and the old the new."[23]

We can therefore respond to the first question: the breakthrough of the *Investigations* consists in leading concepts and objects back to intuition, and thus in radically broadening the scope of intuition itself. The breakthrough implies that intuition gives more than it seems, at least more than it seems to a nonphenomenological gaze. In other words, because intuition is broadened, there appears more than it seems; namely, exactly as much as intuition in its broadened sense gives to be seen by the phenomenological and therefore antinatural, gaze.

2. The Domains of Intuition

But what does the thus broadened intuition give to be seen? A quick response to this corollary of the first question will allow us to conceive exactly how far the broadening, and therefore also the breakthrough, proceeds. In the preface to the *Investigations*, Husserl underscores a second aspect of the unique breakthrough: we know evidently "something objective [*ein Gegenständliches*] that is, without, however, being in the mode of the thing [*Reales*]"; in other words: "'ideas' themselves are and count as objects [*Gegenstände*]."[24] In fact, in 1900–1901, it is a matter of understanding that "ideal objects veritably exist," for example that "the seven regular solids are seven objects just as much as the seven Wise men; the principle of the parallelogram of forces is *one* object just as much as the city of Paris."[25] In order to attain the non-natural orientation that is demanded by the breakthrough, it is necessary to consider as objects those acts taken heretofore as nonobjective—"it is precisely these acts, until now lacking in any objectivity [*nicht gegenständlich*], that must henceforth become the objects of apprehension and of theoretical position; it is these that we must consider in new acts of intuition and thinking, analyze according to their essence, describe and make the objects [*zu Gegenstände . . . machen*] of an empirical or idealistic thought."[26] Objectivity surpasses the mode of Being of the thing, frees itself from reality (*Realität, real*), and therefore is itself also broadened: "I often make use of the vaguer expression 'objectity' [*Gegenständlichkeit*], since here we are never limited to objects in the narrow sense [*im engeren Sinn*], but have also to do with states of affairs, properties, with real forms or dependent categorials, etc."[27] Commenting on the *Investigations* in 1925, Husserl will clearly posit that "there are thus without doubt *irreal* objectities and *irreal truths* belonging thereto."[28] Here it is first necessary to bring up the fact that objectity is extended beyond real objectivity, in a manner parallel to the broadening of intuition beyond the sensible; and it is necessary to note above all that these two broadenings lead to the same—categorial horizon. Moreover, in the note cited from the First Investigation, the broad objectity immediately concerns the categorial forms. It is therefore necessary to understand that to begin with the breakthrough works in favor of and with a view to the categorial, as much through broadened intuition as through broadened objectity.

The broadening of intuition is opposed to its Kantian finitude, according to whom "our nature is so constituted that our intuition can never be other than *sensible*."[29] It is therefore a matter "of submitting the very concept of intuitiveness [*Anschaulichkeit*], against its Kantian acceptation, to an essential broadening [*wesentliche Erweiterung*],"[30] a matter of admitting that the concept affects us, and therefore that the concept is given to us, in its categorial figure. The transgression of the Kantian prohibition is accomplished in three moments; each of these sets into operation a new meaning of the categorial as such, with the result that we can suppose that for Husserl *all* intuition is to some degree categorial.

1. Kant clearly stated it: sensible intuition would remain "blind" if no concept subsumed it. Husserl uses this as a reason to posit that "the goal, true knowledge, is not mere intuition, but adequate intuition that has assumed a categorial form and that perfectly adapts itself thereby to thought, or conversely, the thought that draws its evidence from intuition."[31] The most elementary intuition, hence the sensible, would not have any validity unless to begin with it had a signification whose fulfillment it assures; its function is deployed only in being restricted to the fulfillment of a categorial form. It can presuppose it only if this categorial form is given.

2. This givenness is itself realized in the mode of intuition, at least in "the evident [*einsichtige*] ideation, in which the universal is given to us 'in person.'" For "one and the same intuition" in fact delivers to us two objects that are irreducible to one another: indeed, "on the basis of the same intuitive foundation [*desselben anschaulichen Untergrundes*],"[32] two acts, and not one, are accomplished. On one hand, intuition serves as a foundational presentation for an act of individual intention—we aim at *a particular* house, or *a particular* shade of red, a *particular* little patch of yellow wall and not another,

according to a singularity that is so irreplaceable that in order to reach it one must go "directly before the model" ["*sur le motif*"] at the risk of thereby dying like Bergotte; intuition then functions, as in its first acceptation, by fulfilling a singular aim. But on the other hand we can also aim, through the first intuition utilized as a simple medium, at *the* house as the essence of any empirically possible or impossible house, *the* universal color of red which no shade among all the reds in the world could exhaust or approach, since *this* essential red never shines therein, even though all the particular reds shine on the basis of it. In this way, upon sensible intuition rests "an act of apprehension and aim directed to a species [*spezialisierenden*]," such that "a new mode of apprehension has been built upon the 'intuition' of the individual house or of its redness, a new mode that is constitutive for the intuitive datum of the idea of *red* [*intuitive Gegebenheit der idée*]."[33] Of the categorial, as universal essence, there is datum and intuitive datum: the first intuition is used in order to render the categorial intuitive because it allows itself to be turned away from the individual (and therefore from itself, which is first given *hic et nunc* in the mode of a 'this' [*dieses*]), under the possessive fascination of the categorial. "On the other hand, ideal objects truly exist . . . we also apprehend *evidently* [*einsichtig*] certain categorical truths that relate to such ideal objects."[34] Evidence [*Einsicht*] completes, in ideation, the intuition of essences. The Kantian limit yields to evidence—evidence of the essences that are *intuitively* given. We do not need to insist on this well-known point, but on what makes it possible. The intuition of essences becomes unavoidable by mobilizing already—which is absolutely remarkable—the couple of founding and founded acts, anticipating the Sixth Investigation.[35] Above all, it mobilizes the instance of the categorial. Thus, the difference between particular (founding) acts and universal (founded) acts is "categorial," for "it pertains to the pure form of possible objects of consciousness as such. (See also the Sixth Investigation, chap. 6)." Thus the "nonsensuous acts" have to do with "categorial" thought. And thus above all, when it envisages the "categorial functions," the First Investigation defines the different significations that are attributable to one *same* intuition with variations solely in the "categorial point of view.[36] (In other words, the orientation of intuition toward the universal categorial forms (the essences) rests entirely on the itself categorial interpretation of intuition—heretofore taken as sensuous. As early as the opening of the *Investigations*, the decisive step of a broadening of intuition is accomplished only on the basis of the authority of the "categorial," and thus on the basis of the Sixth Investigation. Once again, the breakthrough remains incomprehensible and unjustifiable if the whole is not read on the basis of its end. This reversal of the order in which to read the *Investigations* does not simply correspond to the methodological paradox of their "zig-zag" movement; it answers above all to the phenomenological paradox of the return to the things themselves, such as Heidegger will formulate it again in 1925:

> These acts of ideation, *of the intuition of the universal,* are categorial acts which give their object. They give what is called an idea, *species*. The Latin term *species* is the translation of eidos, *the aspect under which something shows itself* [*Aussehen von etwas*]. The acts of universal intuition give what is seen in the matters first and simply. When I perceive simply, moving about in my environmental world, when *I* see houses, for

example, I do not first see houses primarily and expressly in their individuation, in their distinctiveness. Rather, *I* first see universally: this is a house.[37]

I see *the* house, *as* house, before seeing (and in order to see) *a* house; or rather, the *as* of the house precedes a particular house and allows it to appear as such. The intuition of essences does not double sensuous intuition by a weak extension, but precedes it in rendering it phenomenologically possible.

3. Whence the last step: categorial intuition in the strict sense. In following the precise moment when, in §45, the Sixth Investigation completes "the broadening of the concept of intuition," and thus the initial (and unique) plan of the breakthrough of 1900–1901, the manner of proceeding cannot but surprise, as much by its economy of means as by the rapid conclusion. Hence a principle: "the essential homogeneity of the function of fulfillment"; in other words: whatever be the intentions of signification, they all require, in principle, at least the possibility of their intuitive fulfillment. A question is connected to this principle: In an expression like *the gold is yellow*, can all the categorial forms receive the corresponding fulfilling intuition, if we stick to the two types of intuition already recognized? It is clear that sensuous intuition (and therefore the founding acts) cannot fulfill the categorial forms of essences, like *gold* or *yellow*; therefore they receive their intuitive fulfillment only from intuitions of essence. There remains the simple *is*. Now the *is* "is itself placed under our eyes is not only thought, but precisely *intuited* [*angeschaut*], perceived." In fact, we do not mean here only *gold*, and then *yellow*, but indeed their connection, and therefore we affirm their unity; more than that, we affirm that the predicative unity is doubled by an existential declaration: we do not mean simply *the gold* (is) *yellow, yellow-gold*, but also *the yellow-gold is*. Therefore we can note that these strictly categorial aims require an intuition and a corresponding fulfillment. We finally obtain confirmation that *is* is properly meant and therefore awaits its own fulfillment when this aim does *not find* an adequate intuitive fulfillment: just as the signification *the yellow-gold* obviously does not coincide with the signification *the yellow-gold is*, so the absence of the intuitive fulfillment of *is* is clearly distinguished from its presence—which would give us the *yellow-gold being* in person. Both positively and negatively, the ultimate categorial form sets into operation the play of intention and of intuition, of aim and of fulfillment. Thus all significations, even categorial, in the end "unavoidably come upon 'intuition' (or upon 'perception' and 'object')."[38] Categorial intuition does not at all impose itself through some mystical initiation that would open a suspect third eye of the mind. It results from the pure and simple return to the things themselves, which verifies that the *is* itself also offers a signification and therefore requires an intuition. It therefore constitutes one particular, though polemically remarkable, case of the "great class of acts whose peculiarity it is that in them something appears as 'actual,' as 'self-given' [*etwas als 'wirklich,' und zwar als 'selbst gegebenen' erscheint*]."[39] Categorial intuition marks the determination of all intuition by the categorial requirement of the givenness in person of the phenomenon. Intuition results from givenness without exception. Another confirmation of this dependence comes from the curiously "analogical" status that is reserved for categorial intuition—analogy with all the other intuitions in relation to the requirement of a universal givenness of the phenomenon.[40]

The limit fixed upon intuition by Kant must be transgressed in various ways—but for one reason: the phenomenological requirement of the givenness in presence of every phenomenon with neither remainder nor reserve, the categorial not being an exception. We thus come upon the last corollary of the first question: Does the breakthrough of 1900–1901, now identified with the broadening of intuition, concern, directly or indirectly, metaphysics—itself definable by the primacy of presence?

3. The Completion of Presence

If metaphysics is defined by the absolute and unquestioned primacy of the presencing of beings, and if that presencing is never completed except through intuition, then one must conclude, without beating around the bush, that metaphysics was never completed as perfectly as with the breakthrough of 1900–1901, since it ends up, at the end of the Sixth Investigation, opening the field of *universal intuition* [*der allgemeinen Anschauung*]—an expression which no doubt will not seem better to many than "wooden iron."[41] Presencing covers a field with neither limit nor remainder, because the intuitive placing-in-evidence becomes universal. The powerful originality of the Husserlian institution of phenomenology can be imagined only if one measures the audacity of the thesis of the *Investigations*: nothing constitutes an exception to intuition, and therefore nothing escapes its reconduction into the full light of presence; neither the sensuous, nor essence, nor the categorial form itself—nothing will remain invisible from now on, since a mode of intuition tracks and hunts down each of these objects as so many modes of presence. Less than seven years after the breakthrough, the Göttingen *Lessons* enumerate at the end of their itinerary "the diverse modes of authentic givenness"; the list is stretched so far that it becomes obvious that no remainder of darkness or withdrawal resists the evidence of appearing [*l'apparaitre*]. Husserl indeed takes an inventory successively of "the givenness of the *cogitatio*," the givenness in recent memory, the givenness of the phenomenal unity in flux, the givenness of the variation of the latter in flux, the givenness of the thing exterior" to the flux, the givenness specific to remembrance and imagination, the givenness of logical entities, the givenness of the universal, and even the givenness of absurdity and of logical nonsense. Hence the ultimate but inevitable consequence that "givenness is everywhere *überall ist die Gegebenheit*]."[42] Like the flow of a tidal wave, givenness submerges all beings and all thought, since the invisible (ἀόρατον) par excellence, the intelligible as λόγος and *idea*, allows itself in a sense to be staged by an intuition that from now on is without limit (in the Kantian sense), without condition (in the Leibnizian sense), and without reserve. Without reserve here means: without keeping anything in the invisibility of withdrawal, but also without maintaining the least self-restraint. Intuition inspects everything and respects nothing; it fulfills the theoretical requirement with a strange sort of barbarism—the flood of presence. One should not be mistaken about the ever more programmatic character of Husserlian phenomenology: it is not a question of any indecision concerning the final direction, nor concerning the means to reach it; the direction is presencing; the sole means is universalized intuition. If the undertaking becomes programmatic, it is because the excessive scope of givenness delivers such a material to constitution that the *Sinngebung* discovers a task that is almost truly infinite—in the measure of the continent opened by the breakthrough. Hence Husserl's troubled and almost anguished appeal to "teams" of investigators, to "generations" of phenomenological workers who would busy themselves in all the available "regions." In this extremely sober way, phenomenology reaches a sort of ὕβρις before the presence that is overabundantly given by intuition. We should cite as confirmation not only what the Second Investigation evokes under the title of the "divine intuition of all [*göttliche Allerschauung*]"[43] but also a text from 1925, which, after having recalled "the task and the significance of the *Logical Investigations*," defines the "method of intuitive generalization [*intuitiven Verallgemeinerung*]" in the following way:

> First it is necessary to disclose what is experienced as a world only in a narrowly limited way [*nur eng begrenzt*] and with unclarified horizons, in such a way that we put possible experience into play, progress from possible evidences to ever new possible evidences and, so to speak, form for ourselves a total picture [*ein Gesamtbild . . . bilden*], an actually explicated though also openly progressing *total intuition of the world* [*Gesamtanschauung der Welt*]: namely as how it would look all in all [*alles in allem*] and would have to look [*aussehen*] if we fill out the open indefinite horizons with possibilities of experience which fit together harmoniously, whether it be by actually experiencing or by immersing ourselves in any experience by fantasy.[44]

Intuition does not only make objects of the world present, it makes *the* world itself present; intuition does not simply fill in the world, it superimposes itself on the world in order to coincide with the whole worldliness of its presentification. Intuition covers the world only in totalizing it according to a *Gesamtanschauung* which shows its total picture (*Gesamtbild*) in forming it (*bilden*): it fills the world with presence only inasmuch as it is itself constituted as a world. It makes (*bilden*) the world only in making itself a world. The world is worlded through intuition, which one must therefore recognize as literally universal. Intuition deposits the world into presence, without withdrawal, without remainder, without restraint. The metaphysics of presence is completed in absolute appearance (*Aussehen*)—the world as intuition of the whole, the intuition of the whole as a worlding.

The breakthrough therefore opens only onto the completion of the metaphysics of presence. We rediscover, by a different path, the interpretation proposed by Derrida. On this path, which was not his, the comparison of Husserl with Nietzsche becomes unavoidable, at least in a late (1888–89) and essential fragment, strangely entitled "Wherein I recognize my twin [*meines Gleichen*]."[45] Nietzsche claims to reveal therein "the hidden [*verborgene*] history of philosophy," not without some similarity to Husserl, who sets up phenomenology as "the secret [*geheime*] nostalgia of all modern philosophy."[46] Why has there been such a secret, such a hidden face in philosophy up until now? Because in both cases the last metaphysician makes obvious what metaphysics could not, and did not dare, allow to appear. Nietzsche defines his own innovation in quasi-phenomenological terms: "Philosophy, as I have hitherto understood and lived [*erlebt*] it, is a voluntary quest for even the most detested and notorious sides of *Dasein*." Now, does not Husserlian phenomenology aim at the frenzied investigation of the most hidden faces of *Dasein*, in order to submit to the presentifying evidence of intuition what previously no philosophy had even been able to *see* face to face? This undertaking in Nietzsche often passes for negative and, in one sense, rightly so: "Such an experimental philosophy as I live [*lebt*] anticipates experimentally even the possibilities of the most fundamental nihilism; but this does not mean that it must halt at a negation, a No, a will to negation." Similarly, in order to see, and therefore in order to return to the things themselves, Husserlian phenomenology already in 1900–1901 must negate any presupposition, to the point that it soon will carry out, under all its forms, the reduction of thought to the evidence of the given. In both cases, plenary presence first demands the destruction of the shadows that restrict or limit it and therefore obfuscate it. But just as the reduction—that other nihilism that is in the first place negative—leads to constitution and the *Sinngebung*, so Nietzsche completes the "no" with a "yes," the great *Amen*: "It wants rather to cross over to the opposite of this—to a Dionysian affirmation [*Jasagen*] of the world as it is, without subtraction, exception or selection—it wants the eternal circulation—the same things, the same logic and illogic of entanglements. The highest state a philosopher can attain: to stand in a Dionysian relationship to *Dasein*—my formula for this is *amor fati*." For its part, the phenomenological breakthrough wants "universal intuition," which makes the totality present in an "overall intuition of the world." The evidence of Husserlian givenness also brings about the "sunrise," and leaves but "the shortest shadow," and even eliminates all nonevidence from the world. To the Nietzschean noon corresponds phenomenology's intuition without remainder, just as to Zarathustra's "uncanny and unbounded Yes and Amen [*ungeheure unbegrenzte Ja-und Amen-Sagen*]" there corresponds the originary givenness of the "principle of principles."[47] For in the principle that fixes the highest state that a phenomenologist might attain, it is indeed a question of maintaining that *everything originarily offered* to us in '*intuition*' (so to speak, in its carnal actuality) *is to be accepted simply as it gives itself;* but also *only within the limits in which it is given there.*"[48] To receive what is given in the noon of intuition as it is given, neither more (Husserl) nor less (Nietzsche)—exactly, according to the sole "legitimate source of cognition," intuition, in both without limit, remainder or withdrawal. Also, in another fragment devoted to the "highest will to power," and therefore echoing the "highest state," Nietzsche explicitly thinks "'being' as phenomenon ('*Das Seiende' als Schein*),"[49] not without announcing Husserl's end point: "Under the blow of the reduction . . . all the ontologies fall," such that "pure phenomenology as well seems to harbor within itself all the ontologies."[50] Beings find their "legitimate source" only in allowing themselves to be reduced to intuition, and therefore made present, with neither remainder nor withdrawal, in the (just) measure that they are given—in short, in appearing as phenomena. Destruction and monstration are spoken equally by the ambivalence of *Schein,* "mere semblance" but also "appearance." Nothing is that does not appear, nothing appears that is not. Therefore the "broadened" intuition and/or the "unbounded yes" set the norm for the Being of beings by ensuring its perfect presence. In order to complete the metaphysics of presence, Nietzsche can therefore recognize as his most strange but no doubt most unavoidable twin—Husserl.

At least in outline, we have thus attained the answer to our first question: the breakthrough of the *Investigations* completes the "metaphysics of presence" by broadening intuition to the point that it manages, in an echo of Nietzsche's "great *Amen*," to place the totality of beings in presence.

4. A Misunderstanding of Signification?

There remains a second question: the completion of the primacy of intuition as universal presentification, a primacy that indisputably characterizes the breakthrough of the *Investigations*, a primacy that we have underscored even more clearly (if that is possible) than did Derrida, a primacy, finally, that affiliates a nascent phenomenology with a Nietzsche coming to his end—does this completion suffice to make the breakthrough of 1900–1901 fall entirely, immediately, and forever back into metaphysics, itself understood as a "metaphysics of presence"? This question can be understood correctly only by adding two remarks to it.

1. The definition of metaphysics by the primacy of presence in it and the claim to identify metaphysics as a unifying form of all philosophy sends us back to Heidegger's thought, without which these ideas would have remained unworkable; therefore, any use of these notions implies taking a position with respect to their initiator. Now it happens that, in returning the breakthrough of the *Investigations* to the closed field of metaphysics, Derrida makes use of the Heideggerian notions without justifying their tactical reprise and without admitting their intrinsic pertinence. Should we speak in general of a "metaphysics of presence"? Should we speak of one in Husserl? Can we speak of one as early as the *Investigations?* These prejudicial questions are not posed. Nor would they so much need to be if Derrida took up the entire Heideggerian strategy for his own use. But precisely, Derrida himself thinks too originally to do so without reservation. For if he accepts the notion of the "metaphysics of presence," he rejects just as radically Heidegger's understanding of the *Investigations:* far from seeing in them the first fruits of a "new beginning," he unveils in them the pure and simple completion of metaphysics—as, precisely, the unveiling of beings in presence. This double and strongly contrasted usage of Heideggerian theses is surprising; it can without any doubt be justified, but it also no doubt does not receive an explicit legitimation in *Speech and Phenomena.*[51] In other words, one needs to ask about this paradox: In reading the *Investigations*, how can we play one Heideggerian thesis (the "Metaphysics of presence") against another (the categorial intuition of Being as the outline of a "new beginning")? We will not claim to resolve this paradox, but we will allow its strange light to illuminate our argument.

2. Besides, Derrida's interpretation largely escapes the simplism that we are attributing to it. For Derrida, the *Investigations* in fact fall back into metaphysics only inasmuch as they have first attained the outer edge of the field of presence; they return to metaphysics only because they fail to transgress that field for "Husserl describes, and in one arid the same movement effaces, the emancipation of speech [*discours*] as nonknowing." By such a "speech as nonknowing" one must understand more precisely—and this distortion might appear as surprising as it is remarkable—the status of signification (*Bedeutung, meinen*), which is valid without the confirmation of an intuition and therefore without the foundation of a presencing; Husserl was no doubt the first (which, by the way, Derrida does not specify) to have understood that "it belongs to the original structure of expression to be able to dispense with the full presence of the object aimed at by intuition"; or again, that "the absence of intuition . . . is not only *tolerated* by speech, it is *required* by the general structure of signification, when considered *in itself.*"[52] Husserl's step forward

would liberate signification from presence. The step back—for Husserl would recoil before his own audacity within the *Investigations* themselves—would reestablish for signification an obligatory confirmation by intuition, and therefore it would censure the autonomy of signification, or rather, to say it with Derrida, "the sign would be foreign to that self-presence; the foundation of presence in general." In order thus to reconstruct the double but simultaneous movement of a breakthrough (toward ideal signification) and of a retreat (before the originally nonoriginal *différance* of the sign), Derrida must implicitly introduce, skillfully, two crucial decisions. First he must lead the definition of signification back to that of the sign or of "speech" [*discours*]; this equivalence, moreover, governs his interpretation much more profoundly than that to which he nevertheless gives priority between the sign endowed with signification (*Zeichen*) and the indication deprived of any "quality of figuration" (*Anzeige*); for before deciding whether indication constitutes the ultimate truth of the significant sign, or the inverse, it remains to be demonstrated that the essence of signification plays first and completely in the figures of the sign. This is self-evident for Derrida but not for Husserl.[53] Next, Derrida must presuppose that intuition governs the "metaphysics of presence" through and through, and therefore that intuition alone completes presencing. But does intuition constitute the last word concerning presence, at least for Husserl?

It seems to us that these two decisions sustain Derrida's entire reading of the *Investigations*. They would equally merit a close discussion. Nevertheless, since they in fact first determine the point of departure proper to Derrida's itinerary (if "property" didn't sound *here* like the impropriety par excellence), and since we are concerned only with the assignation of its stakes to the Husserlian breakthrough, we will occupy ourselves only with the second of these decisions, without concealing how much the first is worthy of question, and without forgetting it entirely. Indeed, the equivalence maintained by Derrida between intuition and presence raises a formidable difficulty in situating signification within phenomenology itself. What status can Husserl grant to signification when, on the one hand, he establishes it apart from any confirming intuition, and when, on the other hand, thanks to its "broadening" to the level of a "total intuition, *Gesamtanschauung*," intuition becomes the universal presencing? In other words, if signification signifies without intuition (such would be the breakthrough according to Derrida), if presence is given universally through intuition (such seemed to us Husserl's breakthrough), what remainder of presence, what mode of Being, in short what place would still belong in particular to signification? The step back would result almost necessarily from this aporia, which Derrida renders unavoidable, whereas Heidegger seems not even to divine it. It is necessary to pose *one* question to the *Investigations*: Does the "broadening" of intuition to the dimensions of a world not radically contradict the autonomy (the ideality) of signification? What presence can still accommodate "intentional" and especially significant "nonexistence" when intuition exhausts all presence? In short, since signification dispenses with presence, and therefore with Being, signification could do without intuition only in doing without itself. This is the aporia. Derrida leads us to it, and Derrida alone. Nevertheless, it seems to us that he responds to it with an elegance that is in some way too quick and too easy to do justice to the question which thus arises. According to that response, encountering "the *différance* . . . that is always older than presence," Husserl would have "turned away from" the "consequences" thereof, as one turns away from an obstacle. The "intuitionist imperative," the authentic categorical imperative of metaphysics, would have held back the breakthrough at the threshold of *différance*, and from the beginning "the originality of meaning as an aim is limited by the telos of vision. To be radical, the difference that separates intention from intuition would nevertheless have to be *provisional*."[54] Do such a self-contradiction on Husserl's part and such a half-conscious repentance offer the only possible picture? No doubt, at least if intuition constitutes the last word of presence; within this hypothesis alone signification must either turn toward *différance* or else fall back under the intuitionist yoke. This hypothesis—which Derrida indisputably presupposes as the horizon of the aporia that he constructs—characterizes metaphysics precisely as a "metaphysics of presence": Being amounts to being present, and presence amounts to intuition. Before this hypothesis, two paths still open up for interpretation. Either Husserl can only go back on his decision in contradicting the autonomy of signification by the "broadening" of intuition; and he would admit thereby to recognizing as unsurpassable the metaphysical hypothesis of presence through intuition, or else Husserl would confront the status of signification only because he would have *already* transgressed the primacy of intuition with regard to presence in a manner all the more decisive in that it would liberate signification from intuition only after having completed the most metaphysical "broadening" of the latter; in this case, the irreducibility of signification to intuition would not contradict the universality of the mode of intuitive presence but would attest, by transgression, that intuition, as universal as it might be, does not constitute the ultimate name of presence. Even without being seen through intuition, signification could still *be*. Could Being therefore be made manifest, already in the *Investigations*, otherwise than through intuition, even categorial, in a mode that is attested above all in signification? Since this interpretative path was not followed, even by the one who *a contrario* renders it possible, let us take it.

5. Presence Without Intuition

Whatever the universality of intuition might be, it admits an exteriority that is all the more irreducible in that it is preserved by "a phenomenologically irreducible difference," which, through a "total separation," leads to "the opposition between intuition and signification."[55] Of all the oppositions to which the *Investigations* lead, that which separates signification from intuition precedes those that follow, all three of which concern the diverse forms of intuition alone. The couples of sensuous/categorial intuition, adequate/inadequate intuition, and general/individual intuition do not place in question the isolation of signification; they place it, in evidence, inasmuch as they presuppose it. The intuitive extraterritoriality of signification is indicated at the end of the *Investigations*, when the last investigation has just gained the categorial intuition, which, far from bringing signification back under the intuitionist yoke, underscores, in extending itself to the most extreme significations, that it never "fulfills" and "coincides with" them except in granting them the a priori right to delimit the spaces to be saturated thus with presence. The phenomenological possibilities of error and deception, of adequate or partial fulfillment, etc., imply that signification precedes intuition and that, even when filled with an intuitive given, it receives therefrom first a confirmation of itself, and therefore of its sense. The convenient formula $i + s = I$, with its extreme variations according to whether $i = o$ or $s = o$, should not lead us into error: signification does not vary in inverse proportion to intuition; intuition can give only what it has, and it can give that only to what it is not—the always earlier signification.[56] Thus the irreducibility of signification to intuition is affirmed as early as the First Investigation, which announces "important [distinctions] that concern the possible relations between signification and the intuition that illustrates it and perhaps renders it evident." It next recognizes that in this way "there is constituted . . . an act of signification which finds support in the intuitive content of the representation of the word, but which differs in essence (*wesentlich verschieden*) from the intuitive intention directed upon the word itself."[57] Signification is opposed irreducibly to intuition and therefore, by that negation, is itself defined as the other of intuition, from the beginning to the end of the *Investigations*. Before intuition, as universal as it may be, there remains, irreducible, signification. How was this actual decision thinkable?

Because an act of signification "is constituted without need of a fulfilling or illustrative intuition," signification displays an autonomy of which intuition offers only an "eventual" complement.[58] In expression or in perception, signification is always fulfilled, and contrary to the convictions of natural consciousness, intuition either lacks totally or else is partially missing and, in any case, comes to offer itself as an addition. "Each assertion, whether representing an exercise of knowledge or not—whether or not, i.e., it fulfills or can fulfill its intention in corresponding intuitions and the categorial acts that give them form—has its intention [*ihre Meinung hat*] and constitutes in that intention, as its specific unified character, its signification [*die Bedeutung konstituiert*]."[59] Intention depends so little on intuition to complete itself as the aim of a signification that it precedes fulfillment; intention dispenses with intuition and therefore can "eventually" render its addition possible. The clearest confirmation of the "inadequacy [*Unangemessenheit*] of illustration [*Veranschaulichung*] even in the case of consistent significations,"[60] comes with examples from geometry: no mathematical ideality can find an adequate fulfillment in actually experienced space; inadequacy, and therefore the surpassing of intuition by intention, and its being exceeded by signification, far from constituting an exception, announces an absolute rule: the signification of *straight line*, or of *curve of the equation ax + b*, or even of *triangle*, will never meet an adequate fulfillment in the experiences of intuition that are actually realized by a consciousness. No doubt, the equation will continually find fulfilling intuitions, but in each case that will be for a particular value of unknowns, never for its abstract, universal essence as such. As for figure, it is clear that no empirical line will ever come to fulfill its signification intuitively; even more, it will very quickly become impossible even to have an imaginary presentification of it (the chiliagon that Descartes can no longer imagine and that he must simply understand). Mathematical understanding, on the contrary, is properly characterized by its capacity to think significations that remain irreducible to any intuition. This capacity is all the more remarkable in that the paradox grows deeper: not only is it a matter of thinking mathematical idealities as such, and therefore as significations that in principle extend beyond any intuitive fulfillment, but even more, it is a matter of thinking them as evident and as more evidently thinkable than intuition could ever make them; not only are mathematical significations thinkable, or better thinkable *only* without adequate intuition, but they are so in full evidence:

> we are appealing [*in Anspruch nehmen*] to this state of things as to an immediately graspable truth, following in this the evidence [*Evidenz*] that is the final authority in all questions of knowledge. I see evidently [*ich sehe ein*] that in repeated acts of representation and judgment I mean or can mean [*meine, bzw. meinen kann*] identically the same [*dasselbe*], the same concept or proposition; I see evidently [*ich sehe ein*] that, for example, wherever there is talk of the *proposition* or *truth* that "π *is a transcendental number*," there is nothing I have less in mind [*in Auge*] than an individual experience, or a feature of an individual experience of any person. I see evidently [*ich sehe ein*] that such reflective talk really has as its object what serves as a signification in straightforward talk. Finally, I see evidently [*ich sehe ein*] that what I mean [*meine*] in the mentioned proposition or [when I hear it] what I grasp as its signification [*als seine Bedeutung*] is the same thing, whether I think and exist or not, and whether or not there are *any* thinking persons and acts to think them.[61]

Phenomenological evidence is realized, at least here, without a fulfilling intuition or an intuition-experience, because the ideality of the object—in fact and in principle, the ideality of any signification—depends neither on an intuition nor on an intuiting agent. As early as the First Investigation, signification attains an evidence that is strictly autonomous because definitively ideal and intentional. Does not the "confusion of signification with fulfilling intuition" that is stigmatized by Husserl in Erdmann and Sigwart, for example, anticipate more clearly the diagnostic that Derrida thinks himself able to formulate—"The originality of meaning is limited by the *telos* of vision"?[62] Doesn't Husserl immediately criticize as nonphenomenological the confusion that Derrida nevertheless attributes to him, according to an anachronism that is as exemplary as it is ideal?

The autonomy of intention, of meaning, and therefore of signification can even find an indisputable confirmation in the very text that Derrida invokes to denounce the "subtle displacement" through which, finally, for Husserl "the true and genuine meaning [*vouloir-dire*] [would be] the will to say the truth [*le vouloir dire vrai*]." At issue here is a passage from the First Investigation, § 11, which, by the way, is significantly entitled "The ideal distinctions between expression and signification as ideal unities." In fact, the passage quoted by Derrida contradicts the presumed ideal status of signification, which it is supposed to illustrate; let us therefore cite the chosen sequence: "If 'possibility' or 'truth' is lacking, an assertion's intention can only be carried out symbolically: it cannot derive any 'fullness' from intuition or from the categorial functions performed on the latter, in which 'fullness' its value for knowledge consists. It then lacks, as one says [*wie man zu sagen pflegt*] a 'true,' a 'genuine' *Bedeutung*."[63] From this Derrida immediately concludes that *for Husserl* signification holds its genuine and final truth, at least *here*, from the fullness of the intuition that serves as a foundation. But Husserl's text seems to us to say just the opposite, as the following points prove. (1) The thesis stated here is not that of the phenomenologist, but indeed that of natural consciousness, explicitly named in a central phrase: "as one says [*wie man zusagen pflegt*]." (2) The terms brought up by Derrida to establish the subjection of signification (meaning) to signification fulfilled by intuition (true meaning) only appear in quotation marks: "true," genuine," "symbolic," "possibility," and "truth" are here used *wrongly* by those who, precisely, do not follow the ideal distinctions; *Husserl's* thesis will therefore consist, conversely, in refusing to refuse a signification its "truth" under the pretext that it lacks a fulfilling intuition. (3) Moreover, this is precisely what he does in the immediately following text, which is omitted by Derrida's quotation. He does this first in announcing the next developments: "Later we shall look more closely into this distinction between intending and fulfilling signification. To characterize the various acts in which the relevant ideal unities are constituted, and to throw light on the essence of their actual 'coincidence' in knowledge, will call for difficult, comprehensive studies." As is often the case in the First Investigation, here we find a reference to the Sixth, in this case to the first chapter of the first part, actually entitled "Signification-Intention and Signification-Fulfillment." Next, and in anticipation of the complete argument, Husserl dogmatically posits his own thesis, which absolutely contradicts the opinion of natural consciousness and therefore also the thesis that Derrida wrongly attributes to him: "It is certain, however [*Sicher aber ist*], that each assertion, whether representing an exercise of knowledge or not—whether or not, i.e., it fulfills or can fulfill its intention in corresponding intuitions, and the categorial acts that give form to these—has its intention [*ihre Meinung*] and constitutes its signification [*die Bedeutung konstituiert*] in that intention as its specific unified character." Unless one wants to claim that Husserl contradicts himself word for word within a couple lines, one must acknowledge that if, finally, it is "certain" that every expression has an intention, and therefore a signification, whether *or not* it has an intuitive fulfillment, then the converse opinion, mentioned above in an intentionally loose language— signification becomes "true" only by finding its foundation in intuition—must be taken not as Husserl's conclusion but as the error that he criticizes. (4) The passage whose integrity we have just reestablished is framed by formulas that leave no room for any doubt. A few lines lower, Husserl invokes "the evidently, grasped ideal unity" that one must not confuse with real judgment. A few lines higher, he evokes the "ideal content, the signification of the statement as a unity in diversity," in order to add the decisive point: "we do not arbitrarily attribute it to our statements, but discover it in them [*sondern finden sie darin*]."[64] We conclude therefore that if "displacement" there must be in § 11 of the First Investigation, it is not "subtle" but on the contrary fairly crude, as is suitable to a position that is explicitly *rejected* by Husserl.

If this text leads to what must indeed be called a misinterpretation, the reason for it could not be a run-of-the-mill oversight. On the contrary, it is through an overly selective attention that Derrida isolates the antithesis in order to turn it into one of Husserl's own theses; indeed, he proceeds starting from the interpretation of another text of decisive importance and difficulty: §26 of the First Investigation, which is dedicated to "essentially occasional and objective expressions." Husserl here stresses that any expression including a personal (or a demonstrative) pronoun ceases to intend *one* signification; for the meaningful sign there is substituted a meaningless sign, whose "indicative [*anzeigende*] function," or whose "universally effective indication [*allgemein wirksames Anzeichen*]," indicates an infinity of possible significations only because it does not signify (and show) any that are self-identical. Here the sign lacks signification. Husserl adds a sequence that

Derrida privileges: "The word *I* names a different person from case to case, and it does so by way of an ever new *Bedeutung*." But then can one legitimately ask about the source of a signification that is always arising because never given in the statement? Husserl's answer is cited immediately by Derrida: "What on each occasion constitutes its *Bedeutung* can be gleaned only from the living discourse [*lebendige Rede*] and from the intuitive data [*anschaulichen Umständen*, intuitive circumstances] that are a part of it. When we read this word without knowing who wrote it, we have a word that is, if not lacking *Bedeutung* [*bedeutungslos*], at least foreign to its normal *Bedeutung*." Signification therefore does indeed depend here on intuition; and it is Derrida who concludes that "Husserl's premises should sanction our saying exactly the contrary."[65]

And yet this objection seems to us weak for several reasons. (1) The absence of signification, in fact indisputable here, and therefore the eventual recourse to intuition to fix it, here has to do with a very particular case: the indeterminacy of the *this* (or of the *I*), such as Hegel, for example, already pointed it out; this type of expression is characterized not by the reduction of signification to intuition, but by the absolute and radical absence of signification itself; it is called an "essential" absence by Husserl, who makes of it less a particular and privileged case of *all* expression (as is supposed by the generalization undertaken by his critic) than an exception to the normal system of expression, or even a veritable nonexpression; if there is no expression without signification—for "the essence of an expression lies solely in its signification"[66]—the essentially occasional expressions must be understood as essentially *non*expressive. They therefore could not call the doctrine of expression into question because they simply do not pertain to it. (2) One should be surprised that the *I* cannot in itself have a signification at its disposal all the less insofar as, in the *Investigations* at least, the *I*, reduced to a simple "complex of experiences," has no ideal signification (as transcendental *I*), with the result that "there is nothing to remark" about the I as the meeting point of completed acts.[67] One would have to oppose another paradox to the alleged paradox denounced by Derrida: Husserl's premises concerning the status of the *I* would have to force us to acknowledge the essentially nonexpressive character of the occasional expressions where it occurs. (3) The weakness of the signification of the *I* irremediable in the First Investigation, is nevertheless not Husserl's last word in 1901; interpreters cannot remain silent about the resumption of the same question in § 5, addendum, of the Sixth Investigation, which explicitly retrieves § 26 from the First Investigation; in this text, which we will not take up here in all of its difficulty, Husserl attempts at least partially to reintroduce signification into indication. He does this first by opposing to the hearer of the *I*, who receives only a "universal and indeterminate thought" and therefore depends on an intuition to constitute signification, the speaker who himself receives the indication as given and immediately possesses "the 'indicated' signification [*die 'angezeigte' Bedeutung*]": he does not have the indication of a signification that is not given, but the givenness of a signification in the sole mode of indication; in short, indication does not always exclude signification, inasmuch as indicated. He does so next by sketching a phenomenology of "indicated intention," as much in mathematics as in the simple deictics of the *this*.[68]

In short, the text privileged by Derrida, while certainly difficult, does not fundamentally call into question the ideal autonomy of signification; it would even be necessary to stress that, at the very moment one meets an objection that is as old (Hegel) as it is formidable, Husserl—even if he concedes at first (and how could he avoid it?) that the expression including an *I* does not offer by itself any "normal signification"—warns nevertheless, even before this step back, that it is in any case not a matter of a "meaning-less word [*nicht ein bedeutungslos*]."[69] Without, obviously, claiming to exhaust all the arguments that would support it, and without refuting all those that would challenge it, we will hold to a single thesis: in the *Logical Investigations*, signification is given evidently without depending on fulfilling intuition. Even without intuition, "we find it there," to speak like the First Investigation. Similarly, it does not owe anything either to the "phonic complex," to speak like the Sixth Investigation, for "signification cannot, as it were, hang in the air, but for what it signifies, the sign, whose signification actual we call it, is entirely indifferent."[70] "Without intuition, signification is nevertheless not disseminated according to the anomic rhythm of the differences of the signifier. In other words; signification offers a "content" that is sometimes characterized as an "ideal content," sometimes understood "as intending sense, or as sense," sometimes identified with a "theoretical content" or a. "logical content"—in all cases, "the essence of signification is seen by us, not in the meaning-conferring experience [*bedeutungverleihenden Erlebnis*], but in its 'content,' which presents [*darstellt*] an identical intentional unity."[71] Signification has a content (*Inhalt, Gehalt*); it holds it in itself and by itself; it does not hold this content like the tenure it possesses so much as it maintains itself in it, and in order to maintain itself in it, it holds in and to it alone. The maintenance of signification, without intuition, indication or enunciative act, is sufficient for it to present itself (*sich darstellt*) in presence. But is it really legitimate to speak here of presence, 'without any presentation instituting it? Perhaps it would be suitable to reverse the question: What mode of presence is deployed sui generis when signification, by itself and itself alone, presents itself?

6. The Evidence of Givenness

Thus, according to a mode of presence that is still undetermined and that, for this very reason, might not be defined exactly by the Word "presence," "each signification can be thought completely [*vollzogen*] without the least correlative intuition." This thesis from the Sixth Investigation is confirmed by another that explicitly takes up again the conclusions of the First Investigation: "*What is here the act in which signification resides?* I think we must say, in harmony with points established in our First Investigation, that: it does not reside in perception, at least not in perception alone."[72] In other words, "signification cannot first [*nicht erst*] have been acquired [*sichvollzogen*] through intuition," because, conversely, "first there is given, and given for itself, the signification-intention; only then [*dann erst*] does the corresponding intuition come to join in."[73] The anteriority of signification over any intuition, ensured by signification's independence, alone explains the *last* word of the First Investigation: whatever be the broadening of intuition, "there are [*es gibt*] ... countless significations which ... can never be expressed."[74] The signification that "we find there" is constituted by itself, in a mode of advance that is without condition because, even though pure of intuition, it attains "the final authority in questions of knowledge: evidence." The decisive point here is this: as an actual though non-real object, signification ultimately appears in full evidence, in the form of "an evidently [*einsichtig*] grasped ideal unity . . . which evidently stands before us [*mit Evidenz . . gegenübersteht*] in its unity and identity [*als Eine und Selbige*]."[75] Phenomenologically, evidence can allow itself anything—in the capacity of final authority—and therefore it can also allow anything—in its capacity as universal choreographer of the visible. It allows itself to make known that significations "must necessarily *exist*, that is, present [*darstellen*] a unitary sense." The autonomy (*Selbige*) in which the unity of sense culminates stems from its sufficiency for entering into visibility (*darstellen*); therefore, since Being is phenomenologically reduced to evidence, signification exists insofar as it signifies by itself: "significations that actually are—that are as significations [*wirklichseiende Bedeutungen— seiend als Bedeutungen*]." In his breakthrough, Husserl reaches Being *before* the Sixth Investigation, and therefore before the categorial intuition, when the Fourth Investigation manages to distinguish the "independent [*selbständigen*]" significations in their specificity; for because of its independence, "signification itself exists in person."[76] The phenomenological placing-in-evidence reaches Being as existence as soon as it reaches signification as independent, precisely because its independence qualifies it as an actual being. Signification is broadened not only to meaning offered without intuition, but even to its acceptance as the actuality of a being. Meaning, as such, has the validity of a being, which consecrates the absolute independence of signification against any presupposition— including and especially intuition. Would it be necessary to go so far as to take intuition as a presupposition to be reduced, in order that there appear the final given of signification?

We thus approach what nevertheless could indeed open up an understanding of the breakthrough of 1900–1901. If it is definitively established that the breakthrough first accomplishes the universal broadening of intuition, we would nevertheless have to envisage the hypothesis that signification also (even especially) is broadened to the point of actually existing as a strictly autonomous being. Everything happens as if intuition were liberated from sensuousness only—according to a paradox still to be considered—in order to allow signification then to be liberated from intuition. And natural consciousness no doubt puts up as much resistance to this second broadening as to the first. Nevertheless, it is necessary to yield to the evidence—to the evidence of evidence—that a text confirms: "*The realm of signification is, however; much wider* [*sehr viel umfassender*] *than that of intuition*."[77] The difficulty of such a thought does not result from its lack of evidence but, quite the opposite, from an excess of evidence in it. There is an excess first of the evidence of intuition over the limits of sensuousness, so far as to be established as a total universal intuition (*Gesamtanschauung*). Next there is an excess of signification that exists beyond intuition, with which it essentially dispenses—the "draft drawn on intuition" is regularly honored by signification all the less insofar as, in principle, the latter is not held to draw it. Finally, and especially, there is an excess of the second excess over the first: incomprehensibly, signification surpasses—by far—the total field of intuition; but how can a field that is *already* broadened and *already* total be transgressed? How are we to avoid the contradiction between the broadening of intuition and the broadening of signification? "The unresolved tension of the two major motifs in phenomenology: the purity of formalism and the radicality of intuitionism"[78] becomes insurmountable as soon as one admits that, in principle if not in fact, intuition here completes metaphysics by no longer tolerating any remainder—any fringe still available to mark the vastness of the realm of signification. To where would this realm extend itself if intuition already covers and discovers everything, including the categorial, in evidence alone? For, precisely, evidence could seem here to spring from *two* sources: intuition or signification—two sources that are autonomous to the point of competing for primacy. In the last phase of his own continual reinterpretation of the *Investigations*, Husserl characterizes them according to a feature that, through its very indeterminacy, easily lends itself to such a contradiction:

> What is new in the *Logical Investigations* . . . is found not at all in the merely ontological investigations . . . but rather in the subjectively directed investigations (above all the fifth and sixth, in the second volume of 1901) in which, for the first time, the *cogitata qua cogitata*, as essential moments of any conscious experience come into their own and immediately come to dominate the whole method of intentional analysis. Thus "self-evidence" (that petrified logical idol) is made a problem here for the first time, freed [*befreit*] from the privilege given to scientific evidence and broadened to mean original self-giving in general [*zur allgemeinen originalen Seibstgebung erweitert*].[79]

That evidence is freed from the limits of natural consciousness for the first time with the breakthrough of the *Investigations*, very well; that it is broadened to the point of coinciding with any self-givenness, originally and universally, very well again; but must the ultimate "broadening" of evidence be understood as the "broadening" of intuition (to the categorial, such as the mention of the Fifth and Sixth Investigations invites us to believe) *or* as the broadening of the realm of signification, "more vast—by far—than that of intuition"? The broadening seems so wide—an unconditional amnesty that would free indiscriminately everything that, like so many captives, metaphysical requirements had fettered—that it "does not want to know" what it frees, or at the very least does not identify or declare it. To what exactly does the "broadening" give free rein? The simple mention of a universal *Selbstgebung* does not answer this question: to the contrary, the indeterminacy of the universality in it underscores the unresolved ambiguity of the evidence. Does the breakthrough of 1900–1901 remain obscure due to an excess of evidence? Would phenomenology, far from resolving the conflict between them, merely exacerbate the irreducibility of formality and intuitionism, by confusing them within an obscure evidence that is universal but vague?

The same interpretation of the *Investigations* that confirms the aporia no doubt also opens the way out. A little beforehand, in fact, a note from the *Krisis*, a note that is decisive in other respects, fixes the breakthrough of 1900–1901 in its origins: "The first breakthrough of this universal correlational a priori of the object of experience and of the modes of givenness [*dieses universalen Korrelationsapriori von Erfahrungsgegenstand und Gegebenheitsweisen*] (while I was working on my *Logical Investigations*, around 1898) struck me so profoundly that, ever since, my whole life's work has been dominated by this task of elaborating the correlational *a priori*." The body of the paragraph confirms this interpretation: "Never before (that is, never before the first breakthrough [*durch-*

bruch] of 'transcendental phenomenology' in the *Logical Investigations*) has the correlation of the world (the world of which we speak) with its modes of subjective givenness [*subjektiven Gegebenheitsweisen*] provoked philosophical amazement." The *Investigations* accomplish their breakthrough not first by broadening intuition or by recognizing the autonomy of signification, but by being amazed, as by a "wonder of wonders," by a correlation. Which one? One should not rush here to find the noema/noesis correlation (dominant in the *Ideen*), nor the intuition/intention correlation (prevalent in the *Investigations*); these correlations, decisive as they are, are rendered possible by a more essential relation, about which Husserl belatedly discovered that it governed the breakthrough of 1900–1901 from the beginning: "the correlation between *appearing and that which appears as such*."[80] Appearing (*Aussehen*) no longer counts as a datum [*une donnée*] for the single conscious subject, but first as the givenness of what thus appears: the appearing, through the correlation that merits the full title of "phenomenological," *gives* that which appears. Or again, that which appears, nothing less than an actual being, appears in person in the appearance, because, according to a necessity of essence (the correlation), it gives itself therein. Phenomenology begins in 1900–1901 because, for the first time, thought sees that which appears appear in appearance; it manages to do this only by conceiving the appearing itself no longer as a "given *of* consciousness," but indeed as the givenness *to* consciousness (Or even *through* consciousness) of the thing itself, given in the mode of appearing and in all of its dimensions (intuition, intention, and their variations): "Beings, whatever their concrete or abstract, real or ideal sense, have their own modes of self-givenness in person [*Weisen der Selbstgegebenheit*]."[81] The phenomenological breakthrough consists neither in the broadening of intuition, nor in the autonomy of signification, but solely in the unconditional primacy of the givenness of the phenomenon. Intuition and intention, as liberated as they may be, are so only through the givenness that they illustrate—or rather that never ceases to illuminate them—and of which they deliver only modes—the "modes of givenness" of that which appears. Intuition and intention would give nothing (and therefore would not have themselves to be given) if everything did not have first, by virtue of the principle of correlation, to be given in order to appear. Givenness precedes intuition and intention because they make sense only for and through an appearance, which counts as the appearing of something that appears (a phenomenon being) only by virtue of the principle of correlation—and therefore of givenness. From now on, seeing [*paraître*] no longer belongs to the domain of semblance [*apparence*], since, in the capacity of an arrival at seeing [*paraître*], it issues from appearing [*apparaître*] and therefore from something that appears. This thing that appears, correlated to its apparition [*apparition*] through the appearing itself, does not deceive in its apparition—as tenuous as the appearance may be (partial intuition, empty intention)—because it gives itself therein. Givenness alone—as it operates in the correlation—loads semblance [*apparence*] with its seriousness as an apparition: there is never an appearing without something that appears, and there is never something that appears (something appearable, if we might risk the neologism) without an apparition. Givenness is thus executed phenomenologically through the strict play of the correlation between what appears (given to give) and the apparition in the semblance. Givenness alone is absolute, free and without condition, precisely because it gives. In 1907 Husserl will say it clearly: "Absolute givenness [*Gegebenheit*] is an ultimate." Or, reciprocally: "The 'seeing' or grasping of what is self-given in person [*Selbstgegebenes*], insofar as it is actual 'seeing,' actual self-givenness [*Selbstgegebenheit*] in the strictest sense, and not another sort of givenness [*Gegebenheit*] which points to something that is not given—that is an ultimate. That is *what is understood absolutely by itself* [*Selbstverständlichkeit*]." The reduction itself would exercise no priority if it did not lead the phenomenon to its final givenness: "*the givenness [die Gegebenheit] of any .reduced phenomenon is an absolute and indubitable givenness.*"[82] In 1913, the "principle of principles" privileges intuition only to the extent that it interprets intuition first as "originarily giving" and admits as one of its formulations a definition that starts directly from givenness: "We see indeed [*Sehen wir doch ein*] that each theory can only again draw its truth from originary data (or: givennesses? [*Gegebenheiten*])."[83] Already in 1900–1901 givenness preceded ("eventual") intuition as much as it did signification, since "for consciousness the given remains essentially equal [*das Gegebene ein wesentlich Gleiches*], whether the represented object exists, or is made up and even perhaps absurd."[84] For both must allow themselves to be reinterpreted as two modes of the one givenness which alone is originary.

Intuition is opened to its "broadening" only inasmuch as it is given first as a mode of givenness: "Thus, when the signification-intention is fulfilled in a corresponding intuition, in other words, when expression, in the current operation of naming, is related to the given object [*auf den gegebenen Gegenstand*], the object is then constituted as 'given' [*als 'gegebener'*] in certain acts, and in truth [*zwar*] it is *given* to us in them—if at any rate the expression actually fits the intuitive given [*dem auschaulich Gegebenen*]—in *the same mode* according to which it is aimed at by signification."[85] In such a text, givenness very clearly marks its anteriority by defining each of the terms to be considered: the object, already "given" in signification, is found "given" anew by intuition, in "the same mode" as the latter; the subtle play of quotation marks alone indicates the divergence between two givennesses, as discretely as is required by the unique dative character of the originary phenomenality. The "object at once intended and 'given,'" or the "meant objectity (which is 'given' to us in evident cognition)"[86] always remains given in the fulfilling intuition because it was in fact *already* in the signification. The "broadening" of intuition does not contradict the autonomy of signification but rather implies it: in both cases it is a question solely of the originary givenness, which can increase one of its modes only by increasing the other—which conditions the first. Intuition can be broadened only by broadening its fulfillment, and therefore by depending on the meant spaces to be fulfilled. If intuition must give, it is therefore already and especially necessary that significations be released, and therefore that they be already given, without intuition and in full autonomy. And in fact, "first there is given, and given for itself, the signification-intention; it is only then that there intervenes, in addition, the corresponding intuition," for "there are significations [*es gibt also . . . Bedeutungen*]."[87] Nothing precedes givenness, which is modulated in all the modes of the phenomenon, whatever they might be. More "broadened" than intuition, more autonomous than signification, givenness gives the phenomenon through itself because it falls thoroughly to givenness to deal the thing in person. In their ultimate advance, the *Investigations* will equate the *Selbstdarstellung* or the *Selbsterscheinung des Gegenstandes*[88] with its *Selbstgegebenheit,* where "something appears as actual and as *given* in person [*als selbst gegeben*]." We should understand the syntagm *aktuelles Gegebensein*[89] in its strictest acceptation: only given Being is fulfilled, as a presencing in the metaphysically insurmountable mode of the act. To the question concerning the mode of presence that is irreducible to intuition, or even concerning the legitimacy of the term "presence," we can therefore outline a response: already in the *Investigations* Husserl determines presence by going beyond intuition to the point of attributing it to signification only because he passes beyond both in favor of givenness. Everything that reveals itself as given, inasmuch as already given, appears, because inasmuch as given to seem, it is. To be—to be in presence, since in metaphysics the two are equivalent—amounts to the givenness that gives to the given the opportunity to appear. One must no doubt recognize here one last figure of the "metaphysics of presence," and confirm Derrida's interpretation. But with two small remarks. (1) Presence is nevertheless not reduced to intuition, to the detriment of autonomous signification; presence triumphs as much in signification as in intuition; the whole of the *Investigations* therefore belongs to the domain of metaphysics. Derrida's interpretation remains, paradoxically, *not* radical *enough* (supposing signification to be broken off from presence, and therefore excepted from metaphysics), because it still contributes to an overly narrow understanding of presence which misses the properly Husserlian deepening of presence as a givenness. It remains the case that, without that interpretation, the Husserlian deepening of presence as givenness would itself have no doubt remained unapproachable. We must therefore confirm Derrida's conclusion—phenomenology remains a "metaphysics of presence"—all the while contesting its principal argument—the reduction of presence to intuition alone. *Here*, and precisely because it is realized in the name of all metaphysics, presence yields to givenness. (2) But if presence culminates in a givenness where the given appears, if therefore the "metaphysics of presence" is completed without remainder with the breakthrough of the *Logical Investigations*, how are we to understand the fact that Heidegger was able to recognize in them his own point of departure, as much during his Marburg courses as during his last seminar, in 1973? Would he have missed givenness as the completion of the primacy of presence? Would he have taken for a break with metaphysics that which seems to us, with Derrida, its unreserved realization? Thus arises the last question.

7. Givenness as a Question

Heidegger himself at least twice recognized in the breakthrough of the *Investigations* the necessary (although insufficient) condition of the "new beginning" that as *Sein und Zeit.* In 1925, in his summer semester course, he salutes "what is decisive in the discovery of categorial intuition" in the fact that it "gives a ground." In 1973, in the final so-called Zähringen seminar, he confirms that "by this *tour de force* [of Husserl] I finally had a ground."[90] It thus seems to be self-evident, as much for Heidegger as for his interpreters, that categorial *intuition,* by fixing the Being itself at work in the expression, defines the hyphen—tenuous but obstinate—between the last metaphysician and the first "thinker."

If such is the case, then Derrida's critique would be victorious: even with Heidegger, presence, ceaselessly reinsured by the primacy of intuition, would discover the Being proper to every being, and it would therefore cover over the originarily nonoriginary *différance*.[91] But the sanctioned interpretation (or indeed self-interpretation) of Heidegger, as right as it seems literally, perhaps masks the essential. According to these two texts, what is essential does not have to do with the intuition of categorial Being, which, moreover, neither one formulates in these terms. For, in fact, categorial Being is never said here to be intuited, nor intuitable, but only and more radically *given* according to categorial intuition. In 1973, categorial intuition is thought explicitly by *analogy* with sensible intuition, an analogy that is rendered inevitable by the fact that Being *is given* as much as the sensible: "For Husserl, the categorial (that is, the Kantian forms) is *given* just as much as the sensible. Therefore there is indeed CATEGORIAL INTUITION. Here the question bounces back: by what path does Husserl arrive at categorial intuition? The answer is clear: categorial intuition being *like* sensible intuition (being giving), Husserl arrives at categorial intuition by the path of analogy." According to Heidegger, the Husserlian path would be reconstructed as follows: givenness surpasses the limits of sensible intuition, and therefore, by analogy, one must admit a giving intuition that is nonsensible, that is, categorial. The decision that leads to categorial intuition therefore *does not* arise from intuition itself, but from the excess of givenness over the sensible, over the giving intuition in the sensible. If intuition becomes categorial, it is because Being gives itself, and not because Being is given by virtue of categorial intuition. Categorial intuition does not give Being, but Being makes inevitable the admission of something like categorial intuition due to its own givenness. Let us reread the decisive passage in order to be convinced: "In order even to develop the question of the meaning of Being, it was necessary that Being be *given,* so that one might question its meaning. Husserl's *tour de force* consisted precisely in this presencing of Being, phenomenally present in the category. By this *tour de force,*" Heidegger adds, "I finally had a ground: 'Being' is not a simple concept, a pure abstraction obtained thanks to the work of deduction. The point that Husserl nevertheless did not pass is the following: having more or less obtained Being as *given,* he does not question any further."[92] The decisive step of the *Investigations* consists in reaching "Being as *given.*" Husserl manages to take it, at least "more or less." What constitutes the weakness? No doubt this: that he contents himself, too easily, with naming that givenness without truly thinking it. How does he name it? Through the finally very rough analogy of a categorial intuition, which, by a new (or rather very old) syntagm, dissimulates the abyss of the givenness of Being. Could one risk saying, without declaring it, that Heidegger opposes categorial intuition to givenness? The breakthrough goes as far as the givenness of Being, but recoils in face of its abyss, by closing it again through the unquestioned because problematic, but structurally traditional, concept of categorial intuition. If categorial intuition results from givenness, then far from provoking givenness, the thought that does no more than stand in categorial intuition flees the enigma of givenness. Heidegger, as opposed to Husserl, will seek to think givenness, and therefore he will destroy categorial intuition—indeed, he will no longer evoke it either in *Sein und Zeit* or later.

This paradoxical conclusion finds confirmation in the 1925 course. Analyzed as one of the "fundamental discoveries" of the "*fundamental book of phenomenology*" that ensures its "breakthrough," categorial intuition is there thought straightaway as an intuition, and therefore as a *"pure and simple grasp of the given in the flesh [von leibhaftig Gegebenem], such as it shows itself,"* it being well understood that *"the flesh is a signal mode of the self-givenness of a being [der Selbstgegebenheit eines Seienden]."* It imposes itself, beyond sensible intuition, as soon as one notices that some categories, like "totality," "and," "but," etc., in fact arrive at an *"originary self-givenness [originären Selbstgebung]"* in the same way as significations fulfilled through sensible intuition.[93] Categorial intuition can be admitted only in response to a categorial givenness, and therefore in being thought first as giving. The categorial acts, "in regard to their character as giving [*gebende*] acts . . . are intuitions, they *give* objectity [*sie geben Gegenständlichkeit*]"; and therefore the categorial act "brings the being in this new objectity to givenness [*zur Gegebenheit*]," precisely because that objectity is defined by self-givenness, as "self-giving [*sich gebende*] objectity."[94] Categorial intuition is never—and this is already true in 1925—directly related to being (still less to Being) as some "intuition of Being"; it always mediates its relation to being through givenness, which originarily determines them both. The breakthrough does not consist here, either, in the broadening of intuition alone, but in the broadening of the concept of reality or of objectity to the dimensions of givenness: "Rather, by way of understanding what is present in categorial intuition, we can come to see that the objectivity of a being is not absolutely exhausted by reality in the narrow sense, and that objectivity [*Objektivität oder Gegenständlichkeit*] in the broadest sense [*im weitesten Sinne*] is much richer than the reality of a thing, and what is more, that the reality of a thing is comprehensible in its structure only on the basis of the total objectivity of the purely and simply experienced being."[95] The stake of the *Investigations*, particularly of the Sixth, has less to do with categorial intuition than with what it points to without itself realizing it—the broadening of presence, understood as objectity, according to the excessive measure of givenness. The broadening must be understood not only as an extension (*Erweiterung*) of intuition and of signification through givenness, but especially as "the demand for a liberation of the [phenomenological] ground [*Freilegung des Bodens*]."[96] Givenness broadens presence in that it frees it from any limits of the faculties, as far as to let beings play freely—eventually beings in their Being. And only such a liberating broadening will be able to claim to surpass the "metaphysics of presence," which, in fact, does not cease to *restrain* the present and to *hold back* its givenness.

The privilege thus accorded by Heidegger to givenness over categorial intuition allows one first of all to free his interpretation of the *Investigations* from Derrida's objection. It also allows one to free Husserl himself, at least in a certain measure, which it will suffice for us to point out without going any further (we have already advanced *too far* on uncovered terrain). Heidegger in fact does justice to the Sixth Investigation on two decisive points. (1) Husserl never declares in it that Being or beings are intuited by the least "intuition of Being" or its equivalent. On the other hand, the evidence of the "object given [*gegebener Gegenstand*] in the mode of the meant" implies that "here *Being* in the sense of truth . . . is realized, here the truth in person is given [*gegeben*], to be seen [*erschauen*] and grasped directly," such that even the "little word *is*," finally, "is *itself given* or, at least, presumed given . . . in the fulfillment." For each correlate of representation, even its Sensible correlate, requires that one name "its actual 'Being given,' or even its appearing inasmuch as 'given' [*sein aktuelles 'Gegebensein,' bzw. als 'gegeben' Erscheinen*]."[97] The completed apparition gives what appears in it in person; now, the expression claims to give even in the copula, or indeed the position; it is therefore necessary to admit that the *is* is given in person since it appears as such. Categorial intuition does not itself give the *is*, nor does it even see it: it marks, as an index (such would be the paradox), the in fact anonymous givenness of the *is*. (2) Husserl always infers categorial intuition starting from sensible intuition, by analogy and in order to respect the advances of givenness: "If 'Being' is taken to mean *predicative* Being, some *state of affairs* must be given to us, and this by way of an act *that gives it—the analogue of ordinary sensible intuition* [*einen ihn gebenden Akt—das Analogon*]."[98] Categorial intuition remains in need of givenness, far from givenness being in need of it in order to be achieved as a givenness of the *is*, and therefore of being in its beingness. Categorial intuition only allows one to take the measure—henceforth without measure—of givenness. It marks the open abyss of givenness, without covering it over—at least in Heidegger's eyes, if not in Husserl's. For here, the one who is most sober before the fascination of overabundant and unconditional presence is doubtless not the one expected. Husserl, indeed, completely dazzled by unlimited givenness, seems not to realize the strangeness of such an excessiveness and simply manages its excess without questioning it. That is, unless bedazzlement doesn't betray—by covering over—a fear before the broadening of presence by givenness.

It is here no doubt that there arises the question that Husserl could not answer, because he perhaps never heard it as an authentic question: What gives? Not only: "What is that which gives itself?" but, more essentially: "What does giving mean, what is at play in the fact that all is given, how are we to think that all that is is only inasmuch as it is given?" It seems permissible to suppose that Husserl; submerged by the simultaneously threatening and jubilatory imperative to manage the superabundance of data in presence, does not at any moment (at least in the *Logical Investigations*) ask himself about the status, the scope, or even the identity of that givenness. This silence amounts to an admission (following Jacques Derrida's thesis) that Husserl, leaving unquestioned the givenness whose broadening he nevertheless accomplished, does not free it from the prison of pr6sence, and thus keeps it in metaphysical detention. Heidegger, to the contrary, seeing immediately and with an. extraordinary lucidity that the breakthrough of 1900–1901 consists entirely in the broadening of givenness beyond sensible intuition, assumes precisely the Husserlian heritage by making the entire question bear on what such a givenness means—and therefore in being careful not to reduce it too quickly to presence, even under the figure of categorial intuition. It will be a question—much further on—of understanding how and why that which is is only inasmuch as given: Being comes down to Being given, from a givenness that is achieved only in the play of the phenomenon with itself—of the appearing with what appears. Such a question, however, presupposes two preliminaries: (1) a step back in face of givenness itself—simply in order to come to consider it worthy of question, instead of forgetting it by dint of inhabiting its evidence; (2) the recognition that, in the henceforth universal givenness, what is at issue is the Being of what thus appears in the very measure that it is given. These two preliminaries amount to asking (1) whether a phenomenological reduction would achieve the step back that allows one to consider givenness as such, and (2) whether the breakthrough of givenness does not inevitably and immediately lead phenomenology toward the question of Being. In fact if not in principle, these two questions amount to one: Does the reduction lead phenomenology to see Being as a phenomenon?

Sketch of the Saturated Phenomenon

§21. The Horizon

According to Quantity—Invisable

I will sketch a description of the saturated phenomenon by following the lead of the categories of the understanding defined by Kant. But the saturated phenomenon exceeds these categories (as well as principles), since in it intuition passes beyond the concept. I will therefore follow them by inverting them. The saturated phenomenon will be described as *invisable*[1] according to quantity, unbearable according to quality, absolute according to relation, irregardable[2] according to modality. The three first characteristics put into question the ordinary sense of horizon (§21); the last, the transcendental sense of the I (§22).

First, the saturated phenomenon *cannot be aimed at* [*ne peut se viser*]. This impossibility stems from its essentially unforeseeable character [*son caractère essentiellement imprévisible*]. To be sure, its giving intuition ensures it a quantity, but such that it cannot be foreseen. This determination can be made clearer by inverting the function of the axioms of the intuition. According to Kant, quantity (extensive magnitude) is declined by composition of the whole in terms of its parts. This "successive synthesis" allows for the representation of the whole to be reconstituted according to the representation of the sum of its parts. In effect, the magnitude of a *quantum* implies nothing more than the summation of the *quanta* that make it up. From this homogeneity another property follows: a quantified phenomenon is "(fore-) seen in advance [*schon . . . angeschaut*] as an aggregate (sum of the parts given in advance) [*vorher gegebener*]."[3] This sort of phenomenon would always be foreseeable, literally seen before being seen in person or seen by procuration, on the basis of another besides itself—more precisely, on the basis of the supposedly finite number of its parts and the supposedly finite magnitude of each among them. Now these properties are precisely the ones that become untenable when the saturated phenomenon is at issue. That is, since the intuition that gives it is not limited by its possible concept, its excess can neither be divided nor adequately put together again by virtue of a finite magnitude homogeneous with finite parts. It could not be measured in terms of its parts, since the saturating intuition surpasses limitlessly the sum of the parts by continually adding to them. Such a phenomenon, which is always exceeded by the intuition that saturates it, should rather be called incommensurable, not measurable (immense), unmeasured. This lack of measure, however, does not always or even first of all operate in terms of the enormity of a limitless quantity; it is most often marked by the simple impossibility of our applying a successive synthesis to it, permitting an aggregate to be foreseen on the basis of the finite sum of its finite parts. As the saturated phenomenon passes beyond all summation of its parts—which often cannot be enumerated anyway—the successive synthesis must be abandoned in favor of what I will call an instantaneous synthesis whose representation precedes and surpasses that of the eventual components, instead of resulting from it according to foresight.

A privileged example is found in amazement. According to Descartes, this passion affects us even before we know the thing, or rather precisely because we know it only partially: "Only the side of the object originally presented [is] perceived, and hence [it is] impossible for a more detailed knowledge of the object to be acquired."[4] The "object" offers us only one "side" (we could also say only one *Abschattung*) and yet is, at the same time, imposed on us with a power such that we are submerged by what shows itself, most likely to the point of fascination. And yet the "successive synthesis" has been suspended ever since its initial term; another synthesis, instantaneous and irreducible to the sum of its possible parts, is being carried out. Every phenomenon that produces amazement is imposed on the gaze in the very measure (more exactly, in the excess of measure) to which it does not result from any foreseeable summation of partial quantities. The synthesis takes place without complete knowledge of the object, therefore without *our* synthesis. It is thus freed from the objectness that we would impose on it so that it might impose on us its own synthesis, accomplished before we could reconstitute it (a passive synthesis, therefore). Its coming forward precedes our apprehension, rather than resulting from it. The phenomenon's anticipating what we foresee of it is out of keeping: it comes before our gaze at it, it comes early, before us. We do not foresee it; it foresees us. As a result, it is amazing because it arises without measure in common with the phenomena that precede it but cannot announce or explain it—for, according to Spinoza, "Nullam cum reliquis habet connexionem [It has no connection with any others]."[5] Disconnected from the rest of the phenomena and from their already known concepts, it imposes itself without precedents, parts, or sum.

Another privileged example comes from cubist painting, which is built around the observation that in fact and on principle the phenomena to be seen go beyond the foreseen sum of their parts—their adumbrations and their aspects. In other words, for cubist painting, to see the phenomena, one must unfold appearing in an ever finite number of facets, which (as in the basic case of the cube for Husserl) continually proliferate and accumulate. The objects that are supposedly the most simple—violin on a stool, with newspaper and vase—in fact always give more to see, and from afar, more than we can think. What we perceive by momentary intuitions and what we conceptually think of these moments remain incommensurably poorer than what we really have to see there. The concepts, by which we know what there is to see so well that we no longer take the time or the trouble to go and truly see, serve only to sum them up, simplify them for us, so as to mask their exuberant splendor. Most of the time, we want to get an idea of things without having any intention of seeing them, so that we can handle them easily, like equipment. If we were to forget their concepts, we would see that there are so many things to see—so many things to see in this old violin on the simple stool, a rumpled newspaper and sad little vase. If only we could let all the facets of each of them appear (distinguished by the variegated plays of color they offer to the light, which modify it so), all the perspectives on each object aligned with the other such that by moving our-selves around them (anamorphosis) we can actually aim at them, and not only the real perspectives but also and especially the unreal ones such as we could imagine and even see them if we could pair the opposite side of one (for example the violin case) with the obverse of the other (for example the newspaper title), the left of the one above (the vase) with the right of the other (the feet of the stool, below), the floor with the ceiling, etc. For all their combinations are by right visible, even though our vision—therefore our intentions and our intuitions—attains only an improbably small number of them. The cubist painter knows this, he who no longer wants to bring into visibility what just anyone—forewarned, busy, practical-minded—sees, excluding all that he does not know in advance, therefore does not recognize, as well as all that does not serve a purpose and therefore is not interesting. The cubist painter wants rather to bring into visibility what could be visible if we tried every intention, every combination of intentions, and even all those that are forbidden to us in the finitude of common intuition, but which we could try to divine. The cubist happily exhausts himself in the endless race toward the impos-sible and ever elusive summation of the visible bursting—for the visible bursts, if one lets it arise in appearing, like a wave crashes with exploding fireworks of water drops, each different in form and color, in time and space, in trajectory and how they glimmer. More radical than the impressionist, who means only to show all that he experiences exactly, the cubist tries, sometimes successfully, to let appear what he could not actually see, but whose least possibility he stubbornly lets ascend into the visible.

In this way, the saturated phenomenon could not be foreseen, for at least two phenom-enological reasons. (a) First, because the intuition, which continually saturates it, forbids it from distinguishing and adding up a finite number of finite parts, thereby annulling all possibility of foreseeing the phenomenon before it gives itself in person. (b) Next, because the saturated phenomenon most often imposes itself thanks to amazement, in which all the intuitive givenness is accomplished by the fact that its possible parts are not counted up, therefore also not foreseen.

According to Quality—Unbearable

Secondly, the saturated phenomenon *cannot be borne*. According to Kant, quality (inten-sive magnitudes) allows intuition to fix a degree of reality for the object by limiting it, eventually to the point of negation. Each phenomenon would admit a degree of intuition, and this is what perception can always anticipate. The foresight at work in extensive magnitude is found again in the anticipation of intensive magnitude. An essential difference separates them, however: anticipation operates no longer in a successive synthesis of the homogeneous, but in a perception of the heterogeneous, in which each degree is demarcated by a dissolution of continuity with the preceding, therefore by an absolutely singular novelty. However, because he privileges the case of the poor phenomenon, Kant analyzes this heterogeneity only in terms of the most simple cases—the first degrees starting from zero, the imperceptible perceptions, etc. This is to say that he approaches intensity only by strangely privileging phenomena of the weakest intensity, precisely where intensity is lacking, to the paradoxical point of basing it on the very absence of intensity, negation: "A magnitude which is apprehended only as unity, and in which multiplicity can be represented only through approximation to negation = 0, I entitle an *intensive* magnitude."[6] Intensity is defined starting from its degree zero. There is no better way of saying that the absolute and unquestioned dominance of the paradigm of a poor phenomenon, indeed one empty of intuition, definitively blocks, in metaphysics at least, every advance toward the liberated phenomenality of givenness. From this perspective, one might not even suspect the opposite case of a saturated phenomenon, in which intuition gives reality (first category of quality) to the phenomenon without any negation (second category) and, of course, without collapsing into limitation (third category). For the intuition saturating a phenomenon attains an intensive magnitude without measure, or common measure, such that starting with a certain degree, the intensity of the real intuition passes beyond all the conceptual anticipations of perception. Before this excess, not only can perception no longer anticipate what it will receive from intuition; it also can no longer bear its most elevated degrees. For intuition, supposedly "blind" in the realm of poor or common phenomena, turns out, in a radical phenomenology, to be blinding. The gaze cannot any longer sustain a light that bedazzles and burns. The intensive magnitude of intuition, when it goes so far as to give a saturated phenomenon, cannot be borne by the gaze, just as this gaze could not foresee its extensive magnitude.

When the gaze cannot bear what it sees, it suffers bedazzlement. For not bearing is not simply equivalent to not seeing: one must first perceive, if not clearly see, in order to undergo what one cannot bear. It concerns a visible that our gaze cannot sustain. This visible is undergone as unbearable by the gaze, because it fills it without measure, after the fashion of the idol. The gaze no longer keeps anything in reserve from free vision; the visible invades all its intended angles; it accomplishes *adaequatio*—it fills. But the filling goes by itself beyond itself; it goes to the brink, too far. Thus the glory of the visible weighs down with all it has, that is to say it weighs too much. What is here weighty to the point of making one suffer is named neither unhappiness, nor pain, nor lack, but indeed success—glory, joy: "O / Triumph! / What Glory! What human heart would be so strong to beat / That?"[7] Intuition gives too intensely for the gaze to have enough heart to truly see what it cannot conceive, only barely receive, or sometimes even confront. This blindness stems from the intensity of intuition and not from its quantity, as is indicated by blindness before spectacles in which intuition remains quantitatively ordinary, indeed weak, but of extraordinary intensity. Oedipus blinds himself on account of having seen his transgression; he is therefore bedazzled by a quasi-moral intensity of intuition. Whoever finds himself smitten by love owes it, most often, only to the silence of a gaze that no one saw except for him. And He Whom no one can see without dying blinds first with his holiness, even if his coming is announced in a mere gust of wind. Because the saturated phenomenon cannot be borne, on account of the excess of intuition in it, by any gaze cut to its measure ("objectively"), it is perceived ("subjectively") by the gaze only in the negative mode of an impossible perception—of bedazzlement. Plato too has described this perfectly in connection with the prisoner of the Cave: "Let one untie him and force him suddenly to turn around [*anistanai*] . . . and to lift his gaze toward the light [*pros to phōs anablepein*], he would suffer in doing all that, and because of the bedazzlements, he would not have the strength to see face on [*dia tas marmarugas adunatai kathoran*] that of which he previously saw the shadows." It is indeed a question of "suffering" by seeing the full light and of fleeing it by turning away toward "the things that one can look at [*ha dunatai kathoran*]." What keeps one from seeing are precisely "the eyes filled with splendor."[8] This bedazzlement, moreover, is valid for intelligible intuition as well as sensible intuition. First, because in the final analysis, the allegory of the Cave concerns the epistemological obstacles to intelligibility, for which the sensible scene offers an explicit figure; next, because the idea of the Good, also and especially, is offered as "difficult to see [*mogis horasthai*]," not by defect, seeing as it presents "the most visible of beings," but indeed by excess because "the soul is incapable of seeing anything . . . saturated by an extremely brilliant bedazzlement [*hupo lamproteron marmarugēs empeplēstai*]."[9] In all these cases, what forbids seeing comes from the excess of the light's intensity, be it sensible or intelligible.

The painter too produces saturation in terms of quality, for he always, indeed first, paints light. But most of the time, he paints it as we see it—always already spread over the things that it makes evident, therefore invisible and, as such, withdrawn from the painting that it opens. Even when Claude (Lorrain) divides his canvas—*The Embarkation of Saint Ursula* or *Dido Building Carthage*—with a blood-red ray of light from the dying sun, he is interested, as much as in this light itself, in registering the subtly shaded effects on the buildings, the boats, and the people who, as if seated on either side waiting to welcome it, end up confiscating it and distracting our attention from it. But when Turner consciously takes up the same theme with the same organization—for example in *The Decline of the Carthaginian Empire*—his essential task is to bring the sun itself to the center of the painting. Or more exactly, so that its light might appear truly as such, not only does he cover the other protagonists in a paradoxical darkness to the point of diluting them; he even ceases to show the sun's flux (*lumen*) directly—which the gaze cannot bear any more than death—in order to "render" only its bedazzling fulguration (*lux*). An unbearable circle diffusing a fiery whiteness, where nothing can any longer be distinguished or staged. To show the sun in effect demands showing what cannot be designated as a thing and what has as its own peculiarity to forbid showing not only anything else, but also itself. This is why in the Venetian canvases (for example, *Venice with Salute*), Turner no longer lets even the slightest flicker of a cupola show through, so much does the unmoving brilliance of the light, saturating the canvas without rest, ravage with whiteness every possible countryside and nullify every project to make even the least *veduta;* nor does he let even the least silhouette subsist, and the church is swallowed in a hazy dark stain, glazed under the deluge of light, like a small remainder of scattered ashes. Thus, the eye experiences only its powerlessness to see anything, except the bursting that submerges it—almost metallic and vibrating[10]—which blinds it. Thus appears the excess of intensive magnitude in the pure and simple impossibility of even maintaining it within the horizon of the visible.

Bedazzlement thus becomes a characteristic that can be universalized to every form of the intuition of an intensity surpassing the degree that a gaze can sustain. No doubt this degree varies with the scope of each gaze (which I have not calibrated here), but the aim always ends up reaching its fulfillment. Now this is not just some exceptional case, which I merely mention as a matter of interest while discussing the poor phenomenon, supposedly more frequent and therefore approximately normative. To the contrary, it is a question of an essential determination of the phenomenon, one that two lines of argument make inevitable. (a) The Kantian description of intensive magnitudes, however original and to the point, massively privileges the degree zero in order to maintain a resounding silence about the notion most characteristic of intensive magnitude—the maximum. For even if it cannot be defined universally, for each gaze and in each case, there is always a maximum, a threshold of tolerance beyond which what is seen is no longer constituted as an object within a finite horizon. Bedazzlement begins when perception crosses its tolerable maximum. The description of intensive magnitudes should therefore prioritize the consideration of their most elevated degrees, therefore the maximum signaled by the bedazzlements. (b) The intolerable, as before with unforeseeability, designates a mode of intuitive givenness that is not only less rare than hasty examination might suspect, but especially one that is decisive for a real recognition of finitude. Finitude is proven and experienced not so much because the given falls short before our gaze as, above all, because this gaze can sometimes no longer measure the range of the given. Or inversely, measuring itself against it, the gaze undergoes it, sometimes in the suffering of an essential passivity, as having no measure in common with it. Finitude is disclosed more in the encounter with the saturated phenomenon than with the poor phenomenon.

Without Relation—Absolute

Neither *visable* according to quantity nor bearable according to quality, the saturated phenomenon appears *absolute* according to relation, which means it evades any analogy of experience.

Kant defines the principle of such analogies in this way: "Experience is possible only through the representation of a necessary connection of perceptions." Mere apprehension through empirical intuition cannot ensure this necessary connection; it will have to produce itself at once through concepts and in time. For "since time, however, cannot itself be perceived, the determination of the existence of objects in time can take place only through their relation in time in general, and therefore only through concepts that connect them a priori."[11] This connection permits three relations: inherence of accident in substance, causality between cause and effect, commonality among several substances. But Kant establishes them only by employing three presuppositions, the contestation of which will again allow me to describe *a contrario* the saturated phenomenon. (a) First presupposition: in all its occurrences, a phenomenon can manifest itself only by respecting the unity of experience, that is to say, by taking place in a network as tightly bound as possible by lines of inherence, causality, and commonality that assign to it, in the hollows as it were, a site. This is a strict obligation: "In the original apperception, the manifold must [*soll*] be unified in terms of its relation in time."[12] In this way, a phenomenon would appear only in a site predetermined by a system of coordinates, itself governed by the principle of the unity of experience. But another interrogation insinuates itself here: *Must* every phenomenon, without exception, respect the unity of experience? Is it legitimate to rule out the possibility that a phenomenon might impose itself on perception without assigning it either a substance in which it resides like an accident or a cause from which it results as an effect, or even less an interactive *commercium* where it is relativized? And for that matter, it is not self-evident that the phenomena that really arise—in contrast to the phenomena that are poor in intuition—can at first and most often be perceived according to such analogies of perception. It could be quite the opposite—that they happen without being inscribed, at least at first, in the relational network that assures experience its unity; and that they matter precisely because one could not assign them any substratum, any cause, or any commerce. To be sure, after a moment's consideration, the majority can be reconducted, at least approximately, to the analogies of perception. But those, not so rare, that do not lend themselves to this henceforth assume the character and the dignity of event. Event, or unforeseeable phenomenon (in terms of the past), not exhaustively comprehensible (in terms of the present), not reproducible (in terms of the future), in short, absolute, unique, coming forward (§17). It will therefore be said: pure event. As a result, the analogies of experience concern only a fringe of phenomenality—phenomena of the type of objects constituted by the sciences, poor in intuition, foreseeable, exhaustively knowable, reproducible—while other levels (and first of all historical phenomena) would make an exception.

The second presupposition (b) concerns the very elaboration of the procedure that allows us to secure temporal and conceptual necessity, therefore the unity of experience. Kant presupposes that this unity should always be accomplished by recourse to an analogy. For "all empirical time-determinations must [*müssen*] stand under rules of universal time-determination. The analogies of experience . . . must [*müssen*] be rules of this description."[13] In short, it falls to the analogies of experience and to them alone to actually exercise the regulation of experience by necessity, therefore to assure its unity. At the precise moment of defining these analogies, Kant himself recognizes the fragility of their phenomenological power. That is, in mathematics, the analogy remains quantitative, such that by calculation it provides the fourth term and truly constructs it; thus the equality of two relations of magnitude is "always constitutive" of the object and actually maintains it in a unified experience; but, Kant specifies,

> In philosophy the analogy is not the equality of two *quantitative* but of two *qualitative* relations; and from three given members we can obtain a priori knowledge only of the relation to a fourth, not of the fourth member itself. . . . An analogy of experience is, therefore, only a rule according to which a unity of experience may arise from [*entspringen soll*] perception. It does not tell us how mere perception of empirical

intuition in general itself comes about. It is not a principle *constitutive* of the objects, that is, of the appearances [phenomena], but only *regulative*.[14]

Clearly, when it is a question of what I have called poor (here mathematical) phenomena, intuition (here the intuition of pure space) succeeds neither in saturating nor in contradicting the pre-established unity and necessity of experience. In this case and in this case atone, the analogy remains quantitative and constitutive—in short, there is an analogy of experience provided that the phenomenon remains poor. But, by Kant's own admission, as soon as we pass to physics (without yet speaking of a saturated phenomenon), the analogy ceases to be capable of regulating anything, except qualitatively. If A is cause of effect B, then D will be in the position (quality) of effect vis-à-vis C without our being able to identify what D is or will be, and without our being able to construct it (by lack of pure intuition) or constitute it. Kant's predicament culminates with this strange use, in the analytic of principles, of principles whose usage remains purely "regulative," which can be understood in only one sense: the analogies of experience do not really constitute their objects, but state the subjective needs of the understanding. Let us suppose for a moment that the analogies of perception, thus reduced to a mere regulative use, should have to treat a saturated phenomenon. The latter already passes beyond the categories of quantity (unforeseeable) and quality (unbearable); it also already gives itself as a pure event. As a result, how could an analogy—above all one that is merely regulative—assign to it, especially with necessity and a priori, a point whose coordinates would be fixed by inherence, causality, and commonality? This phenomenon will by contrast evade relations because it will not maintain any measure in common with these terms; it would be free of them as from all other a priori determinations of experience that might claim to impose itself on the phenomenon. In this sense, I will speak of an absolute phenomenon: disconnected from all analogy with any object of experience whatsoever.

Without Analogy

Accordingly, the third Kantian presupposition becomes questionable. (c) The unity of experience is deployed against the background of time, since "all phenomena are in time."[15] Thus, Kant posits not only time as the final horizon of phenomena, but above all the horizon in general as the condition for the appearing of these phenomena, which it at once welcomes and restricts. This means that before any phenomenal breakthrough toward visibility, the horizon awaits in advance, first; and it means that each phenomenon, in appearing, is in fact constrained to actualize a portion of this horizon, which otherwise remains transparent or empty. When a question sometimes arises about this, it bears on the identity of this horizon (time, Being, *Ereignis*, indeed ethics or the good, etc.). This should not, however, hide another question, one more simple and more radical: could certain phenomena exceed their horizon?

This does not mean dispensing with a horizon altogether, since this would no doubt forbid any and all manifestation; it means using the horizon in another way so as to be free of its delimiting anteriority, which can only enter into conflict with a phenomenon's claim to absolute appearing. Let us suppose a saturated phenomenon, one that wins its absolute character by being emancipated from analogies with experience—what horizon can it still acknowledge? Two phenomenological situations must be distinguished here. (i) Either the phenomenon receives an intuition that exceeds the frame set by the concept and signification that aim at and foresee it. In this intuition, there no longer remains even the slightest halo of the not yet known surrounding the noematic core of the known. The concept or signification of the object coincides exactly with the limits of its horizon, without a significant reserve as yet unfulfilled. Intuition not only attains adequation with signification, but fills it, as well as its entire horizon. Thus is realized the first figure of saturation: intuition, by dint of pressure, attains the common limits of the concept and horizon; it does not cross them, however, and running up against them, it reverberates, returns toward the finite field, blurs it, and renders it in the end invisible by excess—bedazzlement. In this first case, saturation is again accomplished within the horizon, but against it. Fulfilling its horizon, the saturated phenomenon is no longer constituted as object and withdraws behind the bedazzlement it provokes.[16] (ii) Or, having attained the limits of its concept or signification as far as *adaequatio*, then having fulfilled all its horizon and even the halo of the not yet known, the phenomenon saturated with intuition can—in contrast with the preceding case—pass beyond all horizontal delimitation. This situation does not imply doing away with the horizon altogether, but articulating several together in order to welcome one and the same saturated phenomenon. It is a matter of reading this phenomenon, which exceeds all norms in its essentially distinct, indeed opposed, horizons, for which perhaps only an indefinite summation will permit accommodating the excess of what shows itself. Let me emphasize that this hypothesis has nothing strange or uncommon about it, even in rigorous philosophy. Spinoza succeeds in thinking the one and only substance only by such an arrangement. It absorbs all the determinations of beingness and all the individuals corresponding thereto, to the point that it drowns the essentially finite horizon of Cartesian metaphysics in its infinitely saturated presence. To conceive it, it must multiply formally into attributes, all equally and differently infinite, each opening the possibility of an endless interpretation of modes, finite as well as infinite.[17] The substance can thus pass from the horizon of thought to that of extension, without omitting the unknown attributes, other potential horizons. Only this always reversible passage permits calibrating and easing, so to speak, the initial saturation, which would otherwise remain pure and unspeakable bedazzlement. With this, moreover, Spinoza does nothing more than revive, to be sure by overturning, the tactics elaborated by the doctrine of the convertibility of transcendentals. The irreducible plurality of *ens, unum, verum, bonum* (and sometimes *pulchrum*) allowed not only the ordinary phenomenon of a finite being to be translated into a unity (Aristotle, Leibniz), but especially the saturated phenomenon par excellence—the Principle—to be declined in perfectly autonomous registers, where it gives itself to be seen, each time, only according to a perspective that is total as well as partial, conceivable and always incomprehensible: being in the act of Being, one before unity, truth of oneself and of the world, invisible splendor, etc. (Plotinus, Proclus, Dionysius, etc.). The convertibility of these registers indicates that saturation persists, but is distributed into several rival, though compatible horizons. Finitude still describes the saturated phenomenon because it grants it the right to several horizons. Generalizing, I will say that it is fitting to admit phenomena of $n + 1$ horizons, as it was necessary to admit spaces of $n + 1$ dimensions—whose properties saturate the imagination. Here bedazzlement paves the way for an infinite hermeneutic. (iii) We cannot rule out a third case, one that is rare but inevitable (§§23–24): that saturation redoubles the first two cases by lumping them together. If the hermeneutic of an infinite plurality of horizons is by chance not enough to decline an essentially and absolutely saturated phenomenon, it could be that each perspective, already saturated in a single horizon (bedazzlement), is blurred once again by spilling over the others—in short, that the hermeneutic adds the bedazzlements in each horizon, instead of combining them. Then, not only no single horizon, but no combination of horizons, could successfully tolerate the absoluteness of the phenomenon, precisely because it gives itself as absolute, that is to say, free from all analogy with common-law phenomena and from all predetermination by a network of relations, with neither precedent nor antecedent in the already seen or foreseeable. In short, there would appear a phenomenon saturated to the point that the world (in all senses of the word) could not accept it. Having come among his own, his own do not recognize it; having come into phenomenality, the absolutely saturated phenomenon could find no space there for its display. But this denial of opening, therefore this disfiguring, still remains a manifestation (§30).

Couldn't one fear that the very hypothesis of a phenomenon saturating a horizon is a danger—one that should not be underestimated since it is born from the most real experience: that of a totality without door or window, excluding every possible, every other, every Other? But this danger, while no doubt undeniable, results less from the saturated phenomenon itself than from the misapprehension of it. When this type of phenomenon arises, it is most often treated like a common-law phenomenon, indeed a poor phenomenon, one that is therefore forced to be included in a phenomenological situation that by definition it refuses, and it is finally misapprehended. If, by contrast, its specificity is recognized, the bedazzlement it provokes would become phenomenologically acceptable, indeed desirable, and the passage from one horizon to another would become a rational task for the hermeneutic. The saturated phenomenon safeguards its absoluteness and at the same time dissolves its danger when it is recognized as such, without confusing it with other phenomena.[18]

In this way, by giving itself absolutely, the saturated phenomenon also gives itself as absolute—free from any analogy with already seen, objectified, comprehended experience. It is freed because it does not depend on any horizon. In every case, it does not depend on this condition of possibility par excellence—a horizon, whatever it might be. I therefore call it an unconditioned phenomenon.

§22. Sketch of the Saturated Phenomenon: I

According to Modality: Irregardable

Neither *visable* according to quantity nor bearable according to quality, but absolute according to relation, that is to say, unconditioned by the horizon (§21), the saturated phenomenon is spoken of as irregardable[19] according to modality.

We know that the categories of modality are distinguished from all the others in that they determine neither objects in themselves (quantity, quality) nor their mutual relations (relation), but only—Kant insists—"their relation to thought in general." These categories, in contrast to those that Aristotle deduces from, and leads back to, *ousia*, are the operators of the fundamental epistemological relation to the I; in short, they "express only the relation to the faculty of knowledge," "nothing but the action of the faculty of knowledge."[20] In fact, between the object of experience and the power of knowing, it is no longer only a matter of a simple relation, superadded, extrinsic and probably optional, but of the fact that these objects "agree" with the power of knowledge—and absolutely must if they are to be known. This agreement determines their possibility (therefore also their actuality and their necessity) to be and to be known as phenomena solely by the measure of their suitability to the I, for whom and by whom the experience takes place. "The postulate of the *possibility* of things requires [*fordert*] that the concept of the things should agree [*zusammenstimme*] with the formal conditions of an experience in general."[21] The phenomenon is possible strictly to the extent that it agrees with the formal conditions of experience, therefore with the power of knowing that fixes them, therefore finally with the transcendental I itself. The possibility of the phenomenon depends finally on its reconduction to the I. Not only is the phenomenon with an intuitive deficit (poor or common) not assured of its possibility by itself, but it is alienated in an external instance—that of the I—in order that it might perform its own appearing. Far from showing *itself*, it is staged only in a scene set by and for an other besides it, actor without action, submitted to a spectator and transcendental director. The Kantian sense of the categories of modality in the end produces the phenomenon's alienation from itself; far from giving *itself* it lets itself be shown, made visible and staged. In short, it becomes constituted as an object, one that gets its status from a previously objectifying intentionality, like a still and always "well-grounded" phenomenon—therefore, on condition. Such a poor or common phenomenon lacks not only intuition with regard to its concept; it lacks phenomenal autonomy, since it renounces (according to the categories of modality) giving *itself* to whoever happens to see it, and instead lets itself be constituted (constructed, schematized, synthesized, etc.) by whoever precedes and foresees it. The "postulates of empirical thought in general" postulate that the phenomenon never appears except in response to requirements outside and anterior to it, requirements that it can, in the best of cases, satisfy only by submitting to. Alienated phenomenon, exercising a conditioned phenomenality, the poor or common phenomenon perfectly deserves its title—poor in intuition, poor especially in phenomenality.

This same extremity leads to reversing the Kantian situation so as to ask in return: what would happen if a phenomenon did *not* "agree with" or "correspond to" the power of knowing of the I? The likely Kantian response to this question is hardly in doubt: such a phenomenon quite simply would not appear; there would not be a phenomenon at all, but a confused perceptive aberration without object. I can admit that this answer remains meaningful for a phenomenon that is poor in intuition or a common-law phenomenon (which aim no higher than an equality between intuition and concept) though even in these cases, it is perhaps necessary to imagine exceptions, as in quantum physics.[22] But is it still valid for a saturated phenomenon? In fact, the situation is very different here. In saturation, the I undergoes the disagreement between an at least potential phenomenon and the subjective condition for its experience; and, as a result, it does not constitute an object. But this failure to objectify in no way implies that absolutely nothing appears here. To the contrary, intuitive saturation, precisely insofar as it renders it *invisable*, intolerable, and absolute (unconditioned), is imposed in the type of phenomenon that is exceptional by excess, not by defect. The saturated phenomenon refuses to let itself be regarded as an object precisely because it appears with a multiple and indescribable excess that annuls all effort at constitution. The saturated phenomenon must be determined as a nonobjective or, more exactly, nonobjectifiable phenomenon; this denegation means in no way to take shelter in the irrational or arbitrary, since it is a question of a phenomenality that escapes not so much objectivity (one of the characteristics of the object, on the same level as subjectivity) as objectness—the property and status of the object, as it is opposed and abandoned to the gaze of a subject. The saturated phenomenon contradicts the subjective conditions of experience precisely in that it does not admit constitution as an object. In other words, though exemplarily visible, it nevertheless cannot be looked at, regarded. The saturated phenomenon gives *itself* insofar as it remains, according to modality, irregardable.

How does it give itself to be seen without letting itself be looked at? This difficulty is rooted in the presupposition that "to see" and "to gaze" ["*voir*" et "*regarder*"] are exactly equivalent and that the one cannot go without the other. But this is not the case, provided that we read "to gaze," *regarder*, literally: *re-garder* transcribes exactly *in-tueri* and should be understood in terms of *tueri*, "to guard or to keep"—but in the sense of "to keep an eye on, to watch out of the corner of one's eye, to keep in sight." "To gaze" [*regarder*] therefore implies something more or wholly other than simply "to see." In order to see, it is not as necessary to perceive by the sense of sight (or any other sense) as it is to receive what shows *itself* on its own because it gives *itself* in visibility at its own initiative (anamorphosis, §13), according to its own rhythm (unpredictable landing, §14), and with its essential contingency (incident, §16), in such a way as to appear without reproducing or repeating itself (event, §17). On the other hand, gazing, *regarder*, is about being able to keep the visible thus seen under the control of the seer, exerting this control by guarding the visible in visibility, as much as possible without letting it have the initiative in appearing (or disappearing) by forbidding it any variation in intensity that would disturb its inscription in the concept, and especially by conserving it in permanent presence through postulating its identical reproducibility. To gaze at the phenomenon is therefore equivalent not to seeing it, but indeed to transforming it into an object visible according to an always poor or common phenomenality—visible within the limits of a concept, therefore at the initiative of the gaze, enduring as long as possible in permanence, in short, visible in conformity with objectness. And it is not by chance that Descartes entrusts *intuitus* with the role of maintaining in evidence what the ego reduces to the status of *objectum*[23]—the gaze keeps objects in an objected state for the I. Therefore, the gaze sees, but more originally it possesses and conserves—it guards. Consequently it concerns only objects, that is, for the purpose of this study, phenomena whose visibility remains submitted to objectness. And since the excess of intuition over the foresight of the concept and the conditions of the I contravenes objectness, the phenomenon saturated with an excess of intuition can only be withdrawn from the gaze. Determining the saturated phenomenon as irregardable amounts to imagining the possibility that it imposes itself on sight with such an excess of intuition that it can no longer be reduced to the conditions of experience (objecthood), therefore to the I that sets them.

Counter-Experience

In what figure does it appear? For by definition it does appear, since it must appear in the measure of the excess of giving intuition in it. The irregardable saturated phenomenon must appear par excellence, but it also contradicts the conditions for the poor or common phenomenality of objects. If it appears counter to the conditions for the possibility of experience, how could the supposed excellence of its phenomenality not end up as a pure and simple impossibility of experience—not even an experience of the impossible? The response to this difficulty resides in its very statement: if, for the saturated phenomenon, there is no experience of an object, it remains for us to imagine that there might be a counter-experience of a nonobject. Counter-experience is not equivalent to a nonexperience, but to the experience of a phenomenon that is neither regardable, nor guarded according to objectness, one that therefore resists the conditions of objectification. Counter-experience offers the experience of what irreducibly contradicts the conditions for the experience of objects. Such experience to the second degree recovers the peculiarly Husserlian novelty of founded acts: like them, in order to appear, it depends on the very thing that it passes beyond but nevertheless renders intelligible. We could therefore say that, of the saturated phenomenon, there is founded experience. That is, confronted with the saturated phenomenon, the I cannot not see it, but it cannot any longer gaze at it as its mere object. It has the eye to see but not keep it. What, then, does this eye with gaze see? It sees the superabundance of intuitive givenness; or rather, it does not see it clearly and precisely as such since its excess renders it irregardable and difficult to master. The intuition of the phenomenon is nevertheless seen, but as blurred by the too narrow aperture, the too short lens, the too cramped frame, that receives it—or rather that cannot receive it as such. The eye no longer apperceives the apparition of the saturated phenomenon so much as it apperceives the perturbation that it in person produces within the ordinary conditions of experience—in the way that an excess of light is not seen directly on the photographic paper but is inferred indirectly from the overexposure, or else—like the speed of something in motion, unrepresentable in a frozen image—nevertheless appears there in and through the smudge that its very unrepresentability makes on the paper. In these cases, the eye does not see an exterior spectacle so much as it sees the reified traces of its own powerlessness to constitute whatever it might be into an object. It sees nothing distinctly (in particular not an object), but clearly experiences its own powerlessness to master the measurelessness of the intuitive given— therefore, before all, the perturbations of the visible, the noise of a poorly received message, the obfuscation of finitude. It receives a pure givenness, precisely because it no longer discerns any objectifiable given therein.[24] It falls to music, or rather listening to music, to provide privileged occurrences of this sense of the phenomenon. The opening of a symphony—the *Jupiter*, for example—reaches me in such a way that even before reconstituting the melodic line or assessing the orchestral fabric (therefore constituting two objects from two givens), I first receive in my ear the movement (nonobjectifiable because giving) of the sonorous mass, which comes upon me and submerges me, then my very belatedness to the deployment of this coming. A memory of previous performances no doubt allows me to identify the melody more quickly and to assess the orchestral ensemble, but it does not allow me to abolish the arising, therefore the event. The music offers the very movement of its coming forward, its effect on me who receives it without producing it, in short, its arising without real content. Consequently, it comes upon me in such a way that it affects me directly as pure givenness mediated by almost no objectifiable given, and therefore imposes on me an actuality immediately its own. The musical offering offers first the very movement of its coming forward—it offers the effect of its very offering, without or beyond the sounds that it produces. Let me name this phenomenological extremity where the coming forward exceeds what comes forward a *paradox*.

The Paradox and the Witness

The paradox not only suspends the phenomenon's subjection to the I; it inverts it. For, far from being able to constitute this phenomenon, the I experiences itself as constituted by it. To the constituting subject, there succeeds the witness—the constituted witness. Constituted witness, the subject is still the worker of truth, but he cannot claim to be its producer. With the name *witness*, we must understand a subjectivity stripped of the characteristics that gave it transcendental rank. (i) Constituted and no longer constituting, the witness no longer enacts synthesis or constitution. Or rather, synthesis becomes passive and is imposed on it. As with constitution, the giving of meaning (*Sinngebung*) is inverted. The I can no longer provide its meaning to lived experiences and intuition; rather, the latter give themselves and therefore give it their meaning (a meaning that is for that matter partial and no longer all-encompassing). (ii) That is, in the case of a saturated phenomenon, intuition by definition passes beyond what meaning a hermeneutic of the concept can provide, a fortiori a hermeneutic practiced by the finite I, which will always have less givable meaning (concept, intentionality, signification, noesis, etc.) than the intuitive given calls for. (iii) The inversion of the gaze, and therefore of the guard it mounts over the object, places the I, become witness, under the guard of the paradox (saturated phenomenon) that controls it and stands vigilant over it. For the witness cannot avail himself of a viewpoint that dominates the intuition which submerges him. In space, the saturated phenomenon swallows him with its intuitive deluge; in time, it precedes him with an always already there interpretation. The I loses its anteriority as egoic pole (polar I) and cannot yet identify itself, except by admitting the precedence of such an unconstitutable phenomenon. This reversal leaves him stupefied and taken aback, essentially surprised by the more original event, which takes him away from himself. (iv) The witness is therefore opposed to the I in that he no longer has the initiative in manifestation (by facticity), does not see the given phenomenon in its totality (by excess of intuition), cannot read or interpret the intuitive excess (by shortage of concept), and finally lets himself be judged (said, determined) by what he himself cannot say or think adequately. In this way, the phenomenon is no longer reduced to the I who would gaze at it. Irregardable, he confesses himself irreducible. The event that comes up can no longer be constituted into an object; in contrast, it leaves the durable trace of its enclosure only in the I/me, witness constituted despite itself by what it receives. In short, the witness succeeds the I by renouncing the first person, or rather the nominative of this first role. In this witness, we should hear less the eloquent or heroic testator to an event that he reports, conveys, and defends—assuming again therefore a (re-)production of the phenomenon—and more the simple, luminous witness: he lights up as on a control panel at the very instant when and each time the information he should tender phenomenal (in this case, the visible) arrives to him from a transistor by electric impulse without initiative or delay. Here the witness himself is not invested in the phenomenon, nor does he invest it with. . . . Rather, he finds himself so invested, submerged, that he can only register it immediately.

To introduce the concept of the saturated phenomenon into phenomenology, I just described it as *invisable* (unforeseeable) in terms of quantity, unbearable in terms of quality, unconditioned (absolute of all horizon) in terms of relation, and finally irreducible to the I (irregardable) in terms of modality. These four characteristics imply the term-for-term reversal of all the rubrics under which Kant classifies the principles of the understanding and therefore the phenomena that they determine. However, in relation to Husserl, these new characteristics are organized in a more complex way: the first two—*invisable* and unbearable—offer no difficulty de jure for the "principle of all principles"; for what intuition gives can quantitatively and qualitatively surpass the scope of the gaze. It is enough, therefore, that it give without common measure. This is not the case for the last two characteristics: the "principle of all principles" mentions the horizon and the constituting I as the two unquestioned presuppositions of anything that would like to be constituted in general as a phenomenon; and yet the saturated phenomenon, inasmuch as it is unconditioned by a horizon and irreducible to an I, claims a possibility free of these two conditions; it therefore contradicts the "principle of all principles." Husserl, who nevertheless surpassed the Kantian metaphysic of the phenomenon, must in turn be overcome if we are to reach the possibility of the saturated phenomenon. Even and especially with the "principle of all principles," he maintains a twofold reserve vis-à-vis possibility (the horizon, the I). Nevertheless, Husserl's reserve toward possibility can bespeak a reserve of phenomenology itself—which still keeps a reserve *of* possibility so that it may itself be overcome in favor of a possibility without reserve. Because it gives itself without condition or restraint, the saturated phenomenon would offer the paradigm of the phenomenon finally without reserve. In this way, following the guiding thread of the saturated phenomenon, phenomenology finds its final possibility: not only the possibility that surpasses actuality, but the possibility that surpasses the very conditions of possibility, the possibility of unconditioned possibility—in other words, the possibility of the impossible, the saturated phenomenon. Though paradoxical, or precisely for that very reason, the saturated phenomenon should in no way be understood as an exceptional, indeed vaguely irrational (to say it plainly, "theological"), case of phenomenality. Rather, it accomplishes the coherent and rational development of the most operative definition of the phenomenon: it alone appears truly as itself, of itself, and on the basis of itself,[25] since it alone appears without the limits of a horizon or reduction to an I and constitutes itself, to the point of giving *itself* as a *self*. I will therefore name this apparition that is purely of itself starting from itself, this apparition that does not submit its possibility to any prior determination, an auto-manifestation. With this, it is purely and simply a matter of the phenomenon taken in its full sense, in short, of the phenomenon's normative figure, in relation to which the others are defined and declined by defect or simplification.

Three Examples

This is also confirmed by the very history of philosophy, which has long known such saturated phenomena, even if it rarely does them justice. One could even go so far as to hold that no decisive thinker has omitted the description of one (or several) saturated phenomena, even at the price of contradicting his own metaphysical presuppositions. Among many fairly obvious examples, let me select only Descartes, Kant, and Husserl. (a) Descartes, who everywhere else reduces the phenomenon to the idea that the ego has of it, then this idea to an object, nevertheless thinks the idea of the infinite as a saturated phenomenon. It indeed bears all the marks of one. According to quantity, the idea of the infinite is not obtained by summation or successive synthesis, but "tota simul": thus the gaze (*intueri*) becomes the surprise of admiration (*admirari*).[26] In terms of quality, it admits no zero, or finite degree, but solely a *maximum*: "maxime clara et distincta," "maxime vera."[27] In terms of relation, it maintains no analogy with any other idea whatsoever: "nihil univoce"; in effect, it exceeds every horizon, since it remains incomprehensible, capable only of being touched by thought: "attingam quomodolibet cogitatione."[28] In terms of modality, far from letting itself be led back to a constituting I, it comprehends the I without letting itself be comprehended by it ("non tam capere quam ab ipsa capi"),[29] in such a way that even the ego itself could perhaps be interpreted as one who is called. But in any case, wouldn't it be enough to translate "idea of infinity" term for term by "saturated phenomenon" to establish my conclusion? (b) Kant provides an example of the saturated phenomenon that is all the more significant as it does not concern, as does Descartes's, rational theology, but rather the finite exercise of the faculties; for him, it is a question of the sublime. I based my argument above on the "aesthetic idea" in order to contest the principle of the shortage of intuition and to introduce the possibility of a saturation (§20), but already with the doctrine of the sublime, it is an issue of a saturated phenomenon, whose characteristics it bears. That is, in terms of quantity, the sublime has no form or order, since it is great "beyond all comparison," absolutely and noncomparatively (*absolute, schlechthin, bloss*).[30] In terms of quality, it contradicts taste as a "negative pleasure" and provokes a "feeling of immensity," of "monstrosity."[31] In terms of relation, it very clearly escapes every analogy and every horizon since it is literally "limitlessness [*Unbegrenztheit*]" that it represents.[32] In terms of modality, finally, far from agreeing with our power of knowing, "it may appear in such a way as to contradict the finality of our faculty of judgment." The relation of our faculty of judgment to the phenomenon is therefore reversed to the point that it is the phenomenon that from now on "gazes" at the I in "respect."[33] The Kantian example of the sublime would thus permit us to broaden the field of application for the saturated phenomenon.

But without a doubt we owe it to (c) Husserl to have illustrated it in a perfectly universal occurrence: the internal consciousness of time corresponds to, and in a privileged way, the distinctive characteristics of the saturated phenomenon. In terms of quantity first, time proves *invisable* and therefore unforeseeable; that is, the flux admits no homogeneity in its parts, since each consists only in the "continual running-off"[34] of each moment, slipping from the future to the present and from the present into the past, modifying itself without pause. In terms of quality, then, time proves unbearable, since it does not admit degrees. First, because one cannot assign a zero point to the flux; that is, between the original impression and the first retention, nothing ever comes up but "an ideal limit, something abstract," and accordingly, "the ideal now is not something entirely different from the present non-now."[35] Next, because the flux constitutive of temporality has nothing in common with it, has itself "no duration [*kein Dauer*]" and therefore remains "nontemporal [*unzeitlich*]." At best, it would follow a "quasi-temporal order."[36] Degrees of quality (intensity) therefore cannot be set in a time that it precedes, surpasses, and exceeds. In terms of relation, time remains absolute. Nothing shows this better than the doubling of intentionality into, on the one hand, transversal intentionality—which, across the flux, is stubbornly oriented to the object-in-its-how to the detriment of time itself, a mere means or screen for an objectifying aim and of itself indifferent to time—and, on the other, longitudinal intentionality, which pushes from retention to retention so as to constitute without pause the unity of the temporal flux, that is to say, time itself without relation to or aim at even the slightest object. Henceforth, longitudinal intentionality works only in the "the self-apparition of the flux,"[37] before any object, before all real or even intentional immanence; it therefore deploys temporality without applying it to objects or the connection of objects among themselves. Contrary to Kant, time does not first have to ensure the necessary connections among the objects of experience and therefore the analogies. It shows itself in itself and by itself without relation to or among objects, in short, absolutely. In terms of modality, finally, time cannot be gazed at. For, as "original impression," time imposes itself starting from itself as "the absolute unmodified [*das absolut Unmodifizierte*]" which not only "is not produced," but "is the original production."[38] The original impression originally determines consciousness, which henceforth loses its status as origin and discovers itself originally determined, impressed, constituted—transcendentally taken witness.[39]

The saturated phenomenon is therefore by no means an extreme or rare hypothesis. It concerns a figure of phenomenality that is so essential that even barely phenomenological thinkers (Descartes, Kant), like those who are more phenomenological (Husserl), have recourse to it as soon as the thing itself calls for it—that is, when it appears according to excess and not shortage of intuition. In fact, only the saturated phenomenon can mark, by rendering visible to excess, the paradoxically unmeasured dimensions of possible givenness—which nothing stops or conditions.

§23. Topics of the Phenomenon

Poor Phenomena, Common Phenomena

It now seems possible to lay out, if only in outline, topics for the different types of phenomena. In every case, I will maintain the phenomenon's generic definition as what shows itself from itself (Heidegger) and does so only insofar as it gives itself in itself from itself alone; what shows itself does so only to the extent that it gives itself. To give itself means that the aspect that shows itself (shape, schema, species, concept, signification, intention, etc.) should also always give itself in person, though in a measure that varies (intuition, hyletic layer, noema, etc.). Givenness accomplishes manifestation by giving it fulfillment, a fulfillment that is intuitive in the majority of cases, but not necessarily all.[40] The different types of phenomena can be defined as different variations of auto-manifestation (showing itself in and from itself) according to the degree of givenness (giving itself in and from itself).

I will thus distinguish, in terms of their degree of givenness, three original figures of phenomenality. (a) First, the phenomena poor in intuition. They claim only a formal intuition in mathematics or a categorical intuition in logic, in other words, a "vision of essences" and idealities. For this type of phenomenon, what shows itself in and from itself does not need much more than its concept alone, or at least just its intelligibility (the demonstration itself), to give itself—of course, in the empty abstraction of the universal without content or individuation, according to an iterability that is perfect because unscathed by matter (even significative), but nevertheless in fact. Can we imagine, besides these phenomena poor in intuition, others that are absolutely deprived of intuition? The absence of intuition could be understood in two opposed senses. Either as a real shortage, which directly contradicts phenomenality: what in no way gives itself in no way shows itself either. Or, by contrast, as pure givenness coming to relieve intuition (manifestation)—which will demand other distinctions. But with poor phenomena, the essential point is found elsewhere in the privilege that metaphysics has always accorded them over and above all other thinkable phenomena: the privilege of certainty. That is, admitting an intuition that is only formal or categorical, poor phenomena no longer admit anything "that experience might render uncertain,"[41] and therefore their very abstraction guarantees their certainty, therefore objectification. But this epistemological privilege inverts itself and becomes a radical phenomenological deficit—manifestation here does not give (itself), or only a little, since it conveys neither real nor individual intuition, nor the temporalization of an event, in short, no accomplished phenomenality. In opposition to metaphysics' constant decision, we should conclude that the privilege of poor phenomena (abstract epistemological certainty), far from qualifying them, forbids establishing them as secure paradigm for phenomenality in general. (b) The common-law phenomena should be defined by how much they vary in terms of givenness, not by reference to the poor phenomena. In their case, signification (aimed at by intention) is manifest only to the extent that it receives intuitive fulfillment. In principle, this fulfillment can be adequate (intuition equaling intention). At first and most of the time, however, it remains inadequate, and the intention, like its concept, remains partially unconfirmed by intuition, thus not perfectly given. Nevertheless, this deficiency is not enough by itself to disqualify the objectivity of common-law phenomena. By contrast, it alone establishes it. First, because, just as a bank guarantees the loans it makes with reserves that represent only a partial percentage of their total, so too does a weak intuitive confirmation of the concept reasonably suffice to give the corresponding phenomenon provided it is confirmed by being repeated regularly. Next and especially, because the deficit of intuition secures the concept's mastery over the entire process of manifestation, thereby maintaining an abstraction thanks to a weak intuition, or else attaining a degree of certainty comparable (at least tangentially) to that of the poor phenomena. In this way, the common phenomenon can be accomplished according to objectivity. Obviously classed as common phenomena are the objects of physics and the natural sciences. In these cases, it is a question of establishing the objective certainty of conceptual maximums (signification, theories, etc.) on the basis of intuitive minimums (sense data, experimental protocols, statistical accounts, etc.). It should be possible to if not eliminate, at least reduce, "material" understood as the disturbance made by *hulē*. The physical law is true only by accounting for what disturbs it, that is to say only by correcting itself so as to integrate the factors that weaken it—only by calculating what makes an exception to its calculation. For example, Galileo's law of falling bodies is experimentally verified only if one eliminates in thought the friction, the resistance of the milieu, the noninfinity of the space crossed, etc. The objectification of the phenomenon itself demands restricting the intuitive given to what confirms (or rather does not diminish) the concept. The intention thus keeps mastery over the manifestation, and givenness is cut to the size of objectification. But this figure of phenomenality—the common-law variety, with possible but not realized adequation—finds confirmation in the case of technological objects. Here the intention and the concept take on the role of plan, schema, or drawing ("mechanical" or done with CAD), in short, exactly what industry names the "concept" of an object. It is defined by the fact that in principle it renders fully intelligible, that is to say, at least imaginable, the structure of the object, but also by the fact that it already integrates its feasibility (its industrialization) and the calculation of the profitability of its fabrication and commercialization—not only its technical definition (its essence), but also the conditions for its entering production and eventually the economy (existence). The concept (in the sense of the "concept" of a product) renders this product visible before production actually gives it, and sometimes even without any production following the manifestation of its "concept" (simulation, "concept car," etc.). To show in and through a concept (signification, intention, etc.) precedes, determines, and sometimes annuls intuitive givenness (actuality, production, intuition, etc.).

The inadequation between intention and intuition, which Husserl describes in terms of fulfillment by means of the continuous temporal flux of consciousness, is here declined in terms of delay and foresight. Of delay, first. It belongs essentially to the technological object (what I will from now on call the product) that its manifestation in "concept" radically precedes its givenness (its production in and for intuition); its "concept" therefore always gets the upper hand chronologically over whatever intuitive fulfillment might be, that is to say, over this product itself. The technological object would therefore not literally deserve its title "product" since production only completes its "concept" in the sense that, in metaphysics, existence contributes only a mere "complement to the possibility," therefore to essence. For the product never gives itself first, but by contrast always after and following its "concept," which is previously shown and demonstrated. And if it is thus necessary to consider the product on the basis of its "concept," it would therefore be necessary to define it more as induced (on the basis of an anterior "concept") than produced, in advance or before. The incurable chronological gap between the manifest "concept" and its induced (given) production follows, in the field of the technological object, the factual inadequacy between intention and intuition. Above all, it confirms the derived, indeed alienated, phenomenal status of the technological object, which always comes after itself and continually recaptures in an always unequal actuality its own supposedly impeccable intelligibility. Foresight comes next. The theoretical and chronological preeminence of the "concept" of the product, in general of the concept over intuition, allows us to know at the outset and in advance the characteristics of what comes at the end of the chain of production. The product confirms—at best—the "concept," and the intuition, the intention, without any surprise, unpredictable landing, or incident ever arising. What we call, with some naivete in our satisfaction, the product's "total quality" here means this: the "concept" never undergoes even the least variation or incident during the course of its intuitive actualization; manifestation never suffers a counter-blow at the hand of givenness. Thus foreseen, production and intuition (therefore givenness) remain beneath the watchful gaze of the concept. From its vantage point, it sees them coming from afar, without surprise and without expecting anything new from them. The predictability of the technological object, therefore the perfect foreseeability of the product induced on the basis of its "concept," not only confirms that this concerns an alienated phenomenality, but permits (or demands) the product's repetition. That is, since intuition always comes after the fact and plays the role of actual confirmation of the plan's original rationality, and since it should make no difference ("flawless"), it also should not tolerate any innovation, modification, or, in short, any event. Thus the identical repetition of the product becomes possible since it makes no difference. Production already contains the reproduction, which in fact adds nothing to it, since intuition adds nothing real to the "concept." And, quite obviously, the quantity of the (re)production—the number of exemplary products of the product—doesn't add anything to the reproduction, either. It merely declines it. It follows that, like the poor phenomenon, the common-law phenomenon cannot, strictly speaking, be individualized. Wouldn't this happen at a minimum through the "material," the disturbance of *hulē*? But every productive business eliminates this disturbance as far as possible ("flawless," "total quality," etc.). Therefore, the product, common-law phenomenon par excellence, cannot be individualized—it must therefore be reproduced; that is to say, it must continually confirm the primacy of the concept over intuition, therefore the deficit of givenness.

Saturated Phenomena, or Paradoxes

Now it is possible to broach (c) the saturated phenomena, in which intuition always submerges the expectation of the intention, in which givenness not only entirely invests manifestation but, surpassing it, modifies its common characteristics. On account of this investment and modification, I also call saturated phenomena "paradoxes." The fundamental characteristic of the paradox lies in the fact that intuition sets forth a surplus that the concept cannot organize, therefore that the intention cannot foresee. As a result, intuition is not bound to and by the intention, but is freed from it, establishing itself now as a free intuition (*intuitio vaga*). Far from coming after the concept and therefore following the thread of the intention (aim, foresight, repetition), intuition subverts, therefore precedes, every intention, which it exceeds and decenters. The visibility of the appearance thus arises against the flow of the intention—whence the paradox, the counter-appearance, the visibility running counter to the aim. Paradox means what happens counter to (*para-*) received opinion, as well as to appearance, according to the two obvious meanings of *doxa*. But it also means what happens counter to expectation—"praeter expectationem offertur"[42]—what arrives against all that representation or intention, in short the concept, would expect. The paradox therefore belongs, indisputably, to the domain of the truth, with this minor qualification: that its givenness contravenes, in its intuition, what previous experience should reasonably permit us to foresee. That is, here the I of intentionality can neither constitute nor synthesize the intuition into an object defined by a horizon. The synthesis—if there must be one—is accomplished without and contrary to the I, as a passive synthesis, coming from the nonobject itself, which imposes its arising and its moment on and before all active intentionality of the I; for the passivity of the "passive synthesis" indicates not only that the I does not accomplish it actively and therefore suffers it passively, but above all that activity falls to the phenomenon and to it alone. Thus it does indeed show *itself* because it gives *itself* first—in anticipation of every aim, free of every concept, according to a befalling that delivers its self Givenness, now to the measure of the excess of intuition over intention, is no longer defined in terms of what the concept or the horizon assign to it, but can be deployed indefinitely. The concept no longer foresees, for intuition fore-comes—comes before and therefore, at least once, without it. As a result, the relation between manifestation and givenness is inverted. For (a) poor and (b) common-law phenomena, intention and the concept foresee intuition, make up for its shortage, and set limits for givenness; on the other hand, for the (c) saturated phenomena, or paradoxes, intuition surpasses the intention, is deployed without concept and lets givenness come before all limitation and every horizon. In this case, phenomenality is calibrated first in terms of givenness, such that the phenomenon no longer gives itself in the measure to which it shows itself, but shows itself in the measure (or, eventually, lack of measure) to which it gives itself.

But if the paradox clearly emphasizes to the benefit of givenness the principle that a phenomenon shows itself only insofar as it gives itself, we must not conclude from this that it is an exception to the common rule, represented by the first two types. It falls to metaphysics alone to consider the paradox an exceptional (indeed eccentric) case of phenomenality, whose common law it organizes according to the paradigm of the poor phenomenon. With notable exceptions (Descartes, Spinoza, Kant, Husserl), metaphysics always thinks the common-law phenomenon (shortage of intuition) on the basis of the intuitively poor phenomenon (certain, but of little or nothing). My entire project, by contrast, aims to think the common-law phenomenon, and through it the poor phenomenon, on the basis of the paradigm of the saturated phenomenon, of which the former two offer only weakened variants, and from which they derive by progressive extenuation. For the saturated phenomenon does not give itself abnormally, making an exception to the definition of phenomenality; to the contrary, its ownmost property is to render thinkable the measure of manifestation in terms of givenness and to recover it in its common-law variety, indeed in the poor phenomenon. What metaphysics rules out as an exception (the saturated phenomenon), phenomenology here takes for its norm—every phenomenon shows itself in the measure (or the lack of measure) to which it gives itself To be sure, not all phenomena get classified as saturated phenomena, but all saturated phenomena accomplish the one and only paradigm of phenomenality. Better, they alone enable it to be illustrated. This is why one can without much difficulty make each of the determinations of the phenomenon insofar as given (Book 3) correspond with one of the characteristics of the saturated phenomenon (Book 4), precisely because the latter lets the paradigm of the phenomenon as such swing to its full range. (i) Unforeseeability (in terms of quantity), therefore also the nonrepeatability of the saturated phenomenon (§21), consecrates the factuality of the fait accompli, such that it determines every given phenomenon (§15). (ii) The unbearable and intolerable (in terms of quality) character of the saturated phenomenon, therefore also the bedazzlement it provokes (§21), fully develops the unpredictable landing, determination of the given phenomenon in general (§14). (iii) The absoluteness of the saturated phenomenon, outside all relation and all analogy (even that of causality) (§21), demarcates to excess the incident, determination of the phenomenon as given (§16). (iv) Finally, the impossibility of constituting or gazing at (§22) accomplishes in saturation the anamorphosis that already characterizes the given phenomenon (§13). In other words, the two subversions that free the saturated degrees of phenomenality (submerging every horizon, the I reverting into a witness) do nothing other than push the universal determinations of the given beyond their limits—which the poor, common-law, or intermediary (the being given) variants still hide. The saturated phenomenon in the end establishes the truth of all phenomenality because it marks, more than any other phenomenon, the givenness from which it comes. The paradox, understood in the strictest sense, no longer runs counter to appearance; it runs with apparition.

It now becomes possible to trace, within the topics of the phenomenon insofar as given and in order to complete it, a topics of the saturated phenomenon itself The guiding thread will no longer be the degree of intuition (since in all cases, there is on principle saturation), but the determination in relation to which saturation is each time accomplished (quantity, quality, relation, or modality). I will therefore distinguish, without intending any hierarchy, four types of saturated phenomenon. In each case, it will be question of paradoxes, never constitutable as objects within a horizon and by an I. We should not be surprised, then, that we have already seen these privileged phenomena in the previous analyses. With the determinations of the given phenomenon in general, and still more with the sketch of the saturated phenomenon, they were no doubt already at issue.

The Event

The saturated phenomenon is attested first in the figure of the historical phenomenon, or the event carried to its apex. It saturates the category of quantity. When the arising event is not limited to an instant, a place, or an empirical individual, but overflows these singularities and becomes epoch-making in time (delimits a homogeneous duration and imposes it as "a block"), covers a physical space such that no gaze encompasses it with one sweep (not a mappable "theater of operations," therefore, but a battlefield to canvass), and encompasses a population such that none of those who belong to it can take upon themselves an absolute or even privileged point of view, then it becomes a historical event. This means precisely that nobody can claim for himself a "here and now" that would permit him to describe it exhaustively and constitute it as an object. Put trivially, nobody ever *saw* the battle of Waterloo[43] (nor Austerlitz, to be fair). To be sure, it is plain that Fabrice saw only the fire of his own confused erring and barely the fire of the hail of bullets, barely the emperor passing, his horse in flight, or the barmaid in a flutter; but the emperor himself saw hardly more: he saw neither the advance of the enemy reinforcements nor the delay of his own, neither the ditch where his cavalry got bogged down nor the dying among the already dead. In fact, nobody will see more, not Wellington, any of the officers, or any of the men on the field—each will furnish confused and partial reports from an angle of vision taken in by panic or rage. The battle passes and passes away on its own, without anybody making it or deciding it. It passes, and each watches it pass, fade into the distance, and then disappear, disappear like it had come—that is to say, of itself. In history making itself (*Geschichte*), the battle makes itself of itself, starting from a point of view that it alone can unify, without any unique horizon. For those, by contrast, whom it enlists and encompasses, not one of their (individual) horizons will be enough to unify it, speak it, and especially, foresee it. Neither Fabrice, nor Flambeau, nor Chateaubriand, with an ear to the ground, saw it. Consequently, in recorded and transmitted history (*Historie*), the battle will demand additional horizons (this time conceptual) of an indefinite number: military horizons (the strategy adopted since the return from exile, the tactics concerning this place), diplomatic, political, economic, ideological (reference to the Revolution), etc. The plurality of horizons practically forbids constituting the historical event into *one* object and demands substituting an endless hermeneutic in time; the narration is doubled by a narration of the narrations. More: in this hermeneutic labor, the proliferation of horizons implies also the proliferation of the sciences used, as well as of the literary genres. The romantic fiction of Chateaubriand, Hugo, and Stendahl shows as much, better no doubt, than the factual reports of the memoirists or the quantitative historical analyses. The saturation of quantity in a paradox such as the historical event implies, therefore, in order to ensure the indefinite diversification of its horizons (testimonies, points of view, sciences, literary genres, etc.), not only a teleology without end, but above all an interobjectivity—knowledge of the historical event becomes itself historical, like the sum of the agreements and disagreements among subjects partially constituting a nonobject always to be re-constituted, like the history of an intersubjectivity mediated by a nonobject, the paradox itself. The hermeneutic of the (saturated because historical) event is enough to produce a historical community and, through its very inachievability, to render communication possible.[44]

The Idol

The saturated phenomenon appears secondly under the aspect of the unbearable and bedazzlement, insofar as they subvert the category of quality carried to the maximum. I will name this paradox "the idol." The idol is determined as the first indisputable visible because its splendor stops intentionality for the first time; and this first visible fills it, stops it, and even blocks it, to the point of returning it toward itself, after the fashion of an invisible obstacle—or mirror. The privileged occurrence of the idol is obviously the painting (or what, without the frame of the frame, takes its place), not to speak too generically of the work of art. Saturation marks the painting essentially. In it, intuition always surpasses the concept or the concepts proposed to welcome it. It is never enough to have seen it just once to have really seen it, in contrast to the technical object and the product. Totally opposite this, each gaze at the painting fails to bring me to perceive what I see, keeping me from taking it into view as such—so that it always again conceals the essential from visibility. No doubt, I can comprehend, conceptually or by means of information, as a theoretician or historian, a continually increasing part of its given; but the more this part grows, the less accessible givenness itself becomes, as the phenomenon's purely unpredictable landing in its totality and at its own initiative. The givenness of the visible gives rise to other questions. On the basis of what "self" is it given? According to what anamorphosis is it imposed? With what authority does it summon me to come see it? To these questions, all of which are provoked by the surplus of intuition, no concept will ever answer. The painting is definitively given "without concept"—Kant understood this perfectly—or idea (Hegel missed this). This unpredictable landing, whose intuition saturates every possible concept, is attested by the painting in its summoning not only to come and see it, but especially to come and see it again. To see the painting again does not mean adding one intuition to another (to complete one bit of knowledge with another) or reconsidering it (to revise information), but again confronting a new concept or a new intention with an indefinite intuition that the familiar habit of seeing one and the same painting tames. To see again is equivalent to trying to contain and resist the same saturating intuitive given by means of the grill of a new concept (or several of them), a different horizon (or several). The intuitive given of the idol imposes on us the demand to change our gaze again and again, continually, be this only so as to confront its unbearable bedazzlement. In the case of the idol, one point must be noted, which distinguishes it essentially from the previous saturated phenomenon: instead of presupposing an interobjectivity and an at least teleological communication, like the historical event does, the idol provokes an ineluctable solipsism. That is, since the painting summons *me* to see it, since above all I must see it again at the pace of *my* own changing horizon and concept, it shows itself only by arriving to *me,* therefore by individualizing me radically (*Jemeinigkeit* by the idol, no longer by Being). The sequence of gazes that I continually pose on the idol establish so many invisible mirrors of myself; it therefore describes or conceptualizes it less than it designates a temporality where it is first an issue of my ipseity. The idol marks me—traces the mark of the site where I stand—because in it intuition is always lacking the concept.[45]

The Flesh

The saturated phenomenon comes up a third time in the absolute character of the flesh, such that it is torn from the category of relation and carries the fait accompli to its excellence. The flesh is defined as the identity of what touches with the medium where this touching takes place (Aristotle), therefore of the felt with what feels (Husserl), but also of the seen and the seeing or the heard and the hearing—in short, of the affected with the affecting (Henry).[46] For before intentionality opens a gap between the intended and the fulfillment or between the I and its objective and even in order that consciousness might render this ecstasy possible, it must be admitted that it first has to receive impressions, original or derived, whatever they might be—intuitive impressions, but impressions that are significant as well. Now it can do so only inasmuch as, of its essence, it is susceptible to radical affection in itself (self-affection); but it can be affected in itself only inasmuch as its affection presupposes no external or preexisting affect, therefore inasmuch as it accomplishes itself unconditionally. In order to affect itself in itself, it must first be affected by nothing other than itself (auto-affection). Such an affection is at issue each time the paradox not only exceeds every constitutable object, but saturates the horizon to the point that there is no longer any relation that refers it to another object. The affection refers to no object, according to no ecstasy, but only to itself; for it itself is sufficient to accomplish itself as affected. It thus attributes to itself the privilege that *ousia* holds for Aristotle: not to arise from relative terms, *oudemia ousia ton pros ti legetai*.[47] The flesh auto-affects itself in agony, suffering, and grief, as well as in desire, feeling, or orgasm. There is no sense in asking if these affects come to it from the body, the mind, or the Other, since originally it always auto-affects itself first in and by itself. Therefore, joy, pain, the evidence of love, or the living remembrance (Proust), but also the call of consciousness as anxiety in the face of nothing (Heidegger), fear and trembling (Kierkegaard), in short, the *numen* in general (provided that one assigns it no transcendence), all arise from the flesh and its own immanence. Two points allow us to distinguish the saturated phenomenon of the flesh. First, in contrast to the idol, but perhaps like the historical event, it cannot be regarded or even seen. The immediacy of auto-affection blocks the space where the ecstasy of an intentionality would become possible. Next, in contrast to the historical event, but no doubt more radically than the idol, the flesh provokes and demands solipsism; for it remains by definition mine, unsubstitutable—nobody can enjoy or suffer for me (even if he can do so in my place). Mineness (*Jemeinigkeit*) does not concern first or only my possibility as the possibility of impossibility (dying), but my flesh itself. More, it belongs only to my flesh to individualize me by letting the immanent succession of my affections, or rather of the affections that make me irreducibly identical to myself alone, be inscribed in it. In contrast with the interobjectivity to which the historical event gives rise and more radically than the indefinite revision that the idol demands of me, the flesh therefore shows itself only in giving itself—and, in this first "self," it gives me to myself.

The Icon

The saturated phenomenon is accomplished fourth in the aspect of the irregardable and irreducible, insofar as they are free from all reference to the I, therefore to the categories of modality. I will call this fourth type of saturated phenomenon the icon because it no longer offers any spectacle to the gaze and tolerates no gaze from any spectator, but rather exerts its own gaze over that which meets it. The gazer takes the place of the gazed upon; the manifested phenomenon is reversed into a manifestation not only in and of itself, but strictly by and on the basis of itself (auto-manifestation)—the paradox reverses the polarity of manifestation by taking the initiative, far from undergoing it, by giving it, far from being given by it. The saturation of the phenomenon stems first from the silent and probably poor reversal of its flux, more than from its likely excess. And in this way, anamorphosis reaches its ultimate point. It must be observed that intuition here takes an absolutely new turn. The gaze that comes upon me (lands unpredictably, event) provides no spectacle, therefore no immediately visible or assignable intuition; it resides precisely in the black holes of the two pupils, in the sole and minuscule space where, on the surface of the body of the Other, there is nothing to see (not even the color of the iris that surrounds them) in the gaze facing me. The gaze that the Other casts and makes weigh on me therefore does not give itself to my gaze, nor even to be seen—this invisible gaze gives itself only to be endured. The Other is charged to me: strictly speaking, he weighs on my gaze like a weight, a burden. It is the same with the face. To be sure, the Other assigns me by his face, but only if its essential invisibility is understood. This face, nobody has ever seen it, except by bringing about its death—since to see it would suppose at once reducing it to the rank of a constituted spectacle, therefore eliminating it as such—or dying oneself—by transferring oneself to its point of view, thereby nullifying each as individualized monad. The face of the Other is not seen any more than its gaze; it deploys its invisibility over a portion of the flesh where it radiates from the pole of two voids. This face, like this gaze, gives me nothing to see but gives itself by weighing on me. By gaze and by face, the Other acts, accomplishes the act of his unpredictable landing as saturated phenomenon.[88] Such an inversion of phenomenality's polarity evidently implies that the I not only renounce its transcendental function of constitution, but that it pass to the figure of what we have already thematized as the witness (§22): me, insofar as I receive *myself* from the very givenness of the irregardable phenomenon, me insofar as I learn of myself from what the gaze of the Other says to me in silence. And in fact, the concept of witness finds its full phenomenological legitimacy only when related to the saturated phenomenon of the Other, who alone can constitute me as his own because he precedes me in the order of manifestation.

Finally, the icon offers a surprising (or rather, expected) characteristic: it gathers together the particular characteristics of the three preceding types of saturated phenomena. Like the historical event, it demands a summation of horizons and narrations, since the Other cannot be constituted objectively and since it happens without assignable end; the icon therefore opens a teleology. Like the idol, it begs to be seen and reseen, though in the mode of unconditioned endurance; like it, the icon therefore exercises (but in a more radical mode) an individuation over the gaze that confronts it. Like the flesh finally, it accomplishes this individuation by affecting the I so originally that it loses its function as transcendental pole; and the originality of this affection brings it close, even tangentially, to auto-affection, This gathering of the first three types in the fourth and last at least confirms the coherence of the region where phenomena saturate. It would also confirm its phenomenological legitimacy, if the strict correspondence between the determinations of the phenomenon as given (Book 3) and its degrees (Book 4) as far as saturation had not already established it. The definition of the phenomenon as given frees it from the limits of objectness and beingness. It also lets us think that it shows itself in and from itself only insofar as it gives itself in and from itself, indeed by quitting the "self." But it enlarges the field of phenomenality by admitting, beyond phenomena of the common-law type and those poor in intuition, the domain and privilege of saturated phenomena.

The Banality of Saturation

I sometimes see within a banal theater.

—Baudelaire, "The Irreparable"

1

In several steps and not without some stumbling and a few retractions, I proposed a new concept for phenomenology: the saturated phenomenon. This concept will pose the question for my reflections in this essay. The innovation I proposed should be understood cautiously. Formally, at least, it does not mark a revolution but merely a development of one of the possibilities that is by right already inscribed within the commonly accepted definition of the phenomenon. By "commonly accepted definition" I mean that of Kant and Husserl. If not alone, then at least as the first in modernity these two philosophers have saved the phenomenon by according it the right to appear unreservedly.[1] For them, a phenomenon is a representation that ceases to refer, like a symptom, only to its subject (like an inadequate idea in Spinoza) and instead gives access to a thing placed facing it (possibly an object), because some actually given intuition in general (sensible or not, the question remains open) finds itself assumed, framed, and controlled by a concept, playing the role of a category. On these two conditions, the representation is modeled after its objective, concentrated on it and absorbed in it, such that the representation becomes the direct presentation of its objective; its semblance passes through to this object and becomes its appearance. Intuition can then become objectively intentional (like an appearance, no longer a mere semblance) in and through the concept that actively fixes it (according to the spontaneity of the understanding). But reciprocally, the concept becomes objectively intentional (and plays the role of a category) only in and through the intuition that fills it from the outside, by virtue of the passivity that it transmits

to it (according to intuition). Without underestimating the no doubt significant differences in how each philosopher states his case, I therefore assume the compatibility, indeed the equivalence, of Kant's and Husserl's definitions of the phenomenon.

There are then two variations of this initial formulation, according to how one considers the two relations that the two constitutive elements can maintain. Kant and Husserl
each traced one variation. On the one hand, truth is accomplished in perfect evidence
when intuition completely fills the concept, thereby validating it without remainder;
this is the paradigmatic situation, and for that reason the least frequent. On the other
hand, we have the partial validation of a concept by an intuition that does not fulfill it
totally but is enough to certify it or verify it; this is the more ordinary situation (truth in
the common sense of verification, validation, confirmation), even though it can seem
unsatisfying. My innovation intervenes in the wake of these two: it consists only in paying attention to a third possible relation between intuition and concept—that in which
intuition would surpass the concept (in multiple senses) by inverting the common situation where the concept exceeds intuition and the exceptional situation of an equality
between them. In other words, it concerns the situation in which intuition would not
only validate all that for which the concept assures intelligibility but would also add a
given (sensations, experiences, information, it matters little) that this concept would no
longer be able to constitute as an object or render objectively intelligible. Such an excess
of intuition over and above the concept would invert the common situation without,
however, abandoning phenomenality (or the terms of its definition), since the two elements
of the phenomenon are still operative. The ideal norm of evidence (equality between
intuition and the concept) is no longer threatened only and as usual by a shortage of intuition, but by its excess. I named and explained this phenomenon by excess as the (intuitively) saturated phenomenon.

I have not only formally identified this new determination of the phenomenon. I have
also tried to apply it to the task of offering reasons for phenomena that have hitherto
been left in the margins of ordinary phenomenality—indeed, have been excluded by it.
Or rather, not to offer reason, since what is at issue is liberating a phenomenon from the
requirement of the principle of (sufficient) reason, but to offer it *its own* reason, so as to
give it a rationality against all the objections, the prohibitions, and the conditions that
weigh on it in metaphysics (indeed, partially also in phenomenology). What is at stake
here is offering legitimacy to nonobjectifiable, even nonbeing phenomena: the event
(which exceeds all quantity), the work of art (which exceeds all quality), the flesh (which
exceeds all relation), and the face of the Other (which exceeds all modality). Each of
these excesses identifies a type of saturated phenomenon, which functions exactly like a
paradox. I then suggested the possibility of combining, on the one hand, some of these
types and, on the other hand, all four together in order to describe other, still more complex saturated phenomena. The face of the Other, for example, doubtless combines the
transgression of all modality with the surpassing of quantity, quality, and relation.[2] Finally, this combining opens access to a radicalized mode of saturation, one that I designated with the name "phenomenon of revelation." Finally, on the basis of this complexity
of saturations, the case of Revelation might possibly become thinkable. But it would no
longer fall within phenomenology (which deals only with possibility, not the fact of its

phenomenality) to decide about the Revelation, which it could admit only formally. For that, one would have to call on theology.

2

As a general rule, one should neither expect nor hope that an innovation be adopted immediately and unreservedly. Especially if by chance it should be borne out, an assertion cannot lay claim to novelty and to success at the same time. If it meets with no resistance, it is doing nothing more than respond to already-established convictions, which amounts to yielding to the (always) dominant ideology. If instead it incites a reaction, that could be because it is innovative (provided that it is not simply mad). Criticism therefore pays homage despite itself to the innovation that it helps to validate. Even if it does not validate more than it invalidates what it challenges, criticism remains inevitable and indispensable because by its very resistance it lays bare the truly symptomatic points of what is thus advanced. Criticism can hence open a royal road to what is at stake. This seems to be the case for objections addressed to the legitimacy of a saturated phenomenon, for they allow me to identify at least two resistances, therefore two questions. To simplify, I will use two particularly clear formulations of these objections, ones that sum up all the others. The first questions the terms in which the saturated phenomenon is defined; the other, its principle. Although aware of the "appalling uselessness of explaining anything whatever to anyone whatever,"[3] in examining these objections I will try to answer their assault, but above all I will try to extend their lines of attack so as to reach through them once again to the heart of the question.

The first objection points to two contradictions, which lead to two impasses. First, the hypothesis of the saturated phenomenon pretends to go "beyond what canonical phenomenology has recognized as the possibility of *experience* itself," all the while pretending "to be inscribed within an experience."[4] What is more: because "there is no 'pure experience,'" especially not of "full transcendence [and] its pure alterity," it follows that "no Revelation, with a capital R, can be given within phenomenality."[5] In short, we do not have any experience of what passes beyond the conditions for the possibility of experience; yet by its very definition the so-called saturated phenomenon passes beyond the limits of experience; therefore we have absolutely no experience of it. And there is no discussion concerning what cannot (and therefore should not) be thought. Yet who cannot see that this objection, without critiquing or even admitting it, presupposes that experience has only one meaning and that this meaning is the one suited to the experience of objects? In short, who does not see that the objection presupposes the univocity of experience and of objectivity? Now, the entire question of the saturated phenomenon concerns solely and specifically the possibility that certain phenomena do not manifest themselves in the mode of objects and yet still do manifest themselves. The difficulty is to describe what could manifest itself without our being able to constitute (or synthesize) it as an object (by a concept or an intentionality adequate to its intuition). From the outset, by its simple formulation the objection misses the sole and central question, substituting for it a pure and simple fiction—the fiction of a "pure experience," a "full transcendence [and] its pure alterity"—whose absurdity is easy to show. Not only does the description of the saturated phenomenon never use such pompous and deceptive formulations, but it does not even speak willingly of experience (except in the mode of counter-experience). That is, under the guise of modest showiness, the very notion of experience already presupposes too much, namely, nothing less than a subject, whose measure and anteriority define from the start the conditions of experience and therefore of objectification. Consequently, if one wants to contest the horizon of the object in order to do justice to the possibility of the saturated phenomenon, one must also contest the conditions for the subject of experience and therefore the univocal notion of experience itself.

To this first invented contradiction a second is added. Even if one can rigorously admit an experience without object, one cannot think "an experience without a subject."[6] This is why, even if it pretends to stick to an "entirely empty, passive, seized upon, affected, powerless and so on" subject,[7] the saturated phenomenon should maintain intact its role within phenomenality: "yet its function (which is to allow the appearing of phenomena) remains unchanged . . . ; the character of subjectivity is maintained throughout and . . . the promised dispossession or dismissal has not taken place." Thus, I "reestablish, without admitting it, what [I] claim to have dismissed."[8] This contradiction supposes that the (in principle) criticized subject coincides exactly with the (in fact) maintained subject; in other words, it rests on the univocity of the concept of subject. Yet how can one feign not to know that the entire question—and the entire difficulty— consists in seeing whether "subject" cannot and should not be understood in many senses or, in other words, if the critique of the transcendental subject does not free another sense of "subject," or more exactly, of who comes after the subject (to take up a helpful phrase from Jean-Luc Nancy)?[9] I can hardly see why such an equivocity should be dismissed, given that phenomenology has already broached it—if only in passing from Husserl (the transcendental subject) to Heidegger (*Dasein*), indeed, within Heidegger's own thought (from *Dasein* to what succeeds it), not to mention the questioning of the subject who is master of experience in Sartre, Merleau-Ponty, Levinas, and Henry. Anyway, why should the "subject" or whoever comes after it disappear without remainder if it no longer plays any role within the process of phenomenalization except that of response and "resistance" to what gives itself, then of screen where what gives itself would show itself? Why should the "subject" or whoever comes after it be abolished simply because it has lost the activity of the understanding in favor of a more originary receptivity, the spontaneity of representation (or intentionality) to the benefit of a more radical, and perhaps in another mode more powerful, passivity? In not asking these questions, the first criticism betrays an extraordinarily noncritical sense of who comes after the subject— possibly the devoted [*l'adonné*].[10]

The second objection remains. It evidences, at least apparently, a ruthless radicality, since it contests the very principle of the possibility (and therefore the actuality) of a saturated phenomenon: "There remains the (enigmatic, incomprehensible . . .) fact that one could *see otherwise*—that I or the others, we saw otherwise." See what? Saturated phenomena no doubt, but more simply, by a slippage that is as hasty as obsessive, always and already "God." In fact, according to this objection, the one counts for all the others, since in all cases it is a question of denying purely and simply that there is anything whatsoever to see: first, in the saturated phenomenon in general ("one no longer speaks of anything—that is, of nothing that can be assigned"),[11] next, in a phenomenon of revelation in particular ("What will you say to me if I say to you that where you see God, I see nothing?").[12] Indeed, what should I say? Yet the force of the argument can be turned against the one who uses it, for the fact of not comprehending and seeing nothing should not always or even most often disqualify what it is a question of comprehending and seeing, but rather the one who understands nothing and sees only a ruse. Not only does admitting an insurmountable powerlessness to see or comprehend guarantee that something does indeed give itself to be seen and comprehended but the glorious claims of blindness directly and of themselves constitute a theoretical argument against this possibility of seeing or comprehending. To be sure, claiming to see is not sufficient to prove that one saw. Yet the fact or the pretense of not seeing does not prove that there is nothing to see.[13] It can simply suggest that there is indeed something to see, but that in order to see it, it is necessary to learn to see otherwise because it could be a question of a phenomenality different from the one that manifests objects. In phenomenology, where it is a matter only of seeing what manifests itself (and describing how it manifests itself), relying on the authority of one's blindness in order to call a halt to research constitutes the weakest argument possible. Indeed, it is an admission of defeat, to be used only in the last instance. In any case, it is not fitting to flaunt it as a strength, a profound mystery, and a great discovery. After all, blindness can also be explained in the sense that, as Aristotle says, "as the eyes of bats are to the light of the day, so is the reason in our soul to the things that are most visible in all of nature."[14] Until the contrary is proven, it behooves me to persist in making evident what at first appears to offend: "Whether convenient or inconvenient, and even though (because of no matter what prejudices) it may sound monstrous to me, it[15] is *the primal matter of fact to which I must hold fast* [*Ursache die ich standhalten muss*], which I, as a philosopher, must not disregard for a single instant. For children in philosophy [*philosophische Kinder*], this may be the dark corner haunted by the specters of solipsism and, perhaps, of psychologism, of relativism. The true philosopher, instead of running away, will prefer to fill the dark corner with light."[16]

3

The hypothesis of the saturated phenomenon gave rise to a discussion that is still ongoing, despite or because of my detailed accounts.[17] A serious motive must underlie this refusal or at least skepticism. What is this motive, if not the fear that phenomena are saturated only in the case of "exceptional intuitions"[18] and in a "maximalist" mode?[19] Do saturated phenomena touch us only rarely, in an enchantment that is confused and out of the ordinary?

To address this objection, one must distinguish between the *frequency* and the *banality* of phenomena. Common or poor phenomena appear frequently, and this is a consequence of their very definition. First, their constitution as objects requires only an empty or poor intuition, so that the difficulty of comprehending them consists most of the time only in determining the concept or concepts, not in the ordeal of intuition. It follows that their actual production does not mobilize uncommon experiential resources. They therefore appear frequently. Next, if these phenomena with no or poor intuition assume the status of technically produced objects (which is most frequently the case), their mode of production demands no other intuition than that which gives us their material (a material that itself becomes at once perfectly appropriate to each "concept" and available in an in principle limitless quantity). Hence nothing or very little opposes itself to what their production reproduces according to the needs of consumption, itself without assignable limit. The mode of constitution of available objects (*Vorhandenheit*), namely, production, of itself authorizes their reproduction for use (*Zuhandenheit*). Whence follows a frequency of technical objects and their phenomenality that accumulates day by day. It could even be said that the world is covered with an invasive and highly visible layer of poor phenomena (namely, the technical objects produced and reproduced without end), which ends up hurting what it covers over. And what does it cover over, if not other phenomena (e.g., the event, the painting, the flesh, or the Other), which I proposed naming saturated phenomena? In this specific sense, poor and common phenomenality not only guarantees a higher frequency to technical objects, but it makes this frequency inevitable and irrepressible by virtue of its very definition. In this specific sense, saturated phenomena can appear only in less frequent, therefore exceptional cases.

Banality must be understood in a way entirely different from frequency.[20] In the strict sense, what becomes banal, by political and legal decision, concerns all and is accessible to all: all, that is to say, the vassals and their vassals [*le ban et l'arrière-ban*]—the men the lord can mobilize from his own fiefs and then also, in perilous times, from the fiefs of his men for the purpose of waging a war, by derivation, the men in the force who are of age and then the others, the elders. Calling on vassals and their vassals obviously does not happen frequently; at least, all those concerned in this banality hope it will be as rare as possible. By extension, one speaks of the banalization of a forge, a mill, a field, etc., which means that these facilities, properties of the lord, are either used obligatorily (nobody can use another stove, another mill, etc.) or else are used only by those who need them (a field whose pastures are open to those who do not possess their own). Neither banality (obligatory or gracious) has anything frequent about it: only the lord can grant it and one turns to it only in cases of need. Banality, which is open to all, does not equal frequency; indeed, it sometimes opposes it.

To speak of a banal saturated phenomenon therefore does not imply that it becomes current and frequent nor, *a contrario*, that it must become exceptional and rare and therefore be confined to the margins of common phenomenality, which supposedly fixes the norm. The banality of the saturated phenomenon suggests *that the majority of phenomena, if not all* can undergo saturation by the excess of intuition over the concept or signification in them. In other words, the majority of phenomena that appear at first glance to be poor in intuition could be described not only as objects but also as phenomena that intuition saturates and therefore exceed any univocal concept. Before the majority of phenomena, even the most simple (the majority of objects produced technically and reproduced industrially), opens the possibility of a doubled interpretation, which depends upon the demands of my ever-changing relation to them. Or rather, when the description demands it, I have the possibility of passing from one interpretation to the other, from a poor or common phenomenality to a saturated phenomenality. That is, "those things that are the clearest and the most common are the very things that are most obscure, and understanding them is a novelty [*nova est intentio eorum*]."[21] At least that is what I will try to show.

It seems reasonable not to yield to an antitheological obsession, one that would refuse the hypothesis of saturated phenomena en masse for fear of having to admit one particular and exceptional case (God). In short, it seems reasonable not to hide from what is more evident so as to avoid a consequence less evident, though indisputably possible.[22] I therefore suggest that we provisionally disconnect these two questions so as to avoid a voluntary phenomenological blindness. Or, and this amounts to the same thing, before deciding about the possibility of saturated phenomena and the legitimacy of their appearing, it is appropriate first to examine whether such a thing can be found in fact. In other words, when and why must one resort to the hypothesis of the saturated phenomenon? One must do so each time one admits that it is impossible to subsume an intuition in an adequate concept, something always done in the case of a poor or common-law phenomenon—in other words, each time that one must renounce thinking a phenomenon as an object if one wants to think it as it shows itself.

4

There is no shortage of experiences that would permit us to trace the border between these two phenomenalities; one only has to follow the five senses of perception.

Suppose that I perceive, or rather that I undergo, the sensation of three colors arranged one on top of the other—for example, green, orange, and red, it matters little in what figure (circle, horizontal bands, etc.). This intuition, as simple and primary as it is (after all, the color red is literally primary), opens onto two radically different types of phenomena. In the first case, a concept lets us synthesize the phenomenon in an objective mode, and the intuition is inscribed adequately in this concept, which contains and comprehends it all. This is the case when I assign these three colors to the flag of a nation or the signal that regulates traffic at an intersection. In this case, the concept (either the country at issue, here something like Ethiopia or Guinea, or the authorization or prohibition to cross) grasps the intuition without remainder, and the intuition literally disappears in it—to the point that it becomes insignificant, pointless, and even dangerous to concentrate one's attention on the exact form of the colored spots, their intensity, or their nuances. If one does so, one is distracted from the signification, which alone is important to practical knowledge and therefore to the use of this phenomenon. That is, when it is a question of phenomena produced as signs, their intuitions and their forms pass without remainder into their significations, and they appear as signs, thus in terms of their concepts, only on the condition of disappearing as autonomous intuitions of color. This is why it always remains possible to change the intuited colors (of the flag or the crossing signal) arbitrarily, or else blatantly to dispense with them, replacing their visual intuition with a different type of intuition—for example, by substituting the sounds of a national anthem or an alarm. In these cases, intuition plays only a very minor role in relation to the concept (signification, intention), precisely because the phenomenon does not rest first on intuition or appear in its light but is governed and comprehended through and through by the concept. The concept can possibly even be substituted for the lacking intuition because, giving more, it dispenses with intuition radically. In this way the phenomenon of an object is manifest.

Yet there remains a different way for these three colors to appear. Suppose that they are imposed vertically over one another in three horizontal bands in a rectangular frame, as, for example, on Mark Rothko's canvas *Number 212*.[23] Here the phenomenon (this painting) appears with a manifest conceptual shortage or, if one prefers, an evident intuitive excess. Initially, there is no concept in the sense of form. First, each of the horizontal bands resembles a rectangle only approximately. Second, the very imprecision of their edges (in the sense of an ideal and geometric precision) plays the positive function of making the two contiguous colors vibrate in relation to each other (all the more so as a vague and indistinct strip of yellow comes between the green and the red, then between the green and the orange). Third, the arrangement of the three bands of color resembles nothing at all: it shows nothing other than these very colors and the play among them, without making evident anything else in the world, without producing any object, and without transmitting any information. There is no concept in the sense of a signification, still less of a sign that would refer arbitrarily to a second signification. The painting means nothing that we can comprehend; it is not connected to any signification that would assume it; it is not assumed in anything that would permit coding it by doing away with the intuition of its formless colors.

A painting is distinguished from other visibles (objects) in that no signification can comprehend it or do away with our encountering its intuition. A painting consists first in its intuition, which discourages all the concepts that one can mobilize to comprehend it, indeed, which submerges them, although it nevertheless gives rise to them and nourishes them indefinitely. One always has to go see a painting; the *only* thing one has to do is *see* it, without any other "exceptional" intuition besides that of simply, but truly, seeing it. On condition that one should speak only one meaning, all intuition as such, even the most simple, turns out to be exceptional insofar as it and it alone gives (to see). Before this Rothko painting, no form, no signification, no concept, nothing can relieve us from our vigil over its intuition and from responding to its mute summons. And this intuition to be seen resembles nothing besides itself, refers only to the visible itself, and thus it refers us to it. This saturated phenomenon does not have to be constituted or comprehended as an object; it only has to be confronted and submitted to, as it comes upon me.

One undergoes this gap between the objective phenomenon and the saturated phenomenon (a perfect phenomenological difference) not only in vision but also in all the other senses. Consider hearing: What differences arise between the simple sound, the sound as signal, the sound as voice, and the sound as song? In each case, the acoustic experience remains of the same order, and yet the intuition is enriched and made more complex from moment to moment. When the hostess who greets you in the train station or airport makes an announcement or answers a question, she produces an acoustic effect that is pleasant enough as such (she was chosen precisely for the tone of her voice, articulate and yet reassuring, seductive and yet informative), comparable to that of a jazz singer in Chicago or an alto in the aria of a Bach cantata. And yet one voice differs from another as an object differs from a saturated phenomenon. How do we notice this difference? By the fact that, in order to listen to an announcement at the airport, one must comprehend it—that is to say, reduce it immediately to its signification (or to its meaning), without remaining frozen in the sonic intuition used to communicate it. If, instead, I linger over this sonic intuition as such, I would no longer comprehend the information, either because I succumb to the charm of the voice and the woman that I imagine to proffer it or because I do not comprehend the language she is using. In this case, hearing demands comprehending—that is to say, leaping over the sounds and passing directly to the signification. Hearing becomes (as in many languages) synonymous with comprehending, therefore with *not* hearing. In the case of listening to the voice of an alto, however, I can perfectly well not comprehend the text in her song or aria clearly (it might be in German or Italian) or I can know the words by heart without paying the least attention to them because, in both cases, I am not asked to learn a text or gather information but to enjoy the voice, the pure and simple listening to the sonic intuition that it delivers. I listen to *the* Bergenza, *the* Schwarzkopf, almost without concern for what is sung, but because *she* sings it.[24] When the sound is at stake in such an intuition, no clear and distinct signification can subsume it in the role of concept. I could attempt to explain the pleasure I find in listening, to find arguments to blame or praise the song, to discuss the performance with other listeners, and therefore mobilize an indefinite number of concepts (those of music criticism, musicology, acoustics, etc.), but assuming I am not a philistine, I would never imagine that I could successfully include this sonic intuition within the limits of one or several concepts. Not that it pleases without concept, but rather because it calls for all of them, and calls for them because it saturates them all. Thus one listens to a saturated phenomenon.[25]

One can trace the gap just as clearly in the case of touch; for it happens that one touches in two distinct or even contrary manners. In one sense, to touch means to follow a surface in its twists and its turns in order to gain information about the form of an object—as when one fumbles about in the darkness in order to know where one is located and where objects are found, or, more exactly, what objects are there. In this case, one is not seeking intuition (which a flat or rough, hot or cold, convex or concave surface reveals) so much as a signification, comprehended even without anything being seen. I would like to know whether I have run up against a wall or a door to open, whether I am bumping against the corner of a table or perched on the back of a chair, where the light switch is, etc. In this darkness, I therefore do not first touch surfaces or materials; rather, I recognize objects, which is to say that I touch significations directly. Moreover, as soon as these significations are recognized (the room where I am located, the door through which I pass, the chair in which I sit, etc.), I no longer have to touch them by groping with an intuition that touches. Even in the darkness, I can see them directly and spot them in space. To touch here means to see a signification with closed eyes. With Braille, touching allows meaning to be read, significations to be reached, and objects to be known, with nothing being seen in intuition, therefore without intuition par excellence.

By contrast, when I rest my flesh on another's, one that I love because it does not resist me (a gesture that should not be reduced to the convention of the caress), when I touch the one I desire or the one who suffers and dies, I no longer have any signification to transmit, no information to communicate. Often the other does not want to, indeed, cannot hear any. I do not caress in order to know or to make known, as I grope around in order to orient myself in space and to identify objects. I caress in order to love, therefore in silence, in order to console and soothe, to excite and enjoy, therefore without objective signification, indeed, without identifiable or sayable signification. Thus touch does not manifest an object but a saturated phenomenon: an intuition that no concept will assume adequately but that will demand a multiplicity of them.[26]

We can also oppose two modes of phenomenalization in terms of taste. On the one hand, taste can serve only to distinguish two objects—for example, a poison (cocaine) from a food (sugar)—by limiting intuition to the maximum (one does not want to put oneself in danger by exposing oneself to too much) so as merely to anticipate a difference that is ultimately conceptual (two physical bodies, two chemical compositions) and can be expressed exhaustively by numbers and symbols. In this instance, even taste reaches what Descartes would call a clear and distinct idea: "it is so precise and sharply separated from all other perceptions that it contains within itself only what appears to one who considers it as he should."[27] Thus taste can give the intuition of objects and be exhausted in a concept. On the other hand, taste can be exercised over what escapes any concept: for example, when I taste a wine, especially if I participate in a blind tasting (e.g., in the somewhat silly game of recognizing and thereby distinguishing several wines), it is not a matter of leading a clear and confused intuition as quickly as possible back to a supposedly distinct concept. The definition that a chemist can quickly and accurately fix for it offers no response to the vintner's questions: Is this wine worthy of its name and of which one? To answer this question, one must not pass from intuition to the concept or substitute the latter for the former, but rather prolong the intuition to its maximum and plumb its depths. It is a matter not of making the taste of the wine pass away but of following it in time (Does it have a long finish, does it open out at the end?), in density (Does it have body, tannin, bouquet? etc.). It is even necessary to summon sight (its color) and smell (the aroma) so as to reach a precise and exact identification in the end (this grape, this harvest, this plot of land, this year, this producer), yet one that is nevertheless inexplicable in conceptual terms and not transmittable by information. The support provided by custom or by the oenological guide serves only to make it understood that one has not tasted the wine or, having mistasted it, that one perceived nothing or almost nothing. The vintner knows what he or she has tasted and can discuss it precisely with an equal, though without employing any concept, or else with an endless series of quasi-concepts, which take on meaning only after and only according to the intuition that is the sole and definitive authority. This intuition indicates its privilege in that one can never dispense with it. One must always return to it—from one year to the next, from one wine to another, from one moment of the same wine to another moment, it changes, obliging the description to be resumed, all the metaphors to be rediscovered. What is more, this intuition cannot be shared immediately from one taster to another. Accordingly, only one possibility remains to them: to speak of it endlessly—whence a paradoxical conviviality: that of the incommunicable and through it.[28] At issue is an idea that is at once clear and confused for whoever does not participate in wine culture, but clear and distinct for those in the know. In short, tasted wine has nothing objective about it, but appears according to a saturation of intuition, which incites a plurality of quasi-concepts and approximate significations.[29]

The same goes for smell. When I sense an odor of gas or a solvent, of humidity or fire, I am constrained to approach intuitively what could be described by models and parameters (graphs of temperature, pressure, humidity, etc.), if I had the time and the means. I then immediately transform the intuition into obvious significations (danger of flood, of fire, of an explosion, etc.) on which my attention and my activity are concentrated. I no longer remain with my nose in the air, drinking in the smell for pleasure. In other words, in these cases smell refers to a concept (or even a group of concepts) that is, in principle, able to grasp the intuitive totality. It does not merely refer to it, but disappears in it by letting itself be coded in rational equivalents. It is reducible to information concerning the state of things, objective phenomena. But the sense of smell also smells in an entirely different way: when someone with "a nose" for things takes a whiff, as do the experts whose sense of smell is so refined that they can combine fragrances into new perfumes, it is clear that no univocal concept, no signification, will ever succeed in designating this smell or distinguishing it. And yet if it is a success, the perfume thus produced can provoke an experience recognizable by thousands, to the point that even without a label one can recognize Chanel and distinguish it from Guerlain. Arbitrarily and naïvely alterable, the names that we impose on these perfumes do not identify them like a concept or a definition. On the contrary, only their firm and stable intuitions assure them an identifiable signification, although it never rescues them from the arbitrary. The names signify nothing, for the perfumes do not have a univocal signification any more than a definition. They draw their strength from their intuition, ever to be resumed and impossible to comprehend, which provokes new significations, both necessary and provisional, each time: "Perfumes there are . . . Green as the prairies, fresh as a child's caress." The uniqueness of smell stems, no doubt, from the fact that it receives at the outset and almost always saturated phenomena, which can only in exceptional cases and after the fact be assigned to a concept. Before making itself sensed, "the myrrh, or musk, or amber" provokes significations without assignable object. They have straightaway "the expansiveness of infinite things."[30] As soon as its vapors rise, perfume makes something other than itself appear, a pure unforeseeable: "Languorous Asia, burning Africa, And a *far* world, *defunct almost, absent*, Within your aromatic forest stay! As other souls on music drift away, Mine, o my love! still floats upon your scent."[31] Thus the relation between common-law and saturated phenomena is reversed: though the former arise most often and from the outset, the latter, by virtue of their very banality, offer a more originary determination of phenomenality.

Thus considering each of the five senses opens a gap between the phenomenon as object and the phenomenon that "fills the soul beyond its capacity."[32] And in this gap saturated phenomena become visible. Thus the hypothesis of a saturation of the visible by intuition proves to be not only possible but inevitable: first, of course, in order to do justice to "exceptional intuitions" that saturate from the beginning all thinkable significations of certain phenomena that are nonobjective from the outset; but next and especially to do justice to the belated saturation of phenomena at first glance banal, yet more originally irreducible to an objective constitution. This hypothesis therefore has nothing optional about it, since the range of the "everyday banality"[33] that gives itself to appear calls for it and confirms it. Without admitting the hypothesis of saturated phenomena, either one cannot see certain phenomena that nevertheless appear banally, or one has to deny what one nevertheless sees. One impugns it, therefore, only at one's own risk. And is there a greater crime for a phenomenologist than not seeing or, worse, not accepting what one sees—in short, an inflicted or voluntary blindness?[34]

5

The question of fact is thus settled. It remains to consider the question of right: In making an exception to the conditions of common-law phenomenality, does the saturated phenomenon not give up the power to claim the name *phenomenon* legitimately?[35] In wanting to be free from the constraint of every phenomenological a priori, do we not find ourselves in the position of the "light dove" that "cleaving the air in her free flight, and feeling its resistance, might imagine that her flight would be still easier in empty space"?[36] Whoever wants to see too much imagines that he can cross all limits of experience; does he not by that very move abolish the conditions of experience and remain sunk in the illusion of seeing more and better, while in fact he no longer sees anything?

Although repeated by many different voices, this objection is not valid. The hypothesis of saturated phenomena never consisted in annulling or overcoming the conditions for the possibility of experience, but rather sought to examine whether certain phenomena contradict or exceed those conditions yet nevertheless still appear, precisely by exceeding or contradicting them. In other words, the experience of saturated phenomena proves, de facto, that the question is not confined to a choice between, on the one hand, an objective experience (in conformity with the conditions for the possibility of experience) and, on the other, a nonexperience of objects (contradicting all the conditions for the possibility of experience). A third option remains: the genuine and verifiable experience of a nonobjective phenomenon, one that would truly appear while contradicting the conditions for the possibility of objects of experience because it would arise with a nonobjective experience. Or, if one shudders at the formulation of a positively nonobjective experience, one can speak instead of the experience of what, contradicting the conditions of experience, appears in the mode of their saturation in a counter-experience.

This other option can already be detected in Kant's own argument, which is often invoked to deny it. How must conditions for the possibility of experience be understood? Obviously in terms of the famous formulation according to which "the *a priori* conditions of a possible experience in general are at the same time [*zugleich*] conditions for the possibility of *objects* of experience."[37] The first consequence that follows is this: the conditions for the possibility of experience concern only objects and therefore are valid only for phenomena understood as objects. For that matter, one can invoke a priori conditions in general and identify the conditions for experience in particular with those of the objects of experience only by referring to these very objects: namely, to that which alone can admit being thought in advance (by contrast to that which comes upon me without warning and counter to my foresight). But as all phenomena are not reducible to conditioned and foreseeable, produced and reproduced objects, a second consequence follows: contradicting the conditions for the possibility (of the objects) of experience means at the same time contradicting the condition of object for the phenomena in experience. It is therefore not enough to object that one risks contradicting the conditions for the possibility of experience in general by admitting nonobjective phenomena. For by what right can one speak of experience in general, or why should experience admit conditions? In other words, on what condition must experience always submit to conditions? Or if experience in general is identified with certain conditions, *what* experience is meant, and is *this* concept of experience self-evident?

It could be that one can legitimately argue against the so little critiqued use of the concept of experience by highlighting the presuppositions that ground it—the first of which might well be the prevalence of a "subject" (or whatever one wants to call it) supposed to know and always already present, whose priority alone can impose conditions on experience. These conditions are imposed only on condition that we cut experience in general to the measure of what the "subject" can receive. But this condition of all conditions is not self-evident, and here the modest, empirical showiness of the *tabula rasa* quite poorly hides the prideful assumption of a consciousness that, in order to remain empty, nevertheless stays always already in place a priori, so as to keep a transcendental posture even in this arrangement, in fact, *especially* in this arrangement.[38] This transcendental posture governs experience with a certain legitimacy only because it understands how to know solely persisting, certain, and constant objects—in short, present (*vorhanden*) beings whose presence is indisputable. Moreover, when one so quickly and so solemnly calls upon experience to be the judge and the last bastion of defense against other possibilities that phenomenality holds in reserve, one doubtlessly does so only to assure oneself of the enduring presence of being, which constitutes the sole privilege of objects. It could be that this assumption, far from closing the debate, sets its terms and therefore opens it. I ask: Is experience limited to the experience of objects, or does the constitution of objects define only one particular and restricted field of experience, which contradicts the immense banality of the intuitive saturation of phenomenality? Does it go without saying that presence in the present should determine the Being of all beings? Does it even go without saying that all that appears should first be? This empiricism remains thoroughly rooted in the most ponderous metaphysical presuppositions, and it does not dare to question them because it does not even suspect them (whereas Descartes, Kant, and Husserl, to speak only of the greatest, knew perfectly well that the object constitutes only a species, and not even the most usual, of what appears).[39] There is therefore no authority that could legitimate challenge or even dispute the hypothesis of saturated phenomena and the phenomenology of givenness that renders it thinkable. Nothing proves that experience is reducible to the conditions imposed on it by the concern for objectness and objectivity nor that, when I have the experience of what does not appear as an object, I experience nothing or that nothing appears if it does not appear as an object. A third way remains: to experience what contradicts the conditions of objective experience; to experience, at the very least, what this contradiction leaves always accessible and possible for us—the counter-experience itself.

One must, therefore, set out from this decisive point: the notion of experience is equivocal. It does not always aim at an object, nor is it always determined by a transcendental subject. It can also expose an *I* that is nontranscendental (and nonempirical), but given over to [*adonné à*] a phenomenon that cannot be constituted because it is saturated. Do the conditions for the possibility of experience miraculously disappear in this case? In no way. They remain in place, but insofar as they are contradicted and subverted by phenomena that are not limited by them, that do not bow to them, and that are no longer constituted by them as objects. The conditions for experience (of objects) themselves thus become all the more visible and clear as they are more evidently contradicted. Their contradiction does not annul phenomenality as such; it simply testifies that this phenomenality runs up against the finitude of the devoted (of the "subject"), who undergoes it without possessing the power to objectify it. Far from leading to the denial of finitude, the experience of the saturated phenomenon confirms it and attests it perfectly.[40] From the fact that the saturated phenomenon cannot be said univocally or defined adequately, one should not conclude that it is simply lacking—in short, that there are no such phenomena. This lack itself is not at all lacking. Instead, it raises a question that demands a specific response: either the concept is lacking because it simply is not a question of a phenomenon, or the concept is lacking because intuition exceeds it. To be sure, the lacking concept is not enough to prove that a saturated phenomenon rather than nothing gives itself. Yet this lack is enough to demand that one should investigate its status and, subsequently, that of a possible saturated phenomenon.[41] As a result, it is not a question of deciding on a whim if there is, if there must be, or if there can be saturated phenomena in general. When confronted with this phenomenon, it is a question of seeing whether I can describe it as an object (a common-law phenomenon whose intuition is contained within the concept) or whether I must describe it as a saturated phenomenon (whose intuition exceeds the concept). This affair is not decided abstractly and arbitrarily. In each case, attentiveness, discernment, time, and hermeneutics are necessary. But what else is there in philosophy, and are we still philosophers if we refuse this work?

6

A question remains: Even if one admits the legitimacy of such a contradiction of the conditions for experience, what can it still describe, since it no longer describes objects? If it permits the description of nothing, of what phenomenon are we speaking and what phenomenology are we practicing?

Without going back over analyses conducted elsewhere,[42] I would like to recall briefly the chief characteristic of the experience of the saturated phenomenon: it is always a contrary experience, or rather, one that always counteracts. In contradicting the conditions for the experience of an object, such an experience does not contradict itself by forbidding the experience of anything at all. Rather, it does nothing but counteract experience understood in the transcendental sense as the subsuming of intuition under the concept. It is confined to counteracting the counteracting of intuition by the concept. Thus, far from counteracting all experience, it liberates the possibility of an unconditioned experience of giving intuition. Once again, one should not object that an experience without conditions would become impossible and untenable, since it would be a self-contradiction. The issue is precisely to decide whether the conditions for the experience of objects are always and at the same time the conditions for all experience in general, or whether, by contrast, experience can sometimes (indeed, banally) cross the conditions of objectification. In other words, nothing suggests that the possibility of experience should be equivalent to the possibility of experiencing objects or to what a transcendental subject can synthesize, constitute, and maintain in an objective condition. That experience might also contradict the conditions for the possibility of objects means only this: experience does not always or only give access to objects, but also possibly to nonobjective phenomena. That experience is not limited to the field of objectivity does not suggest that it is *self*-contradictory, but only that it contradicts the conditions for the experience of *objects* by a transcendental subject, therefore that it can sometimes (indeed banally) *contradict its transcendental meaning*. According to this hypothesis, experience would unfurl as contrary, or rather as *counteractive*. The counter-experience does not contradict the possibility of experience, but to the contrary frees it insofar as it counteracts its assignation to an object, therefore its subjection to the transcendental subject.

Henceforth the finitude of the transcendental subject (and therefore of its intuition) is not transposed or declined automatically in a finitude of univocally objective experience but is suffered and experienced as such in the contradiction that the excess of intuition imposes on it with each saturated phenomenon. It imposes on the transcendental subject that it must confess itself a devoted. Such a counter-experience can be recognized by several specific characteristics.

(1) Contradicted by the excess of intuition, intentionality can no longer aim at a signification (or a concept) that would permit it to constitute an object. It no longer reaches any intentional "object," because what it reaches no longer has the status of object. Intentionality is therefore turned back on itself, no longer indicating the signification of a definite object but the limits of its own aim, disqualified precisely by intuitive excess. I always see, but what I see no longer attests anything; rather, it measures the range of my disappointed vision. I no longer achieve any vision, but I experience the limits of my sight: "on an island charged by air not with visions but with sight."[43] As it undergoes the trial of itself inasmuch as refused and rebuked by intuition, the intentional aim less reaches an object to signify or conceptualize than finds itself affected by the rebound off an ungraspable objective, one that no concept permitted it to foresee or foretell. Affected in return by what it intended, intentionality rediscovers itself displaced, beside itself, "moved" (like a rugby scrum by the enemy scrum), in short, *altered*.

(2) Counter-experience is marked by the saturation of every concept by intuition. This saturation can, of course, be translated by a positive bedazzlement,[44] but not always or necessarily. Or rather, bedazzlement can itself be conjugated in *disappointment*: not a shortfall of all signification but the fulfillment of another signification besides that intentionally aimed at, a sort of displaced fulfillment, at an unforeseeable distance from the fulfillment that intention awaited and foresaw; not so much a nothing as an unforeseen signification, a seen not fore-seen by the foresight of any object. Such a disappointment, provoked by no lack but by a displacement of overabundant intuition, proposes to fill *another* concept, one not foreseen, indeed, an unknown and not yet identified concept;

for what it is worth, this characterizes the scientific attitude (at least in the case of a revolution of scientific paradigms).[45]

(3) Above all, the saturation of the aim by intuition can be signaled by the very perturbation induced by the reception of its excess. In the case of saturated phenomena, I no longer see anything by an excess of light; I no longer hear anything by an excess of sound; I no longer sense, taste, or smell anything by an excess of excitations—at least nothing objectifiable, realizable as a thing other than myself and able to be looked at as placed before me. Here it must be emphasized that these excesses never face the danger of being illusory—for example, of imagining there to be excess of intuition while there is "nothing." This is so, first, because the (supposed) illusion of an intuitive excess becomes at once an intuitive excess of the illusion itself, since I undoubtedly undergo this excess (it alters me, perturbs me, disappoints me, etc.) as genuine and verifiable. If I believe I see too much light, even if no excess of "objective" light can be found,[46] I do indeed undergo an excess. Second (and the excess is verified precisely for this reason), the ordeal of excess is actually attested by the resistance, possibly the pain, that it imposes on the one who receives it, and this resistance can no more be disputed than one can doubt undergoing one's own pain (for we "feel our pain" without any doubt or separation). This *resistance* suggests a wholly other sense of objectivity: objectivity would no longer mean access to an objective that is targeted, foreseen, and constructed according only to the demands and possibilities of intelligibility, such that "object" ends up designating precisely what does *not resist* the cognitive intention but yields to it without offering any resistance whatsoever, to the point that the object designates the alienation of the thing from itself and its seizure by method. Inversely, counter-experience is an issue of the obstinate resistance of what refuses itself to knowledge that is transparent without remainder, of what withdraws into its obscure origin (the unseen, unheard, untouched, etc.), as is sometimes the case with the resistance of another gaze to my gaze, which marks the irreducibility of this gaze to my own. What we call "meeting" the gaze of the Other (maintaining eye contact) is in fact equivalent to deadening the blow, to challenging the other's power to annihilate, and to returning the weight of an aim.[47]

Thus counter-experience can be defined precisely according to the *notae* alteration, disappointment, and resistance. The experience counteracting, or more precisely, the contrariety that the saturated phenomenon imposes on the one who undergoes it *etiam invito*,[48] is not only imposed on the side of the experience of objects but resists the reproach of subjectivism by its very overcoming of objectivity. That is, the devoted verifies itself infinitely more when face to face with a saturated phenomenon than before an object, since it experiences itself as such in the counter-experience that resists it. Resistance can go so far as to expose me to a danger, the danger of seeing too much [*l'oeil en trop*], hearing too much, sensing too much, tasting too much, smelling too much. This resistance imposes itself as suffering, and what does one feel more than one's pain?

7

Such resistance can and should be experienced in a couple of senses. (1) It can be experienced as the ordeal of what gives itself in the encounter with finitude, by a definitive excess of intuition over every concept that I could impose on it. In this case, resistance translates the effect of the phenomenon on whoever sees it without, however, objectifying it. It is a matter of the reverential fear of the finite before what surpasses it, frightening and attracting it at the same time. Respect (for the good use of my free will, for the moral law, for the face of the other [*autrui*], for holiness, etc.), the sublime, or enjoyment—all these, which are always accompanied by some suffering or humiliation, are described in this way. This resistance recoils by definition before what it glimpses, precisely because it recognizes its excess. (2) The same resistance can take the form of denying what gives itself to sight, not because we see it poorly [*voit mal*] (indistinctly or doubtfully), but precisely because we see it well [*voit bien*] (clearly if not distinctly, indubitably) and this vision pains us [*fait mal*]. In other words, my resistance does not so much undergo as it represses what doubtlessly affects it precisely because this affection becomes an unbearable suffering. In seeing what I see, I also see the obligatory darkness created by the all too clear excess of light. This obligatory darkness spills over the one who sees the truth because it imposes on him a dark obligation: that of re-vising his own self to the (measureless) measure of the saturating excess of intuition. That is, since the saturated phenomenon cannot be reduced to the measure of objectivity, it demands of the one it affects that she see it and admit it in its very excess, without the security of a concept. It therefore demands of the affected that she give herself over [*de s'adonner*], let herself be (re-)made, (re-)defined, and, so to speak, (un-)measured by the measure of its own excess. Instead of summing up the given within the limits of my own finitude (of my concept), I experience the obscure obligation of letting myself conform to (and by) the excess of intuition over every intention that my gaze could oppose to it. This demand can no longer merely provoke a bedazzlement, a disappointment, or a resistance; rather, it incites a second-order resistance (resistance to the resistance, in order to hide from it or to evade it), to the point of a recoiling, a denial, a refusal. It is possible that the intuitive evidence of the saturated phenomenon might not produce the recognition of its truth or its disclosure, but to the contrary and quite logically, the impossibility of receiving it, therefore the possibility of rejecting it. The disclosure of the saturated phenomenon might forbid its reception because, by dint of excess and bedazzlement, its evidence seems to accuse as well as clarify, challenge as well as illuminate. By dint of accusing the traits of the phenomenon, the truth appears to accuse the one who receives it.

To do justice to this ambivalence, Saint Augustine did not hesitate to offer a radical redefinition of the essence of truth: to its straightforward phenomenality (in the Greek sense), in which the more evidence discloses the thing the more its truth is disclosed, he added and perhaps opposed a counteracting phenomenality, in which the more evidence discloses the thing the more access to it is shut, the more it becomes the object of a refusal, indeed, a scandal. Object? Of course, in the sense of the objective around which denial focuses, the objective to be destroyed precisely because it offers no object but exceeds objectivity and objectness. Here, where the truth concerns the unveiling not of a *common*-law phenomenon (one that is objectifiable within the limits of my finitude) but of a saturated phenomenon, one has to pass from the *veritas lucens*, the truth that shows and demonstrates [*montre et démontre*] in a straightforward fashion, to a *veritas redarguens*, a truth that shows [*montre*] only inasmuch as it remonstrates [*remontre*] with the one who receives it. This "remonstrating" truth inevitably accuses whoever challenges it or whoever excuses him- or herself from it. Thus the criteria for reaching the truth are modified: the love of excess is substituted for the evidence of disclosure. Love (or hate) becomes the manner of truth: "Truth is loved, [but] in such a way that those who love something else would like it if what they love were the truth, and because they do not like to be deceived, they also do not want to be shown that they are deceived. And so they hate the truth for the sake of whatever it is they love instead of the truth. They love the truth insofar as it illuminates [*lucens*], but hate it when it turns its light upon them [*redarguens*]."[49] This text does not concern the demand to love the truth already seen or even the requirement to love the truth in order to see it.[50] Rather, it concerns loving the truth so as to bear it, without faltering or condemning oneself to bear the cruel clarity that its radiance poses and imposes on whoever risks gazing at it and the charge it imposes on him or her, "because glory overwhelms who sees it, when it does not glorify him [*porque la gloria oprime al que la mira cuando no glorifica*]."[51]

Before any moral or religious sense, it is first of all a matter of a strictly phenomenological necessity. The bedazzlement and the disappointment of intentionality by the saturated phenomenon impose on the aim the necessity of confronting the excess of intuition directly—without the mediation of the concept or the screen of the object that it allows to be constituted. This excess that pours itself out over my gaze without intermediary affects it, constrains it, and wounds it. This can, indeed almost inevitably *must*, lead the gaze to refuse what shows itself [*se montre*] only by remonstrating [*en remontrant*] with this gaze and what gives itself without excuse. This *veritas redarguens* turns its merciless evidence upon and therefore against the one who sees it (or rather can no longer see it). It can therefore be defined as a light counter to my sight, a light that goes up against my (fore-)sight, rendering it confused and me along with it. I become confused before this light, in all senses of the term: My sight loses its clarity and grows blurred; I lose my confidence, my good sense, and my security—to such a degree that this truth that accuses me of untruth can indeed be called a counter-truth. But here counter-truth does not at all mean the contrary of truth or the simple lie that I could oppose to it, but *the truth that counteracts the one whom it affects*, me. It counteracts me; for if I am to see it without danger, it requires of me that I love it and lend myself to its radiance by conforming myself to its purity.

8

It now becomes possible to broach a final difficulty, one that bears on the one whom a saturated phenomenon affects. The objections often challenge the devoted by privileging the "subject" (quite possibly "without subjectivity") or, inversely, "subjectivity" (sometimes "without subject"). Often they consider it a subject less or more transcendental or, inversely, more or less empirical, according to their preference for one or the other title. These approximations indicate the difficulty of thinking "who comes after the subject," if not our powerlessness to do so I will limit myself to two basic remarks.

(1) The distinction between "subject" and "subjectivity," a hazy one at best, loses all pertinence as soon as the phenomenon concerned, by hypothesis, can no longer be con-

stituted as an object. Therefore, if there is a saturated phenomenon, it will not affect a "subject" or a "subjectivity," precisely because both one and the other function only in a metaphysical situation, where it is a question of constituting and not of admitting an affection, a question of constituting objects, phenomena poor in intuition or common-law phenomena. What or whom a saturated phenomenon affects no longer precedes it, conditions it, and constitutes it, and therefore cannot claim any "subjectivity" or any "subject."[52] (2) A fortiori, one cannot play on the opposition between a transcendental "subject" and an empirical "me." This is so first because the givenness of the phenomenon (which renders it nonobjective, but perhaps also determines it even when it seems objective) makes it always come upon me, by its own advent [*arrivage*], before, without, or counter to the conditions for possibility that the transcendental instance would impose on it.[53] In principle, a phenomenology of the given frees (or tries to free) the phenomenon from all transcendental subjection. Furthermore, an empirical "me" has no meaning or legitimacy except in opposition to a transcendental *I* that it balances and whose shadow it extends. If one is lacking, the other disappears. As I observed above, the supposed empiricity of such a "me" remains doubtful so long as the concept of experience that it puts into operation remains essentially burdened by a transcendental pretension: that of receiving the empirical given without also receiving itself in this givenness, hence of waiting for it and preceding it. Consequently, it seems to me to be wiser to renounce hypotheses that are as imprecise as they are metaphysically charged. To the novelty of the hypothesis of the saturated phenomenon must correspond, at least as an attempt, a new determination of what or who it affects.

I suggest that here we consider anew the figure of the *witness*.[54] In order to focus on what is essential, let me restate the paradox: the witness sees the phenomenon, but he does not know what he sees and will not comprehend what he saw. He sees it indisputably, in perfect clarity, with all requisite intuition, often with an intuitive excess that profoundly and enduringly affected him, possibly wounded him. He knows what he saw and knows it so well that he stands ready to witness it again and again, often counter to his immediate interests. Witnessing becomes for him a second nature, a job, and a social function, which can end up rendering him tiresome, if not odious to those who have to deal with his "obligation to remember." And for all that, the witness still does not ever succeed in saying, comprehending, or making us comprehend what he saw. Most of the time, he does not even claim to do so, indeed, he ends up plunging into silence. This is, nevertheless, its own explanation, for what he saw remains withdrawn from the complete comprehension of the event, a comprehension that the concept alone could secure. Yet the witness precisely does not have available the concept or concepts that would be adequate to the intuition unfurling over him. He develops *his* vision of things, *his* story, *his* details, and *his* information—in short, he tells *his* story, which never achieves the rank of history. Most of the time, he is wise enough not to claim to produce a global interpretation and gladly leaves that to the labor of the historians. In short, the witness plays his part in the interval between, on the one hand, the indisputable and incontestable excess of lived intuition and, on the other, the never-compensated lack of the concepts that would render this experience an objective experience—in other words, that would make it an object. The witness, who knows what he saw and that he saw it, does not comprehend it by one or more adequate concepts. As a result, he undergoes an affection of the event and remains forever late with regard to it. Never will he (re-)constitute it, which distinguishes him from the engineer, the inventor, or, to use a more recent term, the "designer," who produces objects because he comprehends them in terms of their concept before turning to any actual intuition, indeed without recourse to it at all. And in *this* sense it could be said that the "designer," by contrast to the witness, accomplishes the "creation of events." This oxymoron becomes thinkable only as the denegation of the saturated phenomenon by the power of technology, which attempts to produce objects even where the event unrolls.

Described in this way, the witness escapes the majority of the criticisms, however contradictory, that are often addressed to what or whom a saturated phenomenon affects. (a) Does it remain sunk in pure passivity, reduced to recording the given and submitting to the monstrous excess of intuition? Obviously not, since the witness does not stop thinking this intuitive excess by having recourse to all the concepts available to her, in a labor that can be called an infinite hermeneutic. Writing the history of the historians, but also constructing her own identity (or that of others) by the narrative of her individual story, implies an ongoing effort that, remaining without an end that concepts could set, requires no less the activity of response—the response by concepts delayed behind the precedence of intuitions. The devoted is in no way passive, since by her response (hermeneutic) to the call (intuitive), she, and she alone, allows what gives itself to become, partially but really, what shows itself. (b) Does the devoted, by contrast, exercise a spontaneous activity without admitting it, thus betraying the unexamined persistence of the transcendental attitude? Obviously not, since the witness never exercises the transcendental privilege of fixing conditions for experience in advance, by formatting it within the limits of objectivity and objectness. Her activity always remains that of response, determined and even decided by the advent [*arrivage*, event] of intuition. This responsive posture imposes on the witness not only that she receive herself from what she receives, without any advance warning, precaution, or patrimony, but that she remain always in radical dependence on the event that gave her to herself. The figure of the *hostage*, so often criticized as excessive and hyperbolic, here finds its legitimacy: de facto and de jure, the witness is herself only through an other [*un autre*], more interior to herself than the most intimate within her—more her than she herself, and forever because always already.

(c) Does this figure of the witness abandon phenomenological rigor by importing ethical or theological thinking? This reproach raises more questions than it resolves. First, it presupposes that ethics and theology escape strict rationality or are confined to derivative uses of it. Arguing this way, one fails to see that rationality not only holds sway over all domains but often arises or flows forth where thought did not or no longer expects it. What right does one have to rule out the possibility that the model of rationality might migrate from mathematics and physics to biology or information, but also to the poetic word, the ethical demand, or theological revelation? Next, who can fix limits for phenomenology and by what right? One thing is clear: the real phenomenologists, I mean those who actually made visible phenomena heretofore unseen, never stopped crossing these limits, or rather, ignoring them, so that after them phenomenology became, each time, infinitely more powerful than it had been before. It could be that one defends the limits of phenomenology, its orthodoxy, and its past when one has simply given up practicing it. But perhaps involving oneself in phenomenology does not consist in involving oneself in phenomenological doctrines, their history, and their archaeology, but in what phenomenologists themselves are involved in—the things themselves, that is to say, in the phenomena and their description. As for deciding if (and which) saturated phenomena actually give themselves, how could one decide this for someone else? And yet, one could surmise that some such phenomena impose themselves on everyone—above all, the erotic phenomenon.

The Reason of the Gift

A Contradiction in Terms

We give without account. We give without accounting, in every sense of the word. First, because we give *without ceasing*. We give in the same way we breathe, every moment, in every circumstance, from morning until evening. Not a single day passes without our having given, in one form or another, something to someone, even if we rarely, if ever, "give everything."[1] Also, we give without keeping account, *without measure*, because giving implies that one gives at a loss, or at least without taking into account either one's time or one's efforts: one simply does not keep account of what one gives. Finally, we give without account because, for lack of time and attention, most of the time we give *without* a clear *consciousness* of our giving, such that we give almost mechanically, automatically, and without knowing it.

So, at first glance, the attitude of giving appears obvious enough, since its exercise is imperceptible; it happens without reflection and without concern. It could be that the gift's very evidence renders any consciousness of the gift and its giving almost superfluous. Thus, there would be nothing more to discuss about the gift, and no essence to interrogate; the gift would simply need to be made. The gift would not give something to reflect on, something of which one would need to become conscious. Instead, it would directly determine an ethical demand and a social obligation. If it still presented a difficulty, it would not be the difficulty of its definition, but of its exercise. For there would be nothing to say about the gift; instead, as with love, it would only be a question of making it.

Yet as soon as it seems to give us certitude, this evidence takes it back again. For these three ways of giving cannot be brought together without contradiction. Indeed, the third way of giving without account—to give without being conscious of it—manifestly cancels the preceding two ways. For if we truly give without ceasing and without measure, how could we not be conscious of it in the end? Reciprocally, if we give without being conscious of it, how could we know that we are giving without ceasing and without measure? More exactly, how can we be assured that this "without ceasing and without measure" makes our gift a true gift, if we are not conscious of it? In short, how can we give without account if we give without rendering an account of it?

But, beyond this formal contradiction, another contradiction takes shape that is incomparably more profound and that puts the gift as a whole in question. Indeed, the gift that claims to give without account in fact always accounts and even accounts too much. The gift gives in such a way that it loses nothing, and is never lost, but always finds its account and is recovered as at least equal to that which it would have remained had it never given anything. In fact and in principle, the gift does not give without account, because at the end of the account, it is always accounted for in one way or another. The gift gives cheaply (*à bon compte*) because it remains intact after having given—it recovers itself as it is. In short, it always finds its account and recovers itself. At the very least, we can always interpret a gift in such a way that it seems to collapse inescapably, not because of an obstacle that comes from elsewhere, but because of the simple fact that it occurs spontaneously and is brought about perfectly. It suffices to analyze its three dimensions— the giver (*le donateur*), the givee[2] (*le donataire*), and the given gift (*le don donné*) to see how the gift is abolished in favor of its contrary: *the exchange.*

Let us first consider the giver. In fact, he never gives without receiving as much as he gave in return. If he gives and is acknowledged as the giver, he at least receives the givee's recognition, even if his gift is never rendered to him; and, even in the absence of any recognition from the givee, the giver still receives the esteem of those who witness his gift. If by chance he gives without anybody acknowledging him as the giver, perhaps because the gift remains a strictly private affair (without a witness), or perhaps because the beneficiary is unaware of the gift, or rejects it (ingratitude), the giver will still receive esteem from himself (for having been generous and having given freely). This esteem, which is in fact perfectly well deserved, will provide the giver with a sense of self-satisfaction, and thus with the sovereign independence of a wise man. He will feel—justly—that he is morally superior to the miser that he was able to avoid resembling. This gain will compensate in large part for his loss. But, suddenly, the giver has abolished his gift in favor of an exchange—and disappeared as a giver, to become the purchaser of his own esteem. To be sure, this happens at the price of an asset that is lost but then recovered. "A good deed is never wasted" (*Un bienfait n'est jamais perdu*), according to a French proverb.

Let us next consider the givee. In receiving, he receives not only an asset but, especially, a debt. He becomes indebted to his benefactor and therefore is obliged to render to him. If be immediately gives something back for the good received, he will be even— but precisely because he has canceled his debt by substituting an exchange in place of the gift, and thus canceled the gift, which disappears. If he cannot give something back immediately, he will remain obligated in the future, either provisionally or definitively. Throughout the course of his debt, he will have to express his gratitude and acknowledge his dependence. In this instance, he will bring about his release by repaying his debt with his indebted submission, even to the point of taking on the status of a servant before his master. If, perhaps, he denies having received a gift, at the price of a lie and a denial of justice, he will have to argue that it was only a matter of something that was due to him, or that he received nothing. In each of these cases, the givee erases the gift and establishes an exchange in its place—whether real or fictitious is of little importance, since it always ends up abolishing his status as a givee.

Finally, let us examine the given gift, which inexorably tends to erase in itself all trace and all memory of the gesture by which it was given. Indeed, as soon as it is given, that which is given, whatever it may be, imposes its presence, and this evidence obfuscates the act by which it is delivered. The given gift occupies the whole stage of the giving givenness, and relegates this givenness to the nonactuality of its past. If we must always remind ourselves to thank a benefactor before taking possession of the gift (as we constantly remind small children), this is less because of bad manners than because of phenomenological necessity. The gift captivates all our attention and thus annuls its provenance. As soon as it is possessed, as soon as its receipt is confirmed, the given gift is detached from its giver; in one blow, it loses its status of being given in givenness, appearing instead in its pure and naked market value. The gift is judged in terms of its price, cleansed of the giver's intention, becoming again an autonomous object endowed with its own exchange value: it is ready to return to the commercial circuit (to be resold, exchanged, "cashed in"). As soon as it is given, the gift disappears as a given gift, to be solidified in its value as an object for possible—and hence almost inevitable—exchange.

How can one not conclude that the gift, as soon as it becomes actual and appears in the cold light of day, is inescapably transformed into its contrary, according to a threefold assimilation to exchange and commerce? How can one not conclude that this self-suppression implies a radical phenomenal instability that gives the gift the appearance of a phenomenon but leaves it incapable of being constituted as an objective phenomenon? The gift contradicts itself by a contradiction in terms—a contradiction in terms of exchange.

Either the gift appears as actual but disappears as a gift, or it remains a pure gift but becomes unapparent, nonactual, excluded from the instance of things, a pure idea of reason, a simple noumenon incompatible with the conditions of experience. That which appears according to the real conditions of actual experience must, from the gift that it was, be cashed in as an exchange. Either the gift remains true to givenness but never appears or it does appear, but in the economy of an exchange, where it is transformed into its contrary—to be precise, into an exchange, a given that is returned (*do ut des* [I give so that you will give]), something given for a return and returned for a given, part of the trade and management of goods. Exchange is imposed as the truth of the gift, and cancels it. By submitting itself to an economy, the gift exchanges its essence as gift for exchange. For an economy economizes the gift.[3]

The Economy

Does this critique of the gift—perhaps so effective because so abstract—in turn escape criticism? Obviously, it is open to a counterattack, since it rests on at least one unexamined presupposition: namely, that the gift implies a perfect and pure gratuity, in which it is necessary to give for nothing, without there ever being a return.

However, the postulate of gratuity is debatable. First, because for both the giver and for the givee, to receive or to grant a reward that is moral (esteem or recognition), symbolic (obligation), and therefore unreal (not a thing, nothing to do with value or a price) is not purely and simply equivalent to a real reimbursement (an amount, a thing, an asset). Indeed, to confuse the two kinds of gains—received or given—implies annulling all difference between the real and the unreal, and between the thing and the symbol. Suspended between cynicism (which realizes the unreal) and idealism (which dismisses the thing), such a description simplifies the specificity of the phenomena that are at stake here to the point where it annihilates them.

Moreover, it is not evident that the gift disappears as soon as the least satisfaction accompanies it. One may very well be satisfied as a result of a gift, without that satisfaction having been foreseen and preceding the gift as its motivation, or anticipating it as its prior intention. It is entirely possible to discover that we are happy to have given or received, without that giving or receiving having been done solely with the aim of being happy. It could even be that we receive this satisfaction only because we have *not* looked for it, nor forecast it, nor foreseen it—in short, it could be that satisfaction engulfs us precisely because it happens to us unexpectedly, as a bonus (*par surcroît*). The joy of a gift does not motivate the gift any more than it precedes it; rather, it is added to it each time, as a grace that is unexpected, unforeseeable, and in a sense undeserved.

Finally, how is one to avoid suspecting that to require such a strict purity of the gift would imply its absolute independence from every possible other (*autrui*)? This purity would finally lead to a total independence in which not only exchanges and gifts are prohibited, but also alterity in general. Also, how can one not have the feeling that such gratuity would put in question, along with the alterity of the gift's other (*l'altérité de l'autre du don*), the very selfhood of the ego, which I put at stake as giver or givee? In the end, to give with full gratuity, without desire, would we not have to annul our selfhood—or, on the contrary, claim to be a god? At the very least, wouldn't this so-called gratuity be reduced to a pure and simple indifference that, with eyes closed, gave nothing to anyone and received nothing from anyone?[4]

The aporias of gratuity seem so obvious that we should never have been ignorant of them: if the gift contradicts itself when we impose gratuity on it, why have we made that imposition? Of course, there is an excellent reason to do so: because gratuity seems to be—and, in a sense yet to be determined, actually is—the best defense against the economic process of exchange, its absolute contrary. But in what way is gratuity exempted from the economy? To this first question, a second must be added: Why must the gift disappear as soon as it satisfies the conditions of gratuity, as if being exempted from the economy were the equivalent of being excluded also from experience in general? What could the requirements of exchange and of the economy have in common with the conditions of possibility of experience? In fact, they end up coinciding, provided that we reconstitute several stages of their convergence.

First of all, an economic process presupposes and produces an equality of exchange:

In exchanging, it is necessary that each party should agree to the quantity and quality of each of the things exchanged. In this agreement it is natural that each should desire to receive as much, and to give as little, as he can.[5]

It remains to be understood where the power of this equality comes from and how it almost inevitably extends its empire. It is, of course, not only an issue that concerns formal rigor, nor even the requirements of honesty. Rather, it is an issue of a theoretical possibility. According to Cournot:

Whatever man can measure, calculate, and systematise, ultimately becomes the object of measurement, calculation, and system. Wherever fixed relations can replace indeterminate, the substitution finally takes place. It is thus that the sciences and all human institutions are organized.

Thus, he continues, "as the abstract idea of wealth . . . constitutes a perfectly determinate relation, like all precise conceptions it can become the object of theoretical deductions."[6] Measure (mathematical quantification) makes equality possible, and therefore also makes exchange possible. In these conditions, the gift becomes an object by the exchange that "equalizes" it—an object of exchange, and therefore an object of commerce, according to "the abstract idea of *value in exchange,* which supposes that the objects to which such value is attributed *are in commercial circulation.*"[7] Commerce allows the exchange of goods only by fixing a measure of equality between objects of value. However, it fixes these measures of equality in terms of value only because it has already determined the gift in terms of exchange. Now, these terms of exchange are in turn constituted as objects by a measure that arranges them according to equalities and equivalents, and thus puts them in an order. Consequently, the gift enters into exchange and commerce because it is transcribed in terms of an economic exchange and thereby transposed in terms of an object.

We thus understand how the economy can fix the conditions of possibility of experience for objects of exchange: it deploys and puts directly into play the requirements of the *mathesis universalis,* according to its strictest Cartesian definition. Order imposes exchange, and measure guarantees equality in the field of the gift, which thereby becomes problematic as such, even aporetic, insofar as it is converted into an exchange. Either the gift arrives at its concept—exchange—and satisfies its proper conditions of possibility, or it remains gratuitous—that is, without order or measure—and thus contradicts the conditions of its possibility. The gift can be thought only by being transposed into an exchange—in accordance with the properly metaphysical requirements of rationality.[8]

The abolition of the gift, such that it passes into the (measured) equality of exchange, also defines the conditions of possibility of its appearance in experience. For the equality of exchange matters only to the extent that it renders a reason (*rend raison*)[9] for its possibility and its actuality in experience. The economy thus claims to measure exchange on the level of reason, and to render reason to it. Every exchange will have its reason, for no longer will anything be exchanged in vain. In fact, the "economy strives not to consume anything in vain," since what is at issue in "political economics," as in every other science (even human sciences), is a "way of connecting effects to causes"—in this case by means of exchange, which alone defines value.[10] In an economy, just as elsewhere, to render reason allows one to render account, because reason calculates, restores equality, and provides self-identity—which in this instance is value. Reason renders reason because it identifies the conditions of exchange, and therefore assigns conditions to possibility and justifies wealth (as with so many other phenomena) as an effect, by attributing adequate causes to it.

That the equality of exchange renders reason to the economy was in fact confirmed by Marx *a contrario*. Marx objects to the "jurist's consciousness [that] recognizes in this [comparison between exchanges involving labor and all other exchanges], at most, a material difference, expressed in the juridically equivalent formulae: *Do ut des, do ut facias, facio ut des, facia ut facias* [I give so that you will give, I give so that you will act, I act so that you will give, I act so that you will act]" and insists on a contrary view:

> Capital, therefore, is not only, as Adam Smith says, the command over labour. It is essentially the command over *unpaid labour* . . . a definite quantity of other people's unpaid labour.

In so doing, Marx not only unveils the mechanism of "the secret of profit making" but also, by denying the supposed equality in the exchange between salary and labor, destroys the whole "political economy."[11] Thus, the economy as such consists in restoring equality between the terms of exchange in order to provide this phenomenon—the exchange—with the means of satisfying the conditions of its possibility and thereby actually appearing.[12]

Thus, exchange suffices for rendering reason—rendering its due to the gift (in the economy) and rendering its cause to the effect (in experience). Reason always suffices, and its sufficiency restores equality, intelligibility, and justice. In principle, nothing has the right to exempt itself from the demand of reason. Every pronouncement, every action, every event, every fact, every object, and every being[13] must furnish a response to the question that asks it why? διότι? *cur*? Even the very simplest of ideas must do this, even God;[14] therefore, even—especially—the gift. On the contrary, if the gift rests on gratuity, sufficient reason cannot but economize it, precisely in the name of the economy in which reason carries on. Consequently, sufficient reason owes it to itself to exclude the gift from experience, and therefore from phenomenality: one must render invisible everything for which one cannot render reason—and first of all the gift.

In this way, one can understand the annulment of gratuity by the economy. Rendering reason to the gift means demonstrating that no one gives without rendering account, nor without rendering an account for it—thus, without being reimbursed, in either real or symbolic terms. In short, it means demonstrating that one gives only with an account, and for the sake of satisfaction. Sufficient reason can indeed always seize the gift by assigning a reason of exchange to each of its moments. The gift's self-contradiction, which I have formally indicated above, can then be repeated more concretely, in the form of a threefold response to the demand of sufficient reason. To arrive at this interpretation, it suffices to distinguish between external reasons (or causes) and internal reasons (or motives).

The giver does not give gratuitously because, as we have seen, he is always reimbursed, either in real or in symbolic terms. But most of all, one can cancel the giver's merit by arguing that he has given only what he was able to give, and thus that he has given from his surplus. By definition, he was able to dispose of this surplus, and therefore it did not really belong to him. By giving it, he has merely redistributed an excess of property that he had unjustly confiscated. In principle, the duty of justice obliged the giver to distribute that which—in all justice—did not belong to him. In claiming to give, he has done nothing more than fulfill his duty of justice. Justice, which is the motive (internal reason) for the apparent gift, explains it and commands it as a simple duty. Consequently, the giver's claim to gratuity, and even the gift's entitlement to be called such, collapse in the face of a simple duty of justice—the duty to render to each his account, his due.

Reciprocally, the givee can put forward sound motives for receiving an asset as part of a simple exchange and denying that he is the beneficiary of a gift. It suffices for him to maintain that this supposed gift has come about simply as his due. Consider the case where I find that I am impoverished and in real need—I am destitute. This means not only that I am in need, but that I need that which I lack because my condition as a human being requires it—necessarily and by right. On the basis of human rights, I have the right (and not simply the need) to nourishment, to clothing, to housing, and even to earn a salary. Therefore, that which public or private assistance might give me is delivered as my due, and no longer as a gift. Not only would there not be a question of gratuity, but gratuity would do me injury and an injustice. I claim my due in virtue of a right, and those who give me my due owe it to me by virtue of a duty that is imposed on them in accordance with an objective right . . . in fact, if they abandon me to my misery, they would put at risk not only my life but also my humanity, which they would debase to animality.

By the same token, they would lose their own humanity by abolishing mine. They must render reason to the humanity that is in me, but also in themselves if they do not come to my rescue (by simple solidarity among fellow human beings), they put at risk their own status as human beings and their ethical dignity as subjects with rights. Thus, by giving me what I need in order to remain a human being, others only fulfill their duty. They do not give me a gift, but render to me what is due, which in return guarantees their own human dignity. It is a question of an exchange—symbolic, to be sure—between my humanity and theirs. However, the symbol is here infused with the highest possible reality, for it reunites us in the same equality, the same humanity. The gift is abolished in that which is due, and gratuity is abolished in solidarity. All that is operative is the symbolic exchange of sociality—the ultimate economy.

If we now consider, beyond motives (internal reasons), the causes (external reasons), we can in the same way draw the given gift (the object itself, the thing) back into the economy. Let us take a banal example: when a "humanitarian" organization (to avoid calling it "charitable") or a local community association "gives" (let us accept this problematic term for the moment) food, clothing, housing, or employment ("social" or reserved jobs), that organization certainly distributes these goods gratuitously, without payment or an economic transaction. However, this does not mean that these goods have no value for exchange, no market price. On the contrary, to dispense these goods gratuitously, they must be produced and distributed; that is, procured. How? Obviously, by means of gifts: the surplus of individuals, the unsold stock of businesses, or subsidies from community funds. In each case, it is a matter of consumable goods and equipment, with a market value that is calculable with precision and already inscribed in the economic sphere.

These goods and values are removed from the economic sphere by those who, having acquired or produced them within the economy, part with them at an economic loss (pure gratuity, or gratuity mixed with realism—these goods having become useless, unsalable, depreciated in value, etc.). During the period of time in which they are under the control of "humanitarian" associations—that is, until their redistribution—these goods remain outside the economy, with their exchange value neutralized. However, as soon as they are given, they recover this value; and it is precisely for this reason that they are a real assistance to those in need, in that these people are provided with goods for which they do not have to pay a price, but which nevertheless have an exchange value, a value in the economy. The advantage of the "humanitarian" stage of this process obviously does not lie in a definitive suspension of the exchange cycle, nor in an illusory escape from the economy. On the contrary, the advantage lies in the goods finally being reinscribed in the economy, almost gratuitously, in what is close to a neutralization of the exchange. The short moment in which the exchange is suspended (the gift in a strict sense) is directed solely toward finally reinscribing the gift in the economy, and thus making it *disappear* as a gift.

Moreover, the moment of the gift—which is now to be regarded as provisional—is not the first to suspend the economy. On the contrary, the first to do this is the poverty of the one who is poor, which excludes him from entering into exchange, thus canceling the economy, because it does not operate here (*annulait par défaut l'économie*). Therefore, the gift suspends (in a second and positive way) only the initial suspension (the poverty of the first instance); then, by paying on behalf of the one who is insolvent, it reinstates him in the cycle of exchange. The gift is therefore not a gift, in two senses: first, because in the end it restores the economy; second, because it "buys back" (so to speak) poverty and need by providing them with the means for paying, buying, and exchanging anew. Hence, the gift labors for the economy's reinstatement, and not at all for its suppression. The gift restores the poor person's former unbalanced accounts in order to allow him to render accounts anew—in short, to render reason for future exchanges. Thus we often speak of these "humanitarian" associations not only as an associative *economy* but also as vehicles for integration. Integration into what, if not into the economy? The moment of the gift not only is provisional, but appears in the end as a wayward economic agent—a cause or reason, and so powerful that it restores the economy at the very point where it was blocked.

The gift, in its three figures, can and even must (by virtue of a simple care for social functioning) either allow itself to be drawn back into an exchange (justice between giver and givee) or work toward reinstating exchange (insertion by the gift). Hence, it must be abolished in the economy that it restores, rather than being exempted from it. There is therefore always a motive or cause for submitting the gift to an economic interpretation and rendering it reason according to exchange. Either the gift remains provisional and a simple appearance, or it appears, but as an object and according to an exchange, by satisfying sufficient reason, which assimilates it into the economy. The economy economizes the gift because it renders it reason sufficiently.

Reducing the Gift to Givenness

After all this, is it possible to understand the gift as it is given and spoken—that is, as a gift—without in the end rendering it to economic reason or dissipating it in the phantom of an empty gratuity? Such an understanding would demand, at the very least, preserving the gift from the logic that demands not that it give what it claims to give, but instead that it give *reasons* for giving (or, rather, for *not* giving). In other words: How is it possible to avoid compelling the gift to render itself to a reason that authorizes it only by canceling it? The gift is unthinkable in the economy because it is interpreted there as necessarily being a relationship of giving–giving, like an exchange of gifts, where the first gift is recovered in the gift that is returned for it, and where the returned gift is registered as the return on the initial gift (*do ut des*). Paradoxically, the gift is lost here because it does not manage really to give at a loss—in short, it is lost because it has lost the freedom to be lost. Consequently, how is one to conceive of a gift as such: a lost gift that has lost its head, a loss without return—and nevertheless not without a thinkable meaning, even a certain reason adapted to it?

Evidently, we will not arrive at an answer to this question as long as we investigate the gift in terms of exchange and describe it on the economic horizon. We will succeed only if we stop approaching the gift as a concealed exchange that is yet to be interpreted according to economic reason—either as an unconscious exchange or as a supposedly gratuitous exchange (presuming that this is not a contradiction in terms). In short, we will succeed only if we think the gift as such, irreducible to exchange and economy. However, if the gift is not related to exchange, even as an exception to it, we would have to be able to think it starting from precisely that which exchange abolishes—that is, excess and loss, which are in fact the same thing. But we can do justice to excess and loss, and therefore to the gift as such, only by leaving the horizon of exchange and economy.

But is there any other horizon than this, and how is one to identify it? This other horizon could be discovered—if that is to be done without illusion or arbitrariness—only starting from the gift itself, or rather from the point where its phenomenon wells up just before it is dissolved into exchange, during the fragile moment where its three moments are not yet rendered to the economy's sufficient reason. We can discover this other horizon only by restraining the phenomenon of the gift from sliding down into an exchange, and by maintaining it in itself; that is, by reducing the gift to itself, hence to givenness, which is the gift's own proper horizon.

Givenness is opened as a horizon only to the extent that we reduce the gift to it, in the double sense of drawing the gift back to givenness and of submitting the gift to a phenomenological reduction by establishing it in givenness. Yet, givenness is not self-evident and, because it always precedes the gift, it seems to us that it is even less accessible than is the gift. Nevertheless, we can presume that if givenness opens a horizon for the gift, it will testify to itself at least by not immediately assigning the gift to a social process or an ethical behavior (even if it eventually does this), but rather by allowing the gift to appear without requiring that it be dissolved into exchange. In order to appear, the gift reduced to givenness would only have to be given—no more and no less—without having to render reason for itself by coming back to a revenue and making the least return on investment. That would mean describing the gift without reconstituting the terms of exchange; that is, without the two terms that are the minimum basis for any exchange. For, if the giver were to give without a givee to acknowledge this, or if the givee were to receive without any giver to honor, or even if both the giver and the givee were to exchange no given thing, then in each case one of the conditions of possibility of an exchange would be missing, and the gift would be brought about absolutely and as such. Let us attempt such a threefold description of a gift that is liberated from the terms of exchange.

First, a gift can be brought about as a gift without any giver being rewarded (in either real or symbolic terms), because it can be brought about without any giver at all. To see this, it suffices to analyze the hypothesis of a gift that is received from an anonymous or even nonexistent giver. These two conditions in fact coincide in the case of an inheritance, where death steals the giver, forbidding that anything at all be rendered to him. By definition, I am so much unable to render anything to him that this very impossibility constitutes the condition of the gift that is made to me. Indeed, it needs the testator's death for the will to come into effect; thus, it is necessary that I have no one to thank if I am to be able to receive the gift he gives me. The testator will not receive recognition from me (nor recognition of a debt), since he will no longer be here to enjoy it; and, if I declare my recognition, this will be before precisely that social group that knew him, yet of which he is no longer part. It could even happen that I receive the gift of this inheritance without the testator having wanted that, and even against his intentions, because either he was completely unknown to me up until that point, or I to him, with only a genealogical inquiry having led his executor to me. In each of these cases, the giver is lacking, thus excluding recognition and reimbursement. Nevertheless, the gift is brought about perfectly. Therefore, it appears fully, even though it is unexpected, undeserved, unpaid, without recognition or return. On the contrary, it takes on its full meaning in the very absence of motive and sufficient reason.

Second, the gift can be brought about as a gift without a givee of any sort. To establish this, would it not suffice to take the argument from anonymity again, this time applying it to the givee? Indeed, in the vast majority of cases, when we contribute to a "humanitarian" organization, we do not know the individual person who is going to benefit from our help. The organization mediates our gift, such that we remain anonymous to the givee, who in turn is anonymous to us. The gift is carried out even though no givee is made known, such that, by definition, he or she can never render anything to me. However, this argument from anonymity could be contested by arguing that here, in the final instance, it is not a question of a gift, because the intermediary (the association)—even if it does its work scrupulously (distributing contributions, helping efficiently)—precisely refuses to make a gift by rendering the recipients anonymous and merging them into the crowd of those who are helped. As we have seen in the preceding section, here it is more a question of solidarity and what is due by right than it is a question of a gift.

There is still another case where a gift is brought about perfectly, with a clearly identified givee, without, however, any risk that he will be able to make a reimbursement and thus transform the gift into an exchange: the case where I give to an enemy. Whether an enemy is private or public matters little, since in either case the hate he bears toward me will make him return my gift with an insult, and every claim to generosity with additional humiliation. Not only will he not render a gift in return for mine; not only will he deny that there is even a gift at issue; but he will also foster a still greater hate for me. He will return the favor I give him (*il me rendra la monnaie de ma pièce*), inverting the debt a hundredfold. I will deserve to be even more hated by him, because I have wanted to make him benefit from my wealth, to render him slave to my protection, to overpower him by my generosity, and so on.[15] He will therefore take vengeance on me in order to free himself from the least obligation of recognition. He will kill me rather than acknowledge that he owes me the least recognition. Even so, is my gift compromised by this? Not at all, for a gift that is scorned and denied, even transformed into an affront, nonetheless remains perfectly and definitively given; this desolation even makes it appear with a more sovereign force. It is only to an enemy that I can make a gift without risk of finding it taken up in an exchange or trapped in reciprocity. Paradoxically, only my enemy takes care of the gift by protecting it from a relationship of giving—giving. Whoever gives to his enemy does so without return, without anything coming back, and without sufficient reason—incontestably.

Third, the gift can be brought about without giving any object that can be brought back to an exchange value. Indeed, what can I give that is more precious than such a gift? Without doubt, there is nothing more precious than my attention, my care, my time, my faith, or even my life. And, in the end, the other person expects nothing less and can hope for nothing more. Nor I from him. For in giving these nonobjective gifts, which elude being either understood or possessed, which supply no gain or assignable return, and which really provide *nothing* (*nothing real*; *ne rem*), I in fact give myself in my most complete selfhood. In giving this *nothing*, I give all that I have, because I am not giving something that I possess apart from myself, but rather that which I am. Hence, the paradox that I give (myself) more, the more I give nothing: the given gift does not consist in a substrate or a real predicate. Therefore, from here on, I am giving outside the horizon of possession (and dispossession) of anything whatever, and therefore outside both objectness (*objectité*) and the reason that could render an account for the gift.

It should not be objected that by giving no object, I would give less, or would even dispense with actually giving at all. On the contrary (and here the argument repeats itself), I am excused from really giving—that is, from giving *myself*, me in person—when I settle for giving an object in place of myself. Thus, I give money in order to be excused from giving my time and attention. I pay into an annuity in order to be excused from having to love, and so regain my liberty. What happens, for example, when I give a woman a magnificent piece of jewelry? Two hypotheses: Either I give her this object alone, but in order to admit to her that I am leaving her or that I do not really love her (i.e., to settle accounts); or I give it to her as an indication that I love her irrevocably, thus simply as a sign of the true gift, which remains nonobjectifiable and invaluable—the gift of my time, my attention, my faith, my life—in short, the gift of myself. This is a gift that I can give only symbolically now, since it will require the entire duration of my lifetime to carry it out in reality.[16] In summary, either the object that is given remains alone and signifies the denial of the full gift (the gift of self), or it is presented as a simple indication and marks the promise of the full gift (this Same gift of self), which is always still unaccomplished. Every gift that is given—insofar as it implies more than actuality—must become unreal, nonobjectifiable, and invaluable.

Thus, the gift, in its three moments, can be reduced to the givenness in it and can dispense with itself—and it can do this all the better when it lacks one of the terms of reciprocity and is freed from that to which the economy attempts to debase it in each instance: the giving-giving relation of exchange. The gift is given more perfectly the more it is ignorant either of the giver who is compensated by his (good) conscience, or of the givee who is freed from all consciousness (of debt), or of the given that is recoverable as an exchange value by a (commercial) consciousness. The gift is reduced to givenness by being brought about without any consciousness of giving (*conscience*[17] *de don*)—without the self-consciousness that would make it render reason of its accounts and multiply reciprocity. The gift reduced to givenness has no consciousness of what it does; it has hands to do it with, but it does it only on condition that the right hand does not know what the left hand is doing.

The Case of the Gift: Fatherhood

However, this result may still raise a concern. Does it not prove too much, and too quickly, for it to offer a rational argument—is it not simply a question of a polemical response? Does not bracketing each term of the exchange, aside from avoiding reciprocal exchange, come at the price of the disappearance of all of the gift's real process? Does not suspending the exchange's sufficient reason also entail the abolition of all rationality of the gift itself? For we have arrived at an outright contradiction: instead of being defined in relation to the givee, the giver would give all the better by disappearing (as unknown or deceased) from the givee's view; the givee, far from appearing by dealing with his debt, would appear all the better by denying it (as anonymous or an enemy); and that which is given, far from being concretized in a manifest object, would appear all the better by evaporating into the unreal or the symbolic (as an indication). Under the pretext of clarifying the gift in light of its givenness alone, have we not, rather, dissolved phenomenality? In short, does not the would-be phenomenological reduction of the gift to its givenness in the end prohibit it from even having the dignity of a phenomenon?

This difficulty cannot be dodged, but neither should it be overestimated, for it is the consequence, essentially, of beginning the examination at the wrong point. We began our inquiry into the gift by starting with its contrary—exchange—and we recovered proper access to it only by disqualifying that which prevented it—reciprocity. Having left the economic point of view, and making our way through the debris of exchange, we continue to be entangled there at the very moment when we are doing our best to free ourselves from it. Thus, we may need to attempt a direct description, starting from itself, of a phenomenon of the same kind as the gift, but this time inscribed from the outset on the horizon of givenness: a phenomenon that could never allow itself to be recaptured by the economic horizon, a gift that is always already reduced and drawn back to givenness, free of any degradation into economy, born free of sufficient reason. In short, a gift that is naturally reduced to givenness, an exceptional case where the difficulty would not consist in overcoming the natural attitude so as to carry out the reduction but, rather, in face of a phenomenon that is already (naturally) reduced, in reconstituting it (so to speak), starting from that to which it is reduced. Which phenomenon would be able to satisfy this inverted description of appearing *only as always already reduced*? Let me suggest one: *fatherhood*.

Fatherhood is undeniably a phenomenon, since it appears wherever people live; it is a phenomenon that is regularly observable, since it stretches over the duration of each lifetime; finally, it is unchallengeable; since no human being can claim not to have experienced it. No one can deny it, least of all those who themselves are either fatherless or childless, since the phenomenon is even more apparent in such absences, as we shall see. Fatherhood (provided that we do not bring it down to exchange straightaway) never puts itself forward as a simple biological product of procreation, nor as a primary interest group, nor as an elementary political category. Doubtless, fatherhood is connected to all of these things, but only after the fact, once it is subjected to an economic interpretation in terms of exchange, according to which it is a first stage in a series of increasingly complex communities that lead, in principle, up to the state. However, no matter how powerful and widely accepted this interpretation might be, it still belongs to metaphysics and, above all, it conceals the determinations of the gift, in the form in which it appears on the horizon of givenness.

First of all, as with every phenomenon, fatherhood appears insofar as it gives itself. But it gives *itself*, unlike most other phenomena, *insofar as it gives*.[18] Fatherhood manifests all the given phenomenon's characteristics, though they are exhibited not only in the mode of a given but also in the mode of a giving. For if fatherhood did not give, neither would it give itself as a phenomenon that shows itself: Thus, it gives, but with a style that is absolutely remarkable and proper to it.

Fatherhood does indeed give, but *without being able to be foreseen*; for the intention to procreate is never enough for procreation to happen, any more than the intention not to procreate is a guarantee against its happening. Again, fatherhood gives, but *without cause* and without any univocally assignable reason. This is proved by the inability of demographic science to calculate the evolution of the fertility rate or inability to anticipate long-term population growth or decline. This is so pronounced that demographic science resorts to the unquantifiable consideration of psychological, cultural, and even religious factors that at best allow a simple intelligibility a posteriori but never a serious forecast. Thus, fatherhood produces—or, rather, produces itself—as an *event* and not as a simple fact: welling up from pure possibility, it does not produce a finished result, determined and con, eluded once it is delivered, but rather brings about a possibility (the child), whose future, in turn, cannot be foreseen, nor deduced from causes, nor anticipated, but must be waited for.

All these determinations also characterize the phenomenon in general, considered as given,[19] except for one decisive difference. Here, the phenomenon that is given also gives, and thus lays claim to an exemplary role among all given phenomena: that of the given that itself gives (*donné donnant*). That the given gives not only itself, but also a given other than itself, implies the opening of an uncontrollable excess, growth, and negative entropy, which misery, death, and fear are not enough to extinguish (on the contrary, in fact). Simply put, here the given always and necessarily gives something other than itself, and thus more than itself; it proves to be uncontrollable and inexhaustible, irrepressible and impossible (in other words, it makes possible the impossible), having neither master nor god. But there is more, for the given gives insofar as it phenomenalizes both itself and that which it gives. This means that the visible itself—in fact, nothing less than the sum of all the phenomena visible up until this point—will also grow, with an irrepressible, incalculable, and inexhaustible excess that nothing will conquer. By giving itself and showing itself, fatherhood in principle gives and manifests more than itself; the event of its arrival in the visible thus provokes a phenomenal event that is endless by right. Nowhere else does the given's character (*Gegebenheit*)—in other words, the character of appearing in the mode of the given (which would almost deserve the neologism "givenence" [*donnéité*][20])—announce itself as clearly as here, thus conferring on fatherhood an exceptional phenomenological privilege.

However, this exceptional privilege (the highest form of givenness) is echoed or balanced by another characteristic, which can only be conceived negatively, at least upon first glance. This very phenomenon that gives itself in giving cannot, for its part, give itself without first having been given to itself—that is, received from elsewhere; namely, from a(nother) father. But the father's gift brings about a new the threefold paradox of the gift reduced to givenness.

First, the giver remains essentially absent and bracketed here. For *the father is missing*. To start with, the father is missing because he procreates in only a moment and, having become useless, withdraws immediately—in contrast to the mother, who remains, and in whom the child remains. The mother's immanence to the child stigmatizes the father's unfortunate transcendence. The father is also missing later because he leaves (must leave), and attracts the child's attention by—in principle—being lacking to him. Not that he always leaves like a paradoxical thief, forcibly abandoning mother and child. Rather, he is lacking because he can never merge with the given child (in contrast to the mother, who can, and even must, do this for a time), since he can remain united with the child only by taking leave—precisely so as then to pass on his help: as extroverted provider, hunter, warrior, or traveler; in short, as one who constantly returns, coming back to the hearth from which he must distance himself if he wants to maintain it. In order to live there, the father must be missing, and thus shine by his absence. He appears insofar as he disappears.[21] Finally, and most of all, the father is missing because (in consequence of the previous two absences) his fatherhood can never rely on an immediate empirical confirmation. Even a genetic identification is mediated (since it requires time, instruments, and study), and still results in a juridical process of recognition (or denial) of paternity: inevitably, the father remains putative. This does not mean that he conceals or disavows himself as father, but rather that he can declare himself only by recognizing—necessarily after the fact—the child whom he could, by definition, never know from the outset. He can claim the child as his (therefore also deny him) only with a delay, through a mediate word and a juridical declaration. He can really give a father to his child only by giving to him again—after the gift of biological life that is always somewhat random—this time, a status and a name: in short, an identity. This symbolic identity must be constantly given again, endlessly, in every moment, and can be made secure only by repeating it until the end: The father must spend his whole lifetime giving and regiving identity to his child; this identity is his child's status as gift without return, but also without certainty. Fatherhood, or the redundancy of the gift that lacks. For these three reasons—withdrawal, departure, and redundancy—the father appears as the giver who is perfectly reduced to givenness: the bracketed giver.

Second, the gift reduced to givenness is further confirmed in the phenomenon of fatherhood in that the child, however much he appears to be a givee (par excellence, since he receives not only a gift but also himself as the gift of a possibility), by definition cannot make good on the least consciousness of a debt. Indeed, no matter how deeply he is moved by the feeling of indebtedness, nor how earnestly filial piety is sometimes at work in him, nor how seriously he strives to correspond to the father's gift, an obstacle always stands in the way. It is not a question here of subjective ingratitude or of empirical hate, though these are always possible and at least looming. It is a more radical question of an in principle impossibility. Whether he wants to or not, whether he feels bound to it or not, the child can never "render," and will remain ungrateful, inadequate, and inconsiderate, because it will never be given to him to render to his father what he has received from him—life. The child can render him time, care, and attention (watching over his advanced years, ensuring that he is lacking nothing, surrounding him with affection, etc.), possibly until the very end; but the child will never be able to give him life in return at the hour of his death. At best, the child will render a peaceful death to his father, but he will never give back (or render) him life.

It should not be objected that the child will be able to give life in turn. True, the child may be able to do this, but whomever he may give it to, it will not be to his father. For he, too, will give it to those who, by the same principle, will be able to give it only to their own children, and never to their father. These children will, in turn, be exposed as givees who are absent and, in turn, installed as givers who are missing. This is how the arrow of time is pointed, with a genuinely original differance (from which even the differance of the delay of intuition also derives). The child responds adequately, even justly, to the father—the giver who is missing—only by avowing himself to be a givee who defaults. Genealogy extends onward by virtue of these ineluctable impossibilities of rendering the gift, of closing the gift that is reduced to givenness back into the loop of exchange.

As for the gift that is given in fatherhood, at this point it goes without saying that it can in no way be converted, into an object or a being (whether a subsistent being or a utensil being does not matter). The father gives nothing to the other than life (and a name that sanctions this). The given gift is reduced here precisely to life, which, exactly because it renders possible—and potentially actual—every being and every object, itself belongs neither to beingness (*l'étantité*) nor to objectness (*l'objectité*). Life is not, since nothing is without it; it is not seen, or defined, or grasped as something real—as one thing among others. A corpse lacks nothing real that would allow it to be distinguished from the living—"he almost looks like he could talk" (*il ne lui manqué que la parole*), as one says of someone who has just died. But speech is not one real thing among others; it triggers things by naming them and, making them appear, it never itself appears as a thing. Life that is given does not appear, is not, and is not possessed. It gives us our appearing, our being, and our possessing of ourselves. In it, the gift is perfectly reduced to givenness—that nothing which tears everything away from nothingness. Fatherhood thus lays out, in fact and by right, the whole phenomenality of a gift reduced to pure givenness. With fatherhood, the giver is manifested even insofar as he is absent, the givee insofar as he defaults, and the gift in direct proportion to its unreality. Not only do the phenomenological requirements of a reduction of the given to givenness not contradict the description of the gift as a phenomenon in its own right (*de plein droit*); not only are these demands fulfilled, here at least, almost perfectly; but above all, fatherhood appears as a phenomenon in its own right (given) and even privileged (the given that itself gives [*donné donnant*]) only if the phenomenological view interprets (*déchiffre*) it as always already naturally reduced, by reconstituting (so to speak) that on the basis of which it is discovered as reduced, and in the face of which the models of exchange, procreation, and production definitively show themselves to be impotent (*impuissants*) and inadequate. The contemporary difficulty with conceiving fatherhood follows directly from an incapacity (*impuissance*) to reduce the gift to the givenness in it.

The Gift Without the Principle of Identity

Thus reduced without remainder to givenness, the given and giving phenomenon of fatherhood opens new domains to the phenomenality of givenness (or givenence [*donnéité*]) in general, which we cannot explore here. But we can at least emphasize a characteristic of the gift's phenomenality in the strict sense, which is brought into clear light here.

Fatherhood is clearly distinguished in that it is unfolded without reciprocity and with excess. What importance is to be accorded to these two particularities? It is without reciprocity because the father can give (life) as father only on the express condition of never being able to receive it in return from the one to whom he has given it. The father cannot give in order to receive in return—and is singled out precisely by this privilege. The privilege becomes paradoxical only if one persists in envisaging it on the economic horizon, where it seems to arise from a lost exchange and a disappointed reciprocity; but this privilege is easily demonstrated, on the contrary, as soon as analysis takes the chance to transgress the economic horizon for good and enter onto the horizon of givenness. The father appears without contest as he for whom I, as the child, can do nothing, as he to whom I can render nothing, as he whom I will allow to die alone. However, the neglect in which I must finally abandon him, regardless of what may happen and what my filial sentiments may be, has nothing to do with a bitter impotence or a harsh injustice. For, before all else, it marks the sole indisputable transcendence that all human life can and must recognize in its own immanence; with the result that if we ever have to name God with a name, it is very appropriate to call Him "Father"—and Him alone: "Call no one on earth your father, for you have only one Father, and He is in heaven" (Matthew 23:9).

The father—as him to whom we can render nothing, precisely because we owe him our inscription in the given—makes evident the son, he who could not give to himself that which he has nonetheless received as most his own—and vice versa. For we do not experience ourselves solely as given, like every other phenomenon, but as gifted (*adonné*)—as those who receive themselves in the reception of the given, far from waiting for this given in the position of a receiver who is already available and secure in itself. To what extent does the experience of oneself as a gifted also imply the recognition of filiation in myself? The response to this question perhaps (and no more than perhaps) exceeds the scope of philosophy and possibly touches on a domain that is already theological; but the phenomenology of the reduced gift leads one inevitably at least to pose it as a question.[22]

Beyond the transcendence that it unveils in the gifted's intimate immanence, fatherhood also and especially imposes a strictly phenomenal determination: the invalidation of reciprocity. For if the reduced gift attests to itself as irreducible to exchange, that depends, as has just been seen, on the fact that it has no need to rest on the two (or three) terms of the exchange in order to be brought about; it can give its all, as money thrown away, to receive without being able to render, and to be realized without transferring any reality susceptible of being possessed. Consequently, not only can fatherhood, like every other reduced gift, be dispensed of reciprocity, but it cannot even tolerate it nor give it the least right. The reduced gift gives (and receives) without return or revenue, even on condition of having nothing in common with these.

What does this abandonment of reciprocity signify? This question does not concern ethics, whose operations (altruism, justice, generosity, disinterestedness, etc.) themselves become intelligible and determinant only once reciprocity is overcome, and on the basis of this overcoming. Therefore, this overcoming, coming before ethics, goes back to the fundamental determination of metaphysics, of which it puts a radical principle in question: the principle of identity. This principle supposes that nothing can be, at the same moment and in the same respect, other than itself; in other words, possibility is founded on logical noncontradiction: "We judge to be false that which contains contradiction, and to be true that which is opposed or contradictory to the false."[23] Logical noncontradiction, which founds the formal possibility of each thing on its thinkability, hence on its essence, rests on self-equality. In consequence, reciprocity in exchange reproduces between two beings and their two (or more) essences the single requirement of noncontradiction. The economy extends and applies this requirement to the relations of production, possession, and consumption of objects, which are woven by societies and which support their cohesion. Inversely, not to respect this requirement provokes contradiction, and therefore in the end prevents exchanges and societies. The political ideals of equality and solidarity take up the same requirement at a higher level of complexity. Under all its figures, reciprocity generalizes the same principle of identity and the same requirement of noncontradiction.

Henceforth, if the reduced gift attests to itself only in subverting reciprocity—and thus the self-equality of things—not only does it contradict the economy and its conditions of possibility for experience, but it also and especially contradicts the principle of noncontradiction itself. As the case of fatherhood proves, the reduced gift allows for a thing not being left equal to itself, but becoming (or, rather, giving) more than itself, or as much as it loses in the exchange of being accomplished as gift. The reduced gift always gives (or receives) more (or less) than itself, for if the balance stayed equal, the gift would not actually take place—but, in its place, an exchange. For exchange respects the principle of identity, and so it offers only an elementary variant on the case of a relation between two terms. The father, for example, loses himself in giving a life, which will never be rendered to him; and he contradicts himself in renouncing an equal exchange, precisely to fulfill the office of father; but, moreover, he gives much more than he possesses, in giving a life that in one sense he does not have (in and of) himself, because it is not identified with him, who himself remains the son of another father. Fatherhood manifests the nonidentity of each self with itself, this contradiction of self to self then being unfolded in all the figures of inequality. In general, the gift is produced only by provoking this nonidentity with itself, then in releasing an inequality without end: that of the giver with the gift, of the givee with the gift, and of the gift with itself. These nonidentical inequalities can be described successively and even alternatively as a loss; as an excess, or as an equivocation—but they can never be understood on the model of self-identity.

This essential and polysemous nonidentity, which liberates the gift everywhere it operates, in the end imposes nothing less than a new definition of possibility. Henceforth, it must no longer be conceived as bare noncontradiction—namely, the self-identity of an essence, which attests to its rationality in posing no contradiction for the understanding—but as the excess (or, just as well, the deficit) of the self over the self, which, in giving without return, gives more than itself and provokes an other different from the first self (and hence itself also different from itself). Possibility does not consist in self-identity with the self, but in the self's excess over itself. Following the paradoxical logic of the gift, which excludes exchange and reciprocity, everything always ends up as much more (or less) than itself, without any impossibility being opposed to this. For the impossibility that would have to be opposed to this would remain a simple nonpossibility, in the sense of non–self-identity and the principle of identity, the contradiction of which defines *precisely* the new acceptance of possibility that is set to work by the gift—which, far from perishing from its nonidentity and its inequality with itself, wells up only if these latter are unfolded to their end. This means that no impossibility can prevent the new possibility of the gift, since it is fed on impossibility and on the very contradiction of self-identity, self-equality, and the reciprocity of exchange. To that which gains itself only in losing itself—namely, the gift, which gives itself in abandoning itself—nothing is impossible any longer. Not only does that which does not give itself lose itself, but nothing can ruin (*perdre*, lose) the gift, since it consists in the contradiction even of its possibility.

The Horizon Proper to the Gift: Unconditioned Possibility

Such as we have just reestablished it on its own terms under the figure of fatherhood, the phenomenon of the gift unfolds only by eliminating in itself the terms of exchange, to the point of contradicting the principle of (non)contradiction. This result, supposing that it is admitted, far from solidly establishing the phenomenality of the gift and illuminating its logic, could lead to a reinforced difficulty. First, because the exception made to the principle of identity seems to reinforce the tendency to marginalize the gift, with this extreme case of phenomenality being a contrast that makes clear the common regularity of exchange, which is left conforming to identity and noncontradiction. After all, if the gift in general is exemplified principally by the case of fatherhood, would it not be necessary to confine to this indisputable phenomenal exception (a gift naturally reduced to givenness, a gift responding to the gifted) the possibility of contradicting (non)contradiction, indeed the possibility of impossibility? Only the exemplary gift—fatherhood (hence also the gifted)—could be an exception to the principle of identity, which, for remaining phenomena and even for other gifts, would continue to be the rule. But as reasonable as this evasion may seem, it fixes nothing.

First, because *all* gifts without exception are brought about by contradicting the identity in themselves, because they contradict the equality between their terms. Fatherhood offers an example only because it manifests precisely this contradiction of identity not only in itself but in all possible gifts. Next, because the gift as such (in other words, all gifts) exempts itself not only from the first principle of metaphysics—the principle of identity and noncontradiction—but also from the second: "that of Sufficient Reason, in virtue of which we consider that no fact can be real or actual, and no proposition true, without there being a sufficient reason for its being so and not otherwise."[24] For this principle posits that everything—facts, propositions, and hence (especially) phenomena—must have a reason that justifies its actuality. In other words, for a phenomenon to be brought about, it is not sufficient that the possibility of its essence (noncontradiction) be shown; it is also necessary to justify the actuality of its existence, and that can happen only if a term other than it comes, as cause or reason, to render intelligible this transition. But can we always assign a reason or a cause to the phenomenon that gives itself?

I have shown elsewhere the phenomenological fragility of this claim: the phenomenon, in the strict sense, has the essential property of showing itself in itself and on the basis of itself—hence of not becoming manifest in the way an effect becomes actual, namely, by means of another cause or reason than itself. A phenomenon shows *itself* all the more as itself, in that it gives *itself* on the basis of itself.[25] Is the particular case where the given phenomenon takes the figure of the gift, one in which we could more readily assign to its phenomenalization another *self* than itself? Merely formulating the question is sufficient to see that the gift, even less than any other phenomenon, permits another instance to preside at its phenomenalization. The gift shows itself on the basis of itself because, like every other phenomenon, it gives *itself* on the basis of itself, but also because, more radically than every other phenomenon, it gives its *self* on the basis of *itself.* The gift that gives (itself) gives only on the basis of itself, hence without owing anything to another reason (or cause) than itself. One need only return to the precise description of the gift to verify that this phenomenon manifests itself and gives itself as it gives—*of itself* on the basis of itself alone, without any other reason than itself.

Let us suppose the simple illustrative case where a gift appears to its giver before he gives it (the givee remaining bracketed here). How does the reduced gift come (*advient*) to this giver so that it becomes an actual gift? Let us consider first the uncritical answer: the gift passes to actuality when this same giver decides to give it and lays claim to establishing himself as its efficient cause and last reason. But this response is not valid, for the decision itself remains an appearance. More essentially, we must understand how the giver himself comes to the decision of actually giving this gift, hence how (the decision of) taking the decision happens (*advient*) to him. And the response to this question is not as easily established as one might expect.

For, evidently, the giver does not decide to give some gift because of the object that he is giving. First, because an object as such can decide nothing, in particular it cannot decide between itself and all the other objects susceptible of being considered as what one might give. Next, because the reasons for preferring to give one object rather than another could not result from calculations, which in any case the object would suffer, without producing them or justifying them. Neither does the giver decide on some gift because of some potential beneficiary, who could have begged for it more than the others—the number of needy discourages, and the impudence of the claims disgusts, without allowing one to decide. It must therefore be that the giver alone decides to give, by himself. But he must still decide to *give* and not only to part with an available object following rules that include a benefit for him, nor only to share it out by calculation (even by Justice, which is itself an equality), nor to distribute it following economic laws (an exchange). It must be, here again, that a gift gives itself, reduced purely to the givenness in it. And that can happen only if the gift wells up from itself and imposes itself as such on its giver. It can do this only by coming (*advenant*) to this giver as something to give, as that which demands that one give it (*donandum est*)—by appearing among many other objects or beings like itself, in the midst of which the gift imposes itself of itself: as so useful for a distress close to its actual (and provisional) proprietor, that henceforth he or she must become the leaseholder whose time has expired, and finally the giver; or as so beautiful that it is only fitting for a beauty greater than that of its possessor, who is obliged to pay homage with it; or finally as so rare that its finder feels constrained to convey it to a jewel box more exceptional than himself. The examples of this silent constraint—political (devolutions: Lear to his daughters), moral (renunciations: the Princess of Cleves), religious (consecrations: the stripping of Francis of Assisi), or others—abound to the point of dispensing us from describing them further.

Here, before being given, the gift comes (*advient*) to this point on the basis of itself, on the basis of a *self* that imposes itself doubly. First, it imposes itself as that which must be given—a phenomenon distinguished among other phenomena by a prominence such that no one can legitimately proclaim himself its possessor, as a phenomenon that burns the fingers, and of which the very excellence demands that one be rid of it. Next, the gift imposes itself in imposing on its initial possessor that it be let go to a recipient who is always other; for the gift makes the possessor's decision about to whom it is to be given, hence also demands of this possessor that he make himself the giver and dispossess himself of it (in this order, and not the inverse). Thus the gift reduced to givenness is brought about in virtue of nothing other than its own *givability*: in appearing as givable, it transforms its reality as a being or an object and thus convinces its possessor to be rid of it, so as to allow it to appear precisely according to a perfect givability. The gift decides its givenness by itself and decides its giver by itself, in appearing indisputably as givable and making itself be given. And this phenomenality comes to it from nothing other than itself. It has no recourse to any cause, nor to any reason, other than the pure demand of givenness that it show itself as it gives itself—namely, in itself and of itself. It comes (*advient*) on the basis of its own possibility, such that it gives this possibility originarily to itself.

Inversely, let us suppose the illustrative case where a gift appears to its givee, who receives it (the giver remaining bracketed here). How does the reduced gift come (*advient*) to this givee as an actual gift? Because this same givee decides to receive it and lays claim to establishing himself as its final cause and initial reason. But it still remains to be understood how the givee comes to accept this gift as gift, hence first to decide by himself to accept it. Now the difficulties mount up. First, it is necessary that the final beneficiary accepts the receiving of a gift; but this acceptance implies a prior renunciation—and a considerable renunciation—since it is a matter of abandoning the posture of self-sufficiency and calm possession of oneself and one's world; in short, renunciation of that most powerful of fantasies, which is the foundation of the whole economy and every calculation of interest in an exchange, that fantasy of the self-identity of the "I" (contradicting the principle of identity). Before accepting a gift—which would nevertheless seem easy, since it appears to be a matter of gain, pure and simple—it is necessary first to accept to accept, which implies recognizing that one no longer increases oneself by oneself, but rather by a dependence on that which one is not, more exactly on that which the "I" in one is not.

And this consent supposes that one abandons self-equality; hence, not only that which morality would label egoism, but above all that which the reduction to givenness has stigmatized as exchange and economy. It is a matter of nothing less than abandoning one logic to let oneself take up another, which no sufficient reason governs and no cause controls. Next, it is necessary to distinguish between that which it is appropriate to accept and that which one cannot or should not accept; for not every good is offered as a gift that is to be received—whether it remains the possession of an absent or unknown proprietor (desire for a lost object, abandoned and then found, that belongs by right to another), or whether it can in no way become an appropriable good for the enjoyment of whomsoever (such as environmental goods, which belong to nobody), or whether what appears as a gift ends up proving to be an evil in reality (the horse abandoned to the Trojans by the Greeks), and so on. Whence this conclusion: to discern if and when it is a matter of a gift, it is first of all necessary that the gift itself appear given as such; namely, as given to be received.

The beneficiary cannot, as such, satisfy these two requirements—accepting to accept and knowing what to accept—since he himself becomes a givee only at the moment when they are satisfied in his eyes, and hence before him. Therefore, there remains only a sole hypothesis: the gift itself must make itself accepted by the one who accepts it, and that it must declare itself from itself as a gift to be received. And the gift succeeds in this precisely when, from the innumerable crowd of beings and objects that are available, but undistinguished or ruled by possession, one detaches itself and imposes itself by appearing as the one that I must accept (*accipiendum est*). It appears then as a phenomenon that has welled up under the aspect of *acceptability*. It appears in designating itself as to be received, and in making itself accepted by the one who, at first and most of the time, neither sees it as a gift nor conceives of himself as the givee. Such an acceptability is exerted on the one who, without it, would not recognize himself as a givee; and it is not exerted solely, nor at first, in the manner of a moral pressure or a sensual seduction, but in virtue of a privileged aspect of phenomenality—the phenomenality of that which in itself and by itself gives itself to be received. The gift phenomenalizes itself of itself insofar as it shows itself as it gives itself—as that which none can begin to see without first receiving it. The gift thus received refers back to no cause, nor to any reason, other than its pure logic of givenness, appearing in its own right (*de plein droit*). Presupposing neither its givee nor its giver, it comes (*advient*) on the basis of its own possibility, such that it gives this possibility originally to itself: it shows itself in itself because it gives itself in itself.[26]

At the end of this inchoate description, we arrive at the outline of a result: if one seriously undertakes to reduce the gift to givenness, the gift gives itself on the basis of itself alone; not only can it be described by bracketing its givee, its giver, or its objectness, but above all it gives rise to them all under the two aspects of its own phenomenality—givability and acceptability. Therefore, the reduced gift comes to pass (*advient*) with no cause or reason that would suffice for rendering account of it, other than itself—not that it renders an account to itself, but because it renders itself (reason) inasmuch as it gives itself in and by itself. Actually, it renders itself in multiple senses. It renders itself in that it abandons itself to its givee, to allow him the act of acceptance. It also renders itself to its giver, in that it puts itself at his disposal to allow the act of giving. Finally, it renders itself to itself in that it is perfectly accomplished in dissipating itself without return, as a pure abandoned gift, possible in all impossibility.

Thus, the reduced gift—which is illustrated with the phenomenon of the gift giving itself and making itself received—accomplishes the *self* of the full phenomenon (*phénomène plénier*). That which appears, appears as that which shows itself (Heidegger); but that which shows itself, shows itself and can show itself only in itself, hence on the basis of itself. But once again, it can do this showing of itself on the basis of itself only if, in showing itself, it puts its self in play (which, in short, can happen only if it gives itself in itself). A phenomenon shows itself in itself only if it gives its *self*.[27] And giving itself here signifies giving itself in the visible, without reserve or retreat, hence without condition or measure, hence without cause or reason. Unless it is said that the real reason for appearing, like that for givenness, consists in not having a reason. The gift gives itself of itself without borrowing anything from a possibility that comes from elsewhere, such as the parsimonious calculation of sufficient reason—in short, without any other possibility than its own. The gift reduced to givenness requires no (privileged) rights ([*passe-*]*droit*) in order to give itself or to show itself as it gives itself. It requires no possibility from anything, but gives possibility to all on the basis of that which it opens in and by itself.

The Gift Without Principle of Sufficient Reason

Whence it follows that, in exceeding the requirement for a cause and a reason, not only does the gift not lack rationality but, completely to the contrary, it could also be able to constitute itself as a "greater reason" than the tight *ratio reddenda* of metaphysics. Or again: Could it not be that the gift provides the nonmetaphysical figure of possibility par excellence, and that the possibility that is "higher than actuality" opens itself first of all as gift? In other words, if the phenomenon in the strict sense opens itself in itself and on the basis of itself, welling up from a possibility that is absolutely its own, unforeseeable, and new, then could not the gift offer itself as the privileged phenomenon—more exactly, as the figure of all phenomenality?[28]

That the gift reduced to givenness, and—on its basis—the phenomenon as pure given arise from no other cause or reason, but only from themselves, in no way implies that they lack rationality or that they have a conceptual deficiency. For nothing proves that the highest rationality of a phenomenon is defined by the requirement to render reason for its phenomenality to an instance other than itself. It could be that such a figure of reason—a metaphysical figure of heteronomous reason—suffers from an immeasurable deficiency, and that it compromises and even censures the phenomenality of all phenomena, to the point that, in these nihilistic times, it could be that the only phenomena that can still burst forth into broad daylight are those whose intuitive saturation frees them from the grasp of the principle of reason. And to contest the primacy of the principle of reason over the phenomenon—or, what here amounts to the same, of the economy over the gift—is in no way a misguided undertaking, since one and the other, in their respective formulations, spell out a fundamental contradiction precisely from the point of view of givenness.

For the economy, which is founded on exchange, requires equality and its justice, since it is itself defined thus: "Proprius actus justitiae nihil aliud est quam reddere unicuique quod suum est (The proper act of justice is none other than to *render* to each his own)."[29] But what does *reddere* signify here, if not "render" (that is, "regive," hence first of all "give")? Justice would therefore consist in giving to each, possibly (but not necessarily) in return and by reaction, what is due to him. But then justice is no longer based on exchange, since exchange itself is understood here as a particular (moreover, devalued) mode of the gift! Hence, on the contrary, like exchange itself, justice would presume an original intervention, however dissimulated, of the gift itself. Could the reason of exchange and justice lie hidden in the gift, and not at all the inverse? To be sure, the economy could neither reduce the gift nor be reduced to it, but it could arise from it by simplification and neutralization; in short, it could in the end require it and attest to it as its real reason.

Is it the same for the principle of reason? Actually, Leibniz constantly bases it—the "great metaphysical principle" that he proclaims it to be—on the same surrender to *reddere*: "Axioma magnum. / Nihil est sine ratione. / Sive, quod idem est, nihil existit quin aliqua ratio reddi possit (saltem ab omniscio) cur sit potius quam non sit et cur sic sit potius quam aliter" (The great axiom. / Nothing is without reason. / Or, what amounts to the same: Nothing exists without it being possible [(at least for (one who has) omniscience] to *render* some reason why it is rather than is not: and why it is so rather than otherwise).[30] One can render a reason for everything—but how is one to render a reason for it being necessary to *render* this very reason? Though the solidity of the principle of reason has nothing to fear from attempts to submit it to, for example, the principles of contradiction or identity, and though it can resist the quietist pretensions of gratuity or indeterminism, it nevertheless wavers before the immanence of *reddere* in it. For to provide a sufficient reason, it is necessary that a mind (an omniscient mind, as it turns out, for contingent statements) renders it. But rendering it (*re-dare*) implies that one regives it, that one gives it in return, hence essentially that one gives it. For the French *rendre* (render) derives from the colloquial Latin *rendere*, formed from *reddere* in relation to *prendre* (take).[31]

In the end, it may also be possible to translate "render reason" by "re-presentation" (Heidegger); but this re-presentation neither exhausts nor replaces givenness, from which it arises, and which allows it as one of its derived operations. That even (sufficient) reason—which is so foreign to the gift—needs to be given is plainly no longer justified by the principle of rendering reason, which in this instance is capable of nothing and understands nothing. Since it is even necessary to render reason, it, too, rests on the gift, and not at all on itself. Therefore reason, which does not know how to give, never suffices for *giving* this other "reason" for rendering reason—hence the gift alone can give it. Reason becomes truly sufficient only if the gift (reduced to givenness) gives it (and renders it) to itself. Reason suffices no more for thinking itself than for thinking the gift. In short, if it is necessary to regive reason, this implies that the *ratio* remains, in itself, secondary and derivative from a more originary instance—the givenness that puts it in the position of operating as a complete reason and a final argument. Givenness governs the *ratio reddenda* more intimately than exchange rules the gift, because no reason can be dispensed from being rendered (that is, from a gift putting it on the stage and preceding it). The gift alone renders reason to itself, for it alone suffices for giving it. This time the gift no longer waits for its good standing by right (*bon droit*) of reason, but on the contrary justifies reason, because it precedes reason, as a "greater reason" than reason.

The gift alone gives reason and renders reason to itself. It thus challenges the second principle of metaphysics, just as it contradicted the first. How, precisely, is this privilege of the gift's metaphysical extraterritoriality to be understood, and how is it to be extended to phenomenality in general?

The gift gives reason, and gives it to reason itself; in other words, it renders to reason its full validity, because it gives itself reason, without any condition or exception. In fact, the characteristic of a gift consists in its never being wrong and always being right (literally, having reason): it depends on no due or duty, hence it never appears owing or in debt. Having no presupposition (not even the justice of equality or the equality of exchange), no prior condition, no requisite, the gift gives (itself) absolutely freely. For it always comes (*advient*) unhoped-for and unexpectedly, in excess and without being weighed on a balance. It can never be refused or declined; or, if it is refused (and we have clearly seen that this can often be done), it can never be refused with legitimate reason nor, above all, can it be refused the right to give itself, since it gives itself without price, without salary, without requirement or condition. Always coming in excess, it demands nothing, removes nothing, and takes nothing from anybody. The gift is never wrong, because it never does wrong. Never being wrong, it is always right (literally, has reason). Therefore, it delivers its reason at the same time as itself—reason that it gives in giving itself and without asking any other authority than its own advent. The gift coincides with its reason, because its mere givenness suffices as reason for it. Reason sufficing for itself, the gift gives itself reason in giving itself.

But isn't it the same for the phenomenon in general, at least provided that it truly shows itself in and on the basis of itself, because it gives itself of itself in an accomplished givenness (according to the anamorphosis, the unpredictable landing [*arrivage*], the fait accompli, the incident and eventness [*évenementalité*])?[32] Isn't it clearer still if first of all one considers saturated phenomena (the event, the idol, the flesh, and the icon or the face)?[33] When it shows itself on the basis of itself and in itself, the phenomenon comes to pass (*parvient*) only in giving itself, hence in coming (*advenant*), without any other condition than its sovereign possibility. It shows itself in that it imposes itself in visibility, without cause or principle that would precede it (for if they are found, they will come only after its coming, reconstituted a posteriori). Moreover, it does not simply show itself in the visible, such that its horizon defines it *ne varietur* (without anything changing); it adds itself there at the same time as each new instant; and it adds itself there because it adds a new visible that until then had remained unseen and that would have remained so without this unexpected event. Hence, it redefines the horizon to the measure of its own new dimensions, pushing back its limits. Every painter knows perfectly well that in bringing about a painting, he reproduces nothing in the world, but produces a new visible, introduces a new phenomenon, and makes it an irrevocable gift. The phenomenon is never wrong, but always right (literally, has reason), a reason that appears with its gift—its sole and intrinsic reason.

The Icon or the Endless Hermeneutic

1. The Visible in Default

The object appears—it transmutes its reduced givenness into visible phenomenality. Consider the most simple case, where we cannot reasonably doubt that it is a complete appearance, or that it delivers an effective object, since we do manage to constitute a given in giving to it a complete and coherent sense. Consider (being inspired by the cube, the favorite example of Husserl himself) this simple box of tobacco (say, Capstan) that I take out of my pocket, perhaps in order to fill my Peterson at the end of this conference. I see it, just the same as it was at the shop of the retailer who sold it to me, and similar to many other ones that are found in many tobacco shops (even on Harvard Square) and no doubt will be for some time to come, if legislation is only toughened up slowly. It is nothing but a rectangular, metallic parallelepiped, blue and gilded, of about sixty grams, measuring ten centimeters by five, and about two centimeters high. I know this, and there would be nothing to add, if, indeed, I ever perceived it truly in this way. But what I perceive of it as lived experiences of consciousness will only ever be three of the six sides. I'll want to see the three others, which at the moment I do not in fact see, I would have to turn it over with a movement of my hand, but when I see the three other sides (of course!), the first three will become invisible to me. Therefore I can never, in truth, see this box entirely; I only know it. I constitute it, but always in adding other, noneffective sketches to those that I actually perceive. I associate the apprehension of what presents itself with the apprehension of what does not present itself—I associate effectively given lived experiences with those not effectively given (that have been or will be given, but are not presented at this moment). Therefore, even for a physical body (*Körper*), and not only for another flesh (*Leib*), I must have recourse to what Husserl names "a sort of *appresentation* (*Appräsentation*). There is already such an appresentation in external experience as long as the front face of a thing, which is properly seen, always and necessarily appresents a rear face of the thing, prescribing it a contents more or less determined." Appresentation, then, intervenes as soon as the knowledge of the object occurs, before and independently from access to the other person. Without doubt, in the case of an object of the world, I can always confirm the appresentation of three sides by that of three others a moment later. I can always "think it through" regarding this object (even though I could never do the same with another person), but I would, precisely, have to do it, and I would only manage it in abandoning in turn to appresentation the three sides already presented, in order to present to myself the sides previously appresented. Appresentation can be displaced, but it is never eliminated. Now, as appresentation "represents a *there-with* (*ein Mit-da vorstellig macht*), which is nevertheless not itself there and can never become a self [*un lui-même*] there (*ein Selbst-da*),"[1] we have to admit, then, that all constitution encounters a weakness of the *Selbst-da*. I do not intend to look again here at the question of the failure of "presence" in Husserlian phenomenology—a decisive debate, but complex and overdetermined. I only underline an obvious point: even the visibility of a common object, the constitution of which does not offer in principle almost any difficulty since its reduction to its given is so obvious, already conceals and reveals an invisibility. We can identify it with reference to another trait of constitution. A unity, rendered visible in what it is pictured in the lived experiences of consciousness, must be reconstructed, but by recourse to often appresented sketches, not all present. The lived experiences essentially lack every given before showing themselves, because an essential law [*une loi d'essence*] makes simultaneous manifestations of all their sketches incompatible. Space imposes this law. In rendering impossibly incompatible the appearances of lived experiences, it imposes having recourse to appresentation in order to constitute the least object. The visible only breaks forth into day constrained to finitude—crowned with an invisible by default, *l'invu*.

It will be objected that space, if it makes the thing, composes together with temporality, such that it allows us, at least in the case of a worldly object, to bypass the absence for a moment of certain lived experiences in producing them, after the first are brought into visibility and go out of it. In response: not only does the temporal delay not abolish the impossible incompatibility between the lived experiences inflicted by space, but it consecrates it instead, in forcing the phenomenological look to pass always from one lived experience to the other. This is in such a way that the temporalization of constitution reproduces and even aggravates the burden of *invu* that accompanies the rising of the phenomenon to visibility. It occurs in at least three ways. (a) First, it occurs in the fact that all constitution must admit the undefined character of its object. To see all sides of an object takes some time, which means [both] that it is necessary to learn to see the object as such and that this apprenticeship would be sufficient, even if one supposed it to happen by impossible instantaneousness for the visibility of the object to be necessarily temporalized. (b) But every object that shows itself also temporalizes itself. Directly, this is because this object itself changes. This is evidently true for all natural living things (which rise up, ripen, and come undone); for every produced object (technical, or industrial), which also deploys a history: the time of its conception, its fabrication, its commercial exploitation (the time of fashion, of need, demand and so on), finally that of its functioning (its "lifespan"), and then, in the end, of its destruction (in being recycled or deteriorating). The object therefore only ever gives itself in evolutionary lived experiences and cannot, strictly speaking, ever affect me twice in the same way. So, my look can never be drowned twice in the same lived experience of an object. The ineluctable temporality of its bringing into visibility endlessly surrounds past sketches (and all become so) in *l'invu*. (c) Every object that shows itself also temporalizes itself, indirectly, because all constitution depends on the original impression. First, in the sense that the first lived experience assigned to a constitutable object wells up from the original impression, whence rises up its first present, as a worldly fact as well as a visible sketch. In repeating itself endlessly, the original impression assures the continuity of an object identical to itself, which disappears as soon as it ceases to give it. But what the original impression assures to the constitutable object it also accords to the constituent parts, since consciousness does not cease to originate at each first moment, the present fact of which also provokes the present attention to presence. Husserl, in any case, established explicitly that the two sides of constitution take root equally in the original impression, in deducing from the temporal flux not one but two intentionalities—that of the temporal object ("transverse") and that of intentional consciousness ("longitudinal").[2] Well (it seems useless to insist on it),[3] this original impression of temporality, by definition, escapes constitution radically, which it alone renders possible in return. From that point on, we can debate another characteristic of constitution: the constitutable object does not always offer a permanent end to the intentional aim, since its temporalization always makes it possible that no identical kernel remains. If, even in its temporal course, the object is maintained identical to itself for a moment, this will only be in reducing its lived experiences, its sketches, and therefore its visibility to a smaller common denominator. It will be impoverished, therefore, in crowning itself with *invus*, sunken in a past more rich than its present. The visible phenomenon only appears in piercing the fog of its *invus*.

The central determination of constitution remains—that is, that it operates on an object. Must we consider it indisputable, or distinguish a new reserve of invisibility there? In order to answer, it is advisable to go back from the object to what its object-ness presupposes, that is to say, the intentional aim, and therefore the look. Now, no object can truly appear as such if just any aim whatever is exercised on it. In order to appear as such it requires a particular aim, privileged and adapted, whether to its finality and its usefulness—in the case of a technical object or tool, a common object (an object ready-to-hand, *zuhanden*)—or simply to its definition and its essence, as in the case of a subsistent object (an object present-at-hand, *vorhanden*). Even an object as simple as the box that we were analyzing requires it already. It only appears as the object that it is and demands to be if a precise intentionality is applied to it—the one that aims precisely not at what one could see (a simple parallelepiped, closed and probably empty, given that it is quite light), but what one can do with it, which is not seen at first (a box to open and close again, because it is destined to contain a fragile material). An aim, which would be restricted to picking up what the sketches leave to be perceived, would, indeed, not see this object as such. In order to constitute it in its proper phenomenality, it is not a matter of what is perceived but of what is perceived insomuch as ordered to definition, to essence, or in short, to the sense of the object. Constitution, too, consists ultimately in a gift of sense (*Sinngebung*). In this way the object only phenomenalizes itself in imposing, among all the intentionalities that can aim at it, the one that assigns to it the most appropriate sense. Thus it chooses an intentionality or, rather, fixes a target to it, failing which it does not rise to its proper visibility (anamorphosis). But in addition to this object intentionality (which the object imposes in order to be able to appear) there are nonetheless others, which, concerned as we are to constitute an object, we most often do not follow, but which nonetheless remain accessible. What do they or would they leave to appear, if we followed them? Consider again the same box that serves us as an example. Admittedly, one anamorphosis gives access to it as a usable object (as a container, a receptacle, snuffbox, and so on). But we can also aim at it either with the intentionality of another object (as a metallurgical product equipped with certain properties, such as resistance to pressure, watertightness, and so on); or without object intentionality at all (in terms of the decorative motif of the cover, the combination of the two colors, and so on); or even, finally, in aiming very precisely at its transformation from object to nonobject, as a pure aesthetic visible (following the process of the *ready-made*). From that point on, the same lived experiences according to the same sketches are able either to be constituted according to an object intentionality or to escape all sense, therefore not being constituted in such an object. Now, the two attitudes of the look in front of the same visible given cannot be accomplished at the same time by the same intention. Therefore all constitution of the given in a phenomenon of the object type (to suppose that it can be accomplished without remainder) hides from view, by the very visibility that it conquers, other possible epiphanies, according to other intentionalities, without concept—like aesthetic, ethical, or other visibles. In this way, all constitution shocks, by the type of sense that it confers on phenomenality (most often that of the object), all the other visibilities that the same lived experiences and the same sketches had tolerated, or even demanded. Here again, the phenomenon constituted in the end only occupies the visible in repressing in *l'invu* the phantoms of other flashes.

I have thus clarified three ways in which the visible that constitution elaborates into a phenomenon obscurely gives rise to *l'invu*: according to space (the impossible incompatibility of sketches), temporality (the undefined nature of lived experiences given by the original impression), and constitution (the irreconcilable plurality of aims). From now on, it becomes clear that not all that which gives itself can nevertheless, by an essential law [*une loi d'essence*], show itself. In other words, it becomes clear that in phenomenology *l'invu* increases at the same rate as the constitution of seen phenomena.

2. The Visible in Excess

I have thus removed what does not enter into the visible and have identified these three failures of the visible as clues of *l'invu*. By *invu* I understand purely and simply what, as a matter of fact, cannot reach or yet reach visibility, even though I could in fact experiment with it as a possible visible. In effect, the phenomenality accomplished by constitution gives rise, negatively, to a halo of *invu* around every phenomenon, in proportion to which it renders the phenomenon visible. For when concentrated on the object, constitution must "stick to it." It can only accede to the lived experiences of consciousness as much as the object manages to assimilate them. Now, the object always imposes two unbreakable limits on phenomenality. First, it imposes the limit of its own finitude, which necessarily excludes the infinity of all the lived experiences, sketches, and points aimed at that consciousness does not nevertheless cease to receive concerning it. Next, it imposes the limit of the finitude of intuition in it, which either stays in the background concerning meaning or, more rarely, equals it (it is then a question of the facts), without our ever envisaging that it can go beyond it and in this way be liberated from the horizon of the object.[4] At the end of these analyses, I will therefore conclude that all phenomenological constitution only produces a visible in showing as much *invu*.

Having reached this point, we cannot avoid the question of a "phenomenology of the unapparent (*des Unscheinbaren*)." What relation can be established between the *invu* as I have just uncovered it, andthe enigmatic formula that Heidegger introduced in 1973, at the time of the *Zähringen Seminar*?[5] In order to avoid any hypostasis of the invisible, certain distinctions are asserted. On the one hand, the text of 1973 seems to signal toward a phenomenology perfectly liberated from metaphysics and even from the Husserlian operations of phenomenology, since it designates nothing less than the *Ereignis*: "The *Ereignis ist das Unschienbarste des Unscheinbaren*—the least apparent of the unapparent."[6] Thus, in a radical sense, it signals a thought still to come, which would go back on this side of time and of being and only admit "*unum necessarium* [the one thing necessary]: to bring thought and his thought into the clearing of the appearing [*paraître*, seeming] of the unapparent—*in die Lichtung des Scheinens des Unscheinbaren*."[7] According to this line, a "phenomenology of the unapparent" would imply a transcending of phenomenology itself, beyond the gaps between subject and object, noesis and noema, intentionality and constitution, even beyond the reduction. Evidently I neither acknowledge this ambition as Heidegger's own nor take this risk. The "phenomenology of the unapparent" therefore cannot serve us here as a model. We could, in return, come back to another luminous definition of phenomenology advanced as early as 1927: "And it is precisely because phenomena are, at first sight and most of the time, not given (*nicht-gegeben sind*), that there is a need for a phenomenology."[8] Phenomenology is not first required where phenomena are already given and constituted, but only where they remain dissimulated or still invisible. In this way it is in disengaging *Dasein* (and its existentials, anxiety and care), the manner of being of this being and the *Sinn des Seins* as phenomena by rights (until then remaining perfectly hidden and unthought), that phenomenology, taken as the method of the *Seinsfrage*, works on what remains invisible to metaphysics. It therefore really earns the rank, if not the title, of a phenomenology of the unapparent, or at least of the not yet visible. But another difficulty comes to light here, the inverse of the preceding one. Does not such a conversion (of the not yet visible into a visible phenomenon) define all phenomenology worthy of the name? From Husserl disengaging categorial intuition to Derrida establishing *différance*, from Maurice Merleau-Ponty manifesting the flesh of the world to Michel Henry assigning auto-affection, which phenomenology is not attached to the invisible, in order to bring it into full light? From that point on, Heidegger's formula becomes enigmatic to the second degree: either it announces a post-phenomenological thought, about which we yet know almost nothing, or it characterizes, almost trivially, all phenomenology coherent with itself. In any case, it does not clarify the questioning that we have reached, which asks: what invisible—which mode of invisibility renders possible the assignment of *l'invu* to the visible and, thereby, the visible itself?

It is therefore a question of acceding to an invisible that does not reduce itself to *l'invu*, distinguishing itself from it and preserving it. Well, *l'invu* results from the fact that the intentionality of the object cannot (and, without doubt, must not) give meaning to all the lived experiences and all the sketches nevertheless given to it. The object forces constitution to discern, choose, and exclude a considerable part of the intuition that concerns it. In effect, poverty in intuition, far from making the constitution of the object fragile, assures it, to the contrary, of certitude and permanence. The less the object calls for lived experiences, the more easily intention can find its confirmation, and the more continuously it can repeat its aim in an object which from that point is quasi-subsistent. That is why sciences (that is to say, the metaphysics that made them possible) have always privileged phenomena lacking in intuition, whether poor phenomena like logical statements and mathematical idealities (only formal intuition of space) or common phenomena like physical objects (mechanical, dynamic, and so on, adding to space the formal intuition of time). Moreover, metaphysics has first shown the way in looking for its undoubted point of departure in a subjectivity not seeking any intuition, except, perhaps, intellectual.[9] The Cartesian *ego* rises up from the questioning of all intuition (mathematical and sensory); the transcendental *I* disengages itself in opposition to the empirical me; *Dasein* appears by transgression of all being [*étant*] and by its resolution without object; and so on it is the same for common phenomena, objects constituted in the sensible world: in the majority of cases, intuition remains within intention; and if, in some occurrences, it equals it provisionally and attains the facts [*à l'évidence*] in this way, the concept always controls the given and limits it to its measure.[10] Therefore, the visibility of objects, and thus the privilege of their principles, increases with the measure of *l'invu* that they leave behind them. And no recourse remains open to the invisible.

I am therefore proposing to follow another way to accede to such an invisible and to justify it phenomenologically: to consider phenomena where the duality between intention (signification) and intuition (fulfillment) certainly remains, as well as the noetic-noematic correlation, but where, to the contrary of poor and common phenomena, intuition gives (itself) in exceeding what the concept (signification, intentionality, aim, and so on) can foresee of it and show. I call these saturated phenomena, or paradoxes. They are saturated phenomena in that constitution encounters there an intuitive givenness that cannot be granted a univocal sense in return. It must be allowed, then, to overflow with many meanings, or an infinity of meanings, each equally legitimate and rigorous, without managing either to unify them or to organize them. If we follow the guiding thread of the Kantian categories, we locate, according to quantity, invisible phenomena of the type of the event (collective or individual); according to quality, phenomena the look cannot bear (the idol and the painting); according to relation, absolute phenomena, because defying any analogy, like flesh (*Leib*); finally, according to modality, phenomena that cannot be looked at, that escape all relation with thought in general, but which are imposed on it, like the icon of the other person par excellence. It is also appropriate to name them paradoxes, because they do not give themselves in a univocal display, available and mastered, according to a *doxa*. In effect, before the event, I cannot assign a single meaning to the immensity of lived experiences that happen to me. I can only pursue them by unceasingly multiplied and modified significations, in a hermeneutic without end (chapter 2). Before the idol, where my aim cannot bear the intensity (qualitative), I can only slip away, and this very evasion will remain my only access to what crushes me (chapter 3). Before flesh, which feels and feels itself feeling without distinction, I cannot exactly locate myself outside in order to be in front of it, since it admits no "outside" and since I am irremediably in it and am it. I do not see it as a display, but I experience myself in and as it (chapter 4). There now remains the icon of the face to be considered. I cannot have vision of these phenomena, because I cannot constitute them starting from a univocal meaning, and even less produce them as objects. What I see of them, if I see anything of them that *is*, does not result from the constitution I would assign to them in the visible, but from the effect they produce on me. And, in fact, this happens in reverse so that my look is submerged, in a counterintentional manner. Then I am no longer the transcendental *I* but rather the witness, constituted by what happens to him or her. Hence the paradox, inverted *doxa*. In this way, the phenomenon that befalls and happens to us reverses the order of visibility in that it no longer results from my intention but from its own counterintentionality. Consequently, doesn't the saturated paradox open an access to the invisible to an invisible by saturation of the given, without common measure with *l'invu*, by constitutional default?

3. The Paradox of the Face

Phenomenology might be able to accede to this invisible without losing its rigor or sinking into confusion if it attains it in view of authentic phenomena and not in their obscuration. It is the same with the saturated phenomena of the event, the idol, or flesh, to which one will contest neither the status of the phenomenon nor a certain invisibility by excess of intuition. In order to establish it, I will concentrate my attention on the last type of saturated phenomenon, the face.

The face shares the privilege of flesh: in the same way that the latter only feels in feeling itself feeling, the former only gives itself to be seen in seeing itself. But like flesh, the face becomes problematic when it is a question of recognizing it as the other person. For flesh, Husserl has already formalized the aporia: I can infer unknown flesh (*Leib*) from the other person, starting from his or her known physical body (*Körper*), following the analogy that their relationship forms with the relationship comparing my known flesh and my known body. But even recognized in this way, the flesh of the other person remains unknown as such, since by definition it would be merged with mine if it became immediately intuitable and would therefore disappear in it as other. The analogy, as also the imaginary transposition of points of view (the *over there* of the other person being inverted with my *here*, which in return would pass into his or her *over there*), does not correct this indirect recognition of the flesh of the other person, but underlines it. It is that which definitively stigmatizes the substitution for this flesh of an appresentation to intuitive presentation, common to most phenomena: "my primordial *ego* constitutes the other ego by an appresentative apperception, which, following its own specificity, neither requires nor ever tolerates fulfillment by a presentation."[11] Why can flesh in principle not be presented by intuition? Intuition presents flesh well and truly, nevertheless, but precisely as physical body—it makes me see what I can feel. As for what feels (and feels itself feeling), no intuition can make it seen to any look. It remains only to postulate, as Husserl did, that appresentation "presupposes . . . a kernel of presentation (*einen Kern von Präsentation*)."[12] Flesh escapes phenomenality as such (as feeling), because only the felt can show itself by intuition. And besides, far from my flesh being able to constitute that of the other person, perhaps it [*elle-même*] can only experience its limits (thus its proper sphere) in presupposing the flesh of the other person, which, so to speak, would constitute it. The face offers a similar particularity: it is not seen as much as it [*lui-même*] sees. In effect, how can we distinguish a face from flesh in general (from any other part of an animated body)? If the face shares the privilege of fleshmaking itself (be) felt, but necessarily feeling and feeling that one is felt and that one feels—it adds to it a second privilege by which we evidently distinguish it from flesh—not only to be seen, but, especially, to see. We must not only oppose the facade (visible but inexpressive) to the face (visible and expressive) but also recognize by and on this face the unique characteristic of looking without having to be looked at. But this unique characteristic, which suffices to define the face as what looks at me, dictates specifically that I cannot see it, nor look at it in its turn. An empty or careless look is seen neither less nor more than a look eager to see. The look of the other person remains unable to be looked at. Further still: what do we look at in the face of the other person? Not his or her mouth, nevertheless more expressive of the intentions than other parts of the body, but the eyes—or more exactly the empty pupils of the person's eyes, their black holes open on the somber ocular hollow. In other words, in the face we fix on the sole place where precisely nothing can be seen. Thus, in the face of the other person we see precisely the point at which all visible spectacle happens to be impossible, where there is nothing to see, where intuition can give nothing [of the] visible.

If the face, such as it is—that is to say, as the look posed on me no longer offers anything to look at itself, should we not give up looking for a phenomenon there? In short, do we not cross the limits of phenomenology? Two reasons hold us back from yielding to this conclusion too quickly. (a) *To look at* traces the Latin *intueri*, itself constructed on *tueri*, "to guard," "to watch over," "to keep an eye on." And, in fact, to watch over the visible characterizes well the mode of vision appropriate to the object, where we master by its constitution all the dimensions of its noema in a univocal and exhaustive sense. But to watch over offers only one of the modes of aiming and of possible vision; there are others, since not every phenomenon is reduced to an object, no more than every visible allows itself to be mastered by its intentional aim. We have to admit that certain phenomena—for example, paradoxes—can well escape the look (*intuitus*) and nevertheless appear, but they are unable to be looked at. It remains to be defined how what our intentionality cannot keep under its watch manifests itself. (b) We are indebted to Levinas for having fixed it, in determining for the first time the mode of phenomenality proper to the face. It does not give itself to be seen in a display as one visible situated among others in the indefinite series of worldly inanimate apparitions. The face would not be distinguished from them, besides, if it only claimed to be made seen, since, at the most, it would only establish a simple difference of degree from other spectacles, at the risk of confusion. The mask and the makeup that seek to render the face more spectacular than it would be if it remained naked in fact abolish it because they substitute for it an object to see, which effaces it. No, the face is not phenomenalized as such, as long as a spectacle to be looked at remains [*un spectacle regardé*]. It is therefore necessary to define it in a completely other mode: it is insofar as "the face speaks"[13] that it shows itself. To speak is not necessarily the same here as making use of the physical word and the material sounds that it emits. Besides, this sonorous word never "says" anything, save if a nonsaid sense protects it in saving in it the welcome of an understanding, of a comprehension. Thus the word is played first in the listening and in the silence of the sense [meaning]. In this way the face speaks in silence.

How? The center of the face is fixed in the eyes, in the void of the pupils. A counter-look rises up here; it escapes my look and envisages me in return—in fact, it sees me first, because it takes the initiative. The look of the other person, precisely because it cannot be looked at, irrupts in the visible. Its word renders manifest what we could name an ethical phenomenon (following the magnificent French locution "Look, listen [to me] . . !"): the injunction "Thou shalt not kill!" The face (that cannot be looked at) of the look of the other person only appears when I admit—submitting myself to him or her—that I must not kill. Certainly, I can kill the other person, but then he or she will disappear as a face, will be congealed into a simple object, precisely because the phenomenality of the face forbids its being possessed, produced, and thus constituted as an intentional object. Certainly, I can kill him or her, but then I will feel myself as a murderer, forever, and whatever human justice might say, the look of the other person will thus have taken the initiative and the advantage over me; it will weigh on me even after its physical disappearance. If there must be intentionality here—which can be discussed, since there is no constitution—it will not be a question, in all cases, of mine on that of the other, but of his or hers on me. If there must be intuition—which it is certainly necessary to maintain, since a phenomenon appears—it will fill no aim arising from me but will contradict instead all the object aims that I could foster. The noesis prepares no noema but instead releases an uncontrollable and unexpected noematic super-abundance; since it is a question of "the infinite or face,"[14] the noema appears as infinite and submerges all noesis, intuition submerges all intention. The saturated phenomenon thus appears not visible, but by excess. The injunction "You shall not kill!" is enjoined, in effect, with an intuition that no concept could grasp and objectify. There is an excess of intuition because (as Kantian respect is imposed on moral consciousness) the face is imposed on me. Even and especially if I am diverted from it or if I kill it, I know then that it was a demand and a requirement; I can only despise it because I know it. Further, the face in its injunction obliges me to situate myself in relation to it. I do not adapt it to my visual devices, as I would do with an animal or a tool. I do not approach it following my intention, but following its intentionality, because it is the face that asks me not to kill it, to renounce any mastery over it, and to distance myself from it—"*noli me tangere!* [Do not touch me!]." Thus it is I who submit myself to its point of view and must situate myself in the exact, precise, and unique place where it intends to appear as pure face. An anamorphosis par excellence is substituted for the centrifugal intentionality coming from me—a point of view come from another place, which imposes on me its angle of vision. Intuition therefore does not regulate itself according to any signification known in advance by me, but rises up as a fact of phenomenality (in the sense that Kant speaks of a fact of reason), without prior or presupposed condition. There is also excess of intuition over every meaning and concept: the face, in enjoining "You shall not kill!" does not make me understand what it nevertheless strikes me with in silence. This is, first, precisely because it does not even need to say it out loud in order for me to hear it. Next, it is because this injunction can arouse interpretations, behaviors, and thus diverse meanings, even opposed, and endlessly renewed. I can, in fact, not kill, but go on a spectrum from a contemptuous indifference to neutral respect for humanity in general, to the point of friendship between equals, or even to unconditioned love that sacrifices itself. I can also kill, but for many reasons [significations]: gratuitous barbarism, mistake, the rage of disappointed humanism, suicidal madness, ideological certitude, punishment planned by the law, the supposed "just" (or not) war, and so on. In short, the face, insofar as it appears in "Thou shalt not kill," arouses a diversity without end of meanings, all possible, all provisional, all insufficient. The face does not allow itself to be constituted, but this is because it imposes its phenomenon on me. It appears as not being able to be looked at, as impossible to keep under the gaze.

Nevertheless, if the ethical hermeneutic of the face accomplishes a decisive opening in the direction of its specific phenomenality and remains a definitive piece of acquired knowledge from the thought of Levinas, it must he questioned on one point. In admitting that the transcendence of the "face or [of] the infinite" beyond phenomenalities of the object or of being [*étant*] is really accomplished first in ethics, does it have to depend on it exclusively? Levinas himself, it seems, ended by doubting it.[15] Ethics could simply put to work here a phenomenological deployment more originary than it, and which would consequently render possible the description of other phenomena, or of other descriptions of this same phenomenon—the face. In effect, the injunction "Thou shalt not kill!" is exercised first as an injunction, independently of its contents. One could replace it with other injunctions, just as strong, whether existentielle—"Become who you are!"; existential—"Determine yourself as the being for whom being is at stake"; religious—"Love your God with all your heart, with all your soul and with all your mind"; moral—"Do not do unto others what you would not want done unto you"; even erotic—"Love me."[16] These injunctions would impose themselves just as strongly, no doubt. They could not do so if, indeed, the injunction were not addressing a call to an authority that could hear them. But this call could not resound in this way, sometimes in silence, if it did not proceed from a particular phenomenon, the face, because more than any other phenomenon, it must appear under the form, not of an object spectacle, but of a call. The face, saturated phenomenon according to modality, accomplishes the phenomenological operation of the call more, perhaps, than any other phenomenon (saturated or not): it happens (event), without cause or reason (incident/accident), when it decides so (arrival), and imposes the point of view from which to see it (anamorphosis) as a *fait accompli*. That is why what imposes its call must be defined not only as the other person of ethics (Levinas), but more radically as the icon. The icon gives itself to be seen in that it makes me hear [understand] its call. One can only understand in this way that the face envisages me: its phenomenality never consists in making itself seen as one visible among others—in the face, in this sense, there is nothing to see and it remains perfectly invisible. But its phenomenality is accomplished when it is made heard [understood], when the weight of its glory weighs upon me, when it inspires respect. *To respect*—to attract sight and attention (*-spectare*), of course—but because I feel myself called and held at a distance by the weight of an invisible look, by its silent appeal. *To respect* is also understood as the counterconcept of *to look at*.

4. To Envisage

There are therefore phenomena that I call saturated, where the excess of intuition over signification censures the constitution of an object and, more radically, the visibility of a unified and defined spectacle. Among these paradoxically invisible phenomena, I have privileged the face, because the analyses of Levinas have acquired an exemplary phenomenological status for it already. I have tried, nevertheless, to advance one step further, in thinking the face as icon addressing a call, in short, as envisaging me. I therefore attain in this way a phenomenon that is invisible but which envisages me. The question becomes: Can I, in my turn envisage it? Can I attain, in return, this invisible but envisaging face as such, without lowering it to the rank of a constituted and objectivized visible, in respecting its invisibility and saluting its own phenomenality, in short, in envisaging it as it envisages me? Is it necessary to maintain that the face is envisageable or unenvisageable?

In order to respond to this difficult questioning, we go back to Husserl and to flesh, of which the face offers the extreme figure: "flesh (*der Leib*) is not only in general a thing, but rather the expression of the spirit *and, at the same time, the organ of the spirit* (*zugleich Organs des Geistes*)."[17] The face thus expresses the spirit as its "organ." Now, as for Aristotle at least, spirit is in some fashion all things in potentiality. Its expression cannot be limited to a unique signification, as in the case of poor or common phenomena. The expression of the face expresses an infinity of meanings. This infinity is marked first in the fact that the features and movements of the face, even accompanied by explicative words, cannot be translated into a concept or a finite proposition. Not only do the lived experiences of the other person remain definitively foreign to me, but, even for the other (at least I can, by analogy, infer it from my own experience), these lived experiences remain too complex, intermixed, and changing for a statement, even an elaborate one, to be able to take account of them conceptually. What the face says remains, in the best of cases, an approximation of what is expressed there. In the strict sense, the face does not know what it says, or, more exactly, it cannot say the meaning that it expresses, because it does not know it itself. My incapacity to know what it expresses in a fixed meaning does not first betray my impotence or my inattention to seeing or understanding it, but rather its essential impossibility of understanding and saying itself. The other person cannot know more what his or her face expresses than he or she can see this face (because the mirror only ever sends back an image, and an inverse image). The possibility that this face lies to me or, as happens more often, first lies to itself, results, as one of its possible consequences, in the irreducible gap between expression starting from infinite lived experiences and conceptualizable, sayable, and always inadequate significations.

Only a face can lie, because only it benefits from the dangerous privilege of an inadequate, unobjectifiable, and necessarily equivocal expression. The lie is absolutely not the same, from the phenomenological point of view, as the error. The error concerns an object or a state of fact, where intuitive fulfillment does not correspond with the signification that the intuition aims at. In error, besides the fact that it is a matter of a common third and not of a face envisaged "face on," one always supposes an already intelligible meaning; it is only a question of deciding if it is confirmed intuitively, in part or totally, or if it is necessary to substitute another one for it. In the lie, or more exactly in that of which the lie offers an indication and result, the difficulty proceeds from the fact that the face can never coincide with a meaning, complex or not. Moreover, when a face expresses itself in truth, when it does not lie, this does not imply that it delivers a signification that it would confirm by intuition. It is only a question there of sincerity or of veracity (the will not to deceive). This does not imply, either, that it delivers a signification that my intuition would fill and confirm. There it is only a question of an external confirmation, worldly, provisional for that matter, which attests, in the best of cases, to the coherence of the behavior of the other person. A face only says the truth about what it expresses—truth that in a sense it always ignores—if I believe it and if it believes that I believe it. Confidence, not to say faith, offers the sole phenomenologically correct access to the face of the other person. The impossibility of constituting it in an object and a univocal phenomenon must be taken seriously: the classic definition of truth (adequation, evidence), and even its phenomenal definition (to show oneself starting from oneself), become here inoperative. For the face only shows what it expresses, but it never expresses a meaning or a complex of defined meanings. When it envisages me, it does not manifest itself. Or if it manifests itself—because in envisaging me, one can also say that it manifests itself from itself, starting from itself and insofar as itself, more than any other phenomenon manages to do so—it does not nevertheless ever say its meaning.

One could object that the face, most often and to begin with, nevertheless expresses a meaning—for example, that of its passions, which metaphysics wanted to classify as so many significations of the incarnate spirit (from Descartes to Le Brun). But if I admit that I know and understand the other person in reducing him or her to a state of mind, such that passions reconstitute the other, I only know him or her as a psychological agent, of whom I must measure the strengths, the conduct, and the intentions. I then include the other in a social strategy, constituting one element among others in such a way that I can contain or make use of him or her. But in this situation, it is no longer a question of a face that envisages me and confronts me with its call; it is a question of an animated object, which I see as I want and constitute from my point of view. All the same, when the other person finds him- or herself identified by a professional or social role (technician, notary, doctor, teacher, judge, and so on), no doubt he or she benefits from a definition and I can assign to the other a meaning; I can even consider that the person's conduct and words express this meaning. But straightaway the other disappears as a face: I cease to envisage him or her as a face, because. I have no need of it in order to behave toward the other; he or she does not, besides, expect this much; and asks only to be recognized according to function and profession, which is what I most certainly do. Our reciprocal inauthenticity assures social relations very well, which standardization and effectiveness require, which anonymity guarantees. Now, precisely, social relations differ entirely from the face-to-face with the face that envisages me. The other person only appears to me starting from the moment when I expose myself to him or her, thus when I no longer master or constitute the other and admit that he or she expresses self without signification.

Must the face that envisages me remain an unintelligible phenomenon, because without signification? Not at all. For if the face lacks a conceptualizable meaning, it is not by default, but by excess. The face expresses an infinity of meanings at each moment and during an indefinite lapse of time. This endless flux of significations, which happens to the other according to the present rising up from original temporality, can never itself be reduced to the concept or be said adequately. *A fortiori* [for a still stronger reason] I cannot do it myself, either, I who receive him or her from the outside, at a distance of alterity, as an event, renewed without ceasing. To accede to this face will therefore never consist in closing it up again under the cover of what it expresses, of what it stands for, or of what it means to say, in short, under a noema. To accede to this face demands, on the contrary, envisaging it face-to-face, despite or *thanks to* its absence from defined meaning—in other words, expecting that a substitute comes to give a meaning (to constitute, Husserl would say) and a significance to the expression which, of itself, is lacking from it. This substitute is named the event, in the double sense of what happens and, especially, of what fixes the result of an action or sanctions the unraveling of an intrigue.[18] What a face means to say is not read more in its expressions than in its words, since both can deceive (voluntarily or involuntarily, it does not matter). What a face expresses is recognized in what happens to it—the act or the event that happens to it and that contradicts or confirms the spoken word or the silent expression. The truth of the face is therefore played in its story—not in what it says, but in what it does, or more exactly in what it becomes following what happens to it. To envisage a face requires less to see it than to wait for it, to wait for its accomplishment, the terminal act, the passage to effectivity. That is why the truth of a life is only unveiled at its last instant: "One must not reckon happy any mortal / before seeing his last day and that he had attained / the term of his life without undergoing suffering" (Sophocles).[19] That to love would mean to help the other person to the point of the final instant of his or her death. And to see the other finally, in truth, would mean, in the end, closing his or her eyes.

5. Hermeneutics to the Infinite

In this way, according to time as according to space, to envisage a face demands a hermeneutics of its apparent and infinitely numerous thus contradictory expressions, until the last one manages, perhaps, to strip it of all that would cover it up and deliver it in its naked truth. In fact, nothing guarantees to us that the last figure that the face of the other person takes *in articulo mortis* [in the moment of death] will open the ultimate meaning—or that the last will be the right one. That is why, in the meeting of mortal ideologies, Christian theology has the prudence and the decency to postpone this last judgment to the Last Judgment—to God, who alone can fathom the innermost parts. But at least, while we are unable to accomplish this judgment, the duty to pursue its hermeneutic without end remains to our finitude, blinded as it is by a saturated phenomenon. Or rather—and it is this that confirms our ineluctable finitude—it is once the face of the other person dies that in fact the hermeneutic without end truly commences in it, far from ending it. For it is starting from the instant of his or her death that the work of mourning begins and, indissolubly, of memory: putting together all the documents and all the memories that remain to us of the other person, discovering in them new ones by association, siftingauthenticated facts from false ones, criticizing indirect information inshort, constituting the unconstitutable saturated phenomenon of the other person. Then, most importantly, trying to construct a coherent interpretation of it, or, indeed, not too coherent, in order to avoid simplifications; and then to confront the difficulty that all hermeneutics implies—yielding to an ideology or to a passion, oscillating between hagiography and disparagement, the one and the other systematic, thus insignificant. At this moment, not only can I separate myself into two distinct witnesses, but further, if the face of this other person belongs to the public, other witnesses can propose hermeneutics contradictory to mine. And so on, in such a way that the enigma of the face of the other person is going to darken in the exact measure to which hermeneutics will claim to render finally accessible in it the supposed unitary and knowable meaning. From that point on, the phenomenon saturated according to modality (the face) will cover over the characteristics, equally aporetic, of the phenomenon saturated according to quantity (the event).

In this situation, theology and philosophy follow different paths. For theology, in this world, the face of the other person remains a phenomenon of inaccessible meaning; it cannot thus be attained in the present, as long as this present is repeated and lasts. It is therefore necessary to have recourse to faith—to have faith in faith, insomuch as it is defined as "the substance of what is still hoped for, ἐλπιζομένων ὑπόστασις [*elpidzomenon hypostasis*]"—or, in almost phenomenological terms, "the index of invisible things, πράγματων ἔλεγκος οὐ βλεπόμενων [*pragmaton elegchos ou blepomenon*]" (Heb. 11.1). Plainly, it is necessary for me to wait for the manifestation of the face of the other person as I must wait for the return of Christ. It is normal, besides, seeing that "our life is hidden κεκρύπται [*kekryptai*] with Christ in God" (Col. 3.3). How could the finite face of the other person rise up in the glory of its truth, outside the glorification of the infinite Face? The hermeneutic of the saturated phenomenon of the other person becomes, in Christian theology, one of the figures of faith, thus of the eschatological wait for the manifestation of the Christ. Theological faith imposes itself as the unique correct approach, because always deferred to the end of time, to the face of the other, "my fellow, my brother or sister."

On the evidence, philosophy—as it is, phenomenology—cannot claim this direct and royal way, for it cannot wait for the end of time, but only wait in time, thus endlessly. From that point, what path to follow? I suggest repeating here, while displacing it, the reasoning of Kant in favor of a certain sense of the immortality of the soul in the limits of (pure) practical reason. One is reminded of the postulate: "all the other concepts (those of God and of immortality), which, insofar as simple ideas, remain without support in speculative reason, are now connected to this concept [that is to say, freedom] and acquire stability and objective reality with and by it. In other words, their *possibility* (*die Möglichkeit derselben*) is proven by the fact that freedom is effective."[20] In other words, the ideas without sensory effectivity of God and of immortality draw, indirectly, from the effectivity of the idea of freedom (required by the fact of reason, the categorical imperative) a real, although borrowed, possibility. It remains to be established how immortality is linked with effective freedom to the point that it receives a real possibility from it. Freedom, summoned by the moral law, must aim at its perfect realization (holiness); but it unceasingly proves its powerlessness to attain this perfection, from the fact that it is there a question of a "perfection of which no reasonable *Dasein* belonging to the sensible world is capable at any moment of its existence." It is therefore necessary to envisage an "indefinite progress," a progress "going to the infinite," which must finally emerge in "an ulterior and uninterrupted continuation of this progress, as long as its existence can last, and even beyond this life (*über dieses Leben hinaus*)"—an existence that goes beyond this sentient life.[21] Immortality is required indirectly as the necessary condition of the accomplishment of freedom in its perfect moral status. It is necessary to live "as if, *als ob*"[22] another life, an immortality, were possible to us—in order not to resign ourselves to the imperfect use of freedom in this life. In short, a fact of reason— "Act in such a way that the maxim of your will can at the same time be used as a principle of universal legislation"[23] —imposes the effectivity of an idea of reason, my freedom, but this freedom, which must become holy, can never do so in sentient life. It is therefore necessary to infer the possibility of another idea of reason, the immortality of the soul as place of an indefinite progress from freedom toward moral holiness.

I would like to suggest that it is perhaps possible to transpose this argument in phenomenological terms, suitable to the saturated phenomenon of the face of the other person. (a) The fact of reason becomes, here, no longer the categorical, universal and abstract, but this face, itself, where such another person enjoins me: "Thou shalt not kill [me]!" (b) But it gives rise, on my part, to the same respect as the imperative, in claiming from me, in fact in compelling me to deploy, a way of aiming [sighting] that does not objectivize the other person (does not "kill"). Note well that, in French at least, "to kill" is not limited to putting to death; one also says that an ill-chosen color "kills" other colors in a painting (or in furnishings, or a bunch of flowers, and so on), that one flavor "kills" another, that a rejoinder in a public debate "kills" an interlocutor, that in society, ridicule "kills," and so forth. "To kill" thus indicates the destruction of the other person or thing, its objectivization into an insignificant term, entirely annulled, henceforth without force or proper value. In the physical annihilation of the other person, it is in fact *first* a question of this "killing," of removing the irreducible autonomy of a nonobjectivizable, unknowable other person, the unforeseeable center of initiatives and intentionality. All the totalitarianisms have proved it, which have only annihilated physically certain classes of people in order, first and especially, to "kill" this irreducible humanity in them. The metaphorical sense of the word in fact delivers its proper meaning. (c) But, since it is a question here of recognizing an expression beyond all signification, a noesis without adequately correlative noema, an "idea of infinity" (Levinas), this saturating intuition goes beyond all intentionality. Thus, while it is no longer a question of will, but this time of recognition of the other person, I cannot anymore, here, attain what Kant called "holiness," obedience to the law. All that I would perceive of the other person as regards significations and intentions will remain always and by definition in the background and in deficit in relation to his or her face, a saturated phenomenon. And, therefore, I will only be able to bear this paradox and do it justice in consecrating myself to its infinite hermeneutic according to space, and especially time. For as I have already observed, even after the death of this face, hermeneutics must be pursued, in a memory no less demanding than the present vision. And it will be pursued—or at least should be—after my own death, this time entrusted to others. The face of the other person requires in this way an infinite hermeneutic, equivalent to the "progress toward the infinite" of morality according to Kant. Thus, every face demands immortality—if not its own, at least that of the one who envisages it.

Only the one who has lived with the life and the death of another person knows to what extent he or she does *not* know that other. This one alone can therefore recognize the other as the saturated phenomenon *par excellence,* and consequently also knows that it would take an eternity to envisage this saturated phenomenon as such—not constituting it as an object, but interpreting it in loving it. For "love is without end. It is only love in the infinity of the loving (*in der Unendlichkeit des Liebens*)."[24] The face of the other person compels me to believe in my own eternity, like a need of reason or, what comes back to the same thing, as the condition of its infinite hermeneutic.

PART III

Reading Descartes

Marion started his academic career as a scholar of Descartes. His doctoral dissertation *de troisième cycle* was directed by Ferdinand Alquié and was defended in 1974. This was to become *Sur l'ontologie grise de Descartes*, published by Librarie Vrin in 1975. Also coming from the dissertation, yet published separately in 1977, was Marion's edition of Descartes's *Règles utiles et claires pour la direction de l'esprit en la recherche de la vérité*.[1] A third scholarly work, the *Index des Regulae ad Directionem Ingenii de René Descartes*, on which Marion collaborated with J.-R. Armogathe, appeared in 1976. In *Sur l'ontologie grise* Marion identifies the various Aristotelian theses that Descartes criticizes in the *Regulae*, an attack that is unified by Descartes's constant demonstration that where Aristotle takes an object to be independent of the human mind it is in fact thoroughly dependent on it. Where Aristotle has a robust ontology, Descartes argues for something far weaker: a "gray ontology" in which things depend for their being on the ego. So, for Descartes, being is no longer grounded in metaphysics but in epistemology. "The Ambivalence of Cartesian Metaphysics" first appeared in *Les Études Philosophiques* in 1976. It reflects on the project that Marion undertook, pointing out that, for all the grayness of Descartes's ontology, it would be hasty to conclude that metaphysics and ontology are simply absent from Descartes's work. The essay is included at the end of the English translation of *Sur l'ontologie grise*.

In "The Ambivalence of Cartesian Metaphysics" we find a section devoted to what Marion calls Descartes's "blank theology," and this notion was to become the theme of his *thèse d'Etat* in 1980, *Sur la théologie blanche de Descartes* (1981).[2] In this study Marion attends to Descartes's doctrine of the "eternal truths," those necessary logical and mathematical truths that, he believes, have been freely created by God and therefore might have been created differently or not at all. This peculiar metaphysical doctrine has the consequence of removing God from the reach of language, especially univocal predication. We cannot ascribe logical truths or mathematical truths both to the world and to God. All theology, understood as meaningful talk about God, would therefore be no more than a blank space or a white page in Descartes's writings. Marion analyzes what he sees as a parallel between Descartes's teaching of the eternal truths and the demise of analogical predication in Christian theology as elaborated by Aquinas, Suárez, and Vasquez. In the passage presented here, Marion sets up the question about the eternal truths and the loss of analogy, and then ponders the question about the search for an adequate foundation of metaphysics.

Marion's third work in this vein, *On Descartes's Metaphysical Prism*, appeared in French in 1986 and, in English translation, in 1999. As its subtitle says, it is concerned with "the constitution and the limits of onto-theo-logy in Cartesian thought." This concern follows strictly from the insights of *Sur l'ontologie grise* and *Sur la théologie blanche*: Are the "gray ontology" and the "blank theology" combined, as Heidegger's thought would lead us to think, in a onto-theio-logical structure? *On Descartes's Metaphysical Prism* attends with exemplary closeness to an onto-theio-logy of the ego as *cogitatio sui* and God as *causa sui*. This tight metaphysical system is overcome, Marion believes, by Pascal's "third order," charity. We approach this final, magisterial work on Descartes in this anthology by way of Marion's account of the divine names.

Inevitably, not all of Marion's work on Descartes can be contained within the triptych just described. Three collections of essays have appeared. These are *Questions cartésiennes: Méthode et métaphysique* (French, 1991; English, 1999); *Questions cartésiennes II: Sur l'ego et sur Dieu* (1996), a modified version of which is published in English translation as *On the Ego and on God: Further Cartesian Questions* (2007); and *Sur la pensée passive de Descartes* (2013). From the first collection, I have chosen "Does the *Ego* Alter the Other? The Solitude of the *Cogito* and the Absence of *Alter Ego*." Marion argues here that the *Meditations* give no possibility for the ego to acknowledge another ego, at least as a *mens*, although these other egos may well be represented to it. Yet Descartes elaborates a doctrine of love. How can he do so without affirming the existence of others? "To represent or to love—one must choose," Marion writes, and wonders if Descartes realized this. "The Originary Otherness of the Ego," taken from the second collection of essays, returns to the question whether Descartes remains stuck in the "sterile grip of solipsism" and ventures the proposal that the philosopher passes from thinking of the ego as *ego cogito, ergo sum* to *ego sum, ego existo*, a formulation that indicates that the ego participates in a dialogue with another being. The canonical interpretation of Descartes as a solipsist (based on *ego cogito, ergo sum*) is not necessarily in contradiction with the noncanonical interpretation of Descartes as dialogical (based on *ego sum, ego existo*). Instead, Marion insists, it is a matter of a hierarchy of truths in Descartes, and not of contradiction or even tension.

K.H.

The Ambivalence of Cartesian Metaphysics

1. The Absentee Ontology

Is it legitimate to speak of a Cartesian metaphysics?[1] A positive response would presuppose the presence of another question occupying the Cartesian enterprise and its texts: the question which metaphysics poses—beginning with Aristotle, and predominantly until Suárez's *Disputationes Metaphysicae*—about beings in their being. But does Descartes himself take up such a question? The thinker who closes his response to the final *Objectiones* to his *Meditationes* with the confident claim that the conclusions therein have been proved "*a nemine ante me*"[2] seems to be introducing a caesura, the discontinuity of which signals a rupture with previously held conclusions, but perhaps above all with the questions that provoked them. The interrogation that provides the grounds for a metaphysics is but one of those that find themselves dismantled by Descartes.

In practice, Descartes sidesteps the metaphysical question where he could have faced up to it, that is, within what at the same time began to be called ontology, *ontologia*.[3] I have attempted elsewhere[4] to show that the basis for the *Regulae* is a number of Aristotelian texts, which, when precisely identified, raise among other questions that of the universal and first science, and so of the *philosophia prōtē*. The work of Descartes in response transcribes an interrogation that is properly the(i)o-logical into an epistemological register. A similar transcription succeeds in annihilating the *ousiai* of beings, to install in their place a *complexio* constructed out of simple natures. The transcription of ontology into epistemology is duplicated by an *ekstasis* of the thing which places it outside its own *ousia*. This *ekstasis* is the identifying feature of the object. Perhaps in this respect we can speak of an ontology at the center of epistemology, an ontology of the object—but would we be justified in doing so? This is what we have to establish. The "grey ontology" evokes the Being of beings only to all the more profoundly enshroud it.

The same general idea, developed in a different direction, can be found in what has been called the "negative ontology" of the *Meditations*[5]: science's theoretical object corresponds neither to the *on* in its Being, nor even to the *ontos on*, but only to the well (or poorly) founded phenomenon—the world described in a fable, at times fabulous, whose reconstruction the method undertakes in its *Essais* by means of mechanical models. The known object and the (*ontos*) *on* do not coincide, nor does the being established as the *ontos on*—the being metaphysically discovered—admit of any representation of itself: we have ideas of the *ego* and of God only to the extent that we abandon the effort to read an image of either one in them: "idea enim infiniti, ut sit vera, nullo modo debet comprehendi, quoniam ipsa incomprehensibilitas in ratione formali infiniti continetur [for the idea of the infinite, if it is to be true, can be in no way comprehended, for its very incomprehensibility is contained in the formal reason of the infinite]."[6] The mind as known does not give us any real being to know, while the being that is real does not yield itself up to any representative knowledge. If the Cartesian *on* were the *ontos*, it would elude every *logos* that tried to equal it expressively.—Furthermore, the fact that this *on* remains mute about itself betrays its fundamental *Bodenlosigkeit*.[7] In effect, "With the *cogito sum*, Descartes claims to prepare a new and secure foundation for philosophy. But what he leaves undetermined in this 'radical' beginning is the manner of being of the *res cogitans*, more precisely the meaning of being of the '*sum*.'"[8] By conquering *res extensa*, Descartes secures an ontic and epistemic guarantee that is itself secured in the ontic guarantee of the *ego cogito* and is entirely dependent thereon. Thus, this security is governed by a "negative ontology." But the *ego* itself, the new ontic ground of thought, remains ontologically indeterminate: the task is to show that it exists, without the question "what does 'to exist' mean for it?" coming to the fore. Or rather, Descartes answers the question, but with an equivalence, repeated—"Ego sum, ego existo"—and perfectly empty. In effect, because "nota est omnibus essentiae ab existentia distinctio [the distinction of essence from existence is known to everyone],"[9] existence does not call for any comment and, being itself inexplicit, it is far from being able to explain the *sum*. When Aristotle equates *ousia* and *to on*, he devotes the greatest part of his attention to identifying *ousia* itself. When Descartes transfers the *sum* into an *ex(s)isto*, he hopes to make it even easier to avoid what "being" in *existo* means, insofar as it is a manner of Being. His discourse stops at the *sum*, whereas it is there that the question, far from coming to a close, is laid open in its true dimensions: what meaning of Being permits this being the privilege of precedence?

Insofar as the task of metaphysics is to consider beings in their Being (*metaphysica communis*), the "grey ontology," the "negative ontology," and the "ontological *Bodenlosigkeit*" all exempt themselves from metaphysics. Yet to conclude that metaphysics and ontology are absent from Descartes's work would be too hasty a judgment, too superficially considered.

2. Metaphysics: What's in a Name?

In the first place, let us note that Descartes makes use of the term metaphysics and even defines it: "Metaphysica sive Theologia."[10] In the second place, this use, which we still have to identify precisely, has to be compared with Suárez's systematic use of the same term, not that long before Descartes. Descartes's theology-privileging conception of metaphysics actually stands opposite Suárez's egalitarian division of metaphysics into what will later become *Metaphysica specialis* and *Metaphysica generalis*: "Abstrahit enim haec scientia de sensibilibus, seu materialibus rebus (quae physicae dicantur, quoniam in eis naturalis philosophia versatur) et res divinas et materia separatas, et communes rationes entis quae absque materia existere possunt, contemplatur; et ideo *metaphysica* dicta est, quasi post physicam, seu ultra physicam constituta [This science abstracts from sensible or material things (which are called physical because natural philosophy is occupied with them) and it considers divine things and things separated from matter, and the common reasons of being which are capable of exiting without matter; and that is why it is called *metaphysics*, inasmuch as it is constituted after physics or beyond physics]"; "Dicendum est ergo ens, in quantum ens reale esse objectum adaequatum hujus scientiae. . . . Ostensum est enim, objectum adaequatum hujus scientiae debere comprehendere Deum, et alias substantias immateriales, non tamen solas illas [We must then say that being, insofar as it is real being, is the proper object of this science. . . . For it has been shown that the proper object of this science ought to include God and the other immaterial substances, but not only these]"; "Eadem ergo scientia, quae de his specialibus objectis tractat [de Deo et intelligentiis], simul considerat omnia praedicta, quae illis sunt cum aliis rebus communia, et haec est tota metaphysica doctrina; est ergo una scientia [The same science that treats of these particular objects (God and the intelligences) considers at the same time all the predicates that are common to these and to other things as well and this is the entire branch of learning that is metaphysics and therefore it is a single science]."[11] Meditating in his own way on the relation that Aristotle establishes—or doesn't establish—between the *épistēmē tis hē theōrei to on hē on* (*Metaphysics* Γ, 1) and the *prōtē philosophia* as *philosophia theologikē* (*Metaphysics* E, 1), Suárez forgoes consideration of their unity in the enigmatic *katholou outōs oti prōtē*, in favor of a coexistence where the more vigorously the unity is affirmed, the more it seems to beg the question. At the very least, the double dimension of one metaphysics is clear and clearly maintained. As a student of Suárez, consciously or not, Descartes is incapable of ignoring this attempt at a solution. As a properly metaphysical thinker above all, he cannot separate himself from what is perhaps the feature that identifies metaphysics as such—its onto-theological constitution (*Verfassung*).[12] The Janus character of metaphysics reflects and betrays its way of approaching the question of Being: as the Being of beings or—what amounts to the same thing—as Being taken in its presence; thus, what is unavoidably, yet unknowingly privileged is the being that, before even coming forward to be contemplated as the supreme being, comes to attention as the arena and the privileged manner of Being. What results is an onto-theological constitution in which the science of the supreme being arises out of the science of Being's initial presentation as the Being *of beings*.

Through Suárez and St. Thomas, Descartes comes to take up the Aristotelian question of the unity of the two sciences, the theological one and the science of *on hē on*. By means of this historical debate, Descartes takes on, historically more than anything, the essence of metaphysics—which, with him, acquires a new aspect of its disclosure. And yet, Descartes does not himself ascend to his destiny as a metaphysician, without himself entertaining and entering into onto-theology. Can we then as historians provide the outlines of a Cartesian onto-theology?

We have just taken note of a number of interconnected considerations which would seem to exclude any ontology (explicit or not) from Cartesian discourse. If a metaphysical onto-theology nevertheless appears, it could only be one which privileges the(i)ology—"Metaphysica sive Theologia." And in fact, quite a few of Descartes's uses of the term "metaphysics" focus it on the domain, if not of the supreme being, at least of the supreme region of some beings in opposition to others: "As I have also included something of Metaphysics, of Physics, and of Medicine"; "to press me for my Physics and my Metaphysics"; "without having previously demonstrated the Principles of Physics by means of Metaphysics."[13] As the science of that suprasensible being who surpasses all the beings treated in Physics, Medicine, Moral Philosophy, and so on, Metaphysics in the Cartesian sense might run the risk of being confused, at least partially, with revealed Theology. Descartes thus takes pains to defend himself against such a confusion: "he [H. de Cherbury] appears to be more knowledgeable than usual in Metaphysics, which is a science that hardly anyone understands, but because after that he seems to me to mix religion and philosophy and because that is entirely contrary to my meaning, I did not read it to the end."[14] Yet there would be no need for this denial were the business of metaphysics not particularly connected to the divine. Does the incompleteness of the supposed Cartesian metaphysics discredit it, if theological science enjoys so great a privilege in relation to the science of being as Being? It does seem that metaphysics is moving toward theology with Descartes, yet at the same time theology is being interpreted as first philosophy.[15] What is the significance of this? Perhaps it is this: theology deserves its privileged status within metaphysics only insofar as it affords the opportunity not simply for knowledge of the highest being—in the sense of *philosophia prōtē*—but also and especially for founding the means of knowing on principles. In a word, for Descartes, "first philosophy" expands theology, while "metaphysics," on the other hand, tends to be reduced to it. What first philosophy adds to theology are the principles *of knowledge*. Not only does Descartes understand metaphysical onto-theology in the lights of the *theo*-logical, he also understands—and as of a piece with the former—the theo-*logical* as the first science of the first principles of knowing: "the true Philosophy, the first part of which is Metaphysics, which contains the principles of knowledge, among which are explanations of the principal attributes of God, of the immateriality of our souls, and of all the other clear and simple notions which exist in us"; "I have divided my book in four parts, the first of which contains the Principles of knowledge, which is what one can call first Philosophy, or Metaphysics."[16] The disappearance of any mention of a science concerning *ens in quantum ens* from what goes by the title Metaphysics removes the obstacles to interpreting theology in such a way that its applicability to the highest being can be redirected to the first objects known, or the first principles of knowledge. Ontology disappears into the shadows, less to leave the science of the supreme being in the light than to turn away from it toward a science of the (first) principles of science. Accordingly, we have the explicitly epistemological interpretation of the *philosophia prōtē*: "I sent my Metaphysics yesterday to M. de Zuylichem for him to forward to you . . . I haven't yet given it a title, but it seems to me that the most appropriate would be to put

Renati Descartes Meditationes de prima Philosophia; for I do not write in particular concerning God and the soul, but in general concerning all the first things that one can know by philosophizing."[17] What Descartes retains of metaphysics, under the name *prima Philosophia*, is what will later come to be called *metaphysica specialis*, and more specifically, pneumatology. He eliminates its ontology, apparently.[18] Finally, he introduces a generality, which would seem to contradict this specialization, if we were not to take note of the fact that the generality also pertains to some "first things." Which ones? "All" of them, Descartes answers, anticipating the question. All, because the ones already mentioned—God and the soul—do not exhaust the supply of "first things." Not that it is necessary to introduce other spirits into the pneumatology. On the contrary, it is necessary to conceive of the "first things" as beings "that one can come to know," or even better, as "clear and simple notions," whatever they may be, provided they present themselves first "in us," that is to say, first to "anyone philosophizing in order [cuilibet ordine philosophanti]."[19] The supreme being, then, only obfuscates the *ens in quantum ens* by being rendered obscure itself within the ambiguity of a discourse that is less *theo-logical* than theo-*logical*. And yet, just as, in the *Regulae*, the primacy of epistemology does not hide the necessity of a *metaphysica generalis* (because there the science of the object plays the role, dimly, of an ontology of the thing), so too, in the *Meditations*, the emphasis placed on the principles of knowledge does not act to censor the *metaphysica specialis*. It is just that first philosophy, hesitating between the status of a science of the supreme being and that of a science that is of itself primary, remains undetermined: a function successfully exercised, but anonymous, left blank. A blank theology—like drawing a blank, or a blank check—which could be referred either to the *theion* or to the "principles of knowledge." A similar ambivalence in the *prima philosophia* is brilliantly illumined, for eyes that know where to look, by the juxtaposition of the two honorees—*Dei existentia et animae immortalitas*—of the unique title.[20] Do we in fact have in front of us a *metaphysica specialis*, a discourse pursued, concerning the privileged being (*Deus*), or do we have a discourse pursued by the being whom knowledge privileges (*anima*)? Does the theo-logic follow from the *theion*, or does it depend on a capacity to know that has become primordial?

First philosophy's ambivalence here reflects a modification of the relation between theology and ontology. But this or these relations can only become formalized if an onto-theological constitution has first inscribed them within a discourse that is identified with metaphysics. The question remains whether, following Descartes's nomenclature for metaphysics, we can find the signs of a Cartesian metaphysics that would organically issue both in a theology and—however obscurely—in an ontology, and whether, within this *Verfassung*, the ambivalence is born out.

3. A Metaphysics of the Cause

If an ontology is announced by a pronouncement that holds for all beings, and thus for any being in its Being, then we have grounds to speak of a Cartesian ontology that is explicitly announced on a number of occasions: "However, the light of nature does indeed dictate that there is no thing in existence about which it is not permissible to seek why it exists, either to inquire after its efficient cause, or, if it does not have one, to question why it has no need of one [Dictat autem profecto lumen naturae nullam rem existere, de qua non liceat petere cur existat, sive in ejus causam efficientem inquirere, aut, si non habet, cur illa non indigeat, postulare]"; "No thing exists about which it is not possible to ask what is the cause of its existing [Nulla res existit de qua non possit quaeri quaenam sit causa cur existat]."[21] A thesis concerning the Being of beings is indeed announced, under the form of a *diktat*: a being should exist by its cause and should give itself to be seen in Being to the extent that it is caused. Or, if you prefer, a being should come into Being through its cause—it is this that seems to be the cause that Descartes pleads for the Being of beings. The cause here exceeds (as we will see later) the system of the four Aristotelian causes, for, even if it is most often an efficient cause that is meant, the cause has an anterior point of reference—as if to a ground common and prior to the four causes: a "certain concept common to the efficient and the formal cause [conceptum quemdam causae efficienti et formali communem]," for "between the efficient cause and no cause there is something intermediate [inter causam efficientem . . . et nullam causam esse quid intermedium]."[22] The fact that causality has now been anchored deeper than the previously listed causes does not, however, suffice in itself to justify the fact that Descartes takes up the case of the Being of beings within a discourse concerning the cause. Why add "being," here—indeed "Being of beings"—to what can only be understood as a statement of the principle of causality? Is it not in fact *only* the principle of causality that is at issue here? Yet this in itself is no minor matter. Descartes is indeed thinking only of the principle of causality; his thinking of it is so exclusive, in fact, that it subsumes the question of a being's Being in the form Descartes inherits from Suárez, namely, that of existence. Each of Descartes's statements concerning causality bears on the existence of a thing—"cur existat." In effect, existence and cause come together intimately—in "effect," or rather, within an effect. The effect maintains a relation of exteriority to the cause, even more so when efficiency is the cause's privileged mode of presentation. An effect is exteriorized outside the cause, under the cause's auspices. Ultimately, this exteriority is juxtaposed to the exteriority that existence for its part supposes: "For what else is 'existere' except to stand out of something? [quid est enim existere nisi ex aliquo sistere?]."[23] It follows that the exteriority of existence meets up with the exteriority produced by the cause. The cause controls the being by making the being its effect, exposed before it, at a respectful distance. In matters pertaining to Being, the cause allows the being to be a being under the mode of existence—a defeat or an undoing, in which the thing's essence is *ekstasized*, which is to say, the essence is alienated in being exiled from itself and put to work. Existence thus exists *extra causas*.[24] The *ekstasis* of a being (essence, *ousia*) so that it is outside itself, and therefore outside of another being that becomes more essential to it than its own essence, can equally be spoken of as "existence" (effect) or as "cause." The cause appears as the depositary of existence. And so existence becomes the depositary of a new estrangement, at the very moment when it becomes "known to all [omnibus nota]." Or rather, it is the cause itself, as the cause that a being has to plead in order to justify itself as regards Being, that becomes in its turn obscured by a dazzling and unassailable evidence, by virtue of being so well known: "Moreover its seems to me self-evident that everything that exists either exists from a cause or exists from itself as if from a cause [Per se autem notum mihi videtur, omne id quod est, vel esse a causa, vel a se tanquam a causa]."[25] The two points of entry, instead of revealing their ontological import, hide and are themselves hidden by their own evidence. As a result, the influence of the ontological pronouncement is all the greater, for being less open to interrogation. Each and every being has to assume the guise of existence, that is to say, it must plead its cause. Being turns on the cause: with it, being passes to existence. Yet someone might still object that Descartes's enunciation of the existence-cause relation—rigorous and ontologically determinative though it may be—is not original with him: others (Suárez, for instance) preceded him on the path. Why regard Descartes's formulation as both properly Cartesian and properly ontological? Without claiming to resolve the historical question decisively, let me point out that Descartes's formulation of the relation of existence to a cause is exceptionless and that the strictness of its application is made explicit: "nullam rem." Only such a performance can justify giving the role of a founding principle to the cause. This amounts to saying that the cause only attains its status as a world of Being for beings (ontology, *metaphysica generalis*) by the greatest possible extension of its reach, even to the ultimate regions of being. To prove itself it aims to constitute the supreme being (theology, *metaphysica specialis*) in conformity with the cause, that is, to force it too to plead its cause for Being. Descartes formulates this requirement explicitly: "Now that a consideration of the efficient cause is the first and most appropriate intermediary, not to say the only, that we have for proving the existence of God, is I think evident to all. Moreover we are not able to accomplish this with exactitude unless we have freedom in our minds for seeking the efficient causes of all things, even of God himself: for by what right do we exempt God from this, before it is proved that he exists? [Atqui considerationem causae efficientis esse primum et praecipuum medium, ne dicam unicum, quod habeamus ad existentiam Dei probantum, puto omnibus esse manifestum. Illud autem accurate persequi non possumus, nisi licentiam demus animo nostro in rerum omnium, etiam ipsius Dei, causas efficientes inquirendi: quo enim jure Deum inde exciperemus, priusquam illum existere sit probatum?]."[26] Why propose this principle in such a way that even God is not excepted from the question of the cause? Having done so, Descartes, the professed detester of polemics, leaves himself exposed to an obvious and pertinent criticism: God, since He is *a se*, has no cause, nor does He need one. Yet this is not a case of Descartes's forgetting doctrinal prudence, or religious reverence for that matter. Rather, what is at issue here, more essentially, is another necessity that commands another respect—a metaphysical one—from which the thinker, and he alone, cannot exempt himself: each being must plead its cause, because the cause goes hand in glove with the being's existence—with the Being of the being. No sooner has the cause been extracted from the quadripartite system that limited it to one region of being in order to become a foundation, no sooner has the Being of a being become a foundation within the cause, than the *causa sui*, far from being stuck in an absurd contradiction, pleads the cause of the cause. "The Being of beings is represented fundamentally, in the sense of the ground, only as *causa sui*. This is the metaphysical concept of God."[27] The cause, which makes possible an ontology (*ens quatenus causatum*), cannot attain the plenitude of metaphysical speech except by experiencing the curvature of its reach, except in turning back in upon the grounds for its own activity, in a theology (*Deus quatenus causa sui, causa/causatum*). The conceptual polemic surrounding the legitimacy of a *causa sui* (distinction of cause and effect; simultaneity or anteriority of the terms; *effectus indignatas*; etc.) is of little consequence in comparison with the metaphysical intention it is to serve: to include the supreme being within the onto-theological constitution of a metaphysics of the cause. The cause that God pleads to be founded in Being—as *causa sui*—does not suppose the mediation of an efficient cause exercised by God on himself. Rather it is God himself who in some way or another interprets his essence according to the causal model: "But I entirely admit that something is able to be, in which there is so great and so inexhaustible a power that it was never in need of something in order to exist, nor still now does it need something to be conserved, but it is even in a certain way the cause of itself, and I understand God to be such a being [Sed plane admitto aliquid esse posse, in quo sit tanta et tam inexhausta potentia, ut nullius unquam ope eguerit ut existerit, neque etiam nunc egeat ut conservetur, atque adeo sit quodammodo sui causa; Deumque talem esse intelligo]."[28] Not that God produces a cause whose effect he must also provide; rather, his essence, because it is infinite, communicates a so *inexhausta potentia*, such an *exuperantia potestatis*,[29] that it suffices to plead God's cause for Being without being confused with an efficient cause in the strict sense. God's essence, or power, escapes a cause only to make the unfailing permanence of the causal question more evident. To be able to plead its cause without becoming the exteriorized effect of another-as-cause is the privilege of the supreme being. Yet this privilege has its price: the divine essence has to be interpreted as a *potentia*. That the supreme being transcends a cause coincides with God's inclusion within the causal question. In this sense, God, by allowing himself to be defined as *omnipotens*,[30] confesses his impotence: He remains the supreme *being* only insofar as he is submitted to a metaphysics of the cause—he too has to plead his cause for Being.

4. The Reason of the Cause

Why, though, is God able to plead his cause without admitting any cause whose effect, in the strict sense, he might be? Because, in a sense, the cause is beyond causality, as the principle which imposes a cause on God clearly indicates: "about which it is not permissible to seek why it exists, either to inquire after its efficient cause, or, if it does not have one, to question why it has no need of one [de qua non liceat petere cur existat, sive in ejus causam efficientem inquirere, aut, si non habet, cur illa non indigeat, postulare]"; "about God Himself [it] can be asked . . . on account of wh[at] [cause] no cause is [or should be] required for his existence [de ipso Deo quaeri potest . . . propter quam [causam] nulla causa indige[a]t ad existendum]."[31] What does the cause that beings plead for Being have to become in order to move beyond the reach of the cause? Before we risk giving too pat an answer, let us take a look at some of the places where the strangeness of the Cartesian concept of a *causa* is exhibited.

1. In the *Meditations*, Descartes introduces the principle of the equality of cause and effect before he turns to the existence of God; the role of the former in facilitating the demonstration of the latter highlights its efficacy—before any other being than the *ego*, thus before any other possible effect is assured, the *causa* is already in operation as a

principle. In this sense, just as oddly, the meditator's ideas, even though they are deprived of any existence *extra causas* are submitted to the *causa*: "but [it is true] also of ideas [etiam de ideis]."[32]

2. In the same passage, Descartes speaks of a *causa efficiens et totalis*, a term that accompanies the doctrine of the creation of eternal truths.[33] Strictly speaking, the two qualifiers contradict one another: as efficient, a cause could claim totality only in virtue of the domain of its efficiency (Suárez's understanding seems consonant with this: a cause is total in relation to all other causes *of the same type* as it). For Descartes, who reduces the final and formal causes to the efficient, this stipulation no longer makes sense. It is fitting then to say that the efficient cause as such is total in relation to all causality: thus, the (efficient) cause must grow in scope and depth into a total cause.

3. That a cause must be pled has its greatest influence on causal relations and so on the strict correlation of *causa* and *effectus*. *Rule VI* mentions the *effectus* among the number of *respectiva*, but it maintains the *causa* among the *absoluta*. Why is the *causa* accorded this privilege, if the correlation of cause and effect is so obvious? "[I]ntentionally we have numbered 'cause' and 'equal' among the *absoluta*, although their nature is truly *respectiva*: for according to the Philosophers, cause and effect are correlative; but in fact here, if we are seeking what kind the effect is, it is useful to know the cause first, and not vice versa [de industria causam et aequale inter absoluta numeravimus, quamvis eorum natura sit vere respectiva: nam apud Philosophos quidem causa et effectus sunt correlativa; hic vero si quaeramus qualis sit effectus, oportet prius causam cognoscere, et non contra]" (*Regula VI*, 383, 3–8).[34] As a physical factor, the cause remains truly (*vere*) correlative with the effect, but as a functor of knowledge, since it provides the only access for the thing to give itself to be known as an effect (*causatum*), the cause is called *prius*: anterior to an effect that it makes intelligible, and not vice versa. It is under the auspices of intelligibility, and not of efficacy, that the *causa* is elevated above its correlation with an effect. The cause's growth spurt in relation to the effect stems from its epistemic interpretation. But this would still not explain anything, if the *causa*, interpreted in this way as a functor of truth, were not also installed as a foundation: not only is it impossible for anything that has not been caused to be, or for anything not known by its cause to be caused, but it is in fact this very knowing that yields the *causatum* thus known in its essence, and provides its foundation. Thus understood, the cause supplies the reason of what it is that it founds as its known effect.

Causa sive ratio—the formula is Descartes's, and he introduces it precisely where he makes the cause something that even God has to plead: "For about God himself this can be asked, not that he is in need of any cause of his existence, but because the very immensity of his nature is the cause or reason, on account of which no cause is required for his existence [Hoc enim de ipso Deo quaeri potest, non quod indigeat ulla causa ut existat, sed quia ipsa ejus naturae immensitas est causa sive ratio, propter quam nulla causa indiget ad existendum]"; "that the inexhaustible power of God is a cause or reason on account of which a cause is not required [quod inexhausta Dei potentia sit causa sive ratio propter quam causa non indiget]"; "the formal cause, or reason obtained from the essence of God [causam formalem, sive rationem ab essentia Dei petitam]."[35] When Descartes, at the urging of Caterus and Arnauld, attempts to elaborate the unthinkable common, or intermediary (*medium*), concept under which God might be considered, he aims less to submit God to causality than to the *ratio* which, even in the absence of any identifiable cause, still needs to be pled, by each and every being, as its cause for Being. The ultimate name of the *causa*—that is, *ratio*—is pronounced by Descartes only when consideration of the supreme being forces him to do so. Not that such a reason outstrips the cause and leaves it behind; on the contrary, it demonstrates that the basis of the *causa*—on the basis of which it is also a foundation—is not causality, but the *ratio*. The intervention of the *ratio* thus reveals that the cause no longer suffices to guarantee a metaphysics, or what amounts to the same thing, that the cause suffices only by supplying, as a foundation, the reason of the beings pleading their cause, that is to say, only by "adjusting [them] to the level of reason ['ajustées au niveau de la raison']."[36] The reason becomes that which, within the cause, provides the foundation as a principle. It is the intelligibility of the *ratio* that adjusts the thing to its principle, whether that be its true cause, or simply *tanquam a causa*. And so, it would seem, the discourse that investigated beings in their Being—including the supreme being—by way of a cause failed to attain its proper depth: it did not arrive at a consideration of the cause as a reason. Pleading a cause comes down to supplying a reason, because the cause only becomes a foundation by the presupposition that it is a *ratio*.

If we have correctly identified the relocation that Descartes effects of the point at which metaphysics recedes from clarity—and the confirmation provided by the text suggests that we have—then what we are witnessing is not simply an effect of Descartes's reprise of the major themes (ontology and theology). Rather, it is the result of his identification of intelligibility, which has here become a foundation. A cause could seem to pass along from one being to another (under the correlated term "natural"); the *ratio*, by its intelligibility, anticipates every being, being itself located in none of them. Or rather, by anticipating each being, the *ratio* remains indifferent to it, while each being has, as if by accident, a *ratio* in its charge as its own depositary. The *ratio* leaves blank the space for this or that being to assume possession of it by its signature. As we begin to outline this constitution of a "metaphysics of knowledge,"[37] we need to tackle two questions. Not only must we ask what the *ratio* imposes on the metaphysics of the cause in the way of readjustments (or not), we must also ask which supreme being appropriates this *ratio* to itself, as its own intelligibility.

5. A Metaphysics of the *Cogitatum/Cogito*: The Blank Theology

The cause becomes a *ratio* only if the *ratio* actually subsumes the cause, in keeping with the evidentiary process. In effect, the abundance of the *causa* in relation to an effect—a focal point of *Rule VI*—can be traced to a hierarchy of relations (relation 3: any *respectivum*, for example "effect"; relation 2: of the absolute to the *respectivum*; relation 1: of every object "to the respect of our intellect [respectu nostri intellectus])" organized and dominated by the thing's fundamental relation to knowledge. The *causa* surpasses its effect only by prioritizing intelligibility. The thing's reference to *Mathesis universalis*, which secures its entry into evidence through measure, and especially through the process of ordering, becomes more fundamental to the thing than the thing itself and its *ousia*. That this entry into evidence through the process of ordering is *already* the work of a *cogitatio* is clearly stated in *Rule VIII*: "And it is not an enormous task to wish to embrace by thought everything contained in this universe, so that we may recognize how each one is subject to the examination of our mind [Neque immensum est opus, res omnes in hac universitate contentas cogitatione velle complecti, ut, quomodo singulae mentis nostrae examini subjectae sint, agnoscamus]" (398, 14–17).[38] The thing is submitted to the judgment of a *mens* that examines it by a *cogitatio*. It is therefore possible to say of each and every being that it gains access to Being only by passing through a *cogitatio*, and so by becoming a *cogitatum*. The foundation of the piece of wax is not to be found in its sensible qualities (all of which are altered by the fire), nor even in what will become, later, extension. For, "What is something extended? Is it not the case that even the extension itself is unknown? [Quid extensum? Nunquid etiam ipsa ejus extensio est ignota?]." Extension here remains unknown, or difficult to know, because all that is needed to modify the concrete extension of a body is a temperature variation, not to mention the instability of forms. What then remains of the piece of wax for the *cogitatio* to grasp in its cold light? Nothing. At least, nothing but this: "Superest igitur ut concedam, me nequidem imaginari quid sit haec cera, sed sola mente percipere [It remains therefore, for me to concede that it is fruitless to use my imagination to determine what this wax is, but that I perceive it by the mind alone]," that is to say, that in the midst of the wax's failure to present any fixity of its *ousia*, there remains, fixed on the wax, the *solius mentis inspectio*.[39] Because the *ratio* operates as a *cogitatio*, we can always require a *ratio*, even where there is no cause to plead, there being nothing capable of pleading one. That is why even if for Angelus Silesius, "The rose is without a why; it blooms because it blooms / it is not attentive to itself, nor does it wonder whether one is looking at it," for Descartes, the rose, like the tulip, has a cause: "For what makes it the case that the sun, for example, even though it is the universal cause of all flowers, is still not the cause of the difference between tulips and roses is that their production also depends on certain particular causes that are not at all subordinate to the sun."[40] And if the sun does not suffice to plead the cause of the rose and of its distinction from the tulip, then other "particular causes" must be brought in to assist it. The rose, and every other being as well, has to render the reason for what has no cause—the rose itself. For the rose, before it even opens to the light of day, opens to the *cogitatio*.

We can express the way in which each being, by virtue of its submission to the *causa sive ratio*, enters into *cogitatio* still more precisely, if granted what may seem to be some license. What in fact does it mean to render a reason if the reason is already the foundation of the cause? Is the reason itself faced with the question why? We have grounds for a "no" answer here, provided we pay attention to the sequence in the phrasing: *render* a reason, that is to say, permit the reason to render itself—militarily to surrender. The thing renders the reason for itself in the same way one renders payment in full to a creditor. For a thing, to render reason is to put its cause (or its noncause) on the table, that is, to give it up for representation to deal with.[41] Leibniz takes the principle of reason a stage further than Descartes, showing all the more clearly the intention of his predecessor in a decisive step, which we can perhaps explain as the transformation of *causa sive ratio* into *principium* REDDENDAE *rationis*: it is made explicit that the *ratio* has to become a representation. In Descartes's terms, it has to become a *cogitatio*. The passing of the *causa* into the *ratio*, rather than eliminating the necessity for every being to plead its cause for Being, produces another necessity, that of pleading its cause in conformity with *cogitatio*. Here being in its Being is said according to a *causa sive ratio*, that is, as a *ratio reddenda*, hence as a *cogitatum*. The ontology expressed here strictly coincides with epistemology. Not that the accomplishment of the latter makes manifest the supposed failings of the former in a neo-Kantian way; on the contrary, the epistemology here accomplished takes on the task of enunciating each being in its Being, by thinking it in terms of the reason that has to be rendered for it, that is to say, by representing it as a *cogitatum*.[42]

What then might be the theology that corresponds to this ontology? Taking "theology" here to indicate specifically an act of knowing that brings to light a being (divine or not) as the supreme being, and not the science that treats of God only insofar as it comes from God, the corresponding the(i)ology is one that concerns the supreme being under the *ens*-as-*cogitatum* relation. This being requires the *ego* of the *cogito* for its enunciation. Would the *ego* then be the supreme being, instead of the God whose existence is demonstrated elsewhere? From the point of view of the *ens* as *cogitatum*, no doubt about it. What God is, as *causa sui*, to the being that pleads its cause, so is the *ego*, as *cogito*, to the being as *cogitatum*. The *ego* becomes the supreme being for an ontology of the represented being. Elsewhere, Descartes explicitly attributes to the *ego* this role as principle: "I took the being or the existence of this thought [of our soul or our thought] for the first Principle, from which I deduced very clearly the following ones: that is, that there is a God who is the author of all that exists in the world [j'ai pris l'être ou l'existence de cette pensée pour le premier Principe, duquel j'ai déduit très clairement les suivants: à savoir qu'il y a un Dieu, qui est auteur de tout ce qui est au monde]," and he guarantees its uncontested primacy: "this cognition . . . is first and most certain of all [haec cognito . . . est omnium prima et certissima]"; "a certain first notion [prima quaedam notio]."[43] If knowing-by-representing takes on the Being of being (to make it an object), then it is the task of the principle of knowledge (of the *causa sive ratio*) to present Being in the supremacy of one being. What becomes most supremely a being itself serves as the principle. The requisite confirmation of this is to be found in the following remarks.

Heidegger undertook an interpretation of the *cogito* not simply as an ontic term, but as an ontological principle, by way of a commentary on the formula, apparently not found in Descartes, *cogito me cogitare*.[44] What the *cogito* thinks first of all, more than any specific *cogitatum*, is the very essence of the *cogitatio*: the principle that every being, in order to plead its cause for Being, will have to render reason for itself as thinkable. The *cogito* would be a mere banality (as its numerous historical antecedents attest), were the psychological operation that it sets in motion not invested with the role of a principle—one that determines Being for other beings. When the *ego* as supreme being engages in thinking itself as existing, it is the existence of other beings—an existence thereby made possible, of other beings as *cogitata*—that is at stake. In the *cogito*, it is less a matter of the *ego* establishing its own existence than it is one of permitting beings to render a reason of their existence, by representing themselves to a (re)presenter—that is, the *ego*.

That a tension between two principles—the *ego* and God—underlies the *Meditationes* would seem to be confirmed by the agreement among commentators. They may differ greatly in their manners of accenting, or of mediating, the separation, but they hold in common that the separation exists. Thus, Martial Gueroult identifies an irreducible duality of two series, partially juxtaposed: the first goes from doubt to the perfect *ego*, which, in its perfection, occupies the place of first principle; the second leads from the *ego* to God, the principle that puts the *ego* face to face with its own imperfection. In the juxtaposition of the two series, and by means of a brutal transfer from one line of reasoning to the other, "the self-sufficiency of God is substituted for the self-sufficiency of the me." A similar "schism between two orders of reasons" makes the distance separating the two principles manifest. But other interpreters take an opposite view, emphasizing the continuity between the two, with the assurance that "Descartes's demonstration of God's existence is the movement of the *I*, sounding the depths of its own existence" (Henri Gouhier). They therefore seek to "reinscribe" within the *ego* the distance separating it from God and leading it toward him: "The *cogito* is the idea of God and nothing else. . . . The idea of God is not in consciousness; it is consciousness" (Ferdinand Alquié).[45] Concealed within the *ego* is such an amplitude that it could understandably not know its own reach and so be required to meditate on the amplitude of its direct relation to the divine being. In each of these hypotheses, by the heterogeneity of the two principles or by their continuity, the *ego* claims for itself the status of a first principle, in the name of an onto-theological constitution. It thus encroaches on the privilege of God, insofar as the(i)ological function does not accord this status to anything but God, as the divine and supreme being.

Descartes makes reference to the ambivalence we see here in the *ego*, many times, in fact. Thus, the *facultas ampliandi*, which permits the meditator to magnify human perfections to infinity so as to attribute them to God, is based on the presence in/as "me" of the idea of infinity, hence of the *similitudo Dei* that constitutes, through and through, the *ego*. This innatism in turn supposes that "that similitude, in which the idea of God is contained, is perceived by me by the same faculty by which the *ego* itself is [am] perceived by me [illam similitudem, in qua Dei idea continetur, a me percipi per eamdem facultatem per quam ego ipse a me percipior]."[46] In order to conceive of God (in the instances where God is required in his the(i)ological function), the *ego* needs no faculty other than the one that principally assures it of itself and of the *cogitata*, namely the *cogito*. The two concurrent principles have their source in the ambivalence of a single principle, the *cogito*, which holds perhaps as much for one being (God) as for another (the *ego*). The ambivalence of the *eadem facultas* again coincides, as its very anonymity suggests, with what I call a blank theology.

Further still, let us note that Descartes's first *positive* reference to aseity concerns that of the *ego* and not that of God.[47] As a result, the theology of the *causa sui* seems almost to pass from a metaphysics of the cause to one of the *cogito* (part 3 of this concluding essay, above). But since the ontology of the *causa* (once the *causa* becomes the equivalent of a *ratio reddenda*) penetrates the ontology of the *cogitatum* as well (part 4, above), it seems that the metaphysics of the cause as a whole is equally that of the *cogitatio*. And yet the two do not come together finally as one. Why not? Because what is at issue most evidently (although not most importantly) is expressed in the following dilemma: which of the two, God (metaphysics of the *causa/causa sui*) or the *ego* (metaphysics of the *cogitatum/*

cogito) ought to occupy the the(i)ological role? Descartes shows his own greatness in leaving agape the gulfs that open under his pen. Far from resolving the question (which looms behind the so-called Cartesian circle, threatening the whole project), he maintains it, and in a sense consolidates it (in the *Responsiones* and the *Principia*). Can the *ego*, by means of the intelligibility it confers in re-presenting, assume the the(i)ological role in the place of God and his causality? The attempt, by multiple means, to make these two terms coincide, was the task, the aim, and the downfall of those we call, antiphrastically, the "Cartesians." The greatest contribution of Descartes to the consideration of beings in their Being was without a doubt his uncovering and his employment of the onto-theological ambivalence of his metaphysics, singular or plural.

Paris, January, 1976

The Eternal Truths

§1. A Question about Descartes: The Creation of the Eternal Truths and the Loss of Analogy

A thought does not exert its greatness except as measured by the affirmations it makes possible, but also by the questions it raises—or rather, by those it nourishes; for a question nourishes thought more than an affirmation does. An affirmation is worth what its proofs are worth, and disappears as soon as these proofs are put into question. A question, for its part, survives the placing of it in question; and, far from being weakened by it, is reinforced by its having been put in question. A question by definition is always reborn from itself—provided at least that it is actually deployed as a line of questioning.

A line of questioning: that which an answer does not manage to cancel out or to control, but, on the contrary, what the answer extends and that which, in the answer, is fulfilled. The answer reinforces and completes the line of questioning because it continues it; and an answer that no longer sustains the anxious point of the question veers off into a meaningless dogmatism. For unlike ideology, philosophy, far from masking or destroying the power of anxious concern in a question, advances a thesis only in order to keep this power working. And conversely, one would even have to venture that the theses of a philosophy are worth being studied only insofar as they enable one to go back, through them, to the seriousness of the essential question that brought them forth. The dogmatic answer does not abolish the initial question; it bears witness to it because it comes from it, and it can make it possible to renew it. Yet only the regard of a philosopher can accomplish this route of return; moreover that is why only a philosopher is able to see the history of philosophy as a philosophical act: he alone sees it with a philosophical regard. But whence, for the philosopher, comes the question that answers to the answer? From a questioning that provokes him. This very questioning appears in the landscape already defined by the prior history of thought. Originality is never absolute;

it is all the less so when its innovation truly modifies the conceptual landscape. And who does not know that all the would-be overcomings and the claims to a finally absolute origin soon flounder, orphans of principle, widows of reference—unless they are just naively repeating some forgotten old wives' tales? The only originality of any worth is grafted on to a questioning that unsettles the prior landscape of concepts. Better: it is this very unsettling that makes a conceptual landscape look prior, and strikes it with vanity. The structure of this upheaval determines a gap that, speaking strictly, constitutes the sole originality of new thought. A line of questioning, a gap: thus is a new thought able to be inaugurated.

How is Cartesian thought inaugurated, or rather, how is Descartes inaugurated in thought? He claims an absolute novelty: "nemo ante me [nobody before me]," "a nemine ante me [by no one before me]."[1] And nonetheless he claims—in the same moment and with just as much insistence—an absolute continuity with the whole of the philosophic tradition: "Addo etiam, quod forte videbitur esse paradoxum, nihil in ea Philosophia esse, quatenus censetur peripatetica, et ab aliis diversa quod non sit novum; nihilque in mea, quod non sit vetus [I shall add something that may seem paradoxical. Everything in peripatetic philosophy, regarded as a distinctive school that is different from others, is quite new, whereas everything in my philosophy is old]"; "meam Philosophiam esse omnium antiquissimam, nihilque ab ea diversum esse in vulgari, quod non sit novum [my philosophy is the oldest of all, and there is nothing in the ordinary philosophy, insofar as it differs from mine, that is not quite new]."[2] This means expressly: it is by innovating that Descartes remains ancient; but such a game of novelty with antiquity [ancienneté] does not suppose any repetition. On the contrary, it supposes that the innovation of new theses recovers not only old theses, but old questions, and even that it recovers them better than the old theses themselves that correspond to them. When it comes to ancient themes, new thinkers enjoy more seniority [déploient plus d'ancienneté] than the old thinkers do; "more seniority" here does not mean a greater antiquity [antiquité], but a more rigorous correspondence. How should we measure this correspondence, and what kind of status should be recognized for it? To arrive at an answer, first one would have to determine where the originality of Descartes is most indisputably attested, and secondly, one would have to determine how this thesis corresponds to a more ancient question. Where then is the Cartesian originality attested? The method, the doubt, the *cogito*, the proofs for the existence of God, and so on, obviously stake out radical advances; but all of these theses (at least when taken separately) admit of antecedents: from Mersenne and Arnauld up to the most recent research, passing by way of Blanchet, Koyré, and Gilson, the connections to the sources have been noted and assessed. Similarly, these theses reappear in the posterity of Descartes—with modifications and exceptions, to be sure, but without abandoning them. Indeed, it is rather just the contrary: from F. Bouillier to F. Alquié and G. Rodis-Lewis, the lines of descent have been highlighted and pinpointed. Concerning all of these theses, the originality of Descartes resides less in his formulation or discovery of them than in his ordered arrangement of them, and above all in the respective functions they take on for him. Coming forth in a material way from the prior doxographic tradition, they will become an integral part of all subsequent metaphysical reflection. In a sense, precisely because it has become—for us— "Cartesian," the *cogito* no longer belongs to Descartes, any more than the ontological argument still belongs to Saint Anselm alone. There is nonetheless a thesis that properly characterizes Cartesian thought, one that every other thought has unanimously (or nearly so) rejected or been unaware of, so much so that the prevailing interpretation of Descartes's thought has been able to underestimate it in Descartes himself—namely, the thesis regarding the creation of the eternal truths. According to this thesis, no truth, however essential it may seem to the human mind, has absolute validity for God, because God has created it. In other words, the horizon of rationality owes its pertinence (which for us is unsurpassable) to an instauration, thus to an unconditioned condition that renders the instauration conditioned. Descartes sets forth this thesis for the first time in 1630, in three strange and solitary letters to Father Marin Mersenne; with one accord, all the scholarly critics have emphasized its originality. Some have noted it in relation to Descartes's predecessors: "Of all his metaphysical conceptions, it is perhaps the most original, the one that contains the fewest adventitious elements and is explained best by the internal necessities of the Cartesian system" (Gilson). "Nothing is more opposed to scholasticism than the theory of the created eternal truths" (Alquié).

"The creation of the eternal truths officially registers Descartes' break from every Platonic temptation" (Rodis-Lewis).[3] The originality of such a rupture will have to be noted at some length; an originality also and perhaps above all with regard to Descartes's successors, including those who (no doubt by antiphrasis) are called "Cartesians": "The theory of the creation of the eternal truths is not maintained by the great Cartesians of the seventeenth century, Malebranche and Leibniz; to a greater or lesser extent, they even arrayed themselves violently against it" (Bréhier).[4] This judgment has received full confirmation in the work of Belaval on Leibniz, of Gueroult on Spinoza, of Alquié on Malebranche, of Gouhier on Augustinianism, etc.[5] Moreover, in subsequent research I hope to show in detail the modes and the motives for this refusal. Everything happens, perhaps, as if with the creation of the eternal truths Descartes had not only announced a radically new thesis, but above all, had opened up a question about which everyone after him was silent. I ask: what is the novelty at issue here? What places it in question? What is the meaning of the unanimous censure that, as soon as Descartes dies, disqualifies and excludes it? The violent rupture the thesis brings about implies an essential line of questioning; this essential line of questioning itself has yet to be reconstituted in the oeuvre of Descartes.

And it is here that the final paradox intervenes: even in the Cartesian text itself, the thesis is not given out clearly. Not (as is often claimed, wrongly) that this doctrine remains marginal, half-veiled or overly veiled, or dated too precisely; we will see that on the contrary Descartes develops it clearly and constantly from 1630 to 1649 (see below, §13).[6] Besides, these texts do not pose, as such, any insurmountable difficulties of interpretation, and their theoretical content does not profoundly divide the principal critics. Whence then comes the difficulty? From this, that for these critics the creation of the eternal truths would continue to be treated as if it were on the margins of Cartesian metaphysics: "This conception, as important as it is, does not belong to the body of the doctrine" (Gueroult). It goes without saying that here I must follow (even if only methodologically) Ferdinand Alquié, who recognizes in this thesis "the key to Cartesian metaphysics";[7]

otherwise, the line of questioning itself would be lacking to me. Recognizing that it is a key, however, does not yet suffice; a key does open, but it loses all of its essential interest once the opening has been secured. If the letters of 1630 (even as retrieved subsequently[8]) open thought to "Being," they still constitute but an opening, an overture; and in philosophy as in music, the overture must cease in order for the act to begin. Hence, as such, an opening does not yet say anything, but simply attracts attention, even if only by a grand gesture. In order to give it its true metaphysical status, one must certainly recognize its importance for the creation of the eternal truths, but above all one must give it a central site in the whole of Cartesian thought. If one keeps to the explicit theses of 1630, the later allusions, however constant they may be, will not suffice for it. The principal moments of the *Meditationes* (the doubt, the *ego*, God, etc.) neither presuppose nor cite this doctrine. No continuity can intervene, therefore, between theses that are too diverse; continuity could be established only by starting from an authority more essential than the theses, but which, in its uniqueness, inspires them all: the question. Hence we are looking for a question radical enough to have prompted not just the outburst of 1630, but also the moments of the metaphysics of 1641; and, still more, the absence of special metaphysics in the intervening period. Unifying but dissimulated center, the vanishing point of all perspective, this question should also manifest the place and the rupture, the continuity and the gap, between Descartes and his predecessors. Can we identify such a question? I would like to advance a hypothesis: at issue here is the question of analogy. The letters of 1630 raise the question of analogy directly; they expressly criticize the doctrine of Suárez on a related problem and, by opting against the univocity of being, they push the demand for equivocity so far that they open an infinite chasm between the finite and the infinite, ontically as well as epistemologically. In this overture, the *Meditationes* will play out their theses in order to secure, despite the equivocity, an infinite foundation for human knowledge and for finite being. In short, the question of analogy would inspire the thesis of the creation of the eternal truths in 1630, but also the theses of 1641, which attempt to respond to the somewhat tragic opening of 1630. An unspoken question would inspire the explicit theses, and would assure their seemingly invisible coherence. Descartes, theoretician of analogy: let this be our first paradox, a diachronic paradox, in order to remove the suspicion of a synchronic incoherence.

The moment has not yet come to try to establish this paradox in detail, nor to prove its accuracy. On the other hand, some provisional confirmations are called for. (a) Although, to my knowledge, the Cartesian corpus has never been systematically examined using the problematic of analogy, some of the most authoritative commentators have sensed its importance for understanding the Cartesian decision. Thus Etienne Gilson: "The radical negation of quality is the radical negation of the analogy between the material and the intelligible; and, as analogy was the scholastic method par excellence for going from the world to God, this traditional way is closed off to Descartes."[9] Likewise, Henri Gouhier: "He [sc. Descartes] does not even dream of the possibility of an analogical knowledge, for the same reasons dictated to him by his theory of created eternal truths."[10] "In order to avoid univocity Descartes abandons any thought implying a certain likeness, even one purified (as in Thomist analogy) of anthropomorphic suggestions," and therefore "Descartes must look for something other than analogy," "the opposite of an analogy."[11] These commentators agree that analogy offers an authority all the more determinative because it evokes a radical and multiform critique. Our originality consists in trying to unfold all the implications of this critique; in making this absence appear fully; and in making it talk. (b) The hypothesis that a question rarely or obscurely formulated, and a doctrine expressly refuted, could radically determine the Cartesian problematic, can become legitimate only by admitting as well that analogy, which at that time was a theological concept, could still continue to have some play, anonymously, in a context newly philosophic. Etienne Gilson recognized this requirement perfectly: "The fact that in the seventeenth century Descartes and Leibniz had decided to regard as philosophic theses that up until then had qualified as theological does not change their nature. Either they did not become philosophic then, or they were philosophic already. . . . One of the surprises for the historian is to see, passing into the philosophies of the seventeenth century, in revolt against theology, so many of the conclusions obtained in the thirteenth century by theologians who never wanted to be anything else." It is not only a matter of rechristening theses; it can also be a matter of rechristening questions, so that, with the question of analogy becoming, finally, the question of the relation between the finite and the infinite, the isomorphism of the interrogations survives the change of denominations, while being subjected all the while to its effects. Or rather, that we should allow for the hypothesis of such a continuum is what I am calling for. (c) The extent of the original (and strictly Cartesian) break with this continuum implies that one should tease out conceptual rapprochements with earlier authors. Which ones? First of all, there is Suárez of course, because, as Bossuet declares somewhere, one sees in him the summation of the entire School; a judgment Martin Grabmann will confirm in another fashion: "The *Disputationes Metaphysicae* of Suárez present the most detailed systematic exposition of metaphysics ever found."[12] For that matter the precise study of the texts will confirm (if there were any need to do so) the evidence for such a line of descent, which results in a quasi-contemporaneity, and is supported by the pedagogical course of study adopted in the colleges of the Jesuits. Yet one must also take account of the opinions and the authors Suárez cites and expressly controverts in the *Disputationes Metaphysicae*. There is no need at all to maintain that Descartes read Saint Thomas directly (even though he expressly acknowledges having done so), or Duns Scotus, or Ockham, or other authors, in order to admit that he was acquainted with their essential themes; the intermediary of Suárez and the instruction over which he held sway largely suffices for proving a certain familiarity—but here too study of the texts will provide confirmation. Finally, one must take account of more secondary authors that nonetheless Descartes admits to having read or at least skimmed; thus Eustace of Saint Paul,[13] or indeed Charles-Francois d'Abra (Abra de Raconis).[14] I have also gone through other *minores*, contemporaries from the years of Descartes's academic formation: Goclenius (*Lexicon Philosophicum*, Frankfurt, 1613); Scipion Dupleix (*La Métaphysique ou Science surnaturelle*, Paris, 1606); and of course, besides Galileo, Kepler, and Bérulle, all the works Mersenne published before 1630: the *Quaestiones Celeberrimae in Genesim* of 1623; *The Impiety of the Deists, Atheists, and Libertines* of 1624; and the *Truth of the Sciences contra the Skeptics* of 1625. Descartes no doubt never does confirm that he read these works; he even had the cruelty to ensure that, in the case of Mersenne, he had done the opposite;

but besides the fact that here one must take into consideration the coquettish demurrals authors are often prone to, everyone knows that it is not necessary, today as then, to have read a book in order to be under its indirect influence, or still more, to be under the influence of the movement of thought of which that book offers but a symptom. The cultural milieu of the first half of the seventeenth century weighs heavily on Descartes, who (up until 1630, at the least) finds himself defined by it, willy-nilly. As a general rule, I will credit Descartes with the compliment given him by Mersenne, who was in a good position to give it: "Besides, you have pulled off quite a feat . . . in showing that you do not scorn, or at least do not ignore, the philosophy of Aristotle. . . . This is also what I always assure those who believe you understand nothing of scholastic philosophy; but I make sure to tell them that you know it as well as the masters who teach it and who seem the most puffed up with their own abilities,"[15] an opinion that, when all is said and done, only serves to corroborate Descartes's own judgment about himself: "and I saw that they did not regard me as inferior to my fellow students, even though several among them were already destined to take the place of our teachers" (*Discourse*, Part One, AT VI, 5.10–13 = CSM, I, 113). The continuity, without which it would be vain to want to find a Cartesian echo in the question of analogy, depends therefore on three hypotheses, still to be confirmed: (1) that there is a conscious and unconscious destruction of every doctrine of analogy in the Cartesian texts; (2) that it is possible for a theological question to pass into the philosophical domain under another name, indeed under the same name; and finally, (3) that Descartes has knowledge—a much more precise knowledge than one might care to admit—of medieval traditions.

I am trying therefore to renew the hermeneutic device that I have applied to the *Regulae*. In a previous work I had supposed that a constant reference to the thought and text of Aristotle would make it possible to grant the *Regulae* a less marginal status, and to discover in them neither the sketch of an epistemology (that of the *Discourse on Method* and the *Essays*) nor even a completed epistemology, but the subversion of Aristotelian ontology by this epistemology. Put in this perspective, the *Regulae* constitute the gray ontology of Descartes, his general metaphysics.[16] Today, in a similar but more extensive fashion, I would like to apply to the doctrine of the created eternal truths a hermeneutic strategy in which the question of analogy would furnish the constant point of reference. To be sure, instead of only one textual corpus (Aristotle's), here it is necessary to use a corpus that is more wide-ranging and that, though organized around Suárez, goes back through him to other scholastics; moreover, the corpus of reference must be broadened to include some non-scholastic contemporaries of Descartes who also confront the question of analogy, either as theologians (Bérulle, Mersenne) or as physicists (Kepler, Galileo). The difficulty of handling the references nonetheless does not alter the intention: I want to show that within the perspective of the question of analogy, the doctrine of the creation of the eternal truths becomes a theological stance within philosophy; that it definitively determines not only the entire relation between the human and divine knowledge of worldly beings, but also all that is known by man of what later will comprise the threefold domain of special metaphysics (the soul, the world, and God). Thus, answering to the gray ontology that arises from the *Regulae*'s relation to Aristotle would be a determinate (or indeterminate) white/blank theology, based on analogy.[17] Analogy in this way would make it possible to reprise a question about Descartes—the creation of the eternal truths; but it permits this reprise only by itself disappearing, as such.

§2. A Question About Metaphysics: The Creation of the Eternal Truths and the Search for the Foundation

It remains for another question to be immediately unveiled, one that applies more widely, beyond Descartes, to metaphysics. Or rather, it applies to the event that, within metaphysics, Descartes's thought brings about when it first comes on the scene. Actually the historian of philosophy is presented with a threefold event for his consideration; in anticipation of its unfolding, one can formulate it as a continuity, a closure, and an opening.

Continuity. The explanatory model whereby Descartes radically inaugurates modern metaphysics is a caricature that has long since lost its pertinence; and the threads appear ever greater that weave a continuity (even one ripped apart by ruptures) between Descartes and the thought of the Middle Ages. Usually however (save perhaps in the work of the early Koyré) the filiations do not touch on the theological domain, and are spotted only in metaphysics, epistemology, moral philosophy, etc. For, after all, did not Descartes carefully refrain (in intention at least, if not in fact) from all non-philosophical theology?[18] Whence the risk that the study of particular continuities (and of the gaps they manage) could end up reinforcing the impression that the field of thought has, in general, totally changed. Now the historial veering Descartes accomplishes does concern the whole of thought, but it is able to do so only to the exact extent that this veering plays out, concerning every thought, in the theological domain. This evidently does not mean that Descartes signaled a novel preference for secularization, or for its opposite, since these theses (supposing that such a debate, in the history of philosophy, makes any sense) depend on a common manner of asking the question. This question (which alone permits the modern alternative of responses) could not have been altered by Descartes in its subject matter unless he had entered into dialogue with the way in which it was being asked before him. In short, the continuity must be broadened to the theological domain and, within it, must go all the way to the doctrine of analogy. Within this hypothesis, a crucial result would become possible: the modernity that decisively separates rational theology (special metaphysics) from revealed theology (a modernity that runs, roughly speaking, from Descartes to Kant) nonetheless would always remain determined by a question—analogy—proper to Christian theology, since analogy stems from the divine names. Or again, if Descartes puts in place his (special) metaphysics thanks to a debate with the question of analogy, his final position, whatever it might be (including that of a radical and critical modification of all analogy) will inaugurate the whole subsequent problematic, and thus will render it interpretable as a response to the question of analogy. In other words, if it is his debate with analogy that renders Descartes inaugural, then it is this debate that governs as well the posterity Descartes opens. For this reason, even the period of metaphysics that excludes revealed theology from its domain could very well appear as always secretly ruled by, or at least concerned with, revealed theology. The tendency to univocity that characterizes, in different senses, Spinoza, Malebranche, and Leibniz, and which opposes them to the characteristic Cartesian tension towards equivocity, is inscribed in a problematic proper to revealed theology. At no moment, then, would metaphysics cease to maintain with Christianity a relationship of intimate confrontation, no more after Descartes than before him. Such, at least, is one of the stakes of a hermeneutic that interprets the creation of the eternal truths by starting from the question of analogy.

Closure. Paradoxically, this hermeneutic, which claims to over-evaluate the pertinence of analogy for the seventeenth century—as much in Descartes as in Bérulle, Kepler, Mersenne, Galileo, and others—first of all must admit that none of these authors explicitly elaborated a doctrine of analogy. It even seems that after Suárez, no original thinker will invest anything any longer in this doctrine, which disappears little by little behind definitively settled positions. The thought that thinks will no longer think about analogy, or in response to the question of analogy. How does one account for this paradox? By admitting that the question of analogy, like all real questions, can survive in formulations as also in theses that in one moment seem to exhaust it. This displacement of the name, which extends the question without blunting its sharp edge (at least not immediately) is found already in Suárez, for whom analogy is put on the line as much with the problem of the independence and the eternity of truths and logical identities, as it is with the *analogia entis* proper. One could even say that Suárez's march toward univocity is decided much more in his definition of the *ens ut sic* than it is in the fragile and by all appearances diplomatic compromise at which the analogy of intrinsic attribution eventually ends up. All univocity, hence all analogy as a question, is put on the line with the objective concept of being. As much as Bérulle, spiritual author that he is, remains a stranger to an original dogmatics of analogy, so much does his doctrine of emanation, expression, and exemplarism imply in a manner that differs from Suárez but also inevitably, a kind of univocity. As for Mersenne, Kepler, and Galileo, the necessities of a mathematical reading of the physical world, along with their common refusal to accord this reading a hypothetical status only, require them to speak of a "mathematician God" and therefore to accept a univocity for mathematical truths. For God and man understand these truths in one sense only, since, de facto, they admit of only one sense.

Thus does the question of analogy survive the doctrines of analogy, since it extends into these three marches toward univocity: ontological (Suárez), spiritual (Bérulle), epistemological (Mersenne, Kepler, Galileo). The evolution of the lexicon and the displacement of theoretical contexts do not conceal the question of analogy; they only seem to, for they actually attest to its permanence and its pertinence. Besides, when Descartes encounters it, he too treats it according to these three lexicons, and opposes himself to three categories of adversary—whence, moreover, the finally extreme complexity of the letters from 1630, which intertwine three problematics, at least. But in his own refusal of tangential univocity, Descartes formulates the question of analogy in a new lexicon, his own, dominated by the pairs *finite/infinite, created/uncreated, comprehensible/incomprehensible.* Above all—and this is mainly what will allow the edict of 1630 to be deployed in all the metaphysics of 1641 (and later)—he passes from analogy to the foundation. Descartes closes off the question of analogy by opening it up to the question of the foundation, hence by opening the question of the foundation. How should this shift be understood? By way of anticipation, one can foresee that if univocity should no longer secure for human knowledge any immediate relation to the absolute (by reference or by proportion), the absolute equivocity of every measure would then threaten human knowledge with an absolute impertinence that would disqualify all science, even science which is true. One must therefore secure science by an absolute. To secure it—which is to say: to install a relation founded in convention, since only analogy could enable human knowledge to remain in some sort of continuity with divine knowledge. To secure—which is to say: to guarantee knowledge by an authority external to knowledge itself. This discontinuity of founding is doubly opposed to analogy: by discontinuity, but also by what discontinuity implies, namely the indeterminacy of an authority that remains external to the knowledge it makes possible. Passing to the question of the foundation presupposes the search for the foundation. "Search" means not just that the foundation needs to be won, like any other form of knowledge; but that the foundation, because it guarantees from the outside all possible human knowledge, remains definitively foreign to that knowledge, if not unknown to it. The foundation becomes a question for thought only under the figure of the *sought-after* foundation: ἀεὶ ζητούμενον [forever being sought] if not ἀεὶ ἀπορούμενον [forever in a state of aporia].[19] Henceforth the foundation, like analogy, conjugates knowledge and the unknown but in a radically different mode. Passing from one to the other no doubt characterizes the birth of modernity: closure of analogy (as that which mediates knowledge and the absolute by the unknown); opening of the search for the foundation (as that which relates knowledge to the absolute without mediation or continuity). Descartes more than anyone else accomplishes this transition, which is why, if the question of analogy guides a first approach (one in which Descartes exercises a wholesale critique of all univocity), it is necessary, in a second go-round (one in which he tries to secure, with neither univocity nor analogy, knowledge that is certain) to start listening to the question of the foundation.

Opening. If Descartes poses the question of the foundation, he does so by constructing it; and he constructs it only by not answering it in too simple or too quick a fashion—that is, by allowing all of its dimensions to be unfolded. At first the foundation shows up as that which is lacking; the knowledge claimed consists only in "judica absque fundamenta [groundless judgments]," in "Philosophorum rationes . . . (sc. quae) fundamentis nitantur a nemine satis unquam perspectis [arguments of the philosophers . . . (sc. that) are based on foundations no one has ever thoroughly inspected]."[20] The missing foundation can of course be found in the things themselves, as a *fundamentum reale* [a real basis],[21] but in fact the method teaches us to prefer what the mind thinks up from its own fancy (*ex arbitrio excogitare*),[22] hence to privilege a *fundamentum in intellectu* [a basis in our intellect].[23] Whence, in a second moment, the attempt to situate "the foundation of the sciences"[24] in the knowing subject alone, fit for "building on a foundation that is completely my own"[25]; for even if this foundation remains limited by the capacity of the human mind—"fundulus ingenii mei [the meager foundation of my mind],"[26] this slight foundation my mind affords me—it permits universalizing to all knowledge the self-sufficiency of the mathematician: "ipse Mathematicus tanquam αὐτάρκης et se ipso contentus [the mathematician himself as self-sufficient, and content with himself]."[27] Knowledge is founded on a subject that, sufficient though it claims to be, does not for all that warrant the name or the status of an *ego*.

Finally, in a third stage, the creation of the eternal truths intervenes as the discovery of another foundation for knowledge. For in 1630 it really is a matter of the foundation: "and I can say that I would not have been able to discover the foundations of physics if I had not looked for them along that road."[28] After the *Regulae* but before the *Discourse*, Descartes discovers that what later on he will call the *certissima meae Physicae fundamenta* [the most certain foundations of my Physics][29] depend more essentially on God than on the knowing subject, on metaphysics than on the method itself (see §14 below).[30] Should we discern here an evolution that, abandoning the *ego* as a foundation, would make God the foundation instead? Besides the fact that in principle this trivially chronological harmonization would not resolve the theoretical contradiction, at any rate it does not hold up in the face of a remarkable textual fact: the occurrences of *fundamentum* in the *Meditationes* bring together in a single text the three meanings of the foundation. First, weakening the foundations customarily received: "suffosis fundamentis [having undermined the foundations]" (AT VII, 18.11–12 = CSM, II, 12, modified). The doubt triggers the collapse of the foundations, and with them, the whole of knowledge they claimed to make possible; and it remains possible precisely to doubt everything, "quamdiu scilicet non habemus alia scientiarum fundamenta, quam ea quae antehac habuimus [so long as we have no foundations for the sciences other than those which we have had up till now]" (12.3–4 = 9). Nor however is this a pure and simple repetition of the crisis in foundations marked out by the *Regulae*, since no longer does it open out onto just an epistemological subject, but onto the *ego* itself, as that which is metaphysically principial; the *Second Set of Replies* will expressly describe the *ego* with the name foundation: "exponam hīc iterum fundamentum, cui omnis humana certitudo niti posse mihi videtur. . . . Ex his autem quaedam sunt tam perspicua, simulque tam simplicia, ut nunquam possimus de iis cogitare, quin vera esse credamus: ut quod ego, dum cogito, existam [I shall now expound for a second time the basis on which it seems to me that all human certainty can be founded. . . . Now some of these perceptions are so transparently clear and at the same time so simple that we cannot ever think of them without believing that they are true. For example, the fact that I exist so long as I am thinking]" (144.23–25 = 103; 145.23–25 = 104, modified). Will it be necessary to speak here of a *fundamentum inconcussum*, as Heidegger does?[31] On the whole, the *ego* that in thinking (itself), is, certainly acts as an unshakeable foundation; and Descartes freely says as much: "magna quoque speranda sunt, si vel minimum quid invenero quod certum sit et inconcussum [so too I can hope for great things if I manage to find just one thing, however slight, that is certain and unshakeable]" (24.11–13 = 16), "a primis fundamentis denuo inchoandum, si quid aliquando firmum et mansurum . . . in scientiis stabilire [I must start again right from the foundations if . . . to establish anything at all in the sciences that is stable and likely to last]" (17.6–8 = 12, modified), "aliquid certi atque indubitati [something certain and indubitable]" (20.27 = 14). On the other hand, textually speaking it is necessary to emphasize that although the *ego cogito* does indeed meet the requirements for being a "minimum quid . . . quod certum sit et inconcussum [something, however slight, that is certain and unshakeable]," still, in this text no more than in any other (not even in the *Second Set of Replies*!) does it explicitly receive the title *fundamentum*. In the text of Descartes, one word is missing: *fundamentum*. To come to grips with the enigma of this absence is in a sense the whole purpose of my project. In short, why is it that Heidegger was not wrong to twist the Cartesian text, without necessarily really being right in doing so? Answer: because the *ego* lacks the title *fundamentum* at the very moment when it most indisputably fulfills its function. The ego is valid more as the placeholder for the foundation than as the foundation itself, "tanquam scientiae certae fundamenta [as though the foundations of a supremely certain knowledge]" (*Seventh Set of Replies*, 465.23–24 = 313, modified)—as *though* a foundation, without really or expressly constituting a foundation. Thus do the *Meditationes* themselves only half-admit that the *ego* is enough of a foundation. Why? Because, without any doubt, the essence of God is that which in the final analysis exerts the foundation. Like every other truth, the existence of God is *fundata in re positiva* [founded in positive reality]. What *res positiva* [positive thing] can exert the foundation in this way? "[F]undatam in re positiva, nempe in ipsamet Dei immensitate, qua nihil magis positivum esse potest [founded on a positive thing, that is, on the very immensity of God, which is as positive as anything can be]" (*Fourth Set of Replies*, 231.25–232.1 = 162, modified). The foundation passes from the *ego* to God. Or more exactly, it oscillates from one to the other, for the fact that God completes the foundation does not prevent the *ego* from exercising its lieutenancy. And the same text contains the twofold descriptor. One even should wonder—by way of anticipation—whether in a more radical sense the *Meditationes* do not aim (though without planning to, nor perhaps even knowing that they do so) to open up the foundation. To open it up—which is to say: to divide it, to dissociate it from itself, in short to make such an incision in it that one ends up dismembering it. The *Meditationes* construct the question of the foundation only in order to confront the essence of the foundation as a question; whence the duality of two foundations equally possible and alternately real, the *ego* and God. Their ambivalence reveals much more than a conflict and in no way (despite the unfortunate habit of many a critic) could it be reduced to a conflict. The ambivalence points to a possible double identity for the foundation, indicating thereby its constitutive anonymity. If in one and the same text the *fundamentum* is exerted by two authorities, this is because the foundation, in and of itself, can remain undecided even while being exerted. That the exerted foundation remains undecided; that when encountered it remains anonymous, is exactly the paradox that turns the foundation into an intrinsically sought-after foundation. If Descartes opens up the question of the foundation, this is because first of all he opens up the foundation as a question—a question about the infinite and the unknown. And by opening with, and as, the unknown infinite, the question of the foundation actually reprises in its essentials the legacy of the question of analogy. It would remain to be seen if his successors (if at least up until Kant he has had any real successors) will not hasten to close what Descartes opens up with great difficulty and at great risk; that is an inquiry that will have to be taken up elsewhere.

The creation of the eternal truths would become, in this perspective, at once a question and an issue for all of Descartes's thought and for all of modern metaphysics. Let us then test with careful attention what is promised here by way of intention, through examining the two implications of the creation of the eternal truths: the disappearance of analogy, then the search for the foundation.

The Question of the Divine Names

A great divide thus separates the *ego* from itself; or rather, it separates a strictly meta-physical sense of the *ego*—one in which the *ego* exists in the mode of permanent subsistence—from another, rarer and less easily thematizable sense, in which the *ego* harbors possibility and even impossibility. Before we can identify this second face of the *ego*, and in order that we might succeed in doing so, we have to confirm the reality and the legitimacy of such a separation, which claims to manifest nothing less than the limits of metaphysics. Aren't we attributing to Descartes, quite imprudently, either a damaging incoherence or anachronistic investigations? We must therefore repeat the distinction that we thought we recognized between two senses of the *ego*, with an eye toward af-firming or else nullifying it. And we can in fact do so with regard to another being, God. Several observations suggest this possibility to us. (*a*) We saw that the *ego* achieves its metaphysical status, and thus eventually escapes from it, only by starting from the equivalence of thought and Being, which Hegel posited as a fundamental metaphysical thesis. And yet this equivalence, Hegel often insists, does not concern only, nor first of all, the *ego*, but rather God: "the unity of thought and Being. In the form of God no other conception is thus here given than that contained in *Cogito, ergo sum*, wherein Being and thought are inseparably bound up."[1] In short, the theoretical decision that metaphysically institutes the *ego* also metaphysically enthrones God. Consequently, in the same way that they share a similar metaphysical status, they could similarly modify it and eventually transgress it, at least to some extent, which remains to be determined in both cases. (*b*) There is another reason to suspect that God enters into metaphysics equivocally: the redoubling of onto-theo-logy which was made clear earlier (chapter II). In this redoubled onto-theo-logy, God receives not one but two metaphysical positions—first as the most thinkable being, then as the being *causa sui*. This discrepancy calls for clarification all the more as it grows wider on account of a second disharmony: of these two positions, only the second affords God the rank of the being par excellence, of the *causa sui* that, through its effectivity, carries out the universal determination of all beings *ut causatum*; by contrast, in the first position, God does not carry out the universal determination of beings *ut cogitatum*, since he too is no more than a *cogitatum* submitted, despite his divinity, to the being par excellence—the *ego* as the sole *cogitatio sui*. Our inquiry can thus no longer avoid confronting this multifaceted aporia; it must inquire whether or not the two metaphysical names attributed to God can fit together without contradiction, and thus whether or not they exhaust the Cartesian thought of God and limit it strictly to the metaphysical domain marked out by the redoubled onto-theology. (*c*) In fact, seeing as he claimed to have thought the attributes of God, Descartes can be said to have consciously attempted to determine the nature of God through, and also over and above, his existence: "I proved quite explicitly that God was the creator of all things, and I proved all his other attributes at the same time."[2] Admitting the idea of God necessarily implies that one admits the divine attributes. He who denies this implication contradicts himself: "How could he affirm that these attributes [infinity, incomprehensibility] belong to him, and countless others which express his greatness to us, unless he had the idea of him?" Accordingly, the attributes are as inseparable from the idea of God as the idea of God is from the attributes: "It would be no good saying that we believe that God exists and that some attribute or perfection belongs to him; this would be to say nothing, because it would convey no meaning to our mind. Nothing could be more impious or impertinent."[3] Consequently, the idea of God can be known—and in point of fact we do know it, "Habemus autem ideam Dei [we have an idea of God]" (AT VII, 167, 17 = PW II, 118)—only if the attributes are set forth in the light of clear evidence. In consequence, the *Meditationes* will investigate "de singulis Dei attributis, quorum aliquod in nobis vestigium agnoscimus [the individual attributes of God of which we recognize some trace in ourselves]" (137, 13–14 = 98) by starting from the presupposition that "intelligamus existentiam actualem necessario et semper cum reliquis Dei attributis esse conjunctam [We understand that actual existence is necessarily and always conjoined with the other attributes of God]" (117, 6–7 = 83); thus that, inversely, the existence of God cannot be separated from the other attributes and in fact even demands that they be studied. When the existence of God is established for the first time, it provokes contemplation, but an act of contemplation whose scope is immediately enlarged to include the attributes: "in ipsius Dei contemplation immorari, ejus attributa apud me expender [I should like to pause here and spend some time in the contemplation of God; to reflect on his attributes]" (52, 12–13 = 36). When God's existence is established for the second time, this time by means of a demonstration, Descartes mentions the divine attributes in advance: "Multa mihi supersunt de Dei attributis investiganda [There are many matters which remain to be investigated concerning the attributes of God]" (63, 4–5 = 44). Given that the examination of God's attributes makes up an integral part of the attempt to demonstrate his existence, when Descartes studies them, he should make a decision, a clearer one than we have yet seen, about God's essence; therefore, according to the terms of our investigation, he should also make a decision about the coherence of the disparate definitions applied to God, and, eventually, about their belonging—or not—to the metaphysics designated by the redoubled onto-theology of the *cogitation* and the *causa*. (*d*) A final argument could, though it remains extrinsic, confirm our claim. Descartes once acknowledges in passing that he has "said nothing about the knowledge of God except what all the theologians say too."[4] While in context this statement concerns the possibility of a natural knowledge of God, in general it is also possible to understand this protestation as the sign of a discussion or at least a tacit confrontation with the theologians of his day—in particular a discussion concerning the determination of the divine attributes. How could Descartes have entirely ignored the celebrated theological debates of his time? We here suggest one hypothesis in particular: a Jesuit, Lessius, former student of Suárez, born in Anvers (in 1554) and died in Louvain (in 1623), after a brilliant teaching career not without its share of famous controversies, had published a treatise *De perfectionibus moribusque divinis* (Anvers, 1620; Paris, 1620), then, posthumously, at the same time as the *Meditationes* were being edited, a treatise on the *Quinquaginta nomina Dei* (Brussels, 1640). Without claiming that Descartes was directly influenced by these texts (which no argument could suggest), nor even that he read them seriously, we will not rule out the possibility that he was aware of them, at least indirectly (and experience shows, time and again, that this sort of relation is not the weakest). This rapprochement could have a twofold usefulness: first of all, it would permit a comparison, on certain delicate matters, between Descartes's decisions about the divine attributes and those of an acknowledged theologian; next and above all, it would permit reconsidering the Cartesian project—to give metaphysically rigorous names to God and to the God of the Christian revelation—within the ongoing theological debate that plays itself out in the treatise on the divine names and that, inaugurated thematically by Dionysius the Areopagite, traverses the entire Middle Ages until it finds one of its last notable representatives precisely in the person of Lessius.[5] What appears notable is Lessius's insistence on maintaining the Dionysian distinction between, one the one hand, knowledge of God "by affirmations or positive concepts" and, on the other, knowledge by "negations or negative concepts." This couple allows God to be named

> most sublime, best, greatest, eternal, most powerful, wisest, kindest, holiest, most just, most merciful, most beautiful, present to all things, inward creator of all, the fashioner, conserver, governor, and ordainer of all things to his glory as their first principle and their ultimate end,

just as well as, inversely, he can be named

> infinite, immense, eternal, infinitely raised above all perfection, excellence and magnitude conceivable by a created mind: beyond all substance, all power, all wisdom, all understanding, all light, all beauty, all holiness, all justice, all goodness, all beatitude, all glory; in such a way that he is properly speaking none of these things, like unto none among them and infinitely more sublime and more elevated than them.[6]

This twofold pronouncement defines the horizon within which the Cartesian determination of God's attributes appears not only more understandable (in its innovations as well as its repetitions), but above all as a kind of treatise on the divine names. In short, we propose to try reading the Cartesian discussion of the attributes of God as a metaphysical repetition of the theological treatise on the divine names. Only on this condition will it become possible to answer the crucial question: how and within what limits does God enter, with Descartes's redoubled onto-theo-logy, into metaphysics? More than just an arbitrary appeal, the comparison with Lessius makes up an invaluable landmark. And moreover, it seems to us even less illegitimate since, among other points in common, Lessius and Descartes closely link infinity to incomprehensibility. When Descartes retorts to Gassendi that "idea enim infiniti ut sit vera, nullo modo debet comprehendi, quoniam ipsa incomprehensibilitas in ratione formali infiniti continetur [The idea of infinity, if it is to be a true idea, cannot be grasped at all, since the impossibility of being grasped is contained in the formal definition of the infinite]" (368, 2–4 = 253), he seems to be citing Lessius: "Deum ratione suae infinitatis esse incomprehensibilem [God is incomprehensible by definition of his infinity]."[7] For these four reasons, the determination of God's essence becomes a fundamental task when assessing the Cartesian constitution of metaphysics.

The *Meditationes* evoke the name or the names of God from their very beginning, the raising of universal doubt. However, no explicit definition of God is fixed at that time—for rigorous reasons that will be made more clear below. It is only with *Meditatio III* that, in order to support the proof for God's existence, developed formulations of the essence and the attributes of God appear. As a result, Descartes enters, consciously or not (it matters little), into the debate about the divine names. Let us therefore read the two formulae introduced here. Here is the first definition:

> [1] . . . illa [idea] per quam minimum aliquem Deum, aeternum, infinitum, omniscium, omnipotentem, rerumque omnium, quae praeter ipsum sunt creatorem intelligo [the idea that gives me my understanding of a supreme God, eternal, infinite, omniscient, omnipotent and the creator of all things that exist apart from him]. (AT VII, 40, 16–18 = 28)

Here is the second formulation:

> [2] Dei nomine intelligo substantiam quondam infinitam, independentem, summe intelligentem, summe potentem, et a qua tum ego ipse, tum aliud omne, si quid aliud extat, quodcumque extat est creatum [By the word 'God' I understand a substance that is infinite, independent, supremely intelligent, supremely powerful, and which created both myself and everything else (if anything else there be) that exists]. (45, 11–44 = 31)

These two pronouncements, which we will cite from now on as [1] and [2], are framed by the so-called proof for the existence of God by effects, which opens just before [1]— "Sed alia quaedam via mihi occurrit [But it now occurs to me that there is another way]" (40, 5 = 27)—and closes a little after [2], "Ideoque ex antedictis Deum necessario existere, est concluendum [So from what it has been said it must be concluded that God necessarily exists]" (45, 17–18 = 31). This quite clearly delimited situation immediately gives rise to a difficulty, itself multifaceted: obviously [1] and [2] come up only within the second onto-theo-logy, since [l] appears on the same page in which there also arise, in a tremendous relaunching of the *ordo rationum*, *substantia* (40, 12 = 28) and the principle of universal causality (40, 21–23 = 28). What thread connects these three theses, if their textual proximity is not conceptually just by chance? Is the validity of the divine attributes advanced by [1] and [2] limited to the onto-theo-logy of the *ens ut causatum* alone, or do they exceed it in advance? For that matter, can [1] and [2], which are introduced by one and the same *intelligo*, claim to offer a real definition of God and his attributes, or must they be proposed simply as working hypotheses?[8] In this case, how are we to understand that this idea of God can at once remain hypothetical and be actually given to us— "Si detur Dei idea (ut manifestum est illam dari) [if we do have an idea of God— and it is manifest that we do]" (183, 21 = 129), "Habemus autem ideam Dei [We have an idea of God]" (167, 17=118)? Such difficulties can find neither a rapid nor an easy resolution; they call for a detailed examination of each of the attributes successively mentioned by [1] and [2]. Only once such an examination has been performed will the objection of incoherence (*inconsistency*) be able to receive something more than a formal or superficial confirmation or nullification—a carefully considered validation, historically and conceptually carefully considered.[9] Let us therefore retrace, step by step, the terms attributed to God by [1] and [2], with an eye toward testing their many coherences or incoherences and reconstituting their partial necessities.

Quaedam [*substantia*]. This announces, as the first determination of God, indetermination itself. The two formulae agree in this. *Quaedam* [2] (45, 11) in effect corresponds to *aliquis* [*Deus*] in [1] (40, 16). Though the French translation hides it behind a simple indefinite article (*un/une*, AT IX–2, 32, 5 and 35, 41), this indetermination constantly determines all the previous places where God is mentioned in the *Meditationes*; or rather, all the places where Descartes suggests a definition of what, before the first demonstration of the existence of the true God, could lay claim to this title. Two occurrences confirm this claim. The first is found at the end of *Meditatio I*. When Descartes constructs hyperbolic doubt by invoking, equally and indifferently, the two contrary hypotheses of an omnipotent God and an evil genius, he nonetheless gathers them together in the imprecise phrase "tam potentem aliquem Deum [some God so powerful];" a phrase that is not rendered in the French translation (21, 17–18 = 14 [modified]). Next, when *Meditatio III* in its opening stages recalls the situation at which *Meditatio I* ended up, it again evokes "aliquem Deum [some God]" (36, 11 = 25); "quelque Dieu" translates the French (AT IX–1, 28, 36). The indetermination would not be marked so consistently if it did not have an essential function. In fact, it has several. First, during each moment of the rational proceedings that precede the first proof for the existence of a God, Descartes reasons without yet having a precise concept of God; or to say it more precisely, he hesitates between several hypotheses: a God who can do everything, thus one who also allows me to deceive myself (21, 1–16 14); a *Deus fictitius* (21, 20 = 14) who can be identified indifferently with destiny (*fatum*, ἀναγκὴ) or with chance (*casus*, τύχη) or with the necessary order of nature (21, 20–21 = 14), in short with any mode of deception whatsoever ("seu quo visalio modo [or by some other means];" 21, 21–22 = 14); and finally, an evil genius who is himself indefinite ("genium aliquem malignum [some evil genius]," 22, 24 = 15 [modified], rendered in French by "un certain mauvais genie," AT IX–1, 17, 37). This indefinite evil genius can be imagined only insofar as the concept of God invoked up until now has itself remained fundamentally undetermined. And moreover, the entire second *Meditatio* works within the determinate hypothesis of a de-cidedly indeterminate God; the *ego* found itself certain of itself only by struggling against an uncertain God. Whence these decidedly undecided denominations: "est aliquis Deus, vel quocumque nomine illum vocem [is there not some God, or whatever I may call him]" (24, 21–22 = 16 [modified], translated in French by "quelque Dieu," AT IX–1, 19, 19); by virtue of the same indefiniteness, this can also become "deceptor nescio quis [I know not what deceiver]" (25, 6 = 17 [modified], or "je ne sais quell trompeur," AT IX–1, 19, 30), therefore properly *deceptor aliquis* [some deceiver] (26, 24 = 18, or "quelqu'un qui est," AT IX–1, 21, 3–4). In fact, before the proof by effects, Descartes does not base his reasoning on the hypothesis of God, nor on that of the evil genius, chance, necessity, or destiny; he bases it solely on the determined hypothesis of some-thing undetermined. The sole point that all of these hypotheses have in common is to be found in their very indetermination. Before the proof by effects, the *ego* confronts only an adversary hidden by his very indetermination, one that, for each proper name, is named only with a name so common that it is not even a name: *aliquis*. Therefore, when the definition advanced by *Meditatio III,* in [1] as much as in [2], opens with a marker of indeterminacy, it is not saying nothing: it sums up in a single word the only characteris-tic proper to the previous hypotheses—their radical impropriety. *Aliquis* in [2] does not add indetermination to the subsequent list of qualifiers so much as it opposes the inde-termination previously established as the sole determination to the determinations yet to come. About what he attempts for the first time to define categorically as God (and no longer merely as anything whatsoever that can be defined, so long as it is other than the ego), Descartes first says the only thing that experience has, as of now, taught him about it: namely, that it is indeterminate. By God, I mean an undetermined someone, *aliquis*. Here, it is not the *ego* who can say "larvatus pro deo [I come forward masked]" (AT X, 213, 6–7 = PW I, 2), but God who, like Voëtius later, "in me non prodeat nisi per-sonatus [does not come forward against me except in disguiser]" (AT VIII–2, 7–8 = not included in PW). God comes to the *ego* only hidden beneath the mask of the role (persona) that he has until now been playing in the theater of the previous *Meditationes*—that of an *aliquis*. In short, God appears beneath the most dissimulating mask, that of the most total indetermination. In contrast with theology, which proffers negations of God only after having exhausted the affirmations, here the *ego* begins by saying of God that he is named *nescio quis* [I know not what], a *je ne sais qui*: negative philosophy, in which one must acknowledge the echo, no doubt barely conscious, of the negating mo-ment in the divine names: "All things are denied of him because he is higher than all rea-son and all species comprehensible by a created mind," Lessius said.[10] Descartes, however, stands apart from the more common opinion that Lessius has formulated: first because he starts with indetermination, instead of reaching it after affirmations have been denied each in their turn; next because he practices the denegating indetermination with pen-ury, not with excess. That is to say, indetermination holds the place of the affirmations provisionally; it does not correct them after they have been uttered. The negative mo-ment thus loses its theological originality. Far from leading to the overcoming of pred-icative and categorical discourse in general, the negative moment intends such discourse and always strives for it, all the more so when it clearly designates its absence. In this, one has the feeling that affirmations can be established further along, that there is no negation or indetermination that will not be alleviated—thus opening the metaphysical discourse on the essence of God to the threat of idolatry.

However, indetermination is justified by its fulfilling a second function. Hyperbolic doubt can exert its radical *épochè* over genuine science (for it destroys Cartesian science itself)[11] only by confusing two different characteristics. There must first of all be an authority that offers enough omnipotence to disqualify all mathematical and rational logic. Next, it must be the case that this authority, itself absolutely unsurpassable, pass beyond the humanly unsurpassable conditions of science, thus that it be identified, in one way or another, with God. And yet, upon serious reflection, it is seen that these two characteristics are contradictory. In effect, as soon as their utmost consequences have been developed, they can be uttered in the untenable paradox of a deceptive omnipotence, directly (evil genius) or indirectly (omnipotent God who created the conditions of my self-deception). As soon as one poses the question of logical possibility and noncontradiction, the initial hypothesis of the *Meditationes* appears to be not only hyperbolic, but also incoherent. And Descartes does not hide this fact either: outside the strict boundaries of the provisional *ordo rationum*, he will always respond to the objections of atheism by claiming that an omnipotent God can neither deceive, nor let one deceive oneself:

> Et ineptumest quod subjungit, nempe *Deum ut deceptorem cogitari.* Et sienim, in prima mea Meditatione, de aliquot deceptore summe potenti locutus sim, nequaquam tamen ibi verus Deus concipiebatur, quia ut ipse [Voëtius] ait, fieri non potest ut verus Deus sit deceptor. Atque si ab eo petatur unde sciat id fieri non posse, debet responderese scire ex eo quod implicet contradictionem in conceptu, hoc est, ex eo quod concipi non possit.

> (He claims that in my philosophy) "God is thought of as a deceiver." This is foolish. Although in my First Meditation I did speak of a supremely powerful deceiver, the conception there was in no way of the true God, since, as he [Voëtius] himself says, it is impossible that the true God should be a deceiver. But if he is asked how he knows this is impossible, he must answer that he knows it from the fact that it implies a conceptual contradiction—that is it cannot be conceived.

Or, according to Burman's testimony, "Loquitur hīc auctor [Descartes] contradictoria cum summa potential malignitas consistere non potest [What the author (Descartes) says here is contradictory, since malice is incompatible with supreme power]." Finally: "auctor contradictoria loquitur, si dicat potentis simum et malignum, quia potentia et malignitas simul consistere non possunt [If he calls it both most powerful and malicious, the author contradicts himself since power and malice are incompatible with each other]."[12] And yet it is precisely this conceptual contradiction that is called for, at least provisionally, by the unfolding of the *Meditationes*; but to make such a notion bearable, simply as a hypothesis not yet contested, it must be toned down, indeed dissimulated. This is precisely how the indeterminacy of an *aliquis* functions. The debate about the omnipotence of God being opposed (or not) to the merely very great power of the evil genius—however much it might be highly instructive—has in the end only something very limited at stake in it;

and the same is true of the general distinction between these two engines of hyperbolic doubt. For despite their being incompatible by right, a single indetermination is enough for them to be confounded in the same role, as provisional as it is unified.[13]

But there is more. The indetermination also permits, though again provisionally, another difficulty to be removed. One could and even should raise an objection to the primacy of indetermination as the first determination of what lays claim to the title *God*. In effect, the evil genius, the *Deus fictitius*, chance, necessity, and destiny come up only on account of a single common point—namely, the function of omnipotence, through which, whatever they might be, they could disqualify the evidence of order and measure. Omnipotence would thus precede indetermination, and nothing would be submitted to indetermination except for the sake of coming under the sway of power. In fact, as we will soon see, omnipotence constitutes an essential qualification of the Cartesian God. But one must ask what right it has to enter—before all clear and distinct knowledge of the essence as well as the existence of God—the *ordo rationum*. Whence comes the fact that before envisaging God in the strict sense and as such, it is already possible and even permissible to mobilize the idea of an omnipotent God? Descartes's response is always the same: "Verumtamen infixa quaedam est meae menti vetus opinio, Deum esse qui potest omnia [And yet firmly rooted in my mind is the long-standing opinion that there is an omnipotent God]" (21, 1– 2 = 14) says *Meditatio I*, which the parallel text in *Meditatio III* will take over: "haec praeconcepta de summa Dei potential opinio [my preconceived opinion as to the supreme power of God]" (36, 8–9 = 25 [modified]). Omnipotence qualifies something like God, but only by way of an opinion; and for that matter, it could even be demonstrated that such an equivalence finds its origin in the nominalism of William of Ockham.[14] But the only thing that is important to us here is the modality according to which a positive doctrine, thus one foreign to the *ordo rationum*, can get mixed up in this *ordo*. It enters in the mode of *opinio*, that is to say, of a confused, not rationally determined thought having neither origin nor reason—in short, it enters as an undetermined thought. Omnipotence thus only apparently precedes indetermination, since in fact only its indetermination can permit omnipotence to enter into the *ordo rationum*, as an opinion with neither genealogy nor status.

Thus, by opening the list of divine names and attributes with the reticence of an *aliquis/quaedam*, Descartes is not simply signaling the inevitably provisional character of a definition that still awaits an answer to the question *quid sit* as well as *an sit*. To understand this, one has only to compare his work to that of Suárez. To be sure, when Suárez comes up against the impossibility of defining God, he too will immediately have recourse to a *praeconceptio* in order to continue his reasoning: "nevertheless, for us to be able to reason about God, it is certainly necessary to presuppose and have a preconception (*praeconcipere*) as to what this word means." But for Suárez, the *praeconceptio* has a function that is the inverse of the role it plays for Descartes: it precedes and introduces a correct and universally admissible nominal definition of God, far from making provisionally possible an inadmissible contradiction: "For this name signifies a certain (*quoddam*) very noble being, one who surpasses all the others, and all depend on it as on their first author, who, for that very reason, must be served and worshipped as the supreme divinity. This is in effect the ordinary and so to speak first concept that we all form when we hear the name of God."[15] No doubt Suárez's pre-comprehension, like the Cartesian *praeconcepta opinio*, introduces a vague and indeterminate concept of God. But while in Descartes this indeterminate concept is contradictory, provisional, and false, in Suárez it is already correct, thus, in this sense, definitive and established. In the context of Descartes's thought, indetermination makes up an integral part of the concept, which would collapse without it. Accordingly, the genuine concept of God, if one can be found, will have to be won by starting with an already constitutive and forever irreducible indetermination. Imprecision belongs to the concept of God, intrinsically— either for the sake of dissimulating its impossibility during hyperbolic doubt or for the sake of permitting its sudden irruption in the renewal of the *ordo rationum*. Thus a new task imposes itself on us: it is no longer a matter of interpreting the indetermination that constitutes the concept of God as the condition for the possibility of a logical and theological impossibility; rather, it is a question of interpreting this indetermination as the path to a new conceptual situation. The fact that formulas [1] and [2] show up in the same passage where the first occurrence of *substantia* appears now takes on its full meaning: indetermination, preliminary determination of God, in effect opens onto substance.

Does the *Ego* Alter the Other?

The Solitude of the Cogito *and the Absence of* Alter Ego

"Since my supposition there [in my Meditations*] was that no other human beings were yet known to me"* (PW II, 102)

1. From the Egoism of the Self to the Primacy of the *Ego*

"The self is hateful . . . if I hate it because it is unjust that it should make itself the center of everything, I shall go on hating it."[1] Pascal's abrupt pronouncement is rarely given the conceptual consideration it deserves. One may undoubtedly detect in it the thought of a moralist or even perhaps a theologian, but that would be limiting its relevance; for even when one does not go so far as to denounce it as some sort of "pessimism" supposedly deriving from a conventional "Augustinianism," his thesis is not granted any validity outside the realm of practical reason. Pascal would seem to condemn, judiciously though perhaps excessively, the egoism of a self that claims itself as the center of love. Now the strength of Pascal's pronouncement stems, on the contrary, from the fact that this is not a moral attitude assumed by the self in a free decision that it could reverse by means of a little altruism; such an inversion, Pascal states in advance, would suppress, by means of courtesy, the "inconvenience" but not the "injustice." The self makes its unjust claim—to be the focus of everyone's love—less inconvenient but on the contrary more real. The more the self manages to be loved by all without constraint and by using seduction, the more it commits an injustice—for it obviously does not deserve to be loved by all, insofar as it remains finite, imperfect, hateful, etc. The self cannot cease to be unjust, even if it may cease to be inconvenient; a free decision can alter the inconvenience, but not the injustice of the egoism of the self. In other words, the self is not free to entirely free itself from its own egoism: Morally, it may overcome the inconvenience of egoism—that is to say, the external appearance it offers to the gaze of others (which, in this regard, is real) but not its injustice, that is to say, the intimate constitution of the self by itself (and according to which it appears to itself). Relative and moral egoism conceals an absolute egoism, to be taken in the extramoral sense of the term. The self suffers from and enjoys, indivisibly, an original, extramoral, and premoral egoism that is both involuntary and constitutive, one that we can "always" stigmatize for it "always" precedes the purely moral denunciation. I am not free, nor is the self within me, to be unjustly egoistical, for if I were not egoistical, I would simply not be, since I exist only through the *ego*. Pascal stresses that the egoism of the self does not simply, or primarily, result from a secondary and "moral" decision of the "subject," but that it radically amounts to the definition of man as "subject" or more precisely (for the "subject," far from directing it, undergoes this revolution) as *ego*. If man defines himself to himself as an *ego* that relates to itself constantly through its *cogitatio*, he must establish himself as the single and necessary center of any possible world. "Of any world" signifies, first and foremost, of the world of the objects of a now unified science, but also of the world of the supposed "subjects," more often termed the world of the "loved objects." In short, the self-referential establishment of the *ego cogito* (*me cogitate rem*) is not only a concern of the theoretical realm of knowledge (as explicitly developed by Descartes), it also is the arbiter of the so-called practical realm (which may in fact be just as theoretical) of acknowledgment of and by others. Pascal, in the curt and misunderstood pronouncement quoted above, refers the usual worldly and moral egoism to its contemporary and Cartesian foundation: The determination of man as an *ego* determines all his behaviors from the start. Moreover, while this ensures the unity of the *mathesis universalis* in the theoretical realm, it imposes on man an egoism of principle in the practical domain. In short, moral egoism necessarily results from an extramoral determination; Pascal's condemnation is aimed not at a perverted liberty but rather at a metaphysical necessity. For metaphysics does not remain a neutrality that cannot be apprehended by Pascal's gaze: Egoism, if it results from the theoretical establishment of the *ego* as definition of man, nevertheless affects negatively the very possibility of an access to the other as such. The metaphysics of the *ego*, as elaborated by Descartes, radicalizes egoism and deepens the inaccessibility of the other, by transposing egoism and inaccessibility from moral liberty to the extramoral necessity of the first principle. The fact that egoism has now deepened toward the extramoral status of a metaphysical foundation does not void the legitimacy of an axiological questioning; on the contrary, the metaphysical foundation as such seems subject to the examination of a new authority. In Pascal's own terms, we should say that metaphysics, understood as the second order—of minds organized starting from the figure of the *ego* of the *cogito*—finds itself exposed to charity, understood as the third order.[2]

I will not outline here the complex connections between Pascal and Descartes. But by using Pascal's statement concerning any *ego* in general, it is possible to reach the theoretical locus where a question concerning the communication between consciousnesses in a subjective realm would become intelligible and correct. This question could be formulated as follows: As soon as the *ego* (*cogito*) guarantees, independently and definitively, the "one thing . . . that is certain and unshakeable [minimum quid . . . quod certum sit et inconcussum]" (AT VII, 24, ll. 12–13)[3]—as soon, therefore, as any other certain knowledge depends upon the cogitating *ego*, as one of its *cogitationes* in the realm of the already transcendental subjectivity—do other minds remain conceivable in general and accessible to the *ego* in particular? Put differently, does the *ego*, which enjoys an uncontested metaphysical and epistemological primacy, acknowledge other "subjects" that are not directly dependent on it as so many "objects"? In short, is not the reproach addressed by Pascal to the self—namely, that it exercises a radical injustice by establishing itself at the center of everything—fully confirmed in the case of the *ego*, which defines itself in principle as the center of what it now reduces and constructs as its objects? For, in order to permit communication between minds (*mentes*), each mind must appear as such—that is to say, as prior to and radically distinct from any object that it knows and constructs. *Mens* can appear as a mind only if it does not immediately disappear in the common self-evidence reserved to directly visible objects; *mens* remains invisible in the light of representation, precisely because it exercises and produces this light to bring objects into focus. For the *ego*, gaining access to other minds (*mentes*) implies moving beyond the usual light of the *intuitus* (*mentis*) so that, aiming beyond the visible, it may reach, in a light that is opaque to any objectifying representation, other *mentes* seen as such, that is to say, as they themselves also see.[4] In more directly Cartesian terms, we may ask whether and how the *ego* (*cogito*) sees other minds, if not other *ego*s. In order to pose this question and attempt to answer it, we will proceed in a very straightforward manner—by examining whether the *ego* (*cogito*) admits and encounters other *mentes* throughout the *ordo rationum* of the *Meditations*. It is therefore a question of reading the *Meditations* again—not according to the goal it sets for itself, but according to the goal that by definition surpasses objectivity, namely, the otherness of the mind, the mind of the other.

2. The Reduction of Others

The *Meditations* explicitly sets out to demonstrate with certainty the existence of God and the immortality of the *mens humana* (or at least its actual distinction from the body); this acknowledged aim is characterized from the outset by an omission, that of separate intelligences, which typically found their place in contemporary treatises on special metaphysics. Now, these separate intelligences included other human minds as well as angels: Why does Descartes eliminate, from the very title of the *Meditations* onward, such a privileged access to intersubjectivity? A factual answer can be proposed immediately: Descartes correctly rejected the title of *Metaphysica* (which implies separate intelligences) for that of *prima Philosophia*, since in his mind the latter does not "confine [the] discussion to God and the soul but deals in general with all the first things to be discovered by philosophizing" and, he adds, "by philosophizing in an orderly way."[5] This answer, however, simply raises the question anew: How can it be that the existence of other, separate intelligences (separate from the body, like the *mens humana*) is actually not one of the "first things to be discovered by philosophizing in an orderly way"? The existence of the other would therefore not find its place among the priorities of first philosophy. Before we can even begin to attempt to solve it, this radical paradox needs to be confirmed by texts, for it seems utterly improbable that the *Meditations* would remain silent on the existence of the other—of a subject other than the one who says *ego* (and says that it is an *ego*). Actually, minds other than the *ego* do appear in the *Meditations*, in *Meditation I* in particular, but they do so only to disappear immediately when radical doubt is brought to bear. Others emerge, first as madmen (AT VII, 18, I. 26) who are immediately rejected as mindless (*amentes*, 19, 1. 5). Unlike the demented (*demens*, 19, I. 6) who put their damaged mind (*mens*) to poor use, they have no mind, they have lost it, and with it, almost their humanity: As *amentes*, they do not exhibit other minds that could be compared to mine, which thereby remains unique. Do others emerge in the painters (19, 1. 31) mentioned next? No, for this is only an epistemological model, designed to allude to the Cartesian doctrine of perception, and not an existential observation establishing the existence of other *egos*.[6] Do others surface in those (*nonnulli*, 21, 1. 17) who prefer to escape hyperbolic doubt by admitting any lower principle other than an omnipotent God? Obviously not, for this is the doxographic origin of other theses and not an existential assumption. There remain those who are mistaken, and truly mistaken: "others [who] go astray in cases where they think they have the most perfect knowledge" (21, II. 8–9). The fact remains that they go astray, especially insofar as they are not aware of their own errors, and therefore they forfeit all certainty about what they believe they see as well as about what they are; they thus disappear completely from the theoretical horizon now opened by doubt and its constraints. *Meditation I* thus mentions four potential figures of the other, only to reject them one after another; others are acknowledged only to be eliminated. Outside of myself, there are "no minds [nullas mentes]" (25, II. 3–4).

Yet one might object that the elimination of others in *Meditation I* could be a temporary negation that prepares for a subsequent restoration, similar to the restorations enjoyed successively by the *ego* (in *Meditation II*), God (in *Meditation III*), mathematical truths (in *Meditation V*), and the physical world (in *Meditation VI*). This would be the most elegant and satisfactory hypothesis; yet it is flawed, because it is not supported by the texts. *Meditation IV*, although it sets forth a doctrine of error by invoking the finiteness of my understanding, does not attempt even a sketch of an intersubjective definition of truth: The mention of the "whole universe [omnis universitas rerum] (55, 1. 28 = 61, 1. 21) in no way announces an intersubjective constitution of the world. *Meditation VI*, which could reestablish others, as it reestablishes the world of the senses and sensation dismissed by *Meditation I*, remains astonishingly silent on the occurrences of other *mentes* that were called into doubt: Madmen, mistaken folk, even painters are not mentioned; the case of the man afflicted with dropsy is discussed, but only insofar as it represents a human body in general—"the body of a man [hominis corpus]" (84, 11. 19–20), "a body suffering from dropsy [corpus hydrope laborans]" (85, 11. 18–19). The human body proper is admitted as self-evident, but never another person; the other *mens* is conspicuous by its complete absence. If the order of reasons restores to reason what it had earlier called into doubt, it does not restore everything; one thing at least has definitively disappeared, the only thing that precisely cannot be called a thing: the other as such, as *mens* other than *ego*. The other has lost *mens*, and insofar as it was, based on the hypothesis, exhausted in *mens*, it is entirely lost. The exclusion of *amentes* from *Meditation I* not only represents the potential exclusion of "madmen" from the newly delimited realm of reason, it also amounts to the disappearance of the very mention made by the order of reasons of minds other than that of the *ego*. More than simply "madmen," it is "others" who lose their mind. Is *amens* the only name under which *ego cogito* acknowledges others, thereby monopolizing for itself the title of *mens humana* by reducing it to the nominative singular? In other words, does not the warning of the *Second Set of Replies*—"in my *Meditations*, since my supposition there was that no other human beings were yet known to me" (142, 11. 26–28; see 361, II. 16ff = IX, I, 112, ll. 15–17)—describe a final situation, the irreversible suspension of any otherness, rather than simply a temporary episode?

Confirmation of the refusal to acknowledge the other as another *mens* can come only from the examination of the few texts in which Descartes confronts the gaze of the other, obliquely, and as a result of other questionings. These texts are few, but they converge toward the same thesis. Let us follow them.

(a) *Meditation II* establishes the anteriority of *inspectio mentis* over sentient sensation in any perception; it adds a second experiment after the famous analysis of the piece of wax: "And this might lead me to conclude without more ado that knowledge of the wax comes from what the eyes see, and not from the scrutiny of the mind alone. But then if I look out of the window and see men crossing the square, as I just happen to have done, I normally say that I see the men themselves, just as I say that I see the wax. Yet do I see any more than hats and coats which could conceal automatons? I *judge* that they are men. And so something which I thought I was seeing with my eyes is in fact grasped solely by the faculty of judgment which is in my mind" (32, ll. 4–12; original emphasis). The *ego* sees men, "real men." Should we then conclude that it acknowledges their presence in all otherness? The opposite is true, and for several reasons.

First, since seeing men (*homines respicere*) is here a strict parallel to seeing the wax (*ceram visione oculi*), the difference between the extended and the animate in no way affects the single action of seeing, which is accomplished by the *ego* in the same way for the human and for the nonhuman. Second, and especially, seeing men and identifying them as men does not result from the appearance in the visible realm of the otherness of other consciousnesses—truly other, for they are themselves *egos* and, as such, irreducible to the consciousness of the *ego* who sees them. On the contrary, those who are here supposed to be others appear only through a decision that the *ego* pronounces on its own, and by which it identifies them unilaterally; men are men not because they make themselves known to the *ego*, but because the *ego* decides that they are men, and decides for them and in their absence, according to the same procedures by which it establishes that the wax is what it is. Men are like wax for the *ego*'s gaze—wax without extension. Or, rather, men and wax are summed up in what the *ego* decides about them.

Third, more loosely, we could thus comment on the Cartesian reduction of "men": Wax, which is absolutely malleable, has just been subdued by the *ego*; the *ego* uses wax a second time to think "men"—exactly as if it modeled in wax the face to be added to automatons to create the illusion of living beings. Wax and clothing: These are in fact what museums use to exhibit *false* persons. Gazing at these models with almost human faces, these dummies of wax, we indeed have to use our judgment to reestablish the truth—that they are not real persons. That which allows us to unmask wax dummies also lets the *ego* judge that the automatons are actually real persons. Humanity is established in the court of reason, by an arbitrary and irreversible sentence: "I *judge* that they are men [judico homines esse]" (32, l. 10). Humanity is indeed conceded to these men, but at the price of their otherness, since the *ego* grants it to them *proprio motu*, in a sentence that turns them into objects like wax and therefore denies their intrinsic and irreducible otherness. Others may indeed enter into the field of vision of the *intuitus* and find their humanity confirmed there, but they will have to undergo the treatment common to all the potential objects of the *ego*: to let themselves be judged by "this mind itself, that is . . . me myself" (33, ll. 1–2), in order to let themselves be put on display with "[their] clothes off [*vestibus detractis*]" and "naked" (32, ll. 25–26). Men receive the title of "real men" (AT IX = I, 25, 20) because the *ego* strips them of their coats and hats, and above all of their otherness; upon entering the field of the *intuitus*, they become objects, they inherit their identity from it and lose their originating phenomenal initiative that by which they discover themselves to be what they think they are. Their humanity remains borrowed, a concession, a restoration—like a face made out of wax that lends itself to our gaze but that cannot see. People have no more of a face than wax does. This is a reduction of otherness to objectivity, whereby the other becomes even more invisible insofar as it is masked by the visible evidence of its judged objectivity. Can we know others without accepting also to be acknowledged by them? Can we be acknowledged without losing control of knowledge? Descartes does not envisage this for a single moment, which is why Pascal's attack touches him so directly.[7]

3. The Composition of the Other: *Nulla Difficultas*

But how can the *ego* grant itself in this way the right to reduce the otherness of others to common objectivity? And if Descartes seems never to pose this question of right, is it because he ignores it, or rather because he confuses it with, and encompasses it in, a question of fact: Is the *ego* aware of its theoretical power to produce the idea of others, yet without admitting any otherness, therefore without altering its self-sufficiency as unique *ego*? In short, the reduction of otherness to objectivity implies, at the very, least, the power if not the right to reproduce the other without acknowledging its otherness.

(b) A second text clearly asserts this power. After having reiterated its earlier doubt, *Meditation III* undertakes, according to the demands of the ordering of exposition ("considerations of order appear to dictate," 36, I. 30), to classify the *cogitationes* of the *ego* in definite categories ("*certa* genera," 37, line I = AT X, 450, ll. 16 and 18). Among those which properly (*proprie*) deserve the name of idea appears the idea of man, of another man: "when I think of a man, or a chimera, or the sky, or an angel, or God" (37, ll. 5–6). A famous argument then tries to determine whether the *ego* suffices, in each case, to produce as efficient cause both formal and objective reality for each of the ideas thus listed—in other words, whether the *ego* can produce from within itself, without recourse to any other, thus without altering itself with any otherness, each of its *cogitationes*. We shall not dwell on the conclusion—that only the idea of God goes beyond the causal power of the *ego*—or on the detail of the other productions of ideas. Instead, we will concentrate on only one point: How can the idea of man, of another man, arise without the *ego* acknowledging the existence of any otherness? Descartes first notes that, in addition to the idea by which the *ego* represents itself to itself ("which gives me a representation of myself," 42, ll. 29–30)—which he claims, with a remarkable phenomenological intrepidity, presents no difficulty ("which cannot present any difficulty in this context," 42, ll. 30–43, line I)—other ideas represent inanimate things, angels, animate things, "and finally other men like myself," 43, ll. 3–4).[8] Let us mention, in passing, that Descartes places all manifestations of otherness exactly on the same plane, whether otherness is endowed with a soul or not, incarnate or not, finite or infinite. Otherness is envisaged at the lowest degree only: other is that which cannot be reduced to *ego* and its *cogitationes*; otherness is reduced to diversity in light of the universal *mens*, for which all that is not itself belongs to the reality of *res, res a me diversae*. Descartes gives an answer, as brief as it is enigmatic, to the now clear question of the cause of these ideas: "As far as concerns the ideas which represent other men, or animals, or angels, I have no difficulty in understanding that they could be put together from the ideas I have of myself, of corporeal things and of God, even if the world contained no men besides me, no animals and no angels" (43, ll. 5–9). The argument can be formulated as follows: The idea I have of myself is enough to make me an efficient cause of the formal and objective reality of the ideas which apparently belong to others but are actually mine—of animate beings, be they lesser (animals), equal (others), or greater (angels) than me. As pure *ego*, I produce ideas of them by composition of that which derives from my own idea, the idea of (inanimate) corporeal things, and the idea of God. Yet this argument is valid only if the *ego* actually has at its disposal these three required components (this of course without discussing the legitimacy of such a composition). Let us examine them. Can the idea of myself be combined with others so as to generate a new idea? Nothing is less certain—first, because this idea is performative and offers nothing to be considered outside its performance, according to Malebranche's thesis that we do not have a clear idea of our own soul;[9] second, and consequently, because the idea of *ego cogitans* does not belong to the same type as the other ideas of *cogitata* and therefore cannot join them but can only render them thinkable. Yet does not Descartes in fact carry out this combination, in spite of any exegetic scruples? He does indeed, but by interpreting the *ego* as a substance ("I am a substance [ego autem substantia]," 45, l. 7); regarded in this way, the idea of myself has something in common with the second of the three components—namely, the ideas of corporeal things—for extension and thought agree, insofar as both are substantial: "they seem to agree with respect to the classification 'substance,'" (44, ll. 27–28). The idea of another man nevertheless remains *mei similis* (43, l. 4), since it is composed of the substantiality that was already common to two other ideas that were available for the *ego*, the idea of itself (thinking) and the idea of corporeal things (thoughts), assembled under the title of substances. The third component—God—remains: How can the idea of God join the preceding two ideas to compose the idea of the other? This idea is infinite, while the other two remain finite, and incommensurably irreducible to any verifiable composition. And how can Descartes invoke it here, while he does not know it yet in its exceptional singularity? Or should we suppose that the properties of the idea of God that remain to be discovered are already acting implicitly here in the composition of the idea of the other? Let us examine this hypothesis: The idea of the other includes the idea of substance (common to the idea of *ego* and of *res corporales*), on the one hand, and the idea of God as it is examined shortly afterward (45, ll. 9–14), on the other hand. What does the idea of God introduce to the idea of another person who is like myself (43, 1. 3)? Attributes, which are suitable for the *ego* and for humanity, such as the intelligence and the power of a substance, but also infinity and independence ("a substance that is infinite, independent," 45, ll. 11–12). The idea of the other would imply, in light of its composition on the basis of God, two determinations that actually prevent its dependence, as finite object, with regard to the *ego*; by following the route of the argument that Descartes uses to establish that the *ego* can compose the idea of another person without knowing or acknowledging any such—"even if the world contained no men besides me" (43, ll. 8–9)—we should reach, on the contrary, the following paradox, which is equally damaging for Descartes: Either such composition remains impossible because the idea of God remains in vain; or it can occur, insofar as the idea of God is already accepted, although in this case it requires the acknowledgment of an actual *other*, independent from me, in the idea of (another) person, and the acknowledgment of another infinite similar to me in the idea of a person who is similar to me. In brief, if the argument proposed by Descartes—i.e., to reduce the other to the composition that the *ego* has of it—is satisfactory, it leads not to the submission of the other to the *ego*, but instead to the insubordination of the other, which remains infinite and independent from the *ego*. Why has Descartes not *seen* the ultimate consequence of his argument—namely, that it prevents the reduction of the otherness of another to the constitution by the *ego* of another of its *cogitationes*, that on the contrary it forces the acknowledgment that every other is honored with the independence and the infiniteness with which the idea of God infuses it?

While admitting that this is a true inconsistency on the part of Descartes, we must also recognize that our objection itself presupposes a thesis—namely, that the otherness of the other may be grounded in the otherness of God, and that far from contradicting God's otherness, it can be strengthened by it. In other words, the infinite that characterizes God encompasses any otherness, even finite; the otherness of the "wholly Other" ensures and qualifies any other. Does Descartes share this presupposition?

(c) One last text from *Meditation III* proves otherwise. It is one of the rare mentions of humans other than the *ego*—its parents. Does the *ego* acknowledge the existence of a father and a mother, or, like a new Melchizedek, does it reject all genealogy? The question is in fact explicitly posed: "From whom would I derive my existence? From myself presumably, or from my parents, or from some other beings less perfect than God" (48, ll. 3–4). The hypothesis of a positive derivation of the self from the self is quickly excluded, following the understanding of my own imperfection. The last two remain, which amount to a unique acknowledgment of other people who are real and irreducible to the *ego*: "perhaps I was produced either by my parents or by other causes less perfect than God" (49, ll. 21–23). They are eliminated by means of a well-known argument: In order absolutely to produce myself, I am required to produce as efficient and total cause not only my own empirical existence (which at this stage still remains in doubt), but especially the *res cogitans* that constitutes me. Now, this *res cogitans* thinks, among other ideas, the idea of God, which my cause will therefore also have to be able to produce, but it will be able to do so only if it is in actuality as real as the reality that my idea of God presents objectively to me. Therefore, only God will be able to give rise to the idea of God in me. The hypothesis of a parental mediation has only delayed the direct conclusion without weakening it. The contingent parents are not a cause: "As regards my parents, even if everything I have ever believed about them is true, it is certainly not they who preserve me; and in so far as I am a thinking thing, they did not even make me. . . . So there can be no difficulty regarding my parents in this context" (50, 1. 25–51, 1. 2). To eliminate the otherness that would cause the *ego* by generating it presents here no difficulty ("hic nulla difficultas") exactly as, above, the idea of the *ego* presented no difficulty ("hic nulla difficultas," 42, 1. 30).

4. The Solitude of the *Ego*

We thus come to a radical conclusion: The *Meditations* renders conceptually impossible the acknowledgment of another person—at least in the sense of another *mens* who would function as an *ego*. It undoubtedly admits, implicitly at least, that other people, or possibly other souls, may be represented objects for the *cogitatio*; but in this case, far from sharing in it, these people ratify the privilege of the *ego* who alone exercises *cogitatio*. Could we not, however, object that the order of reasons, at least once, acknowledges otherness as such? For the demonstration of the existence of God does in the end reach an other, and even the other par excellence, who stresses his irreducible independence from the *ego* by positing himself as its creator—i.e., as other, but above all, as prior: "I depend on some being distinct from myself" (49, ll. 19–20). Even if Descartes, like Husserl, fails to define the conditions for the emergence and the acknowledgment of the other as such, he does not miss otherness altogether, for—unlike Husserl—he admits its possibility for the single case of God. Besides, he manages to do so by adding to the first ontotheology of the *cogitatio* a second ontotheology granted to the *causa*, for which Husserl offers no equivalent.[10] Yet, if we have to grant that the existence of God undoubtedly introduces a kind of otherness in the order of reasons, we have to resolutely challenge the assumption that it is sufficient to even begin to outline the acknowledgment of the other as such by the *ego*. Indeed, two arguments prevent it from doing so.

(a) Divine otherness renders the outline of an acknowledgment of otherness possible on one condition only: that Descartes conceive of the situation of the finite *mentes* on the model of the divine. Now, not only do the two problematic never overlap, but Descartes opposes one to the other, at least once: Either the *ego* acknowledges the otherness of the parents (begettal), or it admits the otherness of God (creation); otherness has to decide between an empirically accessible and finite other, and a transcendentally disengaged, infinite (wholly) other, but otherness cannot indiscriminately encompass both cases. No texts of Descartes suggest that divine otherness even allows, not to mention requires, the acknowledgment of finite otherness; the finite other does not correspond, univocally or even analogically, to God in the relation of otherness, of personhood, or of consciousness (moral or not).

(b) At any rate, it would then remain to be established that the acknowledgment of God as the other par excellence for the *ego* already amounts to a meeting with the other. For, although God is absolutely distinct from the *ego*, must we conclude, based on *Meditation III*, that He constitutes the other for the *ego*? As *idea infiniti*, God is not an idea of the finite nor the *idea mei ipsius*, as a last term in a continuous and homogeneous series; rather, He appears as the transcendental presupposition of every finite being, and thus of the *ego*. Consequently, the infinite radically determines the *ego*, to the point of stamping it with a mark that becomes indistinguishable from it ("not . . . *distinct* from the work itself," 51, ll. 17–18; PW II, 35 [emphasis added]) and even of conceding it a formally infinite will (56, 1. 26–57, 1. 2I). Rather than opening onto a true other—"a man like myself" (43, 1. 3; PW II, 29)—the otherness of God opens a transcendental horizon; the otherness of a person other than me who would also be another person for me, finite and cogitating as another *ego*, is still missing.

The other is therefore still missing, not because of a temporary lapse but because, from the beginning, the *ego* defined itself in terms of itself alone. Its solitude is not anecdotal, temporary, or superficial. The *ego* becomes itself by refusing all exteriority: "I am here quite alone" (18, ll. 1–2), "conversing with myself alone" (34, 1. 16; PW II, 24 [modified]). This return onto itself leads to a circle that defines the *ego* as such: "the human mind, when directed toward itself, does not perceive itself to be anything other than a thinking thing" (7, 1. 20–8, line I); "when the mind understands, it in some way turns toward itself" (73, ll. 15–16). Thus emerges an essential and quasi-transcendental solitude of the *ego*, which defines the place of the *ego* as the *ego* faces the world (rather than being in it) and God: "I am not alone in the world, some other thing . . . also exists" (42, ll. 22–24); "I can easily understand that, considered as a totality" (61, ll. 17–18), which the French translation intelligently glosses as "inasmuch as I consider myself alone, as if there were no one but me in the world" (AT IX, I, 49, ll. 5–6). The enterprise of first philosophy according to Descartes is defined by and from the *ego*, in order to bring all back to it. It therefore requires, at every turn, that the otherness of an other, finite and human, be reduced, or—what amounts to the same thing—be entirely composed from the *ego*. If an *ego* emerges, only one will emerge; the *ego* is unique, or it does not exist; it therefore shall be alone or shall not be. Fundamentally, the *ego* excludes any *alter ego*.[11]

5. Love or Representation

This rather extreme conclusion may seem too abrupt to remain balanced and equitable. Besides, it opens itself to a massive counter argument: If the *ego* did in fact exclude any acknowledgment of an *alter ego*, and hence if transcendental subjectivity on principle denied any intersubjectivity, then Descartes should have refrained from elaborating a doctrine of love. Yet not only did he provide a thorough and subtle doctrine, but he also elaborated it starting from the passions of the soul; thus from the *mens* and the *ego*. Intersubjectivity is therefore deployed against the background of subjectivity, and the *ego* does indeed acknowledge an alter *ego*. We shall have to accept this refutation if Descartes's doctrine of love actually reaches an alter *ego* and contradicts the autarkic solitude of the *ego*. This is what we now have to examine.

Love is one of the passions. And passions are defined as "confused sensations," "sensations or very confused thoughts," "a confused thought, aroused in the soul by some motion of the nerves"—in other words, *animi pathemata* and *confusae quaedam cogitationes*.[12] Interpreting the passions in general as thoughts and *cogitationes*, even confused ones, signifies that the *ego* still determines that which it nonetheless undergoes. In fact, the passions, although confused, depend on the *ego* just as much as the other *cogitationes* do, and actually doubly so. On the one hand, passions depend on the *ego* simply because of what they represent and the eventual confusion of the represented (*cogitatum*) does not alter this dependence in the least. On the contrary, the absence of an object distinct from the *ego* increases the dependence of the passions on the *ego*. Not only do the passions share the passivity of intellection—"understanding is the passivity of the mind"[13]—but also, since they are caused by "some movement of the spirits" in the soul, they do not belong to worldly things (perception) or to the body itself (sensation), but rather only to the soul: Passions, since they occur in the soul, never leave it and are entirely absorbed in it; hence passions dwell in the *mens*, and, more than any other *cogitatio*, they are confined to it insofar as they admit no other object or subject. Passions thus multiply the overall dependency of the *cogitatio* on the *ego*: Thoughts not only stem from the *ego*, they also "refer" to it.[14] Yet the specific passion called love raises to the next power this dependency that had already been squared. For love is defined as the conjunction of (loved) objects with the *ego*, on the basis of the criterion of agreement: "Love is an emotion of the soul caused by a movement of the spirits which impels the soul to join itself willingly to objects that appear to be agreeable to it." Why reintroduce the will in this way in order to define its exact opposite, a passion? Because it is a question here of introducing the last dependence with regard to the *ego*: After originating as thought, after the delay as a passion, love finally depends on the *ego*, insofar as the *ego* enables it to "join" other objects or even to "join" itself to them, according to the "assent by which we consider ourselves henceforth as joined with what we love in such a manner that we imagine a whole, of which we take ourselves to be only one part, and the thing loved to be the other."[15] Love reintegrates in the same whole, by means of the will, the *ego* and the objects that would have remained outside of the *ego* under the aegis of representation alone; the will joins with the *ego* what representation already brought back to it. In actuality, the definition of love follows word for word the definition of the *res cogitans*. "A thing that thinks. What is that? A thing that doubts, understands, affirms, denies, is willing, is unwilling, and also imagines and has sensory perceptions" (28, ll. 20–23; PW II, 19): The *cogitatio* even reappears, with its opening up onto the other par excellence. "Love is a movement of the soul caused by the movement of the spirits"; the couple "is willing/is unwilling" (*volens nolens*) is at work in the sequence "which impels it to join itself willingly"; "and also imagines" specifies the mode under which appears that which is aimed at by the will of the *ego* ("to objects that appear"); "has sensory perceptions" (*sentiens*) finally justifies the choice of some objects among others ("agreeable to it").[16] The determinacy of love does not open up the *ego* onto an otherness that would be radically outside of the *cogitatio* as such, since, on the contrary, it limits itself to putting into play simultaneously all the possible figures of the lone *res cogitans*, which is self-referential by virtue of its very intentionality. Love does not contradict the *res cogitans*, but powerfully orchestrates all its possibilities, and hence clearly manifests the submission of the *res cogitans* to the *ego*. By loving, the *ego* does not transgress the *cogito* and its realm, but instead fulfills them. This is why the French version legitimately renders the sequence that describes the ego ("I am a thing that thinks: that is, a thing that doubts, affirms, denies, understands a few things, is ignorant of many things, is willing, is unwilling, and also which imagines and has sensory perceptions [Ego sum res cogitans, id est dubitans, affirmans, negans, pauca

244 ■ **Reading Descartes**

intelligens, multa ignorans, volens, nolens, imaginans, etiam et sentiens]," 34, ll. 18–21) by a translation that adds and includes love, although it is absent from the Latin original: "I am a thing that thinks—that is to say, that doubts, affirms, denies, knows a few things, is ignorant of a great many, *loves*, *hates*, is willing, is unwilling, and also imagines and has sensory perceptions" (AT IX, 1, 27, II. 9–12 [emphasis added]). Love does not break from the primacy of the *cogitatio*, but rather completes its emergence to finally assume its place alongside the other modes of thinking.

Consequently, any experience of otherness by love should deploy itself without altering the *ego*-ness (*égoïté*) that transcendentally determines it entirely. Further, this is also why Descartes is able to think love first as a love of oneself, and then as a foundation: "Anger can indeed make people bold, but it borrows its strength from the love of self which is always its foundation, and not from the hatred which is merely an accompaniment" (AT IV, 616, ll. 1–5). But the foundation is the very characteristic of the *ego*, which is, metaphysically speaking, originating (*originaire*) (AT VII, 107, 1. 2; 144, 1. 24; AT VI, 558). By loving someone else, the *ego* reestablishes itself.[17] And Descartes explicitly confirms this in his doctrine of love, by means of two essential traits.

(a) To love means to join willingly with an object, so as to form a whole with it; who is it that thus joins with (an object), and for whom there is an object? For the *ego*, naturally, who considers other objects only insofar as it first "considers itself," either as alone, or as joined into a whole and imagining "that he and they [other objects] together form a whole."[18] The *cogitatio*, which is transcendentally ordered by the *ego*, precedes any type of love and immediately regulates it, by interpreting it as a behavior of the will toward an object that is thought and represented; thus any declaration of love begins with the restatement of the *cogito, ergo sum*, now transposed in terms of desire: "imagining that it . . ." Hence, it becomes impossible to distinguish between a concupiscent love and a benevolent love, for given that the essence of love implies the representation of its "object" by an anterior, prior *ego*, it seems illusory or contradictory to demand the disappearance of the self; as is the case, for instance, in the Augustinian opposition of *uti* to *frui*. Moreover, the antinomy that opposes "love of self to the point of scorn for God" to "love of God to the point of scorn for the self" would also become untenable, insofar as it questions the anteriority of the *ego* in any and all love, as a result of the primacy of representation. For Descartes, benevolence and concupiscence concern only "the effects of love and not its essence,"[19] which is invariably determined by the *ego cogito*.

(b) Thus follows what can be called the formal univocity of love. From the standpoint of the *cogitatio*: "[Consider, for example] the passions which an ambitious man has for glory, a miser for money, a drunkard for wine, a brutish man for a woman he wants to violate, an honorable man for his friend or mistress, and a good father for his children. Although very different from one another, these passions are similar in so far as they partake of love."[20] In what way are they similar, in spite of what opposes them to one another? They are similar insofar as they all partake of the single definition of love. But how can a single definition a supposed definition of *love*—encompass such heterogeneous passions, and according to what common characteristic? For in all cases it is a question of forming a whole with an object, at times desiring only to possess it (thus considering oneself superior to it) and at other times desiring the well-being of these objects (thus considering oneself to be inferior to them). In both cases, esteem, thus the *cogitatio*, determines, starting from the *ego*, whether the union of the whole must benefit the *ego* or instead its "object." Thus the unity of the figures of love, even extreme ones, still rests upon the representational primacy of the *ego*; thus the abstraction of "objects" becomes possible from the single standpoint of the *ego*, "no matter whether the object is equal to or greater or less than us."[21] Besides, the fragility of the distinctions introduced in the end by Descartes to hierarchize the very dissimilar passions to which he grants the name of love is clear. On one hand, the four lower forms are supposedly easily distinguishable insofar as they aim only at "the possession of the objects . . . not the objects themselves." On the other hand, when it is a question of maintaining the possibility of loving God, whom we indeed do not comprehend, Descartes had previously maintained this position, not as the mark of a failure but as the way to success: "For although we cannot imagine anything in God, who is the object of our love, we can imagine our love itself."[22] This is an astonishing thesis, for two reasons. First, because it defines the possibility of loving God by means of the same attitude it stigmatizes in the ambitious man, the miser, the drunkard, and the rapist: to love not the object, but the possession of the object, which shows how far the univocity of Descartes's doctrine of love goes—in spite of the restrictions he visibly attempts to introduce in it. Second, and especially, because the foundation of this univocity is clearly brought to light: Any and all love, regardless of its "object," depends on its representation and thus presupposes the primacy of the *ego*; however considerable that "object" may be, however disinterested the devotional love for it may be, they must both always submit to the consideration of the original *ego*. If the *ego* cannot adequately represent them (by means of the imagination), it will at least be able to substitute the representation of its relationship (union, possession, etc.) with the object; representation is so univocally dominant over any lovable "object" that it can even substitute a representation of representation (of union, of possession, etc.) for the object itself. To love is the equivalent of wanting what one represents to oneself—i.e., an object; but wanting and representing lead back to the *cogitatio*, which stems from the *ego*.

But did not Descartes specifically acknowledge that to love implies surpassing the solitary *ego* in the direction of an *alter ego*? For instance, he writes: "the love of a good father for his children is so pure . . . [that] he regards them as other parts of himself, and seeks their good as he does his own, or even more assiduously. For he imagines he and they together form a whole of which he is not the better part, and so he often puts their interests before his own and is not afraid of sacrificing himself in order to save them."[23] The difficulty here resides in one point: Can we truly call *alter ego*, "other self," what we continuously regard and imagine in the manner of an object, whereas, in actuality, the very characteristic of the (*alter*) *ego* is the exercise of consideration, of representation, in short of the *cogitatio*? If the *ego* is defined as a *cogito*, can the *alter ego*, which is always a *cogitatum*, free itself from the status of an "altered *ego*," and thus an objectified *ego*? The Cartesian doctrine of love seems to fully confirm the negative answer to this question, which had already arisen from the examination of the situation of otherness in the *Meditations*. We encounter here an immense difficulty, which we can provisionally state as follows: When metaphysics in its modern period posits the *ego*—that is, the *ego* as it exercises *cogitatio*, as foundation and first principle—does it not then essentially and on principle cut itself off from any and all access to the other as such, and substitute for that access the other as it agrees to let itself be represented, thus the other constituted as an object? Historical confirmation for such an impossibility is easily found in Spinoza, who reduces the idea of the other to a simple modification of my own idea of myself; in Malebranche, who defines love simply as the "relation to the self" (*rapport à soi*); in Leibniz, who interprets love as an expressive variation of monadic solitude. But the most surprising confirmation perhaps comes from Husserl, at the very moment when he establishes what we must call, along with him, intersubjectivity; the *alter ego* has never been reduced and submitted to the *ego* more than at this moment: "The second *ego*, however, is not simply there and strictly presented; rather is he constituted as 'alter ego'—the *ego* indicated as one moment by this expression being I myself in my ownness." And again: "In myself I experience and know the Other; in me he becomes constituted appresentatively mirrored, not constituted as the original."[24] Starting from the *ego*, the *alter ego* will never be reached as original, in its original state. Should we then question the primacy of the cogitating and constituting *ego*, so as to open an access to an originating, and therefore authentic, *alter ego*? Must we choose between the *ego* and the other? Must we go back to Pascal and view the self as, literally, "hateful"? Hateful means here that when it is a question of loving or simply of reaching the other, the *ego* loses the privilege of being the first to be loved and much more than that, it actually becomes the last to be loved, since it is the first to prevent love. Did not Merleau-Ponty go back to Pascal's objection when he cited and critiqued phenomenologically (although against Husserl) the Cartesian aporia of the "men crossing the square" (AT VII, 32, l. 7)? "For a philosophy that is installed in pure vision, in the aerial view of the panorama, there can be no encounter with another: for the look dominates; it can dominate only things, and if it falls upon men it transforms them into puppets which move only by springs." The allusions to Descartes are obvious: One gazes "out of the window" (AT VII, 32, ll. 6–7), men can perhaps be reduced to "automatons" (32, I. 10). Thus it is a question here of nothing less than overcoming the *ego*. Merleau-Ponty goes on:

> Vision ceases to be solipsist only up close, when the other turns back upon me the luminous rays in which I had caught him . . . attracts me into the prison I had prepared for him and, as long as he is there, makes me incapable of solitude. In every case, in the solipsism as in the alienation, how would we ever find a mind, an invisible, at the end of our look? . . . The other can enter into the universe of the seer only by assault, as a pain and a catastrophe; he will rise up not before the seer, in the spectacle, but laterally, as a radical casting into question of the seer. Since he is only pure vision, the seer cannot encounter an other, who thereby would be a thing seen; if he leaves himself, it will only be by a turning back of the vision upon himself; if he finds an other, it will only be as his own being seen.[25]

This remarkable attempt by Merleau-Ponty to open an access to the other that would not submit the other, in advance, to the conditions of representation, thus of the hold of the *ego* over the other, indicates, by inverting it, the radical aporia of Descartes and, through him, possibly of any transcendental philosophy—the better the *ego* knows the other, the more it alters it. The *alter ego* itself is altered as an *ego*: The *ego* remains unique, and any other *alters* itself.

Yet this conclusion opens itself to two contradictions. They should be mentioned here more as possibilities for arguments still unexploited than as genuine objections, more as directions for future research than as a presentation of results.

(a) Did not Descartes at times also attempt to reach the other not as a represented object (an other altered from its own otherness), but actually as an original subject? Perhaps, since he did sometimes define the other by means of the figure of the irreducible origin of causality: "when our esteem or contempt is directed upon some other object that we regard as a free cause capable of doing good and evil, esteem becomes veneration and simple contempt becomes scorn" (*The Passions of the Soul*, §55, AT X, 374, ll. 5–8). To grant the status of free cause to "anyone" (§152, 445, l. 13), rather than to the *ego* only, implies that we subtract the other from the function of represented object, and thus that we assimilate it, at least analogically, to a true *alter ego*—which cannot be represented since it represents, and thereby can be assigned as a pure cause. Facing the *cogitatio* of the *ego*, the other would then no longer play the role of a simple, objectified (passive) *cogitatum*, but in an unavoidable parallel with the causality exercised by the *ego*, it would hold the rank of (active) cause and no longer simply of an effect (passive and representable). This new rank granted to the other would thus imply that we need to reinterpret the moral philosophy and the doctrine of the passions of the later Descartes from the standpoint of the ontotheology of causality and no longer—although this is what we have done all along here—from the single standpoint of the ontotheology of the *cogitatio*.[26] An in-depth study alone will be able to test the accuracy of this hypothesis.

(b) During his polemic with G. Voet, Descartes at the very least sketched a motif—namely, charity—that would justify the inversion mentioned above from the other viewed as a represented object to the other acknowledged as a "free cause." He defines charity as follows: "haec Charitas, hoc est, sancta amicitia, que Deum prosequimur, et Dei causa etiam omnes homines, quatenus scimus ipsos a Deo amari."[27] That is, the charity by means of which we seek God causes us, because of God himself, to also seek all [other] men; and we do so only as a consequence and imitation of the love that we know God has for them. Thus, loving others does not result from a direct relation between the *ego* and others since, as we have seen, this relationship is regulated by the logic of representation, which reduces the other to a simple represented object, thus an alienated one, and prevents the strict love of an other. Loving others results from an indirect relation, mediated by God, between others and the *ego*: The *ego* loves God and knows that God loves other men; thus, imitating God, the *ego* loves these other men. We should therefore be less surprised now with Descartes's recourse to charity as an essential concept of any social and political relationship.[28] Rather, we should stress the theoretical function of charity: The other can be loved only if the *ego* gives up trying to represent it directly and accepts aiming for it indirectly through the unobjectifiable par excellence—that is, God. The *ego* loves the other precisely insofar as it successively gives up trying to represent it, loves the incomprehensible, and then comes back to the other as it is loved by the incomprehensible. Thus the function of charity is to enable the *ego* to pass beyond the ontotheology of the *cogitatio*, in order to finally reach the other as such.

These two possible arguments indicate at the very least that an essential part of Descartes's moral doctrine has yet to be examined and understood. They indicate also that his strictly metaphysical situation still remains to be determined. To represent or to love—one must choose. Did Descartes in the end detect this?

The Originary Otherness of the Ego

A Rereading of Descartes's Second Meditation

§1. The Scission and the Closure

The question of the subject always comes back into play, reinforced even by the condemnations that desperately attempt to exile it. Too quickly convinced by the charge of "metaphysics," subjectivity persists all the same, at least as a place for interrogation. This obstinacy is easily explained: any discourse requires, if not always a point of origin, at least a point of impact, toward which to orient itself and on which to operate. Even if I do not speak in terms of an origin, even if I do not think with a transcendental status, even if I am not in the posture of a substance [*substantia*], it is still necessary to speak of an "I" that at least hears, at least empirically experiences the world, at least notices a beingness [*étanité*], albeit a derived and relative one. If the figure of the "I" must pass away, it will do so only for the benefit of and before that which will still say "I." Announcing the disappearance of the subject thus comes down to a self-destructive enunciation, if, in this crisis, it concerns no more than the fact of the "I," of an "I" in fact: because, in fact, the "I" is there by definition.

The real difficulty, however, plays itself out elsewhere or otherwise—not with regard to the "I" itself, but with regard to the status of the one who speaks this "I." Modern metaphysics, that is to say, what Descartes inaugurates and what does not cease to develop its possibilities, even and above all when it believes itself to pass beyond him, commences when the existence of the finite thinking thing receives the dignity of "the basis on which it seems to me that all human certainty can be founded."[1] Fundamentally, the "I" does not become worthy of being put into question until it pretends to attain or to posit [itself as] a foundation. Only this pretension institutes subjectivity as the "first principle of the philosophy I was seeking" (AT VI:32, 23; CSM I:127). Yet in coming about, by the same gesture this pretension exposes the "I," which henceforth is inasmuch as it thinks, to two aporias—a scission and a closure.

The scission follows directly and in principle from the function of founding. The foundation cannot emerge as such except in the capacity of principle—as that which implies the rest (ontically and epistemologically) and therefore makes it possible. Thus, the "I" has a transcendental function as foundation: it defines the conditions of possibility of experience, which it opens because it precedes experience. Certainly, such a transcendental priority decidedly confirms the exceptional singularity of the "I," but it also imposes a restriction on the "I": if the "I" determines the conditions of possibility of experience and of the objects of experience, it hence does not belong to this experience and does not count among its objects. Strictly speaking, it excludes itself from experience, precisely because it makes experience possible: a nonobject of experience, it will never appear in experience, held this side of all categorical determinations of the object; it eludes even space and time, since it opens the field of the one and the flux of the other. As transcendental, the "I" remains invisible, undetermined, and universally abstract. It would thus enter into visibility only in determining and individualizing itself according to experience, thus by way of the object. From here on, the transcendental "I" is doubled by an empirical "me," definable and individualized because visible, but deprived of all function and anteriority in principle. If the ego pretends to the rank of principle, it must thereby endure a scission with itself, into a first transcendental (hence abstract) "I" and an empirical (real, but second) "me." Does this scission, which reigns explicitly from Kant to Husserl, already affect the Cartesian ego? Must it already choose between its phenomenological visibility and its primacy in principle? This is the first question.

Yet this intimate scission of the ego from itself is accompanied paradoxically by a closure: the character of the first principle, which makes [rend] experience possible precisely because it does not surrender [rend] to it, pushes the ego back into an absolute phenomenological singularity—that of a condition of possibility of experience without the possibility of being itself experienced there. This empty sufficiency leads to the solution of a continuity between it and all thinkable phenomena—the heterogeneous relation between the gaze and its object, known only by objectifying. It follows that, knowing only the object that it produces, the ego would not be able to access any other ego as such, but only that which it objectifies in itself, an altered ego, a simple other "me." Altering[2] the other [autrui] into an other [autre] object, the ego is hence closed in on itself, without door or window, in the aporia of solipsism. Consequently, it compromises all access to an originary ethics: the provisional morality remains definitive and definitively insufficient. Does the ego instituted by Descartes remain stuck in this sterile grip of solipsism?[3] This is the second question. And the majority of arguments against Descartes's institution of the ego can be led back to one of the following: either an objection of transcendentality (Hume, Nietzsche, Wittgenstein) or an objection in the name of ethics (Pascal, Levinas).

Can one describe or even surmount this scission and this solipsism? One will not be able to do so except by going back to the emergence of this "I" that precedes, provokes, and exploits them. According to this hypothesis, one would have to go back from the transcendental "I" to what makes it possible—the ego, understood in general (and in particular by Kant and Husserl) as essentially an *ego cogito*, that is to say, all the way back to Descartes. We will therefore examine two "trouble spots" of this unique stake. (a) Did

Descartes assume and privilege the figure of such an *ego cogito*? Although this question seems to call forth an obviously positive response, we should not presuppose that it admits of a univocal signification. (b) Above all, does Descartes's enterprise imply by itself the ego's scission into a transcendental "I" and an empirical "me," hence a solipsistic closure without ethics?

§2. The *Ego Cogito, Ergo Sum* According to the Canonical Interpretation of Metaphysics

The historical interpretation of the *ego cogito, ergo sum* remains to be written, and we will not claim to do so here. But it is at least possible to follow the emergence of a dominant and continually corroborated tradition that thinks the ego by equating it with the self through the intermediary of its thoughts, thus identifying the ego with its own being.

(a) Malebranche posits this double equivalence clearly: "Of all our knowledge, the first is the existence of our soul: all our thoughts make incontestable demonstrations of it, because there is nothing more evident than that what actually thinks is actually something."[4] The soul (the ego) identifies itself with its thoughts by an act of thought, thus in the act identifying itself with its existence. Without a doubt, Malebranche does not grant us the clear and distinct idea of this equivalence but only a simple internal sensation. Yet this denial makes it even more visible that in a normal case (to know, without the theological disturbance of the laws of knowledge), the self's transparency to its own existence through its ideas would remain the rule and by right would remain their paradigm.

(b) Spinoza also radicalizes this double equivalence when he transcribes the Cartesian formula into another, which is apparently non-Cartesian: "Man thinks" (*Homo cogitat*). In fact, this axiom of *Ethics* 2 resumes a clearer transposition, fulfilling the *Principles of Cartesian Philosophy* (*Principia Philosophiae Cartesianae*): "So *I think, therefore I am* is a unique proposition which is equivalent to this, *I am thinking*."[5] By "unique proposition" one must understand here not only a proposition that is not divided (contrary to that of Descartes, which turns on an *ergo*) but even a unified proposition, whose terms all pass into each other by the mediation of a third, following a restless equivalence: *ego* implies *sum*, inasmuch as it implies *cogitans*, and so on, according to all the dispositions of the three terms. With a remarkable economy of means, Spinoza extends the Cartesian formula to the simple statement of these three terms. Thus he opens the road to a mechanism of crossing confirmations: where *cogitans* mediates *ego* and *sum*, then *sum* mediates *ego* and *cogitans*, and finally *cogitans* mediates *ego* and *sum*.

(c) Kant undertakes a radical critique of paralogisms of pure reason according to rational psychology, to which he assimilates the *ego cogito, ergo sum*. However, even this critique finally only accuses this argument of not sufficiently consolidating the equivalence between being and thought with which the dominant interpretation credits Descartes. Let us consider the Kantian argument: the *I think* remains a simple empirical proposition, containing in itself *I am*; but as I cannot affirm that all that which thinks exists (a statement that far surpasses the field of possible experience), one must conclude more modestly that "my existence then can no longer be considered, as Descartes had believed, to be deduced from the proposition *I think* (since otherwise it would be necessary to have it proceed from this major premise: *all that which thinks exists*), but rather is identical with it [*mit ihm identisch*]."[6] But even if it does not attain an existence verifiable by intuition (which, moreover, would furnish only an *a posteriori* existence, conforming to the perceptible status of all intuition),[7] the Cartesian proposition remains understood [by Kant] as a proposition of identity (in Leibniz's sense, but also that of Spinoza): *I think* amounts to *I am*, according to a strict tautology: "The Cartesian reasoning *cogito ergo sum* is, in fact, tautological in that the *cogito* (*sum cogitans*) [already] names the effective force."[8] Put simply, this tautology remains a logical one. It is thus intuitively empty and does not result in positing any individual existence as an effect. Thus, Kant does not separate himself from the Spinozist interpretation of the *ego cogito, ergo sum* as a tautology of identity concerning existence and thought in the ego—he only stigmatizes its impossibility. Far from putting the common model in question, his critique reproaches it only for not having the means to assert itself; that is to say, it leads only to an indeterminate principle, open to a simple dilemma: whether to remain a transcendental principle, but one that as noumena is unknowable, or to determine itself empirically and lose the rank of principle.[9] But the tautology remains unchallenged.[10]

(d) It comes down to Hegel to fix this tautology clearly. Starting in 1807, he posits that it goes "back to the concept of Cartesian metaphysics, that being and thought are in themselves the same."[11] This thesis, in fact the thesis par excellence of the common interpretation, accentuates the entire account, otherwise absolutely brilliant, of the *Lectures on the History of Modern Philosophy*: "The determination of being is immediately connected to the I, the pure I, this *cogito* to which it is immediately connected. . . . Such is the celebrated *cogito, ergo sum*, thought and being are there inseparably connected."[12] Thus understood, the Cartesian ego does not end up only with its own existence, one among others, even though exemplary or primary, but in an equivalence (which Kant rejects straightaway) between all thought, at least that which is elevated to the concept, and being. The tautology becomes universal, and the being of all beings is settled in and according to the determination of thought. The ego is not in play only for itself and its existence, but for all existence, insofar as that ought, at one moment or another in logic, to pass through the concept.[13]

(e) Not until Nietzsche, paradoxically, was the canonical interpretation put in question. Without a doubt, at first his challenge seemed more radical in that his critique was not directed—unlike all his predecessors—at the immediate identity of *cogito ergo* and *sum*, but rather at the connection between the *ego* and the *cogito*: the simple fact that thoughts loom up and impose themselves on the conscious subject does not imply that it falls on the subject to think them. These thoughts prove that "it thinks," but not that *I* think these thoughts, choose them, and produce them. "'It thinks, consequently there is a thinker': It is there that Descartes's whole argumentation rests." Thus, this concerns only a grammatical habit, a metaphysical idol supposing a cause where one can imagine an effect. On the contrary, an exact description of the process of thought establishes what it deploys without or despite the acts (or illusions of acts) of a pretended thinking subject. One knows the fortunes of this critique, taken up by psychoanalysis and the Marxist theory of ideology. It must not, however, conceal what is essential for our purpose: Nietzsche does not doubt for an instant that Descartes did not at bottom conceive his *ego cogito, ergo sum* as the immediate and tautological identity of the ego and of its *cogitationes*: "In that one reduces the proposition to 'That thinks, consequently there is thought by it' one obtains then a pure and simple tautology [*blosse Tautologie*]."[14] By this he is content to repeat negatively the positive assumption of previous criticisms that Descartes saw a tautological identity between *cogito* and *sum*. A single difference remains: Kant contests the passage of thought to existence, while Nietzsche contests the passage from the *ego* to thought; but both criticisms are addressed to a tautology that is presupposed.

What we will call the canonical interpretation thus obstinately deploys these two decisions: (a) to privilege the formulation *ego cogito, ergo sum* in preference to all others; (b) to read it as a tautology. It remains all the more in place because even the attacks against it are organized around its way of presenting the issue.

§3. *Ego Cogito, Ergo Sum* as Formulation Privileged by the Commentaries

It would seem necessary, then, to conclude with Husserl that the *ego cogito, ergo sum* defines itself as "a resolutely solipsistic philosophizing [*ein ernstlich solipsistisches Philosophieren*]."[15] It would be all the more necessary since the most scrupulous historians of philosophy confirm the interpretation followed by the metaphysicians. Let us give two examples.[16]

(a) Heidegger, whose *coups de force* most often throw a great light on the texts that he examines, remains here strangely imprecise. Not only does he privilege the formula *ego cogito, ergo sum*, but he glosses it in the direction of a representational interpretation: "The *cogito me cogitare rem* of Descartes"; "Descartes says: all *ego cogito* is *cogito me cogitare*, all 'I represent something to myself' represents at the same time 'me,' me representing it."[17] He does not seem to have any suspicion of the plurality of Cartesian formulae, or that the *cogitatio* could exceed the representation, or, above all, that the *cogitatio* of a thing could not serve as the norm of the *cogitatio sui*. Here the research into a genealogy of nihilism through the emergence of the principle of reason, hence of thought as foundation, obfuscates patent textual facts.

(b) One would scarcely suspect M. Gueroult, whose claims long remained absolutely uncontested, of speculative fantasy, and yet he maintains that with the ego "one reaches something which in certain respects already resembles the Kantian 'I think' or the Fichtean Myself."[18] On what ground does he ratify the canonical interpretation? In fact, Gueroult finds so few texts to justify this that he makes them up unconsciously, sliding from slip to slip. Descartes certainly never describes the *cogito* as reflexive awareness, nor does he admit a "reflexive awareness of the *cogito*"; on the contrary, he explicitly rejects this interpretation: "It is further required that it should think that it is thinking, by means of a reflexive act, or that it should have awareness of its own thought. This is deluded."[19] Furthermore, Descartes does not set aside the reflexive repetition of the *ego cogito, ergo sum*, only because he refuses from the start to make it a representation. Even the term *repraesentare*, although often used to define *idea* in general,[20] to my knowledge never appears in connection with the *ego cogito*. This fact does not restrain Gueroult, who does not hesitate to introduce here "a representation: that of a 'spiritual thing' by which 'I represent myself to myself.'"[21] What textual support justifies this resistance by the interpreter to what he is interpreting? For his whole argument Gueroult refers only to one text, a passage from the Third Meditation in de Luynes's translation: "among my ideas, besides that which presents me or makes me manifest to myself."[22] But one notices immediately that he quotes only a snippet of text, in a context that no longer concerns the *ego cogito* (which has been explicitly left behind). One might then point out that Gueroult doubles the simple formula "me représenter moi-même" to "me répresente[r] moi-même *à moi-même*"; that is to say, he substitutes for one representation of myself a reflexive representation of myself by myself. But this way of making the French citation doubly awkward is added onto an earlier modification of this same French translation— "me répresente à moi-même" from the original Latin "Ex his autem meis ideis, praeter illam quae me ipsum mihi exhibet," which one could better translate as "besides that which presents me or makes me manifest to myself."[23] The original Latin is then wholly unaware of a representation and *a fortiori* of a reflexive representation of self to self. These derivative additions result in transforming what Descartes understands as an exhibition of the ego, and thus as a pure eruption into appearance, into a reflection of self on self and so an equation I = I. A pure phenomenological manifestation becomes an abstract logical identity, a factual happening falls back on an atemporal principle. This textual inexactness by one of the most authoritative interpreters attests in fact to the fragility of every hermeneutic of the *ego cogito, ergo sum* as a guiding thread for the "reflection enveloped by the constituting process of the cogito,"[24] thus for the equality of self to self and, in short, for the canonical interpretation.

But we should emphasize that, to avoid a metaphysical, reflexive, and representational interpretation of the *ego cogito, ergo sum*, it is not enough to return to a purely logical or pragmatic analysis. Indeed, to interpret it as a syllogism (or an *intuitus*), as an inference (strict or not), as an existential affirmation (or not), as a performative linguistic act (or not)—these interpretations all suppose that it serves to pass from an *ego* to a *sum* by means of logic alone in its deductive (or inductive) or even pragmatic form.[25] But, precisely, regarding the self, must one deploy, whether analytically or synthetically, a unity that first off swathes together subjectivity and existence to validate (or invalidate) a logically legitimate self-positing? Is it simply a matter of a self-positing of the ego in existence justified by formal operations? Clearly we do not deny that the formulation *ego cogito, ergo sum* can be interpreted in these terms, even ought to be so interpreted. That has been done brilliantly, and it will happen again. This is not the issue. We ask only whether this formula (and so also the privileged position that it induces in favor of reflexivity) exhausts the Cartesian concept of the *cogito*; in short, whether the canonical interpretation remains the only acceptable one.

Let us consider here a curious remark, otherwise left without consequences, by an excellent commentator [Edwin Curley]: "The Second Meditation is notoriously an exception."[26] A notable exception in respect to what? In that, by contrast to the *Discourse on Method* ("this truth: *I think, therefore I am*"; "cette vérité: *je pense, donc je suis*"), to the Second Replies ("*I think, therefore I am, or I exist*"; "*ego cogito, ergo sum, sive existo*"), to the *Principles of Philosophy* ("this piece of knowledge—*I am thinking, therefore I exist*—is first and most certain of all"; "haec cognitio, *ego cogito, ergo sum* est omnium prima et certissima"), to the *Conversation with Burman* ("cogito ergo sum"), even to the Third Rule ("everyone can mentally intuit that he exists, that he is thinking"; "uniusquisque animo potest intueri, se existere, se cogitare"), the Second Meditation introduces a different formula: "must finally conclude that this proposition, *I am, I exist*, is necessarily true whenever it is put forward by me or conceived in my mind," or again: "this [thought] alone is inseparable from me. I am, I exist."[27] What difference does this other formulation imply? We have shown elsewhere, following J. Hintikka, that it takes us from a passage of reasoning (of whatever sort it may be) to a performative.[28] This point remains incontestable: I am certain insofar as I say that I am because the thought does not occur in the statement but outside of it—it precedes it inasmuch as it brings it about. The *cogitatio* does not "speak" itself in the statement, since it "speaks" the statement: thus it remains absent from the statement precisely because it verifies it. All the other statements—those which favor the canonical interpretation—remain within reasoning, constatives of an act that they do not "speak" or perform. Only the statement in act of the Second Meditation does what it says. It is appropriate, then, to admit the statement privileged by the canonical interpretation only on the basis of and under the condition of the performative statement of the Second Meditation, which alone justifies it.

But one other point remains to be worked out: How and why can Descartes abandon, in 1641 and only in the Second Meditation, the statement *ego cogito, ergo sum*, which all the canonical interpretation has validated as brilliantly sufficient, in favor of a statement that is at once more performed (since performative) and more enigmatic: *ego sum, ego existo*? And by what right might one privilege the formulation of 1641, rather than the canonical formulation, which is employed more often? In short, how could one justify that, precisely in the text of reference, the *Meditations on First Philosophy*, the formulation that has always been privileged by the canonical interpretation disappears? Is it a matter of an inexact stylistic variant? Is it not more likely a matter of the irruption of an essentially different argument? And, since the canonical interpretation results in solipsism, could one not envisage that the formulation of 1641 goes beyond a solipsism of the ego?

§4. *Ego Sum, Ego Existo* as the Formulation Privileged by Descartes

We offer the hypothesis that the formulation *ego sum, ego existo* reveals an acceptance of the first principle of philosophy radically different from that permitted by the canonical formula *ego cogito, ergo sum*. In other words, we accept without reservation one of Husserl's most extraordinarily pertinent remarks: "Behind the apparent triviality of the celebrated proposition *ego cogito, ergo sum* there lies, in effect, a dark yawning chasm."[29] What abyss is this? Our hypothesis will be the following: while the formula privileged by the canonical interpretation leads necessarily to solipsism, the second brings about an originary otherness of the ego.

We are not unaware of the paradox of this hypothesis, especially since a recent critique, which also underlines the privileged formula of the Second Meditation, leads to the confirmation of solipsism—in contrast to our approach. Indeed, as Etienne Balibar astutely notes, this formula is clarified in the phrase "But I do not yet have a sufficient understanding of what this 'I' is, that now necessarily exists." Now, this phrase is easily reduced to *sum ego ille, qui sum*, or to *I am that I am*; that is to say, it imitates closely the *sum qui sum* of Exodus 3:14.[30] And in this divine name—the Name—the identity of the self with itself is fulfilled at the highest level. This is the only identity that could justify a solipsism.

Appearing in this brute form, the interpretation is, literally, unacceptable. We oppose it for two reasons. First, for a philological reason: the privileged passage that we have just cited does not exactly contain the formula *ego sum, ego existo*; on the contrary, it points out its limits, since the performative fact of my existence is not sufficient to establish what (or who) I am: in short, the inference from existence to essence is not valid. One would indeed only be able to comment on what the formula covers (my existence, my being), leaving out what it acknowledges is not covered (what I am, my essence). Second, at no time does the cited text assert the identity of the ego with the ego, or of the ego with its being; on the contrary, it explicitly demands that one distinguish the certain knowledge of the fact that I am from the "rash" [literally "imprudent"] assumption of the "quid aliud . . . in locum mei," of something else taken in the place and instead of what I am.[31] Thus, nothing permits us to talk about solipsism where "the space of the ego" is missing. If there is, then, an interpretive model for the formula of the Second Meditation, the assumed identity of Exodus 3:14 does not exactly capture it, since it leads back to the equivalence of the ego with the ego, and then to solipsism, establishing again the canonical interpretation. This new interpretation offers less first aid than final distraction.

It remains, then, to read the *ego sum, ego existo* proper to the Second Meditation in an altogether different way—to read it for and from itself. This means reading it neither from a later sequence of lines (Balibar), nor from parallel passages (the canonical interpretation), but from the text that precedes and leads up to it.[32] This sequence unfolds a complex argument whose subtitle is sometimes misleading. We will attempt to follow it in four stages.

The first sequence (AT VII:24, 19–26 = IXA:19, 17–22; CSM II:16) tries to contest the preceding conclusion, namely, knowing that all that I see is false, that "nothing is certain [*nihil esse certi*]" (24, 18). To this end, one asks whether there might not be "another different thing [*quelque autre chose différente/diversum*]" (AT IXA:19, 17 = AT VII:24, 19) that I absolutely could not doubt. What does "different" signify here? Certainly, it concerns all that cannot fall into doubt, such as bodies and simple material natures (24, 16–17), and then other *things*; but there is more: it concerns not only an other, but, more radically, an other as little identifiable as the rest, "Some God, or whatever I may call him."[33] Hence this first surprising result: the other emerges hence as hypothesis *before* the ego, from the first attempt at overcoming doubt. It is indeed a question of an other [*autrui*] (and not of another [*autre*] in general) since one accepts for it the name of "God." Certainly, this interlocutor remains masked by its indeterminacy; the French translation thus makes it equivalent to "some other power [*quelque autre puissance*]" (AT IXA:19–20), and the subsequent development of the argument underlines the anonymity ("I know not who"; *nescio quis*; AT VII:25, 6; CSM II:16–17) and later "some one" (*aliquis*; 26, 24). God also advances masked—"enchanted before God [*larvatus pro Deo*]" becomes an "enchanted God [*Deus larvatus*]."[34] But this anonymity does not eliminate completely the essential character of such an other, reinforced by its very indeterminacy. On the one hand, I indeed name it as an other (*nomine illum voco*; 24, 22); on the other hand, in return it "puts into me the thoughts I am now having."[35] It sends them to me (*immittit*; AT VII:24, 23; CSM II:16). God, or what here takes his place (as one might name it), is from the beginning imposed as the interlocutor of the ego; without existing, without showing any essence, without name, it suffices to deceive me and to interrogate me—unconditioned because perfectly abstract, it has no need of reality in order to place into doubt reality by and for me. Far from doubt deploying itself in the solipsism of an abstract and doubled thought (in the sense that the skeptic finds nothing certain besides the absence of certainty; 24, 12–13), it thus deploys itself in a space of interlocution—the ego and the indeterminate other. No doubt the reasoning immediately reverses itself: if the other sends me these thoughts, why not consider that it is myself, directly, who produces them ("maybe that I am capable of producing them myself"; AT IXA:19, 21–22; *ipsemet author*, 24, 24)? But this substitution changes nothing in the space of interlocution, since the ego, in becoming the cause of the ideas that reach it, only pretends to assume, over and above its own role, that of the other. It is a matter of the first use of a hypothesis; Descartes never shrinks from the contradiction implicit in it—to be the cause in me, unknown by me, of the idea of an other than me.[36] Here I would be both ego and its other. Moreover, the first rough sketch of my existence— "In that case am not I, at least, something?"—opens itself to a simple and powerful objection: if I have neither senses nor body, that is to say, I cannot access what is other than myself through the sensible, which has been put in doubt as not being a (sensible) other than me, then I am not able, in place of the other, to cause my own ideas.[37] In consequence, I am not the other and, by the same movement, I am not myself and not even me. Astonishingly, I have not accessed being at the very moment in which the indeterminate other no longer gets through—to this extent the horizon of the first coincides precisely with the second.

The second sequence (AT VII:24, 26–25, 5 = IXA–:19, 30; CSM II:16) seems, on first reading, to weaken the hypothesis of an interlocutory space for the ego, since it inquires about the ego's identity alone and attempts only to object to (*haero tamen*; 24, 26) (i) the objection that I am not *aliquid*, since there is no body and nothing that can be sensed. The counterargument validly runs: (ii) Am I at this point reducible to my body and to the senses, so that I cannot exist without them? But this counterargument immediately produces its own counter: (iii) I am convinced that there is in the world neither earth nor heavens nor bodies nor spirits. This echoes nearly literally the argument from hyperbolic doubt in the First Meditation. The Second Meditation omits the simple material natures (extension, shape, size, place, etc.). Their putting in doubt alone makes possible doubt about the "heavens and the earth," but the text adds *minds*, which do not fall under hyperbolic doubt. This change has only one goal—to include in the doubt even the *cogitationes* and the *ego*.[38] Controversial though it may be, this argument is thus able to claim to challenge whether "I am something" (*ego aliquid sum*; 24, 25). Spirits, like bodies, give rise to doubt, so that even I (*etiam me*; 25, 4) am not.

One expects here the theoretically best reply, that the argument is invalid because it enlarges doubt from bodies to spirits without any justification. Descartes prefers another reply. He recalls that the argument (iii) rests on my conviction of the (controversial) universality of hyperbolic doubt—"I have convinced myself" or "I am persuaded" (*je me suis persuadé*; *mihi persuasi*; AT IXA:19, 25–26 = VII:25, 2; CSM II:16)—and instead of replying with regard to the content (improperly enlarged) or the propriety of this conviction, he examines its form. Whatever may be the content of which I am persuaded, at least I am myself persuaded of this content, thus (iv) "No: if I am persuaded of something, then I certainly existed" (25, 5),[39] which the French glosses: "Non certes: j'étais sans doute, si je me suis persuadé" (or only if I have thought something; IXA:19, 28–30). In short, the conclusion of argument (iii) "I do not exist" (*me non esse*; 25, 4–5), "I was not" (*je n'étais point*; IXA:19, 28), contradicts itself like an inverted performative. If I think (or say) that I am not, I am, because the act producing my nonexistence (content) establishes my existence/being (performance). One finds oneself already before a performative like the one that is explicitly achieved some lines later.

Nevertheless, before we consider the motives for this anticipation (or this delay), we ought to confront another difficulty, argument (iv): "I certainly am, if I am persuaded."[40] Does this not illustrate perfectly, contrary to our thesis, the solipsism of the canonical interpretation? Does not the sequence "*je me* suis persuadé"[41] bring to full visibility the identity with self implied by the formula *ego cogito, ergo sum*? The contrary seems immediately true for two basic reasons. (a) First, because the persuasion received by the ego, at least in the First Meditation, which sets the horizon of the whole argument, at this point in the Second Meditation precisely does not come from the ego, but from a "*long-standing opinion in my mind*" (*meae mentis vetus opinio*; AT VII:21, 1–2; CSM II:14), which suggests an omnipotent God. This opinion imposes itself—whether culturally, historically, or religiously, matters little—on the mind, which discovers it has always (*vetus*) been fixed (*infixa*) on itself. It thus determines the ego by virtue of its facticity ("preconceived . . . opinion," *praeconcepta . . . opinio*, as one can read at AT VII:36, 8–9; CSM II:25). The ego thus enters into doubt only according to its facticity (its "already there" [*déjà là*], which is originarily nonoriginary). It finds itself early on situated before a fait accompli, however indeterminate. One can identify this fact [this "fait"] as the opinion itself, or as God who can do all, or as an indefinite deceiver—it matters little, since in any case the ego finds itself preceded, on the road to a solipsism that should identify it with itself alone, by a certain other. It does not access itself in a monologue but in an originary dialogue. One must then conclude that argument (iv) simplifies to a self-persuasion of the ego, the persuasion that, according to the order of reasons, the other first exerts on it.[42] We will see that Descartes quickly rejects this simplification.

Let us suppose that argument (iv) does reach existence by pure self-persuasion. Is it a matter of a solipsistic identity with the self? Clearly not, because if *ego* and *mihi* identify themselves empirically, they distinguish themselves radically by their illocutionary functions. Descartes follows the following schema: the existence of that which remains in the position of subject (*ego eram*) depends here essentially (*si*) on the persuasion exercised on it (*mihi*; 25, 5) by something indeterminate, whatever it may be, provided that it persuades me. This implies: (a) that the existence follows from the persuasion, and so from the rational discursiveness; without a self-positioning in existence; (b) that the *ego* existing in the nominative itself results from a *mihi* in the dative, whose privilege consists only yielding passively to the persuasion, thus to a *quid* distinct from itself without solipsism; (c) that the *mihi* does not then play the same character as the *ego*, which effaces itself before it, but that two voices play two roles in real dialogue: *I* am in response to the fact that it brings to me a persuasion. This persuasion does not identify itself to me or in itself identify the ego with *mihi*, because it is at play in the irreducibility of a *quid* that is done and contained.[43] In short, at this point the persuasion opens a dialogical space at this point both constraining and originary, in which the *ego* must, in order to maintain its character, change itself into a *mihi*. Argument (iv), "if I convinced myself of something then I certainly existed" (*imo certe eram, si quid mihi persuasi*), confirms, then, not the solipsistic identity of the ego but, on the contrary, its unfolding under the double billing of *ego* and of *mihi*, according to an originary dialogical space in which it doubles itself to receive a guarantee of existence.

The third sequence (AT VII:25, 5–10 = IXA:19, 30–34; CSM II:17) confirms this dialogical arrangement by replacing the formula "if I convinced myself of something then I certainly existed" (*certes ego eram, si quid mihi persuasi—si je me suis persuadé*) by another that is equivalent but explicitly dialogical: "In that case I too undoubtedly exist, if he is deceiving me" (*haud dubie igitur ego etiam sum, si me fallit*, AT VII:25, 7–8; CSM II:17; *point de doute que je suis, s'il me trompe*, 19, 32). Certainly "I am persuaded" [*je me suis persuadé*] is opposed to "I am deceived" [*je suis trompé*] as the certainly true to the false. In fact, the inversion of truth value in no way changes the formal identity of the two syntagma (to persuade *me*, to deceive *me*) and, especially, one and the same result holds for the one (positive) as well as for the other (negative): I am ("I was," *ego eram*; "I also am," *ego etiam, sum*). What signifies my existence follows indifferently from my self-persuasion and my error.

How can we explain this paradox? By admitting that the contents do not matter but that only the permanence of the unique structure counts. What structure if not that of a dialogue? This dialogue supposes an other speaker who challenges the ego and precedes it. In fact, when the ego admits that it is, it admits first that it is only second, that it comes after an other (*ego etiam sum*). If it is only an *also*, what then is the first?[44] The answer is obvious—that which deceives me with great cunning and power but of whose identity I am ignorant (*deceptor nescio quis*, AT VII:25, 6; *je ne sais quel trompeur*, IXA:19, 30; "I know not what deceiver," CSM II:17, trans. mod.). No doubt its existence has not yet been demonstrated, no doubt also when another existence is demonstrated it will involve only a supreme power purified of all deception. It still remains the case that only this interlocutor, with an existence uncertain but anterior to my own, can allow me to prove my own existence and put it to the test. Perhaps it is necessary that he deceive me for me to know with certainty that I am. I am if he deceives me; this implies that I am only if he deceives me, thus he addresses me, challenges me, and assists me. Certain existence results from my challenge by what, although uncertain, nevertheless precedes it. Whether what deceives me exists or not, so long as it addresses me (or assaults me), I am. I am to the exact degree and at the very time that I am challenged. Existence does not follow from a syllogism, from an intuition, from an autonomous performance, or from a self-*affection*, but from my being acted on (from "my affection") by an other than me.

Descartes goes further. In supposing that his deception is not able "ever to bring it about" (*jamais faire*, AT IXA:19, 33; *numquam tamen efficiet*, VII:25, 9) that I am not, does he not suggest that this other even "provokes" my existence *efficiently*? One can do no more than underline that I am not by (means of) myself but, paradoxically, by (means of) this other who deceives me (maybe even in not deceiving me) and who, possibly, is not. Cartesian argumentation inscribes itself in an originarily dialogical space, where the ego finds itself caught before it even exists, brought about from the outset by an other, of whom it knows only this: that the other assaults it and so addresses it. I am an other, certainly—but because it is it by an other. [*Je est un autre, certes—mais parce qu'il est par un autrui.*]

The fourth sequence (AT VII:25, 10–13 = IXA:19, 34–38; CSM II:17) at first seems to contradict this conclusion. Indeed, it reestablishes the short circuit of the ego without mentioning "I know not what deceiver." *Ego sum, ego existo* is put forward and performed by me, exclusively *a me* (AT VII:25, 12). Is it a matter of a reprise of argument (iv) of the second sequence, *ego eram, si quid mihi persuasi* (25, 5)? Without a doubt. In both cases the other is relegated to the second level to shorten the argument and make it more forceful. But we have already established that in this case the dialogical situation, far from disappearing, is displaced and is in play between the *ego* (*mihi*, me) as interpellated and the ego as interpellating (like the other [*autrui*] of itself). We have then shown, with respect to persuasion, that it is in play as an illocutionary act. Can we now extract a plausible interlocution by which the ego would carry out an interpellation of the ego? No doubt, since Descartes uses here the characteristic vocabulary of the performative. It is a matter of a linguistic act ("proclaimed," "put forward"; *pronuntiatum, profertur*) given a temporal dimension as such ("wherever," "as often as"; *quoties*) in a dialogue in which the ego is born out of its own interpellation. This dialogue between self and self ought not only to be understood as a reflection on the self—"mind turning around on itself" (*mens in se conversa*), "I withdraw alone" (*solus secedo*), "mind, while it understands, in a way turns around upon itself" (*mens, dum intelligit, se ad ipsum quoddammodo convertat*),[45] in short, as a representation of the self. One must, rather, recognize here an address to the self, an act of speech toward (even against) the self. "And conversing only with myself" (*meque solum adioquendo*; 34, 16; CSM II:24, trans. mod.), me taking the side of myself challenging myself. I, who am not, make the me foreign to myself, in order, by the me preceding myself, to speak and put forth this other existence (nevertheless my own) and in the act to guarantee it. In this hypothesis, auto-affection and ecstasy no longer contradict each other: I affect myself (and experience myself as being) in the exact measure to which I allow myself to be addressed, interlocuted, and finally thought by a still undecided alterity, either the illusion of a deceiver, or the opinion of an omnipotence, or my own thought remaining other than me. Alterity would thus be in play before the distinction between auto-affection and hetero-affection, between the same and ecstasy, is even established.

We conclude, then, that the formulation *ego sum, ego existo* achieves, in the Second Meditation, and only there, an argument that is absolutely original and irreducible to the canonical interpretation, which privileges the formulation *ego cogito, ergo sum*. Here the ego guarantees its existence by its originary inscription (before which it does not exist), in a dialogical space in which an illocutionary act—to be deceived—by an other who is first, indeterminate, and anonymous recognizes it as such and assigns it being.

Solipsism and a sealed identity of self with self do not, then, define either necessarily or always the Cartesian *ego sum*, even if they can do so on occasion (in the canonical interpretation). This *ego sum* can (and on occasion should) receive itself from an originary interlocution, which operates first on an other. That this other remains empty and problematic makes the constitutive function that it performs for the ego all the more emblematic. Before being a thinking thing, the ego exists as deceived and persuaded, thus as a thought thing (*res cogitans cogitata*), hence the first truth, *ego sum, ego existo*, does not have the first word. It hears it.[46]

§5. The Ego as *Finitus* or the Reestablishment of an Originary Alterity

This noncanonical interpretation can deal with such arguments as have been brought against it. It remains then only to present, albeit summarily, some other arguments that confirm it. The first concerns the formulation of the ego's existence in other statements. Thus the *Discourse on Method* reaches the canonical formulation without any reference to an interlocutor whatever, but in doing so it puts the weight of the argument exclusively on the I, which becomes redundant to the point of excess: "But immediately I noticed that while I was trying thus to think everything false, it was necessary that I, who was thinking this, was something. And observing that this truth '*I am thinking, therefore I exist*' was so firm and sure that all the most extravagant suppositions of the sceptics were incapable of shaking it, I decided that I could accept it without scruple as the first principle of the philosophy I was seeking."[47] It has been correctly emphasized that the *Discourse* is still unaware of hyperbolic doubt due to omnipotence (F. Alquié). It should be added that consequently it is also unaware of the illocutionary relation between, on the one hand, the ego, deceived, interrogated, and hence thought before thinking, and, on the other hand, the originary interlocutor, who is indefinite and anonymous but the first to speak and to think [it]. The intervention of the canonical formulation is here marked by the absence of the originary interlocution—there occurs only the communication of I with itself, which sees itself existing for its own reasoning. The *Principles of Philosophy*, which equally privileges the canonical formulation, also ignores the interlocution, which is replaced, at lesser cost, by a logical contradiction: "For it is a contradiction to suppose that what one thinks does not, at the very same time when it is thinking, exist. Accordingly, this piece of knowledge—*I am thinking, therefore I exist*—is the first and most certain of all to occur to anyone who philosophizes in an orderly way."[48] An "I know not who" (*nescio quis*) no longer intervenes, and the ego owes its existence only to the logical contradiction that would be there if that which thinks was not at the moment in which it thinks: thus the text does not envisage the essential point—Am I then certain that I think?—and does not mobilize the only argument that establishes it: I think because, more originarily, I am thought by a *nescio quis*. And if the canonical formula excludes interlocution, it confirms thus, *a contrario*, that the formula of the Third Meditation itself has to rest on an originary interlocution.

But such an access to the *ego sum, ego existo* from an other different from the ego finds further confirmation in the Third Meditation. (a) When at the beginning of this Meditation Descartes reviews the truths already acquired,[49] he repeats explicitly the first truth to proceed from an originary interlocution: "Yet when I turn to the things themselves which I think I perceive very clearly, I am so convinced by them that I spontaneously declare: let *whoever* can do so *deceive me, he* will never bring it about that I am nothing, so long as I continue to think I am something."[50] Remarkable here is the coordination within the same sequence of two formulations that can be distinguished. Certainly one finds the thought of the self by itself ("to think I am something"),[51] following the canonical formulation, but it occurs only in the second place, preceded by and subordinate to the formulation of the originary interlocution "deceive me who will,"[52] and here the ego does not occur first in the nominative but in an oblique case (*me*, "me"), subordinate to whoever or whatever thinks and determines it. I am thought by the other before I think myself as first existing.

(b) The conclusion of the Third Meditation radicalizes this dependence by articulating explicitly the dependence of the knowledge of self on the knowledge of the other who thinks me not only before I think it but even before I think *me*. This other is here finally recognized as God. Descartes extracts an argument from the similitude and likeness of God that I carry in myself, insofar as I am his creature. It does not reduce to a real image, hence to a limited "part" of my substance, which could be detached from it or at least distinguished by reason. On the contrary, the similitude with God determines me according to the totality of the thinking thing (*res cogitans*) that I am. I have, then, the idea of God (by image and likeness) by the very fact that I think not necessarily God but first and solely myself. It is not that I have the idea of God, among other ideas: I am radically and exclusively this idea itself. The ego *is* the idea of the infinite. Put otherwise, "I perceive that likeness, which includes the idea of God, by the same faculty which enables me to perceive myself."[53] The Latin further emphasizes this paradox: "illamque similitudinem . . . a me percipi per eandem facultatem per quam ego ipse a me percipior."[54] Put otherwise: the faculty by which I myself perceive myself, that is to say, the canonical formulation of my existence resulting from the thought of myself by myself (and the Latin does not shrink from a nearly incorrect redundancy of *egoité*—*ego ipse a me*—which the French does not succeed in rendering), is also equivalent in the same stroke and "at the same time" (*en même temps*, AT IXA:41, 18; *simul etiam*, AT VII:51, 27) to the knowledge of the idea of God. The convertibility of the one into the other rests on a principle evident to Descartes—the positive infinity of God is conceived immediately from the awareness of its finitude by the created (in the circumstance of the ego that doubts): "but I also understand at the same time that he on whom I depend has within him all those greater things [to which I aspire]."[55] In discovering itself "a thing which is incomplete and dependent on another" (*rem incompletam et ab alio dependentem*; AT VII:51, 24–25; CSM II:35) the ego does not merely repeat the perception of its existence in reflective doubt, it founds it in its dependence and its aspiration toward the infinite that it thinks. That is to say, it recognizes that its existence results from an interlocutionary intrigue, from an interior dialogue, and this time no longer with *nescio quis*, the eventual deceiver, but with "actually God" (*revera Deus*; 52, 2), who is not "subject to any faults" (*sujet à aucuns défauts*; AT IXA–:41, 29). The originary dialogical situation of the *ego sum, ego existo* disengages itself at last from the fiction of a God supposed to be a deceiver (because truly all-powerful) to play in the full light of the connection between the infinite, first thinker and speaker, and the finite, first existent but earlier thought because even earlier spoken to. And it is in this framework, finally reestablished as such, that the following Meditations are situated.[56]

(c) In this context, one could even interpret the letters of 1630 on the creation of the eternal truths as a first example of the original interlocution of the mind thinking the finite by the infinite. Indeed, if the "eternal truths" (AT I:149, 21, 152, 5; CSMK III:24, 25) "depend" (145, 9; 150, 7, 17; CSMK III:23, 25) on God in the same way as the "other creatures" (152, 25–26; CSMK III:25) and "the rest of creatures" (145, 9–10; CSMK III:23) that he has "established" (145, 14, 29; CSMK III:23), then they are imposed on the finite spirit as an accomplished fact, other and from the outside. Yet, precisely because they come to it as "eternal truths," as henceforth immovable and fundamental, they do not remain exterior or extrinsic to it, as one object among others; rather, they define nothing less than the finite conditions of rationality; thus they are identified with the thinking, or more exactly calculating, ego: "There is no single one that we cannot grasp if our mind turns to consider it. They are all inborn in our minds" (*mentibus nostris ingenitae*; 145, 18–19; CSMK III:23). The innateness of these truths implies that they are confused with the very conditions of finite rationality, hence with the ego. In consequence, one must conclude that "our soul being finite" (152, 12; CSMK III:25), it receives an infinite institution of the conditions of rationality and of itself. The institution and exercise of the ego thus results from a more original interlocution—"of which the power surpasses the limits of human understanding" (150, 18–19; CSMK III:25).

These texts offer, finally, a last teaching: the two formulations that we have separated—on the one hand, *ego cogito, ergo sum*, on the other, *ego sum, ego existo*—are not opposed so directly that the canonical interpretation of solipsism (which is based on the first) contradicts the dialogical interpretation (which follows the intrigue where the second appears). On the contrary, the two interpretations, the two formulations articulate each other perfectly: the ego's return upon itself actually becomes in effect always possible and legitimate (even pedagogically preferable) as a result of the more radical interpellation of this ego (under the title of "me," *mihi*) by whatever interlocutor in a space of originary interlocution. Provided that the common formula remains subordinate to and dependent on the formulation proper to the Second Meditation, there is no serious incentive to declare a tension, even an inconsistency, between the Cartesian texts. It is sufficient to maintain a hierarchy and so, primarily, not to mask the difference between them.

§6. Augustinian and Cartesian Formulations

There is a final problem: it would be premature to remark that Descartes's argument against the skeptics concerning the immaterial existence of the ego can be authorized by Saint Augustine. Of course, Descartes knew and recognized Augustine as someone who would have been included among the greatest authorities for his readers and for his possible adversaries: "I am grateful to you for pointing out the places in Saint Augustine which can be used to give authority to my views. Some other friends of mine had already done so, and I am pleased that my thoughts agree with those of such a great and holy man."[57] Why, therefore, did he decline such a profitable alliance? Formally, because he preferred the bare force of his own arguments to those of external authorities, even those of Augustine: "I shall not waste time here by thanking my distinguished critic [Arnauld] for bringing in the authority of Saint Augustine to support me, and for setting out my arguments so vigorously that he seems to fear that their strength may not be sufficiently apparent to anyone else."[58] Nevertheless, the question appears more complex.

(a) In fact, Mersenne, having read a manuscript of the *Discourse on Method*, drew Descartes's attention to "a passage of St. Augustine."[59] But to what "passage"? In all likelihood, it was *De civitate Dei* 11.26: "So far as these truths are concerned, I do not at all fear the arguments of the Academics when they say, What if you are mistaken? For if I am mistaken, I exist. For he who does not exist surely cannot be mistaken; and so, if I am mistaken, then, through this, I exist. And since, I exist if I am mistaken, how can I be mistaken that I exist, when it is certain that I exist if I am mistaken?"[60] From this parallel (25 May 1637), one may conclude, first, that even before the appearance of the *Discourse on Method* (licensed on 8 June 1637), Descartes knew that his first principle could be read in the light of Augustine, and second, that he distanced himself from the "passage in Saint Augustine, because he did not seem to have put it to the same use as I have."[61] But no explication is given here to illuminate this apparently evident difference in usage.

(b) By contrast, in a later commentary, dating from the time of the completion of the *Meditations*, Descartes clarifies this distancing: "I am obliged to you for drawing my attention to the passage of Saint Augustine relevant to my *I am thinking, therefore I exist*. I went today to the library of this town to read it, and I do indeed find that he does use it to prove the certainty of our existence. He goes on to show that there is a certain likeness of the Trinity in us in that we exist, we know that we exist, and we love the existence and the knowledge we have. I, on the other hand, use the argument to show that this *I* which is thinking is *an immaterial substance* with no bodily element. These are two very different things."[62] The argumentation should surprise us. In fact, (i) the Second Meditation never employs *substance* or *immaterial* with regard to the ego,[63] (ii) nor does it use the formulation *ego cogito, ergo sum*; (iii) as for the image (and resemblance) of God (if not the Trinity), that is indeed the concern of the conclusion of the Third Meditation. The differences that Descartes invokes to distinguish himself from Augustine rest, in fact, only on inaccurate citations of his own text: however, to avoid the risk of a hermeneutic of dissimulation or—worse—of erroneous auto-interpretation, we shall draw the minimal conclusion that, here at least, Descartes does not rationally justify the difference between his *ego sum* and Augustine's.

The story is otherwise after the *Meditations*. (c) At the beginning of his objections, Arnauld suggests another comparison, this time explicit, with *De libero arbitrio* 2.3.7: "And to begin from those things which are most evident, I ask you first of all if you yourself exist. But perhaps you are afraid of deceiving yourself in this matter, and yet you absolutely could not deceive yourself if you did not exist at all."[64] To justify this comparison, Arnauld links this text with the central passage (for our purposes) of the Second Meditation: "But there is I know not what deceiver, of supreme power and cunning, who is deliberately and constantly deceiving me. In that case I too undoubtedly exist, if he is deceiving me."[65] Yet, although thanking Arnauld for the support of this authority, Descartes declines under the pretext (as we have seen) that an appeal to any authority would suggest that his own arguments could not support themselves.[66] This is a strange response: for if appealing to an external authority never reinforces a weak argument, it cannot weaken a strong one. Yet is not another reason concealed behind this polite refusal, this time a profound reason for Descartes's refusal to align himself with the sympathies of a professed Augustinian? Such appears to be the case, if one even rapidly compares these two texts. Augustine deduces existence directly from self-deception (*fallaris* has primarily this sense), hence from self-reflection, by the simple identity of oneself with oneself [*soi à soi*]: to be mistaken presupposes existence and, here, these are tautologously equivalent; the Augustinian argument accepts, therefore, the identity of the mind with the self. By contrast, the text of Descartes's argument begins with a deceiver-as-interlocutor, one who deceives *me* inasmuch as he presents himself as different from me and persuades me as something external to my being (*fallaris* is radicalized here into *me fallit*). So, contrary to Arnauld's claim (*similia . . . verba*),[67] the issue involves very different kinds of reasoning: in one case a tautology, in the other an interlocutor—an identity or, better yet, a dialogue.

Descartes, therefore, had a profound reason for challenging the authority of Saint Augustine, even if he preferred to offer a diplomatic dodge: it is nothing less than the distinction between the two formulations, where *ego sum, ergo cogito* harkens back to Augustine's tautology (noncontradiction, logical identity) *si non esses, falli omnino non posses*, while *ego sum, ego existo* rests on Descartes's own 1641 interlocution *sum, si me fallit*. When one looks at it this way, one can finally understand how Descartes secures the originality of his thesis *against* Augustine's (and *against* his own expositions of 1637 and 1644). One understands in a flash why he did not stop insisting, almost with contempt, "In itself it is such a simple and natural thing to infer that one exists from the fact that one is doubting that it could have occurred to any writer," to the point of posing the equivalence "this cliché: I think, [therefore] I am [*hoc tritum: Cogito, sum*]."[68] How can we explain that Descartes himself considered *cogito sum* such a truism (and found an indefinite number of precedents in addition to Augustine), if not by accepting that this formulation of his first principle does *not* correspond precisely to the one he favors: *ego sum, ego existo*?[69]

In short, if Descartes challenges the patronage of Saint Augustine, it is because the latter maintained the canonical formulation and—rather strangely—ignored the illocutionary formulation: the otherness that originally makes possible the ego, which is insofar as it is thought. Not only does the comparison between the Cartesian texts and the possible Augustinian sources of the *ego sum* not contradict the distinction (or the hierarchy) that we have established between the two Cartesian formulations, it permits a better reconstruction of Descartes's progression. He commenced by adopting from the tradition (Augustinian or otherwise) a formulation relatively common, if not already banal—*ego cogito, ergo sum*. Next he substituted the noncanonical formulation, well suited for his more speculative writing (the *Meditations*) and placed it in the context of an interlocution, no longer as a tautology—*ego sum, ego existo*. Saint Augustine (and the Augustinians in Descartes's entourage) played, without a doubt, an essential role in this evolution, but not at all the role one might have expected: the interlocution did not replace the tautology because of the influence of the most authoritative theologian of the seventeenth century (who, precisely, remains caught up in the identity of thought with being and of the ego with itself, fastened to the canonical interpretation, just like the later metaphysicians), but in spite of it. Descartes did not accede to the originary interlocution of *ego sum* in yielding to theology; instead he resisted it with a polemic as stubborn as it was diplomatic. It remains to be seen if, in the end, the best theologian will be the one who is opposed to the greatest theologian.

§7. The Otherness of the Ego

I hope to have shown, if not completely to have proven, that one ought to question the exclusive priority of the canonical formulation *ego cogito, ergo sum*. Descartes distances himself from it in a very explicit way: *hoc tritum: Cogito, sum*. The ego does not attain itself except by the interlocution whereby an other than itself establishes it prior to every self-positing. This other is exercised first under the mask of an omnipotent God, at one time confused (against all coherence) with the evil genius who deceives, and, in any case, maintained in anonymity with a *nescio quis*. He proclaims himself finally in the idea of the infinite, the first Cartesian divine name, which cancels the first phantasm. Between the two instances there is only one common point—an unconditional otherness that precedes the *ego* of the *cogito* first chronologically and finally by right to the point where this *ego* reveals itself first as a *cogitatum*, persuaded, deceived, brought about. I am thought by another, then I am: *res cogitans cogitata*. An important consequence follows upon this. I have shown elsewhere that the *ego sum* displays itself as supreme being only insofar as it extends the onto-theo-logy of the *cogitatio* (under the heading of *cogitatio sui*—"thought of itself") but it becomes again a second being (created, derived) since the onto-theo-logy of the *causa* imposes God as supreme being (under the head of *causa sui*—"cause of itself"). This thesis can be confirmed by a new argument here: while the *causa sui* exercises its primacy by a pure tautology—effect and cause, existence and essence make only one, in the same "superabundance of power" (*exuperentia potestatis*; AT VII:112, 10)—the *ego sum, ego existo* does not attain itself by a simple tautology (and here our syntagma *cogitatio sui* could induce an error) but rather in exposing itself to an originary other (who deceives and persuades), hence in a space of interlocution. The *causa sui* would then only be able to assume rightfully the tautological circularity that would privilege the canonical interpretation of the *ego sum* by the whole modern metaphysic, and that is doubtlessly why this last has not ceased to assimilate the *ego* to *causa sui* (positively with Spinoza and Hegel, negatively with Kant and Nietzsche). On the contrary, the properly Cartesian formulation—*ego sum, ego existo*—not only confines itself to the onto-theo-logy of the *cogitatio* and thus admits its finitude but grounds itself in an originary otherness: challenged by an other, the ego is itself only by an other than itself. The distinction of these two onto-theo-logies within Cartesian metaphysics then strengthens itself by the strict assignment of the tautology to God and the otherness to (the) finite mind.

This subversion of the canonical interpretation to the profit of the illocutionary interpretation, if it is an innovation in the history of philosophy, is otherwise nothing novel in philosophy. It was already perfectly described by Levinas: "The I in the negativity manifested by doubt breaks with participation, but does not find in the *cogito* itself a stopping-place. It is not I—it is the other that can say *yes*. From him comes affirmation; he is at the commencement of experience . . . . To possess the idea of infinity is to have already welcomed the Other."[70] Even and especially the ego, first being, has its existence from the call of an other, whoever that may be, even if anonymous. Transcendental idealism does nothing but simplify and mask this originary dialogical intrigue.

Let us risk a conclusion in the form of an answer to the two initial questions. (a) Descartes has posited the ego in its indubitable existence, but not univocally: alongside the identitary model A = A, let us say *ego cogito, ergo sum*, which has always been privileged by the canonical interpretation of modern metaphysics, he has constructed another, illocutionary model in which the ego accedes to its primordial existence only by virtue of a thought that first thinks itself—a *res cogitans cogitata*.

(b) The aporia of solipsism, in which the very conditions of thought would deny to the ego on principle the least access to the other, hence does not result from the canonical formulation of an auto-referential and tautological ego identical to itself. (In this precise case, our previous analyses on the alteration of the other by the ego remain valid.) Descartes hence really does anticipate the impasses of Husserl's "Fifth Cartesian Meditation," which is thus even more Cartesian than Husserl supposed. But this aporia is found surpassed, or at least displaced, if one considers the original formulation of the Second Meditation (and the connected texts), for the *ego sum, ego existo* here presupposes that an original interlocution of the other alone posits the ego in the existence of its thought, hence in the thought of its existence. Henceforth, the other thinks me before I think myself—or causes me not to think myself except on the condition that at the same instant he himself thinks me more originarily. Even more essentially than as *res cogitans*, the ego is experienced as *res cogitans cogitata*. The ego appears always already taken and instituted in an alterity with itself, which, before the encounter of any finite or intramundane other, identifies the ego as different from itself, or rather as deferring the appeal by the delay even of its response. In this sense, Descartes anticipates what one can call the self-alterity of subjectivity according to Husserl.[71]

(c) A final hypothesis emerges from this: Could not the originarily interpellated ego of Descartes conceal a figure of subjectivity other than the transcendental one and allow us to surmount the scission between the transcendental "I" and the empirical "me"? Indeed, the "first principle" itself arises insofar as it always is first behind the origin that thinks it—and it does not remain first despite this being behind, but, on the contrary, by it and in virtue of the evocation that it receives from it. In this way the ego only accedes to the rank of first thinking, hence of "first principle," to the extent to which it discovers itself as first thought, interpellated, interlocuted. It is not a matter of a primacy of second rank, conditional or delegated, but of a primacy instituted by the event itself of experiencing itself originarily thought. The distinction between I and "me" would then lose all pertinence, since in a sense the I takes its possibility from what (who or what that might be) thinks me (*me*), "me" [*moi*]. The "me" no longer consigns, afterward, the empiricity that would posit the "I," but the "I" arises in original facticity where it experiences itself as a "me" thought. The "me" and the "I" exchange their functions only in not confusing them—they are organized following another logic, that of the original interlocution.

In this hypothesis, far from having only instituted the metaphysical era of objectifying and objectified subjectivity, whose traces fade before our very eyes, might Descartes also—and throughout—have anticipated without knowing it, or at least without having signified it explicitly to us, that which comes after the [transcendental] subject and which we have not ceased to sketch and to await?

PART $\boxed{\text{IV}}$

Revelation and Apophasis

Philosophers have often found difficulties in the idea of divine revelation. Both Fichte and Kant launched powerful critiques of revelation in the late eighteenth century, and in the twentieth century Levinas took pains to elaborate how God comes to mind without recourse to the question of his existence or nonexistence. "What is sought," he says, "is the *phenomenological concreteness* in which this signification ['God'] could or does signify, even if it cuts across [*tranche*] all phenomenality."[1] Yet there has also been positive interest in revelation: Schelling's lectures in Munich and Berlin on the philosophy of revelation provide a major instance.[2] The twentieth century has also witnessed bold attempts to affirm divine revelation: Karl Barth reacted strongly against liberal theology (without thereby rejecting all its currents in his own work) and vigorously affirmed the self-revelation of God in his *Church Dogmatics*, and Hans Urs von Balthasar also places a great emphasis on divine revelation in his theology.[3] Kataphatic theologies, in which God is revealed in Jesus Christ, Scripture, and Tradition, usually call forth apophatic theologies, in which we seek God by approaching him in the darkness of unknowing. Revelation is descent, and apophasis is what is required of us in ascent. Yet there are exceptions to this model: one does not find a significant apophatic strain in Barth's theology or, for that matter, in evangelical Protestant theology in general.

It is no surprise that phenomenologists are interested in revelation, for the main impulse of phenomenology is manifestation. (Henry and Levinas are exceptional; the one is drawn to the phenomenality of nonintentional consciousness, and the other to the nonappearance of the face.) At the same time, though, more classical phenomenologists are cautious about revelation. First, revelation is at once a revealing and a reveiling of God (the Father remains hidden even while sending the Son in the Spirit), and therefore quite different from manifestation as it is used in phenomenology; second, divine revelation completely resists being made immanent, as Husserl requires for his phenomenology; and, third, revelation calls forth commitments in the sphere of faith, outside philosophy. In his work, Marion distinguishes between "revelation" and "Revelation." The former is an eidetic possibility that the philosopher can entertain, while the latter turns on an act of faith. So Marion respects the border that runs between philosophy and theology, and he proposes to approach the question of divine revelation only from the side of philosophy. His reservations about the "I" and the "horizon," fully developed in *Being Given* and *In Excess*, orient the question of divine revelation for him, and he poses this question from the side of philosophy. In the end, as philosopher, he is closer to Kant and Fichte than to Barth and von Balthasar. And yet he is a practicing Catholic who personally accepts the revelation of God in Jesus Christ, and one who often cites Scripture in his philosophical writings. What is the status of those citations? The question presses on all readers of Marion, whether they are believers or nonbelievers.[4]

For a philosopher, Marion is unusually well versed in the writings of the Church Fathers, especially the Greek Fathers.[5] I have already noted the use that he makes of icons in his thought, and in "The Prototype and the Image" he reflects further on the holy images. He does so by referring back to Nicaea II (787), the Seventh Ecumenical Council. The veneration of icons had been suppressed within the Byzantine Empire, and the Council sought to restore the liturgical honoring of holy images. As Marion shows, the arguments of Nicaea II resonate with contemporary philosophical concerns about the nature of the image. Yet the icon is not an image, Marion argues, and in fact it "contradicts point by point the modern determination of the image." Only in the icon do we find the visible and the invisible in a harmony.

As we have seen, in *God Without Being* Marion objects to the rerouting in the tradition of thinking of the good as the first of the divine names. It is Saint Thomas Aquinas, he maintains, who has us think, rather, of being as the first of the divine names. Marion's reading of Aquinas has come under attack from various quarters, perhaps most sharply by David Burrell, and in "St Thomas Aquinas and Onto-theo-logy" Marion seeks to clarify his position to his critics.[6] For Marion, Aquinas's notion of the divine being is not metaphysical, at least not in Heidegger's sense of metaphysics as having an onto-theological constitution.[7] This essay benefits from being read in conjunction with "What Cannot Be Said," a study of apophasis that is tightly tied to the concept of divine love. The essay looks back on Marion's engagement with Derrida on the theme of "negative theology" (a formulation he rejects) while also prefiguring Marion's discussion "Words for Saying Nothing," published in *The Erotic Phenomenon*.[8]

We can have no intuition of God and no concept of God: Phenomenology confirms apophasis. Yet if God is impossible for human beings, he does not thereby become impossible for himself. In "The Impossible for Man—God" Marion explores the notion of the impossible with respect to God, and does so in a quite different sense of "the impossible" than is ventured by Derrida in his studies of the gift, forgiveness, and mourning.[9] On Marion's understanding, the angel's announcement to Mary that nothing is impossible with God (Luke 1:37) is not a pre-philosophical statement of divine omnipotence but rather an index of divine love. God's transcendence, his distance from all possibility, is marked not by power but by love; and nowhere is this more apparent than in the divine forgiveness of sin, for all sin is ultimately against God.

K.H.

The Prototype and the Image

I

If, with respect to an image, it was a matter of demanding that it render visible the holiness of the Holy, would that not instead demand iconoclasm? For the holiness of the Holy par excellence is marked by being outside of every determination that would compromise its unconditionality or limit its infinity. The Holy, that protégé of immense separation, evades all comprehension, with respect to both mind and meaning. "Neither flesh, nor blood, nor human will" (John 1:13) is able to force into visibility "that which eye has not seen, not ear has heard, nor has entered into the heart of man" (Isaiah 64:4 = 1 Corinthians 2:9), precisely because it is what "God has prepared for those who love him" (ibid.). But how can God himself prepare the invisible for visibility to every spectacle of its own glory? The iconoclastic [*iconomaque*][1] temptation does not cease to be revived and to seduce, in our own epoch more than any other certainly, because it obstinately reiterates an incontestable, though limited, fact: The Holy is never seen [*s'aperçoit*], since only the visible is seen, according to the measure of the sight granted to our reach. And yet every spectacle reaches visibility only by submitting itself to the conditions of possibility of objects of visual experience, that is to say an intuition, intelligible or sensible; in either case, the intuition itself is proportionate to the consciousness that receives it and is thus defined by finitude. On this principle, phenomenology and critical philosophy are agreed: no phenomenon enters into the visibility of a spectacle unless it first submits itself to the conditions of this visibility itself: the givenness [*donation*][2] to a finite consciousness. Consequently, the most basic piety should hold to this inevitable dilemma: either the Holy maintains itself as such, in which case it refuses itself to every visible spectacle, and the holiness of God remains without either image or visage; or the image that delivers the Holy to the visible simply abandons it as a victim to the torments of its executioners—and the image, widow of all holiness, fills the role of an obscene blasphemy.

Either the invisible or the impostor. Retrieved in our time, the iconoclastic [*iconomaque*] alternative thus schematized gains a remarkable pertinence. We live—this is an indisputable platitude—in a world of images, where moreover the same flux of images perhaps strips us of a place in the world and an approach to the image. This situation reinforces the iconoclastic suspicion: among all these images—indefinitely renewed because absolutely vain, uniformly unseemly by virtue of their banality—what virgin space remains given to the possible visibility of holiness? Does not the imaginary torrent occupy every possibility, to the point of obfuscating, without the least remainder, the more modest reserve where the Holy can begin to appear, if only in the sketch of an enigma? Still further: If images, as today, no longer have only to submit to the conditions of possibility of experience but also still must be conformed to the conditions of the setting in spectacle [*la mise en spectacle*], should not the incompatibility between holiness and the lesser image provoke a fight to the death? The image, henceforth governed, beyond the conditions of its reception (intuition, finitude), by the conditions of its production (spectacle, message, diffusion), is directly and radically established as an idol—indeed, claims the title. And yet the idol constitutes only an invisible mirror delimited by the measure of the first visible that our gaze can aim at being filled by, thus the last visible that it can support without failing; the idol indirectly gives to be seen by the viewer's gaze the scope of his own gaze, by the mirror of an extreme spectacle; it closes itself to every other, because it shuts up the gaze in its finite origin. Only in such a world of images, thus of idols, could iconoclastic [*iconomaque*] violence appear as the unique defense against the universal blasphemy of spectacles—and first of all those that claim to exhibit in our visibility the glory of the Holy, which no one can see without dying.

II

The excess of the image did not characterize the epoch of the Second Council of Nicaea any more than our own, to be sure. Nevertheless this council delivered a theoretical decision for us, whose inspired audacity can enlighten us, even more than we, as historians, could enlighten ourselves. Understanding the Second Nicene Council demands, through but also beyond the hermeneutic labor of its text, that we interpret it for ourselves with the help of its fundamental concepts. These concepts are all ordered toward a decision: since the image, understood according to its usual logic, leads to an iconoclastic dilemma, the holiness of the Holy thus demands, in order that we receive there the revelation in visibility, that we construct a theoretical model absolutely other than that which leads to the idol—the model of the icon. Between the idol and the icon, the rupture tolerates not a single compromise. It remains to bring out how, phenomenologically, the icon escapes the catastrophic (iconoclastic [*iconomaques*]) consequences of the idol—that is, to elucidate in what way and within what limits Actio 7 of the Second Council of Nicaea opens up, for us also, an access of the invisible to the visible. The first decision is thus announced: "We define with all accuracy and rigor that, concerning a manner [of] approaching to the type of Cross (παραπλησί ὥς τῷ τύπῳ τοῦ . . . σταροῦ) worthy of honor and invigoration, it is necessary to set up (ἀνατίθεσθαι, *proponere*) [for God] holy and respectable icons, [made] from colors, mosaics, and other suitable materials."[3]

Icons are thus opposed to idols by two qualifications: first because they alone deserve and can demand the veneration of the faithful; second because they alone keep and manifest a trace of the brilliance of the holiness of the Holy. The second determination evidently guarantees the first: the icon can receive veneration only insofar as it visibly bears on its face the holiness of the Holy. The debate should thus first he concentrated, above all, on the mode of fidelity of the icon—which remains an aesthetic object, made from the explicitly mentioned materials—toward the glory of the Holy. What is this fidelity based upon? How is this fidelity founded? What are the criteria for determining this fidelity?

The canon[4] invokes a "manner [of] approaching," which it is not necessary (despite the emphasis of the Latin translation, *sicut . . . ita*) to understand as a comparison, even less as a similarity [*similitude*]: παραπλησίως indicates approximation, the point of approach [*le fait de s'approcher de*], without either confusion or assimilation. Between which terms does the approximation play? Between the τύπος τοῦ . . . σταροῦ, the mark of the Cross, on the one hand, and the icons on the other. One would thus understand, following the most neutral reading, that the worship of icons should be restored by being elevated approximately to the degree of dignity of the worship of the Cross. But this reading (besides the fact that ἀνατίθεσθαι can be translated as "restore" [*restaurer*] only with difficulty) ignores a fact that is essential, although in part concealed by the canon itself: On the one hand, the Cross is always called a type: τύπος τοῦ . . . σταρου [a type of the cross], the council twice iterates.[5] On the other hand, the icon itself always receives the title of τύπος; if the canon does not explicitly confer it, it suggests it while quoting *in fine* what would become the normative principle of Saint Basil: "The honor given to the icon passes to its prototype, ἐπί τὸ πρωτότυπον":[6] in the face of a πρωτότυπον, the icon can barely appear as a τύπος. But above all, at least since John of Damascus, the icon should be understood, equally, as a τύπος: "The prototype, this is what is put in the icon (εἰκονιζόμενον), from [*à partir de*] what produced it. [Otherwise] by virtue of what did the people of Moses prostrate themselves around the tabernacle carrying the icon and the type (εἰκόνα καὶ τύπον) of what is in heaven?"[7] Very systematically, John of Damascus considers the relation of the icon to that which it shows according to the possibilities of the *typical* [*la typique*]: "icons are the visible [terms] of invisibles and nontypes, [henceforth] corporeally types (ἀτυπώτων σωματιχῶς τυπουμένον) in order to permit a confused knowledge [*une connaissance confuse*]"; in short, icons are "the types of that which has no type, τύποι τῶν ἀτυπώτων."[8] The icon, like the Cross, is equivalent to a type. The canon [Actio 7] presupposes this equivalent status, precisely in order to ground the dignity of icons theologically: they should also be received as types, according to a mode that approaches the type par excellence: the Cross.

The approximation that renders the icon—as τύπος—of the Cross as also τύπος—can moreover go as far as the interpretation of the sign of the Cross—the crucifix—directly as an icon. Thus John of Damascus risks the pure and simple assimilation of the two τύποι: "And indeed often, while we do not have the spirit of the sufferings of the Lord, by viewing the icon of the crucifixion (εἰκόνα τῆς σταυρώσεως) of Christ, these sufferings return to us in memory, and falling to our knees, we venerate what is set in the icon (τῷ εἰκονιζομένῳ), not the material of which it is made"; here, with the Cross as τύπος, it is very much a matter of venerating the ἐκτύπωμα made accessible by an icon. And he confirms the iconic status, thus typical status, of the Cross by adding that it has no need of any reproduction of its original: "For what difference does it make whether or not the Cross bears the ἐκτύπωμα of the Lord?"[9] Thus the conciliar declaration establishes a first point concerning the status of the icon: it holds the rank of τύπος, but this τύπος should itself be taken as an approximation of the first τύπος, that of the Cross where Christ died, such that the crucifix and all icons of the Cross render it accessible to us. The icon bears the glory of the Holy—"The icon is a triumph, as well as a manifestation"[10]—but it faithfully bears such by attesting only to a type, and really only the type of a type, *typus autem Crucis*. The first type is revealed, before the icon, in the Cross. The Cross indeed accomplishes first and perfectly the trait that distinguishes a type from, for example, an image: it does not reproduce its original according to degrees of similitude but rather refers itself paradoxically to a prototype more indicated than shown. The Cross does not offer any spectacle or image of Christ; it does not resemble it any more than it differs from it; simply, it should not be regarded according to any register of either similitude or dissimilitude. What it exhibits to everyone's gaze defers [*differe*] in such a way that it visibly speaks from itself; born as "the most beautiful of sons of men" (Psalms 45:2), he dies "a worm and not even a man" (Psalms 22:6), in such a way that "he no longer appeared human" (Isaiah 52:14). Christ, on the Cross, holds no more than a typical relation, outside of similitude or dissimilitude, with himself. Never the image as such, he is only more radically disqualified when the absolute Face—far from just letting his glory be completely submerged in the space of the visible in a permanent and unlimited transfiguration—submits to the violation not so much of his divine visage but more of his lesser human visage (for no one from among us would want, as visage, what men have given to Jesus). On the gallows of the Cross, nothing is more exhibited than the unnamable, than what cannot be named in any language (and that is why Pilate had to employ no fewer than three idioms to attempt to identify it). Christ kills the image on the Cross, because he crosses an abyss without measure between his appearance and his glory. He definitively disqualifies the least pretension of an image to produce or reproduce what it might of the glory of the original, and thus he fulfills—even within his Incarnation, by it and not despite it—the Old Testament prohibition: "You shall not make for yourself any idol (εἴδωλον), nor any likeness (ὁμοίωμα) of what is in heaven above or on the earth beneath or in the waters under the earth" (Exodus 20:4). Thus the τύπος τοῦ τιμίου καὶ ζωοποιοῦ σταυροῦ [type of the precious and life-giving cross] well deserves these qualifications; it testifies to its honor (τιμιός) by deposing in it every idolatry; it gives life (ζωοποίος) by liberating us.

But, by accomplishing the type par excellence, does not the Cross immediately prohibit every other type? And this for two reasons: the Cross gives a figure of Christ only under the paradox of a secret glory, thus a concealed visibility; further, the Cross, renouncing for itself any similitude, cannot be guaranteed, even "approximately," by similarity to other types, thus to other icons. Would not the interpretation of the Cross as the type par excellence lead to an iconoclastic [*iconomaque*] disqualification of every other image of Christ? Even more, would it not be fitting, since every τύπος refers back to a πρωτότυπον, to renounce, in addition to icons, even the Cross itself? This objection is strong only in appearance and, from the outset, if admits its weakness: it operates entirely within the horizon of similitude or a logic of *mimesis*, since it concludes from nonsimilitude to pure dissemblance, and from this dissemblance it concludes the illegitimacy of every image. And yet, every question that opens the type of the Cross (thus consequently other possible types) comes back to a demand: Is it possible for an image to remain bound under a ruled relation to a prototype without having to obey the laws and demands of the mimetic? And yet, in place of the mimetic, icons substitute an approximation (παραπλησίως) toward the prototype; in order to understand it, it is thus appropriate to see if and how the type par excellence—the Cross—relates to its possible prototype. For the icon only gives Christ to be seen in his holiness in the same way that the Cross gives to be seen—renders visible—the divine holiness of Christ. The question thus remains to be asked: Just what does the Cross actually give to be seen? Does it offer the type of a prototype?

This fitting together of two pieces of wood raised up as a gallows gives nothing as such to be seen of the least holiness or the least divinity—except a human body that one may have perhaps already seen before he had been put to death. As such, the Cross does not produce any new spectacle: neither the dying body nor the infamous crosspiece adds anything to the visible that was not available before. For the passersby and pilgrims going up to Jerusalem, the ones dying on the crosses probably offered—given the harshness of the time—only a spectacle that would have been, in the end, banal and common; the Roman soldiers would have dispersed the crowd with a simple "Keep it moving, there's nothing to see!" more truly still than the intention of "making an example." However, there were some spectators there, the ones cursing, the others lamenting; admittedly, but do these really constitute spectators? No, since in the face of the same sinister exhibition their comportments toward the state of affairs differs because, though they see the same visible, they do not discern the same evidence. Or rather, in the same visible, they recognize, on the basis of different marks, different meanings, which are equally invisible even though all informed and organized by this visible. The invisible meaning recognized by enemies and unbelievers construed it as the failure of a false Messiah; to the compassionate, it is the death of a just man abandoned by God as well as men; finally and above all, the invisible meaning recognized by the "centurion who was standing right in front of him," the dying Christ—this visible nonspectacle of a fleeing life—is "truly the Son of God" (Mark 15:39 = Matthew 27:54). The centurion saw (ἰδὼν) the same thing that everyone else saw—the same sinister yet visible spectacle. However, he alone recognized there the visible trace of the invisible God; he interpreted this corpse as a sign of God—or better, as the one who is God. The transition turns not on an illusion but on a hermeneutic of all vision, even the most profane and banal, already implied; it simply reaches a climax in this case, to the point of a paradox; indeed the distance between the invisible sense and effectively visible spectacle is never so ruptured as it is here, where it is a matter of crossing from this exhausted corpse to the glory of the living God. If, however, the centurion crosses any such abyss, it is because he grounds his interpretation on the Cross itself, or rather on its function as τύπος: it brings right into the visible the type and mark of the invisible; the corpse of Jesus bears the marks [*les stigmates*] of the living God. The invisible admittedly does not deliver itself in a visible spectacle to everyone, directly and without the mediation of a hermeneutic, but it does give itself to he recognized through a certain visible, which it invests overabundantly and as the sign of its mark without remainder. In order to contemplate Christ as such—as Son of the Father—it is never enough, neither before nor after nor during the Cross, [merely] to see Jesus of Nazareth;[11] it is always necessary to recognize in *this* visible spectacle, this visage and shape, these gestures and words, the definitive and incomparable mark that the invisible holiness imposes upon common visibility, the τύπος in and as which God condescends to be made seen as well as seen poorly, allowing itself to be both known [*connaître*] and misunderstood [*méconnaître*]. The type of the Cross—the sign of the Cross—bears the mark where the invisible Holy is given with such little reservation that the immediate rupture of its glory is there abandoned. The irremediable mark of the invisible in the visible thus takes the shape of the Cross.

Why the Cross precisely? Because the τύπος where the invisible holiness demeans itself [*s'abaisse*] should be put together with what the visible offers to it in return: the type so receives the mark of the invisible *ad modum recipientis*. And yet the history of men coincides with the history of murder and of hatred toward God and the innocent; as a result, the visible receives the mark of the invisible in it only according to the mode of its own murderous hatred for the invisible itself—according to the mode of refusal, even to the point of killing it. In this struggle, the invisible remains innocent: it is thus not the invisible that will forcibly brand the visible; it is on the contrary the visible that will mark the invisible with a fatal blow; and even while receiving a mark, it will be only to the second degree: the indelible mark of the blood of the innocent, of the blood of the invisible, marked first by the hatred that the visible has for it. The τύπος of the invisible on the visible will at first exhibit the murderous mark that the visible inflicts upon the invisible that loves it: in short, the wounds of Christ on the Cross. In order to recognize the holiness and innocence of the invisible God, man henceforth has at his disposal a visible mark—the wounds he has inflicted upon the body of God. Thus appears the type of the Cross: not a sacred image imitating the divine and exhibiting in itself a spectacle, but the imprint paradoxically received by the invisible in the manifest wound that the invisible imposes on it. The spear-pierced side of the visible Christ is there made to appear suddenly as the type of the invisible. So also the τύπος τοῦ σταροῦ [type of the cross] on which the Second Council of Nicaea grounds the icon, if it can he authorized only by a single occurrence of τύπος in the Gospels, is precisely the site of the death on the Cross: "The other disciples [*sc.* Thomas called Didymus] were saying to him, 'We have seen the Lord!' But he said to them: 'Unless I shall see in his hands the mark of the nails (τύπον τῶν ἥλων), I will not believe'" (John 20:25). The mark of the nails could never have been inscribed in the hands—practically the holes of the invisible within the visible flesh—if the holiness of the Holy had not first consented to suffer the mark of its being refused by the hatred of men. The mark of this refusal would not itself become thinkable unless the invisible holiness first made it visible thanks to the exposure of its advance. The icon thus finds its logic and its unique legitimacy only in the repetition—this time between the face of the resurrected Christ ("colors, mosaics, and other suitable materials") and an irreducible approximation (παραπλησίως)—of the paradox of recognition without spectacle which sees the visible tool of torture as the invisible holiness of a Living One, who nevertheless died there. Such a repetition breaks here with every imitation, since the one moves from the visible to the visible by resemblance, whereas the other moves from the visible to the invisible by recognition [*reconnaissance*].

To regard the Cross as a type and not merely as an object of sight it is thus necessary to see (thus recognize and confess) in the marks made upon his body the stigmata of the invisible attested by the sin of humanity; the gallows exhibit only a corpse, which, according to the logic of the mimetic, would resemble nothing—but the Cross, like the sign of the Cross, offers to the one who will confess, according to the logic of the type, the Son of God. Thus the Cross, when thus sighted, becomes an icon. On this model and by repeating this hermeneutic transition, we can "approximately" specify the icon— admittedly, here, the visible tool of recognition is adorned with various materials ("colors, Mosaics, and other suitable materials") and no longer by the wood of the gallows; but the invisible remains in both cases, the holiness of the Holy and the glory of the Son. The common icon thus no more imitates the Cross than the Cross imitates the invisible holiness; the common icon repeats the transition from the visible to the invisible that made the Cross the sign of the glory of the Holy. Just as Thomas recognized his Lord in the very type that offered the trace of the nails, so also the faithful can recognize their Lord in the visible types that are drawn by artists. In both cases, it is not necessary to see the visible as a spectacle, but necessary rather to pick up the trace that there records the tracks of the invisible. So the icon can be contemplated with honor only by a gaze that venerates it as the stigmata of the invisible. Only the one who prays can thus climb from the visible to the invisible (according to the logic of the type), whereas the spectator can only compare the visible to the visible (according to the logic of the mimetic). To the saints these things are holy: only the one who prays crosses the icon, because he alone knows the function of type.

III

The recognition, without imitation, in the τύπος of the One who is marked should not be taken as a mere recording in this imprint itself. The τύπος, even the one of the Cross, draws nothing of the invisible in it, but, by an effect of inverted perspective,[12] does not cease to let itself be drawn by it. The second characteristic of the icon determined by the Second Council of Nicaea follows from this: precisely to recognize and so to confess the holiness of that of which it bears the mark. And yet the holiness does not reside in the icons any more than it lives in the Cross under the mode of being one visible spectacle among others. The type of the icon, like the type of the Cross, owes its holiness, transitively, to Christ; but Christ himself holds his invisible holiness only by virtue of his return, permanent and total, to the invisible Father; it is to the Father that he visibly gives his spirit (παρέδοχεν τὸ πνεῦμα, John 19:30), who alone is holy. By this return he truly accomplishes his title of "holy one of God" (Mark 1:24 = John 6:69): Christ testifies to his righteous [*juste*] holiness only by testifying to the unique holiness of the Father; it is by never claiming his own holiness or his own glory, therefore it is only by giving back absolutely to his Father that he takes up that holiness that is given back to him in order to be glorified; Christ attains his holiness by coming undone [*se défaisant*] for the sake of the Father, by making sure that henceforth, all holiness finds its fulfillment in its transfer by itself toward the invisible Holy. The Cross bears the τύπος of holiness only insofar as it exemplifies this transfer. From then on it becomes clear that the common icon can merit any fragment of the glory of the Holy only insofar as it returns all holiness to that One of which it visibly beats the mark, "approximately," just as the Cross bears the mark of Christ's own return of all holiness to One other than himself, the Father. The icon repeats, to a degree largely disseminated, the return of holiness to the Holy One; and this return alone testifies to the holiness of the One that thus casts off holiness. The icon thus displays, in the humility of time and space, the unique act of return which, accomplished on the Cross, revealed economically the original return of the Son to the Father in the Spirit, according to eternal theology. The logic of this return alone qualifies an icon as holy, whether an icon made by human hands, or the Son, the "icon of the invisible God" (Colossians 1:15).[13] Returning—or better, being returned—to the only Holy One, the icon finds its fulfillment in definitively relinquishing any claim to imitate the Holy One to which it returns and which returns in it [*auquel elle se remet et s'en remet*]; if an appropriateness can be ascribed to it, this would be due to unmerited grace and by virtue of a communion of will, never due to the adequacy of any intrinsic correspondence; for the imitation always tries to revert to a model that constitutes an ideal, in order to glorify itself as much as possible; but the icon has nothing that it has not received. It renounces, by an aesthetic asceticism, any mimetic rivalry with glory. Whereas in imitation, the more the derived image is perfected, the less it depends upon the glory of its model, to the point that the tangential autarchy of the glory inevitably drives it to the self-reference of an idol, the icon, on the contrary, glorifies itself only by returning all glory to the invisible. Iconoclasm criticizes the supposed idolatrous derivation of icons, because it persists in interpreting according to the logic of similitude and mimetic rivalry, without ever suspecting—or accepting—that the τύπος has categorically broken away from any imitation of an original. The icon does not represent; it presents—not in the sense of producing a new presence (as in painting) but in the sense of making present the holiness of the Holy One. The icon is ordered to holiness by never claiming it for itself And, since holiness is indicated in the prayer that it returns to the invisible, one will say with the Second Council of Nicaea, "the more often [Christ, the Virgin, and the saints] are looked upon through their iconic mark (δι' εἰκονικῆς ἀνατυπώσεως ὀρῶνται), the more those that contemplate them testify (διανίστανται), in kissing them, a respectful veneration (προσκύνησις), but not a true adoration (λατρεία), which is reserved for the divine nature."[14] The icon admits and calls for veneration, but it is nevertheless exempt from any idolatry, and on two grounds.

First, this veneration is not to be confused with an adoration. Since adoration is reserved exclusively for the divine nature, it is necessary to conclude that the icon does not claim either to represent or above all to constitute the divine nature; this is equivalent to saying, following common patristic distinctions, that it aims only at the person (ὑποστάσι) and face (προσώπον) of Christ.[15] The Incarnation, which delivers the person of Christ and the divine nature, only prolongs the presence of this nature in the Eucharist, where no face accompanies it, and vice versa: it grants legitimacy to the icon, a perpetual visage of Christ waiting for his return, with the sacramental accompaniment of the divine nature. It is precisely this distortion of the economy that prevents the danger of the idol: the Church can never identify the nature and the hypostatic visage of its Christ in a single liturgical performance, nor yield to the ultimate temptation of summoning as a demon that which it should dominate. Hence the importance of not including the common icon under the title of "sacrament." The icon thus strictly retains its paradoxical legitimacy as τύπος: a sign and not (a) nature of the invisible—appearing at a distance from the invisible, precisely because the invisible marks it all the way through.

Consequently, the icon, by refusing to receive adoration for the sake of a simple veneration, thus already accomplishes the same by returning this veneration to the invisibility of the unique Holy One. The icon never ceases to (be) return(ed) to the crucial τύπος of Christ, not only because it is not by nature the Christ, but above all because its very function is to help believers to give back veneration to Christ alone. The icon proclaims itself a useless servant of a veneration that it does not touch, but before which it effaces itself to the point of transparency. The icon is not the idol of Christ precisely because it returns (and is returned) to him: the τύπος uniquely points to its πρωτοτύπων. In order to clarify the importance of the "memory of prototypes (πρωτοτύπων)," the Second Council of Nicaea cites the celebrated formula of Saint Basil: "The honor given to the icon is transferred (διαβαίνει) to the prototype."[16] What prototype deserves to have the icon exile itself in this way? Canon 7 immediately responds: "and he who venerates an icon venerates in it the hypostasis of the One who is there depicted." The icon, by refusing the role of being merely a mimetic image, reaches the person of the other as such the visible opens not onto another visible but onto the other of the visible—the invisible Holy One. The icon does not fight against any original by imitation; it reaches the invisible by never ceasing to transgress itself, according to the paradox of ἀνατυπώσις. In the icon, the gaze walks along itself toward an invisible gaze that envisages it from glory.

IV

The icon steps outside of the mimetic logic of the image by what it accomplishes entirely in its reference to a prototype—an invisible prototype. This definition, however, is open to an immediate objection: Can the invisibility of the prototype guarantee the visibility of the icon? By renouncing the relation of similitude, does not the prototype abandon the icon to a common and unpretentious visibility? From this follows a second objection: If veneration should pass through the visible icon in order to be referred to the invisible of the prototype, would it not be appropriate to dispense with such an ambiguous and certainly misleading intermediary, and instead go directly to the thing itself? The hypothesis of an iconic veneration of an imperceptible original comes down to, and thus recovers, the temptation of a mimetic relation between two homogeneous spectacles; both oppose the icon with an iconoclastic [iconomaque] reaction more powerful still than the one condemned by the Second Council of Nicaea, since it unites the entire history of metaphysics normally held as two extremes: Plato and Nietzsche. What metaphysics opposes to the icon is nothing other than its own aporia before the invisible secret of the visible.

According to the established Platonic position, what we are tempted to understand as an icon has a function only of addition, which later ends up doubling what alone is: this ὕστερον γεγονὸς εἴδωλον [need for idols] (*Republic*, II.382c), under the belated activity of the worker (painter, artisan, project manager, etc.), argues with what is (the thing existing outside of its causes); indeed, this production thus redoubles a first redoubling, the one that the existing thing imposes upon what should already be present to the consciousness of the worker/artist: the ideal model—οτὸ εἶδος . . . ὃ δή φάμεν εἶναι ὃ ἔστι κλίνη (*Republic*, X.597a), that is to say, the essence and pure form of the thing still to come, which alone is in nature (ἡ ἐν τῇ φύσει οὖσα, ibid., 597b). According to the example chosen by Plato, there are three couches: the ὄντως couch, the only real one, imperceptible [*insensible*] but nevertheless obvious [*evident*]; next, the actual, individual couch; and finally the imitation of the imitation, the image painted by the artist. Here the logic of imitation increases visibility in direct proportion to sensibility, thus in inverse proportion to truth and reality. Access to the original and essential being [*l'étant*] requires canceling out the visible and sensible intermediaries as so many distorting filters (literally: those that deform the form, what we might call "enemies of the *eidos*" ["*eido-maques*"]), whose most elaborate colors mix only to obfuscate the anterior light; thus the invisible reality will reappear only when the brilliant luminosity of things and images fades. When Hegel defines the work of art as a "sign of the idea" ("Signs of the Idea," *Encyclopedia of the Philosophical Sciences*, §556), he once again radicalizes the Platonic decision; basically, art is thus reduced to presenting in the sensibility of intuition (thus in the abstract) what is discovered in and by the self only in the accomplished rationality of the idea (which alone is concrete); art assures a mediated, provisional, and mimetic access to the invisible of pure intelligibility. In the two dominant figures of its dogmatic accomplishment, metaphysics thus admits (to being) iconoclastic [*iconomaque*]: the image imitates the original, which alone *is*; it remains sensible (thus aesthetic) with respect to the original, which alone is intelligible, thus imperceptible and invisible (science and absolute knowledge); the weight of glory must directly relate to the original, by deserting images as mere idols. The original cancels out [*annule*] the image (at least in the end): the invisible, equivalent to only the intelligible, effaces all evidence of itself from every sensible image, just as the light of day blackens a photographic film that is exposed out in the open. Being iconoclastic, metaphysics condemns the image to the rank of an idol.

But we no longer belong to the dogmatic epoch of metaphysics; we inhabit the era of nihilism, where metaphysics draws to a close under the mode of a disappearance. Has not iconoclasm—from Platonism to Hegel—disappeared in the epoch of what Nietzsche defined as the inversion of Platonism and the devaluation of all values? On the contrary, it is necessary to recognize that the idolatrous status of the image has never attained its ultimate consequences more than with Nietzsche. Several arguments can be advanced to establish this point.

First, Nietzsche disputes the notion that an intelligible and imperceptible original precedes and rules the sensible as reducible to the rank of imitation, for the presumed original maintains its purity at the price of negations so complete that it can no longer attest to its reality; neither visible nor actual nor efficacious, it is reduced to a shadow of the reality that it flees by believing it precedes it. But is this "otherworld [*arrière-monde*]" imitated by what he names its image, or, on the contrary, is it not the other that imitates it and, as a result, liberates it as the only actual reality? The unequal relation between the original and the image remains, but it is inverted: the image alone *is*, it alone deserves praise, and it alone accounts for the inexistence of the original. We can point out already that, even inverted, the relation of mimetic rivalry here always remains operative: even more, the same inversion confirms that this rivalry dominates the entire debate concerning the visible and the invisible. Is it, however, necessary to conclude that the image, in being liberated from the yoke of its original, has necessarily escaped the status of an idol?

Second, and on the contrary, Nietzsche radicalizes the idolatrous interpretation of every image. Indeed, if he liberates the image from the original that supposedly devalued it, he subjects it to the person who sees it and evaluates it. The image depends all the more upon a spectator when it is divorced from its original. In Nietzschean terms, one might say: to see a visible involves defining (and producing) a spectacle. This definition ultimately comes down to an evaluation, but every evaluation points, before the evaluated, to an evaluator. Every evaluation is performed by a will to power that attests to and thus recognizes this or that evaluation: "Therefore he calls himself 'man,' which means: the esteemer. To esteem is to create: hear this, you creators! Esteeming itself is of all esteemed things the most estimable pleasure" (*Thus Spake Zarathustra* I, §14).[17] By taking on the status of a value evaluated by a will to power, the image is liberated from its intelligible original only in order to be subjected to man, the estimator—which henceforth becomes the unique original, thus taking the place of all originals. To put this in more phenomenological terms: the visible that a gaze keeps under its view represents (*vorstellen*) less an original invisible and more of a representing (*vertreten*) in the sensible of the scope of this gaze itself; if this gaze stops at this visible, it is because there it discovers the maximum or optimal extent of spectacle that it can support or desire; this gaze no longer transgresses the visible, because it is precisely there that it recognizes itself. From that point on the image imitates its viewer first and does not open onto any original other than its solitary spectator; the gaze is said to be in the visible "which tells it something." The image becomes the idol of man—"man is the original of his idol" (Feuerbach)[18]— but even more, man is self-idolized in the visible that he chooses himself in a spectacle. Thus the inversion of Platonism does not put an end to metaphysical iconoclasm; it radicalizes it. It is no longer a matter of a provisional, amendable idolatry of images, imitating at a distance the intelligible that itself remains pure; rather, here we have a self-idolatry, where man, as estimator of all values, can or should, as regards the world, live only on images of his obsessed will to power. Man becomes obsessed by only ever being able to see the images modeled on himself; by virtue of seeing without being seen, he can see nothing but the mirror images of his own gaze. The besieged obscenity of a universe of idols does not permit a single exit, since the gaze will always only reproduce its idols. And on the forestage [*l'avant-scène*] that does not overhang any "otherworld," the sacrifice will execute the very one that it means to glorify—man, original invisible of haunting images.

With this self-idolatry—where the image is reduced to its spectator as its only original—not only do we bring out the coherence of the two extremes of metaphysical iconoclasm; we also reach our world in its accomplished state of idolatry. For what one calls, very often without thinking about it, an "audiovisual civilization," thus a "world of images," presupposes precisely this self-idolatry. Indeed, a "world of images" becomes possible only if images can still open onto their supposed contrary, the actuality of an original in which to dwell. How did the "world of images" not go stale in a mere world of paper? Because, of course, the images themselves are henceforth valued as actualities [*effectivités*]. How can the distinction between the image and the actual be thus abolished? Because a new term mediates them: man, who actually creates these visible products (things [*perceptibles*] in general), in which, however, he gives only himself to be seen, under a million different roles and by a million and one different schemes. This equivalence can go from the image to the actual reality: the image produces itself with an ever-increasing technical perfection (well said to be a "hologram"), in a way that gives rise to the most efficacious of actual effects in the souls of men (propaganda, publicity, pornography, etc.). What makes these images effective is their ability to satisfy the imaginary needs of their "targets"; thus, in the end, it is their ability to be conformed, precisely as idols, to the expectation and the supposed scope of their spectators. The same equivalence can go, inversely, from the actuality to the image: perhaps the will to power should not only evaluate but be evaluated, thus pushed forward [*se faire évaluer, donc se faire valoir*]; what comes back is made seen by being transposed as completely as possible into an image; but "to create an image" requires that I first reduce myself to an idol measured exactly to the gaze that I want to capture; "public idols" secure veneration only by exhausting themselves in the public's gaze and desire, thus strictly by idolatry in every case. In both operations, the mediation fully rests on the idolatrous function. But in order for it to be put to work, it is necessary that a gaze want to see itself in the desire, pleasure, or fear of other gazes. It is not a matter there, first of all, of either a prostitution or a thirst for power; or rather, these are themselves already derived from self-idolatry.

Thus the objections addressed by the mimetic logic of the image to the doctrine of the icon do not define a past debate. Some indications have sufficed to establish that they renew themselves in the most contemporary situation of the visible—the disaster of the image. As a result, if the icon can resist metaphysical iconoclasm, it would be necessary to infer that it covertly responds to our current situation.

V

According to mimetic logic, the image doubles in the visible what the original keeps in the invisible. A number of aporias result from the simplicity of this opposition: what "is" is neither seen nor perceived nor given; what is seen, perceived, and given "is" not. If the icon is to escape from such aporias, it could be known only by moving beyond, or at least displacing, what appears to be a clear-cut opposition. The question thus becomes: How do the visible and the invisible organize themselves between the τύπος and the προτοτύπος [prototype]? Consider the most trivial occurrence that of an icon, an object of worship, before it is lost in "a work of art": the visible surface of the wood there gives to be seen, surrounded by a face, two eyes; these two painted eyes, however, permit themselves to be intentionally pierced (thus under a mode that is irreal) by the invisible weight of a gaze; in short, in these two dots of basically black paint, I discern not only the visible image of a gaze that is (like all gazes) invisible but, provided that I acquiesce to it, this gaze in person, which, in fact, envisages me. Through the merely painted icon, I discover myself visible and seen by a gaze that, though present in the sensible, remains invisible to me. How then do the visible and the invisible coincide? We have already indicated the answer: intentionally. But how can intentionality here traverse from the visible to the invisible and from the other to myself, while in strict phenomenology it exerts itself from a visible intended object [*un visible visant*] to a visible aim [*un visible visé*] and in the field of an aim in terms of myself [*à partir de moi*]? Without a doubt because here the aim is inverted: it comes in no way from my gaze, but from an invisible gaze that engenders the visibility of its face and then envisages me as visible. This paradox demands a more complete justification; we borrow it from Christology, following the hypothesis concerning the intentional unity of the visible with the invisible in the icon, as an object of the world, aesthetically repeating what the hypostatic union of natures indeed accomplished in Christ, as a paradigm of the universe. Briefly: the visible humanity gives to be recognized in the person of Christ the invisible divinity; this divinity, however, was not in any way directly visible in the humanity of Christ, just as his gaze is not immediately given as a spectacle on the painted wood of the icon. If Christ constitutes, as εἴκων τοῦ θεοῦ τοῦ ἀοράτου [icon of the invisible] (Colossians 1:15), the paradigm of the aesthetic icon, this is in no way because he dispels the ambiguous commerce between the visible and the invisible; it is, on the contrary, because he fulfills its most extreme danger. In his person, human nature becomes, entirely, the type whose prototype consists of nothing less than the divine nature. Thus the aesthetic relation still limited to a visible spectacle (a painted face) is radicalized to its prototype, type of an invisible counter-intentionality (a gaze in person). The difficulty of recognizing on the painted wood of the icon the invisible gaze of Christ precisely reproduces the absolute difficulty of confessing that on the wood of the Cross the divine nature of the Son of God dies according to his humanity, the mortal sufferings of invisible holiness in the horror of visible sin. But the hypostatic union guarantees the intentional unity only by the strictly divine equivalence that enables Christ to say: "The one who has seen me has seen the Father" (John 14:9). Only the intratrinitarian communion, according to the Holy Spirit, between the Son and the Father, legitimates it, as a permanent transition from an eternal type to an eternal prototype that cannot be circumvented—a transition from the hypostatic transitivity of the natures in Christ (from that point eternal) to the intentional transitivity of the visible and the invisible in the aesthetic icon (henceforth a derivative icon). The Trinitarian basis opens up a definitive and unsurpassable distance, which only the Spirit can cross without respite and yet without movement. And this is moreover why He alone renders possible the confession of Christ and the veneration of the icon. Certainly the aesthetic icon manages a remarkable commerce between the visible and the invisible; certainly, contrary to iconoclastic logic, it does not freeze these two terms in two sites, separated by imitation. But precisely the visible and the invisible should not move from one extreme of the icon to the other (and back), since they do not circulate as such at first even within the hypostatic union of natures. And this is only mobilized and brought under the control of only the perichoric relation of the persons of the Trinity: the ultimate icon is thus revealed as a "living icon of charity," according to the salutary formulation of Maximus the Confessor.[19] From this comes a consequence, in fact the principle of the icon: the icon breaks with the rigid distribution of the visible in the sensible and the invisible in the intelligible, because it substitutes for an imitation that divides them a transition that does not cease to exchange them. This transition does not manage the visible and the invisible but organizes them with a view to revealing what neither one of them can manifest on its own: the charity that provides the impetus for the transition itself, a movement from the Son to the Father before any passage from type to prototype or from visible to invisible. According to this transition, charity reveals that the Father is given in and as the Son, that the prototype is opened in and as the visible. But these kenotic transitions never testify to charity. They can thus appear only for the one who goes back to them, according to the same kenotic transition by which charity is offered in a paradox. The idol culminates in the visible glory that it appropriates for itself; the icon is completed in the paradox of an invisible holiness, from which it is torn. Thus the icon also overcomes the metaphysical iconoclasm of our time.

VI

The resolutions established by the Second Council of Nicaea find their conceptual scope in the contemporary debate. They call into question, in the name of the icon as an "icon of charity," the logic of the idol right up to its last mode, self-idolatry. We can note these oppositions point by point.

First, the icon objects to every reduction of the visibility in it to the rank of a mere spectacle; it is not exhausted in an object opened to the gaze of a spectator who is able to see it for himself. For before being viewed and seen [être vue et à voir], the icon silently demands from its visitor that he be seen by it and that, through the visible object, the invisible gaze of the visitor be opened to see the sudden appearance of another invisible gaze. The icon wants its interlocutors to envisage it, face to face, whereas the idol is satisfied with merely satisfying a gaze obsessed with its own spectacle.

Next, the icon liberates the image from the mimetic rivalry between the visible and the invisible, definitively frozen in two extremes: it substitutes the original, or the invisible exhausted in the intelligible, with the prototype. The prototype strikes the image with its mark and testifies to it without similitude, so that in response the mark thus made itself testifies in the movement of its return to the prototype; for similitude (and the rivalry that it provokes), the icon substitutes fidelity (and the intentional communion that it permits). The mark [marque], like every sign, does not claim to (be) give(n) to be seen, but intends to be recognized (and recognize itself) as the prototype that marks it. This transition of recognition plays out just as well within the visible (common sign) or the invisible (between the Father and the Son) as at their limit (in the aesthetic icon or in the face of Christ). Rather than being merely an object, the image then becomes the site of a reciprocal transition, thus the instrument of a communion.

Then, letting itself be pierced by another gaze, the icon requires it to render a gaze—the alms of a gaze—which envisages it as it envisages. In order that the gaze thus rendered not become, again, the setting of a pure spectacle (idol), it is necessary that the gaze given by the icon admit new modality of operation: veneration. For the προσκύνησις [veneration] comes from a gaze that is bent toward the sun and thus neither sees head-on nor is able to object to what it welcomes; this gaze does not see at first, but is exposed to being seen without seeing, thus recognizing in the painted visible the anteriority and real alterity of an other-than-itself. Thus the icon leads us to question the objectification, production, and consummation to which iconoclasm reduces the modern image.

Finally, the icon receives and expects a veneration that, however, it never appropriates for itself. The praise received is immediately transformed in a paradox of glory transmitted and lost; indeed the icon deserves veneration only insofar as it shows an other-than-itself and thus becomes the pure type of the prototype, toward which it does not cease to return absolutely. The image extricates itself from idolatry by constantly destroying the screen of its visibility, in order to become impoverished, as the pure sign of that which marks it; the visible is opened, as an abyss or sky that transpierces the obsession with the world. Our imprisoning "world of images" would not admit a single escape to the least bit of freedom if it weren't for the once and for all piercing of the spear that opened the side of Christ.

The icon thus contradicts point by point the modern determination of the image, following the ruthless demands of metaphysical iconoclasm. Far from managing a new spectacle, it allows it to point to another gaze. Far from comparing the visible to the invisible by a mimetic rivalry, it bears the mark of the blow of a prototype by which it is recognized. Far from prostituting itself in a self-idolatrous spectacle, it solicits a veneration that it does not cease to transmit to its prototype. It thus defines itself as the other gaze of a prototype, which demands the veneration of my own gaze climbing, across this type, toward it. The icon has as its only interest the crossing of gazes—thus, strictly speaking, love. In contrast to dogmatic metaphysics the icon saves the image from the status of illusion, alienated from an invisible and intelligible original. In contrast to metaphysics in a state of nihilism, the icon saves the image from self-idolatry, thus from the foreclosure of the "world of images." Neither orphan of the invisible nor prisoner of the visible, the image that takes up the role of the icon again becomes the bond of a communion. The image-affirming [iconodoule] doctrine of the Second Council of Nicaea concerns not only nor first of all a point in the history of ideas, nor even a decision of Christian dogma: it formulates above all an—perhaps the only—alternative to the contemporary disaster of the image. In the icon, the visible and the invisible embrace each other from a fire that no longer destroys but rather lights up the divine face for humanity.

Thomas Aquinas and Onto-theo-logy

Hoc ipsum esse, secundum quod est in creaturis ab ipso removemus; et tunc remanet in quadam tenebra ignorantiae.

—*In Sententiarum Libros* I, distinction 8, question 1, answer 1, ad 4m

The Construction of the Question

Whatever the relevance of the thesis claiming the radical historicity of truth, the greatness of a thought may be measured by its ability to transcend the historical conditions of its appearance and disappearance to go on reappearing in debates and disputes which, at first glance, should not have called it up or welcomed it. In brief, a great thought manages to survive its own epoch so that, as timeless or at least as stubbornly reoccurring, it takes part in epochs that are no more its own and makes itself anachronically contemporary. The thought of Saint Thomas illustrates this paradox in a preeminent way. It has not ceased, from rebirths to rediscoveries, to compel recognition, even during centuries in which it should not have, in principle, seemed able to enter the scene. In a word, Thomism in the strict sense, consists solely in an almost uninterrupted series of "returns to Saint Thomas," which are expressed as much in the alleged fidelity as in the unquestionable diversity of the interpretations. And our time is no exception to this reflex, which, like the others, claims (at least in outline) "to return" to Thomas in order to better invest, today, debates as unknown to him as they are unavoidable for us.

What debates are we talking about? We can name several that have followed each other chronologically: realism against criticism, the issue about the *analogia entis*, then the question of being itself, without even mentioning any debate over "Christian philosophy." To these common threads of discussion in which Thomism never ceases to redefine itself, we add another: the running debate on onto-theo-logy. With this concept, Heidegger has cast into play a new definition of the essence of metaphysics; but he has also established a hermeneutic of the history of philosophy so powerful that it could not be matched, but only by the one used by Hegel. In effect, to the degree that the concept of onto-theo-logy strictly defines all metaphysics and that each metaphysics is necessarily characterized by its impotence to think the difference between entity and being, it is necessary to conclude that, by its very onto-theo-logical constitution, no metaphysics has any access to being as such but only to being(s) as entity(ies).[1] Metaphysics is thus defined as the thought that asserts being only so long as it does not think it, which is to say that it does not reach it. The best indication of this impotence typically comes from the fact that the formula "being inasmuch as it is being" does not disclose in our real understanding much more than "entity inasmuch as it is entity" precisely because when we claim, too quickly and too superficially, to think and to speak being, in reality. We never reach "to be" but, instead, stick to nothing but the subsistence and enduring presence of an entity (one out of the beings). It is not enough to invoke being in order to think it otherwise than as an entity and its properties (e.g., subsistence, independence, act, eternity, etc.), which obviously never define being ("to be") but always nothing—no *thing*—else than entity alone, that is, precisely a thing. This much we can agree on: the facility in qualifying entity with the title of God neither affects nor improves in the least the result that it is still a question of entity, to which being remains wholly irreducible and God completely foreign.

Consequently, if it might happen that the thought of Thomas Aquinas were also to share the common lot of philosophies belonging to onto-theology (directly or by reliable historical mediaries), it would suffer profound harm. First, because it would become once again precisely what all Thomistic philosophers have always intended that it not be: just one more metaphysics among all the others, so that it would have to give up the claim of dominating, from its speculative height, all previous metaphysical schemes and their derivations in subsequent metaphysics (to assume the strongly normative typology of the history of philosophy asserted by this point of view, e.g., by E. Gilson). Moreover, since onto-theo-logy by definition never thinks of being except in relation to entity, that is, confusing being and entity, this hypothesis, if it were true of Thomas Aquinas, would prevent his thought from assuming to have achieved the act of being (*actus essendi*) as the correct definition of God, for, if it were applicable to God, He could remain only as a supreme entity, but it certainly would not be a question of being. If Thomas's doctrine could be assimilated into an onto-theo-logy, it would lose its privileged position in relation to other metaphysics since it would have to renounce any pretense of having achieved *esse*; whether divine or not matters little, because in the first place even the distinction between *ens* and *esse*, or at least the irreducibility of *esse* to its ontic interpretation, would become problematic. Thus, in addition to the theological suspicion of having given in to idolatry by having reduced God to the rank of *esse*, there would also be this time the philosophical accusation of having confused being with entity and claiming most imprudently to have achieved the former, while having treated only the latter. The truth of this question is, then, a debate that is absolutely decisive for the present and future validity of all thought that would like to call itself Thomistic, as much in theology as in philosophy.[2]

Nevertheless, as essential as it may seem today, this debate has long remained foreign to Thomists, occupied as they have been whether with internal quarrels (types of analogy, the concept of entity, the real composition of *esse* and *essentia*) or ritual polemics against modern philosophy as "subjectivist" and/or "idealist." Even when this debate was taken up, it was most often in the form of a dilemma: either the term "onto-theology" was playing the role of a pure and simple sign of infamy, sufficient for pure ideology to disqualify any Thomistic engagement or, tactically, indeed by bravado, it became a title of glory that one assumed not without courage although often without discernment. Both of these attitudes seem to me equally inadequate and ineffective because they omit two indispensable precautions: first, to define exactly the characteristics of ontology according to Heidegger, then, to measure precisely whether the theses of Thomas Aquinas exemplify certain of those characteristics and how far. Only if these two conditions are fulfilled will it become possible to give a different response to the question or, at least, to measure its dimensions and implications.

The Characteristics of Onto-theo-logy

Since one must understand the question correctly before answering it, it is necessary to define (or redefine) onto-theo-logy. Heidegger, in his lecture titled *The Onto-theological Constitution of Metaphysics*, given and published in 1957, elaborates on such a definition: "The onto-theological constitution of metaphysics stems from the prevalence of that Difference, which keeps Being as the ground [*Sein als Grund*] and entity as grounded [*Seiendes als gegründet*] and what gives grounds as a cause [*begründendes*] apart from and related to each other; and by this keeping, perdurance [*Austrag*] is achieved."[3] This determination indicates, then, a double intersecting foundation. (1) Being—inasmuch as it differs definitely from every entity—is proclaimed not an entity, thus as having nothing of entity and especially nothing of that particular entity called God.[4] On the contrary, insofar as it is a negation of entity, it is able to ground each and every entity, including that named "God," because it makes them both thinkable (according to entity, indeed to a concept of entity) and possible (conceivable as noncontradictory in a concept). (2) Reciprocally, entity, in particular the first entity proclaimed in each metaphysics, not only grounds the other beings in the name of the first cause that gives an account as well but also grounds the being of an entity by bringing it to perfection and even by bringing into existence the formal characteristics of entitativeness. These two principal foundations (the second one doubling itself) remain, however, intersected by the difference, which distinguishes them as being and entity and, for the same reason, reconciles them.

Such a pattern implies two types of consequences, some explicitly taken up by Heidegger, the others carried on by historians of philosophy. The first implication is that, according to its onto-theological constitution, any metaphysics has to be organized around the multiple meanings of its single foundation because it is decidedly according to the foundation that the two terms are defined—whether it be the conceptual foundation [*Gründung*] of the entities in being or the causal foundation and sufficient reason [*Begründung*] of the entities by a supreme entity. Moreover, it is also this single foundation that makes it possible to link together these two intersecting foundations, conceptual and causal. In fact, if it happens that being itself (and not only entities) could prove to be grounded in a supreme being, it is because the latter fulfills being by exemplarily achieving its characteristics of being in general among entities—that is, by actualizing possible being. But no doubt there is room here not only for redoubling the second foundation, as Heidegger suggests it, but to justify, too, a third foundation: this would deal not only with the other entities but even with being itself (and its conceptual foundation) as grounded by the supreme entity (and its causative foundation). By way of example, let us select the case, neutral because paradoxical, of one of the two Cartesian onto-theologies. (1) We shall say that, if being is defined on the basis of thought (as *cogitare*), then being would ground entities conceptually by distributing them into a well-known dilemma: "to be is to think or to be thought" [*esse est cogitari aut cogitare*].[5] Now, obviously, all entities without exception rely on this foundation through being, including in the first place the entity that plays the role of first or supreme entity, "God." (2) Then, we could emphasize here that the preeminent entity, that is, the *ego* that thinks (itself) as *res cogitans* and thus first grounds its own existence (*ego sum, ego existo*), also grounds in reason and produces efficaciously, too, those other entities, which are, only insofar as they are thought by it, considered as an entity that thinks first of all itself before any other. (3) Finally, we may conclude that the conceptual foundation of every entity by thought [*Gründung*] is grounded, in turn, in the causal foundation that the *res cogitans* achieves on all thinkable thoughts, thus fulfilling the being of entities.[6] From this first implication, we shall thus conclude that we could not speak accurately about onto-theo-logy without three foundations being at work: the conceptual foundation of entity as such by being [*Gründung*], the foundation of entities by the supreme entity according to efficient causality [*Begründum*], and finally the foundation of the conceptual foundation by the efficient foundation. Of course, the question remains open (although Heidegger did not determine it explicitly) whether onto-theo-logy requires that these three foundations work simultaneously or just one, or two at a time and, in such a case, which ones. We will have to keep in mind this indecision.

A second implication follows, which was more explicitly drawn out by Heidegger himself. The preeminent entity exercises a foundation on all other beings—indeed upon being and its own foundation—but it cannot do it but by acting immediately as causality and efficacy. It must, therefore, turn back on itself the efficient and causal foundation that it exercises on all other entities; it is defined, no matter what name it bears, by its principal function as *causa sui*: "The Being of entity is represented fundamentally, in the sense of the ground, as *causa sui*. This is the metaphysical concept of God."[7] The fame of this statement has, without any doubt, at times masked some of its features. First, in the strict sense, so long as the very term *causa sui* does not appear before Descartes used it, one could not be allowed to speak properly of *causa sui* unless after him (except carefully to make explicit the implicit, which does not happen of itself). Next, the *causa sui* points essentially to a function of foundation by a supreme entity in a metaphysical system, which does not always or necessarily turn out to be God. Thus the supreme entity that grounds by grounding itself through itself can also take the face of "self-thinking thought" (Aristotle) or of the "Eternal Return of the Same" (Nietzsche), as well of that of the divine *causa sui* or that of the "intelligible Word" (Malebranche) and the "ultimate reason of things" (Leibniz). Heidegger marks this clearly by emphasizing that the *causa sui,* when it brings God into philosophy, first assigns him the name of Zeus and that, even so, "before this God man can neither pray nor offer sacrifice."[8] What used to be called God here thus refers, first of all, to a mere function in the onto-theo-logical constitution, that of the causal foundation grounding itself in the manifestation of a first entity. From this perspective—although historically questionable—the God revealed in Jesus Christ would offer only one case, one candidate, or one claimant among many others (neither the first, nor the last, nor even the best) for the function strictly, indeed exclusively, metaphysical of the *causa sui.* Just one condition rules all of them, however: that they should ground entities and being in the name of the preeminent entity, thus that they could be inscribed precisely without exception or remainder within the onto-theo-logical frame of the ontological difference, which is itself thought in a metaphysical manner, starting with and for the exclusive benefit of the entity.

Thus onto-theo-logy is defined according to some extremely precise characteristics, without which we would remain unable to identify any philosophical thought as metaphysical: (a) the "God" must be inscribed explicitly in the metaphysical domain, that is, to allow itself to be determined by the historical determinations of being, inasmuch as it is entity, perhaps beginning with the concept of entity; (b) it must establish there a causal foundation [*Begründung*] of all the common entities for which it is the reason; (c) to achieve this, it must always assume the function and perhaps even the name of *causa sui,* that is, of supreme founding entity, because it was supremely founded by itself. To ask the question of the relationship of Thomas Aquinas's thought to onto-theo-logy thus amounts, beyond prejudicial and ideological polemics, to examining whether it meets these requirements.

The Object of *Metaphysica*

The definition of metaphysics according to onto-theo-logy implies that God, whatever He is, precisely is only under the condition that He ensures the universal establishment in the being of entities (as it were "launched" into being). Thus we need first to measure how far the Thomistic acception of God, assuming the function of a foundation, as he does, would give him the rank of a "God" of metaphysics.

Let us note first that Thomas Aquinas, even if he already uses the concept of *metaphysica,*[9] still uses it with parsimony, without surmising from its usage that the commentary tradition was just attributing to Aristotle. Contrary to the majority of his successors, even the immediate ones, he made of it neither the title of a work nor the focal point of his thought. There is an excellent reason for this prudence: in his eyes, *metaphysica* designates, although not without ambiguity, a strictly philosophical and natural discipline. Defining the title of the books called the *Metaphysics* of Aristotle, he left that word, until this point, undefined or called it simply "haec scientia" and attributes to "this science" no less than three names, none of which, therefore, completely satisfy him: (1) "scientia divina sive theologia," inasmuch as it considers separate substances; (2) "prima philosophia," insofar as it considers the first causes of things; and, (3) finally, "metaphysica" strictly speaking, insofar as it considers entity and what belongs to it ("inquantum considerat ens et ea quae consequuntur ipsum"), that is, inasmuch as it has for its object "ipsum solum ens commune."[10] Nevertheless, could not one raise the objection that we are thus meeting, once again, the reciprocal play between a science of entity in general (*metaphysica*) and a science of the divine inasmuch as it exercises the function of a first cause (*theologia*)? And is that not precisely onto-theo-logy?

This hasty conclusion, however, would lead to a complete misinterpretation because the *theologia* included here in *metaphysica* does not at all amount to the entire notion of theology. Indeed, it is necessary to recognize that "the theology which deals with sacred doctrine" differs generically from the theology that is part of philosophy ("theologia quae ad sacram doctrinam pertinet differt secundum genus ab illa theologia quae pars philosophiae ponitur") or, again, that "theologia sive scientia divina est duplex."[11] In what is this duality rooted? Only theology in the sense of "sacra doctrina" can claim to know divine things in themselves, since it alone receives them "according as they reveal themselves" [*secundum quod ipsae seipsas manifestant*] and "according to what the manifestation of divine things requires" [*secundum quod requirit rerum divinarum manifestatio*]. More precisely, it can take them "as the subject of its science, because it receives them from the outset as such" [*ipsas res divinas, considerat propter seipsas ut subjectunt scientia*], for "it is that theology which is transmitted in Sacred Scripture" [*haec est theologia, quae in sacra Scriptura traditur*]. With regard, in contrast, to "the theology that philosophers deal with and that, by another name, is called metaphysics" [*quam philosophi prosequuntur; quae alio nomine metaphysica dicitur*], it is not able to attain divine things except through their effects ("secundum quod per effectus manifestantur"), which are the only legitimate subject of *metaphysica*, that is to say, the *ens in quantum ens*: "Divine realities are treated by philosophers only insofar as they are the principles of all things. This is because they are expounded in that part of the doctrine where are assigned the things common to all beings that have for their subject *ens* inasmuch as it is *ens*."[12] The science of entity as such is able to deal with divine things, strictly speaking, but only through their effects as entities and according to their entitativeness. Since their effects (and not the divine things themselves) are said only according to entitativeness and as entities, it is necessary to conclude that divine things *are* not directly inscribed in the theology of metaphysics as its subject as it would be if they were revealed completely by common entity. Rather those divine things intervene only indirectly as the principles of things (or *substrat*) and not as the things themselves, "non tanquam subjectum scientiae, sed tanquam principia subjecti." In other words, separate substances and divine things are recognized as subjects only to the *theologia sacrae Scripturae,* which can alone reveal them and make them directly accessible. At the same time, the *theologia philosophica* must limit itself to taking note of the effects of divine things in *ens in quantum ens* and to approach them only as the principle of these effects, whereas revealed theology deals with them as its subject.[13] Divine things exceed the theology of metaphysics exactly inasmuch as the principle of the subject exceeds the subject of a science. And as metaphysical theology deals with divine things according to entity inasmuch as it is entity, it is necessary to conclude that the theology of revelation exceeds entity as entity. To sum up, God does not belong to metaphysical theology precisely insofar as He remains the principle of the subject of metaphysics, that is, of entity inasmuch as it is entity.

In this way, according to Thomas Aquinas, God as such does not belong to metaphysics, or to theology, or to *ens commune,* or to *ens in quantum ens.* By making such a radical theoretical decision, Aquinas sets himself, in advance, against his successors, who quickly invert this choice in order to reintegrate God in metaphysics and its object—that is, entity, and shortly thereafter the concept of entity, too. This will be the case as early as Aegidius of Rome, who states it without ambiguity: "Its subject [metaphysics] can be called God because the principle of entitativeness is reserved to God more than to other beings. On account of this, it is said that metaphysical science is divine and of God."[14] Here, metaphysics deals (or claims to deal) with God as such because it does not have the least doubt that entitativeness has the right and the power to rule God. Despite its alleged privileged entity, God plays exactly the same game as all other entities: he goes into the subject of metaphysics and becomes, therefore, able to undertake there an onto-theological function. "When you say that God escapes entitativeness, I reply that this is false and, even more, that it is entirely true that God is an entity."[15] God can neither flee nor escape from the entitativeness—which deprives Him of his transcendence and which clasps Him in the common net where all beings, so to speak, swarm. The privilege of an exceptional entitativeness that is granted Him makes, in fact, no difference since He is rewarded by inscribing Him into the uniform regime of entity.[16]

Duns Scotus will give a more solid foundation to this thesis by stating that "God is thought only under the reason of entity" [*Deus non intelligitur nisi sub ratione entis*] and, moreover, that *ens* can only be understood univocally because "God is naturally knowable to us only if entity is univocal for the created and the uncreated" [*Deus non est cognoscible a nobis naturaliter nisis ens sit univocum creato et increato*].[17] It is indeed, therefore, the object of metaphysics—the entity radically conceived as univocal both for the created and uncreated—that includes God at the same time into the *ens commune* (with only the correction of infinity) and into metaphysics, so that this concept makes metaphysics for the first time fully acknowledgeable.

Far from remaining marginal, this inclusion will be consecrated definitively at the end of medieval scholasticism by Suárez. Replacing the customary commentary on the *Sentences* or the *Summa* with the literary form characteristic of *Disputationes metaphysicae,* he started immediately by defining the *objectum metaphysicae:* "Entity insofar as it is real entity must amount to the adequate object of this science" [*ens in quantum ens reale (debet) esse objectum adequatum hujus scientiae*]. This formula, in appearance harmless enough, is nevertheless supported by a radical ontic and noetic reduction: entity is defined as an objective and, above all, formal concept that grips it in a completely abstract representation. A drastic consequence follows from this: because this concept is understood as universally as its abstraction allows, it may come before God himself ("aliquam rationem entis, quae sit prior natura Deo") and must therefore embrace God. However, the distinction between finite and infinite will come along to mark a distance (and a very real one, as the Cartesian revival will show) and soften the claim made on God, but the infinite remains nonetheless always inscribed within the realm of entity and within the grasp of metaphysics so that the distinction reinforces the submission of God rather than makes an exception of it. From that moment on, God is included within metaphysics and definitively becomes a part of it: "The adequate object of this science [metaphysics] must include God" [*objectum adequatum hujus scientiae* (mainly *metaphysicae) debere comprehendere Deum*].[18] The univocal concept of being implies, requires, and achieves, both in fact and in right, the inclusion of God in metaphysics. To oppose that inclusion was precisely the unique achievement of Thomas.

In contrast to the apparently irresistible development of the greatest number of his commentators and followers—who all are inclined to understand God within the concept of entity in order to inscribe Him into the object of metaphysics, thus producing the conditions of a genuine onto-theo-logy in theology through ontology–the unmatched position of Thomas Aquinas appears forcefully. For him, God as such does not belong to the subject of metaphysical theology: He remains only the principle (or creator) of common entity, but alone does not fall under it. "First, inasmuch as other existents depend on common esse, but God does not, even more does common esse depend on God. . . . Next, inasmuch as all existents are contained in common *esse*, but God is not, even more is common *esse* contained under His power, since this divine power goes beyond created *esse* itself."[19] God embraces metaphysics but cannot be caught within it. This thesis will seem paradoxical only so long as one fails to recognize Thomas Aquinas in his true historical situation, which was essentially opposed to the main trend of Thomistic commentary. Paradoxical or not, it denies an essential requirement of all onto-theology—that "God" (or whatever may exercise the function of grounding) should imply being as much as all the entities that He founds and in the same way.

Esse Commune and the Analogy

Let us consider this thesis further, then: is it simply a matter of uniqueness in conceptual nomenclature, or is it a decisive choice that determines the entire thought of Thomas Aquinas? Is it supported elsewhere in his thought, or is it an isolated doctrine that does not seriously call into question the onto-theology ruling the whole issue?

The onto-theo-logical interpretation of the thought of Thomas Aquinas implies, beyond the inscription of God within metaphysics, that the same concept could govern "God," the supreme entity, just as much as the entity insofar as it is entity: only this intermediary link could secure the foundations that join the one to the other. Can one recognize any similar concept in Thomas Aquinas in such a way that one could anticipate those of Duns Scotus and Suárez? This seems to be the case from the moment that *ens* is so very often defined by its primacy from the point of view of knowledge: "That which is first offered to the conception of the understanding is being, because it is only insofar as it is in act that a thing is knowable . . . and entity is the proper object of the understanding and it is thus the first intelligible."[20] Thus *ens* is known, or is better defined, by the fact that it is known before every other determination because nothing is known that in some manner is not. What, therefore, distinguishes this position from those of Duns Scotus and Suárez? Two fundamental points.

First, the conception of *ens* thus disengaged does not define here the subject of metaphysics, or that of theological metaphysics, or a fortiori that of revealed theology but only the known object: the priority remains strictly noetic, without claiming to impose itself as a universal or ontical one.

Next and above all, this conception of *ens* does not affect God, and for at least two reasons. (1) Primarily, this conception does not affect God because the divine *esse* cannot be assimilated to *esse commune;* the *Summa Theologiae* demonstrates this by distinguishing two ways in which *esse* is said "without addition": either because its definition implies it without any addition (the *esse commune* of finite entity negatively understood) or because its definition. implies positively that it entails without any possible addition [*divine esse*].[21] The *Contra Gentiles* goes further by emphasizing that the abstract universality of knowledge does not affect God: in effect, since what is common is obtained only by "the understanding that apprehends form . . . stripped of all its individualizing and specifying characteristics" [*intellectu qui apprehendit formam . . . exspoliatam ab omnibus individuantibus et specificantibus*], if God were identified with this abstract *esse commune*, it would be necessary that "there were no existing thing except that alone which is present in the understanding" [non *(esset) aliqua res existens, nisi quae sit in intellectu tantum*]; now God is by definition outside understanding alone; therefore he cannot be confused with *esse commune* such that only representation by understanding suffices to distinguish Him. On the contrary, Aquinas will say that "the divine *esse* is without addition not only in thought, but even in reality; and not only is it without addition, but it cannot even receive addition."[22] Such a rejection of represented *ens* and/or of *esse commune* as the point of departure in the knowledge of God is enough to disqualify in advance all attempts by Duns Scotus and Suárez. Above all, it removes God from the domain of entity that metaphysics claims to open and to delimit. It is precisely because the *esse* proper to God alone is stripped away from metaphysics that it gets free, too, from metaphysical intelligibility, even to the point of appearing from that perspective as altogether completely unknown: "Since the argument [the identity in God of *esse* and essence] understands *esse* as that by which God subsists in Himself, His *esse* remains as unknown to us as His essence."[23] Nothing could be more rigorous and consistent than this conclusion: if, on the one hand, the *esse* of metaphysics, which pertains to created entities, borrows its primacy from any (human) intelligibility; and if, on the other hand, the divine *esse* escapes from metaphysics, then the divine *esse* should and could also be disengaged from its intelligibility. By this essential dichotomy, Thomas Aquinas not only rejects in advance any kind of univocal concept of entity but, more important, he denies the core of every onto-theo-logy that the theological and ontological functions may ground one another thus within a common determination, which the duality of foundations (conceptual and efficient) cannot threaten but, rather, reinforces. The *esse/ens commune* cannot, according to Thomas Aquinas, introduce anything common and, above all, nothing intelligible between entity inasmuch as it is entity and God.

The analogy of being—about which it makes sense to emphasize once again that Thomas Aquinas scarcely uses the term *analogia entis*—has other function than to dig the chasm that separates the two understandings of *esse* (and not to bridge it).[24] It is even more necessary to underline that, coming from Duns Scotus unto Suárez by means of Cajetan, the inflation of this doctrine has had no other aim than to submit it to the growing empire of the univocal and intelligible concept of *ens*. For Thomas Aquinas, analogy by contrast intended to emphasize that no name, no concept, no determination should be applied in the same sense to the creature and to God, especially *esse*. Analogy does not mean the tangential univocity of *esse commune*, but, on the contrary, it opens a space where the univocity of being must be exploded. To do so, Thomas Aquinas proposes a radical distinction in *esse*: "*Esse* is said in two ways: in the first, to signify the act of being, in the other to signify the composition of a proposition, an act of the soul joining a predicate to a subject"[25] Like the composition of subject and predicate, that of esse and essence determines without exception all the field of created entities, but it disappears in God, and in this case alone, essence is no longer distinguished from the act of being: "God is not only his essence but his *esse* as well."[26] This mode of being belongs properly to God and separates Him from every other entity or, rather, from entitativeness in general. God alone, Thomas Aquinas does not cease to emphasize, has nothing in common with entity: "In God alone, His essence is his *esse*" [*soli Deo cujus solius essentia est suum esse*]; or: "It is proper to God alone that the mode of being is his subsistent esse" [*Solius autem Dei proprius modus essendi est, ut sit suum esse subsistens*]; and "God alone is His *esse*" [*Solus Deus est suum esse*].[27] The difference between being and essence, what one could call the ousio-ontical difference, that goes "horizontally" through all created entities is not simply nullified in God but becomes the instrument for enforcing a complete difference, which one could call "vertical," between the ousio-ontical difference taken globally, on the one hand, and, on the other, the ousio-ontic indifference of God. This new difference becomes obvious by creation: "It is necessary, therefore, that in which *esse* is other than its essence have *esse* caused by another" [*Oportet ergo, quod illud, cui esse est aliud ab essentia suet, habeat esse causatum ab alio*]—the essence differs from the *esse*, then the entity shows itself to be caused. Reciprocally, "to create belongs to God according to His *esse*, which is His essence" [*creare convenit Deo secundum suum esse, quod est ejus essentia*].[28] The identity of essence with *esse* becomes here the basis for the power and the character of the creator. This difference (cause/creation) is not identical to the real distinction and composition (*esse*/essence), but its distinct mark is to oppose the real distinction—as well as every *conceptus entis*. The analogy between these two differences does not cease to deepen their dissimilarity in order to guarantee that never will the being of creatures be taken for the *esse* of God.

Thomas Aquinas ensures this, further, through two characteristics given to analogy. (a) First, it is a matter of *proportio* and not of *proportionalitas*: "analogiam idest proprotionem."[29] Whereas *proportionalitas* translates and thus recalls a proportion of four terms, which entails a defined, commensurable, and intelligible: relation between them, *proportio*, by contrast, has no further ambition than to refer several terms to a focal point without the necessity of any common measure between them. The choice for *proportio* thus implies that one admits the epistemological legitimacy of an incommensurable, undefined, and in this sense unintelligible relation between the connected terms. By having preferred an analogy of *proportio*, Thomas Aquinas would have thus marked that he has *not* confused mathematical analogy with the analogy of reference; rather he has repudiated the commensurability of mathematical analogy in order to establish a reference between incommensurable terms (immeasurable because one term remains immense). The analogy of reference leaves "the reality signified outside every limit and overflows the signification of the name" [*rem significatam, ut incomprehendam et excedentem nominis significationem*].[30] (b) Furthermore, *proportio* does not refer to a term standing by its own (*ad aliquod unum*): this pole of reference must not be understood as neutral and abstract, taken outside the series of analogues (as health for sickness, medicine, remedy, etc.), so that it could refer each of them at the same title; rather it refers to another term (*ad alterum*), itself within the series, or even to one of the real terms in the reference (*ad unum ipsorum*), as an effect to its cause or principle, as accidents to their substance.[31] This primary analogical term, a real term, remains at the same time different from its analogues and yet intrinsically constitutive of them. The created thus does not support or claim any commensurable proportion (according to the common concept of entity) with God; but Thomas refers to that *proportio* even to the point of bringing in it this *esse commune* on the same level as any created essence, both being thus trespassed according to the exteriority intrinsic to God.

Analogy thus strongly confirms what the exception of God toward the *esse commune* was already suggesting: if God should happen to be, it would never be as taking the part of any object (or subject) of *metaphysica*, above all as yielding to any kind of univocal concept of entity. The univocity that makes, as a principle and a method, the onto-theology possible (and by the way the metaphysics too, that sometimes embodies it historically) is in advance dismissed by Thomas, who refuses in general the first criterion of onto-theology—that is, the inclusion of "God" in the metaphysical realm unified by and for the sake of entity and, possibly, by one and the same concept of entity One can guess, nevertheless, the price that God must pay in order to remove Himself from this constitution of metaphysics: since onto-theology holds its authority by a concept of entity that makes it intelligible (by definition, since *ens* is the first intelligible), God, in order to distance Himself from this, will have to make Himself known as incomprehensible. But, then God is not first of all incomprehensible in Himself but precisely in order to escape onto-theo-logy—or to free *us* from it.

Cause and Foundation

Such foreignness of God with regard to a metaphysical concept of entity, even supposing that we grant it, would not yet allow, however, to establish that He eludes onto-theology completely. For the second criterion of onto-theo-logy obviously seems to affirm the contrary, since it defines the metaphysical God by his efficient foundation of all other entities, indeed by the efficient foundation of being in general. Now this seems indisputably the case for what Thomas Aquinas views under the name of cause: "It is then necessary to pose a first efficient cause which all call God."[32]

It hardly seems worthy of discussion that the relations of creation and hence of intelligibility between creature and creator are treated here perfectly in terms of foundation—and of foundation by an efficient cause. For not only does efficient causality make created entities get into the entitativeness (from God into the world), but it also opens in return (from the world to God) a knowledge of the creator as a cause and in relation to causality: "We cannot know God naturally except by arriving at Him through effects."[33] Thus God is only named by the name of the cause and because of the cause ("Deus nominari dicitur a suis causatis"); the names attributed to God only make sense as effects from whence they come; they can be applied to God with this minimum of nonimpropriety, which separates them from pure and simple equivocity only to the degree that the causal relation guarantees that they bear the mark of their cause, at least by virtue of its efficient causality. "Good," "beautiful," "true," and so on doubtless tell us nothing of divine goodness, truth, and beauty except that they proceed from it by an indisputable efficient causation but abstractly and without real content. It is only with regard to this relation of what is caused up to its cause that the community of the names of God is generally founded: "These names have nothing in common, but that they follow the order assigned by the cause to what it causes" [*in hujus modi nominum communitate ordo causae et causati*].[34] In short, causality rules the two meanings of the relation: first the entitativeness of the created through God and then the knowledge of God through the created entities. In addition, the empire of causality even extends to the relation of analogy, which, as understood as *proportio*, seems only to offer a particular case of it: "The proportion of the creature to God is the same as that of the caused to the cause and of knowing to the knowable."[35] This hypothesis being granted, there may be a great possibility of contradiction between the analogy, the function of which consists of opening and maintaining the difference of a radical ignorance of God according to *esse commune*, and the causality, whose relation of abstract intelligibility extends as far as its efficacy produces effects, that is, universally. Does not the foundation that assures that "God" bears the name of "cause" endow Him with an intelligibility whose withdrawal was precisely what analogy aimed at? Is not the metaphysical intelligibility of God, undermined by the limitation of the *esse commune* to the created and by the difference of analogy, entirely restored by the assignment of the function of foundation through efficient causality to God?

To the very degree that this question imposes itself, to that same degree so does its denial. In fact, Thomas Aquinas does not so much submit God to efficient causality in the way in which subsequent metaphysics has understood its concept as he reinterprets the causal relation between the created and uncreated according to the demands of analogy, that is, by imposing consideration for the gap of ignorance on it so that causality does not amount to a mere foundation, the terms of which could reciprocally ground one another. Several arguments permit us to establish that the issue consists in redefining causality. (*a*) First of all is the fact that *causa* cannot be understood in Thomas Aquinas as the "totalis et efficiens causa," which Descartes crudely assigns to the creative act of God.[36] For Thomas, on the contrary, divine causality, even if it privileges efficient causality, does not become total since it is achieved also according to finality and form. Far from reducing causality to efficient causality, a restriction that *metaphysica*, with the exception of Leibniz, will massively ratify, Thomas Aquinas confirms the Aristotelian multivocity of causes. (*b*) Above all, he adds a more theological precaution to this properly philosophical reluctance by understanding the *causa* also along the lines of the meaning of Dionysius: "God is the universal cause of all things that occur naturally" [*Est autem Deus universalis causa omnium quae naturaliter fiunt*].[37] In this context, the cause appears to be less what produces than what happens to be required by the thing in order for it to be (as already for Aristotle) and, more radically, what happens to be asked on the mode of prayer (αἰτία from αἰτεῶ) by the creature to the creator, as the request that the petitioner makes to the petitioned. This petitioner has less the status of an effect than that of a *causatum*, of something caused that keeps within itself the full mark of the *causa*, according to a relation less transitive than immanent.

From these two corrections to the concept of causality, an important consequence follows: abstract intelligibility, transparent and eventually univocal efficient causality gives way, for Thomas Aquinas (and the contrary is true for his successors), to a causality co-determined by the relation of creation. Thus, if the caused effects remain really grounded in the cause, they are at the same time infinitely exceeded by it ("prima omnium causa excedens omnia sua causata"). Although completely determined by it, or by that very fact, they remain "definitely inadequate" [*effectus Dei virtutem causae non adaequentes*].[38] Such inadequacy of caused effects to the excessive cause—which results directly from the pattern of creation—obviously implies a unilateral not reciprocal foundation: it goes up to the caused from the cause but never back to the cause from the caused. Creation imposes an essential asymmetry on causality (a mixed relation), which, in return, forbids any attempt to establish a reciprocal foundation of being by entity or of entity by entity. Here, God, whether understood still as entity (*ens*) or already as *esse,* grounds entities but does not in any event receive any counterfoundation, neither from entities (since He creates them) nor from entity as such, from entity in general or *esse commune* (since He creates these as well). The cause can thus certainly remain unknown as such, because, even if it can be known as grounding its effects, it nevertheless gets back no foundation that would make it reciprocally intelligible. This Thomistic reform of causality allows the cause to produce the *esse commune* while transcending it completely. Not being contained within it, this kind of cause defeats, before the fact, the metaphysical system in which causality is only exercised within the limits of the field (and of the concept) of the entity: that is, at first effectively grounding the privileged entity on the derived entities, then exposing itself to the (logical) counterfoundation of the privileged entity by entity in general. Here, according to Thomas Aquinas, causality does not return to God, who achieves it using inasmuch as he keeps off of it.

We can now sketch the relation of causality to the *esse commune.* Contrary to the disposition that *metaphysica* is supposed to have imposed, causality does not unfold the very meaning of being (or of entity) according to Thomas Aquinas but, instead, presides over it—it determines it as another than itself, as its debtor, not as its rule. Causality is not set to work by setting being (or entity) in motion, but it determines that being (or entity) as relying on itself and by distinguishing itself from it. While Heidegger supposes that causality, by exercising onto-theo-logical foundation, completes (itself) at one blow (as) the being of entity, we must suppose that, for Thomas Aquinas, causality is exercised *upon* the being of entity, therefore from outside of it, without being exercised *by* or at least according to it. May one suggest that this exceptional causality arises from its nonmetaphysical meaning? Between the two theses, then, a radical difference is drawn: a distance that distinguishes by itself causality and the being of entity rather than identifying them, as *metaphysica* never stopped to do. We may explain this difference with some new arguments.

(a) God explains himself as *esse* only by exercising a causality toward entities, which affects their *esse* as much as their essences: "He is in all by essence insofar as He is present to all as *causa essendi*" [*Est in omnibus per essentiam, in quantum adest omnibus ut causa essendi*]. This *causa essendi*[39] strictly speaking causes common entitativeness: "The *ens commune* is the proper effect of the highest Cause, namely God" [*ens commune est proprius effectus cause altissimae, scilicet Dei*].[40] What being can mean for entities is now to be seen apart from God (and from what "to be" may mean for him) by the distance of a cause. The cause works only according to that distance, and not playing any more for the *esse commune* but, rather, against and before it—distance upon being, therefore without it.

(b) Thomas thus takes up once again a major argument of the Dionysian tradition. In fact, the *Divine Names* had not only defined God as the principle of entities—ἀρχὴ ἐστι τῶν ὄντων ἀφ᾽ ἧς καὶ αὐτὸ τὸ εἶναι καὶ πάντα τά ὁπωσοῦν ὄντα—but above all as that on which being depends and which, conversely, does not depend on it. Consequently, it is necessary to go so far as to say that God precedes entitativeness and the entity (as already for Plato) because, more radically, He achieves the role of a principle on being as such, verbal and different from entity: καὶ αὐτὸς ἐστι τοῦ εἶναι . . . ἀρχὴ . . . πρὸ οὐσίας ὤν καὶ ὄντος.[41] As the principle of the *esse* of created entities, and in this sense the only *universalis provisor totius entis*, God does not go back to being and, for this very reason being goes back to Him.[42] An essential discontinuity occurs between the possible being of God and the entitativeness of the entities that He causes as its principle: not merely between God and entities but also between God and the being of entities. Thomas Aquinas thus looks as the direct heir of a line of thought that the *Liber de causis* illustrates: if "the first cause is beyond every name with which one names it," its transcendence can neither be asserted nor categorized within being: therefore it exercises itself upon being: "First among created things is being and before it there is no other creature."[43] Or also for Albert: "The first is not created by anyone it is itself the source and cause of every being"; or also: "As for the *esse* that this science considers . . . it is rather the first effusion of God and the first creature."[44] Here again it goes without saying that if the being of entities emanates from the Primary or First, this latter, God, does not depend on it, is not inscribed within it, and is not comprehended in it.

(c) If God, as nonreciprocal cause, exceeds *esse* in the guise of a first creature, it is necessary to realize that being, as original as it remains to us, despite or rather just because of this, is still *a parte Dei* second, regional, hypothetical, conditioned, in short that it befalls us as the known effect of an unknown cause. Created *esse* remains definitively still an effect—"the proper effect of the first agent, God" [*proprius effectus primi agentis, scilicet Dei*]—held at a distance by the cause.[45] The intimacy of the *esse* to each entity does not so much open this latter to the transcendence of the cause as it emphasizes, on the contrary, that the most intimate for us does not exceed the rank of a created effect: "*Esse* itself is the first and most common effect, effect more intimate than all the others."[46] What is most intimate in us nevertheless remains in itself an effect, first to be sure, but for this very reason that much more common. The most essential, most internal, most profound in created entity certainly remains *esse*, which it receives from the *actus essendi* of God, but this *esse* befalls it already as a created *esse*. The created entity doubtless receives its *esse* from the divine *esse*, but, precisely because it receives it by virtue of being created, it receives it as created. *Esse* "clears" from the created to the uncreated not as one transfers a sum from one account to another (without really modifying it), but as a face or a sky clears from one tonality to another—by being essentially modified. The *actus essendi* sets the created *essentiae* in act, and it is precisely for that this *esse* befalls them in the relation, aspect, and condition of an effect. Causality has to be seen throughout from creation.

Such causality does not contradict distance but fulfills it. Causality, according to Thomas Aquinas, does not assign God to the system of metaphysics still to come; rather, it separates Him from it. (*a*) Causality distances at first because it does not tolerate any epistemic univocity: if effect can only be understood in reference to the cause, the cause, in return, even if its existence can be inferred from the effects as *viae*, nonetheless preserves an absolutely unknown essence. (*b*) Causality distances, furthermore, because, if it permits and imposes a foundation of entities by a cause (*Begründung*), nonetheless this foundation does not come from an entity, supreme or par excellence, since God is properly called *esse* and not *ens*; consequently, this foundation is not limited to created entities but ascends to their being, at least in the meaning of their *ens commune*, a hypothesis that the Heideggerian topics do not consider. (*c*) Above all, this foundation does not allow any reciprocal foundation in return, using the conception of the foundation (*Gründung*) of the supreme entity (although lacking) by and according to its being because the *esse commune* has nothing to share with such a divine *esse,* and the latter neither admits nor requires any foundation.

Just as we had already established that Thomas Aquinas does not include God within the metaphysical field of a common concept of being and hence that he refuses in advance the first of the fundamental determinations of all onto-theo-logical interpretation of God, should we not also admit that he nullifies the reciprocal causal foundation of entities and being, because he goes back to the analogy between them and does not submit *esse* to the necessity of a foundation by thinking causality from creation and ignoring any "principle of sufficient reason"? According to this double hypothesis, neither of the two first characteristics of onto-theo-logy finds the least confirmation in the thought of Thomas Aquinas. But before finally drawing this conclusion, which still needs essential qualification, it is necessary to consider the pertinence of the last characteristic of onto-theo-logy.

The *Causa Sui*

We could now discuss the third characteristic of every possible onto-theology—that is, that God is featured in it according to the function of *causa sui*. There is certainly no reason to doubt that Thomas Aquinas refused the legitimacy of assigning what he understood by God to this function of *causa sui*, but the difficulty is rather a matter of understanding his arguments.

The first one looks obvious, as is the logical contradiction that it denounces. God cannot be defined as *causa sui* because nothing can cause itself, since it would then not only have to differ from itself but, above all, to come (and to be) before itself.[47] But this logical argument does not tell enough to disqualify the *causa sui*: Descartes was perfectly aware of it nonetheless admitting its validity, without withdrawing from the obligation of introducing a concept that looked, from the very inception, contradictory.[48]

No doubt it is for this reason that a second argument, implicit but more powerful, takes over for the first. It is expressed as follows: for God fully to exercise the cause that distance demands, He must withdraw Himself from causality.[49] The divine *esse* admits of no cause precisely because it exercises causality toward *entia* alone. "The *ipsum esse* cannot, in fact, be caused by the form itself or the *quiddity* of the thing—I mean as an efficient cause—because then a thing would be cause of itself and a thing would produce itself into being, which is impossible. It is thus necessary that everything whose esse is other than its nature receive its esse from an other."[50] Causality may play here a role too, but only for entities whose *esse* differs from essence, therefore, by definition, not for God. Furthermore, the second of the *viae* can only reach up to God as cause insofar as causality is suspended as soon as it comes to God, who simply stops it—not only because "it is necessary for it to stop" there as it may be elsewhere but, above all, because this stop alone allows the second *via* to hold fast there and to hold fast within God. Without this limitation, no *via* would end in God because none would end at all but would go on from effect to cause, in its turn interpreted as an effect, indefinitely. Only the limitation of the causal chain makes the argument of causality conclusive. An indefinite causality would produce no conclusion, since it would never obtain but a provisional cause, always susceptible of being converted once again into a simple effect. In short, for Thomas Aquinas, the infinite and final cause can (i.e., God) only conclude a finite causality. Which implies a rejection not only of all causality without an end but also of all reciprocal causality. Hence also a rejection not only of reciprocal foundation between being and either entity as such or supreme entity (determination of onto-theo-logy) but, above all, of the foundation of oneself as effect by itself as cause, without any further ontic separation (*causa sui* in the strict sense). The logical argument thus certainly goes beyond any formal evidence. In fact, it sustains the whole speculative edifice.

However, the central point is not to be found here. Had Thomas Aquinas admitted, in anticipation of Descartes, the legitimacy of a determination of God as *causa sui*, he would have also and at first assumed the thesis that makes this determination possible and necessary—that is, that nothing makes an exception to the principle of causality, not even God. This thesis could be formulated with an almost tiny appearance, as with Suárez. Since, one might agree that "there is no entity that is not either effect or cause" [*nullium autem est ens, quod non sit vel effectus, vel causa*], God being well known as an entity and a cause, it is necessary to admit this law without exception: "Causality is as it were a property of entity as such: there is no entity that does not participate in causality in some manner" [*ipsa causalitas est veluti proprietas quaedam entis ut sic: indium et ens, quad aliquam rationem causae non participet*].[51] As a consequence, causality being assumed as an intrinsic exigency of entity should rule God as every other entity. The fact that they oppose each other as the first cause and the final effects does not make any difference according to this universal and univocal law—since the first cause here draws its possibility from the essence of causality itself: From now on, the more radical formulation of Descartes becomes inevitable: "Nothing exists of which one cannot ask by which cause it exists. And that can be asked of God Himself"[52] Here the metaphysical claim raised by the *causa sui* becomes obvious: God gets to existence as the supreme entity only insofar as he no longer makes an exception to the metaphysical rule, the rule that asserts that all existence requires a cause. The stake of the *causa sui* amounts at first to the fact that God, by submitting to a universal rule of entity, renounces his exception to the common regime of entities whose essence differs from *esse*. For Descartes, it will henceforth be the divine essence that will play the role of cause for the divine existence, at the risk, at least implicit, of only existing at the price of the transcendence of its irreducible *esse*. But the stake also amounts to the dispute with (or confirmation of) the prior decision made by Thomas Aquinas to except God from the *esse commune* and hence from *metaphysica*, since it is a matter of submitting or not to causality understood as the common feature of *esse commune*. If one agrees here to this implicit claim (God according to causality [Descartes]), it will be necessary afterward to assign such a God to all the other principles that *metaphysica* will dictate: God according to the principle of order (Malebranche), according to the principle of sufficient reason (Leibniz), according to a priori principles of experience (Kant), and so forth. One also sees the importance of Thomas Aquinas's rejecting (as do, in fact, the majority of the medievals) any a priori proof of the existence of God: such proofs, as Spinoza will deliberately note, imply considering God as a simple part and a simple particular case of the doctrine of the entity."[53] By rejecting the *causa sui*, Thomas Aquinas does not merely reject *a* metaphysical name of God, but, as Heidegger has seen so well, *the* metaphysical name of God, which, by submitting him to a first a priori (causality), constrains him in advance to yield to the "great metaphysical principle" of sufficient reason and hence to all those implied in it.

So, the third and last characteristic of the onto-theo-logical constitution of metaphysics—to assume the name of *causa sui*, that is, of the entity supremely grounding and grounded—gets from Thomas Aquinas the same censure as the two prior ones: God cannot ever be lowered to the function of a *causa sui*. It thus seems consistent to conclude that the thought of Thomas Aquinas does not at all match the requirements of the onto-theo-logical constitution of metaphysics, at least as understood in the strict sense of Heidegger's postulate.

The Horizon and the Name of Being

As well argued as it stands, this conclusion could still appear to be imprudent and hasty as soon as one considers a last objection. The onto-theo-logical constitution in fact requires, beyond the precise features that we have discussed and just put into effect, that the question of God be able to be asked and answered within the horizon of being. In any case, Heidegger has described this constitution only with the opened intention of explaining how God (and especially the Christian God) has come into metaphysics, that is has agreed to take up the role of the grounded grounding God: He yielded to it to the exact measure where—to start with—He lets Himself be set within the horizon of being. In other words, in order to gain supremacy over entity, God must pay a price—no less than to become subjected to the a priori of being. From this moment on, the possibility of inscribing God, such as Thomas Aquinas understands Him, within one of the manifestations of the onto-theo-logical constitution cannot be imposed (and be discussed in detail), but on the presupposition that God, in general and in principle, has to do with being—and that the horizon of being could fit Him as the adequate space for his manifestation.

But this point precisely should not be taken for granted and the majority of Christian theologians prior to Thomas Aquinas had given preference either to the horizon of the Good, in line with Neoplatonism, or to that of love, while subordinating to them in both cases that of being. Thomas Aquinas established, if not the first, at least in the most emblematic way, that the knowledge of God, even theological, can and must be achieved within the privileged horizon of being.[54] The exemplary and radical hermeneutics of Exod. 3:14 definitely does not lead to any "metaphysics of Exodus," since Thomas Aquinas was not, properly speaking, dealing with metaphysics, any more than he would suggest that Exodus could have been aware of metaphysics. Nevertheless, Thomas thus undeniably ends up by closing the theological exodus of God out of metaphysics, or inversely, by making God come out of its reluctance with regard to what would soon take the title of *metaphysica*. In assuming as its first name that of *esse* or *actus essendi*, the Thomistic God does not manifest himself only *in* being (which, even when starting from other horizons, theology has always ended by conceding), but in fact *as* being. The counterargument that this manifestation amounts precisely to being (to be), and not as entity (assuming at least that this ontological difference is still found without loss in the distinction between *esse/actus essendi* and *ens/essentia*, which one could reasonably doubt), takes nothing out of the difficulty but makes it worse: not only is God inscribed in being, but He identifies, singularizes, in a word achieves Himself in the role of making being possible—in such a way that being in act would be enough to accomplish God as such. This decision, absolutely without precedent (and a recent commentator willingly prides himself on it) does not only imply a U-turn in the history of the determination of the divine essence but makes possible for the first time, at bottom, an onto-theo-logy.[55] Consequently, in spite of the concise disagreements, Thomas Aquinas would turn out to be the first and most radical advocate of onto-theo-logy, in the two principal meanings of this word. (*a*) Following Heidegger's meaning, God enters metaphysics to the extent that He speaks of Himself and allows Himself to be spoken of according to being, insomuch as being opens a site where the divine and God could assume their own but designated function. (*b*) Following Kant's meaning as well, for, if one defines as onto-theo-logical the proof that "believes to know His existence [mainly God] on the basis of simple concepts, without any regard to experience," should we not conclude that Thomas Aquinas has given a foretaste for this, since he deduces the being (existence) of God from His definition (concept of essence) as *actus essendi*?[56]

As a consequence, our essay should completely reverse his conclusion. However, if one focused attention only to the internal features of onto-theology as Heidegger has defined it, Thomas Aquinas does not have a connection to it, any more than, in the strict historical sense, does he find a place in metaphysics. But, if we consider the preliminary condition for the possibility of an onto-theo-logy—that is, that God would inscribe Himself without restraint in the horizon of being, in essence and in existence, as an act and by definition—then Thomas Aquinas would become not only the first of the onto-theo-logians but one of the most radical, if not the most radical ever, to the very extent to which he holds neither to a supreme entity (Spinoza, Leibniz, Kant) nor to an indeterminate being (Avicenna, Duns Scotus, Malebranche) but to pure *esse* as such (which Aristotle had only approached). One can see better the blindness of some commentators:

not doubting for a moment that being would count enough to express and keep the transcendence of God, not even guessing that one could prefer to affirm it according to another of the transcendentals, they do not furthermore suspect that inscribing the divinity of God within being henceforth imposes on this God to take part in the destiny of being; now being has quickly passed from *esse*, where Thomas Aquinas claimed to lift it up, to a *conceptus univocus entis*, which leaves unthought the infinite divinity of God (Scotus, Ockham, Descartes), then reintegrates it in its common rule on the basis of *ens supremum* or *perfectissimum* (Spinoza, Malebranche, Leibniz, Kant); and it could, keeping the same definition, end up with the "death of God," according to the very movement where the *ontologia* finally exhausts itself into nihilism (Nietzsche). If, since Thomas Aquinas, the destiny of being identifies itself with that of God, this identification remains for the better (Thomism) and for the worse (*metaphysica*). It is not enough to claim in response that one has only to go back to the "authentic" Thomistic conception of *esse* to escape this contract—it would also be necessary to be able to do so. And we may imagine that such an access to the "authentic" *esse* would be for us today neither that easy nor powerful enough to have us resist the inexorable attraction of nihilism, the danger of which consists precisely in the extent to which it devalues the "authentic" *esse*. (In fact, if it were to dissolve only an "inauthentic" *esse*, what would this matter to us?) Not to listen to a question, this is not enough to prove to have already answered it, still less to have gone beyond it. In a large part of "Christian philosophy," being remains the last resort, the supposedly unshakable rock on which apology would always lean. But does not one see that being can also become—and historically has already become—a stumbling block, a millstone attached around the neck of one's enemy before throwing him into the water? Should we blind ourselves to the point of asking being—in a full era of nihilism—to save God? Should we absolutely set aside the opposite hypothesis—only a god, and possibly God could save what, in being, could rise again and without doubt under a totally other aspect than the one metaphysics has inflicted on it? In a word, to free ourselves from onto-theo-logy should we again and always break away from Thomas Aquinas to start with?

Nevertheless, I suggest following a totally different way: Thomas Aquinas might, on the contrary; have left God *out* of being, taken not only in the meaning of *metaphysica* but also in the meaning of onto-theo-logy (and indeed of *Ereignis*), inasmuch as he has displayed an *esse* as radically foreign to *ens* and to *conceptus univocus entis* as to the being foreseen by Heidegger.[57] To put it clearly, the Thomistic *esse* cannot be understood starting from ontological determinations, whatever they might be, but only starting from it distance with regard to all possible ontology, following instead the claims imposed by the transcendence of God on entity as well as on his own being. This being of entity maintains its distance from *esse*, because this *esse* assumes in fact and before anything else the features of the *mysterium tremendum fascinandum* of a God making Himself conceptually manifest. If *esse* truly offers the first name of God according to Thomas Aquinas, this thus signifies for him in the first place that God is called *esse* but as to name only and not as such. For in good theology, the primacy of *esse* implies especially that it is to be understood, more than any other name, starting from God, and not that God can be conceived starting from *esse*. To think *esse* starting from God, but not in inverse order (in the way of *metaphysica* and of Heidegger as well), allow Thomas Aquinas to free the divine *esse* from its—tangentially univocal—comprehension starting from what philosophy understands by being, entity being of the entity, in a word to mark the distance—an "infinitely infinite distance"—from the creature to God (Pascal).

This distance gets evidences through many precise arguments, which bring out as many differences.

(*a*) The first deals with the difference between God and entity and, therefore with entitativeness in general: "The divine *esse* that is His substance is not the common *esse*, but it is an *esse* distinct from all other entity. This is why by His *esse* in itself, God differs from all other entities."[58] One could certainly be inclined to merge, at least formally, this difference with the ontological difference, if a second argument did not intervene.

(*b*) The difference between *ens* and *esse* must be thought through and from creation; in fact, according to this radicality, it plays with three and not two terms: the divine *esse* really only causes the entities because he causes also their entitativeness (their *esse commune*), their *esse* as created. But if the divine *esse* creates the *esse commune*, as well as being, according to onto-theo-logy (and to *metaphysica*) takes the place of *esse commune*, we should conclude that the *esse* that stays at a creational distance from the *esse commune* refers neither to this one, nor to the one of *metaphysica*, nor to the one of onto-theo-logy, Or again, one could say that such *esse* keeps within itself the transcendence that opposes the act of being to the *esse commune* of entities. It is necessary to suggest, against the first evidences but, we think, according to the intention of Thomas Aquinas—what the *esse* assigned to God excludes itself from the common and created being and consequently from all what we understand and know under the title of being. Therefore, God without being (at least without *this* being) could become again a Thomistic thesis. And to go beyond, unto the *esse* of which God fulfills the act, it would be necessary to think without ontological categories but according to truly theological determinations—as, for example, that of "intensive being."[59] Being taken according to this excellence would thus find itself already outside of being.

(*c*) But another argument definitely emphasizes how the excess of the proper *esse* of God disqualifies all metaphysical (conceptual) meaning of being. Thomas Aquinas brings this out either directly or indirectly. He does it directly by identifying the divine essence with *esse*: "God does not have an essence that would not be His *esse*."[60] Or, "The essence of God is His own proper *esse*."[61] Following this path, God does not have any other essence than *esse*, which stands for it, thus excluding any composition of *esse* and essence, which is required everywhere else. But, indirectly, the same result is expressed even more radically, especially in two texts. (i) "One thing exists, God, whose essence is his proper *esse*, that is why one finds certain philosophers who say that God has neither quiddity nor essence, since his essence is nothing else than his *esse*."[62] There is no question that Thomas Aquinas does not here literally ratify the thesis of the absence of essence in God; but the simple fact that he suggests this absence by alluding to the noncomposition in God of *esse* and essence suggests his accord with those "some philosophers." (ii) "Some say, as Avicenna and Rabbi Moses [Maimonides] do, that the thing that God is is some *esse subsistens*, and that there is in God but only *esse*: as a result they say that He is without essence."[63] What does it mean not to have an essence? Obviously this can only amount be the identity between *esse* and essence. But in its own way what does this identity display? For sure, no essence (or quiddity) can be fitting here for the *esse* of God, who, as a result, remain absolutely and formally without essence. But if we were to admit that it belongs by definition (Aristotle) to metaphysics to bring the questioning about what entity is back around to the question about essence[64] how can we not understand the obliteration of essence with respect to God as a new argument forbidding that God could be taken and thought about according to being, in the meaning which metaphysics uses to give to it? In fact, an *esse* irreducible to an essence signifies an *esse* irreducible, too, to the metaphysical essence a being—as elaborated in onto-theo-logy.

A last argument confirms without the slightest ambiguity the metaphysical exclusion of this *esse*: God's unknowability. In fact, the irreducibility of *esse* to any essence argues for the impossibility of articulating anything about God in a predicative way and, therefore, of speaking of it discursively or, in a word, of understanding it. Thus this pure *esse* reveals itself in principle as unknowable as the God it names. God known as unknown—this implies that his *esse*, remains knowable only as unknowable, in sharp contrast to the *esse* that metaphysics has essentially set in a concept to make it as knowable as possible. We are not short of textual evidences. For example, "Just as the substance of God is unknown, so it is for His *esse*." And, "God is known through our ignorance, inasmuch as this is to know God, that we know that we do not know what He is." Or, "The highest and most perfect degree of our knowledge in this life is, as Denys said in his book *On Mystical Theology* (I.3), to be united to God as unknown. This is what happens when we know about God what He is not, since what He is remains profoundly unknown." Or then, "With the exception of a revelation of grace we do not, in this life, know about God what He is and therefore that we are united to Him as unknown."[65] As a pure act of being, without any reference to the ordinary composition proper to the metaphysical entity, the divine *esse* remains as unknown as God, precisely because "being is meant in two ways: in a first, to signify the act of being; in another, to stress the composition of a proposition, which soul works out by joining a predicate to a subject. According to the first meaning, we can no more know the being of God than His essence, but only according to the second."[66] The meaning of the *esse* proper to God is strictly characterized by His unknowability, in contrast to the categorical meaning, perfectly integrated to the metaphysical plurality of meanings of entity according to Aristotle. To be excluded from being in the metaphysical sense and to remain by definition unknown turns out to be perfectly equivalent in God and in God alone.

To be sure, it seems that a powerful objection could still contain these arguments. God certainly receives, according to Thomas Aquinas, a name that is proper and directly conformed to being: "Qui est." But, as it should be noticed, it happens that the text itself that affirms more clearly this privilege confirms equally clearly that God excludes himself from being (according to metaphysics) by his unknowability. (*a*) First, given that we should consider "Qui est" as "the name that is most proper to God" [*maxime proprium nomen Dei*], it is appropriate to immediately specify that *maxime* emphasizes without equivocation that it remains still comparable to other names and, therefore, does not count absolutely. (*b*) Second, even knowing this name, we still do not know the divine essence: "Our understanding, in this life, cannot know the essence itself of God as it is in itself, but whatever it determines that it understands about God, it remains short of what God is in Himself?" (*c*) Third, the name "Qui est," finally and especially, manifests its most precise property only in the strict measure in which it recognizes also the incommunicability of God: "The name most proper is the Tetragrammaton, used to signify the incommunicable and, if we can speak thus, singular divine substance itself."[67] Thus follows an obvious paradox: the uniqueness and superiority of the name borrowed from Exod. 3:14 come precisely from the insular incommunicability it manifests in God, therefore from the definitive exclusion with regard to all knowable and common being—in short, with regard to the metaphysical concept of *esse commune*. It must be admitted that it is specifically the naming of God according to the being of the so-called metaphysics of Exodus that offers the best argument for the metaphysical exclusion of God according to Thomas Aquinas.

One can then conclude that he does not think of God in a univocal way within the horizon of being. Or simply: the *esse* that Thomas Aquinas recognizes for God does not open any metaphysical horizon, does not belong to any onto-theo-logy, and remains such a distant analogy with what we once conceived through the concept of being, that God proves not to take any part in it, or to belong to it, or even—as paradoxical as it may seem—to be. *Esse* refers to God only insofar as God may appear as without being— not only without being as onto-theology constitutes it in metaphysics but also well out of the horizon of being, even as it is as such (Heidegger). The statement "God without being" not only could be understood as fundamentally Thomistic, but it could be that no contemporary interpretation of Thomas Aquinas could retrieve its validity without assuming the unconditional exclusion of *esse*—therefore without the wise imprudence of such paradoxes.[68]

Answer to the Question: *Esse* Without Being

To the questions originally asked (as to the features of onto-theo-logy), we can now attempt to give an answer. Thomistic thought without any doubt rejects the three features of the onto-theo-logic constitution of metaphysics. (1) God does not go into the field (subject or object) of metaphysics or, a fortiori, into the concept of entity. (2) The foundation for entities and for their being (*esse commune*) in God depends without doubt on causality, but it has nothing that is reciprocal, so that being certainly does not ground (conceptually) God, whose *actus essendi* escapes all concepts, to the strict extent that an act determines being in Him. (3) This is confirmed in the fact that, free from any causality or ground (not even His proper essence, directly identified with his act of being), God denies for Himself the metaphysical figure of self-foundation, for which the *causa sui* designates the paradigm. Yet Thomas Aquinas does not take away all the ambiguities implied by two features of the onto-theo-logic constitution of metaphysics. First, is the nonreciprocity between God and created entities enough to get away with a metaphysical interpretation of creation? Second, and in particular, would not the causal grounds of entities as well as that of the being of entities (as created *esse commune*) by God identify themselves with the metaphysical causation of entities by the supreme entity in metaphysics? One immediately recognizes that the answer to these two questions depends on knowing, first, to what extent God remains tangentially *ens supremum* and, then, to what extent the act of being relies on being itself (4) Hence the last question: if God, as act of being, transcends all real composition of *esse* and *essentia*, thus the whole of created entitativeness, and if in Him *esse* also transcends all concepts, thus if He remains essentially unknown, must we conclude that His *esse* still belongs to what we can understand as "being" (in its metaphysical meaning as well as in its non-metaphysical meaning), or can we admit that it goes beyond any understanding of "being"? In the first hypothesis, the *esse* assigned to God would still impose on Him the onto-theo-logical burden of causal grounding (of the entities and their *esse* commune); while in the second, the meta-ontological transcendence of esse without essence or concept would free Him—even under that name of *esse*—from all connection to onto-theo-logy.

Thus all the answers to the question focus the attention to a precise dilemma: Can *esse* be exclusively understood according to a (historically) metaphysical sense, that is, according to a reopened "question of being," or must it be clarified by a meta-ontological meaning—in a word, be understood as *esse* without being? In fact, since one usually admits that the divine *esse* remains, for Thomas Aquinas, if not for his school, deprived of any concept of being, without an essence, without a definition, without knowability—in a word, amounts to a negative name—why pretend to treat it as an affirmative name, giving the equivalent of an essence, the equivalent of a concept, the equivalent of a knowledge? Why not admit that Thomas Aquinas only held onto this *esse* with the intention of tactically leaning on the term preferred by his philosophical interlocutors, without ever assuming it affirmatively, or raising it to eminence, but by certifying it through apophasis? Obviously, we cannot doubt that Thomas Aquinas did designate God as *esse*. But one must doubt that, once appropriately assigned to God, *esse* could mean only what metaphysics, and even the "question of being," succeeds in conceiving it—and not, on the contrary, aim beyond being itself, whatever it might be. This transgression would not in fact imply ontic, or ontological loss, or any irrationality. It only takes into account that nothing is rationally appropriate to God except what matches infinity.

My hypothesis, I know, might surprise the defenders of Heidegger as much as some among the disciples of Thomas Aquinas. For the former, my hypothesis assumes some points that are hardly acceptable: first that *metaphysica*, taken historically, amounts to metaphysics as a determinant of the history of being; then that *metaphysica*, to speak honestly, starts after Thomas Aquinas (and not much before); and also that the Thomistic attribution of *esse* to a Christian God indicates more an assumption of being in a radically nonontological field than the assignation to God of a place in the metaphysical destiny of being; and finally that an impoverishment of metaphysics by excess can occur at any moment in its history. For the latter, the unacceptable remains that, under the guise of liberating Thomas Aquinas from the burden of *metaphysica*, we could pretend to underline the reshuffling in him of the Dionysian (and "Neoplatonic") subordination of *esse* to a cause, going so far as to interpret in a nonontological way the transcendence of *esse*. These two hesitations may in no way surprise, nor do they lack good arguments: besides the shortcomings in our own knowing, one must admit the weight of traditions and personal commitments as well as the indispensable pluralism of interpretations. It would be enough, therefore, as a first step, if our hypothesis could only be taken in consideration in spite of its obvious limits and its apparent paradox.

But does it go without saying that we could improve our knowledge of God today if we persist in understanding Him starting from what we know—or believe we know—about being? Does taking Thomas Aquinas seriously require that we should think of God starting with being or think of being starting with God? For a long time, it seemed to be out of the question that God, for Thomas Aquinas, had to be thought from being—in debates dealing only with specifying what this being stands for: existence or concept, intrinsic or extrinsic analogy, metaphysics or transcendentalism, and so on. It also seemed, at the same time, to go without saying that the questioning of the primacy of being, as transcendental or as horizon, implied the questioning of the fundamental position of Thomas Aquinas concerning God. We foresee that from now on these two arguments could be articulated quite differently The debate on the determination of the *esse*, and first of all of its irreducibility to the concept of entity and its exit out of the object of *metaphysica*, gets its importance only from its result: to allow—or more often to forbid—thinking of this *esse* by starting with the distance of God. It is no longer so much the issue to decide whether it is necessary or not to name God by the title of *esse*, but if we can get such an understanding of *esse* that it could reasonably claim not to reach to but at least to aim toward whatever it might be that we name God. It is not a matter of deciding whether we should speak of God in the name of being, but if being (taken as *esse* or otherwise) still has sufficient quality or dignity to enunciate whatever it might be about God, which would be more of value than straw. Reciprocally, if Thomas Aquinas does not belong to the onto-theo-logy problematic, it is also necessary to give up our claim of him to bridge its characteristic insufficiency—that of never thinking of being, except by starting with and in the light of entity: it seems no longer to the point to try to read the *actus essendi* as an anticipation either of *Seyn* or of *Ereignis*, which prior to this would have conceived of being as such.

The *esse* that Thomas meditates on may deal not with metaphysics, or ontology, or even the "question of being" but, instead, with the divine names and on the "luminous darkness."

The Possible and Revelation

1

Can phenomenology contribute in a privileged way to the development of a "philosophy of religion"? In other words, can "philosophy of religion" become a "phenomenology of religion"? The context in which the present contribution first appeared presupposed this without a doubt.[1] One might also attempt to establish it by looking at the many works devoted to religion that (methodologically or thematically) claim to go back to or call upon the spirit of phenomenology. Yet these arguments do not suffice. First, facts (even when there are many) do not justify applying phenomenology to religion, as if by right, or recognizing phenomenological method as in any way particularly suitable for religion. Furthermore, there is only one legitimation for phenomenology, namely, return to the things themselves. To confirm that religion could offer a possible field for phenomenology, one would have to show that it uses the phenomenological method to make manifest phenomena that without it would have remained masked or simply missing in the religious domain. Phenomenology could then be applied both to religion and to potential phenomena. This double requirement—justifying religion to phenomenology as a possible phenomenon, justifying phenomenology to religion as a suitable method—imposes a single instruction: the use of a possible phenomenology of religion cannot be surreptitiously presupposed but must be deduced, in the sense in which Kant defines deduction: "the explanation of the manner in which concepts can thus relate a priori to objects."[2] How, then, can phenomenological concepts be related to objects of religion a priori? How must one proceed phenomenologically in order to return to "the things themselves" of religion?

These two questions doubtless share a special difficulty: the possibility of acknowledging a concept of revelation. I presuppose two points here. (a) Religion attains its highest figure only when it becomes established by and as a revelation, where an authority that is transcendent to experience nevertheless manifests itself experientially. Such an experience, effectively beyond (or outside of) the conditions of possibility of experience, is affirmed not only by its affidavit from privileged or designated individuals, but by words or expositions rightly accessible to everyone (e.g., the Scriptures). Revelation takes its strength of provocation from what it speaks universally, yet without this word being able to ground itself in reason within the limits of the world. As long as this paradox is not admitted, or at least thought honestly, the phenomenon of religion remains misunderstood. (b) Understood as metaphysics, philosophy is accomplished by continually (from Descartes to Hegel) radicalizing the implications of the principle of sufficient reason: all that is (being, *étant*) exists to the extent to which a *causa* (actuality) *sive ratio* (concept) gives an explanation either for its existence, for its nonexistence, or for its exemption from any cause. The emergence of the principle of reason forces metaphysics to assign each being its concept and its cause, to the point of dismissing any beings irreducible to a conceptualizable cause as illegitimate and hence impossible. It is therefore no fortuitous coincidence that the thinkers of the *causa sive ratio* (Spinoza, Malebranche, Leibniz, etc.) also disqualified the possibility of miracles and revelation in general. In this context, religion remains admissible only by renouncing revelation in the full sense. Consequently, it remains thinkable for metaphysics only by deserting its ultimate accomplishment. On the one hand, religion may be understood to remain metaphysically legitimate. In that case, it must submit to the requirements of the principle of reason, in short, be content with the limits of simple reason, and thus finally repudiate revelation inasmuch as the latter by definition eludes the grasp of the concept, of cause, and of reason. Or, on the other hand, religion may be understood to remain faithful to revelation, which excludes it from the world. But then it must first renounce concept, cause, and all reason, to the point where it comes to be expelled from metaphysical rationality under the nickname of *Schwärmerei* [religious enthusiasm, or fanaticism].

This is not an artificial dilemma. In fact, it indicates the two principal positions that metaphysicians who do not simply cede to irreligion sustain in face of the hypothesis of a revealed religion. The second part of the dilemma is illustrated by Kant's thematic in *Religion Within the Limits of Reason Alone* (1793) and Fichte's in *Attempt at a Critique of All Revelation* (1792). For them, only the universal has the value of a priori truth in the practical domain. Yet this universal is implemented by the categorical imperative and the moral law. Any revelation's claim to decree moral duty must hence be measured by the norm of the universal moral law. Unless it renounces leaning on revelation altogether, religion will only call upon revelation by submitting it to a moral hermeneutic exercised by the categorical imperative. Any other hypothesis would betray fanaticism.

> For the theoretical part of ecclesiastical faith cannot interest us morally if it is not conducive to the performance of all human duties as divine commands (what constitutes the essence of all religion). Frequently, this interpretation may in the light of the text (of the revelation), appear forced—it may often really be forced; and yet if the text can possibly support it, it must be preferred to a literal interpretation which either contains nothing at all [helpful] to morality or actually works counter to moral incentives.[3]

Revelation will be reduced to an imperative, hence to the moral law, or it will founder outside of all reason, hence outside of all possibility. In either case it disappears as such.

The first moment of the dilemma is exemplified in a theme in Hegel (if not the early Schelling): here revelation is no longer opposed to reason, but by contrast it essentially contributes to reason. In God's incarnation, revelation actually reveals that the absolute dwells among humans, hence that spirit is reconciled to its proper negativity. Revelation reveals that spirit manifests itself absolutely. "Consequently, in this religion the divine Being is *revealed* [*geoffenbart*]. Its being-revealed [*Offenbarsein*] obviously consists in this, that what it is, is known. But it is known precisely in its being known as Spirit, as a Being that is essentially a *self-conscious Being*."[4] The fact of revealing or even of being revealed goes back to manifesting or to being manifest. Revealed (*geoffenbarte*) religion exhausts itself in the end in the manifest (*offenbare*) evidence of the spirit to itself. Revelation finally has no other content than the manifestation and the consciousness of the concept. It is hence only justified by being abolished in manifestation in general. Revelation escapes being disqualified by metaphysics when it limits itself strictly to what admits of reason (Kant) or identifies itself simply with the work of the concept (Hegel). In both cases, it must renounce its specificity: announcing an event, explicating a word that surpasses the conditions of the possibility of experience and submitting to the requirements of the principle of reason.

Without a doubt, numerous classical aporias in the philosophy of religion result from its presupposition and (what shows up here again) from its method, namely, knowing that it is not possible to test the possibility of an impossibility. For the possible possibility of impossibility would imply that possibility cannot be limited to what sufficient reason ensures, hence possibility cannot be restricted to the actuality that produces the cause. Not to limit possibility in the sense in which, since Aristotle, "it is obvious that actuality precedes potentiality [φανέρον ὅτι πρότερον ἐνεργεία δυνάμεως ἐστίν]"[5] would, by contrast, force us to understand how "*possibility* stands higher than actuality [*höher als die Wirklichkeit steht* die Möglichkeit]"; or, following Heidegger, "understanding phenomenology consists in nothing other than seizing it as possibility."[6] If by recognizing phenomena without the preliminary condition of a *causa sive ratio*, but in the way as and insofar as they are given, phenomenology is able to return to the things themselves, then does it not become the highest priority to free the thought of revelation in general? Phenomenology would hence be the only appropriate philosophy, not only for religion in its essence but also for knowledge as revelation.

2

Phenomenology goes back to the things themselves. This watchword would remain a slogan even if detailed procedures did not make it explicit. From the *Logical Investigations* onward, Husserl clears a decisive path toward the things themselves. Despite Kantian prohibitions, he recognizes the given as such by the simple fact that it is given. Essences are given invariable and in themselves, for example, although they are so only through a vision of essence and not by a sensible intuition. Without a doubt Husserl maintains the Kantian equivalence between givenness and intuition, but he doubles its scope. (a) What is intuited is at the same time given: thus signification is verified if sensible intuition fills the directed intention. (b) But inversely (against Kant), what is given testifies also, in the same measure, to what is intuited, even if no sensible intuition notices it: the founding acts that permit us to apply the categories imply a (categorial) intuition, since they are effectively given to consciousness. "In general, whether a givenness [*Gegebenheit*] manifests what is merely represented or what truly exists, what is real or what is idea, what is possible or what is impossible, it is a given in the cognitive phenomenon, in the phenomenon of a thought in the widest sense of the term."[7] In other words, givenness precedes intuition and abolishes its Kantian limits, because the fact of being given to consciousness (in whatever manner) testifies to the right of phenomena to be received as such, that is to say, as they give themselves. To return to the things themselves amounts to recognizing phenomena as themselves, without submitting them to the (sufficient) condition of an anterior authority (such as thing in itself, cause, principle, etc.). In short, it means liberating them from any prerequisite other than their simple givenness, to which consciousness bears witness before any constitution. Since it makes possible the return to the things themselves, the principle of all principles should perhaps be understood as a suspension of the principle of sufficient reason insofar as the phenomenon is not indebted to any reason, because its givenness itself justifies it: "The *principle of all principles, that every originarily giving intuition* [Anschauung] *is a source of right* [Rechtsquelle] *for cognition*, that everything that offers itself to us originarily in 'intuition' ["Intuition"] is to be taken quite simply as it gives itself out to be, but also only within the limits in which it is given there."[8] Intuition counts here as a source not only de facto but also de jure (*Rechtsquelle*). Why this change? Intuition is exercised as a de jure source [*source* de *droit*] because the source *of* right [*source* du *droit*], namely, givenness itself, is exercised in it more originally. What gives itself (inevitably by intuition of whatever type), in the measure and the limits within which it gives itself (inevitably to consciousness), must be accepted simply and purely (*einfach*) for what it is. The question *cur existat?* should not be answered with another *ratio* or another *causa* but only with: *es gibt das was sich gibt*; "there is [lit. it gives] what gives itself"; hence, this gives what this gives. Not only the rose, but any phenomenon is without *why*, since any phenomenon is as it gives itself.

Such a breakthrough opens the imperial road of access to the things themselves inasmuch as phenomenology attains the received phenomenon as it gives itself without prerequisites. Yet it would not make sense to assume that a phenomenon could happen without cause or reason, since at the very least it would be given to consciousness, and inasmuch as given, it would exist. By thus lifting the prohibition of sufficient reason, phenomenology liberates possibility and hence opens the field possibly even to phenomena marked by impossibility. Among other possibilities, religious phenomena would reappear again in philosophy, as *facts* justified de jure since given *in fact*: the lived states of consciousness and the intentionalities of praise, of demand, of veneration, of repentance, of reconciliation, of confidence, etc., beliefs (from theological faith to various "holding as true"), the volitions of charity, of fraternity, of peace, of sacrifice, etc., not scientific but experiential types of knowledge (vision, "presences," internal dialogues, words said in the heart, etc.)—all these lived experiences of consciousness would hence appear as phenomena by full right, at least to the extent to which they are given to consciousness.

When an allegedly adequate explanation is missing for them, that is to say, in fact their cause or sufficient reason, their legitimacy as phenomena is not thereby put into question, but only their objectivity beyond the limits of immanence. Givenness remaining immanent does not prohibit a phenomenon's actually being given: first because phenomenality cannot be reduced to objectivity; then because an intentionality can aim at an object correctly without intuition fulfilling intention adequately (that is even the most frequent case) or without intention being defined exactly by a formalized signification (as is the case in natural language). Without a doubt, a similar broadening of phenomenality does not fail to raise particular difficulties in the case of lived experiences and specifically religious intentions. Are these lived experiences really intentional (that is to say, are they really focused on an object), and, reciprocally, can these intentional aims of objects lay claims to merely partial intuitive fulfillment? Nevertheless, these questions can legitimately be examined in a phenomenological framework that respects their possibility.

What appears is as and according to how it gives itself. In other words: "As much appearance, so much being (whether it is recovered or falsified by its fact)." This equivalence as it is formulated by Husserl, although it contradicts classical metaphysics in a revolutionary way, will be taken up again literally by Heidegger: "As much appearing, so much being."[9] He will take it up in order to radicalize it, since it is now a matter of widening the concept of the phenomenon beyond the limits Husserl fixed for it. In order really to open access to a "phenomenon of Being,"[10] or, in other words, in order to include Being [*l'être*] inasmuch as different from being [*l'étant*] in phenomenality, one must admit that the absence of being gives itself.[11] From the ontic point of view, Being as such strictly amounts to nothing. Hence it gives itself inasmuch as it gives nothing, indeed gives the nothing. This paradox of a givenness without given is repeated for visibility: if it is a matter of making manifest, Being can manifestly not manifest itself visibly; just as easily, Heidegger will later speak of a "phenomenology of the unapparent."[12] Being can therefore only reach phenomenality if phenomenology also concerns what, at first glance, precisely does not manifest itself. In the case of the nonphenomenon of Being, phenomenology hence will attempt to include even what does *not* give itself phenomenally: "And it is precisely because phenomena are proximally or for the most part *not* given, that there is need for phenomenology."[13]

With this intention Heidegger will restore "indication" among the other meanings of the phenomenon (*Schein, Phänomene, Erscheinung*): for the indication announces (*anmelden*) a term that can make itself known while remaining invisible—in this way Being will announce itself in *Dasein* as a privileged being. By understanding the phenomenon as the *Sich-an-ihm-selbst-zeigende*, the phenomenological concept of the phenomenon also includes within it referral by indication, in such a way that, despite the unapparent nothingness of Being, it "means, as that which shows itself, the Being of being, its sense, its modifications and derivatives."[14] Husserl therefore had restored any intuited given inasmuch as intuited to the phenomenon and hence had legitimated the validity of religious lived experience inasmuch as it is given intuitively. In the same way, Heidegger integrates into phenomenality all that shows itself (*sich zeigt*) only by indication (*Anzeige*), inasmuch as the "showing itself" is still accomplished "from itself"—and hence he legitimates the possibility of a phenomenology of the unapparent in general. Certainly, the analytic of *Dasein* already discovers several unapparent phenomena (Being-for-death opened by anxiety, the *Nichts* by the *Gewissen*, possibility by being-in-the-world, etc.). Yet by beginning with the same *Dasein* or with another determination of privileged being, other analyses could make visible other unapparent phenomena. More precisely, one of the objections most often posed by metaphysics to the possibility of revelation and, in general, of religious phenomena is raised here: that through its lived experiences consciousness aims intentionally at an invisible object of the sort that could never be given directly. Nevertheless, this objection fails, because, on the one hand, even the most subjective or the most abstract intuition suffices to establish an actual givenness (Husserl) and, on the other hand, because even the invisible can be considered to be an authentic phenomenon, provided that it show itself beginning from itself, even if indirectly (Heidegger). The two constitutive terms of any phenomenon (lived experience, signification) are broadened in such a way that they allow revelation to enter into phenomenality. If one maintains the provisional definition of revelation introduced above—to know an instance transcendent to experience that nevertheless is manifested experientially—then one must admit that it is inscribed among phenomena, hence in experience (Husserl) of an intentional object that would be invisible and indirect, hence transcendent to experience (Heidegger). And transcendence must be understood here both in the sense of Kant and that of Husserl. The so-called religious lived experiences of consciousness give intuitively, but by indication, intentional objects that are directly invisible: religion becomes manifest and revelation phenomenal. What philosophy of religion tends to close, phenomenology of religion could open. Phenomenology offers a method not only to ontology (Heidegger), but to any region of phenomena not directly visible and hence immediately invisible—hence exceedingly to religion inasmuch as it concerns revelation. In short, phenomenology would be the method par excellence for the manifestation of the invisible through the phenomena that indicate it—hence also the method for theology.

3

One question nevertheless remains: If, when it recognizes religion as legitimate phenomenon, phenomenology gets beyond the limits of metaphysics' "Platonism" by radically broadening the conditions of givenness in presence, it thereby merely broadens what is given in presence.[15] Does such a broadening of manifestation really amount to a liberation of revelation? Furthermore, can (at least Husserlian) phenomenology not always pursue the enterprise of metaphysics with other means, namely, by leading every given back to givenness *in presence*? In this case, would not the conditions of possibility for presence always determine in advance the very givenness of phenomena? Would not such presuppositions merely reverse the metaphysical prohibitions regarding revelation, in such a way that, despite or because of its broadening of givenness, phenomenology would equally forbid the possibility of revelation by assigning to it a determined possibility? If that so, it would be necessary to show that certain presuppositions of phenomenology restrict revelation. To achieve this, I will examine three of them, in order to clear three potential obstacles to the possibility of revelation.

By definition, phenomenology carries out a reduction—or rather, multiple reductions. For Husserl, it is a matter of reducing [*réduire*], or of leading back [*reconduire*], the world to the things themselves, that is to say, to what the *I* effectively experiences as given in the flesh: any possible phenomenon must be led back to one or several lived experiences of consciousness, hence to the *I* as intersection of these lived experiences (at least). No phenomenon can escape this automatic requirement: all that is, is experienced as *Erlebnis*, and what is not experienced in this way (even in the smallest manner) absolutely does not reach phenomenality at all. For Heidegger, reduction can become operative as soon as one transposes the *I* into *Dasein* and recognizes an analogy to lived experiences in the *Stimmungen* [moods or attunement], which give rise to *Dasein* as the fact of being-in-the-world. Following the opening of *In-der-Welt-sein*, nothing is constituted as a phenomenon that does not allow itself to be led back to *Dasein*, affected by diverse *Stimmungen* from the beings of its world. In short, the givenness of phenomena presupposes the point of reference that accommodates their givenness. As broadened as this givenness may appear, it nevertheless only allows things to appear to an *I*. It matters little that the *I* has different statuses (immanent, transcendent, constituting, constituted-constituting, *Dasein*, etc.), since it always precedes the phenomena as their condition of possibility regarding lived experiences.

What is the import of this for revelation? A question can at least be outlined here: Does whoever receives a revelation constitute it as one would constitute any other phenomenon? Obviously, one must doubt this: revelation really only merits its name if it surprises any anticipation of perception and surpasses any analogy to perception. The *I* has not the slightest idea, notion, or expectation regarding who or what is revealed. Furthermore, not only does what revelation reveals without a doubt shy away from being constituted by any sort of *I*, but occasionally it is possible that no lived experiences of the I correspond to it. What is experienced in revelation can be summed up as the powerlessness to experience whatever it might be that one experiences. The recipient of revelation does not retain common measure with what revelation communicates; otherwise, revelation would not have been necessary. In this way, whether due to excess or due to deficiency, the *I* in its finitude cannot register all that happens to it as a lived experience of consciousness. What is revealed is not necessarily experienced, because it transgresses the dimensions of *Erlebnis*. What one so improperly calls an exstasis in fact goes back to the "night of the senses," where the revealed imposes itself precisely because it cannot be experienced.

The dysfunction of *Erlebnis* in revelation is also confirmed *a contrario*, since revelation is annulled when *Erlebnis* persists in exhausting it. Thus Rudolf Bultmann, at the time of his greatest familiarity with Heidegger, attempted to define revelation by beginning with the *I* and its lived experiences, and by underlining that, if *fides ex auditu*, the event of Jesus comes to me by the word that "it announces" to me today: "Preaching itself is Revelation." Hence preaching, as actually experienced, counts as a lived experience. Yet what intentional object is the aim of this lived experience of the revealed? Or rather, what does the revealed lived experience reveal? No other revelation than the *fact* of Jesus: "Jesus is sent as the one who reveals [*als Offenbarer*]; and what does he reveal? That [*dass*] he is sent as the one who reveals." The revealed lived experience reveals the empty fact of revelation, which then, far from opening onto absolute possibility, sends lived experience back to itself: "Outside faith, Revelation is not visible; nothing is revealed in what one believes."[16] The lived experience of faith remains because the *I* that experiences it first believes; but it cannot reach Jesus historically as its intentional object because the received lived experience (preaching), as a screen, returns the spirit of the *I* to itself in a repeated lived experience (faith). The phenomenological method here is applied to theology only by reducing the revealed to the lived experience of the revealed, hence obscuring the revealed revealing itself. The phenomenological reduction provokes demythologization, and *sola fides* reduces revelatory transcendence to real immanence in consciousness. Although it believes, consciousness does not reach any transcendent (thus revealed) object but is nourished by the immanent lived experience of its solitary faith. In 1929, Bultmann merely draws the consequences of the phenomenological definition of theology given by Heidegger in 1927. As Christian religion remains regional by relation to the analytic of *Dasein*, faith must be understood as a tonality of *Dasein*: "Faith is a mode of existence of human *Dasein*." Revelation hence cannot be understood as the communication of information to *Dasein* (thus of other intentional objects) but only as a participation in an event, that of faith itself. Revelation is confused with "the existence that Revelation has encountered."[17] This entails two possible consequences. On the one hand, if the thought of revelation is subjected to the phenomenological requirement of being reduced to the immanence of lived experience (or to modes of existence), hence to the *I* (or to *Dasein*), then the revealed is confined to revealed lived experience (faith, etc.), without any possibility of receiving the revealed revealing itself. Or, on the other hand, if thought claims to remain open to Revelation as such, it must be liberated from its immanence in the *I* (or in *Dasein*). Because it institutes the *I* (or *Dasein*) as the originary instance of phenomenality, the very concept of reduction damages the possibility of revelation as such.

Phenomenology presupposes a horizon for presenting the phenomena it reduces and constructs. Among other possible forms, this horizon assumes that of Being (Heidegger). In this exemplary case our guiding question could again be tested: Does phenomenology tolerate the general possibility of revelation? By establishing the unconditioned priority of ontological difference over any other question, Heidegger always includes God within it: as one among beings, even if the highest, God is given ontic appearance by the opening arranged by Being itself, the truth of Being precedes the light of the being-God: "Only from the truth of Being can the essence of the holy [*Heiligen*] be thought. Only from the essence of the holy is the essence of divinity to be thought. Only in the light of the essence of divinity can it be thought or said what the word 'God' is to signify."[18] The condition for thinking and saying the word "*God*" does not belong only to God, but depends finally on Being alone through the intermediaries of the divine, of the holy, and of the "whole" (*Heile*). Therefore, since thinking and saying the word "*God*" does not depend first and solely on God, one must conclude that God cannot be said or thought directly from himself, in short, that he cannot reveal himself. Without a doubt the being-God is seen as always granting the right to manifestation, but to a manifestation determined a priori according to the dimensions of a horizon, the horizon of Being: "But the holy [*das Heilige*], which alone is the essential sphere of divinity, which in turn alone affords a dimension for the gods and for God, [the sacred] comes to radiate only when being itself beforehand and after extensive preparation has been cleared and is experienced in its truth."[19] In other words, God (placed among the rank of the gods!) cannot appear (*ins Scheinen kommen*), that is to say "become phenomenon," except by entering into a *Wesensraum*, a "space of manifestation," which is measured by the dimensions of Being and not those of God. Hence here (*zuvor*) as in the previous text (*erst*), Being precedes God, for whom it limits manifestation in advance as his horizon. The *Wesensraum*, the *Dimension*, even the *Aufenthalt*,[20] define the parameters of the necessarily finite horizon of any manifestation of God. God can no longer reveal himself freely, but must manifest himself according to the conditions superimposed by the whole, the sacred, and the divine, thus finally by Being. Container [*Écrin*] of any being, Being plays, in the case of God, the function of a screen [*écran*]. It precedes the very initiative of revealing, it fixes the frame of revelation, and it imposes the conditions of reception on the revealed gift.

Even Christian theology can be tempted to reduce the Revelation of God by God to the measure of the ontological horizon of manifestation. Thus Karl Rahner radicalizes what may have been one of Heidegger's profoundest intuitions by constructing an "ontological Christology" (*ontologische Christologie*), not a "squared circle" but a transcendental demarcation of the dimensions of Christology according to the a priori of Being. Any revelation legitimizes itself by beginning from a *Vorbegriff auf das Sein*, because love and knowledge of God have as their condition an *ontological* mediation operated by Christ: "Self-mediation according to Being must be comprehended in advance as the condition of possibility for the immediate personal knowledge of God and for love of him."[21] The possibility of loving God admits a condition of possibility: ontological self-mediation (identified with Christ). Furthermore, this self-mediation must legitimate itself and, in turn, be legitimated according to a being: "An intimate understanding and an ontological legitimacy of such a concept of self-mediation is to find in the transcendental experience of the return of each finite being an absolute Being and the secret of God." Mediation in the person of Christ is hence inscribed into the horizon of Being according to the transcendental dimension of being. This dimension manifests him in his truth, according to the "ontological essence of this self-mediation,"[22] but does not reveal itself in its proper infinite. Put differently: Does Christology reveal God's free charity or does it manifest the transcendental (a priori, ontological) conditions of finite being? The ambiguity results from assuming that a phenomenological horizon is necessary for revelation. Without a doubt, this ambiguity would be confirmed by other instances of phenomenological horizons. By imposing an a priori dimension or abode and therefore a limit for revelation, the concept of the horizon itself disqualifies the possibility of revelation, while at the same time making any manifestation possible.

The obstacles to revelation thus coincide with the conditions of manifestation. One of Husserl's doctrines confirms explicitly that the reduction (to the *I* or to *Dasein*) and the presupposition of a horizon (of Being, etc.) lead to closing phenomenology to the proper conditions of possibility. An absolutely given truth (in conformity with the "principle of principles") imposes itself on any consciousness whatsoever without any restriction: "What is true is absolutely, intrinsically true: truth is one and the same (*identisch*

Eine), whether humans or non-humans, angels or gods apprehend and judge it." The conditions of evidence impose the evidence of their condition on any mind whatsoever, even on God: "Thus we see that not only for us human beings *but also for God* . . . whatever has the character of a spatial thing, is intuitable only through appearances, wherein it is given, and indeed must be given, as changing 'perspectively' in varied yet determined ways, and thereby presented in changing orientations."[23] Givenness to presence—the principle of all the principles—is absolutely essential: if God knows, he must see according to given appearances. It follows that he would not be able to give himself to see except according to the requirements of this same principle. Revelation will either be impossible or it will come down to a common law phenomenal manifestation. A second aporia confirms this first one, namely, the Husserlian impossibility of justifying knowledge of the other as such phenomenologically (at least in the *Cartesian Meditations*). The other cannot appear as other because the phenomenological conditions of appearance (reduction to the *I*, horizon, and constitution) allow only the appearance of an object or the assumption of an *alter ego*. The other either amounts to another object still constituted by an *I* or will be reached only indirectly (*appresentation*), as invisible observer of the same object as *I* am. The horizon of objectivity and the reduction to an *I* confine givenness in the manifestation of objectivity to the point of excluding revelation of an Other [*Autre*] who is authentically such.

Givenness in presence, by which phenomenology surpasses metaphysics and the principle of reason, nevertheless does not permit it to attain the givenness of revelation. The principle of principles presupposes the primacy of the *I* or of *Dasein*. Phenomenology does not liberate the possibility of a theology. "My immediate aim concerns not theology but phenomenology, however important the bearing of the latter on the former may indirectly be"[24] (Husserl). "There is no such thing as a neo-Kantian, or axiological, or phenomenological theology, just as there is no phenomenological mathematics"[25] (Heidegger).

4

Phenomenology cannot give its status to theology, because the conditions of manifestation contradict or at least are different from the free possibility of revelation. Yet the result is not necessarily a divorce, since a final hypothesis remains conceivable: could theology not suggest to phenomenology certain modifications of method and processes in virtue of its own requirements and only for formulating them? In other words, could one not inquire into the (unconditional) conditions to which the phenomenological method would have to subscribe in order to attain a thought of revelation? Inversely, could not the requirements of theology permit phenomenology to transgress its proper limits, in order finally to attain the free possibility at which it has pretended to aim since its origin?

Phenomenology refuses to admit the full possibility of revelation, because it imposes two limits on possibility in general: the *I* and the horizon. Hence even the question of a phenomenology of religion, like that of a phenomenology of revelation, suggests calling into question the axiomatic character of these two presuppositions. In at least one way, the Husserlian *I* persists in Heideggerian *Dasein* despite all their polemics: With

Being-in-the-world intentionality does not disappear but is radicalized, since in both cases only the originally possibilizing opening of the *I* (or of *Dasein*) can take aim at, reach, or experience either an object or, more generally, an intra-mundane being. Intentionality opens a world; *being-in-the world* "worlds": whether as objectivity or as world, such opening is decided in a center that always reverts back to the *I*. This presupposition raises two difficulties within phenomenology itself.

(a) The *I* constitutes objects according to its axis of intentionality. Yet supposing that the constitution of the world is accomplished without remainder (hence that a revelation could be demarcated a priori), one would still have to ask whether the *I* is constituted by itself, to what extent and by what authority. Husserl himself constantly confronted this multiform difficulty although he never resolved it. Merleau-Ponty and Sartre attempted to split the *I* in two, one aspect constituted (transcendence of the ego), one aspect not constituted (prereflexive). Although Heidegger shifted the emphasis from the question of constitution to that of *Entschlossenheit*, he possibly did not, for all that, surpass it. But if the inherent locus of constitution according to the intentional axis remains itself undetermined, does not the very ground of reduction begin to shift?

(b) It does so because a different property of the *I* turns out to be problematic in a parallel fashion: Does the *I* define itself essentially as the origin of intentionality? Even *Dasein* keeps the privilege of opening (on) beings from itself. This polarization of the *I* according to the intentional axis can nevertheless be contested phenomenologically: either by challenging absolutely the intentional ecstasy (subject-object split) from the self-affectivity of the *me*, an original and self-immanent passivity;[26] or by deforming the constituted and the constituting *I* all the way to the givenness in person (*Selbstgegebenheit*) of the original flesh (*Leib*), in such a way that it would precede the gap between immanence and transcendence, constituting and constituted, and hence all intentionality;[27] or, finally, by invalidating the intentional axis through the ethical injunction, which the I no longer exercises but which it receives and suffers from the face of the other—without representation, passively, forever the other obliges the *I* to relinquish any *Jemeinigkeit*, any intentional source, any constitution, in order to become an *I* in the accusative (*me*, not *ego*) convoked, summoned, affected by the other.[28] A single paradox is outlined in these three attempts: one of the instances that restrict phenomenology's acceptance of the full possibility of revelation, namely, to know the *I* (and its equivalents), does not offer any certain phenomenological guarantee. What phenomenology opposes to revelation—the *I* as origin—is perhaps not phenomenologically legitimate: Who is the *I*? Is the *I* original or derived? If it is derived, from where, from what—from whom? Consequently, would it not be suitable to reverse the relation and the dependence? Far from the *I* restricting the possibility of a revelation phenomenologically, would one not have to venture that maybe the *I* can only attain its proper phenomenological possibility from a givenness that cannot be constituted, cannot be objectified and is prior to it—maybe even from a revelation?

Phenomenology returns to the things inasmuch as it makes them visible or phenomenal. It presents the things themselves. This presentation is deployed within a horizon. The horizon can vary: objectivity (Husserl), Being (Heidegger), ethics (Levinas), the body of the flesh (Merleau-Ponty), etc. The principle of horizon always remains. This requirement raises a double question. (a) What sort of horizon could allow for a revelation? While the horizon of objectivity quickly and generally has been recognized as inadequate and theology consequently is acknowledged as a nonobjectifying knowledge, must one therefore uphold the horizon of Being as the indisputable frame for any possible revelation? Fundamental ontology's neutrality—and especially its "appearance of an individualistic and radical atheism to the extreme"[29]—closes down the possibility of revelation, first by leading revelation back precisely to the manifestation of a being, but especially by prejudging that revelation already concerns a being. Of course, one can object: Can revelation retain any meaning without the horizon of Being? Certainly, since the substitution of ethics for Being as horizon already opens phenomenology; no longer is it closed to the invisible phenomenon of the face of the other. The injunction inverts intentionality, and concrete morality appears. But for all that, it is not certain that by passing from Being to ethics (or to the body's flesh) phenomenology has made sufficient progress in the direction of the possibility of revelation, of possibility as revelation. In any case, possibility actually submits straightaway to the restriction of a horizon. Any horizon that determines the scene of incoming phenomena in a priori fashion delimits the possible, hence limits (or forbids) revelation.

(b) Thus the second question: Does revelation admit of a horizon (still to be identified), or does it exclude being presented by any horizon whatsoever in principle? The difficulty of the dilemma increases as soon as one notes that neither of these hypotheses is acceptable. If revelation admits of a horizon, it acknowledges the horizon a priori and therefore renounces possibility. It really then renounces itself and regresses to the rank of a simple constituted manifestation. If revelation excludes any horizon on principle, it can no longer present itself anywhere, to no gaze nor as any phenomenon: thus it would lose any relation with phenomenology and its presentation, certainly with phenomenality as such (*schlechthin*). How should one therefore think the relation of revelation to the horizon (thus to phenomenology), if the two extremes cannot be admitted? Revelation entails a presentation. Hence it condescends to assume a horizon, but it nevertheless challenges any a priori condition imposed on its possibility.

Even so these paradoxical requirements indicate the correct response: revelation presents itself in a horizon only by *saturating* it. Without a doubt, a horizon remains acquired and all visibility takes place within the measure of its scope—revelation can allow itself to be refracted on the horizon of Being, of the other, of the body's flesh, etc. Yet what is thus revealed fulfills at this point the dimensions and the possibilities that this frame imparts to it, so that the resulting phenomenon damages itself. The strength and the scope of what allows itself to be presented can enter the limits of the phenomenological horizon only by disrupting it: each line of the phenomenon interferes with all the others, as if they crossed or reflected each other or interacted within their respective frames.[30] This confusion does not indicate any disarray internal to revelation, but only the incommensurability of any revelation with any phenomenological horizon whatsoever. The confusion of the horizon by revelation marks, as saturation, the *correct*, that is to say, the paradoxical relation of one to the other: revelation does not enter phenomenality except under the figure of a paradox—as saturated phenomena that saturate the entire horizon of phenomenality. "Saturated phenomenon" means: instead of common phenomenality striving to make intuition adequate to intention, and usually having to admit the failure in givenness of an incompletely intuited though fully intended object, revelation gives objects where intuition surpasses the intentional aim. Under the regime of revelation, intuition offers neither as much nor less than but *infinitely more* than intention, hence than the significations elaborated by the *I*. Similar intuitions (still) without intention, without signification, even without expressible objectivity thus play freely (*imaginatio vaga*), interfere with each other, escape constitution, saturate the horizon. Thus revelation forces phenomenology to question that truth could be boiled down to the lived experiences of truth—to know that "evidence would be the 'lived experience' of truth"[31] (and this lived experience would refer unreservedly to *Dasein*'s opening). "Being true, as much as being revelatory, is a mode of the being of *Dasein*."[32] Truth, at least the truth given without restraint by revelation, does not discover (itself) so much as it recovers from intuition all intentions, inundates significations with (albeit extravagant) objectivities, and saturates the horizon with its givenness without measure. In this situation, truth no longer comes from δόξα, (true or false) appearance, but from παραδόξον, an appearance that contradicts opinion or appearance, and above all saturates the horizon.

The conditions under which phenomenology would be able to do justice to the possibility of revelation (to possibility as revelation) can hence, at least summarily, be expressed in this way: (a) that the *I* admit its nonoriginal character and think it all the way to an inherent givenness; (b) that the horizon allow itself to be saturated by givenness instead of insisting on determining it a priori, and that truth accordingly change from the evidence of δόξα to the παραδόξον of the revealed. A definitive response to these two conditions could only be possible after long and difficult investigations, which are to a great extent still to come. If phenomenology would at least begin to approach and to confront them candidly, it might accomplish what previous philosophy of religion has never more than outlined: freeing the possibility of revelation, hence possibility as revelation, from the grip of the principle of sufficient reason, understood as the a priori condition of possibility (hence of impossibility) for any event to come. Certainly, freeing the possibility of revelation doubtlessly would force phenomenology to liberate itself from its pretensions to self-constitution (*I*, the horizon), but this requirement is so radical that it merely confirms how radical the liberation in question will have to be.

What Cannot Be Said

Apophasis and the Discourse of Love

1

What we (wrongly, as we shall see) call "negative theology" inspires in us both fascination and unease. In it, we actually encounter a mode of language or even a language game that claims (perhaps deservedly) to express what cannot be experienced. It fascinates us, first, because it claims to express an event, or better an ineffable advent. But it also makes us uneasy with its assurance that the inexpressible can really be experienced according to the frequently attested paradox: "What no eye has seen, nor ear heard, nor the human heart conceived" is, Paul announces, precisely "what God has prepared for those who love him."[1] In short, this language game occurs only in circumstances where "what had not been told them they shall see, and what they had not heard they shall contemplate" (Isaiah 52:15). Hence it is something unseen, unheard of, ungraspable. To give an extreme but unavoidable example, at stake is the paradox of seeing in human flesh him "whom no one has ever seen" (John 1:18), for "no one shall see me and live" (Exodus 33:20).

The language game of what is called "negative theology" all too quickly claims not only to speak the unspeakable but to phenomenalize it, to experience what cannot be experienced and to express it inasmuch as it remains inexpressible. In philosophical terms, one can thus say (as did Descartes) that "in effect, the idea of the infinite, in order to be true, must in no way be comprehended, for incomprehensibility itself is contained in the formal reasoning of infinity [*idea enim infiniti, ut sit vera, nullo modo debet comprehendi, quoniam ipsa incomprehensibilitas in ratione formali infiniti continetur*]."[2] In more theological terms, one can say of God that "we thus call him . . . the inexpressible, the inconceivable, the invisible, and the incomprehensible, he who vanquishes the power of human language and surpasses the comprehension of human thought" (John Chrysostom).[3] Since the two conditions of this speech exercise are unambiguously extreme (to experience what cannot be experienced, to express the inexpressible) one can hardly avoid looking for an alternative, when faced with such claims. On the one hand, one could simply challenge all "negative theology" as a language game that is both impractical (after all, one cannot experience what one cannot experience) and contradictory (one cannot, after all, express what one cannot express). In this case one chooses to respect the double prohibitions by Kant ("by means of principles to show the specific limits [of reason])"[4] and by Wittgenstein ("Whereof one cannot speak [*sprechen*], thereof one must be silent").[5] On the other hand, one could accept "negative theology" but restrict it to the domain in which it claims its validity, that of the purest and most extreme religious experience, the domain attributed to the "mystical." This acceptance would amount to a marginalization, since this domain remains inaccessible to most of us—certainly to most philosophers. Even if admitted in principle, "mystical theology" would thus remain an unfrequented territory, willingly abandoned by those who attempt to ignore it to those who are willing to lose themselves there, at the risk of irrationality. This refusal in principle is thus reiterated by a refusal in fact. Metaphysics has amply confirmed these two attitudes, as is proven indisputably by its modern history—which can be described as a rejection (indeed, a tenacious elimination from thought) of what cannot be comprehended as one of its objects.

Or rather, this situation has preceded us, for modernity itself has found its limits and is attempting to identify them. Thus the theme of "negative theology" has resurfaced in philosophy in recent years, at least in a vague manner. Among other indications, one can cite Heidegger, who was unable to avoid "comparing" the step back of the thought of presence toward that of giving (*Geben*) "with the method of negative theology."[6] Or Wittgenstein, who states, with a different accentuation: "There is the ineffable [*es gibt allerdings Unaussprechliches*]. It *shows itself.* It is the mystical."[7] It remains simpler, however, to rely on the most explicit testimony—Derrida's arguments (which, moreover, were elaborated in response to my own publications), for a new pertinence for "negative theology" in the forum of contemporary philosophy.[8] As we know, Derrida revived this theme in order to subject the apophatic moment of "negative theology" to deconstruction. He did so by establishing that it inverts itself and, in the end, achieves a second-order kataphasis so as to reestablish the metaphysical primacy of presence, a goal that was in fact never abandoned by theology. To say of God that he is and then that he is not in the long run would aim only at thinking of this nonbeing as the ultimate and finally unchanging figure of his being—a being beyond being. Because, having undergone the ordeal of its negation, the being of God is thus able to prevail not only in transcendence but in presence over the being of all other beings: "apophasis has always represented a kind of paradoxical hyperbole."[9] In this way, the "metaphysics of presence" annexes "negative theology" without any other form of trial, reducing it to the ranks of a pure and simple auxiliary of metaphysics without too much circumspection. Hence deconstruction finally triumphs, by getting rid of a possible rival that is all the more dangerous in having preceded it and having come from elsewhere. One can nonetheless show that this interpretation deals a double blow—and the more violence it exerts, the more fragile it becomes.

(a) First, it denies the patience and suffering of the apophatic negation, without taking into account the seriousness and the work of the theologians involved. One need only think of a very explicit remark made by John Scotus Eriugena on the irremediable nature of negation, which can be neither abolished nor mitigated by a final naming:

> For, when we declare "God is super essential," we imply nothing other than a negation of essence. Whoever declares "God is super essential" explicitly negates that God is essence. Consequently, although the negation is not found in the words themselves, its meaning does not escape the understanding of those who think about it seriously. In this way, in my opinion, I am constrained to admit that the divine names enumerated below, though at first they seem to imply no negation, belong more to the negative part of theology than to the positive part.[10]

In fact, the negation remains as radical and definitive for language as kenosis does for its referent.

(b) But in order to bring everything back to the "metaphysics of presence," this attempt to reduce apophasis to kataphasis must also cancel the third path, often called the path of eminence. How is one to understand, in effect, that everything is predicated of God while at the same time nothing is predicated of him—other than by recognizing that a third path surpasses the first two and only thus does away with the contradiction? Of course, it remains to be seen whether there is a language game that could dispense with affirmation and negation like this, and thus dispense with truth and falsity. Would we still be dealing with a meaningful assertion and, more particularly, with a predication? Without a doubt, but as Aristotle foresaw, not all assertions refer to truth and falsity following the model of predication: "Prayer [is] certainly a discourse [λόγος], but it is neither true nor false."[11]

Even before answering these questions, one can already point to evidence in this direction: First, the phrase "negative theology" does not describe the situation we are dealing with correctly, for the moment of negation (admittedly with variable positions) is inscribed within a triple determination that articulates discourse into (i) *via affirmativa*, (ii) *via negativa*, and, especially, (iii) *via eminentiae*, radically other and hyperbolic. It does not mirror the negation with another superior affirmation (whether disguised or admitted), but tears discourse away from predication altogether, and thus away from the alternative of truth or falsity. Two consequences follow. First, I will no longer say "negative theology," but rather, following the nomenclature of the Dionysian *corpus*, "mystical theology." And second, one will come to realize that "mystical theology" (when it claims to be following the third path) no longer has the ambition of making constative use of language; its ambition is, rather, to be freed from such use. But what type of language use can replace it? I have suggested that it involves moving from a constative (and predicative) use of language toward a strictly pragmatic usage.[12] This has yet to be proven. What follows is an attempt to do just that.

2

But, just as "negative theology" is finally not really negative, it is also possible that it cannot be confined to the theological—at least understood in the narrowest sense. Indeed, one must not exclude the possibility that the pragmatic system used by mystical theology extends to other states of affairs and to other utterances. Nor can one exclude that these other uses may allow us to establish with greater clarity the true function of the third path, which is neither affirmative nor negative. I will thus choose a privileged case of pragmatic language outside of theology, one that illustrates the third path indubitably. I propose considering the erotic event and its corresponding utterance: "I love you!" The question then becomes that of determining what it is one says when one says "I love you!" supposing that one says anything at all. Let me take a famous example from *The Charterhouse of Parma*, when Clélia meets up with Fabrice after years of separation: "'It's me,' a dear voice told him, 'I've come to tell you I love you, and to ask you whether you will obey me.'"[13] Are we dealing with a constative utterance here? Is Clélia really saying something? And is she saying something about something? And in this case, is it a predicate of herself or of Fabrice? I will attempt to respond to these complex questions by emphasizing successive difficulties.

One can first reduce her utterance to its central nucleus, "I love you," and ask what "I love you" says. If, first hypothesis, one reads the formula as it stands, it falls in the domain of pure private language: neither Fabrice nor anyone else can understand what Clélia is saying. Of course, if I were to make an analogy with my personal experience, I could conjecture that she is describing her subjective attachment to the person of Fabrice. Yet one cannot exclude that she may be pretending or lying, either to Fabrice (to seduce him), to a possible witness (to embrace her standing), or even to herself (to love loving, without loving anyone in particular). In order to defend the constative character of Clélia's utterance, one can also reduce her sentence, "I've come to tell you that I love you" to a quasi-predicative proposition in the style "Someone exists—*X*, me, Clélia—such that she is in love with another—*Y*, you, Fabrice" (let me allow for the moment that the identification of *X* and *Y* with Clélia and Fabrice is not problematic). What signification does this utterance offer? One that is revealed by its method of verification. Here two possibilities open up.

(a) "I love you" could perhaps be verified by precise interactions between things and actors (to approach, to speak to, to watch, to take care of, to serve, etc.). Yet can one locate them, and then establish which and how many are sufficient to give a meaning to the predication "*X* is in love with *Y*"? Clélia undoubtedly invests herself—"It is I who have come to tell you," just as she has undoubtedly given sufficient proof of her devotion in the past, helping Fabrice in prison, helping him escape, thinking of him, etc. Yet one cannot say that "I love you!" exactly signifies "I helped you in prison, I helped you escape, I abandoned myself to you, I thought of you," etc. Not only because all of this is far from proving "I love you" (a lot is missing here), but also because one can oppose to these facts other, at least equivalent, facts: Clélia has in the meantime married someone else (Count Crescenzi), she has promised the Virgin never to see Fabrice in the light of day, she has avoided meeting him, etc. Thus, reduced to behaviors and states of affairs, the declaration "I love you!" remains ambiguous, precisely because it doesn't describe anything with precision.

(b) A second possibility remains: since the reduction of "I love you" to a predicative proposition does not guarantee its verification, it remains possible to trust in Clélia's sincerity by considering that the meta-narrative "It is I who have come to tell you" guarantees what she says in the phrase "I love you." But how is one to recognize and prove this sincerity? All the facts and actions that one could inventory belong to the world. They cannot say anything, nor can they determine the validity of someone's sincerity, which in principle remains both out of this world and absolutely foreign to things. At its best, sincerity pertains to the private sphere and thus cannot be described or verified any more than lying can. One cannot even invoke private language in this situation, because the private sphere is precisely deprived of it. What is more, as soon as someone claims to speak and prove his or her sincerity by speaking utterances of the type "I am sincere," "you can trust me," experience has taught us that we should rather hear an indication of deceit, such that the utterance "I am lying" would suggest that I am in fact not lying. Thus Clélia is saying nothing about nothing to Fabrice when she says "I love you!"

Another interpretation is possible, however. Even if Clélia says nothing to Fabrice, she speaks to him as herself. "I love you" perhaps states nothing concerning any state of affairs and predicates nothing at all, but this utterance nonetheless speaks this nothing *to* someone, Fabrice, and it speaks it *on behalf of* someone else. Let me look once more at the example: "'It is I,' a dear voice told him, 'who have come to tell you that I love you, and to ask whether you will obey me.'" Especially if Stendhal is saying nothing about nothing, it is clear that he insists on the speaker and the person spoken to, to the point of saturation: first the speaker, for she says "it is I," "I have come to tell you," "I love you"; then the person spoken to, for he hears "tell *you*," "love *you*," "ask *you*." Clearly, predication and proposition fade away, leaving the naked intrigue of the two speakers, that is to say, the interlocutors, in the foreground. Could we not describe "I love you!" as a strict dialogue, without an object but perfectly intersubjective?

Several arguments compromise this position: (a) Understood in this way, Clélia's declaration to Fabrice is in effect reduced to a pure dialogue between "I" and "you," in other words, between two pronouns labeled personal and thus, properly speaking, both impersonal and improper. Not only could Clélia rightfully make the same declaration to someone other than Fabrice (and what proves that she has not done just that or that she will not do so?), but Fabrice could equally well receive it from someone else (why not from Sanséverina or from "little Annetta Marini," who faithfully listens to his sermons?). The roles could also be reversed. Yet, most importantly, anyone (not only Clélia and Fabrice) can take on these two roles, like characters in a play, or on the spontaneous stage of everyday life. In "I love you!" "I" and "you" remain empty terms, which essentially produce occasional expressions (occasionally significant) and nothing more.[14] Simple pronouns, they suffice neither to bind people, nor to attribute names, nor to create lovers out of them. Thus Clélia does not speak herself to Fabrice, for purely logical reasons. (b) What is more, if "I love you!" is not sufficient to establish a true signification or even the identity of the person one thus claims to love, that is not only because I can love anyone but especially because I can love someone who is not present or who remains anonymous. In fact, the more I sincerely love (or think I love, which amounts to the same for me), the less the identity of the presence of the loved one is required. I can love a woman or a man whom I know only superficially, or whom I do not know at all (based on his or her name or reputation), or even about whom I know nothing. I can love someone who is absent most of the time and who will probably always remain thus, and I can even love someone absent who has never yet been present, not even for a moment. I can love a woman whom I have lost or whom I have left. I can love someone dead out of loyalty and a child not yet born out of hope. Because I love, what I am in love with does not have to *be* at all, and can thus dispense altogether with maintaining the status of a being. Not only does this absence not stop us from loving and desiring, it reinforces this desire. For the loved one, the person to whom "I love you!" is spoken, it is no longer about being or not being, or about being or not being this or that, but only about the fact that one is loved. Thus (and this time for motives that are not only logical, but also erotic), what Clélia says to Fabrice does not designate Fabrice and is not even addressed to him. "I love you," then, neither produces a proposition with a reference (a signification), nor does it predicate a meaning, nor does it even mobilize identifiable interlocutors. It thus does not constitute a locutionary act.[15]

3

And yet, even if it is not a locutionary act, "I love you" remains a speech act. To see this, we can consider a second hypothesis: that "I love you!" constitutes an illocutionary act, in other words, a performative. By pronouncing "I love you!" the speaker does not in effect say anything (neither meaning nor reference), but accomplishes what he says, puts it into practice simply by saying it; the force of the utterance enforces what is said.[16] This hypothesis, one must admit, seems convincing. It would justify the fact that, strictly speaking, "I love you!" offers neither meaning nor reference, without, for all that, saying nothing, since in saying "I love you!" it is not a matter of communicating information or making a predication but of loving in act and in force. So when I say "I love you!" to someone, or when I hear it spoken by someone else, an act is accomplished immediately: whether my lover and I rejoice (as occurs with Clélia and Fabrice) or are worried (like Phaedra and Hippolytus in another context) is due to the fact that this love, simply because I declared it, becomes an effective and unquestionable fact, which modifies inter-subjective reality and which one must, from now on, take into account. One can add to this: because this illocutionary act is a performance, it intervenes in a precise time and place and thus attaches a precise and identifiable signification and precise, identifiable speakers to what hitherto remained an essentially occasional expression: here and now, it is a question of Clélia accomplishing this speech act once and for all and definitively for the benefit of Fabrice and for no one else except her and him. In the same way, the "I don't know what inexplicable and fatal force" that seals the friendship between Michel de Montaigne and Étienne de la Boétie (as if according to a performative) identifies them absolutely and determines the reference to them: the famous but difficult utterance "because it was him; because it was me" thus eliminates at least the danger of an essentially occasional expression and ensures that we are dealing with them, in Bordeaux and in 1554, and no one else, nowhere else.[17]

However, the speech act "I love you!" cannot be analyzed as a performative or illocutionary type. Moreover, so far as I know, neither Austin nor Searle mentions it among the latter (in fact, they seem to ignore it entirely, no matter what heading one gives to it). To understand this impossibility, one need only address Austin's conditions for all illocutionary acts and measure whether or not "I love you!" satisfies the requirements under each heading.

(1) "There must exist a conventional procedure having a certain conventional effect, a procedure that includes the utterance of certain words by certain people in certain circumstances." If by such a conventional procedure one is to understand a ceremony, whether public (marriage, contract, social pact, etc.) or private (engagement, marriage proposal), then "I love you" is not appropriate: I can say it or hear it in all circumstances, sometimes even in a semi-unconsciousness (pleasure, sleep, etc.), even almost in silence. (2) "What is more, the particular people and circumstances in a given case must be suitable to invoke the particular procedure they would invoke." "I love you" satisfies this criterion so long as it implies two people capable of communicating and possessing at least a certain freedom of feeling. But it does not comply, inasmuch as it ignores all "particular procedures" and can be performed in all circumstances and in all language games. (3) "The procedure must be executed by all participants both correctly and" (4) "completely." But "I love you" can very well remain unilateral (this situation is all too common) and thus does not necessitate that "all" (the protagonists of the action) satisfy this requirement: one is more than enough. As for the requirement of a "completely" executed "procedure," it has no pertinence, not only because in this case no "procedure" is required but especially because a "complete" utterance either would change nothing, or by changing something would weaken "I love you!" rather than reinforce it: to add to "I love you!" something like "a lot" or "very much," amounts to saying much less than simply "I love you!" and even insinuates that "I don't love you!"

Let me look at the two remaining conditions: First, (5) "when, as is often the case, the procedure is meant to be used by people having certain thoughts and feelings, or to trigger a certain behavior having consequences for any one of the participants, then a person who participates in this procedure and claims to have certain thoughts and feelings must in fact have them, and the participants must have the intention to behave accordingly; what is more" (6) "they must in the future so behave."[18] It is clear that "I love you" can satisfy these last two requirements even less than the preceding ones. First, as Stanley Cavell has judiciously remarked,[19] I cannot say "I love you" unless motivated by passion, or at least from a passion. Yet no one can verify this passion, not even (or rather especially not) the person who is supposed to benefit from it. Thus my "intention" remains utterly unverifiable. Here one finds the aporia of sincerity: it is a totally private mood, ineffable in everyday language. Thus to say "I love you" guarantees my sincerity no more than it presumes the acceptance (or refusal) of the other or, for that matter, his or her own sincerity. Following Cavell once more, one must next recognize that the freedom and fragility of "I love you" have no ambition to be of any value for anything other than "now," certainly not "in the future": How can I guarantee to someone that I love him or her, if I myself have no certitude? One could answer that I can very well promise to love someone in the future, in spite of the fickleness of my heart and my moods. Of course, but then one is dealing with a promise ("I promise to love you"), and thus with a completely different speech act from "I love you!" The promise is, in fact, the perfect illocutionary act, even the epitome of the performative, satisfying all the enumerated conditions, precisely those that "I love you!" does not satisfy (conventional procedure and effect, fixed circumstances, formal and complete fulfillment, guarantee of reciprocity and the future, etc.).[20] Thus, the promise differs essentially from "I love you!"; it can only be added on, and this supplement confirms that by saying "I love you!" I do not perform an illocutionary speech act.

4

Admittedly, then, "I love you" cannot be considered an illocutionary act, since it respects neither the conventions nor the conditions of such an act. However, the one who pronounces these words does indeed accomplish an act, even if it is not the act of actualizing what he or she says. One does not do what one says by saying it, but in saying it one nonetheless does do something. What can it be? By saying "I love you!" I do not thereby factually or actually love, but I nonetheless radically modify the intersubjective relation between me and my interlocutor; from now on nothing will be the same, for better or for worse. Wherein lies the difficulty, then? Perhaps in this: whereas the illocutionary act effectively accomplishes what it says (to promise, condemn, curse, bless, etc.), the act that says "I love you!" accomplishes something other than what it says: for example, to be fond of someone without sincerely loving him or her, or to admit to holding someone in affection without hoping for the return of that affection, or else to satisfy a preliminary request or to gain a moral advantage by virtue of my sincerity, etc. When I pronounce "I love you!" I do not prove that I love (as with an illocutionary act), but I nonetheless always produce an effect on my interlocutor: returned love, saddened or fearful refusal, placing the other in a position of power over me, fear, gratitude, surprise, etc. The act therefore does not accomplish what it says, but it says what it says in order to have on the interlocutor an effect that is other than what it says—even if it is simply to draw his or her attention and to constitute the other as my interlocutor in an erotic dialogue.

Now this is exactly what is called a perlocutionary act, as defined by Austin: "an act that we instigate or accomplish by saying something: to convince, persuade, frighten, etc."[21] Searle usefully specifies: "If we consider the concept of the illocutionary act, we must also consider the consequences, the effects that such acts have on the actions, thoughts, or beliefs of the *listeners*, etc." That is, by saying something, we elicit a different effect: to persuade, convince, but also frighten, make aware of, lead to act in a certain way, etc.[22] Cavell gives us a perfect example: "the [perlocutionary] effect [brought about by Iago] of helping to drive someone [Othello] mad with jealousy."[23] When I say "I love you!" I try (and in fact always manage) not necessarily to perform the love that I speak but to move, to influence, and, at the very least, to summon my listener to consider my declaration. I declare my love as one declares war: it is not yet to engage in it, but already to oblige my adversary to mobilize him- or herself, and thus to determine him- or herself in relation to me. The declaration of Clélia, if we understand it as a perlocutionary act, must be reorganized: the sequence "to tell you that I love you" must be understood in terms of the sequence that precedes it—"I have come to"—because together they try to produce another effect than that of the declaration itself, an effect that Clélia renders perfectly explicit: "to ask you to obey me." By saying "I love you!" I do not love for all that, but I in effect ask the other to love me or at least to answer me sincerely. I thus accomplish neither a locutionary act nor an illocutionary act, but rather a perlocutionary act.[24]

In fact, other characteristics of this type of act fit what I do when I say "I love you!" (a) The perlocutionary act produces its effect by saying something, but this effect acts, beyond the *dictum*, on the other speaker or the speakers thus provoked; to be more precise, it "produces certain effects on the feelings, thoughts, and actions of the listeners, the speaker, or *other persons*; and it can be done with the goal, the intention or the will to produce them."[25] Instead of doing what I say, I say *in order to* do something to someone, in the same sense in which, in everyday French, as in English, "faire quelque chose à quelqu'un"—"to do something to someone"—means to provoke, to intrigue, to move, to overwhelm, and eventually to seduce someone. Instead of saying something about something, or bringing about what I say, it is rather, for me, about saying *to* someone, not necessarily what I say, since I mean for my listener to understand something *other* than what I say, but that I am here, that I am speaking to him or her, imposing my will or having his or her will imposed on me. Contrary to the illocutionary act, the perlocutionary does not involve itself so much with the utterance as with the person spoken to, and the speaker always takes the initiative: "The speaker is on his or her own to create the desired effect."[26] (b) Perlocutionary acts prove to be nonconventional, or at least "it is difficult to say where convention begins and ends."[27] We have seen that "I love you!" dispenses with almost all conventions proper to locutionary acts, in particular that of reciprocity. This does not signify the disappearance of such conventions in principle, but that in this case they belong neither exclusively nor primarily to logic or language theory, although they do come within the scope of such theory: they arise out of the space of dialogue itself and from the pragmatics that ensue. To sum up, if there must be conventions, they will first depend on the originary fact of the other. In this way, when I say "I love you!" what I say produces an effect that depends not so much on the obvious meaning of my utterance as on the identity, the situation, even the state of mind of my interlocutor. And I can predict this effect, because my interlocutor's moods follow from language conventions: for example, Don Giovanni plays better than Leporello, when it is a question of speaking to Elvira in particular and to women in general. (c) Indeed, in the perlocutionary act what essentially matters is not what I say (the intention and the meaning) but to whom I say it (others, an audience, or a specific someone); the listener is thus privileged over the speaker. Hence the pedagogical rule of thumb that, to teach math to Pierre, one must know mathematics, and above all Pierre. The decisive factor, according to Cavell, consists in the fact that "in perlocutionary acts, the 'you' comes essentially into the picture,"[28] while in illocutionary acts, everything depends on my capacity, as the speaking "I," to perform what I say. And of course, with "I love you!" more than in any other act, what takes center stage is called "you," which constitutes the perlocutionary act par excellence. (d) One last point, decisive for my inquiry, must be addressed: because one is dealing here not with what I utter but rather with the "responses" to it, hence the effects produced when "I have an effect" on my interlocutor, these effects (emotions, thoughts, reactions, etc.) taken in themselves "can be accomplished additionally or entirely by non-locutionary means." In short, there is nothing contradictory or unthinkable about a "non-verbal response."[29] Not only do perlocutionary acts accomplish intersubjective effects (which lie outside the particular utterance) and contradict what is said, but what is more, the responses arrived at in this way can be given in silence (outside of language). Who does not see that "I love you!" can, once its effect is produced, receive a response all the more satisfying in that it remains silent? It could even be that silence constitutes, if not the best response, at least always the first, and that, without this first silence, the following verbalization would not be convincing. Since all these characteristics are reunited in the utterance "I love you!" one can thus conclude that one is dealing with a performative of the perlocutionary type. And, granting it this status, I am justifying, against its omission by Austin and Searle, what Cavell specifically calls a "passionate utterance."[30]

5

It has now become possible to describe the perlocutionary act that I accomplish when I say "I love you!" or at least to trace a sketch. It is a matter of acting in which not only the fact *that* I speak is more important than *what* I say but in which the fact *that* it is spoken has an effect on *the person to whom* I said it. This characteristic, which goes beyond the field of language [*langue*] and its use [*langage*] to give preponderance to individual speech [*parole*], establishes a structure that is essentially pragmatic, and in this case dialogic. This act speaks inasmuch as it calls out. This call elicits a response and possibly a response to the response, without there necessarily being an end in sight. Thus erotic discourse unfolds according to a call, a response, and a counter-call that can be seen as following three paths.

Let me consider the first and affirmative path. How can I make an affirmation if I am, strictly speaking, not saying anything when I say "I love you!"? As we have seen, this proposition does not offer any reference that can be verified, either by myself (I promise nothing—it is not an illocutionary act) or by the person to whom I am speaking (I can lie, and even if I don't lie, he or she does not know the difference—it is not a locutionary act). It also does not offer a precise meaning (to love can mean to possess like an object, to desire, or, on the contrary, to want the best for and even to sacrifice oneself for someone).[31] Yet as a perlocutionary act, "I love you!" does affirm something: the effect that it produces as a speech act. But this effect is split. First, by affirming to someone that I love him, I choose him as my interlocutor; not only do I distinguish him from the crowd of others who remain anonymous or at least indifferent but, by placing him in a prominent singularity, I individualize him, name and compromise him along with myself, whether he wants this or not: I identify myself through him by identifying him with me. Then, in the dialogical space that has thus been opened, I impose upon my interlocutor a decision regarding whether or not he loves me in return. This decision comprises two questions: Does he accept that I love him, or does he refuse to accept it? but also Does he love me in return, or does he hate me? Even a refusal to answer one or the other of these questions would be equivalent to a response (negative in this case). No affirmation can impose itself as powerfully as "I love you!" but, paradoxically, it imposes itself as a question whose contours are almost impossible to trace, as the most radical question that one can perhaps ever ask. Put otherwise, if my affirmation *that* I love him neither promises nor teaches him anything, it nonetheless forces him to answer a question, a question that is formulated from my point of view as "Does he love me?" while he hears it as "Do you love me?" It follows that the initial affirmation "I love you!" as categorical and affirmative as it remains, ends up producing the effect of a "Do you love me?"—a question that leaves room for doubt, for choice, and for a possible refusal. Affirmation thus elicits negation in and of itself; kataphasis becomes apophasis.

One must thus examine the second and negative path. However, can one really consider the question "Do you love me?" to be an apophasis? This assimilation certainly seems paradoxical, but paradoxes are themselves imperative. Let me try to conceive this. To do so, one must remember that, in the case of a perlocutionary act, one does not consider *what* is said but the fact *that* it is said, the effect it has on the listener; but this effect belongs unambiguously to apophasis. By telling her "I love you!" I expect to hear (and to elicit) that she loves me, thus what I want to say is "Do you love me?" and I await confirmation. By this means I find myself in the exact same position as my listener, who, hearing my "I love you!" asks herself and me if I am telling the truth (in other words, if my thoughts concur and if my conduct will reflect what I think and say); she thus asks me as well, in words or in silence, "Do you love me?" Is it possible to give a categorical answer (affirmative or positive) to this double and yet unique "Do you love me"? If it is a question of deciding whether or not (referentially) I am sincere, or whether or not I understand (semantically) what "to love" means, neither she nor I know anything at the moment of the declaration—hence the apophasis. One might answer that what is at stake is not our sincerity but our concrete behavior and coherence: each of us will learn more about the intention of the other over time, which means that if I ask "Do you love me?" at a particular moment t_1, I can hope to obtain the beginning of an answer at moment t_2 or t_3, etc. This, in its turn, implies that the answer to the question is reached, in the best of cases, only in the moment that follows after. Yet if precisely only the *following* moment can affirm something in response to what I asked only the moment *before*, the temporal gap between doubt and confirmation cannot be abolished and will extend from question to response, endlessly. Thus, even in the case of a happy confirmation, the temporal delay and lateness maintain a *différance*.

With all other questions about states of affairs or objects that are in principle characterized by a certain permanence, this *différance* does not seriously compromise the answer. But in the case of the erotic relation, where the fickleness of the heart holds sway even with no intention of lying (and this is precisely why I cannot stop asking "Do you love me?"), *différance* disqualifies the answer, even when it is positive. One need only think of the common experience of receiving a letter in which the sender reassures me, "I love you too!" This answer can never definitively get rid of my anxiety (I who just said "I love you!" and am waiting for a confirmation today), precisely because it was written and posted several days ago, and I know nothing of what the other was thinking during that time, such that today, now, at the exact moment when I read it, it is too late and still leaves me unsatisfied. "Do you love me?" thus remains decidedly apophatic. This is emphasized from the point of view of the speaking I, for whom doubt goes even further (and not, as one might too quickly assume, less far), for by saying "I love you!" I know that I provoke another question in return as the perlocutionary effect: "Do you love me?" And I also know that there is no way for me to respond to this question and that, on the contrary, I have every reason in the world not to know anything about it. Even if I am sincere in the moment, I know very little about my motivations (desire, the vanity of seduction, fear of solitude, moral altruism?) or about their future (for how long?), such that if I confirm, by answering, "Yes, I love you!" I know only one thing—that I am stepping out of bounds and that, at bottom, as far as the moment to come is concerned, I know nothing. The question "Do you love me?" thus effectively establishes an apophasis.

And yet, despite this apophasis, the erotic dialogue is no less persistent. How is this possible? By means of a third path, a hyperbolic redoubling, a sort of eminence. I can really only repeat "I love you!" precisely because the other repeats ceaselessly "Do you love me?"; and for her, it is the same. She and I, we repeat "I love you!" only because her first enunciation (kataphasis) could not avoid giving rise to the apophatic "Do you love me?" And this repetition is prolonged without foreseeable end, because the confirmation always arrives too late for the question. In the same way, we repeat "Do you love me?" although we know that we cannot obtain a definitive response and although we undergo an insurmountable apophasis on its account, because we do not want to renounce the declaration of love that we can never truly promise or act. It follows that the other and I repeat "I love you!" (over and over again) because it cannot be verified. We repeat "Do you love me?" because we do not want to resign ourselves to invalidating it. I keep saying and *repeating* "I love you!" precisely because, on the one hand, I cannot guarantee it, *and*, on the other hand, I cannot give up trying. Short of answering the question, "Do you love me?" I repeat the perlocutionary act that instigates it, "I love you!" It is a question neither of kataphasis nor of apophasis but rather of a temporalizing language strategy, a repetition that affirms nothing, negates nothing, but that keeps alive a dialogic situation.[32] What the present tense sees as impossible (an affirmation cancelled by a negation), and constative language as contradictory (a kataphasis that gives rise to an apophasis), repetition and the future it conquers makes possible, but in a pragmatic, more precisely perlocutionary, sense. I reach the other and the other reaches me because "I love you!" and "Do you love me?" continually provoke a (perlocutionary) effect in us, or to be more exact, incite each of us for and by the other. We tell each other nothing in a certain (constative) sense, yet by speaking this nothing, or rather, these nothings, we place ourselves (pragmatically) face to face, each receptive to the (perlocutionary) effect of the other, in the distance that both separates and unites us. Constative and predicative (locutionary) or even active (illocutionary) speech definitively gives way to a radical pragmatic (perlocutionary) use: neither speaking nor negating anything about anything, but acting on the other and allowing the other to act on me.

6

If we accept the conclusion toward which these analyses have been leading, a few remarks are in order. First, pragmatic usage (which elsewhere I have attributed to mystical theology in order to gain a better understanding of the third and last path) finds a lateral confirmation in the perlocutions of erotic discourse. In both cases there is a pragmatic use of language, in the form of three privileged perlocutions (and all of their variations, which could be itemized): "I love you!" and "Do you love me?" and their repetition, corresponding to kataphasis, apophasis, and hyperbole. In this sense, mystical theology would no longer constitute a marginal and insignificant exception in language theory but, on the contrary, would indicate a much more central and vast domain, where pragmatics, perlocutions, and what they render utterable unfold, among other things. It is no longer a question of a discourse about beings and objects, about the world and its states of affairs, but rather the speech shared by those who discourse about these things when they no longer discourse about them but speak to one another. The suspicion that modern philosophy has bred of the encounter with theology in general and mystical theology in particular differs little from its disinheritance of the question of love in all its forms. One could then interrogate the dimensions of this encounter between erotic discourse and mystical theology. Are we dealing with a formal similitude, limited to linguistics, or a deeper univocity? I cannot answer such a question in this context. I am already satisfied with having been able to ask it. Two comments, marking a convergence, can nonetheless be made

First of all, the following: just like mystical theology, erotic discourse mobilizes three types of names, to name the beloved in three different ways. (a) I love him and thus affirm him using all possible names, predicates, and metaphors in all registers of all possible languages. Consequently, I do not hesitate to attribute to him not only all appropriate names, but also and especially all inappropriate names, names taken from animals, even obscene or religious names, etc. But these excesses are not perhaps perverse at all, no matter how indecent, because they attempt, awkwardly to be sure but perfectly logically, to reach the very limits of the kataphasis that claims the saturated and exceptional phenomenon that is the other in its eroticized flesh. (b) Yet this uncommon phenomenon ends up exceeding all nomination. It thus becomes appropriate to name it precisely as having no name, as resisting all ownership, all character, and all determination. One then has recourse to minimalist designations, childish, animalistic, or silly names, to pure tautology, to deictics and possessive pronouns, or even onomatopoeias, etc.; offering no meaning, they say nothing and thus manifest a strict apophasis. (c) Yet if the flesh of the other remains definitively her own, and mine, my own, they nevertheless accomplish a single common and reciprocal erotics. In *jouissance*, we still speak to one another and, in a certain sense, still give each other names. But *jouissance* can only speak its own repetition, operating it without syntax and managing its temporality: it is a question of articulating together "I love you!" and at the same time "Do you love me?" using alternately "now" (kataphasis), "again" (apophasis), and "come" (eminence). And one could show without difficulty that at least here one is dealing with an analogy from the path of eminence, or more precisely, from the discourse of praise.

In this context (and this is the second comment) one can also question the episode near the end of the Gospels in which Christ asks Peter three times, "Do you love me?" (John 21:15–7). In response to the first questioning, Peter answers, "Yes Lord, you know that I love you." Why does this categorical response not satisfy the initial question? First, because Christ already knows and has always known that Peter does not love him, or at least that at the decisive moment he did not love him as much as he had promised, betraying him (Mark 14:66–72) instead of risking his own death (Mark 14:30). Peter's kataphasis thus actually signifies an apophasis. He denied, in other words, "negated" (Mark 14:68, 69) Jesus' name and even "swore 'I don't know this man *you* are talking about'" (Mark 14:66). He refused even to say the man's name, so that he put the responsibility for uttering it on others. Thus when Christ repeats the question "a second time" (John 21:16), one can assume that Peter hears an allusion to this past lie, also spoken "a second time" (Mark 14:70). Thus he utters his love a second time, as if to compensate for his second denial: this latent confession thus accomplishes the apophasis. Speaking in this way, he either supposes that a locutionary act is expected of him (to inform Jesus of his love and to confirm this information), the stupidity of which is immediately apparent, since Christ knows everything, including this, or else he thinks that by repeating himself it will "sink in" and convince Jesus that today at least he truly loves him. Such an illocutionary act in fact performs nothing, and it is not enough to prove Peter's sincerity. Or else perhaps he finally understands what the third questioning asks of him: it is not about what Peter says about things (first questioning), nor is it about his behaving in all sincerity (second questioning), for Peter knows that Christ knows he knows ("Lord, You know everything, You know [thus also] that I love you"; John 21:17], but rather it is about the perlocutionary effect that Christ expects to have on him: "Tend my sheep." Christ expects neither that Peter should admit not loving him nor that he pretend to love him, but that out of love of Jesus he love the other believers, present and to come. These three stages within a single utterance follow the three paths of mystical theology and of erotic discourse. Is this so surprising, inasmuch as between God and humans everything remains ambiguous except, precisely, love? We repeatedly say, despite all the impossibilities that prohibit it, "The word that resounds even to the heavens, the word, the word of gods and men: 'I love you!'"[33]

The Impossible for Man—God

1. What Transcendence Does Not Transcend

Transcendence—the concept will not take us very far, nor truly "beyond." Not, at least, if we take it in the two ways admitted by philosophy.

First, according to phenomenology, transcendence is defined with respect to consciousness, precisely as what surpasses the immanence of consciousness to itself. In particular, we speak of transcendence with regard to what intentional consciousness targets, when consciousness makes itself the "consciousness of something," namely of something other than itself—"that universal ground-property of consciousness, which is to be the consciousness of something, to carry within as *cogitatio* its own *cogitatum*."[1] What does consciousness reach by aiming for it? It reaches of course a meaning, which appears in the end as a phenomenon in its own right when consciousness is *adequately* filled by intuition. In this case, intentional consciousness transcends itself to grasp the phenomenon of a thing, since indeed "the thing names itself as simply transcendent."[2] The thing transcends consciousness in that it stands outside of consciousness, even though it never stands without it. Far as transcendence of this kind may lead, consciousness never overcomes itself, on this model, except for what remains, more often than not, an object. Taken in this first way (Husserl), transcendence never goes beyond the entitative object. Transcendence therefore remains immanent to the horizon of being. And if we radicalize this first level of transcendence by directing it, not only to the entitative object, but, by reducing being in its totality, to Being itself (Heidegger), then by definition transcendence will never reach beyond Being. On the contrary, erected henceforth as the "transcendent pure and simple,"[3] Being will by right be the term of every intentional aiming and every advance of every possible transcendence.

The transcendence of Being does not disclose transcendence, but instead closes and limits it. The paradox involved does not single out phenomenology. Phenomenology, in all likelihood, may have inherited it from the very first explicit formulations of the concept of *metaphysica*, such as those found, for example, in Duns Scotus. Scotus affirms that the first division of being divides being into finite and infinite, thereby ruling on the distinction between God and creature. It follows immediately from this ruling that whatever complies with *"enti ut indifferens ad finitum et infinitum"*—which is to say *ens*—transcends the difference and is therefore *"transcendens et est extra omne genus."*[4] Transcendentals, of course (as opposed to predication by categories), do not speak of God as belonging to a genus, which God transcends, yet all of them, starting with the chief among them, namely being (or rather entity, *ens*), transcend the difference between finite and infinite: *"sunt talia quae conveniunt enti ut est indifferens ad finitum et infinitum."*[5] Consequently, the transcendence of transcendentals—much as these transcendentals determine God as the infinite being, and therefore determine God in his transcendence—still boils down to being and locks itself inside being: *"de ratione transcendentis est non habere praedicatum supraveniens, nisi ens."*[6] In other words, not only does being as a transcendental still contain God's transcendence within its own boundaries, it is actually called upon to define it—in both senses of the term: It establishes God's transcendence, but at the price of giving it definition. One might, of course, wish to radicalize divine transcendence by increasing its density to the point of *"ipsum esse"* (following St. Thomas) instead of deploying it within the confines of the concept of entity (following Duns Scotus, and later Suárez). One might—and, I suppose, one should. Such a move, however, does not change the fundamental situation with regard to transcendence, since *ipsum esse* cannot itself be conceived, at least from our standpoint (*quoad nos*), except as the real composition of essence and *esse*. This composition defines all that is created positively and, by contrast, defines the divine exception—God, or what is in such a way that in him alone the essence coincides with the act of being—to the point that *esse* absorbs essence and, so to speak, dispenses God of the need to have an essence at all: *"Deus igitur nonhabet essentiam, quae non sit suum esse."*[7] The fact that God's transcendence no longer stakes itself within a concept of entity (which always turns out to be univocal since it is the first transcendental, if not a *supertranscendentalis*),[8] does not suffice to set it free, since it remains coiled within the chasm of essence and *esse* and therefore definitively within the horizon of being.

Thus the two chief meanings of transcendence in philosophy, different as they are, share a common feature: Neither transcends the horizon of entity, much less the horizon of being. Transcendence, in philosophy, even and especially the transcendence that we would like to assign to God as his proper mark, is defined as what does not rise beyond being—into which it runs, instead, head on, as the ultimate transcendental.

2. A Question Outside of Being

This ultimate transcendence, however, must be transcended if God is whom we have in mind, supposing at least that we have not buried the question beforehand in onto-theology, but are prepared to let it exercise its privilege—namely, its freedom with regard to being.

Of course, we may tailor the question of God to fit common usage and frame it on the model of questions concerning the things of the world—according to their being. We typically feel that we do justice to what we call "God" when we reduce the question of God to an inquiry into God's existence. Hence the widespread formula: "I believe in God if he exists; but if he does not exist, I reserve the right not to believe in him." Yet it should be immediately apparent that transposing *this* particular question to the realm of existence, innocent and rational as the move may seem, fails to hold up to analysis. The reasons are many. First, our mode of reasoning may turn out, in the privacy of our decisions, to be the inverse of what it presents itself to be, so that the true form of our argument actually is: "Since I don't believe in God anyway, I will conduct myself as though he did not exist." Or, conversely: "Since *I* have decided to believe in God regardless, I will conduct myself as though he existed." Adhering to one or the other position no longer *results* from the reasons invoked but precedes them and makes instrumental use of them: When it comes to God, the relationship between belief and existence is likely to invert itself. It follows from this that being, insofar as it claims the title of horizon or transcendental, offers no privileged access to the question of God and provides no grounds for a decision procedure. Rather it disconnects God and being absolutely. Hence a new alternative emerges, paradoxical perhaps, but perfectly rational. In *this* particular case, it might well be that God (to my knowledge) exists without my believing in him or, conversely, that God (to my knowledge) does not exist, without this preventing me from believing in him. There is nothing absurd about this way of framing the problem: For indeed, if God by definition surpasses the regime of common experience and the conditions it sets on what is possible in a worldly sense (and God would not, otherwise, deserve the title "God" since he would be a worldly phenomenon among others), in what way would his existence (which is to say his being inscribed among phenomena existing in the world) serve as the criterion for my belief or rejection? Moreover, identifying the question of God with my belief is by no means self-evident. To do so is characteristic of a very peculiar theoretical stance, which assumes that the question of God requires that a preliminary question first be answered regarding his existence, and therefore that a proof of his existence be supplied. The underlying assumption is nothing less than the perfect hegemony, without exception, of the horizon of being, such as metaphysics understands it, based on the principle (which does not take over before Suárez) that *"absolute Deus cadit sub objectum hujus scientiae [metaphysica . . .] quia haec scientia est perfectissima sapientia naturalis; ergo considerat de rebus et causis primis et universalissimis, et de primis principiis generalissimis quae Deum ipsum comprehendunt."*[9] We need only articulate this principle to see the opposite hypothesis spring forth: Natural science can only include natural entities among its general causes and universal principles, taken according to their conditions of intelligibility to finite intellects. Far from metaphysics being able, however *transcendentalis* (or rather precisely because metaphysics is transcendental according to transcendental *ens*), to define conditions of intelligibility and possibility for "God" by means of a glaringly unquestioned univocity, God can only be insaturated as God on the basis of his pre-ontological condition and pre-transcendental freedom. As long as the *"Differenz zwischen Sein und Seiendem erscheint dann . . . als die Transzendenz, d. h. als des Meta-Physische,"*[10] transcendence remains metaphysical, even when it overcomes metaphysics. Transcendence that is taken according to *these* meanings does not open up transcendence but instead slams it shut. Before the world comes into being, and thus before being unfolds its horizon, God poses the question of God—a question that no one is free to avoid since God defines himself, prior to any proof of existence, as "the one whom everyone knows, by name."[11] It follows that the end of metaphysics and even the repetition of *Seinsfrage*, far from ruling out or relativizing the question of God, bring instead and by means of contrast its irreducible character to light: Do we have access to a transcendence without condition or measure?

But then the difficulty deepens and mutates. If, on the one hand, the horizon of being does not allow us to stage what is properly at stake in the knowledge we have of God's name; if, on the other hand, nothing appears within this horizon that is not a certificate-bearing entity: Must we not conclude that there is no possible phenomenalization of God and, moreover, that this very impossibility defines God? Are we not, in the era of nihilism, led by our inner fidelity and devotion to thought to admit God in philosophy strictly as what is empirically impossible and lies outside phenomenalization as a matter of principle?

3. The Impossible Phenomenon

We must ask, first: What do possible and impossible mean here? The terms refer to experience, namely to what experience allows and excludes—therefore to what *may* or *may not* appear and let itself be seen, the phenomenon. How, in turn, is a phenomenon defined? It seems reasonable here to privilege the answers, for the most part convergent, that Kant and Husserl have given us, since these two thinkers have almost single-handedly established the only positive concept that we have of the phenomenon. A phenomenon is defined through the adequacy of an intuition (which gives and fulfills) to a concept or meaning (which is empty and to be filled and validated). Based on this premise, a thing can appear to me in two ways: Either I determine what I have received in intuition by identifying it with some concept that I impose on it, so that it is no longer an unintelligible event of consciousness (or a case of intuition) but precisely such and such an object or describable entity; or the concept that I might have actively formed (through spontaneous understanding or through conscious intentionality) on my own initiative ends up finding empirical validation in some intuition, which conies subsequently to fill it and to qualify it as such-and-such an object or entity. It matters little which one of the two serves as the starting point for achieving adequacy, since in any case the phenomenon only appears by internally conjugating intuition and concept.

What about God? It seems immediately clear that I have neither an intuition nor a concept at my disposal in this case. I have no intuition at my disposal, at least if by intuition I mean what is susceptible to be experienced within the parameters of space and time. For by "God" I mean above all and by definition the Eternal—or at least what no more begins to endure than it finishes enduring, since it never begins at all. I mean, also as a matter of definition, what is nonspatial—what is located nowhere, occupies no extension, admits of no limit (what has its center everywhere and its circumference nowhere), escapes all measure (the immense, the incommensurable), and therefore is not divisible or susceptible of being multiplied. This twofold possibility of entering intuition rests neither on any doctrinal preference nor on any arbitrary negativity, but results from the unavoidable requirements of the simple possibility of something like God. The most speculative theology agrees with the most unilateral atheism to postulate that, in God's case, all formal conditions of intuition must be transgressed: If intuition implies space and time, then there can never be any intuition of God because of the even more radical requirement that there *must* not be any intuition, if God is ever to be considered.

Atheism is not alone in denying even the slightest intuition in God's case, since Revelation also insists that "No one has seen God" (John 1:18). A distinctive mark of God is thus the impossibility of receiving an intuition of him. But there is more (or maybe less). If peradventure I suppose myself to have received an intuition exceptional enough to be assigned to something like God, I would have to have at my disposal a concept that allows me to identify this intuition or, what amounts to the same, a concept that this intuition would validate and which in return would confer on it a form and meaning, But I cannot—again by definition—legitimately assign any concept to God, since every concept, by implying delimitation and comprehension, would contradict God's sole possible definition, namely that God transcends all delimitation and therefore all definitions supplied by my finite mind. Incomprehensibility, which in every other case attests either to the weakness of my knowledge or to the insufficiency of what is to be known, ranks, here and here only, as an epistemic requirement imposed by that which must be thought—the infinite, the unconditioned, and therefore the inconceivable. "*Ipsa incomprehensibilitas in ratione infiniti continetur.*"[12]

While none of the concepts that I use to designate God have the power, by definition, to reach God, all of them nonetheless remain to some extent relevant, insofar as they can be turned from illegitimate affirmations into legitimate negations. Indeed if my eventual concepts designating God say nothing about God, they say something about *me* insofar as I am confronted by the incomprehensible: They say what it is that I am able to consider, at least at a given moment, as an acceptable representation of God; they articulate, therefore, the conception that I make for myself of the divine—a conception that imposes itself on me as the best since it defines precisely what is maximal or optimal for me. In short, the concepts that I assign to God, like so many invisible mirrors, send me back the image that I make up for myself of divine perfection, which are thus images of myself. My concepts of God turn out in the end to be idols—idols of myself.[13]

The radical failure of conceptualization with respect to God gives rise to a double consequence. First, the "death of God," resting as it does necessarily on the premise of a particular concept of "God" (moral God, final cause, *causa sui*, etc.), only disqualifies each time what actually corresponds to the concept, leaving all other concepts (an openended series, but each new concept is as inadequate as the first) still to be revised and critiqued. In other words, every specific form of conceptual atheism remains regional and provisional, while any claim to a universal and final atheism betrays ipso facto its failure to reach the conceptual level in the first place and therefore falls into ideology and violence. In short, the "death of God" gives immediate rise to the "death of the death of God." Secondly, the same difficulty applies, symmetrically, to every form of theism. Whenever theism tries to reach conceptual formulations that are definitive and dogmatic, it condemns itself to idolatry no less than does atheism. The two differ from one another only as a positive idolatry differs from a negative idolatry. Whether or not we decide in favor of God's existence seems at first blush to make a meaningful difference, but the difference turns out, in truth, to be indifferent, as soon as we recognize that in both cases the conclusion is reached only on the basis of defining or conceptualizing God's presumed "essence." Both conclusions thus ratify the same dogmatic idolatry. Both cases also assume that "being" or "existing" signify something that is knowable to us even when applied to "God"—which is not self-evident in the least and betrays a second idolatry, namely the chief idolatry, which is the idolatry of Being itself. The impossibility of assigning a concept to God thus stems from God's very definition, namely that he admits of no concept. Such a conclusion, once again, is not unique to atheism or characteristic of a particular philosophy: Revelation is the first to prohibit the conceptualization of that which "bears the name which is above every name" (Philippians 2:9), which is to say "the love which surpasses all knowledge" (Ephesians 3:19). God therefore is distinguished as well by the impossibility of being conceptualized.

4. The Impossible Experience

Confronted with this double impossibility, we have no choice but to proceed from the common determination of phenomenality to the conclusion that the phenomenon of God is impossible. As we saw, speculative theology admits this result in metaphysics to the same extent as does atheism. Speculative theology, however, which conducts its thought within faith and in view of belief, diverges radically from atheism when it comes to interpreting this phenomenal impossibility. For speculative theology the very impossibility of a phenomenon of God belongs to a real and indubitable experience of God, Indeed if God cannot *not* be thought as beyond phenomenal conditions—unintuitable and inconceivable—this impossibility results directly from his infinity, taken as the hallmark of Isis incomprehensibility. What-belongs properly to God (for philosophy, this is the infinite) characterizes him as what by definition surpasses the finite. Now for us, phenomenal conditions remain at all times finite (the sensory nature of intuition implies its finitude and our concepts belong to our finite understanding), to the point that it has been possible to conclude that Being deploys itself as finite.[14] Consequently, God's infinity can only contradict our finite knowledge of the phenomenon. Translated into epistemological terms, this takes the following form: If incomprehensibility attests to the impossibility of phenomenalizing the infinite, it nonetheless postulates, on a negative mode, a positive experience of the infinite. In other words, the epistemic impossibility of the phenomenon of God (namely his incomprehensibility) is itself experienced as a counter-experience of God.

This inversion—the impossible phenomenon as the paradoxical possibility of a counter-experience—may be contested and has in fact been contested often enough. One can argue for example that incomprehensibility no more offers a formal account of God than does infinity, since it offers nothing to the understanding except the general impossibility of experience as such. The fact that I am unable in this case to comprehend anything is not enough to infer, on the sly, the unverifiable but actual presence of anything whatsoever. On the contrary, and in a more trivial way, the fact that I understand nothing confirms straightaway the ontic inconsistency of an object of any kind. The failure of the *ratio cognoscendi* simply reproduces the failure of the *ratio essendi*. I fail to understand anything because there is, precisely, nothing there generally (*überhaupt*) to understand or even to be conceived. Experience as such becomes impossible. Nor is there any question of a noumenon, since some apparition might well appear (an idol, an illusion) without anything appearing in and of itself.[15]

In short, if we reject the ontological argument because it rests on the simple possibility of passing from concept to existence, must we not a fortiori exclude passing from impossibility (non-concept, non-intuition) to existence?

We will have to conclude, regarding God, that all we ever find is a triple impossibility—impossibility with regard to intuition; impossibility with regard to concept; and impossibility, therefore, with regard to experiencing the slightest phenomenon.

5. The Imprescriptible

There remains nonetheless something that cannot be prescribed[16]—something that remains forever an open question, which cannot be classified away as settled, which asks for its case to be pleaded without cease—the *causa Dei*, as a matter of fact. The question of God has the characteristic feature of always making a comeback, of being incessantly reborn from all attempts to put it to death, in theory as well as in fact. We must recognize as a rational datum that the question of God remains entirely pertinent even if God's existence as such is problematic, or downright impossible to establish. Even on the supposition that a transcendental illusion is involved or that the question is ill-framed, we must still confront it, and confront it all the more. The very fact that the illusion of God survives the phenomenal impossibility of God and any experience of him is what constitutes the question. The question is simply a rational fact, since no rational mind, especially not the most reticent, can pretend not to understand the question of God, even and especially if the inherent impossibility of the question is clearly grasped.[17] The paradox is this: How are we to understand the sense of what we cannot but affirm to be impossible? In other words, we may well proscribe the knowledge of God (of his essence, of his existence, of his phenomenon) but not the question as such of God, which always remains to be inexhaustibly deconstructed every time it makes itself be heard, which is to say at all times. This question alone seems to enjoy the exorbitant but irreducible privilege of having the ability (and therefore the duty) to pose itself to us in spite of (or because of) our impossibility of answering. The question of God survives the impossibility of God. Reason itself requires therefore that we give a rational account of this paradox: We must either explain it, or give up and give in to it.[18]

It goes without saying that having recourse at this point to some psychological explanation or presumed "religious need" would be of no avail. The problem is not to guess how the imprescriptibility of the question is experienced, but to explain how the impossible endures as a possibility—in other words, to conceive bow the thought of the impossible remains, in the end, possible. The whole difficulty lies in the status of this possible im-possibility. The question at stake thus concerns the limits of modality and, therefore, the limits of our rationality.

How can we conceptualize what escapes us? The aporia comes no doubt from the fact that we seek an answer outside of the question itself. Let us stick to our starting point—to the fact, namely, that God's impossibility in no way annuls the possibility of the question of God. How are we rightly to conceive of this paradox? Precisely by recog-nizing God's privilege—*God, and God alone, lets himself be defined by impossibility as such.* Indeed we enter the realm where it becomes possible to raise the question of God, and therefore of the incomprehensible, as soon as we confront the impossible—and only then. God begins where the possible *for us* ends, where what human reason compre-hends as *possible for it* comes to a halt, at the precise limit where our thought can no longer advance, or see, or speak—where the inaccessible domain of the impossible bursts open. What is impossible to human reason does not place the question of God under interdict, but rather indicates the threshold beyond which the question can be posed and actually be about God—transcending, by the same token, what does not concern him in the least. In God's case, and in God's case alone, impossibility does not abolish the question but actually makes it possible.

Now regarding this conclusion, we note a unique convergence: At least three points of view, which otherwise largely stand opposed to one another, explicitly endorse this trial-by-impossibility method of determining the question of God.

1. Metaphysics, to the extent that it constructs the "God, of the philosophers and scientists," construes God as the omnipotent case, the case in which power is possessed over all things, including over what remains impossible for us. Pagan philosophy con-curs: "*Nihil est, inquiunt, quod deus efficere non possit*" (Cicero).[19] Medieval thought agrees: "*Deus dicitur omnipotens, quia potest amnia possibilia absolute, quod est alter modus di-cendi possibile*" (Thomas Aquinas).[20] And both extend into modern metaphysics: "*infixa quaedam est meae menti vetus opinnio, Deum esse qui potest omnia*" (Descartes).[21] This determination has such deep roots that not even efforts to marginalize the question of God fail to endorse and privilege divine omnipotence. Thus Locke: "This eternal source, then, of all being, must also be the source and origin of all power; and *so this eternal Be-ing must be also the most powerful.*"[22]

2. Unexpectedly, moreover, attempts to "destroy" metaphysics have kept intact the determination of God as "the one for whom the extraordinary does not exist" (Kierkeg-aard).[23] Phenomenology (Husserl, Levinas, Henry, etc.) and also the philosophy of his-tory (Bloch, Rosenzweig, etc.)—both of which approach the question of God from the standpoint of possibility and of the future—have abundantly confirmed this choice.[24] Not even the rift cut into philosophy by the "end of metaphysics" seems to jeopardize the paradox that God comes to thought only as the possibility of impossibility, instead, the paradox is radicalized.

3. This first level of agreement, surprising in itself, provokes nothing short of aston-ishment once we recognize a second double-convergence, this time between these two philosophical eras on the one hand, and Revelation on the other (Jewish and therefore Christian). For indeed here as well—or rather here especially—the impossible defines

man's limit with respect to God. Man has his domain and rules his world as far as the possible extends; but as soon as the impossible emerges, there God's proper realm emerges, where holiness reigns (really *his* unique holiness), transcending whatever is possible *for us*. The impossible gives man the only indisputable sign by means of which God allows himself to be recognized: "Nothing is impossible on God's part" (Genesis 18:14). The distance imposes itself so radically that even Christ before the Cross invokes it in the form: "Father, all things are possible to thee" (Mark 14:36). The impossibility for us of seeing the phenomenon of God, and of experiencing it, is precisely and specifically radicalized by the recognition that God alone has power over all that is possible and therefore also over the impossible. His impossibility for us is part and parcel of his own proper possibility: He appears as the "only sovereign (*monos dunastēs*) . . . who alone is immortal and dwells in inaccessible light, whom no man has ever seen or can see" (1 Timothy 6:15–16).

Three standpoints, which otherwise diverge—namely metaphysics, philosophy that overcomes metaphysics, and Revelation—thus agree at least on this one point: The impossible, as the concept above all concepts, designates what we know only by name—God.[25] Impossibility, no doubt, defines the proper place of the question of God only with variations and at the price of equivocity (which will have to be assessed), yet always according to the same principle: The threshold between possibility and impossibility *for us* is strictly what unfolds impossibility as what is possible *for God*. It comes down to thinking what Nicolas of Cusa formulated in a simple and powerful paradox: "*Unde cum Deo nihil sit impossibile, oportet per ea quae in hoc mundo sunt impossibilia nos ad ipsum respicere, apud quem impossibilitas est necessitas.*"[26] To put it another way: Since possibility for us exclusively defines the world and since God's eventual region begins with impossibility (for us and according to the world), then to proceed toward God means to advance to the outer marches of the world, to step beyond the borders of the possible and tread at the edge of impossibility. The only possible pathway to God emerges in, and goes through, the impossible.

In order to embark on it, we must return to the texts that impose this paradox and attempt to think conceptually about three verses of the synoptic gospels. Two of these coincide: "With men, this is impossible, but with God all things are possible" (Matthew 19:26), and "With men it is impossible, but not with God; for all things are possible with God" (Mark 10:27). What is involved is not a simple contrast between certain impossibilities which are supposed to be found on man's side, and other possibilities, found in turn on God's side. Indeed the same exact things change from being impossible with men to being possible with God: "*Ta adunata para anthropois dunata para tō Theō esti*—What is impossible with men is possible with God" (Luke 18:27). What we must probe is how the impossible is converted into the possible when we pass from man to God.

6. God's Operational Name

Before continuing further, let us pause to consider for a moment the still very abstract determination of God that we have reached: God manifests himself in such a way that nothing is impossible with him.

The first implication concerns the inversion of the possible and the impossible, or more exactly the conversion of the impossible *for us* into the possible *for God*. The only region that we have a right to assign to God starts precisely when we run into an impossibility, when we factually stumble against what is impossible for us. Let us be precise: The impossible delineates only the region of finitude—namely ours—and indicates this region alone. The experience of the impossible therefore unlocks as of yet no access to God's own proper region, so long as we have not crossed the threshold. And how could we cross it, confined as we are within finitude? Indeed we cannot do so effectively speaking (we will never accomplish the impossible, nor is this asked of us), yet we cross it by mentally considering what remains incomprehensible for us, namely by conceiving that what is irreducibly impossible for us *can* or *could* become possible in its own right if we were to pass over to God's standpoint. We must mentally conceptualize what remains incomprehensible for us—namely conceptualize that God starts where the impossible translates into the possible, precisely where the impossible appears as though it were possible. Conversely, if any impossibility were to remain irreducibly impossible (for our logic or in our experience), we must not, on this ground, impose closure to the question of God but instead conclude only that we have not yet reached God's own proper region but dwell, still, inside our own. As long indeed as we are dealing with what is impossible, we are dealing only with ourselves, not yet with God. In principle, God cannot come up against the impossible, since, if an impossible remained impossible for him (if it remained possible than anything were impossible to him), *he would not be God*—but some "god" afflicted with impossibility, like us, human beings—for whom alone the impossible remains possible. Contrary to us, God defines himself as that to which (or rather as he for whom) there is no possibility of impossibility. This leads to a second consequence: It no impossibility operates or has sway over God, then nothing can ever make God *himself* impossible. It turns out, as a matter of principle, *that it is impossible for God to be impossible.* We have now reached the point where the objection according to which the impossibility of God is proved on the grounds of intuition, meaning, and therefore phenomenality, collapses: Even once it is granted, the impossibility of experiencing the phenomenon of God obviously concerns us only and our standpoint, where alone the impossible can (and must) impose itself. The impossibility of God has meaning only for us, who alone are capable of experiencing the impossible (in particular the impossibility for us of acceding to the impossible). It has no meaning *for God*. Such an impossibility specifically does not concern *him*, for whom the impossible is by definition impossible. The impossibility of God turns out to be possible only for us, not for God. If we seriously consider that God lets himself be thought only in the form of the impossibility *for him* of impossibility, then it turns out that it is impossible for God not to turn out to be at least always possible and thinkable—if nothing else as the impossible. Nor can anyone object that, in this case, the impossibility of impossibility for God remains inaccessible to us and teaches nothing about him, since we conceive the hiatus, irreducible as it is, by understanding why and how God remains impossible *for us*—which is to say, specifically, *for us but not for him*. We thus conceive God insofar as he is not confused with us and insofar as the difference is forever drawn. Which is what had to be demonstrated.

Finally, it follows that the so-called "ontological" argument becomes subject to revision, which radically transforms it. The argument, in metaphysics and according to Kant's formulation, consists in deducing God's existence from the concept of God's essence and other pure concepts (without recourse to experience).[27] The chief difficulty, contrary to what is stubbornly claimed and repeated, does not lie in the illegitimacy of passing from a concept to existence as a position external to the concept.[28] It lies instead, far more radically, in assuming that a concept adequately defines the divine essence in the first place. The argument inevitably results in forging an idol of "God" (sec. 3, above). How is this aporia overcome? By renouncing all presumed concepts of God and rigorously sticking to his incomprehensibility. Yet how are we to conceive this incomprehensibility in such a way as still to be able to think at all? By conceiving it not only as the impossibility of every concept, but also as the concept of impossibility—impossibility, namely, as the distinctive hallmark of God's difference with regard to man. Concerning God, indeed, we cannot without contradiction assume any concept other than the concept of impossibility to mark his specific difference—God, or what is impossible *for us*. From the moment that we substitute, for a comprehensible concept, the incomprehensible concept of the impossible, the whole argument is turned upside down: It no longer proves God's existence, but the impossibility of his impossibility, and therefore his possibility. God turns out to be the one whose possibility remains forever possible, precisely because it turns out that nothing remains impossible for him, especially not himself. The necessity of God's possibility flows from the impossibility of his impossibility.

Such a reversal of the argument into a proof of the unconditional possibility of God based on his concept (as impossible), strange as it may seem, has already received a formulation—by Nicholas of Cusa. Let our starting point be the thematization according to which St. Thomas Aquinas framed the difference between God and what is created: In the created case, essence always remains really distinct from *esse*, just as potency differs from act; on the contrary, in God, essence is not only always identified in act with *esse* but (at least according to certain passages) disappears into *esse* to the point that in God the whole essence, which is to say the whole power and potency, is accomplished in act, as *actus essendi*. Nicholas of Cusa affirms this distinction, but reverses the way in which it is applied: A created entity can only actualize its potency, which, in itself limited, is an the more exhausted qua potency that it is stabilized in act, which is also limited; consequently no created entity accedes to the level of infinite possibility, since both its essence and its act instaurate its finitude. God, on the contrary, actually is all that he is potentially, according to a double infinity of act *and of possibility*: "*Ita ut solos Deus id sit quad esse potest, nequaquam autem quaecumque creatura, cum patentia et actus non sint idem, nisi in principio.*"[29] God and creature are opposed less by act (relative to essence) than by the privilege in God of possibility, of the possibility of actualizing infinite possibility—in other words, by *possest*. Thus, whereas "*nulle creatura est possest*," God transcends creation first and above all by a definitive, irreducible and eternal possibility, in short by an uncreated possibility—"*increata possibilites est ipsum possest.*"[30] God's omnipotence, which is to say his denomination based on the impossibility for him of impossibility, results in a possibility that is eternal and infinite, originary and ultimate. God's omnipotence means here less an unlimited efficient power than the perfect actuality of possibility as such:

> Esto enim quod Aqua dictio significet simplicissimo significatu quantum hoc complexum; posse est, scilicet quod ipsum posse sit. Et quia, quod est, actu est, ideo posse esse est tantum quantum posse esse act. Puta vocetur possest . . . est dei satis propinquum nomen secundum humanum de eo conceptum. Est enim nomen omnium et singulorum nominum, atque nullius pariter. Ideo dum Deus sui vellet notitiam primo revelare dicebat: 'Ergo sum Deus omnipotens,' id est 'Sum actus ominis potentiae.'[31]

God lets himself be named according to the actuality of the possibility of power, not according to the simple assumption of power in act, even infinite. In God, possibility trumps active efficiency because God's highest efficiency consists in surpassing impossibility (for us) by making it possible—which he does by virtue of the necessity in him of the impossibility of impossibility.

7. From the Impossible as Self-contradictory to the Impossible as Advent

It remains for us to understand the two terms that are inverted in God's case—the possible and the impossible. We will mark the inversion henceforth by writing "the [im-] possible." Metaphysics indeed has its own way, too, of understanding the relation and mutual interplay of these terms.

If as a matter of fact the "highest principle with which we usually start a transcendental philosophy is the standard division into possible and impossible,"[32] God will still be defined in terms of his relationship to the impossible, precisely under the figure of omnipotence. Through a strange reflexivity, this very omnipotence can only deploy itself by letting itself always be bound by the limits of impossibility, not by transgressing them. God can certainly make (effectuate) all things, but on the express condition that things be inscribed within the domain of the possible and not turn out to be contradictory:

> Deus dicitur omnipotens, quia potest omnia possibilia absolute, quod est alter modus dicendi possibile. Dicitur autem aliquid possibile vel impossibile absolute ex habitudine terminorum [praedicatum repugnat subiecto . . .] Quaecumque igitur contradictionem non implicant, sub illis possibilibus continentur, respectu quorum Deus dicitur omnipotens.[33]

The position will quickly show itself to be untenable, for obvious reasons. Namely: (1) In the end it reduces God to the role of an efficient laborer, working on behalf of some possibility, essence or formula "to which, so to speak, God submits himself." The order of Reason imposes itself on God as it does on creatures, law of "all intelligences and of God himself."[34] The road is open to determining God within the limits of ordinary reason, pure and simple. But there is more: (2) If the possible, which limits divine omnipotence, is defined as what is not self-contradictory—adopting Wolff's definition, that *"Possibile est quod nullum contradictionem involvit seu quod non est impossibile"*[35]—then the non-contradictory as such remains to be defined. How does a concept contradict itself?

According, obviously, to the norms, rules, and axioms of conceptualization. One cannot speak of absolute contradiction, but only always of *contradictio in conceptu*.[36] Now what concept other than one of our own representation can be at stake here? "*Nihil negativum, irrepresentabile, impossibile, repugnans (absurdum), contradictionem involvans, implicans, contradictorium*"; therefore "*Non nihil est aliquid:* repraesentabile, *quidquid non involvit contradictionem, quidquid non est A et non-A, est possibile.*"[37] The representable and the non-representable come into play only within *our* conceptualization; therefore within our finite conception; therefore within our finitude. There is no contradiction other than what is conceivable, and nothing is conceivable that is not within our own conceptualization—and therefore *quoad nos*, for us, for our finite mind. If the point is to assign a contradiction (and therefore an impossibility) to God, we must come up with an absolute contradiction, contradictory for an *infinite* understanding. The demand obviously makes no sense, since our understanding is by definition finite. We will never know the slightest thing about what is impossible or contradictory from the point of view of God's infinity. These will remain perfectly undecidable since we will never have access to the conditions of the question. The nation of contradiction as such supposes finitude: Therefore if God is God—which is to say infinite—no contradiction, by definition, can apply to him. With God, nothing is impossible—even, or rather especially, in the sense of a metaphysical impossibility, which does not even concern him.

What sort of impossible is transgressed by God—beyond the impossible that is limited to non-contradiction—remains, however, to be understood. Heidegger unquestionably deserves credit for having challenged the metaphysical distinction between possible and impossible by affirming that, "Higher than actuality stands possibility."[38] The mere inversion of the terms as such does not, however, suffice to redefine them—especially not to redefine possibility. In order for possibility to free itself it must, by definition, escape all condition of possibility that advenes to it externally. This is true to the point that radical possibility must, paradoxically but necessarily, eschew the slightest *definition*, because any finitude limiting it would indeed contradict it. Radical possibility would, as such, transcend all limit and, being thus completely unconditioned, would give us access, finally, to the transcendence which we seek. Formally, such possibility would define itself as the transcendence of all impossibility—taking its point of departure not in some non-contradiction concocted within the limits of representation and positive conceptualization, but negatively, in transgressing these very limits, namely within what remains impossible for conceptualization and representation. Possibility taken in the radical sense would take its point of departure in the impossible, by transcending it, which is to say by annulling it through effectively bringing it about. Radical possibility would start with the impossible and, without passing through conceptualization of a non-contradictory possible for finite representation, would impose it within effectivity. *Radical possibility or effecting the impossible.* In contrast to possibility as defined by metaphysics, radical possibility would not transform possible things into effective things, but *impossible* things into effective things, directly. It would effectively bring about [im-]possibilities hitherto unthinkable.

How can this be, if I know of no such [im-]possible? But am I sure that know of none? No doubt I know of no such [im-]possible as long as I define myself as *ego cogitans*, thinking according to my own representation and concept. By adopting this posture, indeed, I submit everything that can advene through the screen, so to speak, of my own conceptualization and finitude. Hence causality (whether it starts with me as causal agent or with some cause other than myself) never brings about anything, by definition, except what my concept has foreseen for it as possible, according to what is non-contradictory for my representation. I do not, however, define myself always, or even primarily, as *ego cogitans*, according to a conceptual representation. I emerge, or rather I *have* emerged into existence through a very different mode—on the mode of an event in which I myself advene to myself without having either predicted it, or understood it, or represented it, precisely because I was not yet there—nor was I, a fortiori, already thinking at the advent of the event. Before being, in short, I had to be born. Birth, or rather *my* birth, precedes any thought of my own. Consequently, it precedes all possibility as defined by concept and representation.[39] Even if, retroactively, I am quite able, based on someone else's testimony, to reconstitute what came before me and even reduce it to a representable possibility, even a predictable one, such an interpretation does not retroactively establish a non-contradictory possibility that positively precedes the event of my advent. Rather the interpretation starts with the fact itself, without cause or predictability, in order to assign to it, after the fact and always only very partially, a coherence and conceivability through which absurdity is avoided and plausibility insured. What is more, all forms of genealogy and romanticized memories only come after the fact; not only belatedly relative to the event, which advents without waiting for them, but also arrested in their tracks, suddenly mute, before the obscure moment, the silent and inaccessible moment of birth, gestation and conception—period without speech, consciousness or memory. Birth, *my* birth—which delivers me, bears me into the world, and makes me—happens without me. I will never be able to join up with it. Birth made me without me, without my consciousness, or my concept, all of which follow thereafter. Advent of the event because originary, brought about without me. Brought about—advened, rather—without me, my birth advenes from itself without cause, or presupposition, or concept—in short, without possibility. My birth advenes to me in the form of a directly effective impossibility.

Thus I am forced to admit that the case of my birth provides me with the experience of radical possibility—namely the one from which I come and which has effectively made me. Better, by becoming effective precisely as an impossibility, my birth has unlocked possibles for me which are defined, not by my concepts, but by my birth—and which therefore unlock as many concepts in its wake. The impossible, turned effective, imposes possibles and allows concepts of possibles to be produced, in reverse order than the order of non-contradictory possibility.

Still, based on the [im-]possible that is my birth, how is an [im-]possible for God to be imagined? Does the disproportion between the two domains (finite and infinite) not forbid transition and assimilation? It probably does, if we cling to the division that remains internal to the horizon of the concept of being. But not if we focus on the advent of the [im-]possible as such. Indeed what birth accomplishes for each living being, creation brings about from God's standpoint—as long of course as we understand creation here in the theological sense, not as a mere taking of efficient causality to the limit. The point is that *for us* creation thematizes and gathers together the totality of events that advene of themselves—without concepts, without predictions, and therefore without cause—radical possibles, in short, which we not only receive from within it but from which, first and foremost, we receive ourselves. Certainly, for *me,* creation starts always and only with my birth. Yet by the same token my birth exposes rue to the whole of creation, giving me access to every [im-]possible in its primordial [im-]possibility. God, the master of the impossible, effectuates creation by making the [im]possibility of each birth effective, starting with my own.

We thus have access to radical possibility through the [im-]possibility of our own birth. Through it, moreover, we have access as well (by way of an analogy that deserves further scrutiny on some other occasion) to the radical [im-]possibility accomplished by God in the event which, paradigmatically, advenes *for us* from himself, creation. God, who initially aimed at unconditioned transcendence (secs. 1–4, above), for whom nothing remained impossible (secs. 5–6, above), is from now on certified as the one who unlocks radical possibility. As the master of the possible—not as the one who effectually brings about possible things and predicts them, but as he who makes them spring forth from [im-] possibility and gives them to themselves.

8. What God Recognizes (to Himself) as His Own Proper [im-]Possible and Therefore as the Possible for Him

The whole question now bathes in a new light. We remain firmly grounded in God's operational name: With him nothing is impossible that remains impossible with human beings. Since, however, the [im-]possible in question belongs to radical possibility, unconditioned by any possibility of representation or concept (both of which are finite by definition), it can no longer be understood as the outcome of a simple efficient act. God's relationship to radical possibility, therefore, can no longer be thought in terms of omnipotent efficiency. Metaphysically speaking, omnipotence corresponds only to God's knowledge of eternal possibles. Omnipotence as related to possibility in a metaphysical sense is coextensive with the domain of the non-contradictory as represented in concept. It follows that abstract and therefore arbitrary omnipotence no more suits the transcendent God of radical possibility than the representation of eternal possibles defines his overture of possibles. The problem is thus to characterize God's posture with regard to the [im-]possible without *reducing* or *degrading* it to the level of omnipotence. In other words, we must conceive of how God chooses his [im-]possibles for himself. How does the master of the [im-]possible determine what remains impossible for human beings, but is possible for him?

We are all the more entitled to ask the question that it stems directly from biblical texts. Let us consider the difficult narrative of the Annunciation. To the angel who announces the possibility of motherhood to her, Mary responds first with a factual impossibility: "I know no man" (Luke 1:34). Against this factual impossibility, the angel then asserts the principle of radical possibility as a right, pertaining to [im-]possibles: *"ouk adunatēsei pare tou Theou pan rhēma"*—literally, "For on God's part, no saying, no word, shall be impossible" (Luke 1:37).[40] When Mary then accepts the annunciation that is made to her, she emphasizes the "saying" of the angel ("Let it be to me according to your word"), which announced God's "saying, *rhēma.*" Mary's decision and faith concerning the [im-]possible is therefore not addressed to God's omnipotence (which the text never literally invokes) but to God's "saying." In what therefore does she really have faith? She has faith in the "saying, *rhēma*" that God has said, and thus in the commitment he has made. She believes God's word. She takes God "at his word" because she knows that every one of his words commits him once and for all. The point is not to acknowledge simple omnipotence (which commits to nothing and permits, on the contrary, every lie) but to have faith in God's good faith. To have recourse to God's omnipotence is useless, since it still remains immanent to our own finite point of view (like the reverse face of possibility according to represented non-contradiction). Instead, the task is to transcend our own finite point of view in order to pass over to God's point of view—or at least to aim for it, to admit it as an intention. In contrast to us, where saying commits to nothing (we lie), on God's part, saying and carrying out what is said coincide absolutely. More than the power to do anything, God has the power to say anything—not in virtue of his omnipotence but in virtue of his fidelity. God can say whatever and all that he wants because what he says, he does. Thus *rhēma* here signifies indivisibly both word and fact.[41] In the face of the [im-]possible, fidelity in God transcends and replaces omnipotence. God is all-powerful because he always keeps his word, not the inverse. Two details of the text, moreover, confirm this. (1) Rather than a simple assertion, we find a double negation: Negation of the possible, and negation of this negation on the side of God.[42] This implies that nothing will come about that stands opposed to God's word. (2) The verb is conjugated in the future ("nothing shall be impossible" = *adunatēsei*), suggesting that, as soon as Mary gives her consent, God will act, keep his promise, make it his business and that we will see the effect.[43] The possible, or rather the carrying out of the impossible (in the world that human beings know, namely virginal birth) will open up a proper possible for God alone—the Incarnation, which launches Redemption. Not only is the possible not the same for us and for God, the [im-]possible is not either.

We see indeed that the case is not simply one of contradicting, by means of an abstract omnipotence, the laws of the world and of being (even though in fact this happens); but rather to bring into play, at this price, an array of possibilities that are until then unthinkable and unimaginable, possibilities such that only God could foresee them and want them. It is not enough to recognize omnipotence as one of God's proper names— "*Dominus quasi vir pugnator. Omnipotens nomen ejus*" (Exodus 15:4, Vulgate)—rather, we must conceive that God does not will enactments of outlandish and ridiculous monstrosities. In contrast to the sort of omnipotence that we human beings dream of today, the impossibility of the impossibility that God exercises does not bring about just anything—by his power he makes all that he wants, but he wants only by loving.

Recourse to divine omnipotence pure and simple, moreover, struck people from the very beginning as somewhat fragile, abstract, insufficient. Celsius already reproached Christians for "taking refuge in the absurd escape that 'nothing is impossible with God' when they had nothing to answer"—namely, concerning the resurrection of the flesh. Origen, in turn, found himself obliged to specify that "we know full well that we understand all of this [namely, Luke 1:37] to apply neither to what does not exist at all (*adianotōn*) nor to what cannot be thought (*adianotōn*)."[44] The answer is a cautious one, but once again insufficient, since what right do we have to oppose unthinkables and non-existent things to God if "with him nothing is impossible"? More essentially, the question no longer consists in fixing a limit beyond which divine omnipotence would be going too far in some abstract sense (relative to what limit?), but in determining what it is that God can indeed want *as his word*—a word which he commits himself to keep, allowing himself to be taken "at his word." Neither logic, nor contradiction, nor the principle of identity, nor efficacy, nor the principle of sufficient reason, retains the slightest relevancy here, namely when the task is to conceive that to which God's word commits itself and commits God. Obviously, if God is God, he can do whatever he wants—that is not the question. The question, rather, is what God is able to want and wants to be able to do. What does he want, without restriction, to be able to do? What corresponds to him and therefore comes from him. St. Augustine explicates this remarkably:

> Negari se ipsum non potest, falli non potest (2 Timothy 2:13). Quam multa non potest et omnipotens est: et ideo omnipotens est, quia ista non potest. Nam si mori posset, non esset omnipotens; si mentri, si falli, si fallere, si inique agere, non esset omnipotens: quia si hoc in eo esset, non fuisset dignus qui esset omnipotens. Prorsus omnipotens Pater noster peccare non potest. Facit quidquid vult: ipsa est omnipotentia. Facit quidquid bene vult, quidquid juste volt: quidquid autem male fit, non volt.[45]

God does whatever he wants, but the main thing is that he wants only what it becomes him to want—which is to say only what comes from him and answers to his love. God makes what it becomes God to make. Such is the impossible for man—what becomes God.

9. The Radical Impossibility: Forgiveness

In order to determine what it becomes God to want, and then to be able to do—which is to say to determine what God alone is able to have the power to do, since he alone is able to want it—we must turn once again to biblical texts. In particular, we must consider the passages in which Christ himself presents what remains impossible for us but is possible for God. Let us consider, in particular: "With men this is impossible [namely, that a rich man enter God's kingdom], but with God all things are possible—*para anthrōpois touto adunaton estin, para de Theōi panta dunata*" (Matthew 19:26 = Mark 10:27= Luke 18:27, cited in sec. 5, above).

What [im-]possible does Christ here bring to light as the criterion separating man from God? "It is easier for a camel to go through the eye of a needle than for a rich man to enter the kingdom of God" (Matthew 19:24). Physical, worldly impossibility serves here as a sign to expose a much loftier impossibility, but which cannot be directly seen by the human eye or in broad daylight. Why does this specific impossibility for men (and not for God) fail to appear to men (but only to Christ, and therefore to God)? Because as far as men are concerned—namely the spectators of the dialogue, as well as the rich young man—the youth in question has *already* entered God's kingdom, since he has *already* kept the commandments. "All these I have observed"—hence his astonishment that he should fall short. "What do I still lack?" (Matthew 19:20). What indeed does he lack? Strictly speaking, he lacks nothing—except, precisely, having nothing: Owning nothing and keeping nothing outside of Christ himself ("Come, follow me"); which means becoming one with God through Christ, becoming holy like him ("If you would be perfect . . ." Matthew 19:21); and thus fulfilling the highest commandment, "You shall therefore be holy, for I am holy" (Leviticus 11:45; 19:2), in the form in which Christ reiterates it, 'You, therefore, must be perfect, as your heavenly father is perfect" (Matthew 5:48).[46] What is impossible for man ("the rich young man") is the lack of *lack* (the lack of poverty and therefore of identifying with Christ alone)—a lack which cannot appear in a world in which we see only what is ("riches"). The impossible thus remains inaccessible to anyone who lacks the power to lack and cannot even see what he nonetheless knows is beyond his power. Only Christ sees this, even though he points to it only indirectly. We grasp at least that what is impossible here *for man* but *from God's viewpoint,* consists in what men do not even consider—a genuine conversion to God—infinitely more difficult than worldly impossibilities are *for us.*[47]

We read about this reversal of the possible and the impossible for men and for Christ (and therefore from God's viewpoint), namely the very way in which the [im-]possible comes into play, in the story of the paralytic's cure (Matthew 9:1–8; Mark 2:1–12 Luke 5:17–26). A paralyzed man is brought before Christ, but Christ, strangely enough, instead of curing the physical ailment (as everyone expected since he had tirelessly done so before), declares the man cured spiritually. "Your sins are forgiven" (Matthew 9:2). Christ thus accomplishes what is possible to God and supremely impossible to men. Some of the men, or at least some "among the scribes," understand it in precisely this way, but only to denounce it as "blasphemy" (Matthew 9:3)—namely as a claim by Christ to have God's rank. Nor are they wrong in this regard: To claim to be able to do the impossible is, on the part of men, indeed to claim to be God. How is Christ able to sustain his claim before men? When he accomplishes a relative impossibility—the physical and worldly cure of physical paralysis, an impossibility which is both effective *for us* and visible *to us* in the world—he attests that nothing is impossible with him in our world; and therefore that he holds the rank of God, from which in turn it follows that nothing is impossible with him even outside the world. By asking the question "Which is easier, *eukopōteron?*" (Matthew 9:5), he forces men to decide about God in him. Since for men nothing seems more difficult in the world than to cure a physical paralysis, Christ by accomplishing this feat accomplishes the impossible, which is God's prerogative. The choice, then, is either to deny the evidence of the world, which indeed establishes that he comes from God and is God; or to admit the visible evidence that he is indeed God, and therefore admit also that he has power over the true [im-]possible—namely, to forgive sins. Christ thus makes manifest what is impossible *from God's viewpoint,* namely to heal the heart.

What is at stake in the question, "which is easier, *eukopōteron?*" now comes to light. What is harder, indeed what requires, *from God's own viewpoint,* his power and transcendence, does not stem from what appears to us to be most difficult (namely modifying the a priori conditions of phenomenal experience), but what seems *to him* to be least within our reach (even if we are not even able to see this level)—to convert our hearts to God.

The [im-]possible *for God* lies within the stone-hard human heart. God's operational and untransferrable name—his ultimate transcendence—is articulated in his power to convert the hardened hearts of men, to remit their sins, to forgive them. Only God has the power, precisely, to forgive, because only love is able to forgive and has the right to do so. Now "there is only one who is good" (Matthew 19:17), and "No one is good but God alone" (Mark 10:18). Man cannot forgive because he has neither the power to forgive (in his heart, he remains a murderer), nor the right to forgive (every sin is ultimately against God). Evil remains imprescriptible for man, who is powerless to forgive it and therefore must recognize himself to be its prisoner. In order to grasp this more clearly, let us consider an unexpected text: The brutally corrected, almost blasphemous, reformulation by V. Jankelevitch of Christ's words on the cross. "Thus *we* might well say, *reversing* the terms of the prayer addressed to God by Christ in the Gospel according to St. Luke: Lord, *do not forgive them*, for they know what they do."[48] Let us admit that the magnitude here of the evil—that of the Shoah, the genocide of the Jews by the Nazis—explains, even justifies, such a bold reversal. Let us note as well that the reversal amounts to restoring a metaphysical (Aristotelian) definition of moral responsibility—a responsibility which is full and inescapable when we know what we are doing.[49] But we will also, in the end, ratify the correction: Does it not simply recognize as evident that *we human beings*, in fact, *are not able to forgive*—any more than we are able to convert, or free ourselves of our sins on our own? There is a sort of second-order piety in this quasi-blasphemy; namely, the piety of stating clearly and directly that it is impossible in principle for man to forgive or even to ask for forgiveness, and that on the contrary this is possible only with God, as the prerogative of his radical transcendence. Only God has the power to forgive sins—which is to say the sins that all of us (who alone sin) commit in the final analysis against God (even when we inflict them first on other human beings). The impossible for man has the name God, but God as such—as the one who alone forgives the trespasses made against him.

The radical and non-metaphysical transcendence for which we have been seeking thus reveals itself with great clarity in the impossible—but in the only [im-]possible worthy of God, which is charity. Only with love, and therefore with "God who is love" (1 John 4:8,16), is nothing impossible. God's transcendence manifests itself in charity, and only thus does transcendence reveal itself to be worthy of God.

On Love and Sacrifice

Jean-Luc Marion is above all a philosopher of love, and consequently he is concerned with the themes of intentionality, the other, the self, and sacrifice. The first piece reproduced here, "The Intentionality of Love" (1983), is an essay written in homage to Emmanuel Levinas. It is Levinas who, principally in *Totality and Infinity* (1961) and *Otherwise Than Being* (1974), proposed a radical phenomenology of the other person, a project that departs from Husserl's sense of phenomenology as a philosophy of light and manifestation and attends to the nonappearing of the other's face. My relations with the other are asymmetrical, Levinas maintains: The other person always addresses me from on high.[1] The other is not a phenomenon that can be reduced to an item in my consciousness but is rather an enigma whose intelligibility is given by way of a face rather than a concept.[2] At the back of these theses is a critique of intentionality as Husserl conceived it: the relation of noesis and noema is called into question, for example, and attention is given to nonintentional thought.[3] For all his admiration of Levinas, Marion has never been entirely satisfied by the older man's work. In particular, he has pressed Levinas on his hesitancy to speak of love.[4] For in general Levinas prefers to speak of "non-indifference" to the other person instead of love, which, he believes, suggests a fusion of the self and the other.[5]

In "The Intentionality of Love," Marion considers two aspects of Husserl's doctrine of intentionality, the view that consciousness is always consciousness *of* something. The first is the lived experience of consciousness, for love is surely a state of consciousness. The second is the object of intentionality: not the immanence of consciousness but the transcendence of what is intended. The person I love transcends my consciousness and even my intentional aim toward her or him. Yet I cannot regard him or her as a subject of my gaze: were I to do so, I would lose her or him as "other" and gain only an object. Strictly speaking, then, the beloved is always invis*i*ble and invis*a*ble, unable to be seen and unable to be aimed at by my gaze. The other person is always a particular *I*, however, and fixes *me* in her or his gaze. Loving turns, Marion argues, not on seeing the beloved but in a crossing of gazes that is apparent only for those intimately involved in the act of love. Two lovers *live* the invisible crossing of their gazes. Respect and responsibility allow for substitution; it does not matter who stands before me, since I should respect everyone and am responsible for everyone. Not so in love: Marion insists on the individuality of the other's face, one that cannot be substituted for any other.

The Erotic Phenomenon (2003) continues a preoccupation with establishing the weight of love that is first explored in *The Idol and Distance* (1977) and then in *Prolegomena to Charity* (1986). It comes as no surprise that Marion begins his discussion by disagreeing with Descartes's discovery of the *cogito* as the ground of our being in the world. On the contrary, Marion urges, we encounter being in love, not in the ego. The proper formulation should not be "I think, therefore I am" but "I am loved, therefore I am." What Marion calls "the erotic reduction" does not bring us to absolute self-certainty but instead (as he says with a nod to Pascal) "renders destitute all identity of self to self."[6] The section of this book given here, "Concerning the Lover, and His Advance," begins by thinking of the erotic reduction and what prompts it (the question, "Does anyone out there love me?"). The erotic reduction is radicalized, though, by asking a second question, "Can I love first?" If I love first, if I love in advance of being loved, without any assurance that my love will be returned, I love without any principle of sufficient reason. In fact, I follow a principle of *in*sufficient reason, knowing that reason cannot help me when and where I need help. In the erotic reduction the lover bears everything, since he or she gets no support from reciprocity; believes everything, since he or she lives in the "not yet" of a love to come; and loves without seeing, for he or she loves in order to see: what could not be seen before love is now the focus of the one in love.

In the Self's Place: The Approach of St Augustine (2008) is Marion's commentary on Augustine's *Confessions*, and here we see for the first time Marion using the theory of saturated phenomena for reading a canonical narrative work. What is *confessio*? The word appears many times in the *Confessions*, and is used in several distinct senses. It is speech that God has made possible, usually speech that is directed to God. It may be praise (*confessio laudis*), self-blame (*confessio peccatorum*), or avowal (*confessio fidei*).[7] What is the place of *confessio*? In the first part of "The Creation of the Self," reproduced here, Marion argues that creation appears only in terms of the *confessio* of the faithful. To call anything on earth or in the heavens a "creature" is to praise God as creator. No creature is properly defined as a being; strictly, each is a gift that calls forth praise from all other creatures. We do not praise God because we know him; rather, we praise him because he comes to us. But what is the place that he visits? Marion follows this question through various twists and turns, arguing that for Augustine the creature's place is not in itself but in God. What does this tell us about human beings? That "man" is defined by a lack of definition.[8]

The anthology ends with the final essay of *The Reason of the Gift* (2011), Marion's James W. Richard Lectures delivered at the University of Virginia from September 29 to October 1, 2009. "Sketch of a Phenomenological Concept of Sacrifice" extends his theory of the gift giving by way of an exploration of the aporias of sacrifice. Sacrifice is not simply the destruction of a possession, Marion argues, for it presumes the presence of another person. Sacrifice involves privation, not just destruction. Yet the witness of a sacrifice does not fully explain what it is; besides, if sacrifice is truly a gift it must escape the circuit of exchange. It can do this, Marion contends, only if the gift is led back to its givenness, which is masked in each and every gift. Marion takes as an example the sacrifice of Isaac by Abraham as related in Genesis 22:1–19. We are quietly invited to compare Marion's treatment of this canonical example of sacrifice with Derrida's in *The Gift of Death* (1993).[9] Indeed, Marion concludes his analysis with a half-turn back to Derrida when he advises that sacrifice is less a destruction of something than a deconstruction. "Sacrifice destroys the given, by clearing it away in order to uncover that which had made it visible and possible—the advance of givenness itself."

K.H.

The Intentionality of Love

In homage to Emmanuel Levinas

We live with love as if we knew what it was about. But as soon as we try to define it, or at least approach it with concepts, it draws away from us. We conclude from this that love ought not and cannot be conceived accurately, that it withdraws from all intelligibility, and that every effort to thematize it belongs to sophistry or an unseemly abstraction. The inevitable consequence of this attitude is self-evident: we can give love only an interpretation, or rather a noninterpretation, that is purely subjective, indeed sentimental. Consequently, arbitrary individual choice becomes the sole law of love, which remains sunk in an intolerable but inevitable anarchy: we love arbitrarily, or rather, we believe that this arbitrariness still deserves the name *love*. We are thus reduced to the awkward paradox of being unaware of the logic and the rigor of that which we nonetheless continually acknowledge gives the sole flavor and meaning to our life. I love, I do not love, I am loved, I am not loved—without knowing why or, especially, what love is all about. Philosophy, which seemed in its Platonic impetus bound to allow movement beyond this aporia, seems, ever since it interpreted the world as what cognition cognizes exclusively, now to forbid it. Loving, like the rest (knowing, willing, desiring, being capable, and so on), amounts to representing (oneself). The fact that the master of representation has changed identity—*ego*, spirit, will to power—changes nothing with regard to its primal and unsurpassable idiocracy. What can I ever love outside of myself, given that the progress of loving consists in reducing all alterity to myself, under the figure of the represented? Emmanuel Levinas takes up this aporia when he recognizes that "by an essential aspect love, which as transcendence goes unto the Other, throws us back this side of immanence itself: it designates a movement by which a being seeks that to which it was bound before even having taken the initiative of the search and despite the exteriority in which it finds it."[1]

However, when phenomenology introduces its new radicality by positing intentionality, does it not offer a way out of the aporia? We know, since and on account of Husserl, that "the basic character of intentionality" consists for consciousness in "the property of being a 'consciousness of something.'"[2] Consciousness characterizes itself by the strange, although trivialized, property of concerning first and above all what does not concern it. It is paradoxical, if one thinks about it, that we are not only conscious, but also conscious of something other than ourselves. It is one thing to notice that my consciousness never ceases to be affected with sensations, concepts, volitions, and the like; it is something else still more remarkable to notice that these "lived experiences of consciousness" (*vécus de conscience, Erlebnissen*) do not concern uniquely, nor even first, my consciousness, but objects transcendent and exterior to it, everything in it remaining immanent and so to speak coextensive. The lived experiences that weave the fabric of my consciousness nevertheless aim at an intentional object irreducible to my consciousness. Thus, in reading me, you experience experiences of consciousness (signs, already some fatigue, perplexities also, distractions, and so on). However, these lived experiences refer you to intentional objects that transcend your consciousness (the meaning of what I say, the very notion of intentionality that I am summarizing here, or else other notions that mobilize your attention, or other persons, and so forth). We think only intentionally because to think requires leading the lived experiences of our consciousness back to an intentional object other than my consciousness. To say that consciousness is consciousness of something means that it is not first consciousness of itself, but of something other than itself, that it is always outside itself—alienated, so to speak. The question, then, becomes quite clear: does not the intentionality thus sketched furnish the schema appropriate to a conceptual grasp of love, one that tears it away from the common interpretation? Wouldn't what phenomenology says about consciousness in general apply more exactly to love in particular, which would offer the privileged case of an intentional lived experience of consciousness, wholly "alienated" from itself in view of a prevailing intentional object, the other himself or herself that I love? And thus, wouldn't the path open directly toward the understanding of mercy? Let us see.

The Lived Experience of the Other

Love counts indisputably among the states of consciousness. Beneath the figure of amorous passion, it even offers the most intense of all lived experiences of consciousness. If the expression "to fall in love" offers no precise meaning, at least it designates approximately the state of consciousness that Phaedra, standing before Hippolytus, stigmatizes definitively: "I saw his face, turned white! / My lost and dazzled eyes saw only night, / capricious burnings flickered through my bleak / abandoned flesh. I could not breathe or speak. / I faced my flaming executioner, / Aphrodite, my mother's murderer!"[3] For Phaedra, loving Hippolytus amounts to feeling certain lived experiences of her consciousness, immanent to it and as if indifferent to their supposed object. This indifference goes so far that Phaedra can thoroughly reveal these lived experiences of her consciousness to the one she loves by referring them, through an amorous ruse, to the one she ought to love, Theseus. Loving Hippolytus merges so much with the lived experiences of

Phaedra, and so little with the actual singularity of the character Hippolytus, that Phaedra, inverting the same strategy of separation under the impulse of this alleged love, can accuse Hippolytus to Theseus and thus condemn him to death. What Phaedra loves is *not* Hippolytus, but the collection of lived experiences she feels under the name "Hippolytus," and that she moreover interprets lucidly as the effect within her, not so much of the real Hippolytus, as of divine vengeance (Venus). Accordingly, there is no contradiction in hating the very love that one feels in passion: this love does not consist in this or that person—who, from a distance. I could consider; help or curse but in the collection of my own, lived experiences of consciousness—immediately intermingled with my servile consciousness (*conscience serve = servo arbitrio*). The exceptional character of amorous passion is not an objection to this approach. All other love reproduces this characteristic: to love always means first to experience lived experiences of consciousness. Whether it is a question of kindness, friendship, or filial or parental care, I love only through the lived experiences of my consciousness. Even if I accomplish an altruistic duty without any sensible emotion, this absence of emotion already constitutes a lived experience of my consciousness. This analysis also must not be attenuated by the remark that love here only reproduces the universal characteristic of all knowledge—which, quite obviously, must pass through the lived experiences of my consciousness: everything that I perceive and comprehend, I experience first and finally in my consciousness, and not outside of it. Or, to speak like Descartes, "we know for certain that it is the soul which has sensory perceptions, and not the body."[4] For love differs greatly from all perception; perception concerns only things or objects that I can, without their being contradicted, reconstitute, indeed constitute in and through myself; they can without any contradiction be thought as *my* objects; perhaps they even call for this on principle. But with love, it is a matter neither of objects nor of appropriation. In contrast, it is a matter of the other as such, irreducibly distinct and autonomous. If I were somehow to appropriate this other for myself, I would first have to reduce it to the rank of a slave, of an animal object, and thus lose it as other. Indeed, what explains the perception of the object—namely, its constitution in terms of the lived experiences of my consciousness—is the very thing that forbids love, for love should, by hypothesis, make me transcend my lived experiences and my consciousness in order to reach pure alterity. Whence the infernal paradox, universally suffered by all unfortunate loves as their definitive fatality: when I love, what I experience of the other, in the end, in reality arises from my consciousness alone; what I call love of another bears only on certain lived experiences of my consciousness, inexplicably provoked, in the best of cases, by a chance cause that I call the other, but that the other is not. Love appears as an optical illusion of my consciousness, which experiences only itself alone.

Amorous Autism

Let us confirm this quickly. What we might term the autism of love is marked by a paradox already formulated by Pascal[5]: I say that I love somebody, but I love her or him insofar as I experience him or her in my own conscious life as endowed with beauty, loyalty, intelligence, riches, power, affection for me, and the like. If certain, or all, of these lived experiences were to disappear, can I be certain that I would still love him or her? Let us suppose the best of cases: I would continue to love this other without his present beauty, his present intelligence, and so forth; in short, apart from all the glamour that my conscious experiences record; in this (highly unlikely) case, I cannot continue to say that I love her for herself, because I no longer have at band any lived experience of consciousness to permit me to identify her. In fact, even if I love in spite of a withering abstraction from all lived experience and every accidental quality, I simply no longer know *who* I love; properly speaking, I am loving in the void. And this paradox does not concern only the sickly nostalgia of Madame Bovary; it concerns the limit cases of therapeutic relentlessness, where the technique no longer offers anything to love but the abstract of all conscious experience, thus the abstract of the other. Love is identified with the lived experiences of my consciousness, not by an excess of my egoism that a bit of altruism might offset, but by a law of my consciousness; the other cannot appear to me, even to be loved, except through the lived experiences of my consciousness—it is not a matter of morality, but of phenomenology. Thus when I experience love, even a sincere love, for the other, I first experience not the other but my lived conscious experience. Supposing, then, that I still love another than myself, at the very least, I love him *in* me.

At a deeper level, the autism of love belongs to the domain of self-idolatry.[6] For there remains an objection to our analysis: if I love the other in me, I still love the real other, because I do not love just anyone or everyone, but this and that one, this or that one. I love an identifiable, individualized alterity, thus foreign to myself. Even if Proust's Swann could love a woman who was not of his type, he loved her alone, Odette, and not some other, Madame Verdurin or Oriane. But why, exactly, will what I call my love invest this particular figure? Because this figure arouses the most powerful, rich, and abiding lived experiences in my consciousness; that is, this figure fills my desire and my capacity for experiencing, to the point that all the lived experiences issuing from other figures or from the inanimate world are, by comparison, immediately disqualified and as if immaterial. If this figure imposes itself on me, the reason is found less in it, unknown anyway, than in me; I experience in it the maximum of lived experiences that my consciousness tolerates and calls for. Love fills my consciousness because it takes the measurements of my consciousness and submits itself to that measure. Confronted with what I name the other, I see not her but the sum of lived experiences, for which she is only the accidental cause and of which my consciousness is the real measure. In short, if I love this and not that other, it is because the first reflects more exactly the measure of my desire for lived experiences, and therefore of my consciousness. My love is mine only inasmuch as it is for me *less* other than every other love, only insofar as it fills my consciousness with lived experiences, because in fact it reflects my consciousness. I must, then, name this love *my* love, since it would not fascinate me as my idol if, first, it did not render to me, like an unseen minor, the image of myself. If I love *in* myself the other, it will therefore be necessary that I love *myself* in the other—that I love in the so-called other only the idol of myself. Love, loved for itself, inevitably ends as self-love, in the phenomenological figure of self-idolatry. My love always amounts to the love of myself. In other words, because in this love I love myself, I thus love concretely only those who love me. Whence the judgment of Christ: "If you love those who love you, what reward do you deserve? Do not the tax-collectors do as much? And if you hail only your brethren, what have you done that is so special? Do not the gentiles do as much?" (Matthew 5:46–47). If we stick to the definition of love as a fabric woven from the lived experiences of my consciousness, we turn all love back upon ourselves, with a reciprocity that poses no difficulty, because it lacks exteriority. According to the unique presupposition that love plays itself out in my conscious experience and gives me the perfect idol of myself, it attracts what it loves to my consciousness, like the sun attracts the planets, like hatred attracts hatred—necessarily.

The Other, the Aim, and the Object

This paradox marks an impasse, and this impasse results from a unilateral choice: we have used only one of the two terms in the doctrine of intentionality—the lived experience of consciousness. Yet, our concern is precisely with the term that does *not* imply intentionality as such. Intentionality is not identified with the lived experiences of consciousness, but on the contrary identifies them with what they are not—with the intentional object. Intentionality does not have as its object the immanence of lived experiences, but the transcendent object; it aims, through these lived experiences, and by polarizing them toward itself, at the objective of the intentional object. Intentionality renders consciousness intentional of something other than its own lived experiences, namely the object itself. The very fact that the intention most often oversteps intuitive fulfillment confirms the fact that consciousness aims at more than it lives, thus that it aims at an object that is definitively other than itself. Consciousness, by and with its polarized lived experiences, becomes always consciousness of an other, consciousness altered by alterity itself, intrinsically alienated consciousness. Hence, just as the interpretation of love on the basis of the immanence of lived experiences to consciousness brought to light the self-idolatry of passion, its interpretation on the basis of the transcendence of the intentional object should lead to the thought of its authentic alterity. Or, to cite Husserl: "What I demonstrate to myself harmoniously as 'someone else' and therefore have given to me, by necessity and not by choice, as an actuality to be acknowledged, is *eo ipso* the existing Other for me in the transcendental attitude (*der seiende Andere*): the alter ego demonstrated (*ausgewiesen*) precisely within the experiencing intentionality of my ego. . . . 'In' myself (*in mir*) I experience and know the Other; in me he becomes constituted— appresentively mirrored (*appräsentativ gespiegelt*), not constituted as the original."[7] The ambiguity of Husserl's thesis is exposed unambiguously: the other is reached only at the end of an intentionality that, however radical it might be, remains no less the intentionality in and of my consciousness. Alterity completes intentionality, without transgressing it or putting it into question—in such a way that the ego confirms the absolute phenomenological primacy of the "region consciousness," and thus of itself. The other arises as constituted by the ego. Such a constitution of the other can certainly illustrate one of the dimensions of love: namely, that love consists precisely in a dimension that intentionality opens, untiringly decentering the immanence of consciousness and distending without limit its lived experiences, in view of a vanishing point that is by definition always beyond what any intuition will reach. Intentionality implies the never resorbed surplus of intention over intuition, of the object aimed at over its fulfillment, of the dimension over its crossing. Thus it becomes definitively clear that the other, which my love claims to love, will always have to transcend my consciousness by overstepping it, like the horizon whose line recedes in proportion as one draws near to it. The intentional object is not an object, erected after the fact into the object of an intention; on the contrary, it is an intention that gives rise to an objective, without ever doing so adequately and without remaining an object. This point once established nevertheless immediately compels an investigation: the intentional object, if it remains a tangential objective more than a totally constituted object, is no less the objective of the always original ego, of the constitutive *I* that my intentionality assumes. This presupposed condition inflicts on principle a subordination on what it conditions; the fact that the object results from the intention nevertheless does not deliver it from the condition of being conditioned; the fact that it always remains tangentially unknown does not free it from having to depend on an intention awaiting fulfillment. The intentionality of consciousness submits objects, and nothing but objects, to consciousness, as to an *I*. Now, by definition, we are seeking access, via love, to a subject, and thus precisely not to an object—however distant he may be. Intentionality opens only onto the objectivity of intentional objects, and never directly to another subject: in the field of the aim, only one origin, one intentionality, one *I* can be at play. To suppose my intentional aim at the other to be followed by intuition, and thus by success, would for that very reason fail, because intuition can fulfill only an intention toward an object. Every success of intentionality would reach, exclusively an object, and would thus fail to encounter the other as such. If the imperfection of its fulfillment qualifies intentionality and so instructs us in alterity in general, its eventual success disqualifies it from instructing us in the subjectivity of the other. The intentionality of consciousness indeed opens consciousness finitely, but opens it only to the horizon of objects, and thus closes it radically to the encounter with the other subject, with the other as subject, with the other as such.

The Invisible Gaze

The request to think the other as subject offers all the ambiguities of the very term "subject." The reversal of perspective—of perspective itself—will therefore have to be accomplished, if it can be, without recourse to the "subject," to its aporiae and its potentialities. One must give up seeing the other as a subject, and for a radical reason. The other *must* remain invisible so as to offer himself to a possible love, because if, by chance, I saw him (if an intuition adequately fulfilled the intentional objective, a hypothesis that is highly debatable for every legitimate object), he would be ipso facto already disqualified as other. As soon as Orpheus wants *to see* Eurydice, he transforms her into an object and thereby disqualifies her as beloved. He makes her disappear because he does not admit her as invisible. Only the object is visible, and the entrance into visibility qualifies an object as such. The object alone has to be seen, not the other. Why, then, would the other not have to be seen? Because nothing can be seen which does not first have to be intended, and nothing can be intended except as an objective submitted in advance to the gaze that constructs its object. What renders the other decidedly other than me, and first of all other than all the objects wherein I ceaselessly accomplish myself, stems not from a certain quality of its objectivity—but from this: the other is characterized in that she too intends objectives, she too constitutes objects, she too precedes a world. I carry out the function of a transcendental *I* only insofar as I intend objectives, which can thus become visible objects, and inversely, can neither intend me nor see me. If someone other than me—precisely, *the* other—accedes to the function of *I*, he must by hypothesis exert an intention that renders visible the objectified objectives and therefore render himself invisible. The intention, which incites the visible, cannot itself be seen. If the other deserves this title, he necessarily will have to enter into invisibility. The other, as other, irreducible to my intention, but origin of another intention, can never be seen, by definition. This paradox is confirmed in the immediate experience of the exchanged gaze. If I want truly to gaze on the other, I attach myself neither to her silhouette, however pleasing it might be, nor to some voluntary or involuntary sign that her bearing might reveal, but to her face; I face up to her (*je l'envisage*). "Facing up" to her does not mean fixing my gaze on her mouth or some other emblematic element but fixing exclusively on her eyes, and directly in their center—this ever black point, for it is in fact a question of a simple hole, the pupil. Even for a gaze aiming objectively, the pupil remains a living refutation of objectivity, an irremediable denial of the object; here, for the first time, in the very midst of the visible, there is nothing to see, except an invisible and untargetable (*invisable*)[8] void. When "faced up to," the center of the eyes does not shy away, because it does not sustain my gaze; even if this face does not turn away, it hides, in its petrified immobility, within its pupils, the visibility of every possible objective. In not shying away from my gaze, the gaze faced up to or envisaged itself hides the very horizon of the visible. How does it succeed in doing this? Or, which amounts to the same question, why do I insist in gazing on what hides all objects from me?

Against the Current of Consciousness

A single response no doubt suits both questions. Of the face offered to my gaze I envisage only what cannot be seen in it—the double void of its pupils, this void that fills the least empty gazes imaginable—because if there is nothing to see *there,* it is *from there* that the other takes the initiative to see (me). Gazing on the other as such, my eyes in the black of his own does not imply encountering another object, but experiencing the other of the object. My gaze, for the first time, sees an invisible gaze that sees it. I do not accede to the other by seeing more, better, or otherwise, but by renouncing mastery over the visible so as to see objects within it, and thus by letting myself be glimpsed by a gaze which sees me without my seeing it—a gaze which, invisibly, and beyond my aims (*invisablement*), silently swallows me up and submerges me, whether I know it or not, whether or not I want it to do so. The gaze of the other, or better, alterity as gaze, is not "hypertrophied consciousness, but consciousness that flows against the current, overturning the consciousness" (E. Levinas).[9] Consciousness that flows against the current, indeed the countercurrent of consciousness: the other does not become accessible by means of intentional consciousness, but at the price of consciousness's very intentionality. Consciousness, *my* consciousness, should not claim to reach the alterity of the other by diving into its own depths as an intentional consciousness; for intentionality merely radicalizes the irreducible and solitary primacy of the gaze of a subject on its objects. In short, with the best intentionality in the world, consciousness can intend and see only objects, thus forbidding itself the alterity of the other. The other remains invisible to my consciousness, not despite intentionality, but because of it. The alterity of the other transgresses, even and especially, the intentionality of *my* consciousness from the moment that consciousness reverts all the more to me as mine in its spreading out ever more intentionally from me. I never accede to the other on the basis of the consciousness I have of him, but always in opposition to this sudden consciousness (of him by me). I do not reach the other by means of the consciousness I have of him; he forces himself upon me by means of the unconsciousness to which he reduces my consciousness. Of the other, who slips away as visible object, I can only passively experience the invisibility—losing consciousness of him. The other, or my loss of consciousness. But if the very movement wherein my consciousness exteriorizes itself confirms the imperially self-enclosed primacy of my consciousness, that is, if my opening still belongs to me, as the horizon where the sun of my power never sets, is it necessary, if we are to have any hope of loving, to enter into a twilight of all consciousness, to expose ourselves in all unconsciousness to the black sun of an invisible light?

I Is Not Just Anybody

That the other is imposed on me in and through the unconsciousness to which he reduces my consciousness, destitute of intentionality, supposes a paradox: the invisible gaze of the other can actually reach me, in an irreducible exteriority.[10] In order to think through this, it behooves us first to establish the nature of the exteriority here at issue. In the phenomenological attitude as well as in the natural attitude, exteriority only opens out from an originary pole, whose interiority is fixed in the *I*. Intentionality does not modify this presupposition, seeing as it always implies the difference between a "here" and a "there and the flesh of my body can only inhabit a "here." In all cases, I remain an *I*, who defines exteriority on the basis of interiority, transcendence on the basis of immanence, what is intended on the basis of its denominating—and thus dominating—intentional aim. For an invisible gaze to impose its intentional aim on me, it is necessary that the *I* discover itself preceded by a causal authority that certifies its own primacy in dismissing that of the *I*. It is necessary that the denominating domination yield to an uncontrollable anteriority, that of a primary exteriority. Exteriority can, in effect, result not from the interiority of the *I*, but rather destabilize it, precede it, and not proceed from it. For exteriority to be emancipated from the interiority that defines the *I*, it is necessary that it disqualify the denominative power of the *I*. The *I* can falter only if, far from naming the poles of exteriority as its objects (objectives of its intentional aim), it itself finds that it is the object of another aim. In short, only if the nominative *I* dismisses itself in the accusative *me*. Of the forever invisible other, of whom I can never say that I see him as such (precisely, because it is *I* who sees), I know at least that he aims at *me*, as the objective of his invisible intentional aim. His gaze brings out the features of the *I* to the point where no traces remain of it other than a simple and naked *me*. Literally, *I disclose myself*; or more explicitly: the other strips bare the *I* within me to the point of leaving only the *me* exposed. The *I* discloses itself before another gaze and discovers that only a *me* remains. The *me* designates the *I* uncovered, stripped bare, decentered. *I* become *me* by uncovering myself as the simple *me* of an other; *me* indicates not what the gaze of the other aims at and shows (which is said by a *you*), but what the already evanescent *I* experiences of the gaze of an other trained upon it, or better, what the *I* experiences of himself as evanescent beneath the gaze of an other. I become me by discovering myself as the faltering shadow of *I* in the denominating gaze of the other—who came first. The other, hereafter not just anybody (*le premier venu*), says *I* and fixes me as the direct complement, an objective, of his invisible, exterior, and first aim.

The Injunction

This reversal can be made less abstract. Exteriority happens as its most intimate determination to the one who discovers himself in the accusative: if not accused, at least put into question and brought to trial by an anterior injunction. Without any exterior voice compelling me, the injunction brings me to discover myself as obliged by another: I must devote *myself* to . . . it is incumbent upon *me* to . . . this or that, he or she obligates *me* to. . . . I do not read on the other's face the direct visibility of the other in person (and thus an objectivity that, strictly speaking, would be deposited only in a cadaver), but rather my own summons to lay myself open to him. To lay oneself open or expose oneself to the other means first, outside all visible sensibility, to experience ethical responsibility for the other. If I never rejoin him directly, he always enjoins me, indisputably. He makes his invisible gaze felt and weigh upon me by letting the nonsubjective and nonmasterable feeling of respect be born within me. I know and feel, as if in spite of myself, that I am responsible for the fate and the death of my brother. Thus the obligation—which makes itself felt in the feeling of responsibility, inasmuch as the responsibility exceeds the responses that, in the irrepressible feeling of my guilt, are brought by me—summons me in advance before the tribunal of the other. Before being conscious of myself (*Selbstbewusstsein*), I am conscious of my obligation, thus of my fault (*Gewissen*), vis-à-vis the other—the first come (*premier venu*), who makes me the last of the last. The injunction renders me responsible *for* the other (Levinas) and not simply *in front of* the other (Sartre). Even if the other did not see me and thus could not judge me, I would experience, by discovering *me* myself as an accusative dismissed of the nominative, that I owe *myself* to him: in order for him to live, I owe it to him to dedicate myself. I do not measure his right over me by what my existence can, once affirmed, concede him. I experience that my existence will undergo the injunction of the first to arrive and will overdetermine self-consciousness by a bad consciousness (of self), exactly proportionate to the consciousness of the (unfilled) obligation to the other. I lose consciousness of myself because I am conscious of my obligation to the other before and more than I am conscious of myself. Remorse delivers to *me* the sole consciousness of myself, which will not perish, because it delivers the *I* unreservedly, already destroyed before being, to the invisible and silent injunction of the other, whose fate comes down to *me*. The rights of the *I* collapse beneath the infinite obligations that come down to *me*. I can never say anything to the Other except my shortcomings and my belatedness. But it is these very things that open me to him by detaching me from the intentionality of the *I*.

The Crossing of the Gazes

The unconsciousness that we are seeking can therefore be reached. It is not a matter of an unconsciousness wherein the process of a likely love is clouded over with illusory ambiguities; nor is it a matter of simple inversion of the axis of the gaze, where the function of the *I* simply displaces itself from one to the other of the terms at play, thereby reinforcing all the more its validity. Instead, it is a matter of a consciousness that exerts itself on my consciousness, without following it into polarization in terms of the *I*—a consciousness against the grain of the *I*. The moral injunction (*Gewissen*) brings to bear the consciousness of an obligation that imposes itself on the *I* and thus destroys it as originary pole. Still, consciousness is not closed up (*Bewusstsein*) in the indistinctness of the id. The *I* reduced to the *me* retains consciousness, precisely so as to see that it no longer becomes conscious of *itself*, but of an obligation that links it, despite itself, to the anterior other. The moral consciousness forbids the transcendental consciousness to fold itself back over and into an *I* and enjoins it to see itself as consciousness, in itself, of the other than self. The moral consciousness contradicts self-consciousness by counterbalancing the intentionality exerted by the *I*, thanks to the injunction summoning *me*. The injunction constrains and contains intentionality; intentionality objectifies the other on the basis of the *I*; but all the same, injunction summons *me* on the basis and in the name of the invisible other. The invisibility passes from one extreme to the other, the means alone remaining visible to the corresponding aim. Whence comes what we will from now on consider the phenomenological determination of love: two definitively invisible gazes (intentionality and the injunction) cross one another, and thus together trace a cross that is invisible to every gaze other than theirs alone. Each of the two gazes renounces seeing visibly the other gaze—the object alone can be seen, the eye's corpse—in order to expose its own invisible intention to the invisible impact of the other intention. Two gazes, definitively invisible, cross and, in this crossing, renounce their invisibility. They consent to let themselves be seen without seeing and invert the original disposition of every (de)nominative gaze—to see without being seen. To love would thus be defined as seeing the definitively invisible aim of my gaze nonetheless exposed by the aim of another invisible gaze; the two gazes, invisible forever, expose themselves each to the other in the crossing of their reciprocal aims. Loving no longer consists trivially in seeing or in being seen, nor in desiring or inciting desire, but in experiencing the crossing of the gazes within, first, the crossing of aims.

Lived Experience Crossed

Determining love as the crossing of aims gives rise to a clear-cut difficulty: does the crossing itself remain invisible or does it rise to visibility? Put another way, does it become an object, which can actually be seen as a lived experience of consciousness? We will try to argue that the crossing of the invisible gazes becomes visible only for the parties involved, because they alone undergo an experience without recognizing an object in that experience. The intentional gaze, if it crosses the moral injunction, experiences an interdiction, an obligation, or a provocation. It matters little whether it respects them or transgresses them, for in both cases this intentional gaze will actually feel the weight of a counter-aim, a weight that is all the more objective in that, in order to pass beyond, the intentional gaze will require the imbalance of a higher weighing—which would thus be more highly actual. The ethical counter-aim makes its weight felt with the same force whether I transgress it or subscribe to it, whether I resist it or consent to it. But if gazes that are foreign to one another see nothing of the crossing of two invisible gazes, in short if this nonobjective crossing remains decidedly invisible to them, too, things are not the same for each of the two concerned gazes—the two gazes concerned each by the other. The intentionality of the *I* and the obligation to the other (which opposes *me* to him) cross, in that they experience each other; they experience each other in the common lived experience of their two efforts, constrained each to the other, buttressed by their contradictory and thus convergent impetuses. Intentionality and the injunction exchange nothing, especially not two (objectified) lived experiences; yet they come together in a lived experience which can only be experienced in common, since it consists in the balanced resistance of two intentional impetuses. This common lived experience results from the crossed conflict of two invisibles, without one, without the other, without both the one and the other in strict equality, the lived experience either would not be fixed or else would not remain in a lasting equilibrium. The two gazes are balanced in a common lived experience, which does not touch them in their respective origins, but summons them and finally blocks them in their mutual impetuses, to the point of balance in their crossing. With the two invisible aims, this crossing traces a cross, still invisible except to those who suffer its weight in a common lived experience. Thus, in crossing swords, duelists experience something like a single lived experience that communicates a common tension—the pressure that my weapon, and thus my arm, and thus my whole body imposes, contains, and renders to the opposed pressure. Whence I infer an arm outstretched and an entire fighting body, which exerts against me the intention that I exert against it. Arm wrestling, where the two arms cross and where the impetuses of each of the two bodies are immobilized, brings together, face-to-face, the two fleshly faces. What then do each of these two invisibles see of the other? Nothing objective, nor visible (the two adversaries still remain nondead, nonvisible because not cadavers). However, they see their encounter, for they experience the weight of each impetus one against the other, a unique and common weight, balanced and shared. They see, with their always invisible gazes, the lived experience of their tensions. The crossing of gazes here imitates the crossing of swords—what they each see of the other consists in the balanced tension of aims, like two weapons crossed. The crossed encounter is made to stand as a lived experience of the invisible; however, the experienced vision of the lived experience never results in the visibility of an object. The crossing of invisible gazes draws near to being quasi-visible only for the two aims that experience, like a heavy weight falling on the shoulders all at once, the balance of their two impetuses buttressed at full force. Neither the lover nor the beloved encounters the other in passing, dreamily, each in the other. They experience one another in the commonality of the lived experience of their unique tension—the weight of one gaze on the other, crushed by experiencing itself seen, crushing by seeing itself experienced. Two gazes, which seek each other, seek not the invisible site of the other gaze, but the point of equilibrium between my tension and his or her own. The sudden fixity of their common level, like water equilibrated in a lock, does not arouse in them any less inexpressible pleasure than bodily pleasure. For bodily pleasure, perhaps, comes down to generalizing for all flesh the balance of aims, where each attests to its humanity by honoring itself with invisibility—as if with glory. Whence the inverse consequence, that pleasure can answer to the high name of love only as a common lived experience, where two invisibles balance each other; if they fail, the pleasure sinks into insignificance, or, if it claims to overcome insignificance, it sets itself up as an unforgivable posturing as the invisible—an obscene incarnation of the gazes' corpse. The pleasure of the eyes disfigures the pleasure of the gazes, wherein no object—especially not a heart or a face—can bring climax, for climax (*la jouissance*) is born from the inobjectivity that only the tension of the gazes governs. A visible jubilation of invisibles, without any visible object, yet in balance, through the crossing of aims: let this situation count, here, as the sketch of a definition of love.

Ordinary Alterity

To define love as the crossed lived experience of invisible gazes implies, at the very least, that the gaze of the other reaches me and weighs upon my own gaze. We have admitted under the name injunction the advent of a gaze other than that of my own intentionality. The injunction benefits from a noteworthy privilege: it is a lived experience of mine in that it greatly affects my consciousness; I experience the obligation that imposes itself on me and compels me, whether I admit it or not; the obligation affects me directly, inevitably, to the point that I cannot release myself from it by handing it off to someone else, nor even make him experience it (except if he directly experiences a parallel obligation). For the injunction is not received by derived appresentation, in which the originary presence would reside in the other. The injunction does not enjoin the other to me simply because it might come from him; it does not result from a disposition of the other, wherein it would reside first and actually, so as then to pass from an originary presence to a derived presence. The injunction does not come from the other toward me, by an inverted intentionality of the other consciousness acting against my own. It actually arises in me, as one of my lived experiences, which an originary presence assures to my consciousness; yet, as a lived experience of my consciousness, the injunction imposes on my consciousness, without the least bit of intentionality (neither its own, nor another's), the first coming of the other. From the beginning, I experience the rights of the other over me, as more original to me than myself. The injunction makes another gaze weigh on my own, another gaze of which the other knows nothing and, literally, of which he has no idea. In the best of cases, the physical gaze of the other furnishes only the schema of the injunction; or rather, I can regard the other as an invisible gaze (and not see him as an object) only because first of all the injunction imposes him on me, designates him to me and leads me to him—despite thyself, but also despite him. The injunction does not come to me from the other, nor does it push me toward him: it makes me experience, in and through myself, the advent of the other; I experience myself, in myself and as such, obliged to an other who can be entirely ignorant of this obligation. The obligation toward the other is born in the, though it is not born of me; it is born for him. Although it is not born through him. The obligation, really and truly mine, makes the original weight of a gaze that the other does not even have to produce weigh upon me; or rather, the invisible gaze of the other can come to bear on my own gaze only to the degree that the injunction in me precedes it and welcomes it—contrary to all intentionality.

The Means of the Universal

The privilege and the paradox of the injunction alone make possible a phenomenological sketch of love. But in this direction a difficulty also appears: the injunction certainly incites me toward the other, but without my having to or being able to discern love there. If the injunction enjoins to any other whatsoever, indeed to every possible other, simply inasmuch as it offers the face of man, it does not permit the election of such an one, precisely because it enjoins rendering to the other as other what I owe him. The injunction gives rise not so much to love as to duty, for, like duty, the injunction concerns every other, universally. The injunction addresses me to the other in order that I offer him the recognition that he deserves as end, and not as means, or, which amounts to the same thing, the continuation of the particular maxim guiding my action into the universality of a law. The formal universality that determines my behavior toward the other does not in any way depend on the particular identity of this or that other. The formal universality of the obligation becomes thinkable only once persons have been abstracted from it, such that the other opened by the injunction can be played by anyone: the other thus passes from one face to the other, according to the radical substitution that universality imposes. That the particular face here holds the role of the other, without incarnating him definitively, that this face occasionally lends its gaze to the universal injunction, in short that this other remains only the lieutenant of the other (*l'autrui*), finds its confirmation in respect. Without a doubt, the injunction of the law moves me to respect, whether I transgress it or obey it, and thus becomes as particular as my sensibility. But it is precisely this respect, which I experience in particularity, that I do not feel for *this* other, *this* face, *this* individual, but rather for the universal law alone. My individuality submits to affection for the universal, and never for the other who accidentally lends his face to it. Far from my individuality feeling for another, individually unsubstitutable by the mediation of respect for the universal of the law, my individuality instead lets itself be moved by the accidental and substitutable mediation of any individual face in favor of the universal of the law (to the point of becoming, like a free noumenon, itself universal). Accordingly, and paradoxically, the moral law—which states that the other man must always count as end and not as means—never uses the face of an individualized other except as a means for accomplishing the universal. The injunction of obligation toward the other (*autrui*) leads, in reality, to the neutralization of the other as such. The other is neutralized as other, for another can always be substituted who can offer the face of the other (*d'autrui*) that the universal moral law requires:

no face can claim to be irreplaceable because, if it in fact became so, at once, by right, the act accomplished in regard to him would cease to satisfy the universality of the law. The other as such therefore undergoes a second neutralization: to the substitution that is, on principle, always possible, there is added the always required gap between the law and *every* singular individual. Between the letters of the law all possible individuals can and must parade, with equal dignity—which is to say, without any dignity, except borrowed, lent by the law itself. The injunction does not lead to loving *this* other, if only the universality of the law pronounces it; rather, it leads to the law itself, while neutralizing the other in particular (*comme un tel*).

That Face

The injunction therefore must be singularized for my gaze to cross an individually irreducible gaze. It attains this singularization in passing from obligation to responsibility: "It is my responsibility before a face looking at me as absolutely foreign . . . that constitutes the original fact of fraternity."[11] Responsibility inverts the legal arrangement of end and means: I am responsible not in front of the law by means of the other, but directly for the other by means of the injunction itself; the death of the other, or his life, depend directly on my regard for his open face; the other unreservedly constitutes the sole stake of my responsibility; nothing surpasses him, surprises him, or utilizes him. The suspicion of neutralization does not disappear, however. For I am responsible standing before every other, provided that his face exposes itself to my gaze; and it is precisely this provision that enables substitution to remain possible: each of the visible faces enjoins upon me a responsibility which at once prompts and orients my own intention; in order to compel my responsibility, a face suffices, every face, each face, indeed, any face, so long as it opens in an invisible gaze. The unconditioned nature of responsibility implies its universality, from face to face, up until the last, whoever that might be. The neutrality persists because a substitution persists. To be sure, the Neuter, *here,* owes nothing to the Neuter that Levinas stigmatizes in the primacy of the ontological difference; it is not a question of neutralizing the face, nor a being, nor being in its variance with Being; but the face itself neutralizes unsubstitutable individuality; I do not find myself responsible before *such a one* as much as *this such a one* admits of being reduced to *a* face in general, addressee of my gaze, and conjuring of its aim. Now, recourse to a face in general leaves two difficulties unbroached: (1) Where will things stand with the disfigured face? No doubt, it is in just such an undone face (*un tel visage défait*) that the essence of every face must be squarely faced. It nonetheless remains the case that to approach this disfiguration as to a face, one needs to employ a gaze that recognizes and knows how to envisage; not every gaze, even those already affected by responsibility, succeeds. What gap, then, separates the recognition of the disfigured face from its nonrecognition? Responsibility, doubtless, is not enough, not excluding its eventual and explicit deepening. (2) Can the other, designated to me by a face, individualize himself to the point or becoming unsubstitutable for every other other? This question opens out into another question: Why am I enjoined by this other and not that one? And if the reason for this should not be sought, we must then acknowledge that the injunction concerns alterity in its universality, as indifferent as possible to *such* or *such*. No doubt, ethical responsibility cannot, and even must not make distinctions between faces, such that, *with regard to responsibility*, the universality of the injunction implies no return whatsoever of the Neuter. But, if we are seeking to define love as it is distinguished from respect and responsibility, then the possibility of substituting one face for the other constitutes a final obstacle, all the more fearsome because it results directly from love's most advanced approach.

That to Which I Enjoin Myself

In order to bring love back to its conceptual determination, we were obliged to subtract it from representation, even intentional representation, so as to substitute for it the injunction. The injunction itself now remains to be determined, so that it will not settle into any figure of the Neuter. If we want to secure responsibility all the way to the point of love, then the injunction must designate not only the other as such, but *just such* an other as the invisible gaze that crosses my own. That *just such* an other enjoins me implies that he sets himself up as unsubstitutable and strictly irreplaceable. Not only would "The other . . . no longer be now, where I respond for him, the first-come (*le premier venu*)—he would be an old acquaintance,"[12] but he would also no longer be something known at all, if science bears only on the universal, or at least on the repeatable. The other as *such* redoubles his invisibility with a particularity unknowable in itself. Love passes beyond responsibility only if the injunction reaches atomic particularity: love requires nothing less than *haecceitas,* which is also situated beyond essence (unless we must say on the hither side of essence). *Haecceitas* passes beyond beingness (*l'étantité*) in general, but also beyond that which, in the injunction and responsibility, falls under the universal, and thus the Neuter. It pierces all the way through to the unique, which no fellow will ever be able to approach, nor replace. The other as such asserts itself as the other of all the others, and does not reside in itself alone except insofar as it separates from everyone else. *Haecceitas* decides for an absolute separation from every similitude, to the point of provoking the holiness of the other. The other alone singles out himself.

Such a claim immediately gives rise to an objection. Does the singular particularity of the other as *just such* an other—as the sole and unique one—not reproduce, displaced from the one (the I) to the other (the other as such), the fundamental injustice of every self: to insist upon oneself as a basis, which, under the heading of irreplaceable center, centralizes the world into so many interests, to the point of including, as if these interests were reducible to the Same, men to whom this self denies any face? Does not the other win its *haecceitas* as an ultimate and full proprietorship that appropriates the other, starting with my own gaze, which he claims from me with injunction? In short, does not *haecceitas*, as unsubstitutable center and appropriating proprietorship, repeat what Emmanuel Levinas denounced as "mineness," the characteristic of *Dasein* that disqualifies it ethically? This characteristic of the self appropriating itself to itself in the experience of its nonsubstitutability—the egoity of *Dasein*[13]—reappears in the injunction of the other as such, since the *as such* is fulfilled finally (and ever since Leibniz)[14] only in the *I*. The other as such would only open onto an *alter ego*, an alterity still under the figure of the *ego*, and thus an alterity reduced to the Same: this other amounts to the same as me, since we both come back to the figure of the *I*. An *I* displaced still remains an *I*, radically foreign to all alterity as such. And to accede to such an other, simply a displaced *I*, neither love nor ethics would be required—a simple knowledge through analogical appresentation of one monadic ego by another would be enough. In claiming to pass beyond ethics through love, we would only have regressed to ordinary intentionality of consciousness. The objection, however, is less forceful than it appears: it proceeds as if the unsubstitutable other could be understood as a displaced *I*; or more precisely, as if a displaced I still remained, rightfully, an *I*; and therefore as if the unsubstitutable character of the other (what makes him *just such* this other) could be reduced to the egoity of the *I*. But of course a capital difference opposes them: I impose my egoity (or impose myself through it), while the unsubstitutability of the other is not imposed on me by him, but indeed by I who seek it as such (or seek him as *just such* within that unsubstitutability). The other requires his *haecceitas* not because he imposes it on me as his rule, but because *it is necessary for me* that it be imposed in order that the injunction allow me to experience his gaze as such. Inversely, I can and even must renounce my own, my proprietorship of egoity, for the sake of exposing myself to alterity, but I cannot—for that very reason—renounce proprietorship, what is proper to the other, if I want to encounter the injunction of his gaze as such. *Haecceitas* does not reproduce, as a symmetrical reply, the egoity of an *I*; it reverses it. The other resolves himself in the crossing of gazes on the condition of entering this crossing as unsubstitutable, while I enter it only on condition of leaving myself destitute of all intentionality, and thus of all egoity. What is more, intentionality directly contradicts unsubstitutable particularity, because it has as its unique function to permit consciousness to substitute itself for every thing; consciousness is intentionally every thing, thus it itself is counted among none of these things; the unreality of consciousness results from its intentionality and dispenses it from identifying itself among things. *Haecceitas* thus marks the renunciation of intentionality and egoity, and thus stigmatizes the precise act by which the other enters into play as *such*—namely as stranger to an *I*. The injunction that would finally put into play the other as such would, thus, also accomplish the transgression of intentionality by love.

The Invisible Unsubstitutable

But a conditional will weaken this confirmation, as long as we have not established that an injunction actually imposes upon me the gaze of the other as *such*. Can such confirmation ever emerge? Perhaps, if one considers further the injunction itself. (1) The injunction asserts itself upon my gaze because it weighs upon it with the weight of another gaze. Why does this gaze itself weigh in with all of its weight? Because the other in person exposes himself to it. Why then does he lay himself open to it to the point of imposing on me? Because, as we have just seen, the other only becomes absolutely "just such" an other (*tel*) by becoming unsubstitutable for every other other. The other accedes to himself by coming forward in his irreplaceable *haecceitas*; he is thrown off balance, so to speak, by jumping into his alterity with a step that throws him into the final singularity. The other poses his gaze as inescapable injunction only insofar as he weighs into it with all his weight; and he weighs with all the weight of alterity only insofar as he throws himself madly into his alterity. But *haecceitas* is not accomplished as such (does not reach the end of its individuality) unless the other as such becomes unreservedly ecstatic. Now ecstasy, understood in the sense of the Aristotelian ecstasy of time, is summed up in the gaze, which weighs with the weight of *haecceitas* only insofar as *haecceitas* surpasses itself and comes to die in the gaze, as though in a final impetus. The alterity of the other *as such* attains its final individuality because it moves ecstatically, through its *haecceitas*, into a gaze: the other passes completely into his gaze, and will never have a more complete manifestation. Whence a twofold consequence: finally, only the gaze can be called unsubstitutable, and this gaze is simply one with the injunction, since the injunction enjoins for the sake of the other as such. (2) If the injunction that I receive gives me, in a gaze, the last possible ecstasy of the other, it delivers the other to me, without remainder, without reserve or defense, the perfect operative of the unsubstitutable in him. The injunction thus enjoins me to support, with my own gaze, the unsubstitutable alterity of the gaze of the other as such. To support a gaze means to support the invisible unsubstitutable within it. That it can only be an invisible gaze is newly confirmed in the impossibility of an unsubstitutable objectivity—the object is seen, is defined, and is therefore repeatable. The unsubstitutable is fulfilled only in a gaze (ceaselessly other), because it is the operative of alterity itself. The gaze wherein the other is exposed as such can, in weighing on my own, only enjoin him to expose himself in turn to unsubstitutable individuality. The gaze that accomplishes in itself the unsubstitutable can only enjoin me to accomplish, in projecting myself within a gaze, my unsubstitutable. If in his gaze the other risks himself in his last individuality, he can only enjoin me to risk myself, in return, in my ultimate individuality—to risk rendering the unsubstitutable to the unsubstitutable. Note that it is not a matter of reestablishing two self-possessors, and thus two *I*'s. Rather, it is up to each one to let himself be summoned, by another's injunction, to his own individuality, entirely completed in the ecstasy of the gaze—not for the purpose of retaking possession of self by reintegrating what is proper to him, but in order to expose himself in person to the final ecstasy of the other. I owe the other for making me, under his absolutely unsubstitutable gaze to the point of nakedness, also unsubstitutable, individualized, and naked. The other's exposition enjoins me to expose myself, too, in order to shelter it, to maintain it, and to protect it. I receive my unsubstitutable individuality from the advance of the other in his gaze; I receive myself, then, unsubstitutable from his own ecstasy. I receive it as such because it provokes me to make myself an *as such*. The injunction imposes upon me the gaze of the other *as such*, since it imposes upon me to expose myself there, in person, *as such*, by myself moving ecstatically into my unsubstitutable gaze. The other comes upon me as such, because he renders me indispensable—the injunction exerts itself as a summons.

Freed from intentionality,[15] love in the end would be defined, still within the field of phenomenology, as the act of a gaze that renders itself back to another gaze in a common unsubstitutability. To render oneself back to a gaze means, for another gaze, to return there, as to a place for a rendezvous, but above all to render oneself there in an unconditional surrender: to render oneself to the unsubstitutable other, as to a summons to my own unsubstitutability—no other than me will be able to play the other that the other requires, no other gaze than my own must respond to the ecstasy of *this particular* other exposed in his gaze.

But to render oneself other, to surrender this gaze to the gaze of the other who crosses me, requires faith.

July 1983

Concerning the Lover, and His Advance

§15. Reducing Reciprocity

A path closes up all the more tightly as we follow it step by step. The aporia results from the contradiction between the question and the conclusion: in beginning by asking if someone out there loves me ("Does anyone love me?"), I am inevitably led to the hatred of every man for himself, against the background of the hatred of all for all. Whoever wants to get himself loved gains hatred for himself, and then hatred for everyone other than himself, and, finally, self-enrollment in the hatred of all for all.

Can we avoid this conclusion? It is always possible to challenge the logic that leads to it and disclose a simple mistake in the order of reasoning. But this would augment the failure, because then only a fault in reasoning would be able to save my right to have myself loved, as if it would be necessary to forgo hating myself only by recognizing myself as irrational. That is a high price to pay to confirm the prejudice that love is only possible if one gives up thinking correctly. But what other way remains open? At least this one: it is necessary to forgo drawing out a concept of love beginning from the question "Does anyone out there love me?"—that is, to forgo gaining access to a concept by beginning from the demand that one love me—because neither I nor any other can, on this basis, assure myself of anything but their hatred. But then the aporia would not throw into question the general rationality of love, but only the pertinence of the question "Does anyone out there love me?" or at least the way in which we have understood that question up to this point. Put another way, in order truly to accomplish the erotic reduction, it would be necessary to gain access to a question that is much more original and radical. How do we get there?

Let us return to the question "Does anyone out there love me?" Why did we take it up at the outset as a way to gain access to the erotic reduction? There was an obvious motive: this question in effect isolates assurance in confrontation with vanity, by opposing it clearly to certitude in confrontation with doubt; to be is certainly no longer the issue, but rather to surmount the disqualification distilled by the suspicion "What's the use?": to assure oneself of love, and no longer to certify its existence in this precise sense, the question "Does anyone out there love me?" indeed triggers the erotic reduction. And yet, the instance of love does not yet stand forth here except at a very closed angle. Not because it concerns me, the first *ego* waiting for an assurance from out there; for love and assurance could not intervene without a base of support that assigns them, and a stake that calls them forth; the fixing of the erotic reduction upon the *ego* remains absolutely indispensable. Rather, the difficulty arises from what the *ego* allows or does not allow us to glimpse of the erotic reduction. Indeed, with regard to the *ego*, love still only intervenes indirectly, as if negatively, following the search for an assurance against the threat of vanity. Love here plays only the hypothetical and nearly unattainable correlate to my lack of assurance when confronting the question "What's the use?" The erotic reduction still remains partial; as of yet, love only appears there by default. Assurance does depend upon the erotic reduction, but the erotic reduction does not completely achieve it, because the *ego* lacks assurance; and this *ego*, which itself lacks assurance, only apprehends love as a shortfall. The *ego* takes the risk of the erotic reduction under the threat of vanity, and thus in panicked fear of "missing out." Missing out on what? On assurance in love. The *ego* does not venture onto the field of love except in order to escape from the risk of losing itself, thus hoping for an assurance, a return of assurance, the chance to make up the shortfall. It achieves only a narrow and parsimonious pre-understanding of love: it doesn't have any, it needs some fast, and so it asks for it; the more ignorant it is of love's dignity, its power, and its rules, the more frenetically it demands it. The *ego* addresses love like a poor man who, with fear in his gut because he is penniless, never imagines he could be dealing with anyone but usurers, each more pitiless and rapacious than the one before; for him, assurance must be even more costly than certainty, with even more knowledge to sacrifice and more ascesis to endure than in hyperbolic doubt. Caught in this panic at its lack, what does the *ego* hope for when it takes its first step into the territory of love? What does the erotic reduction, in spite of the *ego*, open before it? At best, in the highest estimation of its fearful expectations, the *ego* hopes not to lose anything there—it hopes that love will give it assurance at a fair price. The *ego* is quite willing to pay to obtain assurance, but not if someone takes from it more than it will receive. The *ego*, from the outset, expects from love only a more or less honest exchange, a negotiated *reciprocity*, an acceptable compromise.

Of course, one could immediately respond that reciprocity has nothing to do with love and befits only the economy and calculation of exchange. And in fact the *ego*, still standing at the border of the erotic reduction, naïve and inexperienced in the things of love, is completely ignorant of love's paradoxical logic; it knows little about the lover within that it has not yet liberated; it only reads love as the expectation of and demand for an assurance at a reasonable price. How then does the *ego* calculate this price? Like a wretch, with mistrust and precaution: I want to receive my due—my assurance that someone loves me and only then will I pay and will I love in return. In this way of looking at things, at first it had even seemed preferable to try to make less expensive deals: for example to produce assurance each for his own, without asking for it from elsewhere

(§9), or, if it indeed was necessary to ask for it from elsewhere, to choose the most familiar neighbor, who resembles me the most and bothers me the least—he who hates himself like I hate myself, who hates me just like I hate him, my counterpart (§13). The *ego* had finally to give up on these expedients, but it remains in the same dispositions; the *ego* continues to calculate the smallest margins and holds itself to strict reciprocity; I will only love in return, after the fact, only if someone loves me first and only as much as someone first loves me. I will play the game of love, certainly, but I will only risk the least amount possible, and on condition that the other go first. Love thus is definitely put into operation for such an *ego*, but always out of panic, in a situation of lack and under the yoke of reciprocity—thus love does not really come into play any more than the erotic reduction is truly accomplished. The obstacle that obstructs the opening of the amorous field—an erotic obstacle, not an epistemological or ontic one—consists in reciprocity itself; and reciprocity only acquires this power to set up an obstacle because one assumes, without proof or argument, that it alone offers the condition of possibility for what the *ego* understands by a "happy love." But could such a "happy love," closely controlled by reciprocity, remain happy? In any case, it could not remain a love, because it would fall directly under exchange and commerce. It is for a radical reason that love cannot confine itself to reciprocity nor base its decisions on a determination of fair price: the loving actors have nothing to exchange (no object), and thus cannot calculate a price (whether fair or not); in the realm of exchange, by contrast, the agents deal in objects, the permanent third party lying between them, about which they may make calculations, and the prices of which they may set. Thus it is necessary to reject reciprocity in love, not because it would seem improper, but because in love reciprocity becomes impossible—strictly speaking, without an object. Reciprocity sets the condition of possibility for exchange, but it also attests to the condition of love's impossibility.

This recourse to commerce thus indicates what was blocking the erotic reduction and was shrinking access to the order of love—and I began not so much from assurance itself as from assurance as always already lacking, from my needy *ego*, struck with panic before a shortage and directly taking refuge behind reciprocity. We understand now why the initial question "Does anyone out there love me?" could not until this moment receive an answer, other than the hatred of every man for himself and of all for all: the love that it evoked in fact remained prisoner to the iron law of reciprocity—love, perhaps, but only if I am first of all assured, which is to say under the condition that someone love me first. In short, at this stage, to love means first to be loved. To be loved—to put it another way, to love still refers back to being, and thus merely confirms being in its metaphysical function as first instance and final horizon; once again being determines love, which has no other role than to assure being, as underpinning, against vanity. Love is of use to being, and serves being, but is not excepted from being.

§16. Pure Assurance

This diagnosis suggests a path that might open a way out of the aporia: radicalize the erotic reduction in order to reduce even as far as the demand of reciprocity: To the initial question "Does anyone out there love me?" which limits access to the horizon of love as much as it opens it, it is necessary to add another question, which picks up where the first left off—one that poses the question of love without, however, submitting it to the prior condition of reciprocity, and thus of justice; that is to say, one that does not presuppose that assurance happens first for me. How could we conceive that loving might not first be required to come from somewhere else toward me, but might instead unfold itself freely and without serving me? By admitting the possibility that this event issues from me in view of an other still undetermined—issues from me deep within an elsewhere that is more inward to me than me myself, preceded or validated by no assurance at all. In short, the point is to ask, "Can I love first?" rather than, "Does anyone out there love me?"—which means, to behave like a lover who gives himself, rather than like one who is loved tit for tat.

Now such a possibility—this is the sovereign argument that restarts the entire inquiry—remains by definition always open, and no aporia will ever be able to block it. For the finding (or the simple suspicion) that someone does not love me never prevents me in principle from being able to love first. That no one loves me (whether I know this for a fact or fantasize it is not important) never makes it impossible for me to love the very one who does not love me, at least each time and for as long as I decide to do so. She may not love me as much as she would like, or she may love me as little as she can, but that never prevents me from loving her, if I so decide. They can hate me as much as they want, but they will never force me to hate them, too, if I decide not to. The incomparable and unstoppable sovereignty of the act of loving draws all its power from the fact that reciprocity does not affect it any more than does the desire for a return on investment. The lover has the unmatched privilege of losing nothing, even if he happens to find himself unloved, because a love scorned remains a love perfectly accomplished, just as a gift refused remains a perfectly given gift. What is more, the lover never has anything to lose; he could not even lose himself if he wanted to, because giving without a guarantee, far from destroying or impoverishing him, attests all the more clearly to his royal privilege—the more he gives and the more be loses and disperses, the less he himself is lost, because abandon and waste define the singular, distinctive, and inalienable character of loving. Either love is distributed at a loss, or it is lost as love. The more I love at a loss, the more I simply love. The more I love at a loss, the less I lose sight of love, because love loves further than the eye can see. Accomplishing the act of loving not only allows for not fearing loss, but it consists only in this freedom to lose. The more I lose utterly, the more I know that I love without contest. There is only one single proof of love—to give without return or chance of recovery, and thus to be able to lose and, eventually, to be lost in love. But love itself is never lost, because it is accomplished in loss. Loving surpasses being with an excess that has no measure, because it recognizes no contrary and no inverse. While being ceaselessly demarcates itself from nothingness, and is deployed only with it and struggles only against it, love never meets anything that remains foreign to it or that threatens it or limits it, because even the negative, nothingness, and nothing (what can he imagined that is more opposed?), far from canceling out love, offer it yet another privileged terrain, and allow it to accomplish itself all the more perfectly. Loving loses nothing from the fact of not being, because it gains nothing from the fact of being. Or better, to love consists sometimes in not being—in not being loved, or at least in accepting being able not to be loved. Nothing, neither being nor nothingness, can limit, hold back, or offend love, from the moment that loving implies, by principle, the risk of not being loved. To love without being loved—this defines *love without being*. The simple, formal definition of loving includes its victory over nothing, and thus over death. Love raises from the dead—we must understand this as an analytical proposition.

From this point forward, the old aporia explodes. Not only is reciprocity unable to take the question of love hostage (by bending the question "Does anyone out there love me?") and lead to the hatred of every man for himself (along with the hatred of all for all); but above all, loving only testifies to itself as such by suspending reciprocity and by exposing itself (giving itself over) to losing what it gives, to the point of its very own loss. Either loving has no meaning at all, or it signifies loving utterly, without return. The erotic reduction is radicalized and the question is formulated henceforth in this way: "Can I love first?"

Nevertheless, this radicalizing, fruitful though it has proven to be, gives rise retroactively to a serious difficulty: I was only able, in fact and by right, to glimpse the erotic reduction because there first emerged in me a demand for assurance, such that it disqualified the request for certitude. It was thus in the name and in the direction of assurance that I entered onto the field of love. Now the very logic that first made me pass from the interrogation "Does anyone out there love me?" to "Can I love first?" justifies the primacy of the latter over the former through the freedom to lose and to be lost; but doesn't loss or expenditure without return, as distinctive of love as these may appear to be, forbid me any assurance at all? Doesn't loving signify henceforward being the first one lost, and thus detaching myself from every assurance out there? For the lover that I become, the "out there" itself would no longer authorize any assurance, but would amount to an obligation given by me, to which I abandon myself. The conclusion is clear: as the erotic reduction is radicalized, the demand for assurance loses its legitimacy, and I should give up on it definitively

In fact, this argument is not as good as it first appears, for two reasons. First, because it contradicts the logic of loss and abandonment, rather than illustrating it. Indeed, one reasons as if the act of loving, in giving itself utterly, was lost and abandoned in order to fall away, or even to disappear; but one can only draw such a conclusion by implicitly holding to the point of view of reciprocity and of commerce, where, in a situation of panicked shortage, the loss of what I give would amount immediately to my insolvency as lover and to my annihilation, for lack of the least bit of assurance. On the contrary, if one holds to the strict point of view of the lover, the fact of losing (or the risk of being lost) in no way entails one's disappearance for lack of assurance, but instead the accomplishment of love in its very definition—the more it loses and is lost, the more it attests to itself as love and nothing other than love. The more it loses (disperses, gives, and thus loves), the more it gains (because it still loves). In the erotic reduction, the lover who loses himself gains himself all the more as lover. In fact, the objection still describes the amorous loss from the starting point of the prejudice of reciprocity; it still confuses assurance with the autarkic possession of every man for himself.

Second, the objection fails to understand the essential paradox: the love of the lover always gains, because she has no need whatsoever to gain anything in order to gain (herself), so that she gains even and above all when she loses. Yes, one might respond, but in this game of whoever loses wins, I gain by loving first, without for all of that gaining the least assurance that someone out there loves me; thus one has to admit that love in its essence must give up on any assurance. And the confusion we were trying to clarify by radicalizing the erotic reduction has burst out all over again. Indeed, what is understood by assurance, when, as here, one thinks to deny it to the lover? Evidently assurance from out there, which guarantees the *ego* against vanity; but what is understood by such a guarantee? That vanity will no longer prevent me from loving myself enough so that I can will to be and persevere in my being; thus assurance, at this point, would remain ordered to my being, to the being in me and to me in my being; I thus still dream imperceptibly of escaping from the erotic reduction, which in fact I refuse and would like to flee. Inversely, when I pass on to the question "Can I love first?" what assurance can I legitimately hope for, as a lover? Evidently not the assurance to be able to continue or to persevere in my being despite the suspicion of vanity, but the sole assurance appropriate to the radicalized erotic reduction not the assurance of being [*l'assurance d'être*], nor of being itself [*ni de l'être*] but *the assurance of loving.* By responding to the question "Can I love first?" with the loss of the gift to the point of the loss of self, the lover really does win an assurance—understood as the pure and simple assurance of the precise fact that she loves. When I love to the point of losing everything, I do gain an irrefragable assurance, one that is indestructible and unconditional, and yet solely the assurance that I love—which is enough. The lover finds an absolute assurance in love—not the assurance of being, nor of being loved, but that of loving. And she experiences it even in the absence of reciprocity. Let us suppose that a lover loves—but without return, because someone doesn't love her, or ceases to love her. Has she lost? What has she lost? She will have assuredly lost the assurance that someone loves her; but absolutely not the assurance of loving—provided at least that she persists in loving, without waiting for any love in return. She will keep this assurance as long and as often as she wants—that is, as long as she loves first and, above all, last. When a love rids itself of all reciprocity, who wins and who loses? Within the natural attitude, she who ceases to love wins—in effect, her gain consists in no longer loving; but, in point of fact, she has lost love. Within the erotic reduction, she who continues to love gains, because in this way she keeps love, or indeed, she finds it for the first time.

To the objection, then, one will respond that the point is not to say: "I love, therefore I am certain of my existence as a privileged being," but rather to say: "I love, therefore I have the assurance that I love first, like a lover." Primacy obviously changes status: it no longer indicates the privilege of the greatest surety, or of the greatest certainty, but the risk of greatest exposure. For I only have the assurance that I am loving, for as long as I am loving—that is to say that I assume the risk of loving first; I only have the initiative insofar as I can love, and can make a primary decision to love without return, and can make it so that love, through me, loves. I have the assurance first and foremost of making it so that love loves in me. *I have the assurance that I am making love.* And, as love assures against vanity, I discover myself to be assured by the love that I make, which makes itself in and through me, against the suspicion in the question "What's the use?" This assurance can certainly lead me off track, but like a paradox: it makes me change tracks and start back up on a different route from my first climb toward assurance. Instead of demanding an assurance oriented to my profit, and thus extracted from somewhere else by every means possible (including the hatred of each for himself until it produces the hatred of all for all), I radicalize the erotic reduction in order to receive the assurance in the very gesture of losing what I give, to the point of risking losing myself, without any return on my investment or on my property (my οὐσία, my fund or core, my good). I receive an assurance, but it no longer concerns being, having jumped over it; the assurance only directly concerns love, the love that I set in motion as a lover, not the love that I might lay claim to as the property of one who is loved. Assurance still comes to me, but no longer from an ontic elsewhere that would conserve me in my beingness; rather, it comes from an elsewhere that is more inward to me than myself: the elsewhere that comes upon rue in the very gesture in which I give up what I have (my gift) and what I am, in order to assure myself only of what I truly make in this instant—love. I receive the assurance that I am making love and I receive it only from lovemaking itself and in view of itself alone. I receive from love what I give back to it—the making of it. I receive the assurance of my dignity as lover.

That will suffice for me as long and as often as I make love as a perfect lover. For love grows in loving, a fact that calls for two decisive remarks. First, I do not get beyond self-hatred (or the hatred of every man for himself, or the hatred of all for all) by a frenetic or imaginary excess of love for myself, as recommended by the weighty, authoritative opinions of psychology and psychoanalysis—had I only known, for example, that I have ψυχή, or what is signified by this word, or even that the point is in fact to take care of it and to work on it! No, I pass beyond the hatred of every man for himself by overcoming the hatred in me of all for all, and vice versa. And as I cannot begin with my own case, which remains too close to me, too unknown, and too hostile, I begin by overcoming my hatred for others, who are better known, further away, and less dangerous for me than I myself am. In this first moment of the erotic reduction, even though radicalized, the issue cannot vet be the obtaining of self-love—loving myself, should it ever prove to be possible (and I have some good reasons to doubt it at this moment), would come as a conclusion, as the highest and most difficult of loves, for which I would need infinite help and the borrowed surety of grace, still inconceivable to me at this point (§41).

Second, in moving from the question "Does anyone out there love me?" to the question "Can I love first?" I do indeed receive an assurance the assurance that I love decidedly, that I love as a decided lover. This assurance delivers me so much the more from the suspicion of vanity that not only does it free me from my tense attachment to a being that is preservable by means of perseverance, but above all it leads me back to myself, in my final ipseity. I attain it first of all because, in this way, my assurance no longer depends on an indeterminate elsewhere, at once uncertain (does she truly love me?) and anonymous (can I truly know her?); it is born from a decision that, doubtless, I never make with a full and free consciousness (am I free, am I conscious?), but which at the very least would not be made without my consent, since it is only accomplished if I and I alone make love, I eventually make it without willing it, without foreseeing it, indeed without making it completely, but in the end it is always necessary that I risk myself in making it and that it is I who goes forth, in person and in the flesh, without a substitute or a delegate. When the matter consists of me, this particular other, and my assurance, it is only I who can make love. At the very least, love is not made without me, the lover. The very fact that I make it without any condition of reciprocity, without return and at a loss, confirms powerfully that here, first and foremost, I am at issue, as well as my initiative, or at least my singular and irreplaceable consent. My acts as lover belong to me incontestably, without admixture or apportionment. It might even be that all my other acts, in particular those that come under understanding and representative thinking, may not only be just as well accomplished by anyone, but even must be capable of being accomplished by anyone else, in order to safeguard the universality that is constitutive of interobjective rationality (§7). In this case, I would have no true access at all to my final individuality, nor to my nonsubstitutable ipseity, except through the love that I make, because I can only make love at my expense. It may be that, at the end of my days, I will sum up myself in my acts as a lover.

The erotic reduction, henceforth radicalized, accomplishes—and it alone can do this—the reduction to the proper, for it leads me back to that which I can and must properly assume as my own (§37). Everything else still involves something other than me (the world), or others than me (the other, universal reason, shared understanding). I do not become myself when I simply think, doubt, or imagine, because others can think my thoughts, which in any case most often do not concern me but, instead, the object of my intentionalities; nor do I become myself when I will, desire, or hope, for I never know if I do so in the first person or only as the mask which hides (and is propped up by) drives, passions, and needs that play within me, yet without me. But I become myself definitively each time and for as long as I, as lover, can love first.

§17. The Principle of Insufficient Reason

By loving first, the lover that I become breaks with the demand for reciprocity: my loving no longer presupposes that someone love me first. Love coming down on me from elsewhere no longer constitutes the prerequisite condition for my own decision to love. The lover loves without delay, because he loves without awaiting or foreseeing someone loving him first, and without letting or making another come to him, one who would expose herself first and take the risk of the initial outlay; he loves at once, without waiting for anything in return—neither a real counterlove, nor even the possibility of conceiving a certain hope. Nevertheless, this posture might seem, if not unthinkable, at least implausible, and nearly unrealizable—a formal hypothesis, dreamed up without actual validity It is therefore necessary to consider further how the lover comes to the point of not waiting, or of waiting for nothing, in order to love first.

One does not spot the lover right away: at the outset, she does not see herself, any more than she foresees herself. It is not enough for me to enter into the game of a group of others, nor into a social relation, so that I might glimpse the possibility of becoming or of seeing a lover. Let us suppose first that I inscribe myself within a network of functions determined by readiness-to-hand: all that remains is to put to work some ready-to-hand beings (tools, machines, processes in view of an end); I intervene among these ready-to-hand implements by putting them in motion and to work, by exchanging goods, by communicating information, in short according to the logic of economy. Clearly, reciprocity here determines the totality of these operations and, following the well-understood law of well-conducted business, I will do nothing for free, nor will I ever engage myself in anything without a guarantee. The principle according to which "business is business" forbids, in its exceptionless neutrality, not only my mixing, as they say, business with pleasure, or my doing business with friends, but even more radically my taking into consideration anything that might overflow and muddle the strict reciprocity of commerce. Whether I buy an airline ticket at a reduced price or negotiate a fabulous contract makes no difference: the ritual of exchange hides the partners from one another and masks them behind the transparent clarity of the agreement, the contract, or the settlement. I never deal with particular persons, but instead with substitutable interlocutors, which I eventually put into competition with one another and attempt always to reduce to their pure role as abstract agents of commerce, transparent participants in reciprocity. The less I see an other as a person irreducible to his function in the economy, and the less I venture to accord him a resistant individuality, and thus a privilege of independence or, indeed, of anteriority to me, the more correctly, effectively, and even honestly I will treat the piece of business that brings us together. Economy demands the anonymity of participants in exchange; they accomplish the exchange better above all when they do not try to know one another as such. In this situation, which is by far the most standard, the lover not only may not come forth, but must not.

Let us suppose nevertheless that the social network in which I inscribe myself does not allow itself to be completely reduced to readiness-to-hand or to economy: for instance, a random and provisional encounter, but in principle disinterested, where I go to "relax" (a party, a festival, a gallery opening, a sporting event, etc.). I can perfectly well join in, feel fully at ease, and indeed take pleasure, without ever engaging myself in person. It might even be that the euphoria of my encounters grows the less I engage myself; it may be that I exchange ever more tokens of friendship, of interest, and of seduction the more I never truly give them, distributing them instead according to a strict reciprocity, neither more nor less, as if we were dealing in an immaterial merchandise, invaluable and yet really and truly negotiated in a trade that is more subtle and more enriching than one involving things. I make myself everything for all, but never, above all, someone for someone else. Even if I risk engaging in a little seduction, or even push it a bit further, I am clearly still aiming at reciprocity; I simply practice deferred exchange rather than immediate exchange; I take a first step (or a second, or a third) only in a decided expectation of a return on my investment, all the more delightful because I will have to wait for it, all the more valued because it might return more than I invested. Besides, even if I allow my attention to focus on such or such, to the point of engaging in a more individuated conversation, which, if everything goes well, will produce a thoroughly particular interlocutor, this privilege still doesn't engage me in anything; even if imperceptibly a singles ad scenario—"for friendship, maybe more"—is put into gear, this other and I still retain mastery of the situation, we control, at least through vanity and under social pressure, what is considered to be "going too far." And if we do indeed go too far, even in the flesh, we still are able, following the profitability of reciprocal exchange, to break it off there and leave one another, without any fuss, litigation, or loss (why not stay friends?). Thus reciprocity governs all commerce, even the carnal sort.

When, then, does the lover appear? Precisely when, during the encounter, I suspend reciprocity, and no longer economize, engaging myself without any guarantee of assurance. The lover appears when one of the actors in the exchange no longer poses prior conditions, and loves without requiring to be loved, and thus, in the figure of the gift, abolishes economy. In trade and exchange, only reciprocity reigns—and legitimately so—because it allows us to distinguish good agreements from bad agreements, through the calculation of the reason that suffices in validating the one and invalidating the other. Reciprocity renders economy reasonable, by calculating as exactly as possible what one renders to the other for the service rendered and the payment made. The price fixes the reason of the exchange by guaranteeing its fair reciprocity. The price renders economy reasonable. If the lover decides, then, to love without any assurance in return, to love first, without requiring any security, he transgresses not only reciprocity, but also and above all he contradicts economy's sufficient reason. As a consequence, in loving without reciprocity, the lover loves without reason, nor is he able to give reason—counter to the principle of sufficient reason. He renounces reason and sufficiency. Just as, in the end, a war breaks out without reason, in a deflagration and a transgression of every good reason, the lover makes love break out. He declares his love as one declares war—without any reason. Which is to say that he does so sometimes without even taking the time or the care to make the declaration.

Nevertheless, such a denial of the reason to love, which characterizes the love of the lover, in no way constitutes a banal folly. The issue is not an inability of the lover to find reasons, or a lack of reasoning or of good sense, but rather a failure of reason itself to give reasons for the initiative to love. The lover does not scorn reason: quite simply, reason itself goes lacking as soon as love is at issue. Love lacks reason, because reason gives way before it, like ground gives way beneath our feet. Love lacks reason, like one lacks air the higher one climbs a mountain. Love does not reject reason, but reason refuses to go where the lover goes. Reason indeed refuses nothing to the lover—but, quite simply, when love is at issue reason can do nothing, it can do no more, it is worn out. When loving is at issue, reason is not sufficient: reason appears from this point forward as a principle of *insufficient reason*.

I can verify this insufficiency of reason in love with a few arguments. First, if I love first, without any assurance of return, reciprocity can no more give me reason to love than it can tell me that I am wrong or give me a reason not to love: I remain as free to love as I am free not to love. Second, because I love first, I can sometimes very well not yet know the one that I love; not only because, in a radical sense, I have no need of knowing her and, on the contrary, the anteriority of my initiative dispenses me from having to, but also because the project of knowing this other adequately, without and even before loving her (as an object), has no meaning. Third: if I love without reason or even at times without prior knowledge of the figure or of the facets of the other, I do not love because I know what I see, but inversely I see and I know in the measure that I, the first to love, love. The other appears to me for as much as I love her, for my anterior initiative does not decide solely my attitude toward her, but above all her phenomenality—because I am the first to put it on stage, by loving her.

The lover makes appear the one whom she loves, not the reverse. She makes him appear as lovable (or despicable) and thus as visible within the erotic reduction. The other is phenomenalized in the exact measure according to which the lover loves him or her and, as an Orpheus of phenomenality, tears him or her from indistinction and makes him or her emerge from the depths of the unseen. This allows us to rehabilitate a polemical argument, used as frequently by metaphysics as by popular morality, against Don Juan, but also against the lover as such. The lover would delude himself, it is said, by not seeing the one that he loves as she truly is, but instead, each time, only as his desire imagines her to be. He sees with the eyes of love, which is to say by blinding himself (the large woman is majestuous; the petite, delightful; the hysterical, passionate; the bitch, arousing; the silly, spontaneous; the argumentative, brilliant, etc.—and one can easily transpose these so that they apply to men, too). We reproach desire with deforming and reformulating, in order to desire better. The lover, in this case Don Juan, fools himself, and his confidant, Sganarelle, sees clearly: it is necessary to come back to earth, to look things in the face and not to take one's desire for reality; in short, it is necessary to exit the erotic reduction. But by what right does Sganarelle claim to see better than Don Juan what he himself would have neither noticed, nor seen, if the lover, Don Juan, had not first pointed it out to him? By what right does he dare, with a clear conscience, to reason as the lover, when he cannot, by definition, share either the vision or the initiative? Evidently, because he is completely ignorant of the phenomenological rule according to which the anticipation of loving first allows one to see at last such and such an other, for the anticipation to love first sees her as lovable and unique, while otherwise she disappears into commerce and reciprocity. It is said that Don Juan and Sganarelle see the same other, but with two different gazes—the former with the phantasms of desire, the latter with the neutrality of good sense. This is wrong, for in fact they see two different phenomena. The lover alone sees something else, a thing that no one other than he sees that is, what is precisely no longer a thing, but, for the first time, just such an other, unique, individualized, henceforth torn from economy, detached from objectness, unveiled by the initiative of loving, arisen like a phenomenon to that point unseen. The lover, who sees insofar as he loves, discovers a phenomenon that is seen insofar as it is loved (and as much as it is loved). In contrast, Sganarelle sees nothing of this other and only reasons against Don Juan because he reestablishes reason, of which the lover has just taken leave. It is precisely by reestablishing the economy that Sganarelle compares objectively the qualities and the faults of what the lover loves with other possible loves; he calculates anew the good and bad reasons, the gains and losses; and reason only reappears in order to justify or disqualify a possible reciprocity, a retributive justice. But this restoration has a price: one cannot claim to measure what the lover loves outside of what is for sale except by evoking phantoms alongside this new phenomenon henceforth arisen, crystallized and irrefragable; one cannot measure the lover's beloved except by comparing him or her to the phantoms of other possibilities, to another "he" or another "she"—that the lover could have loved, and should have loved, with better reasons; without seeing what is right in front of his eyes that these phantoms have no rank among true phenomena, that the initiative of the lover has eliminated these very possibilities, and that they have all simply disappeared in front of the evidence of the new phenomenon, henceforth seen and revealed. Reason cannot reason except by comparing, but, from the moment of the lover's declaration, the former possibles collapse when faced with the unique facticity that has come forth, and they fade away, like shadows swallowed up by the light. Of course, one could always see things in other ways than does the lover, with more reason, for instance; but this is precisely the point: the lover has gone beyond the field of validity of comparisons, of calculations, and of commerce; he can no longer see otherwise, nor see anything other than what he sees—and what he sees decidedly no longer has the status of a thing, but of a beloved. The lover's domestic servant can do nothing more for the lover, because he regresses to the hither side of the radicalized erotic reduction that the lover fulfills, or rather, which fulfills him as lover.

Nevertheless, let us once again admit the question, why does the lover commit himself first, without any assurance, to love this one and not that one? If we have understood that, for the lover, no comparison can give a reasonable explanation (because the one that he has seen no longer counts among any other possible), there remains only one acceptable response: the other, become unique, herself occupies, by virtue of her role as focal point, the function of the reason that the lover has for loving her. The lover loves the beloved because the beloved is the one and only, and because the lover makes him- or herself the lover because it was him, because it was me. The lover has no reason to love the one that he loves other than, precisely; the one that he loves, insofar as he, the lover, makes this one visible by loving him or her first. From the lover's point of view (and his alone), love becomes its own sufficient reason. The lover thus makes love by producing the reason according to which he has good reason to go without every other reason. The insufficiency of reason to give love reason thus marks not only the principle of insufficient reason, but erects above all the lover as reason in himself. The *causa sui* that the love of self claimed in vain (§9) transposes itself into a *ratio sui,* but a *ratio sui* that is accomplished, this time, according to the radicalized erotic reduction—no longer by asking, "Does anyone out there love me?" but by exposing oneself to respond in person to the question "Can I love first?" The circle is decentered from the *ego* toward a certain other.

§18. The Advance

I have just followed the same path as Don Juan. For Don Juan knows, perhaps better than anyone else, how to provoke the erotic reduction and impose it upon those who, without him, would have had neither the idea nor the courage to enter into it (not only Sganarelle, but also Anna, Elvira, and Zerlina); he, the first, takes the initiative to love, without any other reason than to accomplish the erotic reduction itself. What is more, his desire does not so much provoke the erotic reduction as result from it; those to whom he declares his love, like those against whom he declares war (often the same people), appear in their increasingly extreme singularity uniquely because the erotic reduction designates them as loved, whether well or badly, but in any case lovable, in a situation to meet the lover. Nevertheless, I will not be able to follow this path any further, because Don Juan does not maintain what he so clearly inaugurates. He takes the initiative by exposing himself continually to the question "Can I love first?" thus continuously provoking the radicalized erotic reduction; but he becomes entangled in reproducing it exactly, almost mechanically, like a forest fire that starts up again with each new outbreak of fire, or rather like a fire in a fireplace that does not catch, and thus needs to be constantly stirred up. Where does this persistent and pitiable repetition come from? Doubtless from the fact that Don Juan practices the reduction solely in the mode of seduction.

Before distinguishing themselves from one another, reduction and seduction (both erotic) come together to put into operation the same advance, the same anticipation—I love first, without any other reason than this one whom I risk loving, without awaiting her response, without presuming reciprocity, without even knowing her. Reduction and seduction each proceed by anticipation—out of balance at first, carried along by their proper impetus into a fall, which remains a race for as long as it catches up with itself by virtue of its prolongation. But their divergence begins precisely with the mode of this advance. In seduction, the advance remains provisional and ends by canceling itself out, because once the other is seduced (led to give consent), I no longer love in advance or to the point of loss, but rather with a return, in full reciprocity: I will simply have made an advance on love, for which I will be reimbursed with interest. Just as the other will inevitably wind up returning to me the love I initially credited to her, my possession will catch up with it and will assimilate it to my *ego*, which will once again become the center of the circle. From that point, seduction betrays the erotic reduction, not because it seduces, but because it seduces neither enough nor long enough; because it ends up reestablishing reciprocity according to the natural attitude; and because it mimics the lover's love in order finally to invert it. This is confirmed by seduction's final moment: not only does Don Juan reestablish reciprocity in the final instance ("elle m'aimera, je le veux"), but he overturns it in his favor ("elle m'aimera et moi, non"), so someone out there loves him without his any longer loving first, or even at all. Seduction wants to make itself loved without, in the end, loving—I only go about the advance with the firm resolution of losing it as soon as possible; I only lose myself in the advance so that someone comes to me and I thus find myself again; or rather so that I find her without her ever finding me again. The advance disappears, like a lure I dangle, assuring me a free gain. In seduction I take pleasure, but the pleasure is solitary.

In contrast, the reduction starts off in an advance that is definitive and without return, an advance that will never cancel itself out, and never catch up with itself; I start off out of balance and I only avoid the fall by lengthening my stride; by going faster, in other words by adding to my lack of balance. The more I do to avoid falling, the more I advance without any hope of return. For even if I reach the other, this does not give me possession, precisely because I only touch her and open an access to her by the impact that I provoke, and therefore according to the measure of the impetus that I take and that I must maintain; the other does not stop me like a wall or an inert and delimited lump, but offers herself to me like a path that opens, always continuing in proportion to my entry forward; the advance thus requires a permanent fresh start, wherein I remain in the race and alive only by repeating my imbalance; each accomplishment asks for and becomes a new beginning. In conformity to the definition of the phenomenological reduction in general, the erotic reduction (radicalized under the form "Can I be the first to love?") is only definitively accomplished in never ceasing to repeat itself. The *ego* will never again become the center; until the end, it must decenter itself in view of a center that is always to come, an other back to whom I lead myself.

Nonetheless, does this still formal opposition between seduction and reduction truly matter, deep down, for the lover? What does the difference between a provisional advance and a definitive advance change in the question "Can I love first?" It touches upon the essential. For with a provisional advance, the other herself remains provisional: a new advance will have to be started, by scaring up any old other, making new advances upon Zerlina, after the declarations made to Elvira, Anna, and the rest of the catalog. By contrast, in a definitive advance a single, unique other suffices in principle super-abundantly; ceaselessly arousing a new start. And yet, even this uniqueness of the other does not tell the essential difference, because already the uniqueness is a result of the difference. For the other only becomes unique for me on the condition that she is confirmed to be infinite that she is able, by herself, not only to support, but to provoke an ever repeatable start of the initial advance, of my initiative to love first. But is there not a patent contradiction at issue here—how can the other, come from this world, and thus definitively finite, open the distance to an infinite restarting of the advance, to an ever repeatable advance of the lover? Put vulgarly, how would the other in the end not overdo it [*saturer*], and the lover not become tired? A vulgar response: Don Juan grows tired, and I grow tired of Elvira or of Zerlina, because we quickly size them up. Put the other way round, we size them up so quickly because, after a certain moment, we do not restart our advance. The other thus appears to me as finite, because my advance toward her has slowed, been extinguished and disappeared, not the inverse. It is the end of the advance that makes the other finite, rather than any finitude of the other justifying the end of the advance. The other becomes finite for me because she enters little by little as my advance diminishes into my field of vision, is immobilized there, and ends up by facing me, massively, frontally, objectively, instead of remaining the vanishing point that I aimed at in advance, without truly seeing it or ever comprehending it. Henceforward seen full frame, like an object, the other is immobilized in a place in the world and I can take her measure—in short, size her up. What we call possession of the other simply exploits her previous objectification; but this objectivity already implies her finitude, and thus the end of the advance. My powerlessness to restart leaves the other to become a thing, my object, the finite that I size up, and from which I eventually turn away. Don Juan does not love too much—on the contrary, he loves too little, too short of the mark, without impetus; he loses his advance. Don Juan loves too little, not because he desires too much, but because he does not desire enough, or desire long enough, or desire persistently enough. He claims to hold his liquor, but he does not hold his love; he does not hold out in his desire, he does not hold out the entire distance. In a word, he does not hold to the erotic reduction. For I, the lover, only hold to the erotic reduction as long as I maintain the advance and restart it. I find pleasure in the other because my advance and her imperceptible delay allow me to avoid the possession of an end.

Thus the advance provoked by the lover, provided that he at least respond to the question, "Can I love first?" definitively characterizes the radicalized erotic reduction—to the point that the reduction is only accomplished so long as the advance is repeated. This advance unfolds and is illustrated by several remarkable postures.

The lover *bears everything*. Indeed, by definition, the other owes no reciprocity whatsoever to the lover; or better, the other only appears as the beloved and only arises as an erotic phenomenon within the situation of the erotic reduction, and thus only at the initiative of the lover, who risks himself first; only in this way does the other escape from the fragile and provisional visibility of the object, which I can size up and, when I'm done, turn away from. Whence comes this paradoxical, yet inevitable, consequence: at the outset, when the declaration of love bursts out, the lover decides everything, and the other nothing—precisely because before the erotic reduction no other could yet be in play, and only objects offered themselves to sight, and thus to possession. The lover thus renders the beloved possible, because he enters first into the erotic reduction. Let us describe the process by which the lover raises an object to the rank of the beloved. The lover presupposes that which he aims at; but, at first sight, what he sees (or guesses at) still only offers an object to the gaze; now, since it is a matter of loving according to an advance and an endless restarting, everything but an object is necessary; and facing me, in appearance, there stands only an object. Whoever admits that only an object is to be found must abdicate the role of lover and, like Don Juan, pass on to another object. The lover, however, does not abdicate: he presupposes that before him, despite the appearances of an object, an other rises up, that is, not only an actual beloved (beloved by me), but also a potential lover. The lover is going to love this assumed other as if he or she already wanted to, knew how to, and could make him or herself be loved, and, in his or her turn, love like a lover. Of course, the lover does not ask for reciprocity or anticipate it, but simply postulates that this other does not have the rank of an object. He attests to this in presupposing—without any guarantee, or certainty, or condition—that he or she too can take the posture of the lover, enter into the erotic reduction, and, in short, love. The lover decides that the other is worthy of the title of other (beloved, not object). Thus he also makes love in the sense that he supposes that the other will end up by making it as well. The lover does not only make love, he has love made (§33).

Next: the lover *believes everything*, endures everything and lasts without limit or help, with the sovereign power of he who loves before knowing himself loved, or worrying about it. The lover makes the difference—he alone differs. He differs from all those who want to love on condition of reciprocity, those metaphysical or natural-attitude *egos* that are obsessed by their equality to themselves, to the point of wanting to enlarge it into a new equality—between what they imagine of themselves, and what they require receipt of from elsewhere. The lover also differs from all the visible objects, and thus from subsistent and ready-to-hand beings, because he loves by advancing himself into a distance, where they must not appear, so that their commerce will not muddle the erotic reduction. Nothing supports the lover, thus it is necessary that he bear everything, in particular that his presupposition—that the other will end up by entering into the erotic reduction—not come, or not come yet; and the very addition of "not yet" amounts to believing everything. The lover believes everything, endures everything and, more precisely, puts up with remaining alone in the situation of the erotic reduction. He alone has as his own the erotic reduction—he remains the idiot of the erotic reduction. But nevertheless the lover assumes this idiotic solitude as a sovereign privilege, acting on a motive that we have already sketched. In the banal, nearly universal case wherein one of the two is no longer in love, or indeed was never in love, who should be designated the least unhappy of the two? It is necessary to make a distinction; in the natural attitude, the least unhappy seems to be the one who loved the least, or who stopped loving earlier—because he has lost less, and suffered less when love disappeared; by contrast, in the erotic reduction, the least unhappy appears as the one who loved the most, because he does not stop loving, even when the other has disappeared, so that he alone maintains love afloat. He has not lost everything, because he still loves. Indeed, he has lost nothing, because he still remains a lover. In the erotic reduction, if one truly wants to win, it is necessary to love and to persist in this advance, without condition—thus the last to love wins the stake. What stake? To love, of course. The winner is—the last lover, the one who loves to the end. For the lover loves to love. That does not turn him away from loving a beloved, but instead allows him to love the beloved, even if the beloved does not love him, or simply loves no one, or indeed even takes exception to her status as other to be loved. The lover loves to love for the love of love. Henceforth, just as he bears everything, the lover can believe everything and hope for everything. To believe and to hope here signify to love without knowing or possessing. Unknowing (which believes) and poverty (which hopes) nevertheless do not indicate any scarcity or shortage, but rather the properly infinite excess of the lover, as he loves without the condition of reciprocity.

Finally: the lover loves, or at least can sometimes love, *without seeing*. Indeed, a lover cannot know what she loves in the way that she would know an object, and in fact she has no need; if she knew it in such a manner, she would be able to constitute it and size it up once and for all; neither does she know it as a subsistent being, whose presence and persistence in identity she could verify at any moment; nor does she know it as a being ready-at-hand, of which she could, at the opportune moment, make a use that is adapted to her needs, her desires, and her projects. She in fact needs to know neither objects nor beings at all, because in order to love, it is necessary for her to practice the erotic reduction of objects and of beings of the world in general, so as to open the distance in which their commerce vanishes and the abandon without return may begin. Properly speaking, she does not know that which she loves, because what one loves does not appear before one loves it. It is up to the lover to make visible what is at issue—the other as beloved, appearing as erotically reduced. Knowledge does not make love possible, because knowledge flows from love. The lover makes visible what she loves and, without this love, nothing would appear to her. Thus, strictly speaking, the lover does not know what she loves—except insofar as she loves it. There follows an incomparable privilege: since she phenomenalizes what she loves in so very far as she loves it, the lover can even (or especially) love what one does not see (if one does not love it)—and, to begin with, the absentee. The absentee in space, certainly: a known living person who for the moment is far away (it matters little here whether voluntarily or involuntarily), or even one who is definitively departed (due to a quarrel). But also the absentee in time, a living being still unknown and potential (the one "who already waits for me," me alone, in the indistinct crowd) and who will identify me; and what is more, a living being only to come, and known by proxy (the hoped-for child, or indeed the child that is feared); and above all the living being dead and gone, whether a known deceased (to whom I may want to remain faithful) or an unknown dead man (who haunts my search for identity). In loving the absentee, the lover in no way succumbs to delirium but instead limits herself to accomplishing exactly the radicalized erotic reduction, which, as we have seen, depends upon nothing belonging to being, or indeed which provokes the nothing itself. At one stroke the lover is freed from the emblematic limit of metaphysics, the difference between being and not being—for she loves just as much what is not as what is; indeed; she loves all the more freely by loving that which is not yet, that which no longer is, or even that which does not have to be in order to appear. She also washes herself of a suspicion weighing upon phenomenology—that of privileging visibility within phenomenality; for the lover loves what she does not see more than what she sees; or rather, she only sees because she loves that which, at first, she could not see. The lover loves in order to see—as one pays to view.

Because the lover possesses nothing, and must do so, it remains for him *to hope*. Hope indicates here a privileged mode of access to that which can unfold within the phenomenality opened by the erotic reduction, precisely because one can only hope for that which one does not possess, and for as long as one does not possess it. In the strict sense hope does not and cannot have an object, because objects call for possession; the more that possession grows, the less it hopes; hope and possession cross one another, inversely proportional. This is suggested by the old expression, "to have hopes"—that is to say, not yet to have the possession of an inheritance, but to find oneself in the position of waiting for it, more or less certain. And the lover has hopes; in fact he has nothing but hopes, which offer the particularity of never converting themselves into so many possessions, not because they go disappointed, but because what he hopes for does not belong to the order of that which one possesses, nor to that which possession governs. He in effect never hopes in objects, but precisely in what surpasses abjectness, or even beingness: the lover, in the very moment of the most headlong advance, which frees him from reciprocity and from economy, still hopes by full rights in assurance, the assurance that someone loves him and defends him from vanity, and thus also from the hatred of each for himself. But this assurance would sink instantly into its contrary if he waited for it like the possession of an object that is certain. For this very possession would contradict itself—possessing the beloved, come from somewhere else like an object, would ineluctably end up in jealousy (§33); it would not even be effective—because the beloved must, in order to assure me against vanity, unfold infinitely, while every object remains finite. Love, coming from out there and going to infinity, can only come upon me if I renounce possessing it and hold myself strictly to the radicalized erotic reduction. Love thus only becomes thinkable according to the mode of the hoped for, of that which can only come upon me as the radically unseen and unwarranted. As such as that which I can neither possess, nor provoke, nor merit, it will remain the unconditioned, and thus that which, on this condition, can give itself infinitely. Hope thus hopes for everything, except that which it could possess. It hopes for everything and, to begin with, the unhoped for. It assists possibility.

The lover bears everything, believes everything, even what he does not see, and hopes for everything. And, now that the erotic reduction is accomplished, he alone remains.

Nothing can triumph over him, because his very weakness makes his strength. Whence comes his advance.

§19. Freedom as Intuition

The lover's advance is nevertheless exposed to an objection that becomes all the stronger as it is multiplied. For the request for assurance, which from the beginning determines the lover in the situation of the erotic reduction, could in the end fail, in several ways. First, because it clearly remains doubtful that someone out there loves me, whether I ask for it naturally, or I pass into the radicalized erotic reduction ("Can I love first?"); the hope to which I have just had recourse confirms me in the assurance that I have none right now, and that all certainty has likewise failed me. And there's more: not only do I have no assurance whatsoever that anyone loves me, but I also have no assurance whatsoever that I love, that I truly love; for, by virtue of the advance, I do not really know whom I love, nor why I love her, nor in fact what loving means; that which makes it possible for me to love—the pure initiative, without sufficient reason—also makes this love of mine enigmatic; whether I love truly without reason (gratuitously, for nothing), or there are in fact reasons within me that I am unaware of that are determining me (reasons that come from the unconscious, from my flesh, or from society), in both of these cases, nothing assures me that it is still I and I alone who takes the initiative to love, because I do not know what "I" and even what "to love" might mean. The danger that most threatens my ambition as a lover doubtless does not consist in my not knowing whether someone loves me or not, but rather in my imagining myself able to love or able to know what loving means. How do I avoid this objection, which weighs all the more heavily because it depends directly upon the erotic reduction, in which loving is summed up by the initiative of loving in advance and without reason? And this objection could threaten even the accomplishment of the erotic reduction—for in the end an assurance received from out there does not go without saying, and the simple fact of demanding it implies neither that one will obtain it, nor that one may legitimately lay claim to it. In short, by taking the initiative to love in the role of lover, in advance and without reason, I would quite simply lack judgment and prudence.

Nevertheless, it could be that this objection only draws its strength from a misunderstanding of the erotic reduction; it boils down once again to the assertion that, in order to love, it is necessary to know whom one is loving, why one loves, and if one is loved in return; all of which are perfectly legitimate demands, but solely in the natural attitude, where nothing is done without sufficient reason, or reciprocity, or knowledge of the other as an object. These reasonable precautions lose all validity as soon as the border separating the natural attitude from the erotic reduction is crossed. And yet, this answer does not prevent the objection from returning under a slightly different form: if the lover only becomes possible beginning with the radicalized erotic reduction, the lover presupposes it; he cannot provoke it, since he results from it. There is a circle here, and it thus becomes more arbitrary to pass on to the erotic reduction, than to pass it by.

Unable to dissolve the objection, I can take support from it. I will thus concede without discussion that I do not have the least assurance that someone out there loves me, nor that I am the first to love, But this lack of assurance does not forbid passing on to the reduction, since the reduction only becomes possible when the very question of assurance, and thus of the lack of assurance, is acknowledged; the lack of assurance does not disqualify the lover from taking an advance; on the contrary, the lack of assurance makes it possible for the lover to advance by opening distance for him, If this is admitted, what results? That I am no longer assured of anything? That in the radicalized erotic reduction my lover's advance leaves me naked and empty? Absolutely not. For, even if I possess no assurance whatsoever that I love first, I at least have the assurance of having decided to do so. Just as love given remains perfectly given even if the gift is refused, since the scorn that the gift suffers in no way interferes with the abandon that the gift accomplishes, so too does the lover who decides to love first acquire the certainty of having decided, even if his advance does not love perfectly without reason, since this imperfection in no way affects the *decision* to advance without reason. Doubtless it is not enough that I decide to love first for me to accomplish without remainder such a love in advance; but it is indeed enough that I decide to love first for me to accomplish without remainder the *decision* of such a love in advance—in short, for me to receive the assurance of acceding to the status of lover. To decide to love in advance is enough to give me the assurance of the lover—the only assurance that I can aim for and hope for—because the decision to love in advance, if it does not decide my actual love, decides at least that I have decided to love in advance. To qualify as a lover, I do not have to perform love's perfect advance: by definition no one can promise that, since it depends on no cause whatsoever, not even my will; but in order to be qualified as a lover, I have only to decide to perform love's advance, a decision that depends only on me, even though it always plays out at the limits of my abilities. To decide to love does not assure loving, but it does assure deciding to love. And the lover attests himself lover precisely through this decision—the first and the purest, without a cause, without return, a pure projection into the erotic reduction, without any other reason than itself. Assurance comes to the lover when he decides simply to love, first, without the assurance of reciprocity. Assurance comes to him when he decides definitively net to wait for it. Or rather, the assurance that comes to him—to love as a lover—no longer coincides with those assurances that he renounces—that someone love him in return, or even the assurance of loving first, perfectly.

In displacing the qualification of the lover from the performance of the advance to its pure decision, one does not lower the requirement imposed upon the lover by the erotic reduction from actuality to simple formal possibility. First of all, because to claim to love first and effectively is, let us repeat, meaningless: at the instant of his initiative, the lover does not know if he acts of his own accord or under an influence, nor under what influences; nor does he know any better what he is truly undertaking, or how far he will succeed. And we cannot ask more from the lover, incomparably more than what his conscious power can cover.

Above all, by leading the advance (to love first) from an actual performance back to the possibility of a decision, the reduction does not collapse, but instead is radicalized. For to decide to love first, in advance, amounts unquestionably to the lover's deciding for and determining his self. In effect, when I ask: "Where am I and who am I?" I am searching for the place where my ipseity plays out and is phenomenalized—which is to say, the place where I make my own decision. But I do not identify myself when I decide for myself alone through an anticipatory resolution, which only anticipates me alone; in this case, I remain the prisoner of the narcissistic mirror of myself, in which I become phantasmagorically at once both spectacle and spectator, actor and judge. On the contrary; I identify myself when I no longer anticipate myself alone, but instead others, the other than myself; for she, who does not coincide with me and who attracts me within the distance that I no longer master, can describe and inscribe me as such—other than myself, henceforward situated under the protection of the other. In making my decision *to love the other in advance* I appear to myself for the first time as I make my decision—exposed to the other for the possibility precisely upon which I decide. Paradoxically, I do not appear when I make my decision by and for myself, but only when I make my decision for the other, because she can confirm for me who I am: in deciding for her, it is through her that I appear. In my decision for the other, my decision to love in advance another than myself, my most proper phenomenality is decided. I do not come to a decision about myself alone, but rather through the gaze of the other; not through an anticipatory resolution without witnesses or grounds, but through love in advance, in the distance wherein I expose myself to the other (§37). The decision to love thus remains valid, even if I do not actually accomplish love in advance, provided nevertheless that I resolve to do so—formally, that I make the decision to decide. Making love in advance perhaps does not depend upon me, but *loving to love* (*amare amare*) does. Nothing can separate me from the freedom of playing the lover.

In this way, we can posit that to love is fully equivalent to loving, and qualifies me already as a lover. We can also note that the distinction between loving the other in fact and only loving to love him or her (or loving to love) here remains imprecise; for I only experience immediately my love for loving, without ever being able to certify to myself that I love the other gratuitously, truly, or sufficiently, and without ever being able to measure it; in order to reach certainty it would be necessary not only for me to love according to the other's measure, which means without measure, but above all for a third party to make him- or herself the arbiter or, what amounts to the same impossibility, for the loved other to assure me; but who among those who share my finitude could claim to decree such a judgment? The transition between the love of love and the love of the other remains tangential and gradual for us, entangled as we are in the flux of our finite and factual affair. No lover claims seriously or easily to love the other purely, beyond his or her conviction of having loved, to love in view of this other: he would like to love, but he never succeeds in proving it, to himself or others. In what, then, do we recognize the radical lover? In the fact that he almost never dares to declare, "I love you!" precisely because he knows what it will cost. Whoever is assured that he actually and correctly loves either does not know what he is saying or is lying (to himself); he would already be doing much if he loved to love without mental restrictions or bad faith. Between loving to love and actually loving the other, we cannot mark a clean difference—we are dealing with a border zone, crossed by comings and goings without any stops, and above all without any stable resting place. Each advances as far as he or she can and as far as he or she wills (as far as he or she can will; as far as he or she wills to be able), hoping to love the other a little, thanks to the love of love.

To love loving comes down to me; in this decision, I come to and come round to appearing to myself as such. Whence arises this liberating paradox: it is enough for me to make *as if* loved to decide to love and thus to acquire a full status of lover. *As if* betrays no regression, no pulling back, no compromise, but instead unveils the privileged space of the initiative reserved for the lover—that which only depends upon him. It depends only upon him to love in advance (with or without the means to accomplish it, it matters little) and thereby to raise himself to the dignity of the lover. In deciding that I love in advance and without reciprocity, without knowing what the other thinks of it, or even if the least other knows anything about it, I have the sovereign freedom to make myself a lover—to make myself amorous. I become amorous simply because I want to, without any constraint, according to my sole, naked desire. Thus the strength of love in advance emerges: I can reasonably love even if I do not know that I am loved (or indeed even if I know that I am not loved), because in deciding to love first, I actually experience that I love. This assurance alone is enough for me. When I "fall in love," I know, at my risk and peril, what I feel and what is affecting me—to wit, that I devolve to the other, whether or not she returns my love, whether or not she knows it, indeed whether or not she accepts it. My being in love with her does not depend on her, but rather on me, alone. And that is enough.

Enough for what? Enough for an intuition to fill me, or indeed to submerge me. There is a paradox here, which could be surprising if, in the end, it did not impose itself: the state of "being in love"—those words define all of its danger, even its injustice—does not depend upon its addressee or recipient; it depends only upon its giver, me alone. It defines me and wells up from me only. In fact, it is only up to me to become loving. The lover experiences it quite lucidly: I do not become loving by chance, at just any moment in my everyday life (happy are those who are the exceptions!), nor by deciding coldly to do it; I know that sometimes there are periods that emerge in which I clearly decide not to become loving deliberately, but eventually to allow myself to become so. For if there are times when I allow myself to be absorbed by the management of objects in the world (the erotic reduction thus remaining impossible), and certain times when I must consent to the work of mourning for a love that has ended (the erotic reduction thus remaining engaged in its negativity), other times open in which I have nothing better to do than to allow myself to love loving, whether because vanity pushes me to ask (myself), "Does anyone out there love me?" or because the erotic reduction radically questions, "Can I love first?" Desire is not yet at issue—it can only come later. At issue is the very condition of desire, which first requires this consent, and the possibility that it opens. More radically: when, in the blur of the first encounter, without any information or the least assurance of reciprocity, I make my decision to go and see, or even to "go for it," this decision depends only on me. In front of a gaze that is not cruel or already misted over, I can very well hold myself back and stay put; I can also allow ambiguity to hover by "just looking"; or I can decidedly attempt to provoke the sparkle that I am hoping for, or that I dread. And, in each of these occurrences, I can make a decision out of simple curiosity, out of a slight sadism, out of playfulness, out of interest, or out of passion. To push my advance or to hold it back, to deploy it generously or to pretend to follow: it all depends on me. No one falls in love involuntarily or by chance, even if only because—all involuntary emotion admitted—he must ratify it after the fact, in order to know when and to what he is surrendering. I know very well when I become loving—at the precise moment in which I ask myself, and reassure myself by claiming that I am not in love ("I am not in love, I have nothing to worry about, I can stop at any moment"), in short at the moment in which it is already too late. Whether I am beginning to become amorous, or I already love loving, or I imagine myself loving, in each case I am willing it and, in this acquiescence, am deciding for it. The affection that I experience at the beginning of my amorous state imposes itself upon me in fact as an auto-affection. And this auto-affection will not leave me for some time, because it comes with my consent, and cannot touch me without it. The amorous state touches me the most deeply (affection for self), because in the end it falls to me alone to consent to it, and thus to decide for it (affection through the self, auto-affection).

When I consent to becoming amorous, and agree that I become loving of my own accord, what is decided is not summed up in a simple subjective emotion that would be individual and prereflexive. Rather, what is decided will invade me with an affective tonality that is powerful, deep, and durable, and which, little by little or quite brutally, will contaminate the totality of my inner life: not only my emotional but also my intellectual life, not only my conscious but also my unconscious life. Or better: more inward than my most inward part, this tonality will overdetermine all of my apparent decisions, all of my public argumentations and all of my private debates; it will ruin the most limpid logic and the interests that are the least questionable; it will eventually drive me to the most extreme social and relational choices, will push me toward the most risky outbursts and the most suspect compromises. What will be at issue in this tonality, for months, for years, perhaps forever, is a horizon encompassing all of my decisions and all of my thoughts. What status can I attribute to it? It does not have to do with an emotion, or a passion, or even less with a delirium, but first of all with what phenomenology calls a lived experience of consciousness [*un vécu de conscience, Erlebnissen*]. But this lived experience, while it is indeed provoked within me by me (insofar as it depends only upon me to love loving), is not limited to my subjectivity; it indissolubly involves the other as its intentional reference, always aimed at, even and above all if I do not yet actually reach, him or her. Insofar as it is aiming at such and such a specific other, who obsesses me even when remaining virtual, this lived experience proves itself to be radically intentional—intentional of this other. Thus the affective tonality that exposes me as amorous, or rather that qualifies me as a lover, gives me an intuition that is polarized toward an other than myself, the one that I already imagine loving, without yet knowing what I am saying. By intuition I here mean that which could fill the signification aimed at by intentionality, so that by eventually becoming adequate to the signification, the intuition allows a strict phenomenon to appear. Nevertheless, it does not exactly work this way; to become loving by my consent, and thus by my decision, amounts to receiving an intuition that is still so vast and so vague that it could fill an indeterminate number of significations, and thus render visible an indeterminate number of diverse phenomena. Effectively, this vague availability is easily verified (by following banal experience and popular wisdom) in the worrisome propensity of the same amorous affective tonality to give rise to passions, intuitions, and thus phenomena of the other that are very different, or even contradictory, and which pass, brutally and apparently without rhyme or reason, into one another; in love, I can fix myself arbitrarily upon one or another other, or swing arbitrarily between them, with about-face reversals as violent as they are sudden; even supposing that I focus myself for a considerable lapse of time upon the same other, I can certainly imagine adoring her, devoting myself to her, or enjoying her, but, if the circumstances disappoint me, I can just as well suddenly come to suspect her, betray her, or indeed even hate her. With the same affective tonality, which functions like an intentional intuition of a potential other, I can will to constitute phenomena that are as precise and visible as they are different and contradictory; which is to say phenomena that in the end are fluctuating, provisional, and nearly phantasmal.

Where does this instability come from? Evidently not from a failure of intuition, since intuition remains ever ready to fill any signification; indeed, my decision to love loving is enough to render intuition available to validate, without reserve or condition, any of the significations that I will, or that the current affair proposes. The danger comes precisely from the abundance, autonomy, and limitless fluidity of my intuition—endlessly restarted by my decision to love loving. The instability of amorous phenomena thus never comes from a poverty of intuition, but instead from the opposite: from my incapacity to assign to it a precise signification that is individualized and stable. Always available and already there, intuition shows itself to be superabundant in front of a signification that is first and foremost lacking (What other?) and most of the time provisional (Will I love a long time before veering into jealousy or hatred?). In short, the affective tonality of loving to love proves itself to be an intuition that is at once intentional toward the other and without an assignable other—an intentional intuition, but without an intentional object; a fulfilling intuition, but without a concept to fill. The intuition that furnishes me with the affective tonality of loving to love arises in excess, but is dispersed without form. It remains a vague intuition, which renders my love of loving vagabond—morally flighty, but above all phenomenally incapable of staging the least identifiable other. A blind intuition, which never sees any other. Saturated with itself, it gives loving to love, without showing anything.

Thus, intuition—in the affective tonality of the amorous state—comes to a decision following the resolution taken by the lover, and, since this resolution always plays out in advance, it gives itself before the other appears as such (supposing that he or she will ever appear). The intuition shows itself as always already given to the lover by himself, provide that he had radicalized the erotic reduction by asking himself, "Can I love first?" As he progresses in the performance of this reduction, the intuition thus provoked by his decision will grow, to become, at the limit, a saturating intuition. And all the more saturating in that, in a first and long moment, it wanders, vague and virginal in an assured, or only assigned, signification. The affective tonality of finding myself in fact in love—of attaining the status of lover—does not yet lead onto any signification: the other does not intervene here. The intuition of loving becomes blinding, because it only depends upon the lover who, once more, makes love first. But, this time, his priority closes the horizon for him.

§20. Signification as Face

As lover, I attempt to rise to the other as a phenomenon, which the radicalized erotic reduction would set forth through the question "Can I love first?" But the ordinary definition of the phenomenon cannot, in this very specific case, remain unchanged. I cannot simply maintain the claim that the phenomenon shows itself when one of my intentional significations finds itself validated by an intuition, which comes to fill it adequately

This is the case for two reasons. First, because, in the radicalized erotic reduction, I alone make the decision to love in advance and, as I love to love, I provoke through myself and by myself alone the intuition (in this case, the amorous affective tonality): this auto-affection actively produces, in immanence itself, intentional lived experiences, which can validate nothing other than myself: my amorous lived experiences only confirm my status as lover, and that I make love; they do not render the other that I love visible or accessible to me (supposing that I really do love *one*). Thus the difficulty here no longer consists in confirming a signification (always available to my spontaneous intentionality, yet still in itself empty) by intuition (eventually lacking, yet forcing itself upon me). Rather, the difficulty lies inversely in fixing a precise signification to the superabundant and vague intuition, which the decision to love in advance provokes; the point is no longer to validate a signification by an intuition, but rather an immanent and available intuition by a foreign and autonomous signification.

Whence comes the second reason: this signification should validate my intuition (my decision to love loving as the other; the sought-for signification must, in fixing my intuition, make the other manifest to me as a full-fledged phenomenon. To allow this to happen, it will not be enough that the signification attempt to represent the other to me, since the signification would degrade the other to the dishonorable rank of an object, which I could constitute at will and modify at my leisure. It will be necessary that this signification make me experience the radical alterity of the other—none other than just such an other—while the vague intuition, which I produce spontaneously by my decision, keeps me from the other and allows me to love (in fact, to love loving) without a fixed point. Signification, here lacking, must above all not represent the other to me, but must prepare me to receive alterity. Since it is precisely the case that I do not experience this alterity in the advance toward loving to love, I will have to experience it in signification's coming upon me. How can a signification ever make me experience the alterity of the other, or more exactly, the alterity of just such an unsubstitutable other? The signification in question will only arrive if it comes upon me from this alterity itself, if it no longer arises as that against which my intentionality would end up knocking, but rather as that which affects me from out there, beginning from itself. By virtue of a signification provoked no longer by my intentionality but instead by a counterintentionality— exteriority's irrefutable shock, contradicting my aim, my forecast, and my expectation. In order for the other to manifest him or herself to me as a whole phenomenon, I must not wait for the contribution of an intuition, but rather the unpredictable arrival of a signification, coming to contradict my intention *with its own*. In order to see the other, I must not attempt to make him or her appear like a phenomenon oriented according to my centrality; on the contrary, I must wait for a new signification to thwart my own significations and impose upon me, for the first time, an alterity that transcends even my advance toward loving to love. For every common-law phenomenon, my forecasted significations await the confirmation of intuitions yet to come. For the other, under the rule of the erotic reduction, my superabundant but vague intuition must continue to await the unforeseeable advent of a signification, which holds it fixed.

Thus the signification of the other, unlike the intuition of loving to love, will not belong to me; it will come from an exterior elsewhere by an advent, the experience of which alone will bring the proof of alterity. How could such a signification ever affect me, to the point of shaking me deeply enough, so as to assign my lover's *ego* to just such an other and none other? I have, in fact, known for a long time how such a signification could affect me—ever since I learned to envisage the face of the other. The face—of the other: there is a tautology here, for only the other imposes upon me a face, and no face opens upon any other ordeal than that of alterity. What does a face show? Strictly speaking, it gives nothing to be seen, at least if one were hoping to see intuitively a new visible, more fascinating or attractive than the others. In effect, the face shows nothing more than does any other surface in the world and, as a source of intuitions, it does not benefit from any privilege over the other parts of the human body. They too offer a surface that is sensible and accessible to all of my senses; I can likewise see its contours, touch its surface, smell its odor, suck the skin, even listen to its being bruised, just like any other thing in the world. What is so special about the face? Nothing, intuitively speaking. Even less than nothing, if we consider that the eyes—in all appearances the most notable characteristic of the face offer to our seeing only the emptiness of the pupils, and thus nothing at all. The face furnishes me with no new intuition. But does it oppose me with its spoken word? Not always, or necessarily: its silence often is enough to immobilize me. And yet, the face stops my gaze and my attention like nothing else, it detains me, precisely because it opposes me with the origin of the gaze that the other lays upon the world and, eventually, upon me.

This hypothesis remains: the other's face holds me with the gaze that it lays upon me, by the counterintentionality that its eyes exert, by a nonspectacle and a nonintuition, and thus perhaps by a signification. But what signification? For I could still lend it one of my own significations—the ones that I impose upon objects and upon beings in the world; and also those that my lover's intuition, which loves to love in advance, deploys endlessly in its wandering: desire, expectation, suffering, happiness, jealousy, hatred, etc. Nevertheless, it is not these significations, my own, that are at issue, because, produced as they are by my spontaneous decision, they impose upon me nothing from out there, but instead impose themselves upon the other; with these significations, I would cover up the other and hide him, or worse, destroy him. In a word, if I follow the significations that I impose upon him, I can ignore him, use him, possess him—even kill him. Kill him? This is the decisive signification—because I must not even conceive of it, because it turns against me, and because it imposes upon me a prohibition, and thus an alterity. To kill him—I cannot impose *that* upon him, without it turning against me, and his face imposing itself upon me, like something that I could neither produce nor refute. Empirically, I can in fact kill this face; indeed I could kill nothing other than such a face, because it alone calls for murder and makes murder possible, just as murder renders the face that much more visible. But why? Because everywhere out there, it is not yet murder that is at issue: for the animal, for example, the issue is only one of passing from life into death. Why, then, is it an issue of murder here and only here? Because the face alone signifies to me, in speech or in silence, "Thou shalt not kill."

By what right and by what authority does the face impose on me such a signification? This question neither admits nor asks for a response, because the only thing that matters is *the fact* that the face signifies to me precisely this signification. It is all about a fact, as constraining as a fact of reason, even more formal than a simple right. For a right only has value if in actuality, it is ratified by force. But the signification "Thou shalt not kill" survives the violation of the right within it—I can kill, but then I become a murderer, and will remain one forever. The consciousness of and remorse for this murder could very well fade—but not the irrevocable fact that I am a murderer, a fact that will mark me forever, everywhere upon the surface of the earth and for the rest of my time. All the perfumes of excuses, of good reasons, and of ideologies can do nothing; nothing could ever kill within me the fact of the murder that I have committed. The face thus imposes upon me a signification, which is opposed to the empire of my *ego*, which up to this point has met no resistance I must not submit myself to the face, and there where it arises I must not go. Strictly speaking, we ought not to speak of the other's face, since the alterity of the other only imposes itself upon me there where a face opposes itself to me; neither should we, following logically, speak of the face in general, nor of the other in general, but only of just *such* an other, designated by *just such* a face—it being understood that I never envisage a universal or common face, but always *just such* a face, which opposes to me *just such* an alterity, in telling me not to kill him—not to come to where he stands.

The face opposes itself to me; it thus imposes upon me a signification, one that consists only in the ordeal of its exteriority, of its resistance, and of its transcendence in relation to me. But, if I admit this result—and how could I not admit it?—shouldn't I necessarily give up on the horizon of love? For I attempt to phenomenalize the other, but as a lover; I try to fix my intuition upon a signification come about from the other by way of counterintentionality, but the intuition here is an amorous one, one of loving to love; I attempt, of course, to accede to the exteriority of the other, but following the advance taken in the radicalized erotic reduction. However, doesn't the signification that rises out of the injunction "Thou shalt not kill" come strictly under the ethical, and not the erotic? How could an ethical signification fix the resolutely erotic intuition of the lover—the vague intuition of loving to love? And more serious: does not the ethical give access to the signification of the other through the universality of the commandment, thereby excluding the individuation that is precisely required by the lover? These two disputes—the ethical or the erotic, universality or individuation—have not ceased to occupy the lover, who only conquers himself by trying to settle them.

§21. Signification as Oath

At this point where the lover now stands, let us consider for a moment the first dispute. We note right away that however powerful and legitimate the strictly ethical understanding of the injunction "Thou shalt not kill" remains, it nevertheless does not exhaust the injunction's signification. For to understand "Thou shalt not kill" solely as an injunction (and formal ethics must understand it in this way) implies referring it back to the one—I in this case—who must respond to and answer for it; thus, by an unforeseen reversal, "Thou shalt not kill" would determine me rather than the other, whose most proper signification it nevertheless delivers. Before understanding this signification within the ethical horizon, then, shouldn't one allow it to open out as the pure exteriority of the other, and ask not what the obligation means for me, whom it clearly obligates, but first of all what it means with regard to the other, who obligates me in it? In effect, how does this signification reach me, if not as the pure advent of an exteriority, by a counterintentionality that keeps me all the more at a distance as it touches my heart? The injunction "Thou shalt not kill" signifies—signifies for me that there, where it arises, I cannot go, except by killing this exteriority. It signifies the pure exteriority that as lover I searched for in taking the advance of loving (to love) first; as pure exteriority, the injunction thus does not contradict the radicalized erotic reduction, but fixes its amorous intuition that up to this point has remained vague. In hearing "Thou shalt not kill," I can and must, by virtue of being a lover, hear "Do not touch me"—do not advance here, where I arise, for you would tread ground that, in order for me to appear, must remain intact; the site where I am must remain untouchable, unassimilable, closed to you in order that my exteriority remain open to you—the exteriority that alone will fix your intuition and make visible to you a full-fledged phenomenon. The phenomenon, which unites your immanent intuition to my definitively distant signification, is born of your retreat in front of my advance. The erotic phenomenon that you want to see will only appear to you if you fix upon this intact signification the excess of your intuition to love loving. You will only receive this phenomenon by not taking hold of it, by not killing it, and thus first of all by not touching it.

I find myself in a radically new situation. And yet it is not a question of a psychological novelty (after all, encountering the other, if possible, would doubtless imply such a duality within distance), but rather of a phenomenological novelty. In the end the erotic reduction amounts to the posing of a single question (encompassing "Does anyone out there love me?" as well as "Can I love first?")—that of knowing if just such an other can by all rights show him- or herself to me, that is to say *beginning from him- or herself.* I perceive henceforward the answer: the phenomenon of the other, following the guiding thread of the erotic reduction, distinguishes itself from all else in that its two aspects—intuition and signification—do not belong equally to my own egological sphere. It does seem to work the same way in all the other phenomena, where intuition (categorial, of essence, or empirical) comes to me from the exterior, to fill (in part or adequately) a signification that is found to be already given. But here, the question is not one of simple exteriority, which in the end never puts into question the lordship of my *ego*, the sole constituent in the final instance. Here, an exteriority that is otherwise originary reaches me, distinguishing itself by absolutely new characteristics.

First, exteriority is no longer accomplished with intuition, since the lover gives rise to exteriority unconditionally by his or her decision to love loving; for the amorous affective tonality, which I thus produce, remains vague, without a point of fixation; it implies and releases in me an alterity; but leaves it still undetermined—an alterity that is purely negative, an exteriority that is unlimited, yet potential, and always anonymous.

Second, exteriority, on the contrary, issues, here and here alone, from signification, which only a given other, singular and definite, can impose upon me by opposing the distance in which I must attempt neither a touch nor a siege.

Third, the exteriority of this signification, even confirmed by an adequate intuition, allows me the evidence of no object whatsoever: here transcendence no longer results from objectivity, because it does not belong to the world, nor is it offered to the least constitution; certainly it gives itself, but according to a mode that is not worldly and not objective; it gives itself beginning from itself, following a counterintentionality.

Fourth, exteriority marks its initiative by speaking; the arising of speech, when it wants and as it wants, to whomever it wants, puts forth an authority that has no common measure with the language it puts to work, its content, its meaning, and its rules; language can become an object again, but not speech insofar as it is the speech spoken by the other, who can take it back.

In all of these characteristics, signification shows that it imposes itself upon me as having come from the other *by giving itself as capable of not giving itself* I only receive it because it very much wants to give itself and because it arises from the ground of an elsewhere (that which I await ever since the question "Does anyone out there love me?") that I cannot even dream of producing, or provoking, or even invoking. Signification does not come upon me here in a way that is like that of all the other phenomena, from the ground of the unseen and thus from the world and from its original opening; signification, when it consents to put itself into play, issues from another world—or better, not even from a world, but from an other more exterior to me than any world, because the other, too, defines a world (or indeed, henceforward he or she is the first to do so). In the erotic phenomenon, it is not solely a question of an inversion of the relationship between intuition and signification; but rather the gift of an unconstitutable signification, unforeseeable and absolutely exterior to my lover's intuition (loving to love in advance), by an *ego* that catches me because I did not foresee it, cannot expect it, and will never comprehend it. The amorous phenomenon is not constituted beginning from the pole of the *ego* that I am; it arises of itself by crossing within itself the lover (I, who renounce the status of the autarkic *ego* and bring my intuition) and the other (she who imposes her signification by opposing her distance). The erotic phenomenon appears not just in common to her and to me, and without a unique egoic pole, but it also appears only in this crossing. *A crossed phenomenon.*

In order for such a crossed phenomenon to be accomplished, the signification that has come through counterintentionality must not fall short of my intuition. How does this signification give itself? Surely not by an intuition in which I ought to see something real—which the other, by definition, can never be. On the contrary, the signification of the other gives itself without ever becoming an available thing, but, rather, insofar as it consents to abandon itself, insofar as it gives itself as being able not to give itself. It gives itself while saying that it gives itself, *as if* it were giving itself and *as capable of not giving itself.* The other can only give her signification of herself by signifying to me, in speech or in silence, "Here I am, your signification." In order to signify to me this signification, a moment is nevertheless not enough, for it must fix over time my lover's vague erotic intuition. It is thus necessary that the other signify to me, "Here I am, your signification" not only in time, but for a period of time that fixes me—thus a time without delay, or restriction, or assignable limit. The signification only imposes itself upon me if it gives itself without foreseeing taking itself back, and thus gives itself in self-abandonment with condition, or return, or prescription. "Here I am!" only gives a signification to my erotic intuition by daring to claim to give itself without holding hack, without return—forever. The other thus must not only say to me, "Here I am!" in the moment, but she must also promise it for every moment still to come. She must not tell me the signification, she must promise it to me. The signification, which alone allows my intuition to make the phenomenon of the other appear to me, arises like an *oath*—or it is forever lacking.

For only this oath allows the full erotic phenomenon at last to be put on stage: henceforward intuition, which is put forth in the immanence of the lover who is in the situation of the radicalized reduction, is docked with the signification that the face of the other assigns to it. In this way a fully achieved phenomenon is constituted, one that nevertheless offers two exceptional characteristics in comparison with the majority of other phenomena. To begin with, this new type of transcendence does not confer upon the phenomenon its fulfilling intuition, but rather its signification. Next, what transcends the immanence of my *ego* here no longer refers back to a region of the world, but still to an *ego*, that of a supposed other; this phenomenon without equivalent no longer plays between an *ego* and the world, but between two *egos* outside of the world. Should we still even speak of *a* phenomenon? What does it manifest, if I not only do not master the signification (the noematic face), but two *egos* frame it and confer upon it two distinct intuitions, so to speak (two competing noeses)? Formally a single response seems possible: neither of the two *egos* can see the other in the strict sense of receiving its intuition as that of a phenomenon of the world, in order to fill the signification that it would have first fixed—as if the other would intuitively confirm the intentional aim that I would have already taken at her beforehand and, eventually; without her; each *ego* must here attempt to fix its erotic intuition, immanent and deployed in advance, upon a signification received from the other. The common erotic phenomenon will thus not consist of a new visible or a common spectacle: since two intuitions of opposed and irreducible origin enter into play, there will appear to each of these two *egos* a different phenomenon, filled with a different intuition and presenting another visible (precisely, the visible *ego*, which inverts the seeing *ego*).

The common phenomenon, instead, will consist in the unique signification, to which two intuitions come to moor themselves—because each *ego* assures the other, by oath, with a unique signification, "Here I am!" Of course, the other does not appear to me as an immediately visible spectacle (she would thus regress to the rank of an object); rather, she appears to me insofar as she lends herself to the function of a signification, which fixes and finally secures my erotic intuition. And reciprocally, I only appear to an eventual other by lending myself to the function of signification, which will assign what has up to that point been a vague erotic intuition to a fixed phenomenal site. The two *egos* are accomplished as lovers, and mutually allow their respective phenomena to appear, not of course according to an imaginary and fusional logic—by exchanging or sharing a common intuition—which would abolish the distance between them, but by assuring one another reciprocally of a signification come from elsewhere—by lending themselves to the play of a crossed exchange of significations—thus, firmly consecrating the distance within them.

Must we still speak of a common phenomenon, or, rather, of two distinct phenomena? Neither: we speak of a *crossed phenomenon*, with a double entry—two intuitions fixed by a single signification. One signification, and not two; for each of the two *egos* lends itself to the same operation and gives itself as one and the same signification, "Here I am!" In effect, no *ego* claims to describe itself empirically like a *me* endowed with such and such properties, but means to reduce itself to the pure assertion "Here I am!" Each of the *egos* assures the other of the same and unique signification—that which my immanent erotic intuition requires and to which I lend myself by assuring in an oath, "Here I am!" The two *egos* do not join together in a common, directly visible intuition, but rather in a common signification that is indirectly put into phenomenality by two irreducible intuitions. A single phenomenon, because a single signification; yet a phenomenon that nonetheless has a double entry, because manifested according to two intuitions.

The lover thus does see the unique phenomenon, which he loves and which loves him, by the grace of this oath.

The Creation of the Self

§38. The Aporia of the Place

Creation does not come at the beginning, but after and within praise because it alone can and wants to interpret visible things as endowed with a beginning, therefore as created. There would not be any possibility of seeing the world as heaven and earth created by God if one did not first consent to praising God as God. Praise thus sets forth the *liturgical* condition for the possibility of recognizing creation—even if afterwards and almost anachronistically, one can obscure the praise and posit creation as an ontic commencement. But this reversal of the real and primordial liturgical order into a cosmological order reconstituted *a posteriori* remains, even if it is convenient to accept, a methodological artifice and as such deprived of even the least bit of legitimacy in the eyes of the *confessio*. Creation does not render *confessio* possible, as the ontic place for its enactment, but it itself becomes possible only starting with *confessio*, its liturgical preliminary. In a word, in and through its praise of God, *confessio* gives its first place to the creation of heaven and earth, not the inverse. Thus we understand the extent to which the question to which creation responds has nothing ontic or ontological about it. This question asks about the liturgical and therefore theological conditions for the praise of God and considers creation only as an output of the hermeneutic operation of praise—in and through the interpretation of heaven and earth *as* created and *as* silently proclaiming not themselves but God.

It is therefore necessary to begin by fixing the place of creation in praise if one wants later, by derivation, to see creation itself as a place. In fact, from the very opening of the *Confessiones* (in I, 1, 1), the issue has always been to deduce a place starting from praise. For if God gives himself as *laudabilis valde*, as he who is par excellence fit to praise, a question arises: how to praise him seeing as we do not know him and, in fact, he must first announce himself to us for us to invoke him: "*Prae*dicatus enim es nobis" [You were said to us *in advance*]? We can therefore praise him (say him) only in response to his own announcement of himself (his prediction), such that praising him amounts to calling him upon oneself: "Quaeram te, Domine, *in*vocans te et invocem te credens te" [I want, Lord, to seek you by invoking you and to invoke you by believing in you] (I, 1, 1, 13, 275). But what does it mean to *in*voke or to praise by *in*voking, if not to call God to come into myself, "*in me* ipsum eum invocabo, cum *in*vocabo ipsum"? This coming of God into myself, which turns out to be the sole posture praise can adopt, supposes that I myself have the status of an open place for God to come into; but who am I to pretend to constitute a place when faced with God? "Et quis locus est in me, quo veniat in me Deus meus? Quo Deus veniat in me, Deus, qui lecit caelum et terram?" [And what place is there in me where my God might come into me? In what corner would God into me, God who made heaven and earth?] (I, 2, 2, 13, 274). A contradiction arises here: I have no other place in me besides the one that God made, therefore God cannot come into me without my first coming into him or discovering myself always already in him: I am not a place for God; rather I take place in him. Praise cannot ask God to come into me, since I do not have a place to offer to him, where he would dwell as in his temple. In fact, of place, I have none other besides him, or more simply, besides the place that he himself has set up for me by creating heaven and earth. If praise there must be, it will call for an impossibility—that I come, myself, into its very own place, God—to wit, into God himself. "Et ego, quid peto, ut venias in me, qui non essem, nisi esses in me? . . . non ergo essem, nisi esses in me, an potius non essem, nisi essem in te, 'ex quo omnia, per quem omnia, in quo omnia'?" [And what is it that I imagine I am asking when I ask that you come into me, me who would not be if you were not in me? . . . For I would not be if you were not in me, or rather I would not be if I was not in you, you 'from whom all things come, by whom all things were made, in whom all things reside'] (Romans 11:36; I, 2, 2, 13, 276). Once again creation does not respond to the ontic or ontological question, since it precedes it and, at best, renders it conceivable, but always as a derivative, in a secondary set of considerations. The metaphysical interpretation of creation in fact supposes that the question of place has already been resolved, and in the basest manner conceivable: as the production of a world of beings by the exercise of an efficient causality. This interpretation quite simply does not see the difficulty, which resides in asking on the basis of what place a praise of the *laudabilis valde* can be set forth. The creation of heaven and earth (once again *not* the creation of the world, nor of beings, especially not subsistent) comes up only in order to respond to the original question, the *confessio.*

The absence in myself of the place for praise by *confessio* is illustrated by at least two aporiae. The first is almost self-evident. Since God created heaven and earth, he is found everywhere where heaven and earth are stretched out; in this sense, I find myself from the outset already in him. This does not, however, resolve the difficulty, which by contrast becomes all the more formidable: in finding myself in heaven and earth which come from him and are in him, I experience how great is the distance separating me from him; for, located in what is of, by, and in God, I do not discover myself exactly in, nor of, nor through God. I must, inversely, notice that God is not contained anywhere, especially not in what he created: "An non opus habes, ut quoquam continearis, qui contines omnia, quoniam quae imples continendo imples?" [Or is it that you have no need that some place contain you, since what you fill you fill by containing it yourself?] (I, 3, 3, 13, 276). As it seems unacceptable to conclude that one part of God is present in heaven and earth while another would remain outside—seeing as one thereby supposes a univocal spatialization of God in his creation, it must be concluded by contrast that "ubique totus es et res nulla te totum capit" [you are entirely everywhere without anything comprehending you] (I, 3, 3, 13, 278). But then even the creation of heaven and earth, far from opening for us a place to receive God, reveals him as all the more *secretissimus et praesentissimus*, at one and the same time the most secret and the most present (I, 4, 4, 13, 278). Hence, the aporia of the place where and whence God could be praised by our *confessio* imposes its utopia.

This way of crystallizing the difficulty in fixing a place by mere recourse to the creation of heaven and earth refers us to a second aporia: the most pressing and the most evident, since it has in fact all along haunted the path we have been traveling, in particular when we were tracking the anonymity of the *ego* and the immemorial (chap. II, §12; chap. III, §16). The utopia of heaven and earth seems, throughout Saint Augustine's itinerary, like a repetition (in Book XII) and an anticipation (in Book I) of the most constant utopia, that of the self: the creation of heaven and earth leaves me without place for praise because, more essentially, I know of no place (*ubi*), permitting me to dwell anywhere, much less in myself. If I do not offer a place where God can come, this is not first or only on account of my sin rendering me uninhabitable to his holiness,[1] but on account of a constitutive utopia of my finitude, that sin only orchestrates. We have already seen this once before in the gaps that sometimes arise between myself and myself to the point of alienating me from myself. For example, when the pain of losing a friend makes me hate all other things ("oderam omnia"), ones which nevertheless make up my own life ("mihi patria supplicum et parterna domus mihi infelicitas" [my homeland becomes a torture and the house of my father a great unhappiness]), to the point of transforming my own evidence into a question to myself—"factus eram mihi magna quaestio" (IV, 4, 9, 13, 422). Or again when the temptation to prefer, in listening to a song, the musical pleasure over the liturgical praise makes me no longer know who I truly am, that is to say *where* I am truly going with my desire, I discover myself once again outside myself: "mihi quaestio factus sum" [I become for myself a great question] (X, 33, 50, 14, 232). I can appear to myself as so frequent a question only because I do not in fact frequent myself—I lack access to myself, there where I truly dwell. My alienation in these crises attests that I do not know where to recover myself because, in fact, I do not have any proper place, because I no longer have *place* for myself nor for a *self*.

The same utopia leads me astray also in the exercise of *memoria*. In its first sense, this faculty offers the *place* par excellence for the mind since, in it, *here*, everything we think is buried ("Ibi reconditum est, quidquid etiam cogitamus") in such a way that, here, I am even able to make reappear at will what is past ("*Ibi* quando sum, posco, ut preferatur quidquid volo," X, 8, 12, 14, 162). I can always therefore, in the normal course of things, encounter myself *here* ("*Ibi* mihi et ipse occurro meque recolo," X, 8, 14, 14, 166). In remembering everything, I dwell in myself, I have a place. But strangely (or, like a stranger) what is proper to my memory, to this *place* more my own than any other, consists also in that I am not always in command of it, since sometimes it dispossesses me of myself and does not come back to me: "Ecce memoriae meae vis non comprehenditur a me" [and look, the strength of my own memory is not something I comprehend], precisely when I do not remember or, worse, do not even remember having forgotten. Hence, I suffer from myself, because I no longer recover myself *here*, because the place is missing precisely there where I find myself, "laboro *hic* et laboro *in* me ipso" (X 16, 25, 14, 184). In other words, I no longer know what I am because I no longer know *where* I am. "Nec ego ipse capio totum, quod sum. Ergo animus ad nabendum se ipsum angustus est, ut ubi sit quod sui non capiat? Numquid extra ipsum se ac non in ipso?" [I do not know myself entirely what I am. The mind is too narrow to contain itself, so narrow that it does not know where to find what is its own [its place]? Would it find it outside itself and no longer *in* itself?] (X, 8, 15, 14, 166). I do not give *place* to myself.

The utopia runs still deeper. For there is still one place, just one, *where* I know that I find myself, at least *where* I would like absolutely to find myself, but this is the one place that I am incapable of reaching. That is, all men desire beatitude, unconditionally, but no one even knows *where* his knowledge of it comes from: "Nonne ipsa est beata vita, quam omnes volunt et omnino qui nolit, nemo est? Ubi noverunt eam, quod sic volunt eam? Ubi viderunt, ut amarent eam?" [Isn't it the good life itself that all men want to the point that nobody, absolutely nobody can be found who does not want it? *Where* then did they know it so that they want it so? *Where* did they see it to love it so?] (X, 20, 29, 14, 194). Not only do I admit as radically my own only the sole *place* that I know I cannot reach by myself, but I do not even know *where* I got the knowledge that I have of it since I absolutely do not know it. I do not even know from *where* it came to me, the *place where* I desire to find myself came to me and *where* I know I cannot find myself.

Now, I who no longer have a place for myself (the *quaestio*), I who no longer give place to myself (*memoria*), I who do not know from where the place of my desire comes to me, I hear it named everywhere, provided that I no longer listen to myself but to heaven and earth *inasmuch as created*. For, if the things of the world remain mute so long as one interprets them as apparently subsisting beings (in fact, even this mindless thick-headedness already demands an interpretation, though it is ignorant of this), they say, in a loud and understandable voice, their place as soon as one succeeds (in fact, accepts) in hearing them as they say themselves, as creatures. At once, "si quis audiat, dicunt haec omnia: 'Non ipsa nos fecimus, sed fecit nos qui manet in aeternum'" [if someone listens, they all say, 'We are not made by ourselves, but he, he alone made us, he who remains for eternity'] (Psalm 99:3, 5; IX, 10, 25, 14, 118).[2] By proclaiming in a silent, but piercing, voice that they do not subsist in themselves, that they do not have a *place* in themselves, heaven and earth make plain that they arise from an other place besides their self, and this tacit yet evident acknowledgment is in fact already equivalent to praise—that is to say, to the mode of *confessio* that is appropriate for them. But, at the same time, heaven and earth, in proclaiming their utopia, overcome it, by recognizing it transform it from *quaestio* into response. Into a response not only to the *quaestio* of their place (the place consists in an other place besides the self), but in general to the possibility of praise. Hence, since the interpretation of heaven and earth as created does not come from them, but from my interpretation of the world as not subsisting in itself and referring to its utopia, creation (its hermeneutic as created) appears as the response to the *quaestio* about my possibility of praise and *confessio*—by no means, once again, a response to the investigation that wants to know why there is something rather than nothing.

The possibility of *confessio* thus opens when the utopia (I no longer have place for myself, I no longer give a place to myself and I do not know from where the place of my desire comes over me) is no longer fixed in itself, no longer closed on itself, no longer withdrawn as aporia, but itself becomes the response: when the *not-here* appears as an other place, or rather an other place, an alteration that displaces the place outside itself, outside even the self, in such a way as to open the *over-there* as my place. "Sed ubimanes in memoria mea, Domine, *ubi illic* manes?" [But where do you reside in this memory that is called mine, O Lord, *where* do you reside *over there*?] (X, 25, 36, 14, 205). For me (therefore, on the basis of my hermeneutic of the world as created, also for all things), the only *here* is *over there* such that I find myself when I head off for *there where I am not.* The desire for beatitude (therefore desire as such, since desire always desire beatitude) saves me only because it enjoins me to leave. To leave from what, if not from the self, which clings to its *here*? Toward what in me, if not toward *over there*? To turn to God (which one calls, without fully understanding what one says, conversion) designates first of all the exodus from the *ubi* toward an *illic*—which means of course that I am only because I arrive in him by praise: "Et ego dico: Deus meus *ubi* es? Ecce *ubi* es. Respiro *in te* 'paululum,' cum 'effundo super me animam mean in voce exsultationis et confessionis.'" [And I say, my God, *where* are you? But look *where* you are: I breathe 'a little' *in you*, when I pour out 'over myself my soul in a voice that exults and confesses'] (Psalms 41:8; XIII 14, 15, 14, 450). But this suggests above all that I am in him only because, in the first place, he is in me and that in this way the *illic*, over-there, precedes and renders possible derivatively an *ubi*, here, for me. For me, every *ubi* becomes an *illic*, which neither remains nor ever becomes again an *ibi*—I am in my place (*ubi*) only by not remaining in it as in a closed *here*, by forever passing elsewhere (*illic*). "Et ecce intus eras et ego foris, et *ibi* quarebam. . . . Mecum eras et tecum non eram." [And behold you were inside [the place to reside], and I myself was outside, and I sought you *here*. . . . You were with me, but I myself was not with you.] (X, 27, 38, 14, 208). The truth resides in my interior, but not in me, because *I am not inside myself,* because my interior remains exterior so long as I do not become interior to my exterior itself. This reversal of the *here* and *over there* is not equivalent to the presence in me of God or a piece of the divine, but indicates that I reach myself only by taking place *over there*—in this case, in God. For I have no place to take place so long as I stubbornly dwell *here*—in other words, stubbornly will that my *ubi* reside where I am, *ibi*: "Non ego vita mea sim: male vixi ex me, mors mihi fui: *in te* revivisco. I am not myself my own life. On my own, I lived woefully, I was a death to myself. I return to life in you" (XII, 10, 10, 14, 358).[3] Life, like the happy life, defines my place, which in both cases is found *over there.*

By converting the place, creation therefore offers, in the form of a hermeneutic of heaven and earth, but also of man, a response to the question of the possibility of praise. With it, the aporia of the place becomes, just like autopia, the very posture of *confessio.*

§39. The Site of *Confessio*

Creation therefore responds to the question of the possibility of *confessio*, and creation gives place to *confessio* by defining *where* those who must do so—in other words, all that is not confused with God—can do so. Creation does not define only what happens to be created, but first of all that in view of which the created is created—accomplishing a *confessio* by praise of the creator. Creation gives place (*ubi*) to *confessio* by opening the dimensions where the created can direct itself toward the creator of a *here* (*ibi*) turning toward an *over-there* (*illic*). Three such dimensions can be specified, and this enables us to designate the site.

The first dimension opens out toward nothingness on the basis of the earth. More exactly, it is detected as early as the first reading of the verse that comments on the beginning ("In the beginning, God created the heaven and the earth") by adding: "And the earth was obscure and empty, *inanis et vacua*" (Genesis 1:2). Or rather, for that is the version of the Vulgate about which he was ignorant (or which he refused), St. Augustine prefers to reproduce literally the translation of the Septuagint: ἀόρατος καὶ ἀκατασκεύαστος, *invisibilis et incomposita*.[4] This choice does indeed seem better since, instead of two redundant terms (giving rise to inevitably loose translations), it lets us distinguish two different characteristics of the earth. First, it appears without form because it remains at bottom unorganized, without structure or composition. If what is at issue is indeed the original, primal earth, truly that of the beginning (*primitus*), then this notion implies logically (*consequenter*) that it is still without form or composition: "ipsa terra, quam primitus facit, sicut Scriptura consequenter eloquitur, invisibilis et incomposita" (*De Civitate Dei*, XI, 9, 35, 56ff). Whence the paradoxical consequence that if we are talking about the earth of creation, but of a "creation birth and without memory" (Péguy),[5] then it is not a matter of the earth such as we see it, since we now see only forms in it: "non erat talis, qualem nunc cernimus et tangimus. Invisibilis enim erat et incomposita et abyssus erat" [it was not such as we see and touch it today, for it was invisible and not composed; it was an abyss] (*Confessiones* XII, 8, 8, 14, 354). But if it is an issue of an "informitas sine ulla specie" [a formless absence of form] (XII 3, 5, 14, 348), then it is no longer a question of our earth, but of "informis material" [formless matter] (XII, 15, 22, 16, 376). The earth such as we know it would not have been created if, more originally and even though the biblical text does not mention it explicitly, matter had not also been and at the same time. The creation of the earth as formless and without composition implies that of matter. This implication has at least two consequences.

First, if primary matter is created, Augustine's doctrine breaks, despite all the similarities one would like to point out, with the Greek position (from Plato to Plotinus), by removing matter from the rank of principle. Whence an argument that proves decisive, though derivative, against the Manicheans: since *materia* comes, by creation, from God, it cannot constitute a principle of evil, because more essentially it does not constitute any principle whatsoever:

Neque enim vel illa materies, quam ὕλη antiqui dixerant, malum dicenda sit. Nam eam dico, quam Manicheus ὕλην appellat dementissima vanitate, nesciens quid loquatur, formatricem corporum: unde recte illi dictum est, quod alterum deum inducat: nemo enim formare et creare corpora nisi Deus potest. . . . Sed ὕλην dico quandam penitus informem et sine qualitate materiam, unde istae, quas sentimus, qualitates formantur, ut antiqui dixerunt. Hinc enim et silva graece ὕλη dicitur, quod operentibus apta sit, non ut aliquid ipsa faciat, sed unde aliquid fiat.

For even this hat the Ancients called ὕλη should not be called evil. I am not speaking of this ὕλην that Manes, in his demented vanity, not knowing what he was saying, claimed was formative of bodies, from which it was correctly concluded that he was introducing another god, for nobody can form and create bodies except God. . . . But I myself call ὕλην a certain formless matter without quality from which the qualities that we sense take form, as the Ancients said. Hence in Greek the wood to be worked is called ὕλη because it is of service to the workers, not because it itself makes something, but on account of the fact that it is that out of which something is made.[6]

Thus the earth presupposes matter, but matter itself presupposes creation. Therefore matter offers no place, neither to the earth nor to the *confessio*, but it receives itself just like all the other things (even if it does not yet have the rank of thing) in itself for the sake of working the *confessio*.

But there is more: since matter has no place in the world and since it gives no place to the world, from where does it get its place? It can get it only from an other instance, yet more empty, invisible, and formless than it, for there is no longer any to be found: "Citius enim non esse censebam, quod omni forma privaretur, quam cogitabam quiddam inter formam et nihil nec formatum nec nihil, informe prope nihil." [I would sooner admit the nonbeing of what had no form than I would think something between form and nothing, neither formed nor nothing, formless next to nothing.] (XII, 6, 6, 14, 350). On the hither side of matter, just at the limit of nothing, ("illud totum prope nihil erat . . . jam tamen erat"), nearly nullified ("de nulla re paene nullam rem"; XII, 8, 8, 14, 354), is found nothing other than nothing itself; and therefore "fecisti aliquid et de nihilo" [you made something even of nothing, out of and *with* nothing] (XII, 7, 7, 14, 352). It is a good idea, in other words, to use the two possible translations of *de nihilo*, for God does not merely create *out of* (*ex*) nothing in such a way as to exit from it and substitute for it being (after nothing comes being); he above all created *with* (*de*) nothingness so as to make being with, in material guise, nothingness itself. Nothingness, in the figure of *de nihilo*, does not hold merely the place of starting point for the created (as that from which it would have exited); it also holds the place of its material (as that of which it will always remain woven). The created does not emerge from nothing except by assuming it again at the heart of its very beingness. It should then be said, in a transitive sense, that the created is its nothingness and that it is so because God gives it to it: the created is its nothingness only because it is so *by* God, "*abs te*, a quo sunt omnia" (XII, 7,7,7, 14, 352). God, in creating the created, does not abolish nothingness in it, but assigns this very nothing to the created in assuming it as created *by* him. The *de nihilo* is understood and thought together with the *a Deo*. The *a Deo* balances, maintains, and subverts the de nihilo. "*De nihilo enim a te*, non de te facta sunt, non de aliqua non tua vel quae antea fuerit, sed de concreata, id est simul *a te* creata materia, quia ejus informitatem sine ulla temporis interpositione formasti . . . . Materiem quidem *de omnino nihilo . . .* fecisti." [*With* nothing, not *with* you, that is things were made *by* you, not *with* a matter not created by you or already there, but *with* concrete matter, because you formed the formless in it without the slightest temporal delay . . . . You truly did make matter *absolutely with nothing.*] (XIII, 38, 48, 14, 516ff).[7] In this sense, creation does not, strictly speaking, confer Being on the created, but permits it to assume its nothingness so as to male it work at the *confessio.* Here what is is not absolutely, as if God remained an optional complement to the act of Being; to the contrary, here what is is only optionally, inasmuch as created and insofar as the *de nihilo* remains thought together with the *a Deo,* therefore is oriented to the *confessio.* The created remains an intermittent being, under contract to time, marching to the beat of a time determined by its praise:

> Et inspexi caetera infra te et vidi nec omnino esse, nec omnino non esse: esse quidem, quoniam ab te sunt, non esse autem, quoniam id quod es non sunt . . . . Si non manebo in illo, nec in me potero.

> I considered the other things beneath you and I saw that they neither are absolutely nor are not absolutely. They are, of course, since they are from you, but they are not, since they are not what you are . . . . If I do not remain in him (God, my good), I will not be able to do it in myself either. (VII, 11, 17, 13, 618)

Creation, which presents itself first as an event and an advent (chap. V, §35), also sets up a condition—the status of what does not take place in itself, but in a nothing that sustains and cuts across an other than itself. In a sense, every created thing says: "Non ergo vita mea sim" [It is not I who am my own life] (XII, 10, 10, 14, 358).

A second dimension can also open a site for the *confessio,* this time in terms of the heavens—or more exactly, the "heaven of the heavens." That is, from his first reading of the verse "In the beginning, God created the heavens and the earth," Saint Augustine read it together with a surprising formulation found in Psalm 113:15–16, which itself already comments on Genesis 1:1: "Domino qui fecit caelum et terram, caelum caeli Domino, terram autem dedit filiis hominum." [Lord who made heaven and earth, the heaven of the heavens belongs to Him; the earth, he gave to the sons of men.] There ineluctably follows an investigation concerning place: "*Ubi* est caelum, quod non cernimus, cui terra est hoc omne, quod cernimus? . . . Sed ad illud 'caelum caeli' etiam terrae nostrae caelum, terra est." [*Where* is the heaven that we do not see, by relation to which all that we see is earth(ly)? . . . But, in relation to this 'heaven of the heavens,' even the heavens of our earth are earth(ly).] (XII, 2, 2, 14, 346). Even if the hypothesis of a τόπος νοητός has a long tradition, it falls to St. Augustine alone to have elaborated this isolated, indeed marginal, biblical phrase into a concept of great importance. Just as the earth, once reinterpreted as *invisibilis et incomposita,* becomes matter and even the *nihil* of the *de nihilo,* in such a way as to give place for praise, so too do the heavens, once overinterpreted as *caelum caeli,* give another place for praise. The difficulty of this place stems from the imprecise, indeed contradictory determinations, which render it all the more strange.[8] It would seem at first that we are dealing with just an equivalent of the (Plotinian, indeed Aristotelian) νοῦς, since the title of a *caelum intelligibile* (XII, 21, 30, 14, 390) is associated with that of *mens pura* (XII, 11, 12, 14, 360) or *mens rationalis et intellectualis* (XII, 15, 20, 14, 372), sometimes in the same sequence: "caelum intellectuale, *ubi* intellectus nosse simul, non 'ex parte, non in aenigmate, non per speculum, sed ex toto,' in manifestatione, 'facie ad faciem'" [intelligible heavens, *where* the understanding goes together with knowing, not 'in part, enigmatically, in a reflection, but totally,' fully manifest, 'face to face'] (1 Corinthians 13:12; XII, 13, 16, 14, 366). It is about the place where the knowledge of God becomes manifest and evident (but evidently not adequate). And yet, the situation proves to be more complex since this intellectual evidence still comes from the created: the intelligible heavens still remain a *creatura aliqua intellectualis* (XII, 9, 9, 14, 356). They contemplate God as such, without sensible intermediary, but always from the point of view and within the essential limits of the created: "profecto sapientia, quae creata est, intellectualis natura scilicet, quae contemplatione luminis lumen est—dicitur enim et ipsa, quamvis creata, sapientia" [wisdom, which is created, intellectual nature to be sure, but wisdom which is light only by contemplating the light—it too is therefore said to be wisdom, though created] (XII, 15, 20, 14, 372).[9] No gnostic temptation can insinuate itself here, therefore, since the contemplation, even purely intellectual, of God remains marked by the distance of the created from the uncreated, a distance that does not so much safeguard the divine privilege as it maintains the created in its possibility of praising. Thus, *confessio* alone unites with God, not mere knowledge, which remains only a means and a mode of it. Consequently, no distinction seems any longer to institute itself explicitly between the intellects united in this place, establishing hierarchies, for example among men and the angels or among the angels themselves, as if their differences blur here in the single office of *confessio*. This function alone is enough to characterize a commonplace *where* the intelligent created (human or angelic) praises God inasmuch as intelligible.

We are therefore dealing with a place, but one that embraces indifferently the angelic choirs (celestial hierarchy), the terrestrial church (ecclesiastical hierarchy), the eschatological mass of the elect, the intelligible heavens, indeed the world of idealities, provided that the *confessio* of God the intelligible is put into operation everywhere by intellectual creatures. Thus this place receives explicitly the title of place par excellence, of *domus tua* and *civitas tua* (XII, 11, 12, 14, 360),[10] that must be understood as the house or the city where God can come and dwell *as* God, without being disfigured, blasphemed, and killed. God can *descend* into the "heaven of the heavens," as one descends into a city, in order to sojourn or holiday there. For this city should not be understood as God's proper place, his everyday residence, nor the city where he would be at home, but as the sojourn where he lets one come and meet or see him. Thus these houses and this city do *not* belong to eternity, for the very purpose that we, we men like the other intelligent creatures, might have access to them. The "heaven of the heavens" draws as close as possible to the eternity of God, but does not enjoy it, neither fully nor directly. This residence of God does not reside in God, therefore does not share his eternity, *domus Dei, non quidem Deo coaeterna* (XII, 15, 22, 14, 374). Between the "heaven of the heavens" and the eternity of God, things are never so intimate as to reach co-eternity, but an exteriority always remains open for participation: "domus Dei non terrena neqe ulla caelesti mole corporea, sed spiritualis et particeps aeternitatis tuae" [the house of God, not terrestrial and not bodily, not even a celestial body, but spiritual and taking part in your eternity] (XII, 15,

19, 14, 370). And yet, this intellectual but not eternal place for the praise of the intelligible manifests a new mode of temporality for the creature. For, though not eternal because not coeternal with God ("nec illa creatura tibi coaeterna est" XII, 11, 12, 14, 360), the "heaven of the heavens" benefits, if not solely at least first of all and in the name of the other creatures, from the privilege of not being submitted to time ("nec in illa invenimus tempus," XII, 15, 21, 14, 374). Or at least to time understood in the derived and devastated mode of *distensio*: "supergreditur enim omnem *distensionem* et omne spatium" [it overcomes all *distension* and space] (XII, 15, 22, 14, 376). The "heaven of the heavens" therefore appears, inasmuch as the place for intelligible praise, as a place free from distraction (from *distenso*). Does its privilege in space therefore bring with it a privilege in time? How to explain this new consideration and formulation?

The text adds that the "heaven of the heavens" is liberated from distraction *and* from space. But why space, since distraction refers in book XI to time? Because, no doubt, distraction is the definition of the time distended by temporal ecstases, ecstases that, themselves obliged to be distended and distending, *spatialize* time, to the point of distending it and dispersing it according to the model of space (see chap. V, §36). It must therefore be understood that while all the other creatures are strictly worldly and decline their temporality according to the most widespread and powerful model—namely, space *partes extra partes*—thereby deploying their time only by dispersing it and distending the mind in it, the "heaven of the heavens" makes an exception—precisely and to the degree that it participates in eternity (without however becoming annexed to it), it succeeds, "sine ulla vicissitudine temporum" [without the least variation in time] (XII, 13, 16, 14, 366), in deploying an intentional temporality ("secundum intentionem," XI, 29, 39, 14, 338). It can do this, however, only by letting itself be affected and taken up by the eternity that it does not possess: "te sibi semper praesente, ad quem toto affectu se tenet, non habens futurum quod expectet nec in praeteritum trajiciens quod meminerit, nulla vice varietur nec in tempora ulla *distenditur*" [holding present to you with all its (creation's) affection, you who always remains present to it, it has no more future to expect, nor past to cross in order to remember, it no longer varies with any change nor is *distracted* and pulled apart into any times] (XII, 11, 12, 14, 360). The "heaven of the heavens" overcomes the distension of time with an intention only insofar as it tends toward the divine eternity, therefore insofar as it adheres to it—tension by adherence: "cohaerentem Deo vero et vere aeterno, ut, quamvis coaeterna non sit, in nullam tamen temporum varietatem et vicissitudinem ab illo se resolvat et defluat" [*adhere to God*, the true and truly eternal, so that without being coeternal with him, it (this sublime creature, the 'heaven of the heavens') is nevertheless never unstuck from him and does not flow out in any alteration or change of time] (XII, 15, 19, 14, 370).

In fact, the privilege of the "heaven of the heavens" explains the situation of all creatures. Distraction (or temporal distension) characterizes them all by virtue of a more essential and all-encompassing, therefore also spatializing, mutability: "quia non *de* ipsa substantia Dei, sed *ex* nihilo cuncta facta sunt, quia non sunt id ipsum, quod Deus et *inest quaedam mutabilitas* omnibus, sive *maneant* sicut aeterna domus, sive mutentur, sicut anima hominis et corpus" [because none of them are made *of* [i.e., *with*] the very substance of God, but *out of* nothing such that *some inherent mutability is still in them*, whether they *settle* like the eternal mansion ('heaven of the heavens') or change like the soul of man and his body] (XII 17, 25, 14, 380ff). For all, the one question becomes how to reach a dwelling place where they settle down despite their natural (created) mutability. That cannot come about through yet another natural immutability (since eternity characterizes the uncreated alone); it will therefore have to happen through a disposition that is not natural but free and decided—an adherence through love: "inest ei tamen ipsa mutabilitas, unde tenebresceret et frigesceret, nisi *amore grandi tibi cohaerens,* tanquam semper meridies luceret et ferveret ex te" [the mutability is still in it ('the heaven of the heavens'), which could make it grow dark and cold, if it does not *adhere to you by a great love,* like a noonday always shining and burning with you] (XII, 15, 21, 14, 374). The creature, following the model of the "heaven of the heavens," should not overcome the distraction of time by trying not to yield to spatial (spatializing, spatialized) changes, through a correction of its nature (Manicheanism), nor by a supernatural knowledge (Gnosticism), but by a loving adhesion to God, in which, as an extra, it will also find cohesion with itself. This does not mean passing beyond time so as to pass unto eternity, but surpassing the incoherence of distraction in and through love of the divine permanence, in a tension that itself still remains temporal. In this way, the "heaven of the heavens" at last, after having been called *domus tua* and *civitas tua,* assumes the eschatological name *new Jerusalem,* which descends from the heavens to the earth: "recordans Hierusalem *extento in eam* sursum corde, Hierusalem patriam meam, Hierusalem matrem meam, teque super eam regnatorem" [remembering Jerusalem *stretched out toward it* with all my heart, Jerusalem my homeland, Jerusalem my mother, and toward you who rules over it].[11] In this way the "heaven of the heavens" provides the paradigm for every place of praise for every creature because, though instituted from the first day of creation, it also takes on eschatological status: place for all confessions, therefore place for all the loving adhesions to God's unalterability, arbiter of my confessions, "arbiter inter *confessiones meas*" (XII, 16, 23, 14, 378).

It now becomes possible to see a third dimension of the place of *confessio.* Or more exactly, to advance an interpretation of the concluding books of the *Confessiones* as themselves constituting a place, opening the place par excellence for every word that would like to be said as *confessio.* These three books are, in effect, organized, at least they can be read as being organized, trinitarily: each of them takes up in one of the figures of the Trinity (*Trinitas omnipotens,* XIII, 11, 12, 14, 442) one of the ecstases of time.[12] In this sense, *Confessiones* XI lays out the present of the past and the immensity of *memoria* in terms of the Father: "Omnia tempora tu fecisti et ante omnia tempora, tu es.—You made all of time, and before all time, you are" (XI, 13, 16, 14, 298). As for *Confessiones* XII, it lays out the present of the present, keeps in its *contuitus* the inaugural now of the creation of heaven and earth: "in Verbo suo sibi coaeterno fecit Deus intelligibilem atque sensibilem corporalemque creaturam" [it is in his coeternal Word that God made the creature endowed with intelligence, sensible therefore and corporeal] (XII, 20, 29, 14, 388), and that "*always* contemplates the face of God" [semper Dei faciem contemplantem] (XII, 17, 24, 14, 380). Finally, *Confessiones* XIII lays out the present of the future, the eschatological *expectatio,* because the Spirit from the beginning watches over our future: "et Spiritus thus bonus superferatur ad subveniendum nobis in tempore oportuno" [and your good

Spirit hovered (over the waters) so that it could come to our assistance when the time comes] (XIII, 34, 49, 14, 518).

"Heaven of the heavens" and creation *de nihilo* therefore attempt to define the place *where*, or more exactly *from where*, the *confessio* can be lifted up. In fact, these places turn out, in the end, to be trinitarian: it becomes possible to praise God as God only if God himself gives the place and time for it. And *where* else would that be except in God himself?

§40. Resemblance Without Definition

So, the creature's place is not found in itself, but always in God, such that the place for the *confessio* of God is determined by and in God, to such an extent that creation consists only in the opening of the place of *confessio*. It is hence a universal rule. What remains for us to understand is how it is specified in the case of man.

The story of creation contains, on the sixth day and in the case of man, several peculiarities. If we admit the story as it is told in the *Vetus Latina*,[13] each created thing was created according to its kind, "secundum genus suum,"[14] in conformity with itself and itself alone. This version even emphasizes the self-identity of the individuation by kind when it adds "secundum similitudinem" (Genesis 1, 11), indeed, when it insists "secundum *suam* similitudinem" (Genesis 1, 11, 12). The created thing bears a likeness to itself; it resembles itself. In other words, the work of creation, which separates and distinguishes in order to open distance (thus setting the conditions for the blessing of the created by God, as well as those for the praise of God by the created), requires referring each creature to itself, such that it resembles nothing other than its own kind, its own species, its own aspect (*species*)—in short, nothing other than itself in its ultimate essence. But, this is not how things go in the case of the creation of man. First, because in the story of his creation, the mention of kind (or of species) disappears: there is no reference of *this* created thing to its own proper essence: "Cur ergo et de homine non ita dictum est 'Faciamus hominem ad imaginem et similitudinem nostram *secundum genus*,' cum et hominis propago manifesta est?" [Why then did he not also say with regard to man: 'let us make man in our image and likeness *according to his kind*,' since man, too, obviously reproduces (according to his kind)?][15] This modification does not involve some threat of no longer being able to reproduce (as a consequence of the first sin, for example) since what immediately follows is the blessing of his fruitfulness (Genesis 1:28: "Increase and multiply"). The sole explanation would come from the appearance of Eve, who shows up on the margins and as an exception to the species of the primordial *man*, so to speak. In order to understand this first peculiarity of the story of the creation of man (and woman), a second, still more explicit one should be considered. In Genesis 1:26, creation no longer happens according to the creature's resemblance *to itself* ("secundum *suam* similitudinem"), but according to its resemblance *to an other* besides itself—and moreover, to an other of maximum alterity, since it is a reference to God: "non jam secundum genus, tanquam imitantes praecedentem proximum, nec ex hominis melioris auctoritate viventes. Neque enim dixisti: 'Fiat homo secundum genus,' sed: Taciamus hominem ad imaginem et similtudinem *nostram*,' ut nos probemus, quae sit voluntas tua." [No longer according to a kind, as if we imitated some precedent nearby or lived under the authority of some man better (than us). For you did not say: 'let man be according to his kind,' but: 'let us make man in our image and likeness,' so that we might know by the trial what your will is] (*Confessiones* XIII, 22, 32, 14, 482). Not only does the phrase *ad similitudinem nostram* literally contradict *secundum suam similitudinem*, but it is also substituted for kind (or species)—that is to say, it holds the place, in the case of man, of any and every definition: "Nec dicis *secundum genus*, sed *ad imaginem et similitudinem nostrum*" [You did not say *according to its kind* [ours], but *according to the image and likeness* (yours)] (XIII, 22, 32, 14, 484). Whence this paradoxical consequence: man constitutes a creature par excellence and even particularly excellent, precisely because he does not have a kind or species proper to him, therefore does not have a definition that would appropriate him to himself. Man is defined by the very fact that he remains without definition—the animal properly without property.

This is not just an incidental remark; it concerns what Saint Augustine does not hesitate to name a *mystery*, in the sense of the *magna quaestio* that man becomes for himself (chap. II, §10) and also in the sense of a sacrament by which God blesses man by creating him. "Sed quid est hoc et quale mysterium est? . . . Dicerem te, Deus noster, qui nos ad imaginem tuam creasti, dicerem te hoc donum benedictionis homini *proprie* volnisse largiri." [But what is this and what is this mystery? . . . I would say, our God, who created us in your image, I would say that you wanted to grant *properly* to man the gift of your *blessing*?] (XIII, 24, 35, 14, 490). However, Saint Augustine hesitates before this conclusion as the issue remains quite subtle. God also encouraged the animals to reproduce; he even blessed the fish of the sea (Genesis 1, 22). What then is particular to the blessing of fruitfulness given to man? No doubt precisely that: man alone receives from God a blessing of fruitfulness, while he did not receive a kind or species thanks to which he could naturally reproduce—reproduce *himself from himself.* This would mean that if man propagates himself over the entire earth to the point of dominating it, he owes this not to his kind or his species (which he does not have), nor to his essence (which remains unknown), but to a direct and ongoing blessing from God. In what does this consist? Evidently in substituting for kind and species the *ad imaginem et similitudinem nostram* in order to hold the place of the absent essence. Thus man does not increase according to his kind, his species and his essence—that is to say according to himself, but by the blessing come from elsewhere that sets him up from the get go in the likeness and in the image of an other than himself, God. Man does not increase by an essential and internal law, but solely by receiving God's blessing, a blessing that consists only in being disposed according to the image and likeness toward God. Man does not have a proper essence, but a reference to an other than himself, who, more intimate to him than himself (than his lacking essence), occupies the essential place on loan to him.

The image, by definition and essentially, can never provide an essence or a definition, which would be obtained by replicating, reproducing and imitating another essence or definition—all the more so here, as the image concerns that for which man does not, by definition and essentially, have the means to constitute the slightest bit of image: God. Here, and in the case of man more than in that of any of the others, the image remains impracticable; consequently, it has to be thought starting from the likeness (*similitudo*).

Obviously man does not bear the image of God as God, the Son, bears it toward God the Father through the connection of the Spirit, for only the Son is the image of the Father while man is found only *in* the image of God:

> Sed quia non omnino aequalis fiebat illa imago Dei tanquam non ab illo nata, sed ab illo creata, hujus rei significandae causa, ita imago est *ut ad imaginem* sit: id est, non aequaliter parilitate, sed *quadam similitudine* accedit. Non enim locorum intervallis, sed *similitudine* acceditur *ad* Deum, et dissimilitudine rededitur *ab eo*.

> But because this image of God [man] was not absolutely equal to him, since not born of him but created by him, so to make this point clear, this image is image *inasmuch as unto the image*—that is, it is not equal to it in a parity of God and man, but approaches it by *some likeness*. It does not draw near *toward* God by degrees of place, but by likeness *toward him* and it grows apart by unlikeness *away from him*. (*De Trinitate* VII, 6, 12, 33, 550)[16]

It is not a matter of keeping or losing the image of God as a content (as if *created in the image of God* can count as a definition as categorical as *rational animal, animal endowed with language*, or *animal that laughs*), but of referring the image *toward* that *unto which* it is like. The image is not compared to a model, like a visible reproduction is to another visible accessible elsewhere: the image is borne only by that which refers itself across the likeness unto an original that remains as such invisible, and only in the measure to which it so refers itself. The image consists only in the tension of referring itself to that *to* which it means to resemble. It appears only as this movement *toward*, and only this *intentio ad* keeps a likeness. Man bears the image of God instead and place of kind, species or essence inasmuch as he resembles Him. But he cannot, except absurdly, pretend to resemble him as a visible image is like a visible model, indeed as an intelligible image is like an intelligible model. This would seem to be the illusion of the Neoplatonists: establishing a positive likeness, one measurable by intervals, between the terms of the likeness. It must be that man resembles God otherwise—which means both in another way and by remaining in alterity. "Sola est autem adversus omnes errores via munitissima, ut idem ipse sit Deus et homo; *quo* itur Deus, *qua* itur homo" [In order to avoid all errors in advance, one thing alone is needed: that the same item be God and man, God *toward* whom it goes, man *through* whom it goes].[17] This means that one must go toward the image through the likeness: man bears the image of God to the degree that he abandons any likeness to himself (*ad suum genus, ad suam similitudinem*) and risks resembling nothing—at least nothing of which he could have any idea or the *species* (ἰδεῖν εἶδος) of which he could see. For man does not resemble God by resembling something visible or intelligible, but mostly by resembling nothing visible or intelligible—in short, by resembling no image, especially not some so-called *imago* of God, but in bearing the likeness of the *style* of God. Man is a God, like a Cézanne is a Cézanne, a Poussin a Poussin—without anything behind or beside them that would be Cézanne or Poussin visible as themselves apart from the painting. No, the paintings of Cézanne and Poussin appear as such, without any other visible mark or signature, but still as paintings that bear all over the inimitable style of Cézanne or Poussin. In this sense, man is a God. He appears as God-made, as a God if he admits bearing God's style, letting his own particular features be suppressed, so that its provenance might come forward. Man is a God only as he returns from where he comes, to his most intimate other.[18]

We should not be misled into assimilating the image to a content of the likeness, for it provides less a content than a container, in the sense of a place where the likeness is at play in its varying degrees: "Ergo intelligimus habere nos aliquid *ubi* imago Dei est, mentem scilicet atque rationem."[19] Of course the rational mind offers the place for the likeness, but it does not offer its content. Of course, one can draw up a table of the images that offer a place in the rational mind of man for a likeness with the Trinity: considering this mind as a whole (*De Trinitate* IX), the triad mind, knowledge, and love (*mens, notitia, amor*), refers to the Trinity; considering man in his relation to the world, one sketches the Trinity with two other triads: first, (according to XI, 2, 2–5), the thing seen, sight, and the intention which connects the one to the other (*res, visio, intentio*); second (according to XI, 3, 6–7) memory, interior vision, and the will (*memoria, visio, voluntas*); finally and especially, one can privilege the triad of memory, understanding, and will (*memoria, intelligentia, voluntas*) following *De Trinitate* X, 11, 17).[20] This last figure specifies the place of the best likeness: "Ecce ergo mens meminit sui, intelligit se, diligit se: hoc si cernimus, cernimus Trinitatem; nondum quidem Deum, sed jam imaginem Dei." [Look, the mind remembers itself, understands itself, loves itself: if we see that, we see the Trinity; not yet God, of course, but already the image of God.][21] But these triadic analogies disclosing an image of the Trinity do not display it in themselves as their stable content, but solely in the degree to which they refer this content to God himself. A major text specifies this:

> Haec igitur trinitatis mentis *non* propterea Dei *est imago*, quia sui meminit mens, et intelligit ac diligit se; sed quia *potest etiam* meminisse, et intelligere, et amare a quo facta est. Quod cum facit, sapiens ipsa fit. Si autem non facit, etiam cum sui meminit, seseque intelligit ac diligit, stulta est. Meminerit itaque Dei sui, ad cujus imaginem facta est, eumque intelligat atque diligat. Quod ut breviusdicam, colat Deum non factum, cujus ab eo capax est facta, et cujus particeps esse potest.

> And therefore this final trinity of the mind *is not the image* of God inasmuch as the mind in itself remembers itself, understands itself, and loves itself, but because it *can also* remember and understand and love he by whom it was made. If it does that, it becomes itself wise. But if it does not do so, it is stupid, even when it remembers itself, understands itself and loves itself. To put it briefly, let it worship the God not made, of whom it was made capable and in whom it can participate.[22]

To be sure, the three faculties make an image of God; however, it is neither the three faculties themselves, nor their reciprocal organization, nor even their possible and distant similarity to the three persons of the Trinity that does so—as the majority of commentators seem to say again and again—but rather their possibility of referring to God, as he who can make them play among the themselves the likeness of the trinitarian game of persons in it. The faculties offer a mere place, which becomes a visible and reliable image of the Trinity only to the degree that they receive (in the sense of *capacitas*) participation in the Trinitarian communion and, thus, play trinitarily, as if by derivation, among themselves. They appear as images only to the degree of their likeness, therefore tangentially, by changing degrees, measured by their participation. "Non sua luce, sed summae illius lucis participatione sapiens erit. . . . Neque enim participatione sui sapiens est [Deus], sicut mens participatione Dei." [It (the mind of man) will not be wise by its own light, but by participating in this great light. . . . For God is not wise by participating in himself, as in contrast the mind (of man) is wise by participation in God.][23] What makes the image (pure place and simple possibility of similitude) a likeness does not stem from some status, a property, or an essence of this image, but from the movement, from the tension and the *intentio* toward God, therefore from the degree of participation allowed by the *capacitas*. In this sense, the absence of a proper definition becomes for man the negative condition of the likeness toward God, but a negative that must forever be increased and confirmed. Not only is man defined by his never fixed likeness with God rather than by a fixed definition; but he is defined by this very absence of definition: it is proper to him not to appropriate himself or be appropriate to himself; it is proper to him *not* to resemble himself because that which he does resemble, God, does *not* coincide with his essence, nor with any essence whatsoever, because, God resembling nothing worldly, man too resembles nothing in this world. There is man only without properties and therefore without definition. To the question "quid sit homo?—what is man?" hasn't saint Augustine at least once answered that he does not have to answer. "Nec nunc definitionem hominis a me postulandum puto" [I think that a definition of man cannot be asked of me now].[24]

The essential indefinition of man should be understood as a privilege. Lacking the power, lacking any obligation to be circumscribed does indeed constitute a privilege—indeed the privilege of God according to the prohibition against "making any graven image, nothing that resembles what is found in the heavens" (Exodus 20:4), nothing therefore that would pretend to represent God by comprehending him. Would man therefore also find himself "in the heavens"? To be sure, first by becoming a nonresident alien (by participation), if not official citizen, of the "heaven of the heavens." But also in the sense that—and this is the decisive paradox—what counts for God (that no name, no image and no concept can pretend to comprehend him) also counts for man; neither one nor the other admits either kind, species, or essence. Man remains unimaginable, since formed in the image of He who admits none, incomprehensible because formed in the likeness of He who admits no comprehension. Strictly speaking, man resembles nothing since he resembles nothing other than He whom incomprehensibility properly characterizes. Or again, if God remains incomprehensible, man who resembles nothing other than him (and especially not himself) will bear the mark of his incomprehensibility. In other words, man, without kind, species, and essence, delivered from every paradigm, appears without mediation in the light that surpasses all light. Of this incomprehensibility bestowed, his face bears the mark precisely inasmuch as it reveals itself as invisible as the face of God.[25] Man differs radically from every other being in the world by an insurmountable difference—one no longer ontological, but holy. He no longer differs as the rational animal, *ego cogitans,* the transcendental I, absolute consciousness, the "valuating animal as such,"[26] or even as "the lieutenant of nothing,

Platzhalter des Nichts"[27] still less as the "shepherd of Being—*Hirt des Seins*,"[28] but as the icon of the invisible God, εἰκον τοῦ θεοῦ τοῦ ἀοράτου (Colossians 1:15)—exactly as by participation in the image and likeness of the incomprehensible icon of the invisible. His invisibility separates man from the world and consecrates him as holy for the sake of the Holy.

In coming to this conclusion, Saint Augustine inscribes himself within an ongoing tradition of Christian theology, whose argument was formalized by Gregory of Nyssa: "The icon is perfectly an icon only so long as it is missing nothing of what is known in the archetype. Now, since incomprehensibility of essence (τὸ ακαταληπτὸν τῆς οὐσίας) is found in what we see in the divine nature, it must necessarily be that every [icon] keeps in it too a likeness with its archetype. For if one understood the nature of the icon, but that of the archetype transcended comprehension, the contrary character of what we see in them would betray the deficiency of the icon. But since the nature of our mind, which is according to the icon of the Creator ὅς κατ'εἰκόνα τοῦ κτίσαντος, escapes knowledge, it keeps exactly its likeness with its lord by keeping the imprint of the incomprehensibility [set] by the unknown in it (τῷ καθ' ἑαυτὸν ἀγνώστῳ)."[29] Knowing man therefore demands referring him to God inasmuch as incomprehensible and therefore establishing by derivation his incomprehensibility, with the name of image and resemblance. Augustine too came to this conclusion. While Saint Paul, for his part, posited that no one "among men knows the secrets of man, except the spirit of men in him" (1 Corinthians 2:11) and thereby assumed that man understood the secrets of man, Augustine is quick to posit the contrary: "tamen est aliquid hominis, quod nec ipse scit spiritus hominis, qui in ipso est, tu autem. Domine, scis ejus Omnia, quia eum fecisti" [and yet there is something in man that not even the spirit of man itself knows, which is (nevertheless) in him, but you, o Lord, you know all of him (man), for you made him].[30] Starting from this self-non-knowledge nevertheless known by another, God alone, the operation of *confession* must necessarily be launched, or rather the duality constitutive of a doubly oriented *confessio* toward my ignorance of myself and toward the knowledge of myself by another:

> Confitear ergo quid de me sciam, confitear et quid de me nesciam, quoniam et quod de me scio, te mihi lucente scio, et quod de me nescio, tamdiu nescio, donec fiant 'tenebrae meae' sicut 'meridies' in vultu tuo.

> I will confess therefore what I know of myself and I will also confess what I do not know about myself, since even what I know of myself is because you illuminate me that I know it; while what I do not know of myself I remain ignorant of as long as my *shadows* do not become *like a noonday* (Psalm 89:8) before your face.[31]

Man differs infinitely from man, but with a difference that he cannot comprehend and that, provided he intends to save it, he ought not comprehend.

In this way, we verify again the principle that guides every itinerary toward oneself and toward God (for there is but one): "Interior intimo meo, superior summo meo" (*Confessiones* III, 6, 11, 13, 382). But we know now that the aporia of *magna mihi quaestio* coincides with the solution: the indefinition of man.

§41. *Pondus Meum*

The indefinition of man, this privilege, implies that I do not reside in any essence but that on the contrary I resemble what has no semblance, God, without shape or εἶδος, indescribable, incomprehensible, invisible—in other words, that I resemble nothing. Or more exactly, that I *re*-semble, that I semble by way of re-flection, like the glittering light of the light that illuminates, I appear as the *re*port of the rapport *to the* likeness of God, *ad similitudinem Dei*. I appear each time myself according as I move up (or down) the invisibly graded scale of my likeness, of my proximity or separation from the invisibility of God, whose invisible accomplishment I reflect more or less in the visible. What remains to be understood is by what scale I could travel from one degree to the other of this re-semblance and if I could, in the end, should there be one, find a stable point in a visible reflection of the invisible. Managing this instability constitutes the ultimate, and the most disturbing, risk in the march toward this outside oneself, lacking which I will never become who I am. If I have to cross the re-semblance and dwell in it, which momentum and drive can lead me there?

To go farther we must go back to our point of departure, to the *confessio*. It has, since the beginning, put into operation the principle of rest and restlessness: "Et tamen laudare te vult homo, aliqua portio creaturae tuae. Tu excitas, ut laudare te delectet, quia fecisti nos *ad* te et inquietam est cor nostram, domec requiescat in te." [And he wants to praise you, man does, this tiny portion of what you have created. You excite him to love and praise you because you made us *unto* you, and our heart knows no rest so long as it does not rest in you.] (*Confessiones* I, 1, 1, 13, 272). The way and the question open therefore with the observation of my restlessness—literally, my disequilibrium: so long as I rest in myself, I do not hold steady nor hold myself together. I cease to vacillate only if I find a place outside myself in God. I cannot not want (and love) to find my repose in God because I cannot settle in myself, nor in anything else, if I do not *settle* myself in God. With perfect coherence, the final moment of the *confessio* describes, in three successive passages, only the three actors of this rest: the one that completes creation, also the one in which creation took place as a place of rest for the created, and finally the very rest in which creatures should end, if they admit an end, by settling as if in their own place. "Quamvis ea [sc. opera tua] *quietus* feceris, *requievisti* septimo die, hoc praeloquatur nobis vox libri tui, quod et nos post opera nostra ideo 'bona valde,' quia tu nobis ea donasti, sabbato vitae aeternae *requiescamus* in te." [Though you made your works while remaining *restful, you rested* on the seventh day, your book told us in advance that we, too, after our works (which are 'very good,' since it is you who gave them to us), in the Sabbath of eternal life, we will find our *rest* in you.] (XII, 36, 51, 14, 522). Put otherwise: "Etiam tunc enim sic *requiesces* in nobis, quemadmodum nunc operaris in nobis, et ita erit illa *requies* tua per nos, quemadmodum sunt ista opera tua per nos" [For then too you *will rest* in us, as now you work in us, and then this *rest*, yours, will be in us, as your actions are yours through us] (XIII, 37, 52, 14, 522). And finally: "Post illa [sc. quaedam bona opera nostra] nos *requituros* in tua grandi sanctificatione speramus. Tu autem bonum nullo indigens bono, semper *quietus* es, quoniam tua *quies* tu ipse es." [After them (some of our works, good ones), we hope to *rest* in your great sanctification. But you, who have no need of any good, you are always *at rest*, because you are unto yourself your own *rest*.] (XIII, 38, 53, 14, 522ff). God alone holds himself at rest because he alone holds himself in himself, such that everything that does not hold itself in God but remains in itself (willingly or not) cannot settle there, therefore does not settle at all or come to remain anymore at rest. God alone gives rest, because he alone has it. And he alone has it because he alone is it. And everything else, all the way until the ends of his creation, takes place (happens and is found) only in this rest. Creation, originally eschatological, consists only in giving place to this coming of each creature into the place of its rest. This place, for man without definition, is found in nothing less than in the rest of God himself: "Nam et in ipsa misera inquietudine . . . satis ostendis, quam magnam rationalem creaturam feceris, cui nullo modo sufficit ad *beatam requiem*, quidquid te minus est, ac per hoc nec ipsa sibi." [For even our unhappy restlessness . . . you show sufficiently how great you made your rational creature, since nothing less than you will suffice for its *rest,* not even itself to itself] (XIII, 8, 9, 14, 438). Short of God, man does not find himself, or find where he is.

Now, and this is a remarkable fact, the text which I just quoted, the one that defined the "heaven of the heavens" as *place* where one settles in the Spirit ("requiesceret in spiritu tuo") and showed that man could find rest in nothing less than God ("magnam rationalem creaturam feceris, cui nullo modo sufficit ad *beatam requiem*, quidquid te minus est") goes on to show how to measure the proximity or distance of each man with regard to this place:

> Corpus pondere suo nititur ad locum suum. Pondus non ad ima tantum, sed ad locum suum. Ignis sursum tendit, deorsum lapis. Ponderibus suis aguntur, loca sua petunt. Oleum infra aquam fusum super auqam attolitur, aqua supra oleum fusa infra oleum demergitur: ponderibus suis aguntur, loca sua petunt. Minus ordinata inquieta sunt: ordinantur et quiescunt. Pondus meum amor meus; eo feror, quocumque feror.

> The body strives with all its weight toward its place. The weight does not push only down, but towards its place. Fire tends toward the higher, the stone toward the lower. They are [both] put into motion by their [respective] weight, [but] they seek their [own] places. The least ordered things remain without a place to settle: as soon as they recover their order, they settle down at rest. My weight, it is my love; wherever I take myself, it is my love that takes me there. (XIII, 9, 10, 14, 440)

This argument looks limpid as well as decisive, for it does not say merely that "Anima . . . velut pondere amore fertur quocumque fertur" [the soul, wherever it takes itself, takes itself there by love as by a weight],[32] but specifies also and above all that it is ultimately for the soul a matter of its will: "Voluntas . . . ponderi similis est" [The will . . . resembles a weight].[33] The details of this have yet to be understood precisely.

The point of departure for this argument does not concern, it is worth noting, the question of love, but the strictly physical problem of the cause of local motion. On this issue, Aristotle reasons in this way: "If each of the simple bodies has by nature a certain type of movement, for example fire upward and earth downward and towards the center, it is clear that the void cannot be the cause of motion."[34] To this distinction between movements up and down, he also adds the possible distinction, for each of them, between those that follow nature and those that contradict it (κατὰ φύσιν καὶ παρὰ φύσιν)—in other words, by force or by nature (ἢ βίᾳ ἢ κατὰ φύσιν).[35] But it is doubtless wise, here and elsewhere, not to exhaust oneself in identifying the supposed Greek sources of Saint Augustine by arbitrarily offering erudite readings; it is enough to stick with Cicero, the common and most credible mediator: "The earthy and moist parts are borne by themselves and by their weight (*suo pondere ferantur*) in perpendicular angles toward the earth and the sea, while the two other parts, fire and animate, in contrast with the two previous ones which are borne by their gravity and their weight (*gravitate ferantur et pondere*) toward the central place of the world, are raised (*rursum subvolent*) in straight lines toward the celestial place, be it because their own nature desires higher things (*ipsa natura superior appetente*), or be it because they are pushed, by virtue of their lighter nature, by the heavier parts."[36]

Indisputably, Saint Augustine assumes as such this principle for the explanation of locomotion—as a physical theory. Several texts testify to this:

> Lege naturae cedunt pondera minora majoribus, non modo cum ad proprium locum *suo sponte nutu feruntur*, ut humida et terrena corpora in ipsius mundi medium locum, qui est infimus, rursus aeria et ignea sursum versus; sed etiam cum aliquo tormento aut jactu aut impulsu aut repulso, eo quo sponte *ferrentur*, vi aliena ire *coguntur*.

> According to a law of nature, the less heavy weights yield to the heavier, not only when *they move themselves* toward their proper place (in this way, the moist and earthly bodies tend toward the place at the center of the world, which is the lowest, while, inversely, the airy and fiery bodies tend upward), but also when *they are compelled to move* in another direction besides that which they would follow *of themselves*, by some mechanism, disturbance, attraction, or repulsion.[37]

He even attaches enough authority to this "law of nature" that he will rely on it as something like an experimental test in narrative form:

> Pondera gemina sunt. Pondus enim est impetus quidam cujusque rei, velut conantis ad locum suum: hoc est pondus. Fers lapidem manu, pateris pondus; premit manum tuum, quia locum suum quaerit. Et vis videre quid quaerat? Subtrahe manum, venit ad terram, quescit in terra: pervenit quo tendebat, invenit suum locum. Pondus ergo illud motus erat quasi spontaneus, sine anima, sine sensu. Namque si aquam mittas super oleum, pondere suo in ima tendit. Locum enim suum quaerit, ordinari quaerit; quia praeter ordinem est aqua super oleum. Donec ergo veniat ad ordinem suum, *in quietus motus* est, donec teneat locum suum.

> There are two kinds of weight. For weight is the impetus of any thing whatsoever insofar as it strives toward its [proper] place: such is weight. Take a stone in your hand; you feel its weight; it presses your hand, for it seeks to reach its place. And do you want to know what it is thus seeking to reach? Withdraw your hand, it goes to the earth and settles there. It has arrived there where it tended; it has found its

place. Therefore this weight was a quasi-spontaneous movement, with neither soul nor sensation. For if you throw water on oil, the water tends by its weight to go downward. It tends, that is, toward its place; it seeks to put itself in order; for water above oil, this is not in order. So long as it has not returned into its order, *movement does not settle and come to rest*, until such time as it has arrived in its place.[38]

The "laws of nature" (almost in the modern sense) abide so firmly that Augustine will even mention them as objections to the possibility of miracles:

> Acper hoc, *inquiunt,* quoniam terra abhinc sursum versus est prima, secunda aqua super terram, tertius aer super aquam, quartum super aera caelum, non potest esse terrenum corpus in caelo; momentis enim propriis, ut ordinem suum teneant, singula elementa librantur.

> And consequently, *they say*, since, in ascending from lower to higher, earth comes first, then the water above the earth, third is the air above the water, and fourth comes the heavens above the air, a terrestrial body cannot be found in the heavens; for these different moments balance each of the elements, such that they [each] find their proper order.[39]

Up until this point, there has been nothing innovative on the part of Saint Augustine; he simply assumes a doctrine that was widely accepted at his time—to the point that one could even legitimate it theologically by the authority of the Book of Wisdom 11:21: "Omnia in mensura et numero et pondere disposuisti" [you arranged all things in order, measure, and weight], with the immense legacy that this verse is known to have.[40] It is thus still only a matter of the laws of local motion, and, in a restricted sense, of the laws of the world.

In fact, the innovation only starts when Saint Augustine no longer deals with a place in the world (neither physics, nor nature, nor local motion), but the *place* of he who *confesses*. How, it will be asked, can one pass from the laws of local motion to the place of confession? By an unforeseen tactical reversal: the laws of local motion will be elevated, transposed, and overtaken at the level of the rules of love; *pondus*, its tensions and its movements, will be displaced into the movements and intentions of *amor*. Saint Augustine undertakes this by bringing the formulation of Cicero (more so than those of Aristotle) together with one from Virgil: "Trahit sua quemque voluptas" [Each is led by his own pleasure].[41] Still more surprising, he introduces it, in fact, in order to comment on a verse from the Gospel of John, "Nemo venit ad me, nisi quem Pater attraxit" [Nobody comes to me, if the Father has not attracted him] (John 6:44), in which he tries to explain how the Father, even if he attracts someone toward the Son, does not compel him and does not contradict his will, even though attracted. And the argument:

> Quomodo voluntate credo, si trahor? Ego dico: parum est voluntate, etiam voluptate traheris. Quid est trahi voluptate? 'Delectare in Domino, et dabit tibi petitiones cordis tui.' Est quaedam voluptas cordis, cui panis dulcis est ille caelestis. Porro, si poetae dicere licuit 'Trahit sua quemque voluptas,' non necessitas, sed voluptas, non obligatio, sed delectatio, quanto fortuis nos dicere debemus trahi hominem ad

Christum, qui delectatur veritate, delectatur beatitudine, delectatur justitia, delectatur sempiterna vita, quod totum Christus est?

How do I believe willingly if I am attracted into belief? As for me, I say: you are only slightly led by your will, but [much more] also by pleasure. What does it mean to be attracted by pleasure? "Take pleasure in the Lord, and he will give you what your heart asks" (Psalm 36:4). There is a certain pleasure of the heart for whomever the bread from heaven is sweet. For that matter, if a poet could say: "each is led by his own pleasure," not necessity but pleasure, not obligation but delight, how much more so should we say that the man is led toward Christ who takes pleasure in the truth, who takes pleasure in beatitude, who takes pleasure in justice, who takes pleasure in life without end, all things that Christ is entirely?[42]

The breakthrough and the boldness consists in calling on Virgil to interpret John 6:44, so as to complete and correct Cicero (and Aristotle). Local displacement (φορα)—in other words, arrival in the proper place—no longer results only from a physical weight, but also from pleasure's inclination, which triggers in the heart the same spontaneity that gravity unleashes in the body. For what takes up and displaces the role of weight in the spirit does not come from (at least not first of all), "the weight of glory" (βάπος δόξης) in Saint Paul's sense,[43] but from *delectatio*. By *delectatio*, we must understand the fact not of taking pleasure (according to the ignoble expression of today), but of *receiving* it: "Delectatio quippe *quasi* pondus est animae. Delectatio ergo ordinat animam. '*Ubi* enim erit thesaurus thus, *ibi* erit et cor tuum': *ubi* delectatio, ibi thesaurus; *ubi* autem cor, *ibi* beatitudo aut miseria." [It is therefore pleasure that is *something like* the weight of the soul. For pleasure puts the soul in order. "There where your treasure will be, there too will be your heart" (Matthew 6:21): *there where* your pleasure is, *there* is your treasure; *there where* your body is, *there* is beatitude or misery.][44] Love is set forth according to a logic as strict as motion and therefore can be understood as rigorously as it.

A comparison between motion and love is thus established, one that ends up at an analogy of proportion, according to which what weight is to the body desire is to love. Sometimes the terms correspond strictly without admitting any difference: "Amant enim requiem, sive piae animae, sive iniquae; sed qua perveniunt ad illum quod amant, plurimae nesciunt; nec aliquid appetunt etiam corpora ponderibus suis, nisi quod animas amoribus suis." [For all souls love rest, the pious as well as the unjust; but by which path to reach what they love, the majority know not at all, and bodies too seek nothing with their weight, except what souls seek with their loves.][45] But more often the terms respond to one another while maintaining a gap, for differences remain. First because the relation between desire (for pleasure) and love serves as paradigm for the relation between natural weights and bodies, and not the other way around, as common sense doubtlessly would expect:

Si essemus lapides aut fluctus aut ventus aut flamma vel quid hujus modi, sine ullo quidem sensu atque vita, non tamen nobis deesset *quasi* quidam nostrorum locorum atque ordinis appetitus. Nam *velut* amores, corporum momenta levitate nitantur. *Ita* enim corpus pondere, *sicut* animus amore fertur, quocumque fertur.

If we were only stones, waves, winds, a flame, and something of this sort, without any sensation or life, we would not however be deprived *of some sort of appetence* in our motions and their [right] order. For, *just like loves*, the pressings of bodies strive on by their lightness. That is, *just as* the spirit is borne by its love wherever it is carried, *so too likewise* the body by its weight.[46]

Motion follows weight, like desire follows love, to the point that the loving drive of the desiring soul becomes the paradigm for movements, even in things.

The drive of love in its desire does not serve as paradigm just for inanimate nature, but even with regard to all the reasonable spirits; even men and the angels see their hierarchy modified according as the weight of love follows the law of nature or that of justice: "Sed tantum valet in naturis rationalibus *quoddam veluti* pondus voluntatis et amoris, ut, cum ordine naturae angeli hominibus, tamen lege justitiae boni homines malis angelis praeferantur." [But it holds among rational natures *like some sort* of weight of the will and of love, which makes it such that, if, according to the order of nature, one should prefer angels to men, nevertheless, according to the law of justice, one should prefer good men to bad angels.][47] When the desire deployed by love is at issue, weight loses the characteristics that it had when only the weight of a body is considered: concerning love, weight weighs even without nature, indeed against it, to the point of becoming a free or voluntary weight, which weighs there where it wills:

> Qui motus si culpae deputatur . . . non est utique naturalis, sed *voluntarius*; in eoque similis est motui quo deorsum lapis fertur, quod sicut iste proprius est lapidis, sic ille animi verumtamen in eo dissimilis, quod *in potestate* non habet lapis cohibere motum quo fertur inferius; animus vero dum non vult, non ita movetur.

> But if one assigns blame to it . . . this movement is no longer natural, but *voluntary*. It is like the movement that carries the stone downward, in that it belongs properly to the mind, like its own to the stone; but it is also unlike it, in that the stone does not have the *power* to contain the movement which bears it downward, while the mind does not move thus unless it wills to.[48]

Love may indeed be explained as a weight, provided that we mean a free weight: free first from the constraints of matter, second from the limits of nature, and therefore, in the end, perfectly voluntary.

Saint Augustine therefore corrects the model of physics that explains local movement by the weight of bodies—not out of a concern to spiritualize or to edify, but instead in order to adapt the paradigm of *pondus* to the theoretical requirements that love imposes on it. For in the case of love, *pondus* must become voluntary and therefore set itself free from natural (and material) determinations, since it implies freedom in two ways. First because nobody can love except voluntarily: even if freedom does not always signify the choice of decision, a lover without freedom inevitably becomes a patient, indeed soon enough a sick soul. Next because love supposes choosing some beloved to love rather than another; consequently, the freedom of love necessitates splitting its weight and accordingly opposing one weight to another in order to do justice to the choice between two loves. There will be at least two loves and two weights: "Amores *duo* in hac vita secum in omni tentatione luctantur: amor saeculi et amor Dei; et horum *duorum,* qui vicerit, illuc amantem tanquam pondere trahit." [*Two* loves contend with one another during this life at each temptation: the love of the world and the love of God; and the one of these *two* loves that emerges victorious will transport the lover as by a weight.][49] Love splits according as the desire of the soul, that is to say its weight, pushes it upward or downward. Love is so determinative of weight, and so loosely bound to the material sense of a bodily displacement, that saint Augustine does not hesitate to assign it the upward movement as well as the habitual (physical) movement downward.

If weight can still make something fall, this fall is no longer physical, since it makes the soul fall and also brings about spiritual falls: "Mane si potes: sed non potes; *relaberis* in ista solita et terrena. Quo tandem *pondere,* quaeso, *relaberis,* nisi sordium contractrum cupiditatis visco et peregrinationis erroribus?" [Settle, if you can; but you cannot; you will *fall back* into your earthly habits. *Under the weight of what weight,* I ask you, *will you fall back,* if not that of the filth you have acquired through the clinging of your desire and the erring of your errors?][50] And therefore, faced with this weight which can make one fall in spirit, in spirit too can another weight operate, one which brings an ascent: "Quomodo enim oleum a nullo humore premitur, sed disruptis omnibus exsilit et supereminet: sic et caritas non potest premi in ima; necesse est ut ad suprema emineat" [As oil is compressed by no other liquid, but escapes them all and wraps around them, so too charity cannot be pressed down to the bottom. It must necessarily rise up and dominate].[51] Here the paradox that appeared earlier finds the logic that structures it: I am to myself a weighty burden when I remain empty of God, who relieves me and lifts me up toward him, as soon as he fills me: "Nunc autem quoniam quem tu imples, *sublevas* eum, quoniam tui plenus non sum, oneri mihi sum" [But now, since you *lift up* the one whom you fill, seeing as I am not filled with you, I am to myself a burden].[52] Filled with God, I undergo the impact of a weight oriented upward, while filled (in fact, stuffed) by myself alone, I undergo a weight oriented downward. Grace, in other words, the love come from God with the aim of returning me to him, exerts a *counterweight,* a weight that ascends, an uplift and an upbraiding.

> Cui dicam, quomodo dicam de *pondere* cupiditatis in abruptam abyssum et de *sublevatione* caritatis. . . . Neque enim loca sunt. . . . Affectus sunt, amores sunt, immunditia spiritus nostri *defluens* inferius amore curarum, et sanctitas tui *attolens* nos superius amore securitatis.

> To whom and how should I speak of the *weight* of cupidity [that leads] toward the sudden abyss and of the charity that *uplifts* . . . ? It is not about places . . . . These are the affects, loves, the impurity of our spirit *plummeting* lower through love of its cares and your holiness *lifting us up* higher by love of assurance. (X, 7, 8, 14, 436)

Love, like the weight from above, which comes from there and leads back, lifts us up toward our place, which is defined precisely by the fact that there and there alone we can settle: "In dono tuo requiescimus: ibi te fruimur. Requies nostra locus noster. Amor *illuc attolit nos*" [It is in the gift that you give that we find rest: here we enjoy you. Our rest, our place. *Here, up to here,* your love *lifts us*] (XIII, 9, 10, 14, 438). That weight not only could lift us toward the heights, but in fact does so first and essentially when the issue is my proper place, this paradox imposes itself and ceases to appear surprising. The bottom line is that the ground always attracts—rather than grounds—precisely because it shows itself above, attracts from on high, weighs on us from *above*. Consequently, Christ constitutes the ground par excellence, the "fundamentum fundamentorum," insofar as he comes from on high, like the heavenly Jerusalem descends from the heavens, descends like the "heaven of the heavens:" "Etenim origo fundamenti hujus summitatem tenet; et quemadmodum fundamentum coporae fabricae in imo est, sic fundamentum spiritualis fabricae in summo est" [And therefore the origin of this ground stands at the summit; and just as the ground of the corporal construction is found below, so is the ground of the spiritual construction found at the summit].[53]

I find my place only there where I truly want to dwell. And I truly want to dwell only there where my love pushes me, transports me and leads me, as a weight leads, transports, and pushes. This weight must be known in order to know what I freely want. "Sed vis nosse qualis amor sit? Vide quo ducat. Non enim monemus ut nihil ametis, sed monemus ne mundum ametis, ut cum qui fecit mundum, libere ametis." [But do you want to know which love it is? See where it leads you. For we are not warning you to love nothing, but not to love the world so that you might love freely with he who made the world.][54] I am the place where I confess; but I rest in this place only because my love pushes and settles me there like a weight. But a voluntary weight, since through it I love. And if I love there, I am there as in my self.

Sketch of a Phenomenological Concept of Sacrifice

I. The Aporia of Sacrifice

Strictly speaking, we should not begin with sacrifice, at least in the sense of a noun, or of a substantive, because sacrifice (*sacrificium*) always results from the action of a verb, of the verb "to make" (*sacrum facere*): a sacrifice appears once an agent has rendered something sacred, has set it apart from the profane and thereby consecrated it. Moreover, *sacrum facere* gave us *sacrifiement* in Old French, which states more clearly the process of rendering something sacred than the result of this process. The question of sacrifice concerns, then, first and above all the act of making something sacred and of wresting it from the profane (the act opposed to that of profanation), an act of which sacrifice is only a result that it limits itself to recording, without explaining it. This clarification nevertheless raises a difficulty: how can we conceive the transition between two terms, the profane and the sacred, while their very distinction becomes, in the epoch of nihilism in which we live, indistinct and confused, if not completely obscured? It is as if the "death of God," and above all what has provoked it—the realization that the highest values consist only in the valuation that confirms them, and thus are only worth what our valuations are worth—have abolished any difference between the sacred and the profane, and thereby any possibility of crossing over it by a *sacrifiement* (or on the contrary, by a profanation). Would not sacrifice disappear along with the sacred that is disappearing?

However, this is not the whole story: We still have a common, if not entirely vernacular, sense of sacrifice: sacrificing is equivalent to destroying; or, more precisely, to destroying what should not be destroyed, at least according to the normal practices of daily life, namely, the useful and the functional. In effect, beings understood as that which I make use of (*zuhanden* beings in Heidegger's distinction) are defined by the finality that links them not only to other ready-to-hand beings but ultimately to my own

436

intention, which gathers the subordinated finalities of these beings into a network of finalities, all oriented toward myself as the center of a surrounding world. This being, not only useful but ready-to-hand (*usuel, zuhanden*), refers to me, and, in so doing, becomes for me my own world: it is good insofar as it is mine, it is a good insofar as it is my good. As a result, doing away with it would amount to my doing away with myself; and if taking a step further in the negation, I were to destroy it, then I would also destroy myself. Such destruction of property as such, and even as my property—thus this destruction of myself—has not disappeared in our own time, and is still designated as sacrifice. Even daily, we are subject to its paroxysm in the form of *terrorism*. Both common usage and the media rely on the semantics of sacrifice in order to qualify terrorist acts: the terrorist, it is said, *sacrifices himself for* his cause, or else, he *sacrifices* the lives of his random victims in order to draw attention to this very cause. Such terms, as approximate and thus misleading as they may be, nevertheless retain some relevance because pure violence, without any moral or even political justification, in its stupidity and its barbarism, in fact elicits a paralyzing dread before an act that in principle is alien to the world of living beings or the community of reasonable people and obeys the logic, absurd to us, of another world which moreover denies and annihilates our own. Terrorism abolishes property, innocent people, and the terrorist himself, because it accomplishes first and radically the destruction of all beings as useful and functional, and the destruction for us of the organization of the world itself in terms of ends and accomplishment. Thus destroyed, the everyday thing (*l'usuel*) becomes the sacred insofar as it no longer belongs to the world in which we can live, and in which it is our purpose or intention to live in the normality of the profane. Now, if we grant that terror under its polymorphous though faceless figures remains today our ultimate experience of the sacred, and that this figure of the sacred, as debased as it proves to be, nevertheless allows us a common concept of sacrifice, then what makes a profane thing sacred, the *sacrifiement*, consists in its destruction. The terrorist produces the sacred (under the figure of absurd horror) by *destroying* life, including his own.[1] The process that makes the profane sacred entails the destruction of the thing thus sacrificed.[2] One access to sacrifice thus remains available to us to the extent that the experience of terrorism guarantees us the experience of the destruction of property as such, and thus of the world as ours.

Nevertheless, this first result, by providing us an indisputable because perfectly negative access to the sacred and to the *sacrifiement*, only reinforces the aporia. For the point is not merely to deplore the fact that destruction is the only remaining figure of sacrifice today, but above all to ascertain the extent to which, even in this form, its intelligibility remains problematic. How, indeed, does destroying something contribute to making it sacred? What does sacrifice do if all it does is undo? What can it consecrate if it limits itself to annihilating? To what or to whom can it give, since it nullifies the content of any gift and nullifies itself as possible giver? The definition of sacrifice as the destruction of a good as such not only explains nothing of sacrifice but could actually explain its opposite—the self-appropriation of autarchy. Indeed, the wise and the strong want to rid themselves of a possession by destroying it and thereby becoming free of it; they alone can do this, and they prove it to themselves by surviving what they destroy in themselves: in making a sacrifice of other goods (by ascesis, renunciation, mutilation, and so forth), they demonstrate their autarchy to others; or rather they prove at least to themselves their autonomy and ataraxy. Sacrifice thus becomes the auto-celebration of the ascetic ideal, in which the *ego* attains a kind of *causa sui* by no longer owing anything to anyone, not even its own person to the world. Sacrifice, understood as the destruction of a good, can be inverted into a construction of the self, which sacrifices nothing of its own, only the world to itself.

II. Sacrifice According to Exchange

Thus we must give up on defining sacrifice only by the destruction of a possession. In fact, it becomes possible to speak of sacrifice only if one introduces a third term, beyond the destroyer and the good destroyed—precisely the third, the other. Even in the most banal understanding of sacrifice, for example the sacrifice of a pawn or a piece in chess, the other already appears, even if only in the most basic guise of the mimetic rival, the alter ego, my opponent: even if, in making this supposed gift to my opponent, my purpose is simply to strengthen *my* position, it is my position vis-à-vis *him*, and I sacrifice this piece *to him*. In short, my sacrifice always assumes the other as its horizon of possibility. Thus it is the other that determines the destruction of a good, either because he benefits from it as its new recipient (I transfer it to him while mourning its loss), or because he shares its loss with me as my rival (I give it up in order to deprive him of it, in order to strengthen my position).

In this new sense, where it occurs within the horizon of the other, does sacrifice become more intelligible than in the previous case, where it is pure and simple destruction of a good? Undoubtedly, because we notice immediately that it is in fact no longer simply a matter of destruction, but also of privation (with destruction, but also sometimes without). And this obtains on both sides of the alternative. On the one hand, I deprive myself of a good, because I can do without it, and in this way assure my autonomy (autarchy, ataraxy, etc.); in other words, I deprive myself of a good precisely in order to prove to myself that it has only a minor importance and that I remain myself even without it; hence by losing a possession that is other than me, I gain a more perfect possession of myself. On the other hand, I deprive myself of a good, not because I would simply destroy it, but because by destroying it or by making it unavailable to me, I want to divest myself of it to the point that, by this definitive loss, another might possibly appropriate it in my stead; in fact, I display this good I have renounced so that it may become available for the other to appropriate it. Nevertheless, these two situations clearly differ. In the first case, it is indeed enough for me to deprive myself of a good (to the extent that I myself survive), in order to prove its dispensable character and in this way demonstrate my autarchy: the sacrifice is accomplished perfectly by itself. The second case is rather different: admittedly, I manage to deprive myself of a good (I indeed sacrifice it) but this renunciation is not *as such* sufficient for some other to take possession of that of which I have nevertheless deprived myself; the sacrifice remains unfinished: my renunciation only allowed for the display of the good, which, though made available, still remains in escheat at this point in the process: less given than just given up. For even when I divest myself of a good, whether or not the other takes possession of it is not up to me; that depends only on the other. By my decision alone, the sacrifice can thus only be accomplished halfway; its realization does not derive from my simple act of dispossession, but awaits the other's acceptance, and thus depends upon another decision, on an *other* decision, come from elsewhere. I can at best act *as if* my dispossession were equivalent to a taking possession by the other, but I can neither assure that nor assume it. Dispossession cannot anticipate reception because the other's acceptance can come only from the other himself, and thus by definition escapes me. Sacrifice involves my dispossession, but my dispossession is not enough for a sacrifice, which only acceptance by the other can ratify. If we assume that giving up is enough to begin the sacrifice, accomplishing it as a gift is contingent upon its acceptance by the other. There is nothing optional or secondary about this discrepancy, which defines and marks the irreducible distance between me and the other, such that neither I nor the other can abolish it. Even when offered (or rather: precisely *because* offered), it is part of the definition of sacrifice that it can nevertheless be refused and disdained by the other—in this specifically lies the other's role. Thus, even if defined within the horizon of the other, the destruction or disappropriation of a good is not enough to account fully for the possibility of sacrifice.

Yet it happens that the most current explanation of sacrifice, produced by sociology and the sociology of religion in particular, presupposes exactly the opposite: that my dispossession of a good is enough for the effective accomplishment of a sacrifice. Sacrifice would consist in effecting the loss of a good (by destruction or by devolution) for the benefit of an other (divine or mortal, most often superior hierarchically), such that he accepts it and consequently renders a counter-gift to the one who initiated the sacrifice—with this reciprocity constituting the decisive presupposition. Obviously, the realization of the sacrifice by its initiator does not imply and does not at all guarantee the acceptance of the good that has been ceded, and still less, the reciprocity of a counter-gift. Nevertheless, this interpretation of sacrifice imposes itself, perpetuates itself, and prevails, even today. How does it manage to do so? By assuming what it cannot prove, to wit, that the acceptance and the counter-gift always (or at least in the majority of cases, as the standard situation) follow from the dispossession (with or without destruction). But, once again, how does this presupposition legitimate itself? By implicitly basing the entire explanation of sacrifice on the model of exchange.[3] Moreover, in the majority of cases, we find the three terms gift, exchange, and sacrifice equated, or even substituted without distinction for one another. Just as the gift consists in giving up a possession in order to obligate the other to give back a counter-gift (*do ut des*), and just as exchange implies that every good that passes from the one to the other is compensated by a good (or a sum of money) passing from the other to the one, in like fashion, the sacrificer (the sacrificing agent) abandons a good (by dispossession, of exposure or destruction), so that the supposedly superior other (divine or mortal) will accept it, and in so doing, enter into a contractual relation, and, by contract, return a good (real or symbolic). In the three cases, under the imprecise (and confused) names of gift, exchange, and sacrifice, the same economy of contract obtains: I bind myself to you by abandoning a possession, *therefore* you bind yourself to me by accepting it, *therefore* you owe me an equivalent item in return. Henceforth, sacrifice does not destroy any more than the gift gives up, because both work to establish exchange; or rather, where sacrifice destroys and the gift cedes, both operate thereby to establish the economy of reciprocity.

We must conclude that destruction or dispossession and the horizon of the other still do not allow us to determine a concept of sacrifice, but only lead us to assimilate it with exchange in the same confusion that undermines the notion of the gift. In this context, at best, one would call sacrifice the imprudence of an incomplete exchange where a gift is given up without knowing whether an acceptance will ratify it, while at worst, sacrifice would be the illusion of a contractual arrangement that no one would ever have entered into with the one who is making the sacrifice. Unless it were a matter of simple deception, of the other or of oneself, claiming to give up unconditionally, hoping all the while, secretly or unconsciously, to receive a hundredfold what one loses only once. It would be better instead to consider the very term sacrifice an impropriety, an empty or contradictory concept, and apply to sacrifice the contradiction that Derrida deplored in the gift: "The truth of the gift [. . .] suffices to annul the gift. The truth of the gift is equivalent to the non-gift or to the non-truth of the gift."[4] We can thus say that the truth of sacrifice culminates in exchange, that is to say, in the non-truth of sacrifice, since it should consist precisely of a relinquishing without return; it also ends in the truth of the non-gift par excellence, that is to say, the confirmation that whenever one believes he speaks of, and makes, a sacrifice, one still hopes for an exchange and a return that would be all the more profitable, since one claimed to have lost everything.

III. The Misunderstanding of the Gifts

Nevertheless, a way could be opened through the aporia itself, and thanks to it. More precisely, the extension of the aporia of the gift to sacrifice might already indicate another path—by making us think sacrifice precisely in its relation to the gift. We would then no longer only think of it as the dispossession (yea, the destruction) of a good within the horizon of the other, but also as a moment of the more comprehensive phenomenon of the gift. For the phenomenon of the gift at the outset manifests much more than exchange: as we have attempted to demonstrate elsewhere, the gift can and thus must be separated from exchange, by letting its natural meaning reduce to givenness. For, while the economy (of exchange) denatures the gift, if reduced to givenness, the gift excepts itself from the economy, by freeing itself from the rules of exchange. The gift in effect proves able to accomplish itself, even and especially, by reducing each of the terms of exchange: without a giver (*donateur*), or indeed without a recipient (*donataire*)—thus freeing itself without reciprocity—and even without a thing given—thus freeing itself from a logic of equality.[5] As reduced to the givenness in it, the gift is accomplished in an unconditioned immanence, which not only owes nothing to exchange, but dissolves its conditions of possibility. The gift so reduced performs itself with an *unconditioned* freedom—it never lacks anything that would prohibit it from giving itself, because, even without invoking the terms of the exchange, it still shows itself, even all the more so. But if the gift proves *unconditioned* in this way, would it not offer sacrifice its most appropriate site, since sacrifice claims precisely (though without at this juncture justifying its claim) to give and to give up *without condition*? In this hypothesis, the solution to the aporia of sacrifice would come from the answer to the aporia of the gift—from the reduction of the gift to givenness. We will need then to proceed to a reduction of sacrifice to givenness in order to formulate sacrifice, as one of its moments, in terms of the phenomenon of the reduced gift.

Where, then, does the most evident aporia arise when the phenomenon of a gift unfolds? Precisely at the moment when the given gift *appears*. For when what the giver gives (a thing, a being, a piece of information [*une donnée*], a present, etc.) comes into full light, the gift as such inevitably starts to become obscured, and then to disappear. Indeed, the gift given, which takes on the consistency of the thing and of a being, occupies the center of the phenomenal stage, so as to conceal or even exclude everything else. Everything else, that is to say first of all the giver: for the giver disappears in his own gift: on the one hand, he must indeed give *something*, whatever may be the actual status of this something (a simple sign of good will or a real gift in itself, useful or useless, precious or trivial, inaugural or reciprocal, etc.); otherwise he would not appear at all as a giver giving. But, precisely to the extent that he gives his gift truly and irrevocably, the giver allows his given gift to separate itself from him, and assert itself as such, autonomous and thus available to the recipient, who appropriates it. The gift not only becomes a phenomenon independent of the phenomenon of the giver, but it excludes him, either by consigning him to the phenomenal background, or by obscuring him completely. This disappearance of the giver does not result from any recalcitrance on the part of the recipient, hut from the very definition of the gift given; it is not ingratitude that causes the exclusion of the giver, yet this exclusion ultimately results by virtue of the very phenomenality of the gift given, in itself exclusive and appropriating. The giver must disappear (or at least his obviousness [*évidence*] must diminish and his presence withdraw) in order for the gift given to appear (or at least for its presence [*évidence*] to increase and for it to announce itself in the foreground). Otherwise, the gift given would not only not appear as such; it would not be truly given at all: its recipient would not dare to approach it or to extend his hand, or even to claim himself the recipient, because the tutelary and overhanging presence of the giver would still cast a shadow of possession over it. The recipient cannot take the gift given for his own, so long as he still *sees* in it the face and the power of its previous owner. The owner must withdraw from the giver, so that the gift can start to appear as given; but ultimately, the giver must disappear completely for the gift to appear as given definitively; that is to say, given up, abandoned.

And there is more. In effect, just as the gift appears only if the giver disappears, the gift thus abandoned ends by masking in itself not only the giver but the very process of the gift. If a gift appears as truly given only from the moment the giver yields it, the abandoning is reversed: the gift given appears because *it* in turn, abandons its giver. But a gift without relation to any giver no longer bears the mark of any process of givenness, and thus appears as alien to what is given in it. Paradoxically, a gift truly given disappears as given, too. It appears henceforth only as a *found* object: a thing, a being or an object, which is found there, in front of me, by chance and without reason, such that I may wonder what status I should grant it: is it here in its own right (like a piece of fruit fallen from a tree), by the voluntary intention of an other (like an installation in a museum, a sign at the edge of the road, etc.), by involuntary accident (like a possession lost by its distracted owner, or stolen from him), or even possibly placed here by an anonymous giver, either for the benefit of some unspecified beneficiary (like the emergency phones on the side of a freeway), or for the benefit of an identified recipient, in which case it could be intended for an other, or for me? The gift-character of the found object is thus no longer self-evident; it is only one hypothesis among others, and not the least plausible. In the extreme, if my hermeneutic does not allow me (or does not wish) to recognize the gift as given, the gift as such disappears completely: What is specific to the gift—once we grant that it implies relinquishment in order to appear—thus consists in disappearing as given, and in allowing nothing more to appear than the neutral and anonymous presence, left without any origin, of a thing, of a being, or of an object, coming only from itself, never from elsewhere—nor originating from a giver or from a process of giving. The major aporia of the gift derives from this paradox: the gift given can appear only by erasing in its phenomenon its giver, the process of its gift, and, ultimately, its entire gift-character.

Two examples unambiguously confirm this paradox. First; the one in which Saint Augustine analyses the case of "a fiancé who gives a ring to his betrothed; but she loves the ring thus received more than the fiancé who gave it to her. Wouldn't we consider her adulterous in the very gift made to her by her fiancé, even while she loves what her fiancé has given her? Certainly, she loved what her fiancé gave her, but if she were to say: 'This ring is enough for me, now I don't want to see his face again,' what would she be? Who would not detest this lunacy? Who would not accuse her of adultery? You love gold instead of your husband, you love the ring instead of your fiancé; if you truly have in mind to love the ring in place of your fiancé and have no intention of seeing him, the deposit that he gave you as the token of his love would become the sign of your loathing."[6] Of course, in the case of this caricatured ingratitude, the issue for the theologian is to condemn the sin in general, as the attitude that leads us to love the gifts of God while rejecting God himself, who gives them to us. But the phenomenological description of the gift remains no less pertinent here: the betrothed first sees the fiancé, the giver, then the gift, the ring; the fiancé intended of course that, by seeing the gift (the ring), the betrothed would not stop seeing his face, the face of the giver. He reckoned to benefit from a phenomenal structure of reference (*Hinweis*): the phenomenon of the ring offering its own visibility and, moreover, conferring it to the (absent) visibility of the giver, who, by this indication, would benefit from a second-degree visibility, by association. In this way, the giver, invisible as such, gives being to the visible gift, but in return the visible gift gives him a visibility by proxy. Yet this exchange (the gift of being for the given exchanged for the gift of appearing for the giver) is not phenomenally valid: in fact, the betrothed sees and wants to see only the ring, and not, by indication and reference, the *facies sponsi*, the face of the giver. The gift given, as such and at the outset (the ring), monopolizes all of the visibility and condemns the giver to disappear from the visible stage. Henceforth, not only does the fiancé/giver no longer enter the phenomenon of the gift, but the gift-character of the given is erased: the ring becomes the possession of the betrothed, who sees nothing more than herself in it, possessing it. Along with the giver, the gift itself disappears.

In an entirely different context, but along the same descriptive line, and in describing the *es gibt*, such that it determines the appearance of time and being (for neither one nor the other *are*, so that with respect to them it is necessary to say *es gibt, it gives*), Heidegger insists on the phenomenal characteristic of the gift, which gives (itself) in this *it gives*: "The latter [*es gibt*] withdraws in favor of the gift [*zugünsten der Gabe*] which It gives. . . . A giving [*Geben*] which gives only its gift [*nur seine Gabe gibt*], but in the giving holds itself back and withdraws [*zurückhält und entzieht*], such a giving we call sending [*das Schicken*]."[7] We understand that the giving can precisely *not* give *itself* more exactly *cannot* give *itself* in person, precisely because it gives its gift (the gift given), makes it appear as such, and in order to arrive at this, must not only remain in the background but must withdraw itself from visibility. The *es gibt*, because it gives (and dispenses) being as much as time, neither can nor should give itself. The *giving* gives only the *given*, it never gives *itself*. The giving cannot return on itself in a *donum sui*, as *causa sui* in metaphysics claims to do. Can we advance in the understanding of this fundamental impossibility? Possibly, by considering difference as such, namely, the difference that Heidegger in this case no longer calls ontological (*ontologische Differenz*), but the different from the same, the differentiation (*der Unterschieden aus dem Selben, der Unter-Schied*). What differs here is called the unique *Austrag*, the accord, which unfolds at once as being and as a being, which are both given in the same gesture, but precisely not in a similar posture: "Being shows itself as the unconcealing coming-over [*zeigt sich als die enthergende Überkommnis*]. Beings as such appear in the manner of the arrival that keeps itself concealed in unconcealedness [*erscheint in der Weise der in die Unverborgenheit sich bergenden Ankunft*]. . . . The difference of being and beings, as the differentiation of coming-over and arrival [*Unter-schied von Überkommnis und Ankunft*], is the accord [*Austrag*] of the two in *unconcealing keeping in concealment*."[8] In fact, nothing is clearer than this phenomenological description of the *es gibt*: when it is given, or more precisely when *it gives* (understood in the trivial sense: when it functions, it works, it performs), the being arrives in visibility because it occupies and seizes visibility entirely (just as the arrival, *Ankunft*, of a train, precisely in the banal sense of the term, fills the station and focuses every gaze upon it). But beings can neither unleash nor prompt the visibility that they appropriate in this way: only being can open and uncover it, because it alone consists precisely in this display, because it alone comes from a coming over (*Überkommnis*), opening the site that an arrival (*Ankunft*) will eventually occupy. This arrival receives its site, but by occupying it, it masks it and also renders invisible the coming-over that had opened it. By occupying the entire stage, beings make this very scene invisible. Being thus disappears in the visibility (*l'évidence*) of the being whose arrival covers up its nevertheless unconcealing coming-over. The being thus hides being from view by a phenomenological necessity which attests that being never shows itself *without* a being nor, moreover, *as* a being, as *Sein und Zeit* has already repeated with decisive insistence. The process of the givenness of the giving thus reproduces, here ontologically, in the agreement of being and the being according to the *es gibt*, the aporia of the gift in general, which Saint Augustine had described in a theological context.

It is characteristic of the gift given that it spontaneously conceals the givenness in it; thus a characteristic of the phenomenon of the gift is that: it masks itself. Is it possible to locate the phenomenon of sacrifice within the essential aporia of the phenomenality of the gift? And, in being articulated there, might the phenomenon of sacrifice even allow us to solve the aporia of the gift?

IV. The Lifting of the Given and the Relieving of the Gift

By virtue of its visibility, the given constitutes an obstacle to that which makes this very visibility possible. What then makes the visibility of the gift possible, if not the process of givenness, whereby the giver turns the gift over as given, by handing it over in its autonomous visibility?

We should here note carefully that the gift given does not mask only (or even first of all) the giver, as an effect is detached from its efficient cause, or as the beneficiary of a favor refuses out of ingratitude to recognize it. The gift given masks the very process of giving givenness, a process in which the giver participates without constituting it intrinsically (he can even recuse himself without the process of giving being suspended). For, as we noted above, a gift (reduced) can remain perfectly possible and complete even with an anonymous or uncertain giver, or indeed without any confirmed giver. In fact, at issue here is one of the cardinal figures of the reduction of the gift to givenness. The question thus does not consist in reverting from the given to the giver, but in letting appear even in the gift ultimately given (in a being arrived in its arrival [*arrivage, Ankunft*] the advancing process of its coming over, which delivers its visibility by giving it to the gift, or, more generally, the very coming-over that delivers the gift phenomenally [the *Überkommnis* that unconceals the visible]). At issue would be the suspending of the gift given, so that it would allow the process of its givenness, namely, the given character of the gift (its givenness [*donnéité*] to translate *Gegebenheit* literally), to appear in its own mode, instead of crushing it in the fall from the given into a pure and simple found object. So it is, not a question of suppressing the gift given, for the benefit of the giver, but of making this gift transparent anew in its own process of givenness by letting its giver eventually appear there, and, first and always, by allowing to appear the coming-over that delivers the gift into the visible. At stake here is the phenomenality of this very return: to return to the gift given the phenomenality of its return, of the return that inscribes it through givenness in its visibility as gift coming from somewhere other than itself. The gift appears as such—in other words, as arriving from somewhere other than itself—only if it appears in such a way that it ceaselessly refers to this elsewhere that gives it, and from which it finds itself given to view.

That the gift given allows the return from which it proceeds to appear: this defines the signification and the phenomenological function of *sacrifice*—such is, at least, our hypothesis. To sacrifice does not signify to relinquish a good (by destruction or dispossession), even if this relinquishing were possibly for the other's benefit; rather, it consists in making appear the referral from which it proceeds, by reversing it (by making it return) toward the elsewhere, whose intrinsic, irrevocable, and permanent mark it bears insofar as it is a gift given.[9] Henceforth, sacrifice presupposes a gift already given, the point of which is neither destruction, its undoing, nor even its transfer to another owner, but, instead, its return to the givenness from which it proceeds, and whose mark it should always bear. Sacrifice gives the gift back to the givenness from which it proceeds, by returning it to the very return that originally constitutes it. Sacrifice does not separate itself from the gift but dwells in it totally. It manifests this by returning to the gift its givenness because it repeats the gift on the basis of its origin. The formula that perfectly captures the conditions of possibility of the gift is found in a verse from the Septuagint, ὅτι σὰ τὰ πάντα καὶ ἐκ τῶν σῶν δεδώκαμεν σοι—"all things are yours and it is by taking from among what is yours that we have given you gifts" (1 Chron. 29:14). To make a gift by taking from among gifts already given in order to re-give it; to "second" a gift from the first gift itself, to make a gift by reversing the first gift toward the one who gives it, and thus to make it appear through and through as a given arising from elsewhere—this is what accurately defines sacrifice, which consists in making visible the gift as given according to the coming-over of givenness. At issue is absolutely not a counter-gift, as if the giver needed either to recover his due (in the manner of an exchange), or to receive a supplementary tribute (gratitude as a symbolic compensation); rather, the point is the recognition of the gift as such, by repeating in reverse the process of givenness, and by reintegrating the gift to it, wresting it from its factual fall back to the rank (without givenness) of found object, non-given, *un-given*, in the end, to make visible not only the given but the process of givenness itself (as coming-over, *Überkommnis*), which would otherwise be left unnoticed, as if excluded from all phenomenality.

Sacrifice does not return the given to the giver by depriving the recipient (*donataire*) of the gift: it renders givenness visible by re-giving the gift. Sacrifice effects the redounding (*la redondance*) of the gift. As a result, sacrifice loses nothing, above all not the gift that it re-gives; on the contrary, it wins—it wins the gift, which it keeps all the more that it makes it appear for the first time as such, as a gift given, finally safeguarded in its givenness (given-ness, *Gegebenheit*). Sacrifice wins, but without even having to play the game of "loser wins" (as in the so-called pure love of God), as if it were necessary to lose much in order to win still more by retribution. Sacrifice wins by re-giving (*redondance*): it conquers the true phenomenon of the gift by restoring to it, through the act of re-giving, the phenomenality of givenness. Sacrifice re-gives the gift starting with the recipient and makes the gift appear as such in the light of its givenness and, sometimes, for the glory of the giver. In this, it corresponds to forgiveness (*le pardon*): forgiveness re-gives the gift as well, but starting from the giver, who confirms it in the light of givenness for the salvation of the recipient. Forgiveness and sacrifice correspond to one another in this way, so as to make the phenomenality of givenness appear by the double redounding of the gift, beginning either from the recipient, or from the giver.

V. The Confirmation of Abraham

Thus we have determined sacrifice according to its phenomenality by inscribing it within the framework of a phenomenology of the gift: its function is to make appear what the gift, once given, never fails to cover over and hide—the process of givenness itself—such that on the basis of a review of this process, the giver eventually becomes visible again as well. Can we confirm this determination of sacrifice by a significant example? Certainly, if we consider the episode of the sacrifice of Abraham, or rather of the sacrifice of Isaac by Abraham, related in Genesis 22:1–19. Without glossing over its radically theological status (indeed, how could one do so?), we shall sketch an interpretation of it first according to the principle of the phenomenality of sacrifice.

Certainly there is a sacrifice involved, specified as such: "[O]ffer [your son Isaac] as a burnt offering upon one of the mountains of which I shall tell you" (22:2)—but it is a sacrifice that precisely does *not* take place, at least if one confines oneself to the common determination of sacrifice (a destruction or dispossession allowing an exchange within the framework of a contract). Understanding this sacrifice presupposes, paradoxically, understanding why Isaac has *not* been sacrificed ("Abraham went and took the ram, and offered it up as a burnt offering instead of his son," 22:13). Or more precisely, it involves understanding why, while there was no sacrifice following the common understanding (no destruction of Isaac), there was indeed, according to the biblical account, fulfilment of the obligation toward God, since God acknowledges: "[Now I know that you fear God" (22:12)]. Now this is possible only if we grant that this account does not follow the common determination of sacrifice, but instead follows its phenomenological concept—that of sacrifice conceived on the basis of the gift, and of the gift reduced to givenness. It is here that we must therefore locate the concept. A first moment seems evident: God demands of Abraham a sacrifice, and even a consuming sacrifice (where the victim is consumed in fire, leaving nothing to share between God, the priest, and the one offering, in contrast to other forms of sacrifices). This demand of sacrifice falls upon Isaac, the one and only son of Abraham. Do we have here a sacrifice according to the common concept? Precisely not, because God asks nothing out of the ordinary of Abraham, nor does he enter into any contractual agreement with him; he simply and justifiably takes back Isaac, who already belongs to him, and even doubly so. First, quite obviously, because all first-borns belong to God by right: "The first-born of your sons you shall give to me. You shall do likewise with your oxen and with your sheep; seven days it shall be with its dam; on the eighth day you shall give it to me" (Exod. 22:29–30). Or again: "Consecrate to me all the first-born; whatever is the first to open the womb among the people of Israel, both of man and of beast, is mine" (Exod. 13:2). The question consists only in knowing what this belonging and this consecration really imply. The answer varies, from actual putting to death (in the case of the plague on the firstborn of Egypt, Exod. 12:29–30), to the ritual sacrifice of animals in the Temple, right up to the redemption of the firstborn of Israel, prescribed explicitly by God (Exod. 13:11–15, 34:19; Num. 18:14), who forbids human sacrifices.[10] In this sense, Isaac belongs first to God, before belonging to his father (Abraham), in the same way as any other firstborn, of Israel or of any other people.

God has nevertheless another right of possession over Isaac, radical in another way: Isaac in effect does *not* belong to Abraham, who could not, neither he, nor his wife, on their own, engender him ("Now Abraham and Sarah were old, advanced in age; and it had ceased to be with Sarah after the manner of women," Gen. 18:11). Thus, Isaac belongs from the beginning and as a miracle to God alone: "Nothing, neither word nor deed, remains impossible for God. At the same season next year, I will return to your home and Sarah will have a son."[11] And in fact, "The Lord visited Sarah as he had said, and the Lord did to Sarah as he had promised. And Sarah conceived, and bore Abraham a son in his old age at the time of which God had spoken to him" (21:1–.2). Thus, by right, Isaac, child of the promise through divine omnipotence, comes to Abraham only as a pure gift, unexpected because beyond every hope, incommensurate with what Abraham would have possessed or engendered himself. But this gift nevertheless disappears as soon as Isaac appears as such, that is to say, as the son of Abraham, or more precisely, as the one whom Abraham claims as his son: "Abraham called the name of his son who was born to him, whom Sarah bore to him, Isaac. . . . And the child grew, and was weaned; and Abraham made a great feast on the day that Isaac was weaned" (21:3, 8). And for her part, Sarah, too, appropriates Isaac as *her* son ("I have borne him a son in his old age!" 21:7), since she drives out as a competitor the other son, natural born, whom Abraham had had with Hagar (21:9–14). And the call that God addresses to Abraham aims only to denounce explicitly this improper appropriation: "Take your son, your only son Isaac, whom you cherish"—because Isaac precisely *is not* the possession of Abraham, who therefore must not cherish him as such. The demand for a sacrifice opposes to this illegitimate appropriation, which cancels the gift given in a possession, the most original right of the giver to have his gift acknowledged as a gift given, which is to say, simply acknowledged as an always provisional, transferable, and alienable usufruct: "Go to the land of Moriah, and offer him there as a burnt offering" (22:2). Abraham hears himself asked not so much to kill his son, to lose him and return possession of him to God (according to the common concept of the gift), as, first and foremost, to give back to him his status as gift, precisely to return him to his status as gift given by reducing him (leading him back) to givenness.

And Abraham accomplishes this reduction in the most explicit and clear manner imaginable. Isaac, who reasons according to the common concept of the gift, of course notices that his father does not have (that is to say, does not *possess*) any possession available to sacrifice (to destroy and to exchange in the framework of a contract): "[Where is the lamb for a burnt offering?" (22:7)]. Abraham, who already reasons according to the phenomenological concept of sacrifice, as gift given reduced to givenness, answers that "God will provide himself the lamb for a burnt offering" (22:8)—which means that God decides everything, including what one will offer him, and thus that neither Abraham, nor even Isaac, will be able to give anything to God, except what God, himself and in the first place, has already given to them; in a word, this means that every gift made to God comes first from God as a gift given to us. The place of sacrifice is thus called "God provides" (22:14). It should be pointed out here that the Hebrew says יִרְאֶה *yir'eh* (from the root ראה *r'h*, to see, to foresee, to provide), but that the Septuagint first understands, for the name Abraham attaches to the mountain, *God saw*, ἔιδεν (second aorist of ὁράω), and then, for the name that it later retains, ὠψθη, *God appears* (passive aorist of ὁράω). Thus, it is as if the fact that God sees and provides, and therefore quite clearly *gives* the offering of the sacrifice, or put another way, *gives the gift to give*, that is, makes the gift appear as such, given by the giver—were equivalent to the appearing of the giver, to the fact that God *gives himself to seeing*. So God gives himself to be seen as he gives originally, as he shows that every gift comes from him. He appears as the giver that the gifts manifest by referring to him as their origin and provenance.

Abraham, and he alone (not Isaac), sees in this way that God alone gives the gift of the burnt offering, such that God subsequently appears to him. But he had already recognized God as the giver of gifts from the moment that he had finally agreed to recognize

Isaac as for him the principal among the gifts given by God, and thus due to God. So it is no longer important that Abraham kill, eliminate, and exchange his son for God's benefit in order to accomplish the sacrifice demanded (according to the common concept of sacrifice); rather, it matters exclusively (according to the phenomenological concept of the gift) that he acknowledge his ˉson as a gift, that he accomplish this recognition of the gift by giving it back to its giver, and, thus, that he let God appear through his gift, rightly recognized *as a gift given*. God clearly understands it as such since he spares Isaac. It is important to note that to the extent that he restrains Abraham from killing Isaac, God specifically *does not* refuse his sacrifice, but nullifies only the putting to death, because the putting to death does not belong to the essence of sacrifice: the actual death of Isaac would have ratified only sacrifice in its common concept (destruction, dispossession, exchange, and contract). In fact, God lets Abraham go right to the end of sacrifice, but understood in the sense of its phenomenological concept: the recognition of Isaac as a gift received from God and due to God. And in order to recognize it, one need only acknowledge Abraham's loss of Isaac, a recognition accomplished perfectly without his being put to death, and from the moment he is accepted as a boundless gift: "The angel said, 'Do not lay your hand on the lad or do anything to him; for now I know that you fear God, seeing you have not withheld your son, your only son, from me'" (22:12). By refusing to let Isaac be put to death, God does not thereby refuse to acknowledge the gift offered by Abraham; he accepts the sacrifice all the more, understood this time in the strict phenomenological sense. By sparing Isaac, henceforth recognized (by Abraham) as a gift (from God), God re-gives Isaac to him, gives him a second time, presenting a gift by a redounding (*don par une redondance*), which consecrates it definitively as a gift henceforth held in common and, ultimately, transparently between the giver and the recipient. The sacrifice redoubles the gift and confirms it as such for the first time.[12]

VI. Sacrifice in Truth

Thus sacrifice requires neither destruction, nor restitution, nor even exchange, much less a contract, because its basis is not the economy (which dispenses with the gift), but the gift itself, whose aporia it endeavors to work through. For the function of sacrifice is only to allow the recognition of the giver and, through him, the entire process of givenness, by reducing the given. In *this* sense, sacrifice can be understood as a destruction, but a destruction taken in the sense of *Abbau*, of the deconstruction that frees by putting into the light of day what accumulation had covered up. Sacrifice destroys the given, by clearing it away in order to uncover that which had made it visible and possible—the advance of givenness itself. This deconstructive and uncovering destruction can thus be better named a reduction: the bracketing of the gift given allows the giver's gesture to rise again to the visible, makes the recipient recover the posture of reception, and above all gives movement back to the coming-over of givenness in each of the three terms involved (giver, recipient, and gift given). Sacrifice is a redounding of the gift originating with the recipient (just as forgiveness [*le pardon*] consists of the redounding of the gift from the giver). In this way one succeeds in raising the epistemological obstacle of an economic conception of sacrifice by recognizing that "to sacrifice is not to kill, but to abandon and to give" (Bataille),[13] to the point that it becomes possible to conceive, as Levinas puts it, an "approach of the Infinite through sacrifice."[14] It constitutes an approach to the infinite because the reduction of the ever-finite given opens the only royal way toward the illumination of a possible infinite—not a being, even one that is given, and even less a necessarily determined and possessable object, but the process of an arrival (*une advenue*), always come from elsewhere and, for that very reason, inalienable and unavailable. Unless the very access to being depends on sacrifice, if, like Patočka (and doubtless in opposition to Heidegger), one decides to think the *es gibt* resolutely, on the basis of givenness, such that givenness requires sacrifice, but also alone renders sacrifice intelligible: "In sacrifice, *es gibt* being: here Being already 'gives' itself to us, not in a refusal but explicitly. To he sure, only a man capable of experiencing, in something so apparently negative, the coming of Being, only as he begins to sense that this lack opens access to what is richest, to that which bestows everything and presents all as gift to all, only then can he begin to experience this favor."[15] Which can finally be transposed into theological terms, for it may be that Saint Augustine says nothing different when he defines sacrifices as "opera . . . misericordiae, sive in nos ipsos, sive in proximos, quae *referuntur ad Deum* [works of mercy shown to ourselves or to our neighbours, and done with reference to God]."[16]

Notes

Introduction / Kevin Hart

1. The notion of "saturated experience" had been proposed by Gabriel Marcel in his *The Mystery of Being* (London: Harvill Press, 1950), 1:55. Marion's notion is considerably more sophisticated than Marcel's, as should become clear later in this introduction.

2. See Jean-Luc Marion, *Sur la théologie blanche de Descartes. Analogie, creation des vérités éternelles et fondement* (Paris: Presses Universitaires de France, 1981), *The Idol and Distance: Five Studies*, trans. Thomas A. Carlson (New York: Fordham University Press, 2001) and *God Without Being: Hors-Texte*, trans. Thomas A. Carlson, foreword David Tracy (Chicago: University of Chicago Press, 1991), chaps. 1–2.

3. See Elizabeth S. Haldane and G. R. T. Ross, trans., "The Principles of Philosophy," I. vii in *The Philosophical Works of Descartes* (Cambridge: Cambridge University Press, 1972), 1:221.

4. See Edmund Husserl, *The Basic Problems of Phenomenology: From the Lectures, Winter Semester, 1910–1911*, trans. Ingo Farin and James G. Hart (Dordrecht: Springer, 2006), 41. Martin Heidegger quotes Husserl's observation in a seminar on the second Meditation: "If Descartes had remained at the second Meditation, he would have come to phenomenology," *Introduction to Phenomenological Research*, trans. Daniel O. Dahlstrom (Bloomington: Indiana University Press, 2005), 206. For Marion's motivation as a historian of phenomenology, also see my comments in the introduction to the second part of this collection.

5. Heidegger, *The Basic Problems of Phenomenology*, trans. Albert Hofstadter (Bloomington: Indiana University Press, 1982), 328.

6. See Max Scheler, "Phenomenology and the Theory of Cognition," *Selected Philosophical Essays*, trans. David Lachterman (Evanston, Ill.: Northwestern University Press, 1973), 137. Husserl proposed his understanding of phenomenology as a strict method in his "Philosophy as Rigorous Science," *Phenomenology and the Crisis of Philosophy*, trans. and intro. Quentin Lauer (New York: Harper & Row, 1965).

7. Consider, for example, the following as an instance of the subjective idealism that the Munich Circle thought that they detected: "Reality is not in itself something absolute which becomes tied secondarily to something else; rather, in the absolute sense, it is nothing at all; it has

no 'absolute essence' whatever; it has the essentiality of something which, of necessity, is *only* intentional, *only* an object of consciousness, something presented [*Vorstelliges*] in the manner peculiar to consciousness, something apparent [as apparent]," *Ideas Pertaining to a Pure Phenomenology and to a Phenomenological Philosophy*, I: *General Introduction to a Pure Phenomenology*, trans. Fred Kersten (Dordrecht: Kluwer, 1998), 113.

8. The Göttingen Circle flourished, and in 1907 Theodor Conrad established the Göttingen Philosophical Society. Adolph Reinarch was of special importance to Husserl in Göttingen, and his conceptions of the a priori and "state of affairs" [*Sachverhalt*] had a decisive impact on his teacher. See, in particular, his essay "Concerning Phenomenology," trans. Dallas Willard, *The Personalist* 50, no. 2 (1969): 194–221. For an introduction to Reinarch, see Kimberly Baltzer-Jaray, *Doorway to the World of Essences: Adolph Reinarch and the Early Phenomenological Movement* (Saarbrücken: VDM Verlag Dr Müller, 2011).

9. The formulation is Robert Sokolowski's, though made more generally than I have done so here. See his *The Formation of Husserl's Concept of Constitution* (The Hague: Martinus Nijhoff, 1964), 137. It should be noted that Husserl first developed his account of consciousness from the work of Wilhelm Wundt, whose lectures Husserl attended in Berlin. See Wundt, *Principles of Physiological Psychology*, trans. Edward Bradford Titchener (London: S. Sonnenschein and Co., 1910).

10. Before Husserl, the word "phenomenology," used without philosophical ambition simply to mean "description of phenomena," was adopted by various significant writers: see, for example, P. D. Chantepie de la Saussaye, *Manual of the Science of Religion*, trans. Beatrice S. Colyer-Fergusson (London: Longmans, Green, and Co., 1891), chaps. 9–27. The word is still used in that sense. See, for example, H. Huegel, *Phenomenology of Plasma Engine Cathodes at Current High Rates and Low Pressures* (Washington, D.C.: NASA, 1984).

11. See, for example, Pfänder's remarks on phenomenology in his introduction to *Logik* (1921), in Alexander Pfänder, *Phenomenology of Willing and Motivation and Other Phaenomenologica*, trans. Herbert Spiegelberg (Evanston, Ill.: Northwestern University Press, 1967), 66.

12. See Martin Heidegger's 1919 seminar, "The Idea of Philosophy and the Problem of World-view," in *Towards the Definition of Philosophy*, trans. Ted Sadler (London: Continuum, 2000). Yet see Emmanuel Levinas, "Reflections on Phenomenological 'Technique,'" *Discovering Existence with Husserl*, trans. Richard A. Cohen and Michael B. Smith (Evanston, Ill.: Northwestern University Press, 1998), 91–110.

13. See Heidegger, "The Question Concerning Technology," in *The Question Concerning Technology and Other Essays*, trans. and intro. William Lovitt (New York: Harper & Row, 1977).

14. Husserl, "Review of Ernst Schröder's *Vorlesungen über die Algebra der Logik*," *Early Writings in the Philosophy of Logic and Mathematics*, trans. Dallas Willard (Dordrecht: Kluwer, 1994), 57.

15. See Husserl, *The Crisis of European Sciences and Transcendental Phenomenology: An Introduction to Phenomenological Philosophy*, trans. David Carr (Evanston, Ill.: Northwestern University Press, 1970), 189.

16. Ibid., 46.

17. Husserl, "The Origin of Geometry," ibid., 368–369. Husserl's reservations about technique are also stated in *Ideas* III. See *Ideas Pertaining to a Pure Phenomenology and to a Phenomenological Philosophy*, III: *Phenomenology and the Foundations of the Sciences*, trans. Ted E. Klein and William E. Pohl (The Hague: Martinus Nijhoff, 1980), 11.

18. See Levinas, "Phenomenon and Enigma," *Collected Philosophical Papers*, trans. Alphonso Lingis (The Hague: Martinus Nijhoff, 1987); Maurice Merleau-Ponty, *Phenomenology of Perception*, trans. Colin Smith (London: Routledge and Kegan Paul, 1962), esp. xiv; Jean-Yves Lacoste,

Experience and the Absolute: Disputed Questions on the Humanity of Man, trans. Mark Raftery-Skehan (New York: Fordham University Press, 2004), esp. chap. 9.

19. See Jacques Derrida, *Of Grammatology*, trans. Gayatri Chaktravorty Spivak, rev. ed. (Baltimore: Johns Hopkins University Press, 1997), 62.

20. See Eugen Fink, *Sixth Cartesian Meditation: The Idea of a Transcendental Theory of Method*, trans. Ronald Bruzina (Bloomington: Indiana University Press, 1995). On the meontology of the transcendental subject, see also James G. Hart, *Who One Is*, I: *Meontology of the "I": A Transcendental Phenomenology* (Dordrecht: Springer, 2009).

21. The program of transphenomenology is announced by Abraham in an unpublished manuscript of 1961, "De la psychoanalyse à la transphénoménologie," and evoked by Jacques Derrida in his introduction to Nicolas Abraham and Maria Torok, *The Wolf Man's Magic Word: A Cryptonomy*, trans. Nicholas Rand (Minneapolis: University of Minnesota Press, 1986), xxx. For heterophenomenology, see Daniel C. Dennett, *Consciousness Explained* (Boston: Little, Brown, 1991), chaps. 3 and 4. See also Alva Noë, ed., "Dennett and Heterophenomenology," a special double issue of *Phenomenology and the Cognitive Sciences* 6, nos. 1–2 (2007).

22. See Michel Henry, *The Essence of Manifestation*, trans. Girard Etzkorn (The Hague: Martinus Nijhoff, 1973), xi.

23. See, for example, Shaun Gallagher and Dan Zavahi, *The Phenomenological Mind: An Introduction to Philosophy of Mind and Cognitive Science* (London: Routledge, 2008).

24. Prominent among West Coast phenomenologists are Dagfinn Føllesdal, Hubert Dreyfus, Ronald McIntyre, and David Woodruff Smith, and among their East Coast counterparts are John Brough, Richard Cobb-Stevens, John Drummond, James Hart, and Robert Sokolowski.

25. See, for example, Maurice Merleau-Ponty, "Cézanne's Doubt," *Sense and Non-Sense*, trans. Hubert L. Drefus and Patricia Allen Drefus (Evanston, Ill.: Northwestern University Press, 1964), esp. 11, 14. Marion evokes Klee in phenomenological terms in *In Excess*, 68.

26. See Husserl, "Husserl an von Hofmannsthal (12. 1. 1907)," *Briefwechsel*, 10 vols, VII: *Wissenschaftlerkorrespondenz*, ed. Elisabeth Schuhmann and Karl Schuhmann (Boston: Kluwer, 1994), 135. See also Dorion Cairns, *Conversations with Husserl and Fink* (The Hague: Martinus Nijhoff, 1976), 59. On the need of phenomenology to supply reasons, and not be merely descriptive, see the introduction to Claude Romano's *Au coeur de la raison, la phénoménologie* (Paris: Gallimard, 2010).

27. See Michel Henry, *I Am the Truth: Toward a Philosophy of Christianity*, trans. Susan Emanuel (Stanford, Calif.: Stanford University Press, 2003), 80. On this claim, see Ruud Welten, "God Is Life: On Michel Henry's Arch-Christianity," *God in France*, ed. Peter Jonkers and Ruud Welten (Leuven: Peeters, 2005), 122, 141,

28. See, for example, Christina M. Gschwandtner, *Reading Jean-Luc Marion: Exceeding Metaphysics* (Bloomington: Indiana University Press, 2007), 83.

29. See J.-L. Marion, *The Reason of the Gift*, trans. and intro. Stephen Lewis (Charlottesville: University of Virginia Press, 2011), chap. 1.

30. Husserl, *Ideas* I, 44.

31. See J.-L. Marion, *Reduction and Givenness: Investigations of Husserl, Heidegger, and Phenomenology*, trans. Thomas A. Carlson (Evanston, Ill.: Northwestern University Press, 1998), 204.

32. See Martin Heidegger, *Being and Time*, trans. John Macquarrie and Edward Robinson (Oxford: Basil Blackwell, 1973), 191–192. Husserl proposed a variation on this theme. See his *Formal and Transcendental Logic*, trans. Dorion Cairns (The Hague: Martinus Nijhoff, 1978), 317.

33. See J.-L. Marion, *Being Given: Toward a Phenomenology of Givenness,* trans. Jeffrey L. Kosky (Stanford, Calif.: Stanford University Press, 2002), 7–10.

34. See Dominique Janicaud, "Phenomenology and the 'Theological Turn,'" trans. Bernard G. Prusak, in *Phenomenology and the "Theological Turn": The French Debate* (New York: Fordham University Press, 2000). For Heidegger's methodological atheism, see his *Phenomenological Interpretations of Aristotle: Initiation into Phenomenological Research*, trans. Richard Rojcewicz (Bloomington: Indiana University Press, 2001), 149.

35. Marion, *Being Given*, 5. Yet the emphasis should be on the phenomenality of Revelation, not the concept of Revelation. For the idea of the "flesh of the world," see Maurice Merleau-Ponty, *The Visible and the Invisible*, ed. Claude Lefort, trans. Alphonso Lingis (Evanston, Ill.: Northwestern University Press, 1968).

36. Not all the new French phenomenologists are interested in religious questions, and Janicaud does not criticize all of them. He finds within his crosshairs Levinas, Marion, Chrétien, and Henry. He excuses Lacoste: See *Phenomenology and the "Theological Turn,"* 100 n. 23. Other contemporary French phenomenologists include Philippe Capelle, Jean-François Courtine, Françoise Dastur, Nathalie Depraz, Emmanuel Falque, Didier Franck, Jean Greisch, Henri Maldiney, Claude Romano, and the earlier work of Jocelyn Benoist. A wide and useful survey is offered by Bernard Waldenfels in his *Phänomenologie in Frankreich* (Frankfurt: Suhrkamp, 1987), although it would need to be updated to take stock of the work of Marion and those younger than him.

37. See Martin Heidegger, *Phenomenology of Intuition and Expression: Theory of Philosophical Concept Formation*, trans. Tracy Colony (London: Continuum, 2010), 23. Also see *The Basic Problems of Phenomenology*, 20.

38. Marion's clearest account of this situation is in "Phenomenology of Givenness and First Philosophy," *In Excess: Studies of Saturated Phenomena*, trans. Robyn Horner and Vincent Berraud (New York: Fordham University Press, 2002), §§ 4–5. Also see *Being Given*, §1.

39. On the different senses of "consciousness," see Husserl, *Logical Investigations*, trans. J. N. Findlay (London: Routledge and Kegan Paul, 1970), II: Investigation 5. Here I have in mind transcendental consciousness, not the empirical ego or its psychic experiences.

40. See Heidegger, *Being and Time*, 60. Also see Heidegger, "Seminar in Zähringen," *Four Seminars*, trans. Andrew Mitchell and François Raffoul (Bloomington: Indiana University Press, 2003), 80.

41. Plato, *Republic, Books VI–X*, trans. Paul Shorey, Loeb Classical Library (Cambridge, Mass.: Harvard University Press, 1935), 129–30.

42. Aristotle, *Posterior Analytics, Topica*, trans. Hugh Tredennick and E. S. Forster, Loeb Classical Library (Cambridge, Mass.: Harvard University Press, 1960), 159.

43. See Gregory Vlastos, *Plato's Universe* (Seattle: University of Washington Press, 1975), 111–112.

44. G. J. Toomer, trans., *Ptolemy's Almagest* (Berlin: Springer-Verlag, 1984), 600.

45. Proclus, *Hypotyposis astronomicarum positionum*, ed. Carolus Manitius (Stuttgart: Teubner, 1974), 5. 10. 3

46. Simplicius, *On Aristotle's "On the Heavens 2. 10–14,"* trans. Ian Mueller (Ithaca, N.Y.: Cornell University Press, 2005), 488: 22–24.

47. See J. H. Lambert, *Neues Organon* (Berlin: Akademie-Verlag, 1990), 2:645–836.

48. Immanuel Kant, "To Johann Heinrich Lambert," *Correspondence*, trans. and ed. Arnulf Zweig (Cambridge: Cambridge University Press, 1999), 108.

49. On this issue, see Frederick C. Beiser, *German Idealism: The Struggle Against Subjectivism, 1781–1801* (Cambridge, Mass.: Harvard University Press, 2002), I: "Kant's Critique of Idealism."

50. See Kant, *Metaphysical Foundations of Natural Science*, trans. and ed. Michael Friedman (Cambridge: Cambridge University Press, 2004), chap. 4.

51. G. W. F. Hegel, *The Phenomenology of Spirit*, trans. J. B. Baillie (New York: Harper & Row, 1967), 134.

52. See Hegel, *The Phenomenology of Spirit*, 135.

53. G. W. F. Hegel, *Lectures on the History of Philosophy, 1825–6*, I: *Introduction and Oriental Philosophy*, ed. Robert F. Brown, trans. R. F. Brown and J. M. Stewart with the assistance of H. S. Harris (Oxford: Clarendon Press, 2009), 261, 58.

54. Cairns, *Conversations with Husserl and Fink*, 22, 52.

55. The concept of intentionality comes to us primarily from Duns Scotus, although Husserl learned of it from his teacher Franz Brentano. See Brentano's *Psychology from an Empirical Standpoint*, trans. A. C. Rancurello et al. (London: Routledge, 1973), 88.

56. Husserl, *Logical Investigations*, II, 540.

57. A fulfilling intention is a full intention that fulfills an empty intention.

58. See Husserl's letter to William Ernest Hocking, January 25, 1903, *Briefwechsel*, 3, 129–130.

59. See, for example, Edmund Husserl, *Ideas Pertaining to a Pure Phenomenology and to a Phenomenological Philosophy*, II: *Studies in the Phenomenology of Constitution*, trans. Richard Rojcewicz and André Schuwer (Dordrecht: Kluwer, 1989), §41. See also Didier Franck, *Chair et corps. Sur la phénoménologie de Husserl* (Paris: Éditions de Minuit, 1981)

60. See Edmund Husserl, *Analyses Concerning Passive and Active Synthesis: Lectures on Transcendental Logic*, trans. Anthony J. Steinbock (Dordrecht: Kluwer, 2001), 467. Clearly, Husserl is not talking of self-conscious, personal immorality, though neither is he talking merely of endless dreamless sleep.

61. Some of these questions are taken up by Maurice Blanchot in his "For Friendship," trans. Leslie Hill, *Disastrous Blanchot, The Oxford Literary Review*, vol. 22 (2001), ed. Timothy Clark, Leslie Hill and Nicholas Royle, 25–38, and Jacques Derrida, *Politics of Friendship*, trans. George Collins (London: Verso, 1997). Of course, the classical account of friendship is to be found in Aristotle, *Nichomachean Ethics*, Book 8. For Marion on friendship, see *In Excess*, 38, and *The Erotic Phenomenon*, trans. Stephen E. Lewis (Chicago: Chicago University Press, 2007), 218–20.

62. Husserl, *Logical Investigations*, I, 252.

63. Martin Heidegger, *Logic: The Question of Truth*, trans. Thomas Sheehan (Bloomington: Indiana University Press, 2010), 28.

64. Immanuel Kant, *Critique of Pure Reason*, trans. Norman Kemp Smith (London: Macmillan, 1933), B303, p. 264.

65. See Husserl's comments on the relation of phenomenology and experiential psychology in *Ideas* III, chap. 2, esp. 38 and 59. Also see, more generally, his *Phenomenological Psychology: Lectures, Summer Semester, 1925*, trans. John Scanlon (The Hague: Martinus Nijhoff, 1977).

66. Husserl, *Ideas* III, 65.

67. Martin Heidegger, *Kant and the Problem of Metaphysics*, 4th ed. enlarged, trans. Richard Taft (Bloomington: Indiana University Press, 1990), 1.

68. Husserl, *Ideas* I, 257. Trans. slightly modified.

69. Yet the word ἐποχή is taken from Greek skeptics such as Arcesilaus. See Giovanni Reale, *A History of Ancient Philosophy: The Systems of the Hellenistic Age*, ed. and trans. John R. Catan (Albany: State University of New York Press, 1985–90), 3:331.

70. Eugenio Montale, "The Eel," trans. Kevin Hart, in *Poems*, ed. Harry Thomas (London: Penguin, 2002), 159–160. For a brief account of poetry as involving bracketing, see Jacques

Derrida, "'This Strange Institution Called Literature': An Interview with Jacques Derrida," in Derrida, *Acts of Literature*, ed. Derek Attridge (New York: Routledge, 1992), 44–46.

71. Husserl, *Ideas* III, 65.

72. See, for example, Husserl, *The Crisis of European Sciences*, 236, 256–57.

73. See ibid., §41.

74. Ibid., 151.

75. Fink, *Sixth Cartesian Meditation*, 144.

76. See Edmund Husserl, *The Idea of Phenomenology*, trans. William P. Alston and George Nakhnikian (Dordrecht: Kluwer, 1990), 8, and *Ideas* I, §§87–90.

77. On contemplation in phenomenology, see Kevin Hart, "Contemplation: Beyond and Beneath," *Sophia* 48 (2009): 435–459.

78. See Husserl, *Ideas* III, 22, 51, 70.

79. Ibid., II, 29.

80. Edmund Husserl, "Foundational Investigations of the Phenomenological Origin of the Spatiality of Nature: The Originary Ark, the Earth, Does Not Move," trans. Fred Kersten, rev. Leonard Lawlor, in Maurice Merleau-Ponty, *Husserl at the Limits of Phenomenology: Including Texts by Edmund Husserl*, ed. Leonard Lawlor with Bettina Bergo (Evanston, Ill.: Northwestern University Press, 2002), 118. For Merleau-Ponty's notes on the essay, see pp. 68, 74, and for a lucid account of the problem, see Anthony J. Steinbock, *Home and Beyond: Generative Phenomenology after Husserl* (Evanston, Ill.: Northwestern University Press, 1995), 109–122.

81. See George Berkeley, *A Treatise Concerning the Principles of Human Knowledge*, in *Philosophical Writings*, ed. and intro. David M. Armstrong (London: Collier-Macmillan, 1965), § 3.

82. Husserl, *Ideas* II, 4.

83. For further elucidation of Husserlian phenomenology, see Rudolf Bernet, Iso Kern, and Eduard Marbach, ed., *An Introduction to Husserlian Phenomenology* (Evanston: Northwestern University Press, 1993), Robert Sokolowski, *Introduction to Phenomenology* (Cambridge: Cambridge University Press, 2000), and Dan Zahavi, *Husserl's Phenomenology* (Stanford, Calif.: Stanford University Press, 2003).

84. For reflections on Marion's personal itinerary, see his *La rigueur des choses: Entretiens avec Dan Arbib* (Paris: Flammarion, 2012).

85. René Descartes, "To Mersenne. On the Eternal Truths (April 15, May 6, and May 27, 1630)," *Philosophical Essays and Correspondence*, ed. Roger Ariew (Indianapolis: Hackett, 2000), 28.

86. See J.-L. Marion, *Sur la théologie blanche de Descartes. Analogie, création des vérités éternelles et fondement* (Paris: Presses Universitaires de France, 1981), 28.

87. See Francisco Suárez, *The Metaphysical Demonstration of the Existence of God: Metaphysical Disputations 28–29*, trans. and ed. John P. Doyle (South Bend, Ind.: St Augustine's Press, 2004), Disputation 28, Section 3 §§ 10, 11. See also Thomas Aquinas, *Truth*, trans. Robert W. Mulligan, 3 vols. (1954; rpt. Indianapolis: Hackett, 1994), I, q. 2 art. 11, and Cajetan, *Commentary on "Being and Essence,"* trans. Lottie H. Kendzierski and Francis C. Wade (Milwaukee: Marquette University Press, 1964), chap. 2.

88. Marion, *On Descartes' Metaphysical Prism: The Constitution and the Limits of Onto-Theology in Cartesian Thought*, trans. Jeffrey L. Kosky (Chicago: University of Chicago Press, 1999), 352. With respect to Marion on destitution, see Vincent Carraud, *Pascal et la philosophie* (Paris: Presses Universitaires de France, 1992), chap. III, esp. §16.

89. See Marion, *On Descartes' Metaphysical Prism*, 228.

90. See Duns Scotus, *Philosophical Writings*, trans. Allan Wolter (Indianapolis: Bobbs-Merrill, 1962), 28.

91. See Descartes, "Meditation" III, *The Philosophical Works*, I, 166.

92. Aristotle, *Metaphysics*, 1003a 21; Suárez, *Disputationes metaphysicae*, 1.1 26.

93. Martin Heidegger, "The Onto-Theo-Logical Constitution of Metaphysics," *Identity and Difference*, trans. Joan Stambaugh (Chicago: University of Chicago Press, 2002), 61. Marion notes, "In effect, from the beginning, our studies have been organized by reference to onto-theo-logy," *On Descartes' Metaphysical Prism*, 5.

94. See Marion, *On Descartes' Metaphysical Prism*, chap. III §15 and chap. IV §20.

95. J.-L. Marion, "The Originary Otherness of the Ego: A Reading of Descartes' Second Meditation," *On the Ego and on God: Further Cartesian Questions*, trans. Christina M. Gschwandtner (New York: Fordham University Press, 2007), 3–29.

96. See Marion, *On Descartes' Metaphysical Prism*, 291.

97. On the three orders see Pascal, *Pensées*, ed. and trans. Roger Ariew (Indianapolis: Hackett, 2005), 142/110, 339/308, 680/423. For a discussion of the three orders, see Dawn M. Ludwin, *Blaise Pascal's Quest for the Ineffable* (New York: Peter Lang, 2001), 7, 14–15. For Marion's view, see *On Descartes's Metaphysical Prism*, chap. 5.

98. See Gianni Vattimo, "*Verwindung*: Nihilism and the Postmodern in Philosophy," *SubStance* 16: 2 (1987), 7–17, and Richard Rorty, *Contingency, Irony, and Solidarity* (Cambridge: Cambridge University Press, 1989).

99. Marion, *On Descartes' Metaphysical Prism*, 351.

100. See Richard Kearney and Joseph Stephen O'Leary, *Heidegger et la question de Dieu* (Paris: Quadrige/Presses Universitaires de France, 2009).

101. See Paul de Man, *Wartime Journalism, 1939–1943*, ed. Werner Hamacher, Neil Hertz, and Thomas Keenan (Lincoln: University of Nebraska Press, 1988), and *Responses: On Paul de Man's Wartime Journalism*, ed. Werner Hamacher, Neil Hertz, and Thomas Keenan (Lincoln: University of Nebraska Press, 1989).

102. Derrida, *Of Grammatology*, 158.

103. See, for example, John Macquarrie, *An Existentialist Theology: A Comparison of Heidegger and Bultmann* (London: SCM Press, 1965).

104. See Pseudo-Dionysius the Areopagite, "The Divine Names," in *The Complete Works*, trans. Colm Luibheid (Mahwah, N.J.: Paulist Press, 1987), chap. 4.

105. See Thomas Aquinas, *Summa Theologiae*, 1a, q. 11, art. 4, *responsio*. Marion modifies his view on Aquinas in his "St Thomas Aquinas and Onto-theo-logy," trans. B. Gendreau, R. Rethy, and M. Sweeney, *Mystics: Presence and Aporia*, ed. Michael Kessler and Christian Sheppard (Chicago: University of Chicago Press, 2003), 38–74. Also see *God Without Being*, xxiii. For Balthasar on distance, see his *Explorations in Theology*, III: *Creator Spirit*, trans. Brian McNeil (San Francisco: Ignatius Press, 1993), 173. Also see Balthasar's brief reflections on *Dieu sans l'être* in *Theo-Logic*, II: *Truth of God*, trans. Adrian J. Walker (San Francisco: Ignatius Press, 2004), 135 n. 10 and 177 n. 9.

106. See Heidegger, *The Question of Being*, trans. William Kluback and Jean T. Wilde (London: Vision Press, 1959), 83.

107. See St. John of Damascus, *On the Divine Images: Three Apologies Against Those Who Attack the Divine Images*, trans. David Anderson (Crestwood, N.Y.: St. Vladimir's Seminary Press, 2002), and St Theodore the Studite, *On the Holy Icons*, trans. Catherine P. Roth (Crestwood, N.Y.: St. Vladimir's Seminary Press, 2001).

108. Marion, *God Without Being*, 7. My emphasis.

109. See Dale M. Coulter, *"Per Visibilia ad Invisibilia": Theological Method in Richard of St. Victor* (Tournhout, Belgium: Brepols, 2006).

110. See Husserl, *Ideas* I, §58.

111. See Husserl, *The Basic Problems of Phenomenology: From the Lectures, Winter Semester, 1910–1911*, trans Ingo Farin and James G. Hart (Dordrecht: Springer, 2006), Appendix XIII, and Cairns, *Conversations with Husserl and Fink*, 47. Also see Angela Ales Bello, *The Divine in Husserl and Other Explorations*, Analecta Husserliana XCVIII (Dordrecht: Springer, 2009) and Emmanuel Housett, *Husserl et l'idée de Dieu* (Paris: Cerf, 2010).

112. See Jacques Taminiaux, *The Metamorphoses of Phenomenological Reduction* (Milwaukee: Marquette University Press, 2004).

113. Martin Heidegger, "What Is Metaphysics?" trans. David Farrell Krell, *Pathmarks*, ed. William McNeill (Cambridge: Cambridge University Press, 1998), 88.

114. Martin Heidegger, *The Fundamental Concepts of Metaphysics: World, Finitude, Solitude*, trans. William McNeill and Nicholas Walker (Bloomington: Indiana University Press, 1995), 63. On Heidegger's account of boredom, see Lars Svendsen, *A Philosophy of Boredom*, trans. John Irons (London: Reaktion Books, 2005), chap. 3, and Elizabeth S. Goodstein, *Experience without Qualities: Boredom and Modernity* (Stanford, Calif.: Stanford University Press, 2005), chap. 5.

115. See Heidegger, *The Basic Problems of Phenomenology*, trans. Albert Hofstadter (Bloomington: Indiana University Press, 1982), 21.

116. See Marion, *Reduction and Givenness*, 192–98.

117. Yet see Marion's comments on Heidegger's account of deep boredom as an attunement in *Reduction and Givenness*, 173–174.

118. Blaise Pascal, *Pensées*, ed. Roger Ariew (Indianapolis: Hackett, 2005), S766. Ariew argues elsewhere that in some respects Pascal was Cartesian. See his "Descartes and Pascal," *Perspectives on Science*, 15: 4 (2007), 397–409. Marion would agree. See his *On Descartes' Metaphysical Prism*, 280.

119. The first full account of "saturated phenomena" is given in "The Saturated Phenomenon," an essay whose theses Marion has adjusted significantly. A translation can be found in *The Visible and the Revealed*, trans. Christina M. Gschwandtner and others (New York: Fordham University Press, 2008), 18–48.

120. Husserl, *The Idea of Phenomenology*, 49.

121. Ibid., 11. Also see *Logical Investigations*, II, 539.

122. Edmund Husserl, *Psychological and Transcendental Phenomenology and the Confrontation with Heidegger (1927–1931)*, trans. and ed. Thomas Sheehan and Richard E. Palmer (Dordrecht: Kluwer, 1997), 218. See also, even more markedly, *Phenomenological Psychology*, 179.

123. Marion, *Reduction and Givenness*, 56.

124. It would be interesting to explore the similarities and differences between Marion and Jan Patočka with regard to phenomenality. See Patočka, *Qu'est-ce que la phénoménologie?* (Grenoble: Editions Jérôme Millon, 1988), 249–261; and *Papiers phénoménologiques* (Grenoble: Editions Jérôme Millon, 1995), 163–210.

125. See Marion, *Being Given*, §19.

126. See Gottfried Leibniz, *Monadology* §32, in *Discourse on Metaphysics/Correspondence with Arnauld/Monadology*, trans. Albert R. Chandler (La Salle, Ill.: Open Court, 1973). Marion is influenced by the Heidegger of *The Principle of Reason*, trans. Reginald Lilly (Bloomington: Indiana University Press, 1991). For the principle of insufficient reason, see Marion, *The Erotic Phenomenon*, §17.

127. See J. F. Herbart, *Hauptpunkte der Metaphysik* in *Sämmliche Werke*, 19 vols., ed. Carl Kehrbach et al. (Aalen, Germany: Scientia, 1964), 2, 187; Husserl, *Cartesian Meditations*, 103; Martin Heidegger, *History of the Concept of Time: Prolegomena*, trans. Theodore Kisiel (Bloom-

ington: Indiana University Press, 1985), 86; and Marion, *Reduction and Givenness*, 203. See also Michel Henry, "Quatre principes de la phénoménologie," in *Phénoménologie de la vie*, I: *De la phénoménologie* (Paris: Presses Universitaires de France, 2003), 77–104.

128. See Marion, "Does the *Cogito* Affect Itself? Generosity and Phenomenology: Remarks on Michel Henry's Interpretation of the Cartesian *Cogito*," trans. Stephen Voss, *Cartesian Questions: Method and Metaphysics* (Chicago: University of Chicago Press, 1999), 99.

129. See Marion, *Being Given*, 5.

130. See Marion, "L'interloqué," trans. Eduardo Cadava and Anne Tomiche, *Who Comes After the Subject?* ed. Eduardo Cadava et al. (New York: Routledge, 1991), 236–245, and *Being Given*, book 5.

131. See Aristotle, *Categories*, 1b 25–2a 5.

132. Kant, *Prolegomena to Any Future Metaphysics*, trans. Paul Carus, rev. James W. Ellington (Indianapolis: Hackett, 1977), 65.

133. Kant, *Critique of Pure Reason*, B 106.

134. For the principles, see *Critique of Pure Reason*, A 148–62.

135. J. G. Fichte, *The Science of Knowledge*, ed. and trans. Peter Heath and John Lachs (Cambridge: Cambridge University Press, 1982), 51. Also see the first introduction to the new attempt to present the *Wissenschaftslehre* (1797), *Introductions to the "Wissenschaftslehre" and Other Writings (1797–1800)*, trans. and ed. Daniel Breazeale (Indianapolis: Hackett, 1994), 27–28.

136. F. W. J. von Schelling, *On the History of Modern Philosophy*, trans. Andrew Bowie (Cambridge: Cambridge University Press, 1994), 99.

137. Hegel, *The Phenomenology of Spirit*, 277.

138. See Husserl, *The Crisis of European Sciences*, §§30–32.

139. See Heidegger, *Kant and the Problem of Metaphysics*, 4th ed., enlarged, trans. Richard Taft (Bloomington: Indiana University Press, 1990), §§15, 34, and *Phenomenological Interpretation of Kant's "Critique of Pure Reason,"* trans. Parvis Emad and Kenneth Maly (Bloomington: Indiana University Press, 1997), §25.

140. Marion, *Being Given*, 199, 278.

141. Honoré de Balzac, *The Alkahest: The House of Claës*, trans. Katharine Prescott Wormeley (Boston: Roberts Bros., 1887), 148–149.

142. See Marion, *Being Given*, §§ 4, 28.

143. See Marion, "The Banality of Saturation," trans. Jeffrey L. Kosky, *The Visible and the Revealed*, 119–144.

144. See Marion, *Being Given*, 215–216.

145. See ibid., §24.

146. Richard Kearney, "On the Gift: A Discussion Between Jacques Derrida and Jean-Luc Marion," *God, the Gift, and Postmodernism*, ed. John D. Caputo and Michael J. Scanlon (Bloomington: Indiana University Press, 1999), 63.

147. See Karl Barth, *Church Dogmatics*, I. i., ed. G. W. Bromiley and T. F. Torrance, trans. G. W. Bromiley (Edinburgh: T. & T. Clark, 1936), 323. Also see Barth's rejection of philosophy as a way of discussing revelation, *Protestant Theology in the Nineteenth Century: Its Background and History,* no trans. (Valley Forge, Pa.: Judson Press, 1973), 307.

148. See Augustine, *Expositions of the Psalms*, 3:51–72, trans. Maria Boulding, ed. John E. Rotelle, The Works of Saint Augustine, Psalm 62, 242–43.

149. Kearney, "Jean-Luc Marion: The Hermeneutics of Revelation," in *Debates in Continental Philosophy: Conversations with Contemporary Thinkers* (New York: Fordham University Press, 2004), 18.

150. See Marion, *Being Given*, 235.

151. J. M. Cohen, ed. and trans., *The Life of Saint Teresa of Ávila by Herself* (Harmondsworth: Penguin, 1957), 188.

152. See Origen, *Contra Celsum*, trans. and intro. Henry Chadwick (Cambridge: Cambridge University Press, 1965), 44–45.

153. See, for instance, Bernard of Clairvaux, *On the Song of Songs*, IV: *Sermons 67–86*, trans. Irene Edmonds (Kalamazoo, Mich.: Cistercian Publications, 1980), 73:2. The expression *modus sine modo* is mostly used in the Christian tradition to indicate how we are to love God, at the extreme of our way of loving other human beings, though it can be read otherwise to suggest how God loves us, in a way without a way, because the deity is within us as well as beyond us. See my essay "Impossible Love," *Archivo di Filosofia* 78: 1 (2010): 267–276.

154. See Marion, "The Banality of Saturation," 140–141.

155. See Fink, *Sixth Cartesian Meditation*, 120.

156. On Fink's Gnosticism, see Steven Galt Crowell, "Gnostic Phenomenology: Eugen Fink and the Critique of Transcendental Reason," *Husserl, Heidegger, and the Space of Meaning: Paths Toward Transcendental Phenomenology* (Evanston, Ill.: Northwestern University Press, 2001), esp. 250.

157. Jocelyn Benoist, *L'idée de phénoménologie* (Paris: Beauchesne, 2001), 102. See Marion, "The Banality of Saturation," 124 and 175 n. 12.

158. On this theme, see Tasmin Jones, *A Genealogy of Marion's Philosophy of Religion: Apparent Darkness* (Bloomington: Indiana University Press, 2011).

159. See Kearney, "Jean-Luc Marion: The Hermeneutics of Revelation," 16.

160. See Jean-Luc Marion, *Figures de phénoménologie. Husserl, Heidegger, Levinas, Derrida, Henry* (Paris: Vrin, 2012).

161. See Wilfred Sellars, *Empiricism and the Philosophy of Mind*, ed. Robert Brandom (Cambridge, Mass.: Harvard University Press, 1997). Claude Romano is one person who is attempting to bring about a conversation between the two schools. Such is one burden of his *Au coeur de la raison, la phénoménologie*. More generally, see Jack Reynolds, James Williams and Edwin Mares, ed., *Postanalytic and Metacontinental: Crossing Philosophical Divides* (London: Continuum, 2010).

162. Henry, *The Essence of Manifestation*, 41.

163. See ibid., §11.

164. Henry, *The Essence of Manifestation*, 240.

165. For more detail on Henry's basic position, see Kevin Hart, "Inward Life," in *Michel Henry: The Affects of Thought*, ed. Jeffrey Hanson and Michael R. Kelly (London: Continuum Press), 87–110.

166. Michel Henry, *Marx: A Philosophy of Human Reality*, trans. Kathleen McLaughlin (Bloomington: Indiana University Press, 1983), 134.

167. The point is made crisply by Henry in "The Critique of the Subject," in *Who Comes After the Subject?* 159.

168. See Henry, "The Critique of the Subject," 166, and *La barbarie* (Paris: Presses Universitaires de France, 1987), 33. For Henry's rejection of Heidegger's account of the *cogito*, see his *The Genealogy of Psychoanalysis*, trans. Douglas Brick (Stanford, Calif.: Stanford University Press, 1993), 78. For Marion on Henry, see "Does the *Cogito* Affect Itself?" *Cartesian Questions*, 96–117.

169. Michel Henry, *Philosophy and Phenomenology of the Body*, trans. Girard Etzkorn (The Hague: Martinus Nijhoff, 1975), 208.

170. See Henry, *The Essence of Manifestation*, 461.

171. See Michel Henry, *I Am the Truth: Toward a Philosophy of Christianity*, trans. Susan Emanuel (Stanford, Calif.: Stanford University Press, 2003), and *La barbarie*. Henry focuses, however, on the synoptic gospels in his *Words of Christ*, trans. Christina M. Gschwandtner (Grand Rapids, Mich.: Eerdmans, 2012).

172. See Michel Henry, *Seeing the Invisible: On Kandinsky*, trans. Scott Davidson (London: Continuum, 2009), and Marion, *The Crossing of the Visible*, trans James K. A. Smith (Stanford, Calif.: Stanford University Press, 2004), esp. chap. 1.

173. Emmanuel Levinas, *The Theory of Intuition in Husserl's Phenomenology*, trans. André Orianne (Evanston, Ill.: Northwestern University Press, 1973), 149.

174. See Levinas, "Intentionality and Sensation," § 4, in his *Discovering Existence with Husserl* for an important distinction that Levinas draws between two modes of intentionality.

175. See Levinas, "Phenomenon and Enigma," *Collected Philosophical Papers*, trans. Alphonso Lingis (The Hague: Martinus Nijhoff, 1987), 61–73.

176. Emmanuel Levinas, *Totality and Infinity: An Essay on Exteriority*, trans. Alphonso Lingis (The Hague: Martinus Nijhoff, 1979), 35.

177. Haldane and Ross, *The Philosophical Works of Descartes*, I, 166.

178. See Levinas, *Totality and Infinity*, 58.

179. Vasily Grossman, *Life and Fate*, trans. and intro. Robert Chandler (1985; New York: New York Review Books, 2006), 407–408.

180. See Emmanuel Levinas, *Existence and Existents*, trans. Alphonso Lingis (Dordrecht: Kluwer, 1988), 57–64, and *Ethics and Infinity: Conversations with Philippe Nemo*, trans. Richard A. Cohen (Pittsburgh: Duquesne University Press, 1985), chap. 3.

181. See Marion, *The Erotic Phenomenon*, 42.

182. See Levinas, *Autrement que savoir* (Paris: Éditions Osiris, 1988), 74–76. Also see Marion's remarks on this in "From the Other to the Individual," trans. Robyn Horner, *Transcendence: Philosophy, Literature, and Theology Approach the Beyond*, ed. Regina Schwartz (New York: Routledge, 2004), 54–55.

183. Marion, "From the Other to the Individual," 43.

184. Marion, "The Intentionality of Love," *Prolegomena to Charity*, trans. Stephen Lewis (New York: Fordham University Press, 2002), 93.

185. See Levinas, "Reality and its Shadow," *Collected Philosophical Papers*, 1–13. A modification of his general view on art may be found in *De l'oblitération: Entretien avec Françoise Armengaud à propos de l'oeuvre de Sosno*, 2nd ed. (Paris: Éditions de la Différance, 1990).

186. On Jena Romanticism and its heritages, see Philippe Lacoue-Labarthe and Jean-Luc Nancy, *The Literary Absolute: The Theory of Literature in German Romanticism*, trans. Philip Barnard and Cheryl Lester (Albany: State University of New York Press, 1988).

187. See Levinas, *Of God Who Comes to Mind*, trans. Bettina Bergo (Stanford, Calif.: Stanford University Press, 1998), xi.

188. Friedrich Nietzsche, *Daybreak: Thoughts on the Prejudices of Morality*, trans. R. J. Hollingdale (Cambridge: Cambridge University Press, 1982), 5.

189. See Jacques Derrida, "Letter to a Japanese Friend," trans. David Wood and Andrew Benjamin, *Psyche: Inventions of the Other*, ed. Peggy Kamuf and Elizabeth Rottenberg (Stanford: Stanford University Press, 2008), 2:2. Also in the background is Husserl's word "de-sedimentation." See Derrida, *Edmund Husserl's "Origin of Geometry": An Introduction*, trans. John P. Leavey Jr., ed. David B. Allison (Stony Brook, N.Y.: Nicolas Hays Ltd., 1979), 50, 119.

190. See Jacques Derrida, "How to Avoid Speaking: Denials," trans. Ken Frieden and Elizabeth Rottenberg, *Psyche*, 2:143–95. Derrida's remarks on Marion are mostly in the endnotes. Also see

Derrida's essay "*Sauf le nom* (Post-Scriptum)" in *On the Name*, ed. Thomas Dutoit, trans. David Wood et al. (Stanford, Calif.: Stanford University Press, 1995).

191. Jacques Derrida, "The Crisis in the Teaching of Philosophy," *Who's Afraid of Philosophy? Right to Philosophy* I, trans. Jan Plug (Stanford: Stanford University Press, 2002), 103.

192. Kearney, "On the Gift," 69, 71.

193. Jacques Derrida, "Différance," in *Margins of Philosophy*, trans. Alan Bass (Chicago: University of Chicago Press, 1982), 6. On Derrida and apophatic theology, see Kevin Hart, *The Trespass of the Sign: Deconstruction, Theology, and Philosophy*, expanded ed. (New York: Fordham University Press, 2000).

194. See Derrida, *Speech and Phenomena and Other Essays on Husserl's Theory of Signs*, trans. David B. Allison (Evanston, Ill.: Northwestern University Press, 1973), 101.

195. Marion, "In the Name: How to Avoid Speaking of it," *In Excess*, 155.

196. Yet see Derrida's response to Marion's essay and the consequent short discussion with Marion in *God, the Gift and Postmodernism*, 42–47.

197. See Derrida, *Given Time* I: *Counterfeit Money*, trans. Peggy Kamuf (Chicago: University of Chicago Press, 1992), 122.

198. See Marion, "Présence et distance: Remarques sur l'implication réciproque de la contemplation eucharistique et de la présence réelle," *Résurrection*, 43–44 (1974), 33; his discussion of Hölderlin in *The Idol and Distance*, esp. 113, 124; and "The Gift of a Presence," *Prolegomena to Charity*, 124–152. See also his reflections on the gift after the engagement with Derrida in *The Reason of the Gift*.

199. See J.-L. Marion, *Certitudes négatives* (Paris: Grasset, 2010).

200. Kearney, "On the Gift," 66.

201. For further general guidance on Marion's writing, see the introduction to Kevin Hart, *Counter-Experiences: Reading Jean-Luc Marion* (Notre Dame, Ind.: Notre Dame University Press, 2007). See also Robyn Horner, *Jean-Luc Marion: A Theo-logical Introduction* (Burlington, Vt.: Ashgate, 2005) and Christina M. Gschwandtner, *Reading Jean-Luc Marion: Exceeding Metaphysics* (Bloomington: Indiana University Press, 2007).

Introduction to Part I: Metaphysics and Its Idols

1. For Derrida's view of *The Idol and Distance* and *God Without Being*, see his essay "How to Avoid Speaking: Denials," *Psyche: Inventions of the Other*, ed. Peggy Kamuf and Elizabeth Rottenberg (Stanford: Stanford University Press, 2008), 2:307–311. Also see Derrida's response to Marion in *God, the Gift, and Postmodernism*, ed. John D. Caputo and Michael J. Scanlon (Bloomington: Indiana University Press, 1999), 42–47. The discussion "On the Gift" is also valuable, 54–78.

2. French readers were introduced to Heidegger's views on the relations of being and God in "Textes de Martin Heidegger," an appendix to *Heidegger et la question de Dieu* (1980), ed. Richard Kearney and Joseph S. O'Leary. This collection featured Marion's "La double idolâtrie— Remarques sur la différence ontologique et la pensée de Dieu," which was later to appear in *Dieu sans l'être* (1982), along with a response to Beaufret and Fédier. The volume was reissued by Quadrige/PUF, with an introduction by Jean-Yves Lacoste, in 2009. For Heidegger's remarks on God and being, see p. 366.

3. Also see, in this regard, "The Icon or the Endless Hermeneutic" and "The Prototype and the Image," both in this collection. For the patristic works on which Marion relies, see St. John of Damascus, *On the Divine Images*, trans. David Anderson (Crestwood, N.Y.: St. Vladimir's Seminary Press, 2002) and St. Theodore the Studite, *On the Holy Icons*, trans. Catharine P. Roth (Crestwood, N.Y.: St. Vladimir's Seminary Press, 2001).

4. See Pseudo-Dionysius the Areopagite, "The Divine Names," in *The Complete Works*, trans. Colm Luibheid (Mahwah, N.J.: Paulist Press, 1987), chap. 4.

5. Jean-Luc Marion, *God Without Being: Hors-Texte*, trans. Thomas A. Carlson (Chicago: University of Chicago Press, 1991), xxiii. See Aquinas, *Summa theologiae*, 1a q. 11 art 4 *responsio*.

6. Marion includes "Saint Thomas d'Aquin et l'onto-théologie" in the second edition of *Dieu sans l'être* (2002).

7. See Friedrich Nietzsche, *The Gay Science: With a Prelude in Rhymes and an Appendix of Songs*, trans. Walter Kaufmann (New York: Vintage Books, 1974), §125.

8. Jean-Luc Marion, *The Idol and Distance: Five Studies*, trans. Thomas A. Carlson (New York: Fordham University Press, 2001), 89.

9. See Dominique Janicaud, "The Theological Turn of French Phenomenology," trans. Bernard G. Prusak, in *Phenomenology and the "Theological Turn": The French Debate* (New York: Fordham University Press, 2000), 51–66. Also see Janicaud, *Phenomenology "Wide Open": After the French Debate*, trans. Charles N. Cabral (New York: Fordham University Press, 2005), esp. chap. 3.

10. Marion, "Metaphysics and Phenomenology: A Relief for Theology," in *The Visible and the Revealed*, trans. Christina M. Gschwandtner and others (New York: Fordham University Press, 2008), 64.

11. Marion, "'Christian Philosophy': Hermeneutic or Heuristic," in ibid., 78, 79. For an overview of the debate, see Gregory B. Sadler, ed. and trans., *Reason Fulfilled by Revelation: The 1930s Christian Philosophy Debates in France* (Washington, D.C.: Catholic University of America Press, 2011).

The Marches of Metaphysics

Translated by Thomas A. Carlson. Reprinted from Jean-Luc Marion, *The Idol and Distance: Five Studies* (Fordham University Press, 2001), 1–26.

1. In this sense, see Saint Paul: "Remember that at that time you were without Christ, excluded from the city of Israel, foreign to the covenants of the promise, without hope, atheists without God in this world!" (Ephesians 2:12). On ἄθεος, see G. Kittel, *Theologisches Worterbuch zum neuen Testament,* the θέος article, s.v., by Stauffer, vol. III, pp. 120–22; French trans., *Dictionnaire biblique*, G. Kittel, "Dieu" (Geneva: Labor et fides, 1968), pp. 120–24.

2. See L. Oupensky, *Essai sur la théologie de l'icone* (Paris: 1960); P. Evdokimov, *L'art de l'icone* (Paris: D.D.B., 1970); and especially C. von Schönborn, O.P., *L'icone du Christ: Fondements théologiques élaborés entre le 1ᵉ et le 2ᵉ concile de Nicée* (Fribourg, Switzerland: Éditions Universitaires, 1976).

3. Wittgenstein, *Zettel*, § 191; French trans., *Fiches* (Paris: Gallimard, 1970).

4. Kant, *Critique of Judgement*, § 87.

5. Saint Thomas, *Summa Theologica*, Ia. q. 2, a. 3. See also *Summa contra Gentiles*, I, 13 and Duns Scotus, *Opus Oxoniense*, I, d. 3, q. 2, a. 4, n. 10.

6. Malebranche, *Entretiens sur la métaphysique et sur la réligion*, VIII, § 1, in *Ouevres complètes* (Paris: Vrin, 1965), vol. XII–XIII, p. 174. See also *Recherche de la vérité*, II, II, VIII, § 1, in ibid., vol. I, p. 456 (Paris, 1962).

7. Descartes, *Meditatio III*, in *Oeuvres*, ed. Adam-Tannery, vol. VII, p. 45, lines 11–13.

8. Spinoza, *Ethics*, I, definition 6.

9. *Phänomenologie des Geistes*, ed. Hoffmeister, p. 529. See also the *Encyclopedia of the Philosophical Sciences*, § 593.

10. *Principes de la nature et de la grâce*, § 8, *Philosophischen Schriften*, ed. Gerhardt, vol. VI, 602. See also "Est illud Ens sicut ultima ratio Rerum, et uno vocabulo solet appelari Deus," in *Opuscules et fragments inédits*, ed. Couturat (Paris, 1903, and Hildesheim, 1966), p. 534.

11. Here, as throughout the translation, the distinction between the capitalized "Being" and the lowercase "being" corresponds to the distinction between the substantive use of the infinitival *être* and the participial *étant*, which itself corresponds to the distinction in Heidegger's German between *Sein* and *Seiendes*. [Trans.]

12. On this point, we should note that the equation of οὐσία and "subject," and therefore also its comprehension as "substance," denotes the properly metaphysical turn that occurs at the very heart of Aristotle's thought. See R. Boehm, *La métaphysique d'Aristote: Le fondamental et l'essential*, translated from the German and presented by E. Martineau (Paris: Gallimard, 1976).

13. Heidegger, *Identität und Differenz* (Pfullingen: G. Neske, 1957), p. 63 = French trans. in *Questions* I (Paris: Gallimard, 1968), p. 305. See also, in addition to the whole of this text, *Wegmarken,* particularly "Einleitung zu 'Was ist Metaphysik?'" (Frankfurt: V. Klostermann, 1967), p. 208 = French trans. in *Questions* 1, p. 41. The translation of *Austrag* by "conciliation" renders almost nothing of the German, except the most common sense (arrangement, organization, etc.), thus concealing the self-withdrawal (*aus*) through which Being sustains beings (*trag*), all the while abandoning visibility to them. For the sake of convenience, I nevertheless keep the usual translation, despite this insufficiency.

14. Heidegger, *Identität*, p. 51, then p. 64 = French trans., pp. 294, 306.

15. Heidegger, *Wegmarken*, p. 208 = p. 40, and *Identität*, p. 47 = p. 290. See also *Questions* IV (Paris: Gallimard, 1976), p. 64; *Vorträge und Aufsätze* I, p. 42 = French trans. in *Essais et Conférences* (Paris: Gallimard, 1958), p. 56; *Wegmarken*, p. 180 = French trans. in *Questions* II (Paris: Gallimard, 1966), p. 131.

16. Heidegger, *Identität*, pp. 64–65 = p. 306.

17. Ibid., p. 45 = p. 289. That same experience is alluded to in the text of *Unterwegs zur Sprache* (Pfullingen: G. Neske, 1959), p. 96, which recognizes in the experience, moreover, as well as an "origin," a "future."

18. Heidegger, *Wegmarken*, p. 208 = pp. 40–41.

19. The right that one can claim to have to submit certain thinkers to a theological approach escapes the danger of a trivial recuperation only if it goes hand in hand with the conviction that a theological contribution can come to us from those same thinkers. That these two movements are not contradictory is certainly what I have learned from H. Urs von Balthasar (particularly *Herrlichkeit*, III/I *Im Raum der Metaphysik* [Einsiedeln: Johannes Verlag, 1965]).

20. René Char, *Recherche de la base et du sommet* (Paris: Gallimard, 1971), p. 8.

21. Here René Char (*Fureur et mystère* [Paris: Gallimard, 1962], "L'Absent"), who says in his own way what the Fathers contemplate in the paradoxical face of Christ: the "paradox of God"; thus Athanasius, *Against the Pagans*, § 42; Cyril of Alexandria, *That Christ Is One* (P.G. 75, 753 a = *Deux Dialogues christologiques*, coll. "Sources chrétiennes" [Paris: Cerf, 1964], p. 430, and 759 b = p. 452).

Double Idolatry

Translated by Thomas A. Carlson. Reprinted from Jean-Luc Marion, *God Without Being* (University of Chicago Press, 1991), 25–52.

1. Bossuet: "That is what is called an *epoch*, from a Greek word meaning to *stop*, because we stop there in order to consider, as from a resting place, all that has happened before or after, thus avoiding anachronisms, that is, the kind of error that confuses ages," *Discourse on Universal His-*

tory, foreword [trans. Forster, p. 5]. One remarkable point: the epoch stops (*epekhō*), suspends, as it were, the flow of time, as the idol stops the gaze, which cannot go beyond the farthest point where its capacity is filled. History as a succession of epoch-making idols? History can function therefore only inasmuch as the idols that make epoch in it still remain possible. Would the icon then institute the only possible end of history—its eschatological transgression (a traverse of distance, once again)?

2. Hölderlin, *Der Einzige*, 1, l 48 f., "Herakles Bruder," 2, ll. 51–52: "Ich weiss es aber, eigene Schuld ists! Denn zu sehr, / O Christus! häng ich an dir, wiewohl Herakles Bruder / Und kühn bekenn'ich, du bist Bruder auch des Eviers," and 3, ll. 50–55 (*Gesamtausgabe* [hereafter *GA*], 2/1, pp. 154, 158 and 162). See my work *L'idole et la distance*, secs. 10 and 11 (Paris: Grasset, 1977).

3. C. Baudelaire, *Fusées*, XVII, in *Oeuvres complètes*, Pléiade (Paris, 1966), p. 1256. See P. Valéry, *Monsieur Teste*: "I confess that I have made an idol of my mind," *Oeuvres*, 2, Pléiade (Paris, 1960), p. 37 [trans. Mathews, p. 35].

4. There is nothing surprising in the transition from an "aesthetic" to a conceptual idol, since in one and the other case it is only a question of apprehension. Hence the famous sequence from Gregory of Nyssa: "Every concept [*noēma?*], as it is produced according to an apprehension of the imagination in a conception that circumscribes and in an aim that pretends to attain the divine nature, models only an idol of God [*eidōlon theou*], without at all declaring God himself" (*Vita Moysis*, II, par. 166, P.G., 44, 337b). On this point Nietzsche defends the legitimacy of an extension to the concept of the idol. Not only does he explicitly define it as an ideal—"Götzen (mein Wort für 'Ideale') umwerfen" (*Ecce Homo*, preface, sec. 2)—but he dedicates *Twilight of the Idols* to the "eternal idols" only inasmuch as he means "great errors," namely, concepts (cause, effect, freedom, etc.), those of metaphysics (*Twilight of the Idols*, foreword). These conceptual idols largely outlast religious idols and the "death of God." Hence their extreme danger.

5. L. Feuerbach, *Das Wesen des Christentums*, in *G.W.* (Berlin, 1973), p. 11.

6. F. Nietzsche *Wille zur Macht*, sec. 55 [trans. Kaufmann].

7. *Das Wesen des Christentums*, 1/2, p. 93–95 [trans. Eliot, p. 46].

8. E. Kant, "moralischer Welturheber." See *Kritik der Urteilskraft* (hereafter, *K.U.*), sec. 87, "Folglich müssen wir eine moralische Weltursache (einen Welturheber) annehmen, um uns gemäss dem moralischen Gesetz einen Endzweck vorzusetzen . . . nämlich es sei so ein Gott. . . . d. i. um sich wenigstens nicht von der Möglichkeit des ihm [sc. a righteous man] moralisch vorge-schriebenen Endzwecks einen Begriff zu machen, das *Dasein* eines moralischen Welturhebers, d. i. Gottes annehmen." ["Hence in order to set ourselves a final purpose in conformity with the moral law, we must assume a moral cause of the world (an author of the world) . . . in other words, that there is a God . . . i.e., so that he (a righteous man) can at least form a concept of the possibility of (achieving) the final purpose that is morally prescribed to him—assume the existence of a *moral* author of the world, i.e., the existence of a God." Kant, *Critique of Judgment* [trans. Pluhar, pp. 340, 342]. The [French] translation by A. Philonenko (Paris: Vrin, 1968) indeed reinforces precisely the idolatrous function of the "concept": "se faire au moins une idée de la possibilité du but final qui lui est moralement prescrit, admettre l'existence d'un auteur *moral* du monde, c'est-à-dire de Dieu" (p. 259). Likewise, "ein moralisches Wesen als Welturheber, mithin ein Gott angenommen werden müsse . . . ein moralisches Wesen als Urgrund der Schöpfung an-zunehmen" (sec. 88) ["moral (being as author of the world), and hence a God . . . a *moral being* as the original basis of creation" (trans. Pluhar, pp. 345, 346)]. And "Nun führt jene Teleologie keineswegs auf einen bestimmten Begriff von Gott, der hingegen allein in dem von einem mor-alischen Welturheber angetroffen wird," sec. 91 ["But in fact physical teleology does not at all lead to a determinate concept of God. Such a concept can be found only in the concept of a

moral author of the world" (trans, p. 346)]. (See, amongst others, *Kritik der praktischen Vernunft*, Ak. A. p. 145 [trans. Beck, p. 150]; *Religion innerhalb der Grenzen der blossen Vernunft*, III, 1 sec. 4 [trans. Greene and Hudson, p. 93], etc.). It remains to ponder over the motive that permits Kant thus to believe himself to have withdrawn from a danger that he expressly mentions, idolatry (*Idolatrie, K.U.*, sec. 89), and defines as "a superstitious delusion that we can make ourselves pleasing to the supreme being by means other than a moral attitude" [trans. p. 351]; for can one not ask how that which the practical attitude cannot not presuppose—that "God" is expressed according to morality, hence by a concept of morality—is still, and always will be, an idol? And his warning would turn on Kant himself: "For no matter how pure and free from images of sense such a concept of the supreme being may be from a theoretical point of view, practically the being is still conceived of as an *idol*, i.e., it is conceived of anthropomorphically in what its will is like" [trans., p. 351, n.57]. And if God did not subscribe to the categorical imperative? Kant's answer is well known: one would have to exclude God, and Christ as well, reduced to the simple role of an example of the moral law.

9. *Religion innerhalb der Grenzen der blossen Vernunft*, III, Ak. A., VII, p. 139 [trans. Greene and Hudson, p. 130].

10. Fichte, *Über den Grund unsers Glaubens an eine göttliche Weltregierung*, in *Fichtes Werke*, III, ed. F. Medicius, p. 130 [trans. Edwards, p. 25].

11. "Gott ist etwas Realeres als eine bloss moralische Weltordnung," *Untersuchungen über die menschliche Freiheit . . .*, ed. Schröter, 1/9, p. 356 ["God is more of a reality than is a mere moral world-order," trans. Gutmann, p. 30].

12. Leibniz, *Textes inédits*, 1, ed. G. Grua (Paris: Presses Universitaires de France, 1948), p. 287. This does not differ significantly from the reiteration by Husserl of "God" as "the subject possessing an absolutely perfect knowledge and therefore possessing every adequate perception possible" since it then is a matter of the pure and simple "idea of God," forged starting from requisites of *our* mind in the role of "a necessary limiting concept in epistemological considerations and an indispensable index to the construction of certain limiting concepts which not even the philosophizing atheist can do without" (*Ideen* I, secs. 43 and 79) [trans. Kersten].

13. M. Heidegger, *Identität und Differenz* (Pfullingen, 1957), p. 63 [trans. Stambaugh p. 71]. See "Insofern die Metaphysik das Seiende als solches im Ganzen denkt, stellt sie das Seiende aus dem Hinklick auf das Differente der Differenz vor, ohne auf die Differenz als Differenz zu achten"— "since metaphysics thinks beings as such as a whole, it represents beings in respect of what differs in the difference, and without heeding the difference as difference." (ibid., p. 62 [trans., p. 70]). And *Über den "Humanismus," Wegmarken, G.A.*, 9, p. 322 [trans. Krell, pp. 202–203].

14. Ibid., p. 63. "Sein als Grund und Seiendes als gegründetbegründendes . . ." [trans. p. 71].

15. Ibid., p. 47 [trans., p. 56 (modified)].

16. Ibid., p. 51 [trans., p. 60], then p. 64 [trans., p. 72]. One must hear in *Ursache* at once the cause [*la cause*], and that which metaphysically assures it, the primordial thing [*la chose primordiale*], *Ur-Sache*. See *Wegmarken, G.A.*, 9, p. 350 [trans. Krell, pp. 228–229]; and *Die Frage nach der Technik, Vorträge und Aufsätze* (Pfullingen, 1954), p. 26 [trans. Lovitt, p. 26]: "In the light of causality, God can sink to the level of a cause, of *causa efficiens*. He then becomes, even in theology the god of the philosophers, namely, of those who define the unconcealed and the concealed in terms of the causality of making, without ever considering the essential origin of this causality." The thinker accepts, in this way, running the risk of reproach for "atheism," since one can wonder to begin with, "might not the presumably ontic faith in God be at bottom godlessness [*im Grunde Gottlosigkeit*]? And might the genuine metaphysician be more religious [*religiöser*] than the usual faithful, than the members of a 'church' or even than the 'theologians' of every

confession?" *Metaphysische Anfangsgrunde der Logik im Ausgang von Leibniz* (SS. 1928), *G.A.*, 26, p. 211 [trans. Heim, p. 165].

17. Ibid., p. 64–65 [trans., p. 72 (modified)]. David, on the contrary, dances, naked, before the Ark. And, psalmist *par excellence*, sings.

18. *Nietzsche*, I (Pfullingen, 1961), p. 366 [trans. Krell, p. 106 (modified)]. See: "The ultimate blow against God and against the suprasensory world consists in the fact that God, the first of beings [*das Seiende des Seienden*] is degraded to the highest value [*zum höchsten Wertherabgewür-digt wird*]. The heaviest blow against God is not that God is held to be unknowable, not that God's existence is demonstrated to be unprovable, but rather that the god held to be real is ele-vated to the highest value. For this blow comes precisely not from those who are standing about, who do not believe in God, but from the believers and their theologians who discourse on the being that is of all beings the most in being (*vom Seiendsten alles Seienden*), without ever letting it occur to them to think on Being itself, in order thereby to become aware that, seen from out of faith, their thinking and their talking is sheer blasphemy if it meddles in the theology of faith [*die Gotteslästerung schlechtin*]" ("Nietzsches Wort 'Gott ist tot,'" in *Holzwege* [1950], pp. 239–240 = *G.A.*, 9, p. 260 [trans. Lovitt, p. 105]). Likewise "when one proclaims 'God' the altogether 'highest value,' this is a degradation (*Herabsetzung*)of God's essence. Here as elsewhere thinking in values is the greatest blasphemy imaginable against Being" (*Über den "Humanismus," Weg-marken*, in *G.A.*, 9, p. 349 [trans. Krell, p. 228]). One question, by way of anticipation: blasphemy against "God" coincides here, and in several convergent ways, with blasphemy against Being; but could one not suspect that this very coincidence between the two blasphemies constitutes by itself a third and not lesser blasphemy, even though precisely it becomes possible, if only to anticipate it, on the exclusive condition of not thinking starting from and in view of Being?

19. J.-P. Sartre, *L'être et le néant* (Paris, 1943), p. 703. The entire work (and therefore no doubt also Sartre's finally vulgar "atheism") rests on the assimilation of God to the *causa sui*, without any prudent distinction (Heideggerian or Pascalian) between the possible "gods." The fascination exercised by the "dignity of the *causa sui*" (p. 714, in a certainly involuntary echo of the debate between Descartes and Arnauld on the *causae dignitas*, *Oeuvres*, VII, p. 242, 5 [trans., vol. 2, p. 168]) invests not only the concept of "God," but even the elementary christology that the rhetoric must here fabricate for itself: "We have seen that desire is lack of being [*manque d'être*]. As such, it is directly *carried upon* the being which it lacks. This being, we have seen, is the *in-itself-for-itself*, consciousness become substance, substance become cause of itself, the Man-God" (p. 664); "the *Ens causa sui* that the religions name God. Thus the passion of man is the inverse of that of Christ, for man is lost as man in order that God be born" (p. 708). But whence comes the naïve and aggressive evidence that the highest name of the divine resides in the *causa sui*, if not from a half conceptual and entirely uncriticized anthropomorphism?

20. Bossuet, *Discours sur l'histoire universelle*, II, 1 [trans. Forster, p. 115].

21. F. Nietzsche, *Werke*, ed. Colli-Montinari, VII/3, p. 323, 17 [4] sec. 5 (and *Wille zur Macht*, sec. 1038) [trans. Kaufmann, sec. 1038].

22. *Uberwindung der Metaphysik*, sec. 12, in *Vorträge und Aufsätze*, 1, p. 75 [trans. Stambaugh, p. 96].

23. *Über den "Humanismus," Wegmarken*, *G.A.*, 9, pp. 351, and 338–39 [trans. Krell, pp. 230 and 218]. The polemic provoked by these texts, or rather by the commentary of them that we persist in making, leads us to cite other parallels (without however pretending, as much as the thesis is constant, to exhaustiveness).

Thus: (a) "The turning of the age does not take place by some new god, or the old one re-newed, bursting into the world from ambush at some time or other. Where would he turn on his return if men had not first [*zuvor*] prepared an abode for him? How could there ever be for the god an abode fit for a god, if a divine radiance [*en Glanz von Gottheit*] did not first begin to shine in everything that is? . . . The ether, however, in which alone the gods are gods, is their godhead [*ist ihre Gottheit*]. The element of this ether, that within which even the godhead itself is still present [*west*], is the holy. The element of the ether for the coming of the fugitive gods, the holy [*das Heilige*], is the track of the fugitive gods" (*Wozu Dichter?*, in *Holzwege*, 1950, pp. 249 and 250 = G.A. 5, pp. 270 and 272 [trans. Hofstadter, pp. 92 and 94]).

(b) "Whether the god lives or remains dead is not decided by the religiosity of men and even less by the theological aspirations of philosophy and natural science. Whether or not God is God comes disclosingly to pass from out of and within the constellation of Being [*ob Gott Gott ist, ereignet sich aus der Konstellation des Seins und innerhalb ihrer*]" (*Die Kehre*, in *Die Technik und die Kehre* (Pfullingen, 1962), p. 46 [trans. Lovitt, p. 49]).

(c) "The default of the unconcealment of Being as such releases the evanescence of all that is hale in beings [*alles Heilsmen im Seienden*]. The evanescence of the hale takes the openness of the holy [*das Offene des Heiligen*] with it and closes it off. The closure of the holy eclipses every illumination of the divine [*des Gottheitlichen*]. The deepening dark entrenches and conceals the lack of God [*den Fehl Gottes*]." Hence the consequence: "Because it is more essential, and older, the destiny of Being is less familiar [*unheimlicher*] than the lack of God [*unheimlicher als der Fehl Gottes ist . . . das Seinsgeschick*]" (*Nietzsche*, II, pp. 394 and 396 [trans. D. F. Krell, p. 248]).

(d) "One could not be more reserved than I before every attempt to employ Being to think theologically in what way God is God. Of Being, there is nothing to expect here. I believe that Being can never be thought as the ground and essence of God, but that nevertheless the experience of God and of his manifestedness, to the extent that the latter can indeed meet man, flashes in the dimension of Being, which in no way signifies that Being might be regarded as a possible predicate for God" (*Séminaire de Zurich* [French], trans. F. Fédier and D. Saatdjian, *Poésie* no. 13 (Paris, 1980), p. 61; see the [French] trans. of J. Greisch, in *Heidegger et la question de Dieu* (Paris, 1980), p. 334).

(e) "*Das Sein ist Gott*, now understood speculatively, signifies: *das Sein 'istet' Gott*, that is to say, *das Sein lässt Gott Gottsein*. '*Ist*' is transitive and active. *Erst dasenfaltete Sein selbst ermöglicht das Gott sein:* it is only *Being* developed unto itself (in the sense that it is in the *Logic*)which (in an aftershock) renders possible: *Being-God*" (*Séminaire du Thor 1968, Questions*, IV, p. 258). No doubt this last text must be utilized with more prudence than the preceding ones, on account of its commentary status and its mode of transmission; in the present context it remains significant.

24. See, before all else, two principal texts: *Der Ursprung des Kunstwerkes*, in *Holzwege*, particularly p. 29ff. = *G.A.*, 5, p. 25ff. [trans. Hofstadter, p. 39ff.]; and the conference *Das Ding*, in *Vorträge und Aufsätze*, I (Pfullingen, 1954), in which p. 51 [trans. Hofstadter, p. 178] "When we say sky, we are already thinking of the other three along with it by way of the simple oneness of the four [*aus der Einfalt der Vier*]. / The divinities are the beckoning messengers of the godhead [*die winkenden Boten der Gottheit*]. Out of the hidden sway of the divinities the god emerges as what he is, which removes him from any comparison with beings that are present. / When we speak of the divinities, we are already thinking of the other three along with them by way of the simple oneness of the four." To simplify things, or rather to exaggerate the formulation to the point of coarseness, one could even state that, since the "appropriating mirror-play of the simple onefold of earth and sky, divinities [*Göttlichen*] and mortals, we call the *world*" (ibid., p. 52 = p. 179; emphasis added), and therefore since the world makes the four of the Fourfold, hence "makes" the gods, then—far from "God" creating the world—it would be up to the world to "make" the gods.

25. Postscript to *Was ist Metaphysik?* in *Wegmarken*, *G.A.*, 9, p. 307 [trans. Kaufmann, p. 261].

26. *Metaphysische Anfangsgründe der Logik* [1928], *G.A.*, 26, p. 20 [trans. Heim, p. 16]. Fortunately, this text radicalizes what the formulations of *Sein und Zeit*, sec. 4, might have held back too much.

27. Ibid., p. 171 [trans. p. 136]; see secs. 10 and 11. These precocious analyses agree with the "neutrale tantum" which characterizes, later, the *Ereignis*, in *Zur Sache des Denkens*, 1969, p. 47 [trans. Stambaugh, p. 43].

28. Respectively, *Metaphysische Anfangsgründe der Logik*, *loc. cit.*, sec. 10, p. 177 [trans., p. 140], and *Prolegomena zur Geschichte des Zeitbegriffs* [1925], *G.A.*, 20, Frankfurt, 1979, p. 109–110 [trans. Kisiel, pp. 79–80]. The purely phenomenological atheism of Husserl, *Ideen* 1, sec. 58, can serve, only to a certain extent, as a reference. On the permanence of the phenomenological method in the project of an analytic of *Dasein*, see the clarification by J.-F. Courtine, "La cause de la phenomenologie," in *Exercices de la patience* 3/4 (Paris, 1982).

29. *Vom Wesen des Grundes*, in *Wegmarken*, *G.A.*, 9, p. 159 [trans. Malick, p. 91]. In fact the text continues, and transforms the reduction of divine transcendence into its constitution on the basis of *Dasein*: "One must first gain an *adequate* concept of *Dasein* by illuminating transcendence. Then, by considering *Dasein*, one can *ask* [*nunmehr gefragt werden kann*] how the relationship of *Dasein* to God is ontologically constituted." The question of *Dasein*, that is to say the question that *Dasein* poses itself in relation to Being, determines in advance the possibility of any question of God: before the "turn," a preliminary already plays before and upon God; that it should be a question here of *Dasein*, and not of *Sein*, changes nothing for our present purposes.

30. Respectively, *Hölderlins Hymnen "Germanien" und "Der Rhein" G.A.*, 39, p. 32; *Grundprobleme der Phänomenologie*, *G.A.*, 24, p. 110 [trans. Hofstadter, p. 79]; *Nietzsche*, II, p. 415 [trans. by Stambaugh p. 15]; *Vom Wesen und Begriff der* φύσις, in *Wegmarken*, *G.A.*, 9, p. 240 [trans. Sheehan, p. 222]. We are not taking account, of course, of the numerous texts that bring in the metaphysical interpretation of "God" as supreme being.

31. *Die Technik und die Kehre*, p. 45 [trans. Lovitt (modified), p. 47].

32. See, among others, *Nietzsche*, p. 324 [trans. Krell, II, p. 68], and *Identität und Differenz*, p. 65 [trans. Stambaugh, p. 72].

33. "[D]ans l'embarras d'une 'poule qui aurait trouvé une fourchette,'" literally, "in the straits of a hen who would have found a fork."—Trans.

34. "[U]n caquet de basse-cour," literally, "the cackle of a poultry yard"—Trans.

35. Report in *Berichte aus der Arbeit der Evangelischen Akademie Hofgeismar*, I, 1954 [trans. Hart and Maraldo, p. 65].

36. "[S]i la poule peut s'étonner de trouver une fourchette," literally, "if the hen can be surprised to find a fork"—Trans.

37. La Fontaine, *Fables*, I, 18, *Le renard et la cigogne.*

Introduction to Part II: Saturation, Gift, and Icon

1. See Jean-Luc Marion, *The Visible and the Revealed*, trans. Christina M. Gschwandtner et al. (New York: Fordham University Press, 2008), x–xi.

2. See, for example, Jean-Luc Marion, *Being Given: Toward a Phenomenology of Givenness*, trans. Jeff Kosky (Chicago: University of Chicago Press, 2002), 225.

3. Jean-Luc Marion, *Reduction and Givenness: Investigations of Husserl, Heidegger, and Phenomenology*, trans. Thomas A. Carlson (Evanston, Ill.: Northwestern University Press, 1998), 203.

4. See ibid., 178–181. Heidegger's discussion of *Angst* occurs in "What is Metaphysics?" (1929), though it is only in the "Postscript to 'What is Metaphysics?'" (1943) that Marion discerns

a clear understanding of the relation of nothing and being. Both texts may be found in Heidegger, *Pathmarks*, ed. William McNeill (Cambridge: Cambridge University Press, 1998). Heidegger's discussion of boredom may be found in his *The Fundamental Concepts of Metaphysics: World, Finitude, Solitude*, trans. William McNeill and Nicholas Walker (Bloomington: Indiana University Press, 1995), §§ 19–41.

5. See Marion, *Reduction and Givenness*, 188–189. See also Blaise Pascal, *Pensées*, ed. and trans., Roger Ariew (Indianapolis: Hackett, 2005), 6, 163. It should be remembered that boredom and vanity were already marked as themes in *God Without Being*, chap. 4.

6. See Marion, *Reduction and Givenness*, 197–198.

7. See Jean-Luc Marion, "L'interloqué," in *Who Comes after the Subject?* ed. Eduardo Cadava, Peter Connor, Jean-Luc Nancy (London: Routledge, 1991), 236–245.

8. See Husserl, *Ideas Pertaining to a Pure Phenomenology and to a Phenomenological Philosophy*, I: *General Introduction to a Pure Phenomenology*, trans. Fred Kersten (Dordrecht: Kluwer Academic Publishers, 1998), §95.

9. See Emmanuel Levinas, *The Theory of Intuition in Husserl's Phenomenology*, trans. André Orianne (Evanston, Ill.: Northwestern University Press, 1973), 57–63, and "The Ruin of Representation," *Discovering Existence with Husserl*, trans. Richard A. Cohen and Michael B. Smith (Evanston, Ill.: Northwestern University Press, 1998), 111–121. Levinas alludes to his own work when he evokes "another phenomenology, even if it were the destruction of the phenomenology of appearance and of knowledge," "Transcendence and Intelligibility," *Basic Philosophical Writings*, ed. Adriaan T. Peperzak, Simon Critchley, and Robert Bernasconi (Bloomington: Indiana University Press, 1996), 153.

10. See Jean-Luc Marion, "The Saturated Phenomenon," in *The Visible and the Revealed*, 18–48. Marion notes that this essay is now "out of date" and he directs us to the version included in this anthology. See *The Visible and the Revealed*, xiv.

11. See Immanuel Kant, *Critique of Pure Reason*, trans. Norman Kemp Smith (London: Macmillan, 1933), 113.

12. See Jacques Derrida, *Given Time* 1: *Counterfeit Money*, trans. Peggy Kamuf (Chicago: University of Chicago Press, 1992), and *The Gift of Death*, 2nd ed. bound with *Literature in Secret*, trans. David Wills (Chicago: University of Chicago Press, 2008). The second volume of *Given Time* was to be devoted to Heidegger's *Time and Being*, but Derrida was not able to write the text before his untimely death.

The Breakthrough and the Broadening

Translated by Thomas A. Carlson. Reprinted from Jean-Luc Marion, *Reduction and Givenness* (Northwestern University Press, 1998), 4–39.

1. *Logische Untersuchungen*, vol. 2, viii, see xiv [Eng. trans., vol. 1, 43; mod.] (from here on we will refer to this work according to the pagination and the volume numbering of the second edition of 1913, reprinted in 1968 [Tübingen: Niemeyer], since the excellent translation of H. Elie, A. L. Kelkel and R. Schérer [Paris: Presses Universitaires de France, 1961–64], keeps it in its margins). See "Die *Logische Untersuchungen* als ein Durchbruchswerk," *Entwurf einer Vorrede zu den "Logische Untersuchungen"* (1913), published by E. Fink, in *Tijdschrift voor Philosophie* (1939), 127 [English translation, *Introduction to the Logical Investigations: A Draft of a Preface to The Logical Investigations* (1913), ed. Eugen Fink (The Hague: Martinus Nijhoff, 1975), 34] (with, however, some reservation concerning the completion of the break, 117, 124)[Eng. trans., 24, 32]. On this prefatory project, see K. Schuhmann, "Forschungsnotizen über Husserls 'Entwurf' einer 'Vorrede' zu den *Logischen Untersuchun-*

gen," *Tijdschrift voor Filosofie* (1972). The expression reappears even in the *Krisis*, § 48, *Hua*, VI, 169, 169 n. 1 [Eng. trans., 166]. Heidegger maintains the expression, in 1925, during his presentation on the "fundamental discoveries of phenomenology," at the beginning of the *Prolegomena zur Geschichte des Zeitbegriffs, GA,* 20 (Frankfurt, 1979), 30, 103 [Eng. trans., 24, 75].

2. See, among others, R. Ingarden, "Bemerkungen zum Problem 'Idealismus-Realismus,'" *Jahrbuch für Philosophie und phänomenologische Forschung, Ergänzungsband* (Halle, 1929), and *On the Motives Which Led Husserl to Transcendental Idealism* (The Hague, 1975) [Eng. translation of a Polish original, Warsaw, 1963].

3. Above all R. Schérer, *La phénoménologie des "Recherches logiques" de Husserl* (Paris: Presses Universitaires de France, 1927).

4. Heidegger, *Questions* IV (Paris, 1976), 35. See also the "Summary of a Seminar on the Lecture 'Time and Being,'" in *Zur Sache des Denkens* (Pfullingen, 1976), 47.

5. J. Derrida, *La voix et le phénomène* (Paris: Presses Universitaires de France, 1st edition 1967; 4th edition 1983) respectively, 57, 27 [Eng. trans., 51, 26] (see 8, 37, 111, 114ff.). On principle we will confine ourselves to this work, which is exemplary and decisive for the whole of Derrida's later itinerary.

6. *LU*, vol. 2, *Introduction*, § 3, 9, 11 [Eng. trans., vol. 1, 254, 256; mod.].

7. Ibid., § 2, 5, 6 [Eng. trans., vol. 1, 251, 252]. See *LU*, V, § 8, 362, and § 12, 367.

8. *Phänomenologische Psychologie* (summer course, 1925), § 4, *Hua*, XI, 46–47 [see Eng. trans., 33–34]. See § 3: "More accurately speaking, the particular investigations of the second volume involved a return of the intuition [*Rückwendung der Intuition*] back toward the logical lived experiences that take place in us whenever we think, but which we absolutely do not see, which our gaze does not take into consideration, whenever we carry out the activity of thinking in the originally natural mode" (ibid., 20–21) [Eng. trans., 14; mod.].

9. *LU*, vol. 2, Introduction, § 2, 6 [Eng. trans., vol. 1, 252].

10. *LU*, II, § 23, vol. 2, 163 [Eng. trans., vol. 1, 384].

11. *Entwurf einer Vorrede*, 333; French trans., 399–400.

12. *Selbstanzeige* of the *LU,* published in *Vierteljahrsschrift für wissenschaftliche Philosophie* 25 (1901), 260, reprinted in *LU*, II, 2, *Hua*, XIX/2, ed. U. Panzer, 782 and translated by J. English, in *Articles sur la logique* (Paris: Presses Universitaires de France, 1975), 208–209.

13. *LU*, vol. 2, Introduction, § 7, 22 [Eng. trans., vol. 1, 266] and *LU*, VI, Appendix 2, vol. 3, 227 [Eng. trans., vol. 2, 856].

14. *Entwurf einer Vorrede,* 116, 131, then 117 [Eng. trans., 23, 39, 24; mod.]. In the same style, see 120, 334 [Eng. trans., 27, 55–56].

15. *Ideen* 1, § 24, Hua, III, 52 [Eng. trans., 44; mod.] (see § 19, 44 and § 20, 46; § 78, 185; § 140, 347). To this *Rechtsquelle* corresponds, in 1901, "an adequate phenomenological justification [*eine . . . Rechtfertigung*], and therefore a replacement by evidence" (vol. 2, 22); in 1913, in the *Entwurf einer Vorrede*, "the right of what is seen clearly" *"dem klar Gesehen sein Recht lassen"* (117) [see Eng. trans., 24]; in 1932, in the *Krisis,* and precisely in order to underscore the novelty of the *Investigations,* "the right" that, "for the first time, the *cogitata qua cogitata,* as essential moments of each lived experience of consciousness" (§ 68, *Hua*, VI, 237) [Eng. trans., 234; mod.] be recognized.

16. *LU*, V, § 8, vol. 2, 362 [Eng. trans., vol. 2, 550; mod.]. See all of § 27, 438ff. [Eng. trans., vol. 2, 606ff.].

17. *LU*, vol. 2, Introduction, § 7, 19, 21 [Eng. trans., vol. 1, 263–264, 265]. Aristotle, *Second Analytics,* II, 19, 100b, pp. 10–11, 13–14 (see *Prolegomena,* § 66. *LU*, vol. 1, 242, which, as it were, cites Aristotle implicitly but literally).

18. *LU*, II, § 26, vol. 2, 173ff. [Eng. trans., 393].

19. Respectively, *Selbstanzeige* (*Hua*, XIX–12, 782, Fr. trans. *Articles*, 208) and the *Entwurf einer Vorrede*, 333 [see Eng. trans., 54].

20. *LU*, VI, Introduction, vol. 3, 5–6 (Eng. trans., vol. 2, 670; mod.), which moreover repeats the announcement of the Sixth Investigation made by the Second, § 26, vol. 2, 173–174. Husserl's italics.

21. Respectively, *LU*, VI, § 37, vol. 3, 120, and § 45, 142, 143 [Eng. trans., vol. 2, 763–764, 785; mod.]. See § 53, 165, "broadening [*Erweiterung*] of the concept of Intuition" [Eng. trans., vol. 2, 803; mod]; and § 66, which identifies, on one hand, sensible intuition and intuition according to the narrow acceptation, and, on the other, categorial intuition and "intuition in the broadened sense [*erweiterten Sinne*]" (vol. 3, 202) [Eng. trans., vol. 2, 832; mod.].

22. Respectively, *Selbstanzeige*, *Hua*, XIX–2, 779, 782, 781 (Fr. trans. *Articles*, 205, 209, 207). See also *Entwurf einer Vorrede*: "the general sense and style of the solution . . . manages to be recognized in *Investigation VI*" (118) [Eng. trans., 25; mod.], "the . . . *most important* investigations—viz., the fifth and, above all, the sixth" (323) [Eng. trans., 45], and above all an attitude that curiously seems to define Heidegger's attitude in advance: "some careful readers of the work (and especially those of the younger generation) have . . . understood its full meaning by taking their cue from the sixth investigation" (330) [Eng. trans., 52]. Such a subordination of the First Investigation to the Sixth indeed seems to contradict the decision (essential for his whole interpretation) of Jacques Derrida, "pointing out in the first of the *Investigations* those roots which will remain undisturbed in Husserl's subsequent discourse" (*La voix et le phénomène*, 8; Eng. trans., 9).

23. *LU*, vol. 2, Introduction, § 6, 17 [Eng. trans., vol. 1, 260–61]. The precept of such a zig-zag remains operative in the *Krisis*, § 9, I, *Hua*, VI, 59 [Eng. trans., 55].

24. *Entwurf einer Vorrede*, respectively, 118, 119 [Eng. trans., 25, 26; mod.]. One should consult the illuminating note by J. English [in *Articles*, 366–367].

25. *LU*, II, §8, vol. 2, 124, and *LU*, I, § 31, vol. 2, 101 [Eng. trans., vol. 1, 352, 330; mod.].

26. *LU*, II, vol. 2, Introduction, § 3, 9–10 [Eng. trans., vol. 1, 255; mod.].

27. *LU*, I, § 9, vol. 2, 38 n. 1 [Eng. trans., vol. 1, 281; mod.].

28. *Phänomenologische Psychologie*, § 3, *Hua*, XI, 24 [Eng. trans., 17; mod.].

29. *Critique of Pure Reason*, A 51/B 75 [Eng. trans., Norman Kemp Smith (New York: St. Martin's Press, 1929), 93].

30. *Krisis*, § 30, *Hua*, VI, 118 [sec Eng. trans., 112]. *LU*, VI, § 66 already explicitly reproaches Kant for having missed the "fundamental broadening [*Erweiterung*]" (vol. 3, 202ff.). On this point see I. Kern, *Husserl und Kant* (The Hague, 1964), §§ 9, 11.

31. *LU*, II, § 25, vol. 2, 168 [Eng. trans., vol. 1, 388; mod.], which is better understood according to Heidegger's commentary on it: "concrete intuition expressly *giving* its object is never an isolated, single layered sense perception, but is always a multi-layered [*gestufte*] intuition, that is, a categorially specified intuition" (*Prolegomena*, § 6, *GA*, 20, 93) [Eng. trans., 68].

32. *LU*, II, respectively, § 15, vol. 2, 145; then § 10, 131; finally § 4, 114 [Eng. trans., vol. 1, 369, 357, 344]. See likewise § 1, 109 and § 25, 171, but also, as early as *LU*, I, § 10, vol. 2, 41 and § 23, 76.

33. *LU*, II, § 1, vol. 2, 109 [Eng. trans., vol. 1, 340]. To be compared with §§ 8 and 15, as well as the *Prolegomena*, § 39, vol. I, 128–129.

34. *LU*, II, § 8, vol. 2, 124–25 [Eng. trans., vol. 1, 352; mod]. See *Phänomenologische Psychologie*, § 9, *Hua*, IX, 86–87, and Heidegger: "The categorial 'forms' are not constructs of acts but objects which manifest themselves in these acts" (*GA*, 20, 96) [Eng. trans., 70].

35. See *LU*, II, § 1, vol. 2, 109 and § 22, 122; or *LU,* I, § 13, vol. 2, 50.

36. Respectively, *LU*, II, § 1, vol. 2, 109 [Eng. trans., vol. 1, 340]; § 22, 162 [Eng. trans., vol. 1, 383]; *LU*, I, § 11, vol. 2, 44 [Eng. trans., vol. 1, 285], and finally §13, 49–50 [Eng. trans., vol. 1, 289; mod.].

37. *Prolegomena*, § 2, *GA*, 20, 90–91 (see 93, 96) [Eng. trans., 66–67, mod. See Eng. trans., 68–69, 70–71]. The interpretation developed in *Speech and Phenomena* always presupposes the self-sufficiency of the First Investigation, and therefore in principle underestimates the Sixth (cited only once, in a note, French, 67) [Eng. trans., 60]; this separation leads to a complete misunderstanding of the intervention of the categorial in the First Investigation itself, which could not but warp any approach to signification as such. Moreover, Husserl later subordinated the First Investigation to the last two, for example in the *Vorlesungen fiber Bedeutungslehre, Sommersemester 1908, Hua*, XXVI, 6, 17, etc.

38. *LU*, VI, § 45, vol. 3, 142–143 [Eng. trans., vol. 2, 785; mod.].

39. *LU*, VI, § 45, vol. 3, 143 (*wirklich*, vol. 3, 156, 146, etc.) [Eng. trans., vol. 2, 785].

40. On the analogical character of categorial intuition, see below notes 92 and 98.

41. *LU*, VI, § 52, vol. 3. 162 [Eng. trans., vol. 2, 800].

42. *Idee der Phänomenologie, Hua*, II, 74 [see Eng. trans., 59]: Word for word: "Everywhere givenness . . . is a givenness in the *phenomenon of cognition*, in the phenomenon of a thought in the broadest sense." To be sure, it is a matter here of givenness, not simply of intuition. But the decisive importance of this gap will only become visible later. For now, we can receive from givenness only the intuited or the intuitable. See below, note 82. A significant repetition of this situation can be found in J. N. Mohanty's essay, "Modes of Givenness," in his work *Phenomenology and Ontology* (The Hague, 1970), chap. 1.

43. *LU*, II, § 24, vol. 2, 168 [see Eng. trans., vol. 1, 388].

44. *Phänomenologische Psychologie*, § 10, *Hua*, IX, 88 [Eng. trans., 66; mod.]. Likewise: "If we were to deny that the world as world is experienceable [*erfahrbar*], then we would have to deny exactly the same for every single thing" (ibid., § 11, 97) [Eng. trans., 73].

45. Nietzsche, *Fragment*, 16 [32], *Werke*, VIII/3, 288 (*Wille zur Macht*, § 1041) [Eng. trans., W. Kaufmann (New York: Random House, 1967), 536]. The question of the relation between Nietzsche and Husserl, although sometimes pointed out (as in *La voix et le phénomène*, 27 n. 1 [Eng. trans., 25 n. 5]) has hardly been posed. R. Boehm's essay "Deux points de vue: Husserl et Nietzsche," *Archivio di Filosofia* (1963), reprinted in *Vom Gesichtspunkt der Phänomenologie* (The Hague, 1968), is not yet sufficient to pull it off.

46. *Ideen* I, § 22, *Hua*, III, 148 [Eng. trans., 142], confirmed by the *Krisis*, § 14, 55, 57, *Hua*, VI, 71, 193, 202ff.

47. *Thus Spoke Zarathustra*, III, § 4, "Before Sunrise" [Eng. trans., W. Kaufmann, in *The Portable Nietzsche* (New York: Penguin, 1982), 277].

48. *Ideen* I, § 24, *Hua*, III, 52, lines 9–13 [Eng. trans., 44; mod.]. Or again: "One must . . . take the phenomena as they are given" (*Philosophie als strenge Wissenschaft*, § 52 = *Aufsätze und Vorträge* [1911–21], *Hua*, XXV, 33).

49. Nietzsche, *Fragment*, 7 [54], *Werke*, VIII/I, 320 (*Wille zur Macht*, § 617).

50. Husserl, *Ideen* III, § 13–14, *Hua*, V, 76–77 [see Eng. trans., 65–66]. Likewise *Philosophie als strenge Wissenschaft*, § 48: "no difference between the phenomenon [*Erscheinung*] and Being" (*Hua*, XXV, 29) [see Eng. trans., 106]; or *Krisis*, § 71: "Through the reduction, this world—and he [*sc.* the psychologist] has no other which is valid for him (another one would have no meaning at all for him)—becomes a mere phenomenon [*zum blossen Phänomen*] for him" (*Hua*, VI, 257) [Eng. trans., 254].

51. Except in outline, *La voix et le phénomène*, 27, note; 68; 83 note, and 93. [Eng. trans., 25–26, 61, 74, and 83].

52. *La voix et le phénomène*, respectively, 109, 100, 104 [Eng. trans., 97, 90, 93]. See: "What is structurally original about meaning would be the *Gegenstandslosigkeit*, the absence of any object given to intuition" (ibid., 107) [Eng. trans., 92]; and: "The possibility of this nonintuition constitutes the *Bedeutung* as such, the *normal Bedeutung* as such" (ibid., 107) [Eng. trans., 96].

53. *LU,* I, § 2, vol. 2, 25. The Husserlian definition of signification, if it begins with the distinction of types of signs, very quickly reaches, as early as the First Investigation, the status of an "ideal unity" (§ 28, 91; § 29, 92); hence the possibility of granting it an *ideal* "content," without intuition, which assigns it apart from the sign. See below, note 71.

54. *La voix et le phénomène*, respectively, 76, 109 [Eng. trans., 68, 97].

55. Respectively, *LU,* VI, § 26: "einen phänomenologisch irreduktibeln Unter-schied" (vol. 3, 93) [see Eng. trans., vol. 2, 742]; then § 5, 21 [see Eng. trans., vol. 2, 285] and § 22, 201 [Eng. trans., vol. 2, 832].

56. The full development of *LU,* VI, § 23, vol. 3, 79ff. [Eng. trans., vol. 2, 731ff.].

57. *LU,* I, respectively, § 6, vol. 2, 32 [Eng. trans., vol. 1, 276; mod.], then § 10, 41 [Eng. trans., vol. 1, 283]. See also *LU,* VI, § 13: "Our analyses have been lightly sketched rather than thoroughly executed, but they lead to the result that *both signification-intentions and acts of signification-fulfillment,* acts of 'thought' and acts of intuition, *belong to a single class of objectifying acts*" (vol. 3, 52) [Eng. trans., vol. 2, 709].

58. *LU,* I, § 10: "without need of a fulfilling or illustrative intuition" (vol. 2, 41) [Eng. trans., vol. 1, 283]; likewise *LU,* VI, § 63, vol. 3, 191. *Eventuell: LU,* I, § 9, vol. 2, 37; § 10, 39. Other texts: *LU,* VI, § 4, 15 (*ohne*); § 5, vol. 3, 15, 18–19, 20 (*ohne*), etc.

59. *LU,* I, § 11, vol. 2, 45 [Eng. trans., vol. 1, 286; mod.]. See § 13, 49; § 18, 66. These are confirmed by *LU,* VI, § 46, vol. 3, 144ff. and § 70, 220.

60. *LU,* I, § 18, vol. 2, 65 [Eng. trans., vol. 1, 302; mod.].

61. *LU,* I, § 31, vol. 2, 100 [Eng. trans., vol. 1, 329–30; mod.], which one can compare with § 11, 45.

62. *LU,* I, § 15, vol. 2, 57 [Eng. trans., vol. 1, 295; mod.] could certainly serve as an anticipated response to *La voix et le phénomène*, 109 [Eng. trans., 97]. We should take this occasion to stress that our own precise subject (the status of signification in the breakthrough of the Investigations) only concerns chap. 7 of Derrida's work. We do not have to examine here the whole of his resumption of diverse Husserlian themes any more than we have to discuss the whole of Heidegger's relation to Husserl (see below, chaps. 3–4).

63. *LU,* I, § 11, vol. 2, 44 [Eng. trans., vol. 1, 285–286], cited in *La voix et le phénomène*, 109 [Eng. trans., 97].

64. Ibid., 44–45 [Eng. trans., 285–86; mod.]. We should note that the phrase "as one says [*zu sagen pflegt*]" finds an echo on the following page: "the fundamental ambiguity of the word 'judgment' habitually leads one [*zu treiben pflegt*] to confuse [*vermengen*] the evidently grasped ideal unity with the real act of judging"—habit here again confuses an evidence, far from defining its nature. § 15 will stigmatize as a typical misinterpretation the "confusion [*Vermengung*] of signification with fulfilling intuition" (vol. 2, 57) [Eng. trans., vol. 1, 295], or again "the tendency . . . to treat *fulfilling intuitions* as [being] significations (in this case one habitually [*man pflegt*] neglects the acts that give them a categorial form)" (ibid., 56ff.) [Eng. trans., vol. 1, 295; mod.]. When § 16 uses quotation marks—exactly like the passage cited from § 11—to evoke J. S. Mill's use of the "name that is meaningful in a 'genuine' and 'strict' sense," it is in order immediately to denounce a confusion and an error therein. Such a confusion must be denounced

all the more in that it is common and leads to an "insoluble enigma" (§ 19, 67) [Eng. trans., 303]. The formula *"Man pflegt zu sagen"* elsewhere characterizes natural consciousness, e.g., in *LU*, VI, § 40, vol. 3, 130.

65. *LU*, I, § 26, vol. 2, 82 [Eng. trans., vol. 1, 315; mod.], cited in *La voix et le phénomène*, 107 [Eng. trans., 96].

66. *LU*, I, § 13, vol. 2, 49 [Eng. trans., vol. 1, 289]. See: "signification is nevertheless nothing other than what we mean [*meinen*] by an expression" (*LU*, II, § 15, vol. 2, 143ff.) [Eng. trans., vol. 1, 368; mod.]. For Hegel, see *Phänomenologie des Geistes*, II, *GW*, 9, eds. Bonsiepen, Hedde (Hamburg, 1980), 71ff.

67. Respectively, *LU*, V, § 14, vol. 2, 386 and § 12, 376 [see Eng. trans., vol. 2, 568, 561]—"nothing to remark"—which speaks of consciousness as a simple "bundle of experiences." Here *I* says the expression but never expresses itself as such therein.

68. *LU*, VI, § 5, addendum, vol. 3, 22–23 [Eng. trans., vol. 2, 686]. See § 60, 184 [Eng. trans., 819], where S and P, as *Anzeigen* in the mathematical formula (notation), refer, in their global signification, to categorial elements that are significant because given. In light of these texts, the lack of *"Gestaltqualität"* which characterizes the *Anzeige* at the beginning of the journey (*LU*, I, § 2, vol. 2, 25) [Eng. trans., vol. 1, 270], can seem destined to be reduced, at least tangentially. At least it is not self-evident that it constitutes a structure that is insurmountable and immediately exclusive of *any* signification.

69. *LU*, I, § 26, vol. 2, 82 [Eng. trans., vol. 1, 315].

70. Respectively, *LU*, I, § 11, ". . . we . . . find them there [*darin*]" (vol. 2, 44) [see Eng. trans., vol. 1, 285], and *LU*, VI, § 26, vol. 3, 92 [Eng. trans., vol. 2, 741] (see § 4, 14ff.).

71. Respectively, *LU*, I, § 11, vol. 2, 44 [Eng. trans., vol. 1, 285]; § 14, 52 [Eng. trans., vol. 1, 291] (intentional sense as one of the possible contents, on the same level as fulfilling sense and the object itself); § 29, 92 [Eng. trans., vol. 1, 323; mod.] (*Gehalt*); § 31, 99 [Eng. trans., vol. 1, 329; mod.] (*logischer Gehalt*); and § 30, 96–97 [Eng. trans., vol. 1, 327; mod.]. See note 53, above.

72. *LU*, VI, § 63, vol. 3, 191 [Eng. trans., vol. 2, 824; mod.], then § 4, 14 [Eng. trans., vol. 2, 680].

73. *LU*, I, § 21, vol. 2, 71 [Eng. trans., vol. 1, 306], then *LU*, VI, § 8, vol. 3, 33 [Eng. trans., vol. 2, 695; mod.].

74. *LU*, I, § 35, vol. 2, 105 [Eng. trans., vol. 1, 333; mod.]. Such are the last words, indeed *the* last word of the First Investigation: the excess of signification and not its lack. One must not, therefore, privilege § 28, 91 [Eng. trans., 321–22] (as does *La voix et le phénomène*, 113) [Eng. trans., 100–101]. This holds inasmuch as this text itself, in its last paragraph (omitted by Derrida), ends with the reminder of having to understand "signification as ideal unities."

75. *LU*, I, § 31, vol. 2, 100 [Eng. trans., vol. 1, 329; mod.]; § 11, 45 [Eng. trans., vol. 1, 286] (see § 29, 94–95).

76. *LU*, IV, § 12, vol. 2, 327 [see Eng. trans., vol. 2, 517]: *"aber die Bedeutung selbst existiert"* (and the combinations of signification also, § 13, 332) [Eng. trans., 521]; § 13, 330 [see Eng. trans., 519]:*. . . die . . . wirklich seiende Bedeutungen—seiend als Bedeutungen"* (see 326, 329, 333, etc.). Likewise already *LU*, II, § 8, vol. 2, 124.

77. *LU*, VI, § 63, vol. 3, 192 [Eng. trans., vol. 2, 824]. Here there must intervene as a response to the "broadening of intuition," the 1925 text that proposes, with and beyond the *mathesis universalis* reached by the *Investigations*, to push "the broadening from a priori and formal logic and mathematics to the idea of a total system [*Gesamtsystem*] of a priori sciences" (*Phänomenologische Psychologie*, § 3f., *Hua*, IX, 43) [Eng. trans., 31]. The *Gesamtsystem* corresponds, in the "broadening" of signification, to the *Gesamtanschauung* in the "broadening of intuition." It is here again

that the *Überschuss* of signification is at play (*LU*, VI, § 40, vol. 3, 131, taken up by Heidegger, *GA*, 20, 77).

78. According to the excellent diagnostic formulated by Derrida, *La voix et le phénomène*, 16 [Eng. trans., 16].

79. *Krisis*, § 28, *Hua*, VI, 237 [Eng. trans., 234].

80. *Krisis*, § 46 and n. 1, *Hua*, VI, 168–169 [Eng. trans., 165; mod.]. On this correlation, see *Die Idee der Phänomenologie*: "The word 'phenomenon' is ambiguous in virtue of the essential correlation between *appearance and that which appears.*" (*Hua*, II, 14) [Eng. trans., 11].

81. *Selbstgegebenheit* in fact demands a double translation of *selbst. Gegebenheitsweisen*, ibid., *Hua*, VI, 169. To be compared with *LU*, VI, § 39, I, vol. 3, 122.

82. *Die Idee der Phänomenologie*, *Hua*, II, respectively, 61 and 50 (where, following A. Lowit, we correct the German punctuation); see above, note 42 [Eng. trans., 49, 39–40; mod.].

83. *Ideen* I, § 24, *Hua*, III, 52, lines 14–16 [Eng. trans., 44; mod.]; see § 19: "Immediate 'seeing' (*noein*), not merely sensuous, experiential seeing, but seeing in the universal sense as an originarily giving [*originär gebendes*] *consciousness of any kind whatever*, is the ultimate legitimizing source of all rational assertions" (44) [Eng. trans., 36; mod.); § 79, 191, etc. For Heidegger also, intuition is originary only inasmuch as it gives: *GA*, 20, 64, 67.

84. *LU*, V, § 11, vol. 2, 373 [see Eng. trans., vol. 2, 559]; see Introduction, § 2, 5.

85. *LU*, I, § 14, vol. 2, 50–51 [see Eng. trans., vol. 1, 290).

86. Ibid. [Eng. trans., 291], then § 29, 92 [see Eng. trans., 323].

87. "*Zunächst ist dabei die Bedeutungsintention und zwar für sich gegeben; dann erst tritt entsprechende Anschauung hinzu*" (*LU*, VI, § 8, vol. 3, 33) [Eng. trans., vol. 2, 695], then *LU*, I, § 35, vol. 2, 105 [see Eng. trans., vol. 1, 333]; see § 9, 37 and *LU*, II, § 31, 183. Conversely, "The act of signifying cannot be fulfilled only by means of intuition" (*LU*, I, § 21, vol. 2, 71) [see Eng. trans., vol. 1, 306].

88. *LU*, VI, § 37, vol. 3, 117, and § 23, 83; see § 38, 121: "*Selbsterscheinung des Gegenstandes.*"

89. *LU*, VI, respectively, § 46, vol. 3, 146, and § 48, 154. See §§ 45, 47 and 52, vol. 3, 142, 151, and 162.

90. Respectively, *GA*, 20, 97 [see Eng. trans., 71] and *Questions* IV, 35.

91. The attribution, without discontinuity, of categorial intuition as Heidegger's point of departure constitutes the paradoxical meeting point between J. Beaufret, *Dialogue avec Heidegger*, vol. 3 (Paris: Editions de Minuit, 1974), 129, and T. Adorno, *Negative Dialektik*, (Frankfurt, 1966), 75, without citing commentators of lesser rank. It is moreover clear that J. Derrida could not ask if "Heidegger's thought does not sometimes raise the same questions as the metaphysics of presence" (*La voix et le phénomène*, 83, note) [Eng. trans., 74) if he did not himself also accept such a continuity.

92. *Questions* IV, 131, 315, respectively. The italics are, of course, from the editors of the seminar held by Heidegger.

93. *Prolegomena*, *GA*, 20, respectively § 4, 30 (103); § 6, 64; § 5, 54; § 6, 80 [Eng. trans., 24, 47, 41, 60]. See *leibhafte Gegebenheit*, 81 and *leibhafte Selbigkeit*, p. 83.

94. Ibid., respectively, § 6, 85; then 87 and 98 [Eng. trans., 63, 64, 72].

95. Ibid., § 6, 89 [Eng. trans., 66; mod.].

96. Ibid., § 8, 104 [see Eng. trans. 76: "the demand to lay the foundation"].

97. Respectively, *LU*, VI, § 39, vol. 3, 123; Introduction, 5; finally § 44, 140 and § 45, 143 [see Eng. trans., vol. 2, 766, 670, 782, 785].

98. *LU*, VI, § 44, vol. 3, 141 [Eng. trans., vol. 2, 784]. See a similar deduction in § 46, 146; § 47, 152; § 52, 163, 164.

1. [*Invisable*, from *viser*, designates that which cannot be aimed at, meant, or intended. —Trans.]

2. [*Irregardable* designates what cannot be looked at or gazed upon. The verb *regarder* has most often been translated "to gaze" while the noun form, *regard*, is rendered as "the gaze."—Trans.]

3. *Kritik der reinen Vernunft*, A 163/B 204 [English trans., p. 199].

4. *Passions de l'âme*, §73, AT XI, p. 383, 7–10 [English trans., p. 354]. See §78: "When it is excessive and makes us fix our attention solely on the first image of the objects before us without acquiring any further knowledge about them" (ibid., p. 386, 14–17 [English trans., p. 355]). See the perfect commentary by D. Kambouchner: admiration (connected to amazement) "which has a corporeal thing for its object has this thing as its object only *inasmuch as it appears*, and only with its 'new,' 'rare,' 'extraordinary,' unexpected character does its apparition become an event. . . . It has as its object *the phenomenon of a thing or the thing in its phenomenalization*" (*L'homme des passions: Commentaires sur Descartes* [Paris, 1995], vol. 1, p. 295, my emphasis).

5. *Ethica* III, appendix, definition IV [English trans., p. 142].

6. *Kritik der reinen Vernunft*, A 169/B 210 [English trans., p. 203].

7. Paul Claudel, *Tête d'or*, in *Theatre* I (Paris: Pléiade, 1956), p. 210. Glory is weighty; Hebrew says this with just one word: *kavod*. Obviously, I am here quite close to J.-L. Chrétien, *L'inoubliable et l'inespéré* (Paris, 1991).

8. Plato, *Republic*, 515c and 517a. The term *marmaryge* originally designates vibration (for example that of a dancer's feet, *Odyssey* 8.265), then the vibration of overheated air, therefore that of the mirage, which provokes bedazzlement.

9. Plato, *Republic*, 517bc and 518a.

10. J. M. W. Turner, at the National Gallery (n. 498) and at the Clore Gallery of the Tate Gallery (for *The Decline of the Carthaginian Empire* and *Venice with Salute*, n. 5487). Here I am indebted to an as yet unpublished study by C. Monjou. See J. Gage, *J. M. W. Turner: A Wonderful Range of Mind* (New Haven: Yale University Press, 1957), chap. 4.

11. *Kritik der reinen Vernunft*, B 218 (see B 219) [English trans., p. 208 (see p. 209)].

12. Ibid., A 177/B 220 [English trans., p. 209 (modified)].

13. Ibid., A 177–78/B 220 [English trans., p. 210].

14. Ibid., A 179/B 222 [English trans., p. 210]. See also A 665/B 693.

15. Ibid., A 182/B 22.4 [English trans., p. 213].

16. In the absolute without analog, we thus come upon bedazzlement, characteristic of the phenomenon saturated with respect to quality. There is no incoherence; here, seeing as, by excepting itself from the analogies of experience, the absolute phenomenon can no longer be compared to another. It shows itself as such, by reference to itself alone. It therefore brings to the fore what individualizes it as such—its unbearable intensity, provoking bedazzlement. As for its characteristic of unforeseeability according to quantity, it is self-evident that the disqualification of external relations (analogies among phenomena) confirms the disqualification of internal relations (summation of the parts of the phenomenon), far from contradicting it.

17. Spinoza, *Ethics* 1, §16: "Ex necessitate divinae naturae infinita infinitis modis (hoc est omnia, quae sub intellectum infinitum cadere possunt) sequi"—almost the correct definition of

the saturated phenomenon. See §17, sc.: "A summa Dei potentia, sive infinita natura infinita infinitis modis, hoc est omnia necessario effluxisse."

18. Whence the importance of a rereading of the *Critique of Pure Reason* that would attempt, though *a contrario*, to define and do justice to the saturated phenomenon, alongside common or poor phenomena. It would be a question of interpreting it no longer in terms of the *Aesthetic* (grossly put, Heidegger), of the *Analytic* (Cohen), or even of the transcendental doctrine of method (J. Grondin), but of the *transcendental dialectic*—taking seriously the doctrine of ideas (aesthetic as well as of reason) and asking after their paradoxical phenomenality.

19. [*Irregardable* designates what cannot be looked at or gazed upon. The verb *regarder* has most often been translated "to gaze" while the noun form, *regard*, is rendered as "the gaze." —Trans.]

20. *Kritik der reinen Vernunft*, A 74/B 100, A 219/B 266, and A 234/B 287 [English trans., pp. 109, 239, 252].

21. Ibid., A 225/B 273 [*zusammenshänge*] and A 220/B 267 [English trans., pp. 243 and 239].

22. See the works of C. Chevalley, in particular his introduction to the French translation of N. Bohr, *Physique quantum et connaissance humaine* (Paris, 1991); and that of W. Heisenberg, *Philosophie: Le manuscrit de 1942* (Paris, 1997).

23. On *intuitus* according to Descartes, see my study in *Règles utiles et claires pour la direction de l'esprit en la recherche de la vérité* (The Hague, 1977), p. 295ff.

24. That givenness (*Geben*) shows itself inasmuch as it remains irreducible to its given (*Gabe*) was established perfectly by Heidegger in *Sein und Zeit*, p. 8 (see *supra*, Book 1, §3).

25. "Das Sich-an-ihm-selbst-zeigende"; Heidegger, *Sein und Zeit*, §7, pp. 31, 12. See "Das an ihm selbst Offenbare von ihm selbst her sehen lassen," *Prolegomena zur Geschichte des Zeitbegriffs*, §9, GA 20 (Frankfurt am Main, 1979), p. 117. The "von ihm selbst her" indicates an apparition "of itself" in the strict sense of "on the basis of itself." What remains is to establish how a phenomenon can be ensured a "self," the ipseity of a *Selbst*. The hypothesis of the saturated phenomenon lets us do this better than Heidegger does, who limits the *Selbst* to the ipseity of Dasein.

26. AT VII, 371, 25, and 52, 15. The infinite is never in potential, but *actu*: 47, 19.

27. AT VII, 46, 8, 12.

28. "Nihil univoce nobis convenire," AT VII, 137, 22 (see p. 433, 5–6, and *Principia Philosophiae* I, §51); *attingere*, AT VII, 139, 12 (esp. pp. 52, 5, and 46, 21, which doubts even this mere "touching": "Nec forte etiam attingere cogitatione ullo modo possum").

29. AT VII, 114, 6–7. This is why here, and here alone, *intueri* does not contradict *adorare*. Emmanuel Levinas recognized the more than normal phenomenality of the idea of infinity so perfectly that he revived it in order to describe the face of the Other: *Totality and Infinity*, pp. 26, 48–50; *Of God Who Comes to Mind*, pp. 26, 62–65, and p. 69. But above all, "The Idea of the Infinite in Us," in *Entre Nous*, pp. 219ff.

30. *Kritik der Urteilskraft*, §25, p. 248 [English trans., p. 306]; *Formlosigkeit*, §24, p. 247; *Unordnung*, §23, p. 246; "Über alle Vergleichung" and *schlechthin*, §25, p. 248 (and §26, p. 251) [English trans., p. 306].

31. *Kritik der Urteilskraft*, §23 [English trans., p. 245]; *Gefühl der Unangemessenheit*, §26, p. 252 [English trans., p. 135 (modified)]; *Ungeheuer*, §26, p. 253 [English trans., p. 136 (modified)].

32. *Kritik der Urteilskraft*, *Unbegrenztheit*, §23 [English trans., p.128]. See "keine angemessene Darstellung," p. 245.

33. *Kritik der Urteilskraft*, §23, p. 245 [English trans., p. 129 (modified)]. See *subjektive Unzweckmässigkeit*, §26, p. 252; *Widerstreit* of the subjective end, §27, p. 258. Respect (*Achtung*) comes up in §27, p. 257. I here follow P. Lacoue-Labarthe, "La vérité sublime," and J.-L. Nancy,

"L'offrande sublime" (in particular: "The sublime totality is beyond the maximum: which is as much as to say it is *beyond all*"), in *Du sublime*, ed. M. Deguy (Paris, 1988), p. 68.

34. *Zur Phänomenologie des inneren Zeitbewusstseins (1893–1917)*, *Hua* X (The Hague, 1966), "ständiges Kontinuum," §10, p. 27 [English trans., p. 48 (modified)] (see "beständliger Wandlung," "stetige Modifikation," p. 63). The very concept of object-in-its-how (*Objekt in wie*) indicates the permanent and perpetual transformation of the object, that is to say, the relation between its (permanent) signification and the corresponding lived experiences (always other), which obey another intentionality, that of their temporal succession without object. This is why one can say, following R. Bernet, that it is, properly speaking, no longer an issue of intentional consciousness, but of a "passive consciousness resulting from an affection" (*La vie du sujet* [Paris, 1995], p. 196).

35. *Zur Phänomenologie des inneren Zeitbewtustsein*, §16, p. 40 [English trans., p. 62 (modified)]. See §32, p. 70 and §36, p. 75.

36. *Zur Phänomenologie des inneren Zeitbewusstsein*, n. 50, p. 334 (twice); §39, p. 82. See "The original time [*Urzeit*], which is not yet really time" (ms. C 7 I.; p. 17, cited by D. Franck, *Chair et corps: Sur la phénoménologie de Husserl* [Paris. 1981], p. 188).

37. *Zur Phänomenologie des inneren Zeitbewusstsein*, §39, p. 83. On the double intentionality of the flux, §39, p. 80ff [English trans., p. 105ff].

38. *Zur Phänomenologie des inneren Zeitbewusstseins*, §§10 and 11, pp. 28 and *29 et passim*; §31, p. 67; and finally *Beilage* I, p. 100 [English trans., pp. 48 and 50 (modified)].

39. On this "pulsional . . . primordiality," see *Téléologie universelle*, ms. E III 5 (September 1933), n. 34, *Hua* XV, pp. 593–97; and the commentaries from E. Fink ("intentional self-constitution of phenomenological time"), *Studien zur Phänomenologie,* and D. Franck, p. 153.

40. See supra, Book 1, §6, Book 2, §12, Book 3, §18. That givenness can sometimes not come to pass in and through its intuition has already been seen in Book 1, §§4–5, and will be confirmed below (Book 4, §23).

41. Descartes, *Regulae ad directionem ingenii*, AT X, 365, 16, cited supra, §20 [English trans., p. 12].

42. Goclenius (R. Göckel): "Paradoxum est inopinatum et admirabile, quod praeter opinionem et expectationem offertur," *Lexicon philosophicum graecum* (Frankfurt, 1615), p. 963.

43. Maurice Merleau-Ponty, *Phénoménologie de la perception*, p. 426.

44. The phenomenology that broaches this type of saturated phenomenon was elaborated in an exemplary fashion by Paul Ricoeur, in particular in *Temps et récit* III: *Le temps raconté* (Paris, 1985).

45. The phenomenology that describes this type of saturated phenomenon, the idol, could be attributed to Jacques Derrida—it being understood that he has inverted it exactly. The difference resides in the on principle irreparable deficit of intuition to intention. But it thus belongs all the more within the thematic of degrees of intuition and saturation: "Hear aright the chance and the necessity of a 'that's sufficient.' It's *enough*, but without satisfaction; and which does not saturate. Nothing to do with sufficiency or insufficiency. The verb *to suffice* will teach you nothing about such a 'that's sufficient'" (*La vérité en peinture* [Paris, 1978], p. 284 [English trans., p. 206], concerning G. Titus-Carmel).

46. One must, without question, attribute the elaboration of a phenomenology appropriate to the paradox (saturated phenomenon) inasmuch as absolute to the remarkably steadfast thought of Michel Henry, from *L'essence de la manifestation* (Paris, 1963) to *Phénoménologie matérielle* (Paris, 1990) and *C'est moi la vérité* (Paris, 1996).

47. Aristotle, *Categories*, 7,8a 14–15. To be sure, this phrase belongs to the formulation of a question, but it immediately receives a positive response, at least concerning the first *ousia*.

The Banality of Saturation
Translated by Jeffrey L. Kosky. Reprinted from Jean-Luc Marion, *The Visible and the Revealed* (Fordham University Press, 2008), 119–144.

1. The reproach, sometimes explicit, often implicit, that I remain within "metaphysics" because I take my point of departure from Kant's typology (and Husserl's) seems to me unjust and inadmissible, for several reasons. Methodologically, even if I do start with a "metaphysical" definition of the phenomenon for the purpose of reaching that of the phenomenon as it shows itself from itself and insofar as it gives itself, I am only repeating the Husserlian and Heideggerian movement of starting with a "natural" or "inauthentic" situation so as to pass, by reduction or destruction, to a "reduced" or "authentic" situation. Historically, in defining the phenomenon for the first time as *Erscheinung* and not as mere *Schein*, Kant indicated a way to overcome all metaphysical senses. Heidegger made no mistake about this, as he took the Kantian definition as his point of departure in constructing the "phenomenological" acceptation of the phenomenon in *Being and Time*, §7. Finally, conceptually, it would be necessary to define, at least once, what one means precisely, therefore *conceptually*, by the term *metaphysics*, a task all the more delicate (as confirmed by Heidegger's successive positions on its use) because the term has perhaps never received a stable or univocal definition. (See my study "La science toujours recherché et toujours manquante," in *La métaphysique. Son histoire, sa critique ses enjeux*, ed. J.-M. Narbonne and L. Langlois [Paris: Vrin, 1999], 13–36.)

2. See my *Etant donné: Essai d'une phénoménologies de la donation* (Paris: Presses Universitaires de France, 1997), §24; trans. Jeffrey L. Kosky under the title *Being Given: Toward a Phenomenology of Givenness* (Stanford: Stanford University Press, 2002), §24. Here, in distinction to my first approach to the saturated phenomenon (see Chapter 2 of this volume), I no longer include revelation in the list of simple paradoxes or saturated phenomena. Supposing that it can enter phenomenality, revelation demands at least a combination of the four figures of saturation, ending up in a radicalized paradox. On this point, see *Being Given*, §25, and *De surcroît. Études sur les phénomènes saturés* (Paris: Presses Universitaires de France, 2001), chap. 6; trans. Robyn Horner and Vincent Berraud under the title *In Excess: Studies of Saturated Phenomena* (New York: Fordham University Press, 2002), "In the Name, How to Avoid Speaking of It," 128–162.

3. Baudelaire, "Three Drafts of a Preface" to *Les Fleures du mal / The Flowers of Evil*, ed. Marthiel and Jackson Mathews (New York: New Directions, 1989), xxvii.

4. Marlène Zarader, "Phenomenology and Transcendence," in *Transcendence in Philosophy and Religion*, ed. James Faulconer (Bloomington: Indiana University Press, 2003), 110. This essay often assumes what it calls a "canonical" phenomenology, which is a puzzling formulation. Would this be a moment in the history of phenomenological doctrines? But then one would need to know who defines the "canon." Husserl? But which period in Husserl's work? And why one rather than another stage? As things stand, none of these questions receives an answer, since not one of them is even posed. Does this concern an abstract and nontemporal model of phenomenology? But what legitimacy can be granted to this? Often the most dogmatic defenders of the (presumed) orthodoxy of phenomenology also seem to ignore its real history and development (it matters little whether this happens voluntarily or not).

5. Ibid., 113, 110, and 118, respectively.

6. Ibid., 114. This is an allusion to Rudolf Bernet, *La vie du sujet. Recherches sur l'interpretation de Husserl dans la phénoménologie* (Paris: Presses Universitaires de France, 1994), who in concluding evokes the question of "an intentional life without subject or object" (297ff). This concession, one that is inevitable in phenomenological terms (not only in reference to the dispute

among Bolzano, Twardowski, Meinong, and Husserl about nonexistent objects, but also in regard to the overcoming of *Vorhandenheit* by *Zuhandenheit* in *Being and Time* §§15–17) already grants a lot, in fact almost everything, to the saturated phenomenon's claim to legitimacy, whose chief ambition is precisely to do justice to phenomena that are irreducible to objectification.

7. Zarader, "Phenomenology and Transcendence," 115. Of course, the devoted [*l'adonné*, see n. 10 below] was never defined in such a way, since it finds itself charged, at the very moment when it receives itself with what gives itself, with the visibility of the very thing that gives itself. Here there is nothing like a simple choice between "activity" and "passivity," with no other option (these are, for that matter, only categories borrowed from Aristotle, radically metaphysical, whose phenomenological usefulness can be disputed). The devoted operates according to the call and response and manages the passage of what gives itself to what shows itself: neither the one nor the other corresponds to these categories. "Passivity" and "activity" intervene only once the characteristics of the devoted are misconstrued. One can make the same observations concerning Charles Larmore's criticisms of the supposed passivity of the devoted in *Les pratiques du moi* (Paris: Presses Universitaires de France, 2004), 221ff.

8. Zarader, "Phenomenology and Transcendence," 114. Obviously the problem consists in deciding not whether the devoted maintains a "character of subjectivity" but *which one*—transcendental, empirical, or something else? The outrageously simplified alternative loses all pertinence. For that matter, why reproach the devoted for *keeping* a subjective function when other criticisms (or even the same ones) give it grief for *losing* this function?

9. Title of the collection *Who Comes After the Subject?* ed. Eduardo Cadava, Peter Connor, and Jean-Luc Nancy (New York: Routledge, 1991).

10. [*L'adonné* designates being "devoted" or "given over" to someone or something and is also used to refer to someone "addicted" to something. Jeffrey Kosky translates the term as "the gifted" in *Being Given* and in his original translation of the present article, but "devoted" seems a more accurate and appropriate translation in light of Marion's treatment. See esp. bk. 5 of *Being Given*. —Trans.]

11. Jocelyn Benoist, "L'écart plutôt que l'excédant," *Philosophie* 78 (June 2003), 89. See "there was nothing to overcome" (ibid., 93). One remark: What does it mean to say "nothing that can be assigned [*rien d'assignable*]"? Is this the same as seeing absolutely nothing? No, without a doubt, since it is specified that what is at stake is challenging "some *absolute* form of appearing" in the name of some phenomenon (89). "To assign" therefore means *not to absolutize the phenomenon* (77), to accord (to *all* phenomena) only a *relative* phenomenality. But, I ask, relative to what or to whom? Such a presupposition should be argued or at least explained more fully. Once it is admitted, no doubt a saturated phenomenon (not to mention a phenomenon of revelation) cannot be admitted. But does not the entire question rest on the legitimacy of this presupposition?

12. Jocelyn Benoist, *L'idée de phénoménologie* (Paris: Beauchesne, 2001), 102. Let me observe that this question, one far too personal to remain purely philosophical, goes on: "I see nothing or something else, for example, the infinite forest of sensible life or the metamorphoses of the divine in our daily affair of being loved, rather than the monotheistic idol?" (ibid.). Or: "[the phenomenon's] intuitive richness and the unbelievable complexity of the forest of the sensible" (Benoist, "L'écart plutôt que l'excédent," 92). This simple addition calls for some remarks. (a) Can one describe the supposedly "infinite forest of the sensible" and its "frightening complexity" without having recourse to one or several saturated phenomena? (b) How can one describe what is here named quite rightly "our daily affair of being loved" without, once again, a nonobjectifying phenomenology, therefore a phenomenology of saturated phenomena (as I attempted in *Le phénomène érotique* [Paris: Grasset, 2003]; trans. Stephen E. Lewis under the title *The Erotic Phenomenon*

[Chicago: University of Chicago Press, 2007])? (c) Finally, with what right and by what procedures can one recognize (once again rightly) "metamorphoses of the divine," indeed, oppose them to a presumed "idol," except by presupposing a rationality of this very divinity, therefore the means to think it, e.g., as paradox of paradoxes (*In Excess*, chap. 6)? But then, if one does not want to remain sunk in platitudes and edifying discourses but reach the level of the concept, what philosophy will allow one to do so? At the very least, one can say it is not a positivism decked out in Husserlian rags, which tries the patience, the diligence, and the effort of the one who describes phenomena as they give themselves in excess and without remaining always in one's measure.

13. I think here of a remark by Husserl: "He [Wundt] refuses to, because he deduces, as the real a priori philosophy, that he can have absolutely nothing like it. Against this a priori, there is no cure. One cannot make oneself understood to someone who both does and does not want to see" ("Entwurf einer 'Vorrede' zu den 'Logischen Untersuchungen' (1913)," *Tijdschrift voor Philosophie* [Louvain, 1939], 335; trans. Philip J. Bossert and Curtis H. Peters under the title *Introduction to the Logical Investigations: A Draft of a Preface to the Logical Investigations (1913)* [The Hague: Martinus Nijhoff, 1975]). I owe this reference to Benoist himself (*L'idée de phénoménologie*, 102), whom I thank.

14. Aristotle, *Metaphysics* 1, 993b 9–11 (or also *Physics* 1, 2, 185a 1–2), commented on by St. Thomas Aquinas, *In Metaphysicorum Libros* 22, n. 282. For the angels, another caution is in order: "Accordingly, just as a man would show himself to be a most insane fool if he declared the assertions of a philosopher to be false because he was unable to understand them, so, and much more, a man would be exceedingly foolish were he to suspect of falsehood the things revealed by God through the ministry of his angels, because they cannot be the object of reason's investigations" (*Summa contra gentes* 1, 3).

15. Husserl refers here to the "I am" as the sole intentional ground of the entire ideal world, even that of the other. I would gladly substitute the saturated phenomenon as the official model of phenomenality, even (as we will see) for poor or common phenomenality.

16. Edmund Husserl, *Formale und Transzendentale Logik, Versuch einer Kritik der logischen Vernunft*, Hua VII, §95; trans. Dorian Cairns under the title *Formal and Transcendental Logic* §95, (The Hague: Martinus Nijhoff, 1969), 237.

17. Efforts that, for the most part, remain in vain, since the criticisms of the saturated phenomenon, while calling for precise and concrete analyses, most of the time do not consider the descriptions offered in *In Excess* (and thereafter) but stick to the still abstract schema in *Being Given*, if not just to the 1992 essay (Chapter 2 of the present work).

18. Benoist: "I believe instead that it is necessary, continuing some Husserlian analyses, and like numerous philosophies today, to recognize the fundamental and relatively uniform *richness of intuition*. What need is there to go looking for exceptional intuitions?" ("L'écart plutôt que l'excédent," 87). This is to say too much and to say it too quickly. (a) What are these "Husserlian analyses" and these "numerous philosophies"? (Are not these precisely ones that the author rejects elsewhere?) (b) Why, finally, could this "fundamental richness" of intuition not exercise an influence in defining the phenomenon itself, perhaps even modifying this definition? (c) Does the "relatively *uniform* richness of intuition" designate some specific characteristic for this uniformity or not? If it is the case, does it not suggest a model common to all phenomena endowed with this "rich" intuition, and would it not therefore join my attempt to establish a new paradigm of phenomenality?

19. Dominique Janicaud, *La phenomenology éclatée* (Combas: L'Éclat, 1998), 69 (though the same author had previously denounced a "watered-down experience," in *Le tournant théologique de la phénoménologie française*, ed. Dominique Janicaud, Jean-François Courtine, et al. (Com-

bas: L'Éclat, 1991); trans. under the title *Phenomenology and the "Theological Turn": The French Debate* (New York: Fordham University Press, 2000), 50.

20. On this apparently unexpected point, see *Being Given* §23 (and in fact also §§3–4), which already sketch this banality without, admittedly, formulating it as such.

21. St. Augustine, *Confessions* 11.22, 28, in regard to time; trans. Rex Warner (New York: Signet, 2001), 270–71, trans. modified.

22. The confusion of these two questions (whether willed or not) weighs heavily on Janicaud's criticism in *La phénoménologie éclatée*, in particular chap. 3, 63ff., to the point of leaving it too confused to be really useful and worth discussing.

23. Reproduced in Diane Waldman, *Mark Rothko, 1903–1970: A Retrospective* (New York: Abrams, 1978), plate 173. See the analysis of other paintings by Rothko (and Klee), as well as other phenomena saturated in terms of quality (idol), in *In Excess*, chap. 3, §2–§4.

24. [Marion uses different examples in the French text. —Trans.]

25. The detailed and argued application of the concept of the saturated phenomenon to music itself (and not just to listening) has been more than sketched by Sander van Maas, "On Preferring Mozart," *Bijdragen: International Journal in Philosophy and Theology* 65, no. 1 (2004): 97–110.

26. Derived uses are attached to the objective sense of touch: touching in the sense of taking possession (money, military equipment) or else of hitting a distant target (i.e., in fact not touching directly, from flesh to thing). To its sense in terms of the saturated phenomenon, other uses are attached: to touch someone in conversation (wound or move him or her, beyond what is said or without saying anything specific to the other), to touch on something or other while with someone (without saying anything, without the intention of saying anything specific, but doing so nevertheless), to stay out of touch (in fact, to lose all contact with society or a group).

27. Descartes, *Principia Philosophiae* [*Principles of Philosophy*], I, §45, in *Oeuvres de Descartes*, ed. Charles Adams and Paul Tannery, 11 vols. (Paris: Vrin, CNRS, 1964–79), VIII-A: 22; trans. John Cottingham, Robert Stoothof, and Dugalf Murdoch as *The Philosophical Writings of Descartes* (Cambridge: Cambridge University Press, 1985), I: 207–8; trans. modified. Hereafter AT and CSM, respectively. Even taste can admit coding in terms of order and measure, insofar as one can assign it causes that, in extension (intelligible and producing intelligibility), determine it as their effect.

28. Signification, in the sense of what can be communicated clearly and distinctly in language, is lacking here, but this shortcoming opens space for public discussion about the least communicable intuition—as if the chasm between common and private language had became blurred.

29. "Hence a perception can be clear without being distinct, but not distinct without being clear" (Descartes, *Principles of Philosophy*, I, §46 / CSM, 209). One could introduce a distinction: certain clear items of knowledge become distinct, though without a unique concept, such that it is indeed clear but not necessarily clear for just anyone. There is an excellent description of the saturation of taste in P. Delerm, *La première gorge de bière* (Paris: Gallimard, 1997). (But why stick with just poor old beer?)

30. Baudelaire, "Correspondances," *Les Fleurs du mal*, 12; trans. modified.

31. Baudelaire, "La chevelure," ibid., 32; my emphasis.

32. Baudelaire, "Le poison," ibid., 62; trans. modified.

33. In the correct formulation of Janicaud (*La phenomenology éclatée*, 112). I am contesting nothing save that such a banality impugns the hypothesis of saturated phenomena. To the contrary, it implies them.

34. One thinks of M. Aymé's character: "Vouturier knew to recognize the evidence and, in the same moment, to refuse its consequences. . . . He gave up the blessed springs of paradise in

favor of remaining faithful to his lieutenant and to his ideal of secularity" (*La Vouivre*, chap. 8 (Paris: Gallimard, 1974), 3:581.

35. An objection often raised, though with very different intentions, among others by: Janicaud, in *La phénoménologie éclatée*, 67; Béatrice Han, in "Transcendence and the Hermeneutic Circle," in *Transcendence and Philosophy of Religion*, ed. James Faulconer, 136ff.; and Ruud Welten, in "Saturation and Disappointment: Marion According to Husserl," *Bijdragen: International Journal in Philosophy and Theology* 65, no. 1 (2004): 79–96.

36. Immanuel Kant, *Kritik der reinen Vernunft*, 2d ed., vol. 3 of *Kants Werke* (1787; Berlin: Walter de Gruyter, 1968); trans. Norman Kemp Smith under the title *Immanuel Kant's Critique of Pure Reason* (London: Macmillan, 1964), A5/B7.

37. Ibid., A111 (my emphasis). See also A158/B197.

38. Leibniz had already seen this: "Does the soul have windows? Is it similar to writing tablets, or like wax? Clearly those who take this view of the soul are treating it as fundamentally corporeal. Someone will confront me with this accepted philosophical maxim, that there is nothing in the soul that does not come from the senses. But an exception must be made of the soul itself. *Nihil est in intellectu quod non fuerit in sensu excipe nisi ipse intellectus*" (*Die Philosophischen Schriften*, ed. Karl Gerhardt [Berlin: Akademie-Verlag, 1962], II.1, §2; trans. Peter Remnant and Jonathan Bennett under the title *New Essays Concerning Human Understanding* [Cambridge: Cambridge University Press, 1981], 110). Even *rasa*, the *tabula* remains a tablet erased and therefore available for the *self*, for the *ego cogitans* before the experience cogitated—in short, it already posits an a priori, in a certain fashion. If empiricism itself already implies a transcendental posture (consciously or not, it doesn't really matter), one can be free from it only by one path: thinking the *ego* as the devoted, for the devoted does not precede the given that it receives (as a *tabula rasa* already there awaiting it still does), since it *receives itself* from what it receives (see *Being Given* §26).

39. Let me refer to the analyses of the infinite (Descartes), of the sublime (Kant), and of the originary impression of time (Husserl) as nonobjective phenomena sketched in *Being Given*, §22.

40. There is no greater misreading than to imagine that I attribute an *intuitus originarius* to the devoted so as to permit it to experience directly, clearly, and distinctly the divine absolute (Han, "Transcendence and the Hermeneutic Circle," 137). There is no better illustration of the devoted's situation of saturation than what Kant identifies with reason as our *intuitus derivativus* because here this finitude is not limited to sensible intuition but determines the entire experience of phenomenality.

41. In the (arbitrarily) privileged case of God, for example, Jocelyn Benoist objects: "But *is it enough not to be a concept to be God?*" (*L'idée de phénoménologie*, 86). Or: "repeating my criticism of your thought, *it is not enough not to be a concept to be God*" (ibid., 96). Let me pass over the fact that respect for the basic rules of mystical (so-called "negative") theology would have resulted in avoiding this syntactical error. To speak more precisely, several remarks are called for. (a) Of course, God is not a concept, but it happens too often that we want to identify him by a concept (albeit only the very concept "God"). (b) Yes, God should not be identified with *a* concept, since his incomprehensibility requires all concepts (*via affirmativa*). (c) Agreed, it is not enough that God exceed each concept (and demand them all), but that nevertheless remains a necessary, though not sufficient, condition; as soon as we invoke a concept, it is no longer a question of God. (d) God *is* not a concept, for a more radical reason: he does not have *to be*, by contrast to everything that this polemic supposes in continually returning to the opposition between "atheist" and "believer" ("I am an atheist, you are not," ibid., 84), without at any time accepting the need to dispute the grounds or even the meaning of this opposition. It could be that "believer" is opposed no more to "atheist" than to "theist," "deist," or what have you, but rather to "nonbe-

liever," designating someone who refuses to believe what he or she already knows well enough, be it only so as to have the power to refuse it.

42. See esp. *Being Given*, §22 and §30, and *In Excess*, passim.

43. Stéphane Mallarmé, "Prose pour des Esseintes," in *Stéphane Mallarmé: Selected Poems*, trans. C. F. MacIntyre (Berkeley: University of California Press, 1957), 63. One can also speak of "the eye exceeded by light" (Emmanuel Levinas, *De Dieu qui vient à l'idée* [Paris: Vrin, 1982], 57; trans. Bettina Bergo as *Of God Who Comes to Mind* [Stanford: Stanford University Press, 1998], 30).

44. On bedazzlement, see *Being Given*, §21. Benoist notes, as an objection, that "the only bedazzlement I know of is that of our organs' sensibility, sometimes submitted to a stimulation too strong for them" ("L'écart plutôt que l'excédent," 91). But who ever asked for a different definition of bedazzlement? I can only suggest the following. (a) The "organs" submitted to this stimulation "too strong for them" cease to give us an object exactly in the sense that I indicated. (I suggest elsewhere that "this bedazzlement counts for intelligible intuition as well as for sensible intuition"; *Being Given*, §21.) (b) In such a situation, "our organs" extend more broadly than to sensation understood in the most sensualist sense, as I have just suggested in §4. (c) Theology itself (to return to the case always privileged by my reader) always considered the "spiritual senses" to be the senses of "our organs," suggesting only that the sensibility of the latter is not limited to sensualism. It is in this sense that one must understand the sensibility of categorical intuition in Husserl (See my *Réduction et donation: Recherches sur Husserl, Heidegger et la phénoménologie* [Paris: Presses Universitaires de France, 1989]; trans. Thomas A. Carlson under the title *Reduction and Givenness: Investigations of Husserl, Heidegger, and Phenomenology* [Evanston, Ill.: Northwestern University Press, 1998]).

45. I owe it to Ruud Welten ("Saturation and Disappointment: Marion According to Husserl") to have drawn my attention to this essential point.

46. Let me note that this hypothesis is quite contrived, indeed inconceivable. Who, how, and by what right could convince me that I do not experience the excess of light that makes me blink, indeed, close my eyes? Descartes's argument (and its exegesis by Michel Henry) are fully valid here: "For example, I am now seeing light, hearing a noise, feeling heat. But I am asleep, so all this is false. Yet I certainly *seem* to see, to hear, and to be warmed. This cannot be false; what is called 'having a sensory perception' is strictly just this" (Second Meditation, AT VII:29, 12–16; CSM II: 19).

47. On this resistance, see *In Excess*, chap. 2, §5, and chap. 4, §5. If one neglects it, the decisive phenomenological gap between "giving itself" and "manifesting itself" disappears. Then one remains stuck in misreadings that give rise to objections concerning the supposed passivity of the devoted or the supposed infinity of manifestation, etc. [The explanatory part of the note is not in the French version. —Trans.]

48. Descartes, *Meditations on First Philosophy*, AT VII:22, 6 (See also 28, 27; 79, 14).

49. St. Augustine, *Confessions* 10.23, 226–27 (trans. modified).

50. In the sense of *gaudium de Deo* or *de veritate* (as in *Confessions* 10.29–22, 33, or *De vita beata* 4.35) or of Pascal's "Truth is so obscured nowadays and lies so well established that unless we love the truth we shall never recognize it" *Pensées* §739 (New York: Penguin Books, 1966).

51. St. John of the Cross, *Llama de amor viva*, 4.11. Hans Urs von Balthasar has commented: "The illuminating light is in the first instance predominantly purificatory," such that we can speak of an "experience of the absolute in the non-experience of all content or finite activity" (*Herrlichkeit*, vol. 2, *Fächer der Style* [Einsiedeln: Johannes, 1962], 527; trans. under the title *The Glory of the Lord* [San Francisco: Ignatius Press, 1986], 138). Kevin Hart offers an

excellent commentary on this formula in "The Experience of Non-Experience," in *Mystics, Presence, and Aporia*, ed. Michael Kessler and Christian Sheppard (Chicago: University of Chicago Press, 2003), 196ff.

52. One should therefore take quite seriously—as is rarely the case, in my experience—the fact that Descartes himself avoids these terms. No doubt because for him, at least, the *ego* (as well as the *mens* or the *anima*, etc.) never exerts itself toward an object, according to the rules of the method, but sometimes admits an affection.

53. See *Being Given*, §1. If only for this reason, there is no occasion for theologians to be worried about the surreptitious reestablishment of a transcendental condition of possibility assigned to Revelation. See, e.g., V. Holtzer, "La foi, ses saviors et sa rationalité: Esquisse des débats fondamentaux en théologie catholique contemporaine," a presentation at the conference L'intelligence de la foi parmi les rationalités contemporaines, Institut catholique de Paris, 5 March 2004; or Kathryn Tanner, discussion at the conference "In Excess: Jean-Luc Marion and the Horizon of Modern Theology," at the University of Notre Dame, 9–11 May 2004. For that matter, *Being Given* already explicitly evokes this possible objection and answers it (235–36 and 243), thereby taking up the analyses of 1988.

54. See *Being Given*, §22.

The Reason of the Gift
Translated by Shane Mackinlay and Nicolas de Warren. Reprinted from Ian Leask and Eoin Cassidy, eds., *Givenness and God: Questions of Jean-Luc Marion* (Fordham University Press, 2005), 101–134.

1. "To give everything [*tout donner*]" is perhaps an odd expression, because on the occasions when I say that I give "everything," most of the time I in fact give nothing (nothing real, no thing—first paradox), and this very fact allows me to give all that I can, namely, to give myself (almost) without reserve or restraint (second paradox). But what is the significance of this gift where I give nothing in order to give myself—precisely not as a thing, but as an "unreal" gift, completely given and yet repeatable? From the very, outset, we find ourselves in an aporia.

2. [The normal English translation of *donataire* is "recipient." However, in *Being Given*, Kosky introduces "givee," which preserves the common root of *donateur, donataire, don*, and *donner*. Because of the parallels between *Being Given* and this chapter, we have followed Kosky's choice. —Trans.]

3. On the question of the gift, its possible contradiction, and the critique of my treatment of it in *Reduction and Givenness*, see, in succession: Jacques Derrida's remarks in *Given Time. 1: Counterfeit Money*, trans. Peggy Kamuf (Chicago: University of Chicago Press, 1992), esp. pp. 12ff. and 50ff.; translation of *Given Time, Donner le temps. 1: La fausse monnaie*, in the series La Philosophie, en Effet (Paris: Éditions Galilée, 1991), pp. 24ff. and 72ff.; my responses *Being Given*, 74ff./*Étant donné*, 108ff; and our debate, "On the Gift: A Discussion Between Jacques Derrida and Jean-Luc Marion," in *God, the Gift, and Postmodernism*, ed. John D. Caputo and Michael Scanlon (Bloomington: Indiana University Press, 1999).

4. It is appropriate here to acknowledge the analyses of Camille Tarot, *De Durkheim à Mauss, l'invention du symbolique. Sociologie des sciences de la religion* (Paris: La Découverte, 1999); and Main Caillé, *Anthropologie du don. Le tiers paradigme* (Paris: Desclée de Brouwer, 2000).

5. Anne Robert Jacques Turgot, *Reflections on the Formation and Distribution of Wealth* (written in 1766, published in 1768–70), in *The Economics of A. R. J. Turgot*, ed. and trans. P. D. Groenewegen (The Hague: Martinus Nijhoff, 1977), §31, p. 57.

6. Antoine-Augustin Cournot, *Researches into the Mathematical Principles of the Theory of Wealth*, trans. Nathaniel T. Bacon, in the series Reprints of Economic Classics (New York: Macmillan, 1927; repr. New York: Kelley, 1971), §2, p. 10, and §6, pp. 16–17.

7. Ibid., §2, p. 8; Cournot's emphasis.

8. Though one could easily refer to Descartes (e.g., *Discourse on Method*, AT, VI, 61–62), Cournot refers more to Leibniz: "We have already sketched elsewhere [*Traité de l'enchaînement des idées fondamentales*, 11, chap. 7] the principles of this *superior dynamic* for which Leibniz had the idea, and which shows us, in the laws that govern the work of machines, a proper example for conceiving the much more general laws under whose empire the perpetual conversion of natural forces into one another is brought about; in the same way, one can establish a comparison between the phenomenon of economic production and the work of machines, so as to adjust [*rendre sensible*] the analogies they present" (*Principes de la théorie de richesses* [1860], ed. Gerard Jorland, in Cournot's *Oeuvres complètes*, vol. 9 [Paris: Vrin, 1981], p. 39; Cournot's emphasis). In his own way, Diderot fully recognized and stated that the "economy" is inscribed in the deployment of a *mathesis universalis* in its strictly Cartesian meaning, on which it depends from beginning to end for the radicality of objectification: "One holds forth, one investigates, one feels little and reasons much; one *measures everything to the scrupulous level of method*, of logic and even of truth. . . . Economic science is a fine thing, but it stupefies us." *Salon de 1769*, in Diderot's *Oeuvres complètes*, vol. 16, *Beaux-arts* III, ed. Herbert Dieckmann and Jean Varloot (Paris: Hermann, 1990), 657; emphasis added.

9. [*Rendre raison* means to give a rational explanation or reason, thereby making something appear reasonable. However, because both "render" and "reason" are important terms in this chapter, *rendre raison* is translated throughout by the somewhat clumsy "render reason." —Trans.]

10. Jean-Baptiste Say, *A Treatise on Political Economy or The Production, Distribution and Consumption of Wealth* (New York: Claxton, Remsen & Haffelinger, 1880), translation of *Traité d'économie politique on Simple exposition de le la manière dont se forment, se distribuent et se consomment les richesses*, 6th ed., ed. Horace Say (Paris: Guillaumin, 1841; 1st ed., 1803), vol. 1, p. 455, and vol. 1, p. 117.

11. Karl Marx, *Capital: A Critique of Political Economy. Book One: The Process of Production of Capital*, trans. from the 3rd German ed. by Samuel Moore and Edward Aveling, ed. Frederick Engels (London: Lawrence and Wishart, 1954), chap. 19, p. 506; chap. 18, p. 500; chap. 6, p. 172; chap. 1, sec. 4, pp. 84ff (emphasis added). The excess of surplus value, which does not appear in the exchange's formulation, destroys its equality. This fact contradicts not only social justice, and Ricardo's or Smith's theory of value, but also invalidates the very notion of a political economy (henceforth dubbed "bourgeois"). Excess—even the invisible excess of surplus value—destroys the terms of exchange, and thus the economy. Certainly, Bataille envisages an economy based on excess: "The solar radiance . . . finally finds nature and the meaning of the sun: it is necessary for it to give, *to lose itself without calculation*. A living system grows, or lavishes itself *without reason*," such that "in practical terms, from the perspective of riches, the radiance of the sun is distinguished by its unilateral character: it loses itself *without counting, without consideration. The solar economy* is founded on this principle" ("The Economy to the Proportion of the Universe," trans. Michael Richardson, in *Georges Bataille: Essential Writings*, ed. Michael Richardson [London: Sage, 1998], pp. 75 and 74; translation of "L'économie à la mesure de l'univers," first published in *La France libre* no. 65 [July 1946], repr. in Bataille's *Oeuvres complètes* [Paris: Gallimard, 1976], vol. 7, p. 10; Bataille's emphasis). But one can question the legitimacy of thinking (and naming) this excess (without reason or measure) of expenditure starting from an economy, unless one assumes an economy deprived

of exchange, price, and calculation; that is, the contrary of what economists understand by this term.

12. Marx relies here on Aristotle's arguments. On the one hand, equality defines justice, and therefore exchange: "Since the unjust man is unequal and the unjust act unequal, it is clear that there is also an intermediate for the unequal. And this is the equal." On the other hand, injustice consists in upsetting equality by appropriating "more" (value): "The man who acts unjustly has too much, and the man who is unjustly treated too little, of what is good." *Nicomachean Ethics*, trans. W. D. Ross, rev. J. O. Urmson, in *The Complete Works of Aristotle: The Revised Oxford Translation*, ed. Jonathan Barnes, Bollingen Series 71:2, vol. 2 (Princeton, N.J.: Princeton University Press, 1984), V.3.1131a10–11; V.3.1131b19–20.

13. Leibniz strongly emphasizes that this universality of the principle of sufficient reason extends to the contingency of the event. "*No fact* can be real or actual, and no proposition true, without there being a sufficient reason for its being so and not otherwise" (*G. W. Leibniz's Monadology: An Edition for Students*, trans. Nicholas Rescher [Pittsburgh, Pa.: University of Pittsburgh Press, 1991], §32, p. 116; emphasis added); or "The principle in question is the principle of the want of a sufficient reason *for a thing to exist, for an event to happen*"("Fifth Letter to Clarke," in *G. W Leibniz: Philosophical Essays*, ed. and trans. Roger Ariew and Daniel Garber [Indianapolis: Hackett, 1989], §125, p. 346; emphasis added). Or again: "Constat ergo omnes veritates *etiam maxime contingentes* probationem a priori seu rationem aliquam cur sint potius quam non sint habere. Atque hoc ipsum est quod vulgo dicunt, nihil fieri sine causa, sed nihil esse sine ratione (It is therefore established that all truths, *even the most contingent*, have an a priori proof or some reason why they are rather than are not. And this is what the vulgar say: Nothing comes to be without cause; or: Nothing is without reason)"; untitled text described on the contents page by the editor [Gerhardt] as "Ohne Überschrift," in Betreff [Untitled, in] der Mittel der philosophischen Beweisführung [Reference to the Means of Philosophical Demonstration] in *Die philosophischen Schriften von Gottfried Wilhelm Leibniz*, ed. C. I. Gerhardt, 7 vols. (Berlin: Weidmann, 1875–90), vol. 7, p. 301; emphasis added.

14. Without repeating the Cartesian *causa sui*, which submits even God to causality (*de ipso Deo quaeri potest* [which can be asked even about God himself], *Ilae Responsiones, AT* VII, 164, 1. 29)—or, in His case alone, to reason—Leibniz nevertheless thinks God as being a reason (His own sufficient reason) for Himself: "Vides quid ex illo theoremate sequatur, *nihil est sine ratione* . . . omnia, quae sibi ipsi ratio cur sint, non sunt . . . ea tamdiu in, rationem, et rationem rationis, reducenda esse, donec reducantur in id quod sibi ipsi ratio est, id est Ens a se, seu Deum (You see what follows from the thesis: *nothing is without a reason* . . . everything that is not a reason for its own existence . . . is to be reduced to its reason, and its reason's reason, until it is reduced to what is its own reason, namely, the Being of itself, that, is, God)." *Confessio philosophi*, in Leibniz's *Sämtliche Schriften und Briefe*, ser. 6, vol. 3, *Philosophische Schriften: 1672–1676*, ed. Leibniz-Forschungsstelle der Universität Münster (Berlin: Akademie-Verlag, 1980), p. 120; Leibniz's italics.

15. Pierre Corneille: "Cinna, let us be friends! An end to strife! / You were my enemy; I spared your life; / Despite your base designs—that plot insane—/ I'll spare my would-be killer's life again! / Let's now compete and time its view deliver / On who fares best—recipient or giver. / My bounties you've betrayed; I'll shower more: / You shall be overwhelmed, as ne'er before!" (*Cinna or The Clemency of Augustus,* in *Le Cid; Cinna; Polyeuct: Three Plays*, trans. Noel Clark [Bath: Absolute Classics. 1993], V, 3. vv. 1701–1708). Admittedly, Cinna receives the gift as it is given— but we are here in Corneille's world and not in ours.

16. See my analysis in *In Excess/De Surcroît*, chap. 5.

17. [The French *conscience* can mean either "conscience" or "consciousness." —Trans.]

18. Fatherhood gives *itself* only to the extent that it gives. Thus it inverts and bears out the definition of "the gifted [*l'adonné*]," who receives *himself* from what he receives. See *Being Given*, § 26, esp. pp. 266ff./*Étant donné*, 366ff.

19. On the phenomenon's determinations as given, see *Being Given*, bk. 3, pp. 119ff/*Étant donné*, 169ff. I mention only some of them here, but fatherhood also validates the others (anamorphosis, facticity, fait accompli, incident, etc.).

20. ["Givenness" is the obvious English translation for both *donnéité* and the German *Gegebenheit*. "Givenness" is, however, already well established as the English translation for Marion's *donation*. To avoid any confusion, "givenence" has been introduced as an alternative. —Trans.]

21. See Roland Barthes: "Historically, the discourse of absence is carried on by the woman: Woman is sedentary, Man hunts, journeys; Woman is faithful (she waits), man is fickle (he sails away, he cruises) . . . It follows that, in every man who speaks of the absence of the other, *the feminine* declares itself: this man who waits and who suffers from it, is miraculously feminised." Roland Barthes, *A Lover's Discourse: Fragments*, trans. Richard Howard (London: Jonathan Cape, 1979), pp. 13–14; translation of *Fragments d'un discours amoureux* (Paris: Seuil, 1977), p. 20; Barthes's emphasis.

22. Michel Henry does this with an exemplary rigor, by opposing reciprocity—"The phenomenon that is at the economy's origin is exchange, the concept of which cannot be formed independently of that of reciprocity"—to that which goes beyond it—"the nonreciprocity of the interior relation that connects us to God signifies the intervention of another relation than that which is established among men," that [relation] precisely where "each person is son of God and of him alone . . . no living being having the power to bring itself into life." *Paroles du Christ* (Paris: Seuil, 2002), pp. 37, 46, 47.

23. Leibniz, *Monadology*, §31, p. 21.

24. Leibniz, *Monadology*, §32, p. 21.

25. See *Being Given*, §§17–18 (and bk. 3, passim).

26. This gift, which imposes itself to be given and received of itself, could be described, with Barthes, as *adorable,* for "*Adorable* means: this is my desire, insofar as it is unique: 'That's it! That's it exactly (which I love)!' Yet the more I experience the specialty of my desire, the less I can give it a name; to the precision of the target corresponds a wavering [*tremblement*] of the name; what is characteristic of desire, proper to desire, can produce only an impropriety of the utterance. Of this failure of language, there remains only one trace: the word 'adorable' (the right translation of 'adorable' would be the Latin *ipse*: it is the self, himself, herself in person)" (Barthes, *A Lover's Discourse*, p. 20 / *Fragments d'un discours amoureux*, p. 27). In fact, the ipseity and the pure self of this phenomenon—that which it is a question of loving, hence of receiving, hence of giving—come to it perhaps from precisely what they liberate from my desire and from its language, which in this adorable, see only fire, only a manifest object of an obscure desire.

27. On the transition from "show itself" to "give itself," see *Being Given*, §6, pp. 68ff.

28. Thus this remark, which Barthes makes in passing, would take on all its weight: "The gift then reveals the test of strength of which it is the instrument" (*A Lover's Discourse*, p. 76 / *Fragments d'un discours amoureux*, 91).

29. Thomas Aquinas, *Summa theologiae*, IIa–IIae, q. 58, a. 11 (emphasis added), referring to Aristotle (*Nicomachean Ethics*, V), who does not, however, use this exact formula.

30. Leibniz, *Elementa verae pietatis* (1677–78), in Gaston Grua, *Textes inédits*, 2 vols. (Paris: Presses Universitaires de France, 1948), vol. 1, p. 13; emphasis added. See also vol. 1, p. 25; and

"Specimen inventorum de admirandis naturae generalis arcanis," in Leibniz's *Die philosophischen Schriften*, vol. 7, p. 309.

31. See Oscar Bloch and Walther von Wartburg *Dictionnaire étymologique de la langue française*, 8th ed. (Paris: Presses Universitaires de France, 1989; 1st ed., 1932), p. 546; Alfred Ernout, *Morphologie historique du latin*, 3rd ed., Nouvelle Collection à l'Usage des Classes, no. 32 (Paris: Klincksieck, 1953; 1st ed., 1914), §207, p. 136; and Antonio Maria Martin Rodriguez, *Los verbos de "dar" en latin arcaico y clásico* (Grand Canary: Universidad de Las Palmas, 1999), *ad loc*. This is confirmed by Vincent Carraud, who emphasizes this "fundamental meaning" (*donner la raison* [to give reason], *ratio redeanda/ratio reddita*, etc.) even in the formulas of the history of metaphysics (*Causa sive ratio. Le raison de la cause, de Suárez à Leibniz* [Paris: Presses Universitaires de France, 2002], pp. 27ff., 436, 462 and n. 1, 492, etc.).

32. On the determinations of the phenomenon as pure given, see *Being Given*, bk. 3.

33. On the analysis of saturated phenomena, see *Being Given*, bk. 4, §§21–23, and *In Excess*, passim.

The Icon or the Endless Hermeneutic

Translated by Robyn Horner and Vincent Berraud. Reprinted from Jean-Luc Marion, *In Excess: Studies of Saturated Phenomena* (Fordham University Press, 2002), 104–127.

1. Husserl, Hua. I, V, §50, p. 139; *Méditations cartésiennes*, p. 158; *Cartesian Meditations*, p. 109.

2. Husserl, Hua. X, §39, pp. 80ff.: *Leçons pour une phénoménologie de la conscience intime du temps*, pp. 107ff.; *On the Phenomenology of the Consciousness of Internal Time*, pp. 84ff.

3. Especially after the works of Klaus Held, *Lebendige Gegenwart: Die Frage der Seinsweise des transzendentalen Ich bei Edmund Husserl* (The Hague: Martinus Nijhoff, 1966), and Didier Franck, *Chair et corps: Sur la phénoménologie de Husserl.*

4. On the penury of intuition for Kant and Husserl, see *Etant donné*, IV, §20, pp. 265ff.

5. Martin Heidegger, *Seminar in Zähringen* (1973), *GA: I Abteilung: Veröffentlichte Schriften 1910–1976, Band 15: Seminare 1951–73*, ed. Curd Ochwadt (Frankfurt am Main: Vittorio Klosterman, 1986), p. 399; *Questions* IV, trans. Jean Beaufret et al. (Paris: Gallimard, 1976), p. 339.

6. Martin Heidegger, *Der Weg zur Sprache* (1959), *GA: I Abteilung: Veröffentlichte Schriften 1910–1976, Band 12: Untervegs zur Sprache*, ed. Friedrich-Wilhelm von Heffmann (Frankfurt am Main: Vittorio Klosterman, 1985), p. 247; French translation: "is, among the unapparent, that which is the most unapparent" (*Acheminement vers la parole*, trans. Jean Beaufret et al. [Paris: Gallimard, 1976], p. 246).

7. Martin Heidegger, Lettre à Roger Munier, February 22, 1974, in *Heidegger: Cahiers de l'Herne* (Paris: L'Herne, 1983), pp. 114 (translation) and 115 (text).

8. Heidegger, *Sein und Zeit*, §7, p. 36; *GA* II, p. 48; *Etre et temps*, trans. and ed. Emmanuel Martineau (Paris: Authentica, 1985), p. 47; *Being and Time*, p. 60 (Macquarrie); p. 31 (Stambaugh).

9. With the formidable ambiguities of this concept, underlined by Xavier Tilliette, *Recherches sur l'intuition intellectuelle de Kant a Hegel* (Paris: J. Vrin, 1995).

10. On this subject of phenomena, see *Etant donné*, IV §23, pp. 309ff., which integrates the last case, here yet to come, of the saturated phenomenon.

11. Husserl, Hua. I, V, §54. P. 148; *Méditations cartésiennes*, p. 168; *Cartesian Meditations*, p. 119.

12. Husserl, Hua. I, V, §55, p. 150; *Méditations cartésiennes*, p. 171; *Cartesian Meditations*, p. 122.

13. Emmanuel Levinas, *Humanisme de l'autre homme* (Montpellier: Fata Morgana, 1972), pp. 47ff.

14. Levinas, *Totalité et infini*, p. 182.

15. See my discussion "D'autrui a l'individu: Au-delà de l'éthique," Actes du Colloque *Emmanuel Levinas et la phénoménologie* (Sorbonne, 11–12 December 1997), appearing under the

title *Levinas et le phénoménologie*, added to *E. Levinas: Positivité et transcendance* (Paris: Presses Universitaires de France, 2000). English translation by Robyn Horner, in Regina Schwartz, *Transcendence* (London: Routledge, 2002).

16. I do not take account *here* of what Heidegger thematized under the title of *Anspruch des Seins* (*GA* IX, p. 319), because he does not proceed precisely from any face or any icon. It remains to be understood how he can nevertheless depend on a phenomenological structure of the call (see my *Reduction et donation*, VI, §6, pp. 294ff.; *Reduction and Givenness*, pp. 164ff., and *Etant donné*, V, §26, pp. 366ff.).

17. Husserl, Hua. IV, §21, p. 96; *Idées directrices* II, p. 144 (modified); *Ideas* II, p. 102.

18. Pascal: "And these prophecies being accomplished and proved by the *event* mark the certitude of these truths and consequently the proof of the divinity of J.C." *Pensées*, §189, p. 524.

19. Sophocles, *Oedipe Roi*, II. 1528–30, trans. J. Grosjean (Paris: Gallimard, 1967), pg. 711.

20. Immanuel Kant, *Critique de la raison pratique*, Preface, Ak.A.V., p. 4; French translation, vol. 2 (Paris: Gallimard/Pléiade, 1985), p. 610.

21. Kant, *Critique de la raison pratique*, Preface, Ak.A.V. p. 122ff.; French translation, pp. 757–758.

22. Kant, *Das Ende aller Dinge*, Ak.A.VIII, pp. 330 and 334; French translation, vol. 3 (Paris: Gallimard, 1986), pp. 313 and 318.

23. Kant, *Critique de la raison pratique*, Preface, Ak.A.V. p. 30; French translation, vol. 2, p. 643.

24. Husserl, *Erste Philosophie (1923–24): Zweiter Teil: Theorie der phänomenologischen Reduktion*, Hua. VIII, ed. Rudolf Boehm (The Hague: Martinus Nijhoff, 1959), §29, p. 14; *Philosophie Première (1923–24). Deuxième partie: Théorie de la reduction phénoménologique*, trans. Arion L. Kelkel (Paris: Presses Universitaires de France/Epimethée, 1972), p. 20.

Introduction to Part III: Reading Descartes

1. Jean-Luc Marion, *René Descartes. Règles utiles et claires pour la direction de l'esprit en la recherche de la vérité. Traduction selon la lexique cartésien et annotation conceptuelle avec des notes mathématiques de Pierre Costabel* (The Hague: Martinus Nijhoff, 1977).

2. Jean-Luc Marion, *Sur la théologie blanche de Descartes. Analogie, création des vérités éternelles et fondement* (Paris: Presses Universitaires de France, 1981). A revised edition appeared in 1991.

The Ambivalence of Cartesian Metaphysics

Translated by Sarah E. Donahue. Reprinted from Jean-Luc Marion, *Descartes's Grey Ontology: Cartesian Science and Aristotelean Thought in the Regulae* (St. Augustine's Press, 2013), chapter 8 (appendix).

1. Originally published in *Les Études Philosophiques* (1976), this essay is the further development of a lecture given at the University of Nice in February 1976, at the invitation of the Société Azuréenne de Philosophie.

2. *Objectiones Septimae*, AT VII, 549, 20–21.

3. See the article, one to which I frequently have occasion to refer, as I do here, by Ernst Vollrath, "Die Gliederung der Metaphysik in eine Metaphysica Generalis und eine Metaphysica Specialis," *Zeitschrift für philosophische Forschung* (1962) vol. 16, no.2, pp. 258–84; if, as we know to be the case, Johann Clauberg is the first to write *ontologia* in Latin (in his *Elementa Philosophiae sive Ontosophia* [Gröningen, 1647], p. 3), other authors before him had used the term in Greek: Abraham Calov, *Metaphysica Divina, Pars Generalis Praecognita II* (Rostock, 1636), p. 4; Alsted, *Cursus Philosophici Encyclopaedia Libri XXVII* (Herborn, 1620), liv. V, I, c.1, p. 149;

and especially Rudolph Gogkel (Goclenius), *Lexicon Philosophicum* (Frankfort, 1613): "*ontologia et philosophia de* ENTE" (p. 16). Descartes could, then, have made use of the term, without having to impose or invent it himself. That his position with regard to this tradition should have remained so marginal, due to a lack of interest, as much as to ignorance, is worthy of note.

4. That is, in *Descartes's Grey Ontology*.

5. Alquié, "Descartes et l'ontologie négative," *Revue Internationale de philosophie* (1950).

6. *Quintae Responsiones*, AT VII, 368, 2–4.

7. Heidegger, *Sein und Zeit*, §61, n.1, p. 320 (n.19 to p. 295 on pp. 411–12 in the English translation by Joan Stambaugh, *Being and Time* [Albany: SUNY Press, 1996]). See my article outlining this point, "Heidegger et la situation métaphysique de Descartes," in "Bulletin cartésien IV," *Archives de Philosophie* 38 (1975): 253–65.

8. Heidegger, *Sein und Zeit*, §6, p. 24, trans. Joan Stambaugh, *Being and Time*, p. 21.

9. *Tertiae Responsiones, objectio XIV*, AT VII, 194, 13. *Existentia*, in particular, counts among the number of terms "quae per se satis nota mihi videntur" because of being "simplicissimae rationes," *Principia* I, §10, AT VIII-1, 8, 4–5 and 8, 14. Elsewhere, *existentia* is included in the list of extremely simple natures (*Rule X*, 419, 22 and 420, 7). Jean Wahl's interesting attempt to give "Un exemple d'une règle inconnue, le verbe *être* chez Descartes," (*Descartes*, Cahiers de Royaumont 2, ed. Martial Guéroult and Henri Gouhier [Paris: Les Éditions de Minuit, 1957], pp. 360–67) after having brought into question the equivalence of *esse* and *existere*, changes its tack, and, for some odd reason, resolutely resists pushing the question its author has so well identified any further (as the rather strange discussion that follows shows).

10. "Descartes à Regius, janvier 1642," AT III, 505, 11–12.

11. Suárez, *Disputationes Metaphysicae*, in *Opera Omnia*, ed. Vivès (Paris: 1866), vol. 25, respectively: *Disputatio* I, p. 2; §1, no.26, p. 11; §3, no.10, p. 25. See in addition: "Scientia . . . quae de primis rerum causis et principiis, et de rebus dignissimis considerat [Science . . . which considers the first causes and first principles of things and the most dignified things]", §3, no. 9, p. 24. The double object of metaphysics is also treated in a similar manner by St. Thomas: *Sententia super De generatione et corruptione*, Prooemium, 2: "Et inde est quod philosophus in m[M?]etaphysica simul determinat de ente in communi et de ente primo, quod est a materia separatum [Consequently in metaphysics the philosopher discusses both being in general and the first being, which is separate from matter]," (whether, depending on the choice of the editor, *Metaphysica* here designates the work or the science, makes no difference to the point I am making); *Sententia super Metaphysicam*, Prooemium: "Secundum igitur tria praedicta, ex quibus perfectio hujus scientiae attenditur, sortitur tria nomina. Dicitur enim scientia divina sive *theologia, inquantum* praedictas substantias considerat. *Metaphysica* inquantum considerat ens et ea quae consequuntur ipsum. Haec enim transphysica inveniuntur in via resolutionis, sicut magis communia post minus communia. Dicitur autem *prima philosophia*, inquantum primas rerum causas considerat [Three names are assigned to it in accordance with the previous considerations that manifest the perfection of this science: it is called divine science or theology insofar as it considers the separate substances, and metaphysics insofar as it considers being and that which follows upon it. These things that transcend physics are found by way of analysis, like the more common is found after the less common. It is called first philosophy, insofar as it considers the first causes of things]." Note that here (as in *Sententia super Posteriora Analytica*, Liber I, l.5, n. 7; l.41, n. 7) metaphysics in the strict sense is a *Metaphysica communis*, contrary to what seems to be the Cartesian acceptation. There remain, however, a number of instances where Metaphysics is concerned *circa res divinas* (for instance, *ST* II–II, q.9, a.2, obj.2, and *SCG* I, 4).

12. We should take care not to speak of, nor above all to understand the *ontotheologische Verfassung* as a "structure," but truly as a constitution. A structure maps the relation between two directly identifiable themes, in one case, the divine in its names, in the other, the *ens commune* in its aspects. A constitution can operate between two poles that are more hidden, unexpected, complicated, where, for example, the divine can only withstand a theio-logic, indeed can only be established in the absence of the divine. This precaution will be useful to us later on. On the ontotheological constitution, see, of course, *Identität und Differenz* (Pfullingen: G. Neske, 1954), English translation by Joan Stambaugh, *Identity and Difference* (New York: Harper & Row, 1969); but also the "Einleitung zu 'Was ist Metaphysik'?" *Wegmarken* (Frankfurt: V. Klosterman, 1976), p. 207 ("Introduction to 'What is Metaphysics?'" *Pathmarks*, p. 287). Heidegger does however sometimes speak of an "onto-theological *structure* of . . . metaphysics," (*Identität*, p. 47, trans. Stambaugh, *Identity*, p. 56). But in fact, his analyses of what we maladroitly attempt to indicate by a "structure" tend to occur when he is exposing the traditional concept of metaphysics (*Kant und das Problem der Metaphysik* [Tübingen: 1929], §1, English translation by Richard Taft, *Kant and the Problem of Metaphysics* (Bloomington: Indiana University Press, 1997).

13. Respectively, "Descartes à Mersenne, [mars 1637]," AT I, 349, 26 (see 370, 25–27 and 564, 14); "Descartes à Huygens, [mars 1638]," AT II, 50, 13–14; "Descartes à Mersenne [27 mai 1638]," AT II, 141, 25–26. Also, "These here are all the Principles that I make use of concerning immaterial or Metaphysical things, from which I deduce very clearly the principles of corporeal or Physical things," *Principes*, "Préface," AT IX–2, 10, 11–15.

14. "Descartes à Mersenne [27 août 1639]," AT II, 570, 17–571, 1. H. de Cherbury had published a *De veritate* in 1624. The rapprochement could also be in the other direction: "I have always considered that two questions, concerning God and the Soul, are preeminent among those which are best demonstrated by Philosophy instead of Theology," *Meditationes* "Epistola," AT VII, 1, 7–9.

15. What does *prima philosophia* signify for Descartes? Vollrath ("Die Gliederung der Metaphysik," p. 267) has rediscovered a text of Pereira, who, oddly and hypothetically, understands *prima philosophia* as a science of being in its Being: "Necesse est esse duas scientias distinctas inter se; Unam, quae agat de transcendentalibus, et universalissimis rebus: Alteram, quae de intelligentiis. Illa dicitur prima Philosophia et scientia universalis; haec vocabitur proprie Metaphysica, Theologia, Sapientia, Divina Scientia [It is necessary that two sciences be distinguished from each other: One which treats the transcendentals and the most universal things; another which treats the intelligences. The former is called first philosophy and universal science; the latter is properly named Metaphysics, Theology, Wisdom, Divine Science]," *De communibus omnium rerum naturalium principiis et affectionibus* (Cologne: 1592), p. 23 (Rome: 1582). If Descartes understood the term in this way, it is hard to understand why the *Meditationes de prima philosophiae* claim to speak of God and the immortality of the soul. If, on the contrary, as Vollrath indicates, Pereira had hardly any influence except outside his order, the Jesuits, and in Protestant Germany ("Die Gliederung der Metaphysik," p. 269, 278), then it would be the more traditional and less bizarre nomenclature of Suárez that Descartes resurrects: "eique [Metaphysica] tanquam uni et eidem attribuit [Aristoteles] nomina et attributa, quae partim illi conveniunt, secundum quod versatur circa Deum et intelligentias; sic enim vocatur theologia, seu scientia divina et prima philosophia; partim ut versatur circa ens in quantum ens, et prima attributa, et principia ejus qua ratione dicitur scientia universalis et metaphysica. *Sapientia* autem vocatur, quatenus haec omnia complecitur, et prima principia, primasque rerum causas contemplatur [and insofar as it (Metaphysics) is one and the same, (Aristotle) attributes to it the names and the attributes which suit it in part following from the fact it treats God and the intelligences

and for this reason it is called theology or divine science and first philosophy; and in part because it is occupied with being insofar as it is being, and with its first attributes and its principles, it is called universal science and metaphysics. And it is called *wisdom* inasmuch as it contains all these things and contemplates the first principles and the first causes of things]," *Disputationes Metaphysicae I*, §3, no. 9, *Opera Omnia*, vol. 25, p. 24. In this sense, *prima philosophia* suits the title of the *Meditationes*. In addition, Vollrath's own reading of the *Meditationes*, that is, as the *metaphysica specialis* of Descartes, only holds if *prima philosophia* here indeed means *theologica*, in contrast to the nomenclature of Pereira ("Die Gliederung der Metaphysik," p. 280).

16. *Principes de philosophie*, "Préface," AT IX–2, respectively, 14, 7–12 and 16, 12–16.

17. "Descartes à Mersenne, [11 novembre 1640]," AT III, 235, 10–18. We can better understand the originality of Descartes's title and what is at stake in it by comparing it with that of Spinoza: *Cogitata Metaphysica, in quibus difficiliores quae in Metaphysicis, tam parte Generali, quam Speciali, circa ens ejusque affectiones, Deumque ejusque Attributa, et mentem humanam occurent, quaestiones breviter explicantur* [Metaphysical Thoughts, in which are briefly explained the more difficult questions that arise in metaphysics, as much in the general as in the special part, concerning being and its modifications, God and his Attributes, and the human mind] (Amsterdam, 1663). Here, metaphysics is, at least in appearance, equally distributed between its two acceptations, maintaining one discourse "circa ens ejusque affectiones," that the *Meditationes* ignores. Vollrath likewise recognizes this: "We can see here in this title that all the elements of the metaphysics of the future are united under the name of First Philosophy," "Die Gliederung der Metaphysik," p. 280.

18. The interpretation of *prōtē philosophia* as a first science makes its debut before Descartes, in Pereira, Conrad Dasypodius, and van Roomenx (texts cited in Crapulli, *Mathesis Universalis*). Just as the *Regulae*, starting from a general epistemology, encounters the question of the supreme science (and so of the supreme being), so too the *Meditationes*, in investigating the supreme being (and thus the supreme science), encounters being in general. The ambiguity that appears here between being and knowledge perhaps reproduces that which runs through the general quasi-metaphysics of the *Regulae* (see chap. 1, §11, to which, in a sense, this concluding essay is only a footnote).

19. *Principia Philosophiae* I, §7 and §10, AT VIII–1, 7, 9 and 8, 10. See §12, AT VII–I, 9, 4–5.

20. The difference that has been the subject of much commentary between the *in qua* of the 1641 edition and the *in quibus* of the 1642 edition is less important than the permanence of the couple formed by *Dei existentia* and *animae immortalitas/distinctio*.

21. Respectively, *Primae Responsiones*, AT VII, 108, 18–22; *Secundae Responsiones*, AT VII, 164, 28–29.

22. *Quartae Responsiones*, respectively: AT VII, 238, 24–25, and 239, 16–17.

23. Richard of Saint Victor, *De Trinitate* IV, 12: "Quod autem dicitur existere, subintelligutur non solum quod habeat esse, sed etiam aliunde, hoc est ex aliquo habeat esse. Hoc enim intelligi datur in verbo composito ex adjuncta sibi praepositione. Quid est enim existere nisi ex aliquo sistere, hoc est substantialiter ex aliquo esse? In uno itaque hoc verbo existere, vel sub uno nomine existentiae, datur subintelligi, posse, et illam considerationem quae pertinet ad rei qualitatem et illam quod pertinet ad rei originem [What is said to exist is understood not only to have being, but to have it from a distinct source; that is it has being from something else. For this point may be understood in the way that the verb 'existere' is compounded with the preposition that is added to its root. For what else is 'existere' except to stand out of something, that is, to be substantially from something? In this one verb 'existere' or in the one term 'existentia' we may understand both that consideration that pertains to the nature of a thing and what pertains to

its origin]," *Patrologia Latina*, 196, 237d–238a. This refers back to the sense in which Aristotle uses *ekstasis/existanai* in the case of *metabolē/kinēsis* (*Physics* 4.12.221b3; 4.13.222b16, b21; 7.3.246a17; 8.7.261a20; etc.), where the *ekstasis* should almost be understood as a *defeat*, the movement by which the thing is undone and annihilated.

24. Suárez: "Nam existentia nihil aliud est quam illud esse, quo formaliter et immediate entitas aliqua constituitur extra causas suas, et desinit esse nihil, ac incipit esse aliquid [For existence is nothing other than that by which formally and immediately some entity is constituted outside its causes and ceases to be nothing and so begins to be something]," *Disputationes Metaphysicae*, XXXI, §4, no. 6, *Opera Omnia*, vol. 26, p. 236; and passim. Even more vividly, Eustache de Saint-Paul: "Antequam enim res existat dicitur esse potestate, et quasi latere in causis suis; tunc autem incipit existere, cum virtute causarum foras prodit [Before a thing exists, it is said to exist in potency and to lie hidden, so to speak, in its causes; it begins to exist, however, when it comes forth into being through the power of its causes]," *Summa Philosophiae*, vol. 4 (Paris: 1609), p. 37, cited in Gilson, *Index*, no. 189.

25. *Primae Responsiones*, AT VII, 112, 3–5.

26. *Quartae Responsiones*, AT VII, 238, 11–18. Also: "Nulla res existit de qua non possit quaeri quaenam sit causa, cur existat. Hoc enim de ipso Deo quaeri potest [No thing exists about which it is not possible to ask what is the cause why it exists. For about God himself this can be asked]," *Secundae Responsiones*, AT VII, 164, 28–165, 1; and "Quomodo enim ii qui Deum nondum norunt, in causam aliarum rerum efficientem inquirerent, ut hoc pacto ad Dei cognitionem devenirent, nisi putarent cujusque rei causam efficientem posse inquiri? [For how is it that those who do not yet know God inquire after the efficient cause of other things so that they may arrive in this way at the thought of God, unless they think that the efficient cause of each thing can be sought?]," *Quartae Responsiones*, AT VII, 244, 21–25.

27. Heidegger, *Identität und Differenz*, p. 51, trans. Stambaugh, *Identity*, p. 60.

28. *Primae Responsiones*, AT VII, 109, 3–7; see also 112, 3–11.

29. *Inexhausta potentia*, AT VII, 109, 4; 236, 9; *immensa potentia*, 56, 4–5; 110, 26–27; 111, 4; 119, 13; 237, 8–9; *exuperantia potestatis*, 112, 10; and from these to the astonishing equivalence, clearly stated: "immensitas potentiae, sive essentiae," 237, 1.

30. God "qui potest omnia," AT VII, 21, 2; *omnipotens*, 40, 17; see 45, 9–14; 56, 4–5; etc.

31. Respectively, *Primae Responsiones*, AT VII, 108, 20–22; and *Secundae Responsiones*, 164, 28–165, 3.

32. *Meditatio III*, AT VII, 40, 21–26, and 41, 3.

33. *Meditatio III*, AT VII, 40, 22. See *Principia* I, §18, AT VIII–1, 12, 1; and the letters "Descartes à Mersenne, [27 mai 1630]," AT I, 152, 2; "Descartes à Elisabeth, 6 octobre 1645," AT IV, 314, 22–24; "Descartes à Mersenne, [31 décembre 1640]," AT III, 274, 20–24. Descartes here reproduces, with the addition of an equivalence with *efficiens*, the Suárezian definition of the *causa totalis*: "causa totalis est illa, quae agit tota virtute necessaria in illo ordine ad talem effectum; ergo repugnat causae totali ut sic, habere consortium alterius causae similis in effectione ejusdem effectus [A total cause is one which with all needed power acts in that order so as to produce such and such an effect; therefore, it is repugnant to a total cause to have the companionship of another like cause in its role of bringing about the self-same effect]." *Disputationes Metaphysicae*, XXVI, §4, no. 4, *Opera Omnia*, vol. 25, p. 930.

34. See §14. It should be noted that the ranking of cause and effect is the same in the *Discours*, except that there the difference may in fact be quantitatively measured; in effect, according to the computerized index compiled by the *Équipe Descartes* (C.N.R.S., Paris, affiliated with the Équipe de Recherches 56; see "Bulletin cartésien III," *Archives de philosophie* 37 [1974]: 453–458),

in the *Discours*, the lemma *effet* registers 13 items and *effets* 5, while the lemma *cause* registers 11 (7 instances of which occur in the phrase "à *cause* de"), *causes*, 10, and *causer*, 3 (P. Cahné, *Index du Discours de la Méthode de René Descartes* [Rome: Edizioni dell'Ateneo, 1977]). In the *Regulae*, on the other hand, the tally is 17 items of the lemma *causa* to 14 of the lemma *effectus* and 5 of the lemma *efficio*, that is to say, the frequencies are comparable (Jean-Robert Armogathe, Jean-Luc Marion, *Index des Regulae ad directionem ingenii de René Descartes, Corpus Cartesianum* I [Rome: Edizioni dell'Ateneo, 1976]). On the imbalance between cause and effect viewed in a slightly different manner, see Martial Gueroult, *Descartes selon l'ordre des raisons*, vol. 1 (Paris: Aubier-Montaigne, 1968), p. 188, n. 79.

35. Respectively, *Secundae Responsiones*, AT VII, 164, 29–165, 3; *Quartae Responsiones*, AT VII, 236, 9–10; 236, 21–22. See the *causandi ratio* of God the creator of the eternal truths in *Sextae Reponsiones*, AT VII, 436, 7. Opposing this view is Yvon Belaval: "the formula *Causa sive Ratio* is in no way Cartesian" (*Leibniz, critique de Descartes* [Paris: Gallimard, 1960], p. 448); in a similar vein are the reservations of Eugenio Pucciarelli, who takes issue with Descartes for having considered the *ratio* only as a *causa*, despite the formula, and never as a sufficient reason ("La causalidad en Descartes," *Escritos en honor de Descartes* [La Plata, Argentina: Universidad Nacional de La Plata, 1938], pp. 196 and 205). The formula (to which Schopenhauer had already called attention, *Über die vierfache Wurzel des Satzes von zureichenden Grunde*, §7, *Sämtliche Werke* [Berlin: 1847], vol. 1, pp. 7–8) is examined by Wahl, *Du rôle de l'idée de l'instant dans la philosophie de Descartes* (Paris: J. Vrin, 1953), p. 53; Röd, *Descartes' Erste Philosophie*, p. 109; and Stanislas Breton, "Origine et principe de raison," *Revue des Sciences Philosophiques et Théologiques* 52 (1975): 45: "first modern formulation of the principle of reason." An even more characteristically Cartesian equivalence has to be examined in tandem with this one, namely, that between *principe* and *cause*: "la recherche de ces premières causes, c'est-à-dire des Principes" (*Principes*, "Préface," AT IX–2, 2, 17–18); "la cause ou principe" (*Principes*, "Préface," AT IX–2, 8, 10; see 4, 23; 5, 21–24; and *DM*, AT VI, 64, 1). On the distinction between cause and principle, see Suárez, *Disputationes Metaphysicae, XII*, §1, no. 25, *Opera Omnia*, vol. 25, p. 385.

36. *DM*, AT VI, 14, 1.

37. Heidegger's phrase, so long as we understand it as a "metaphysics of the object (*Gegenstand*), that is, of beings as object, of the object (*Objekt*) for a subject," "Uberwindung der Metaphysik," V, in *Gesamtausgabe* III, vol. 67: *Metaphysik und Nihilismus*, English translation by Joan Stambaugh, "Overcoming Metaphysics," in *The End of Philosophy* (Chicago: University of Chicago Press, 2003), pp. 86, 89; and Erich Przywara: "bei Descartes, immente Metaphysik der Erkenntnis," *Analogia Entis*, in *Schriften*, vol. 3 (Einsiedeln: Johannes Verlag, 1962), p. 445.

38. See the prior indication of the same, *Rule IV*, AT X, 378, 1–2.

39. *Meditatio* II, respectively, AT VII, 31, 10–11; AT VII, 31, 16–18 (see 19–20); AT VII, 31, 25 (see 32, 5–6; 32, 15–16; etc.). It doesn't seem as if one can really speak of extension here, unless it is "as an idea of my intellect, supplying the condition of the possibility of my consciousness of the material object," (Gueroult, *Descartes selon l'ordre*, vol. 1, p. 130): what supplies the condition of my consciousness of a material object is not at all its extension (which is unknown here), but my consciousness itself, as the inspecting relation 1 (see *Meditatio* II, AT VII, 32, 24–28).

40. "Descartes à Elisabeth, 6 octobre, 1645," AT IV, 314, 17–22. On the distinction between *weil* and *warum*, whereby the former escapes the principle of reason because it escapes representation; see Heidegger, *Der Satz vom Grund* (Pfullingen: Neske, 1957), pp. 71–73, English translation by Reginald Lilly, *The Principle of Reason* (Bloomington: Indiana University Press, 1991). pp. 37–38.

41. Here I transpose, somewhat trivially, Heidegger's analysis of the *reddere* in *rationem reddere* as "zurückgeben, herbeibringen, zu-stellen [to give back, to bring along, to re-render]." "Dies sagt: Der Grund is solcher, was dem vorstellunden, denkenden Menschen zugestellt werden muss [This means that reason is what must be rendered to the representing, thinking person]," *Der Satz vom Grund*, p. 47, trans. Lilly, *Principle of Reason*, pp. 23–24.

42. My earlier conclusion (§31) thus merits both a confirmation and a challenge. Confirmation, because the ontology of the *Regulae* already corresponds to that of the *cogito/cogitatum* and thus is on the way to a definitive status. Invalidation, because the metaphysical position assumed by Descartes as early as 1628 is perhaps not modified in the *Meditationes*, even if it is masked.

43. Respectively, *Principes*, "Préface," AT IX–2, 10, 4–8; *Principia* I, §7 and §10, AT VIII–1, 7, 8–10 and 8, 9–10; finally, *Secundae Responsiones*, AT VII, 140, 19. Likewise, *Meditatio II*, AT VII, 24, 12–13; 25, 23–24; "Epistola ad p. Dinet," AT VII, 573, 14–16 and 602, 20–21; "Descartes à Clerselier, juin–juillet 1646," AT IV, 444, 23–25, completed by 445, 5–8. — Establishing the *ego*'s role as first principle is the task Röd takes on in *Descartes' Erste Philosophie* and in his article, "Zum problem des Premier Principe in Descartes' Metaphysik," *Kantstudien* 51 (1959–60): pp. 142–75. On this point, at least, he and Mahnke, *Der Aufbau*, pp. 136–151, are in agreement. The distinction between the order of reasons and the order of matters does not, however, seem sufficient to resolve the conflict between the principles. Even more radical, in my opinion, are the analyses of Przywara, *Analogia Entis*, pp. 417 and 421; and of Gustav Siewerth, *Das Schicksal der Metaphysik von Thomas zu Heidegger* (Einsiedeln: Johannes Verlag, 1959), pp. 156–57.

44. References and a presentation of the question can be found in my "Heidegger et la situation métaphysique de Descartes," in "Bulletin Cartésien IV," *Archives de Philosophie* 38 (1975): 253–265. Descartes comes close to the formula *cogito me cogitare* at AT VII, 33, 12–14, and 44, 24, and also in AT V, 149, 7.

45. Respectively, Gueroult, *Descartes selon l'ordre*, vol. 1, pp. 222–223; Gouhier, *Essais sur Descartes* (Paris: J. Vrin, 1949), p. 128; Alquié, *La Découverte métaphysique*, p. 236. See also Röd, *Descartes' Erste Philosophie*, Mahnke, *Der Aufbau*, and Rudolf V. Gumppenberg, who believes he has resolved the difficulty, although he has only formulated it, and very well at that: "We are thus able to attempt a Cartesian Ego-ontology here, which does not immediately close us off from the being of the external world, but rather points back onto the absolute itself" ("Über die Seinslehre bei Descartes," *Salzburger Jahrbuch für Philosophie* 12 (1968): 134. Löwith's extremely balanced but perhaps too conciliatory position in *Das Verhältnis* is also worth reexamining.

46. See, respectively, Descartes, *Quintae Responsiones*, no. 4, AT VII, 365, 9–26; no. 9, 370, 113–371, 7; then *Meditatio III*, AT VII, 51, 20–21 (also *IV*, 57, 15); finally, *Meditatio* III, AT VII, 51, 21–23.

47. *Meditatio III*, AT VII, 48, 7–10: "atque ita ipsemet Deus essem [and thus I should be God myself]."

The Eternal Truths

Translated by Derek Morrow. Reprinted from Jean-Luc Marion, *Descartes's Blank Theology* (Notre Dame University Press, forthcoming).

1. Respectively, *To the Curators of Leiden University*, 4 May 1647 (AT V, 9.16 = CSMK, 317); and *Seventh Set of Objections* (AT VII, 549.20–21 = CSM, II, 375, modified).

2. Respectively, *Letter to Father Dinet* (AT VII, 580.16–19; 596.12–15 = CSM, II, 391; 393, modified). See the fragment cited at AT X, 204.2–5.

3. Respectively, Étienne Gilson, *La liberté chez Descartes et la théologie*, p. 157; Ferdinand Alquié, *La découverte métaphysique de l'homme chez Descartes*, p. 91; Geneviève Rodis-Lewis, *L'oeuvre de Descartes*, vol. 1, p. 100.

4. Émile Bréhier, *La philosophie et son passé*, p. 119.

5. See Martial Gueroult, *Spinoza*, passim; Alquié, *Le cartésianisme de Malebranche*, p. 177 f.; Rodis-Lewis, *Descartes et le rationalisme*, p. 36 f., p. 92 f., etc.; Henri Gouhier, *Cartésianisme et augustinisme au XVIIe siècle*, Un cartésianisme sans création des vérités éternelles, p. 156 f.; and the overall judgments of Martial Gueroult in *Descartes, Cahiers de Royaumont*, vol. 56.

6. [Here Marion is referring to chap. 13, "The Arbitrariness of the Code: The Creation of the Eternal Truths."— Trans.]

7. Respectively, Gueroult, *Descartes selon l'ordre des raisons*, vol. 1, p. 24; Alquié, *La découverte*, p. 90. As for Léon Brunschvicg (*L'esprit européen*, p. 97), he was wont to see in this doctrine "the flip-side of Cartesianism."

8. ["même rappelées ultérieurement" (taking *rappeler* here as equivalent to Heidegger's *wiederholen*). —Trans.]

9. Gilson, *Etudes sur le rôle de la pensée médiévale dans la formation du système cartésien*, p. 253.

10. Gouhier, *La pensée religieuse de Descartes*, p. 263.

11. Gouhier, *La pensée métaphysique de Descartes*, p. 231, then 220 and 221. See also L. Laberthonnière, *Oeuvres*, p. 140, etc.; J. Maritain, *Le songe de Descartes*, p. 226 f.; A. Koyré, *Du monde clos à l'univers infini*, p. 99; J. Lopez Garcia, *El conocimiento de Dios en Descartes*, p. 134. L. Brunschvicg's remark that analogy plays no role in Descartes because Gilson's *Index scolasticocartésien* has no article on it, is one that can be turned against itself: analogy disappears from the Cartesian discourse because this discourse never stops expelling it, consciously, in order to avoid the risk of univocity.

12. Martin Grabmann, *Mittelalterliches Geistleben*, vol. 1, p. 535 (citing other judgments to the same effect, pp. 536–539). On the privileged relation of Descartes to Suárez, see G. Siewerth, *Das Schiksal der Metaphysik von Thomas zu Heidegger*, p. 121; L. Gilen, "Über die Beziehung Descartes zur zeitgenössischen Scholastik," *Scholastik* 1957; B. Jansen, "Die Wesenart der Metaphysik der Suarez," *Scholastik* 1940; M. Rast, "Die Possibilienlehre des Franz Suarez," *Scholastik* 1935; and M. Heidegger, *Gesamtausgabe*, vol. 24, pp. 174–175.

13. See *To Mersenne*, 11 November 1640 (AT III, 232.5–7 = CSMK, 156): "I have bought the *Philosophy* of Father Eustache of St. Paul, which seems to me the best book of its kind ever made." See also *To Mersenne*, December 1640 (AT III, 259.19–260.10 = CSMK, 161); AT III, 286.3–6 (= not included in CSMK), and *To Mersenne*, 22 December 1641 (AT III, 470.6–8 = not included in CSMK): "If I had wanted to refute anybody, it is certain that I would have picked Father Eustache's *Compendium* as the best way to do it." Descartes is referring to Eustache's *Summa Philosophica quadripartita, de rebus dialecticis, moralibus, physicis et metaphysicis* (Paris, 1609 and 1626).

14. *To Mersenne*, 11 November 1640 (AT III, 234.7–8 = not included in CSMK) alludes to Charles- François d'Abra (Abra de Raconis), *Totius Philosophiae, hoc est logicae, moralis, physicae et metaphysicae brevis . . . tractatio* (Paris, 1622).

15. *Mersenne to Descartes*, 1 August 1638 (AT II, 287.11–13, then 16–23 = not included in CSMK). On these questions of influence, I maintain the positions first defended in René Descartes. *Règles utiles et claires pour la direction de l'esprit en la recherche de la vérité*, XIV–XVI; and in *Sur l'ontologie grise de Descartes*, §1, pp. 13–23.

16. [Here Marion refers to the thesis of his first book on Descartes, *Sur l'ontologie grise de Descartes*, first published in 1975, six years prior to the appearance of *Sur la théologie blanche de Descartes*. —Trans.]

17. See my sketch "L'ambivalence de la métaphysique cartésienne," *Études Philosophiques*, 1976 (included in this anthology).

18. Here I am thinking of Eucharistic problems, in particular those discussed by Jean-Robert Armogathe, *Theologia Cartesiana. L'explication physique de l'Eucharistie chez Descartes et Dom Desgabets* (The Hague, 1977).

19. [See Aristotle, Meta. Z, 1, 1028b3; —Trans.]

20. Respectively *Rule II* (AT X, 365.13 = CSM, I, 12); and *Rule IX* (401.14–17 = 33).

21. *Rule XIV* (AT X, 448.12, 22; 449.11 = CSM, I, 63).

22. *Rule XIV* (AT X, 448.15 = CSM, I, 63, modified): "ex arbitrio . . . excogitare (dimensiones) [(dimensions) . . . that are arbitrary inventions of our mind]."

23. *Rule III* (AT X, 370.22–23 = CSM, I, 15).

24. *To Hogelande*, August 1638 (AT II, 346.27 = CSMK, 119).

25. *Discourse on Method*, Part Two (AT VI, 15.6 = CSM, I, 118, modified).

26. *To Beeckman*, 17 October 1630 (AT I, 161.6 = not included in CSMK).

27. *To Hogelande*, 8 February 1640 (AT III, 722.7–9 = not included in CSMK).

28. *To Mersenne*, 15 April 1630 (AT I, 144.9–11 = CSMK, 22).

29. *To More*, 5 February 1649 (AT V, 275.17 = CSMK, 364).

30. Here Marion is referring to chap. 14, "The Flip-Side of the Code: Doubt about the Foundation." — Trans.]

31. Martin Heidegger, *Der Satz vom Grund*, p. 29. We owe it to Spinoza for no doubt being the first to have (unconsciously?) altered the Cartesian formula: "firma et inconcussa fundamenta scientiarum [the firm and unshakeable foundations of the sciences]" (*Principia Philosophiae Cartesiana*, I, Prologue). And it is of course no accident that the plural should appear at the same time the substantive does.

The Question of the Divine Names

Translated by Jeffrey L. Kosky. Reprinted from Jean-Luc Marion, *On Descartes' Metaphysical Prism: The Contribution and the Limits of Onto-Theo-logy in Cartesian Thought* (University of Chicago Press, 1999), 206–218.

1. Hegel, *Vorlesungen über die Geschichte der Philosophie, Jubileum Ausgabe*, Bd. XIX, p. 350 [English trans., p. 237].

2. *To Mersenne*, 28 January 1641 (AT III, 297, 15–17 = PW III. 172).

3. *To Mersenne*, July 1641 (AT III, 394, 1–4 then 8–13 = PW 111, 185 then 185).

4. *To Mersenne*, March 1642 (AT III, 544, 17–19 = PW III, 211). Perhaps it is also necessary to consider the formula *Deus est suum esse* (AT III, 433, 9–11 and VII, 383,15 = PW III, 196 and 263), taken directly from Saint Thomas, "Deus non solum est sua essentia . . . sed etiam suum esse [God is not only His own essence . . . but also His own existence" and "sua igitur essentia est suum esse [His essence is His existence" (*Summa Theologiae*, Ia, q. 3, a. 4, resp. [English trans., pp. 17 and 17]).

5. A history of the treatise on the divine names remains to be written. In this regard, we permit ourselves the liberty of referring to the studies in my *L'idole et la distance* (Paris, 1977), chap. III, and *God Without Being*, chap. III.

6. L. Lessius, *Quinquaginta nomina Dei*, respectively: "per affirmationes seu conceptus positivos . . . per negationes, seu conceptus negativos" (chap. I, p. 6—the prologue makes explicit reference to Dionysius, p. 5); then: "Priori modo, concipimus Deum esse spiritum sublimissimum, optimum, maximum, sempiternum, potentissimum, sapientissimum, benignissimum, sanctissimum, justissimum, misericordissimum, pulcherrimum, rebus omnibus praesentem, omnia interius

creantem, formantem, conservantem, gubernantem et ad suam gloriam ordinantem tanquam primum principium et finem rerum omnium" (chap. I, pp. 6–7); and finally:

> Posteriori modo Deus concipitur esse Spiritus infinitus, immensus, sempiternus, infinitus supra omnium perfectionem, excellentiam et magnitudinem a mente creata conceptibilem elevatus: supra omnem substantiam, supra omnem potentiam, supra omnem sanctitatem, omnem justitiam, omnem bonitatem, omnem beatitudinem, omnem gloriam; adeo ut ipse nihil horum proprie sit, nulli horum sit similis, sed infinite sublimior et praestantior. (Chap. I, p. 8.)

7. L. Lessius, *De Perfectionibus moribusque divinis*, 1, 2 (Paris, 1620), p. 11. See the subsequent development:

> Omnis hi modi incomprehensibilitatis sequuntur ex ejus infinitate: sed nos hic potissimum agimus de tertio, quo Deus dicitur *incomprehensibilis* omni intellectui creato. Hoc modo Dionysius et Damascenus Deum dicunt esse ἀκατάληπτον, ἀπερίληπτον, ἀπεριχώριστον [All these modes of incomprehensibility follow from his infinity: but we hold this most especially concerning the third, in which God is said to be incomprehensible to every created thing. This is why Dionysius and Damascene said God is ἀκατάληπτον, ἀπερίληπτον, ἀπεριχώριστον].

(Ibid.) If Descartes's formula depended on Lessius, even from a distance, it would thus go back directly to Dionysius, and through him to the entire tradition of the Church Fathers. Permit us to let this ever so fascinating hypothesis remain open.

8. *Intelligo* introducing a definition of God: AT VII, 50,19; 40,18; 45.11; 109,7; etc. = PW II, 34; 28; 31; 78; etc. Formulas [1] and [2] are directly commented upon by, among others, E. M. Curley, *Descartes against the Skeptics* (Cambridge, Mass., 1980), pp. 127–128 ("Is this definition stipulative or reportive?").

9. H. Frankfurt, "Descartes on the consistency of reason," in M. Hooker, ed., *Descartes: Critical and Interpretive Essays* (Baltimore/London, 1978), p. 36. See also, by the same author, the study "Descartes' Validation of Reason," *American Philosophical Quarterly* II/ 2 (1965), particularly pp. 223–225. Whence my study "The Essential Incoherence of Descartes' Definition of Divinity," in A. O. Rorty (ed.), *Essays on Descartes' Meditations* (Berkeley––Los Angeles, 1986).

10. L. Lessius, *De Perfectionibus moribusque divinis*, 1, 3: "Negantur de ipso omnia, quia ipse est supra omnem rationem et speciem creatae menu conceptibilem" (op. cit., p. 14).

11. On this essential point, see F. Alquié, "Expérience ontologique et déduction systématique dans la constitution de la métaphysique de Descartes," in *Descartes. Cahiers de Royaumont* (Paris, 1957), and my work *Sur la théologie blanche de Descartes*, §14, pp. 323ff.

12. Respectively, *To Voëtius* (AT V111–2, 60, 16–24), then *Conversation with Burman* (AT V. 147, 7–8); finally, AT V, 150, 30ff = PW III, 222 then 333; finally, not included in PW When the *ordo rationum* permits, the *Meditationes* will raise this contradiction: AT VII, 53, 23–29 PW II, 37 (see *Principia Philosophiae* 1, §29); similarly, the *Letter to Buitendijck* from 1643 (AT IV, 64, 1–28 = PW III, 229–30). H. Frankfurt made this point clear: "Descartes does not recognize in the First Meditation, that the notion of a being both omnipotent and evil is logically incoherent. And as long as the existence of the demon seems possible to him, it provides him with what he must take to be a reasonable ground for doubt" (*Demons, Dreamers and Madmen: The Defense of Reason in Descartes' Meditations* [Indianapolis, 1970], p. 48).

13. We are thinking of the famous debate between R. Kennington, "The Finitude of Descartes' Evil Genius," *Journal of the History of Ideas* (1971), pp. 441–46, and H. Caton, "Kenning-

ton on Descartes' Evil Genius," *Journal of the History of Ideas* (1973), pp. 639–641; then R. Kennington, "Reply to Caton," ibid., pp. 641–643, and H. Caton, "Rejoinder: The Cunning of the Evil Genius," ibid., pp. 641–644. See also H. Caton, *The Origin of Subjectivity* (New Haven: Yale University Press, 1973), pp. 115–121. In fact, *summe potens* in 45,12–13 is equivalent to *omnipotens* at least in 40, 17 [1], as well as in *Principia Philosophiae* I, §§14 and 22.

14. For this identification, see *Sur la théologie blanche de Descartes*, pp. 330–333 and 303–305.

15. Suárez, *Disputationes Metaphysicae, XXIX*, s. 3, n. 4: "tamen ut de illo [Deo] ratiocinari possimus, necesse est saltem praeconcipere et praesupponere, quid hac voce significetur" (op. cit., vol. 26, p. 35); then n. 5: "Significat ergo hoc nomen [Deus] quoddam nobilissimum ens, quod et reliqua omnia superat, et ab eo tanquam a primo auctore reliqua omnia pendent, quod proinde ut supremum numen colendum est ac venerandum; hic enim est vulgaris et quasi primus conceptus quem omnes de Deo formamus, audit nomine Dei" (ibid.). Like Suárez, Descartes admits a spontaneous preconception of God; on this occasion, he borrows it from the nominalist tradition (or simply from the first article of the *Credo*). However, while for Suárez this preconception maintains a certain theoretical validity, for Descartes, based on the fact of hyperbolic doubt, the preconception not only loses all solidity, it is also inverted into an argument against all correct thought, as much of God as of *reliqua omnia*. Indetermination is inverted for the same reason as the preconception.

Does the *Ego* Alter the Other?
Reprinted from Jean-Luc Marion, *Cartesian Questions: Method and Metaphysics* (University of Chicago Press, 1999), 118–138.

1. Pascal, *Pensées*, 597.

2. On the inclusion of metaphysics in its Cartesian embodiment in the hierarchy of orders, see Marion, *Sur le prisme métaphysique de Descartes*, chap. 5, §§22–24.

3. The question arises of exactly where, for instance, M. Gueroult thinks he can juxtapose two characters of the *ego* that are, in my view, incompatible. On the one hand, its absolute solipsism: "I alone am known; I alone exist. Do there exist other substances outside of me. . . . I know not, I cannot speak of this." On the other hand, a so-called universalism: "One sees how little this self is individual; for the 'I' of the individual implies the 'you' of the other, that I *exclude* from myself certainly, insofar as I posit myself as substance, but that *I am positing*, at the same time (outside of myself). One sees by this to what extent Descartes is at the ends of a transcendental intersubjectivity" (*Descartes' Philosophy Interpreted according to the Order of Reasons*, vol. I, p. 71). What we actually see is to what extent Gueroult is here closer to Fichte than to Descartes, as is often the case elsewhere.

4. On the fundamental invisibility of what is not in the mode of objectivity, see J.-L. Marion, "L'intentionalité de l'amour," in *Prolégomènes à la charité* (Paris, 1986, 1991).

5. Respectively, *Letter to Mersenne*, 11 November 1640, AT III, 235, ll. 15–18 and 239, l. 7.

6. See the clarification on this point in Marion, *Sur la théologie blanche de Descartes*, pp. 319–323.

7. It is utterly remarkable that Pascal, without doubt purposely, used and reversed the Cartesian example in *Pensées*, 688: No longer does the *ego* inspect men from above in search of identification, but on the contrary the *ego,* from below and reduced to the rank of a seen self, withstands the gaze of another *ego,* which it definitely is not. See Marion, *Sur le prisme métaphysique de Descartes*, chap. 5, §24, pp. 344ff. G. B. Matthews has clearly established that in the episode of the hats and the coats that were (eventually) animated, Descartes was not approaching the question of the otherness of other people, but simply that of the animation or the

pure mechanism of bodies ("Descartes and the Problem of Other Minds," in *Essays on Descartes' Meditations*, edited by A. O. Rorty [Berkeley, 1986], pp. 141–152).

8. Besides, otherness or diversity does not directly concern souls or people (in the sense of the otherness of another person) but "things," *res a me diversae* (39, l. 15; 40, l. 2; 73, ll. 9–10; 75, ll. 8–9), or substances (79, l. 15); similarly, for separation (29, l. 4) and exteriority (25, l. 26; 38, l. 12), it is a question of simple nonidentity rather than a relationship between two *egos*. As for an animated being, its otherness from the *ego* is mentioned only to be immediately refuted: "do not require me to posit a source distinct from myself" (44, ll. 9–10).

9. For example, *Recherche de la vérité, Eclaircissement XI*, in *Oeuvres complètes* (Paris 1964), vol. 3, pp. 163ff. See the analysis in which Alquié brings Descartes and Malebranche together on a point that seems to divide them, in *Le cartésianisme de Malebranche* (Paris, 1974), pp. 91–101.

10. See Marion, *Sur le prisme métaphysique de Descartes*, chap. 2.

11. Besides, if the *we* reappears at the very conclusion of the *Meditations*, it is precisely to point out its weakness: "we must acknowledge the weakness of our nature" (90, ll. 15–16). The weakness of the *we* reciprocally underlines the strength of the *ego*. The same analysis of the solitude of the *ego* and the reduction of others could be conducted from the *Discourse on the Method* and the *Principia*, probably with the same results.

12. Respectively, letter to Chanut, 1 February 1647, AT IV, 606, l. 12; 605, ll. 20–21; 602, l. 27–603, line 1; and *Principles of Philosophy*, IV, §190, AT VIII, 1, 317, ll. 24–25.

13. Letter to Regius, May 1641, AT III, 372, l. 12.

14. *The Passions of the Soul*, §§27 and 29, AT XI, 350, ll. 16, 18, 24.

15. Ibid., §79, AT XI, 387, ll. 4 and 12; and §80, 387, ll. 20–24. See also letter to Chanut, 1 February 1647, AT IV, 603, ll. 9–12.

16. *The Passions of the Soul*, §79, AT XI, 387, ll. 3–6. See §80, 387, ll. 18–24. On the relationship between the theoretical *ego* and the *ego* of affection, see two different approaches: K. Hammacher, "La raison dans la vie affective et sociale selon Descartes et Spinoza," *Les études philosophiques* (1984, no. 1); and, especially, Henry, *Généalogie de la psychanalyse*, chaps. 1 and 2.

17. As stigmatized by D. Dubarle, this is, to say the least, a "lacuna, a serious lacuna in the Cartesian philosophy of the human other" ("Ontologie de la subjectivité," *Revue de l'Institut Catholique de Paris* [April–June 1988]: 126).

18. *The Passions of the Soul*, §80, AT XI, 387, ll. 23–26, and §82, 389, l. 17. See §79, "join itself willingly to objects that appear to be agreeable to it," "things it deems bad," AT XI, 387, ll. 4–6 and 8. It is noteworthy that love mobilizes first a representation and then a will, thereby mimicking the two moments of the true theoretical judgment, as found in *Meditation IV*.

19. *The Passions of the Soul*, §81, AT XI, 388, ll. 10–11.

20. Ibid., §82, AT XI, 388, l. 24–389, l. 6.

21. Letter to Chanut, 1 February 1647, AT IV, 611, ll. 3–4. See *The Passions of the Soul*, §81: "to some object, whatever its nature may be," AT XI, 388, ll. 11–12; §82: "Nor do we need to distinguish as many kinds of love as there are different possible objects of love," AT XI, 388, ll. 22–24. It is noteworthy that the diversity of its objects unifies love rather than divides it, for the same reason that science—according to *Rule I*—remains one, in spite of the infinite diversity of its objects: for it is always a question of a single and same spirit ("mens humana . . . universalissima"), regardless of the objects to which it is applied. Thus the doctrine of univocal love transposes the doctrine of the unity of science from the theoretical to the ethical domain. The fundamental option—the preeminence of the *mens humana* as an *ego*—is still at work in both cases.

22. Respectively, *The Passions of the Soul*, §82, AT XI, 389, ll. 7–8; and letter to Chanut, 1 February 1647, AT IV, 610, ll. 5–8.

23. *The Passions of the Soul*, §82, AT XI, 389, ll. 10–20.

24. Husserl, *Cartesian Meditations*, respectively, §44, p. 125, and §62, p. 175.

25. Merleau-Ponty, *The Visible and the Invisible* (Evanston, Ill., 1968), pp. 77–78. See also other formulations: "The reflection suppresses the intersubjectivity" (p. 48), or "philosophically speaking, there is no experience of the other" (p. 71). See *Phénoménologie de la perception* (Paris, 1945), pp. 41ff.

26. It is assumed here that the division in two of Descartes's ontotheology, which I tried to establish in *Sur le prisme métaphysique de Descartes*, chap. 2, is still valid.

27. Letter to Voëtius, AT VIII–2, 112, ll. 21–29.

28. "The laws of charity [*leges charitatis*]," ibid., 99, l. 23; 114, ll. 6–7; 116, l. 29; 130, l. 27. On this strange return by Descartes to a strictly theological theme and its use in political philosophy, see my remarks in the preface to the excellent edition (based on the translation by V. Cousin) by T. Verbeek of *La querelle d'Utrecht* (Paris, 1988), pp. 7–13; and the remarks by P. Guenancia, "Descartes accusé se défend," *Critique* 510 (November 1989).

The Originary Otherness of the Ego: A Rereading of Descartes's Second Meditation

Translated by Christina M. Gschwandtner. Reprinted from Jean-Luc Marion, *On the Ego and on God: Further Cartesian Questions* (Fordham University Press, 2007), 3–29.

1. "Fundamentum, cui omnis humana certitudo niti posse . . . videtur." AT VII:144, 24–25; CSM II:103. See: "I preferred to use my own existence as the basis of my argument"; "malui tui pro fundamento meae rationis existentia meiipsius." AT VII:107, 2–3; CSM II:77.

2. [The French word Marion uses here has connotations of distortion or falsification. —Trans.]

3. I have assumed this in *Questions cartésiennes* (Paris: Presses Universitaires de France, 1991), chapter 6: "L'ego altère-t-il autrui?" [*Cartesian Questions*, trans. Daniel Garber (Chicago: University of Chicago Press, 1999), chapter 6: "Does the *Ego* Alter the Other? The Solitude of the *Cogito* and the Absence of the *Alter Ego*"]. I ask here the same question anew.

4. Malebranche, *De la recherche de la vérité* 6.2.6, in André Robinet, ed. *Oeuvres complètes*, 20 vols. (Paris: Vrin), vol. 2, ed. Geneviève Rodis-Lewis (Paris: Vrin, 1974), 369. I follow here the interpretation of Ferdinand Alquié, who maintains on this point a fundamental continuity between Descartes and Malebranche: "Reducing the 'I think, therefore I am' to the affirmation of the existence of my spirit, Malebranche hence retains that which is the most profound and the most indubitable in the *Meditations* of Descartes. The I think remains foundation." Ferdinand Alquié, *Le cartésianisme de Malebranche* (Paris: Vrin, 1974), 103.

5. "Ideoque *cogito, ergo sum*, unica est propositio, quae huic, *ego sum cogitans*, aequivalet." Spinoza in *Ethics* 2, ax. 2 and *Principia Philosophiae Cartesianae* 1, Prolegomenon, ed. Carl Gebhardt (Heidelberg: C. Winter, 1925), 144; English translation by Edwin Curley, *The Collected Works of Spinoza* (Princeton: Princeton University Press, 1985), 1:448, 234 (trans. mod.). Henceforth cited as *Works*.

6. Immanuel Kant, *Kritik der reinen Vernunft*, B422, note.

7. Ibid., end of §24, B156.

8. Kant, ibid., A355. See Jocelyn Benoist, *Kant et les limites de la synthèse* (Paris: Presses Universitaires de France, 1996), chapters 4–5.

9. The fortune of this Kantian interpretation of the first Cartesian principle succeeds by way of the Marburg School, in the works of Wolfgang Röd, *Descartes: Die Genese des cartesianischen Rationalismus* (Munich: Beck, 1982), and Franz Bader, *Die Ursprünge der Transzendentalphilosophie bei Descartes* (Bonn: Bouvier, 1983).

10. Fichte's position remains, it seems to us, close enough to that of Kant: "Before him [Kant], Descartes has proposed a similar principle: *cogito, ergo sum*, which is not the result of a different proposition or conclusion of a syllogism of which the major would be *quodcumque cogitat, est*; Descartes can have considered so voluntarily this principle as an immediate fact of consciousness. In this sense, it would signify: *cogitans sum, ergo sum* (or as we say it, *sum ergo sum*)." *Wissenschaftslehre* 1794–95, §1, in *Gesammelte Werke*, 2:262. But this immediate identity is found also exactly in the terms of Spinoza. See the brilliant analysis of Alexis Philonenko in "Sur Descartes et Fichte" (*Les Études Philosophiques* 2 [1985]), which, moreover, does not hesitate to attribute to the Cartesian proposition a "thetic value . . . in the sense of Fichte; it is neither analytic, nor synthetic [but] existential tautology. *Formaliter spectata*, the formula goes back to the principle of identity A = A and one knows how Fichte engenders beginning from A = A, formal proposition, the Me = Me, material proposition." Alexis Philonenko, *Relire Descartes. Le génie de la pensée française* (Paris: J. Grancher, 1994), 237ff.

11. Hegel, *Phänomenologie des Geistes* in *Gesammelte Werke* (Hamburg: F. Meiner, 1980), 9:313. See also Bernard Bourgeois, "Hegel et Descartes," *Les Études Philosophiques* 2 (1985).

12. Hegel, *Vorlesungen über die Geschichte der Philosophie. Teil 4. Philosophie des Mittelalters und der neueren Philosophie*, ed. Pierre Garniron and Walter Jaeschke (Hamburg: F. Meiner, 1986), 93. Let me note that Hegel cites, to my knowledge, only the following texts: the Latin translation (Pierre de Courcelles, *Specimina*, 1644) of the *Discourse on Method* 4; the *Principia Philosophiae* 1, §7; and—taken as a text of Descartes!—Spinoza, *Principia Philosophiae Cartesianae*; the *Meditations* seems entirely ignored—a fact that is even more remarkable since Hegel is without doubt one of the first to devote himself to actually reading the texts of his predecessors. That shows the weight of the canonical interpretation. Moreover, H. G. Hotho, student of Hegel, whose dissertation *De Philosophia Cartesiana* (Berlin, 1826), is cited in the *Encyclopaedia* of 1830 (§64, Zusatz), never mentions anything but the formula "cogito, ergo sum" (11) before concluding that "it cannot be denied that the philosophy of Spinoza is a true consequent and continuation of Cartesian philosophy"; "Spinozae philosophiam veram esse Cartesianae philosophiae et consequentiam et continuationem negari necquaquam potest." (59).

13. Schelling develops a very similar interpretation: "In the *cogito ergo sum*, Descartes believed to have discerned the immediate identity of thought and being." *Sämtliche Werke*, ed. Schröter, 10:9. Here also, the criticism matters less than the interpretation that it presupposes.

14. Friedrich Nietzsche, *Wille zur Macht*, ed. Peter Gast/Elisabeth Förster-Nietzsche, §484 = *Nachgelassene Fragmente* 10 [158], ed. Colli/Montinari, vol. 8:2 (Berlin: W. de Gruyter, 1970), 215. See *Beyond Good and Evil*, §16. See the significant work of Hartmut Brands, *"Cogito ergo sum": Interpretationen von Kant bis Nietzsche* (Freiburg im Breisgau: K. Alber, 1982).

15. Edmund Husserl, *Conférences de Paris*, in *Méditations cartésiennes*, *Husserliana* 1:4; French translation *Méditations cartésiennes et les conférence de Paris* (Paris: Presses Universitaires de France, 1994), 3.

16. [The paragraph on Heidegger is missing in the existing English translation. —Trans.]

17. Heidegger, *Sein und Zeit*, §82, 433, and *Nietzsche* (Pfullingen: G. Neske, 1961), 2:153. Regarding this issue, see my *Cartesian Questions*, 99ff.

18. Martial Gueroult, *Descartes selon l'ordre des raisons* (Paris: Aubier, 1953), 1:116.

19. Ibid.: "It is further required that it should think that it is thinking, by means of a reflexive act. . . . This is deluded"; "requiri ut actu reflexo cogitet se cogitare, sive habeat cogitationes suae conscientiam. . . . Hallucinatur"; "celui qui exige de penser que l'on se pense, ou que l'on ait conscience de sa pensée par un acte réflexif, celui-là délire." Seventh Replies; see AT VII:559, 5–7; CSM II:382. [Translations in this chapter have been assisted by Thomas McLaughlin (Latin) and

Christian DuPont (French).] See Sixth Replies, AT VII:422, 8–14; CSM II:285: "But this does not require reflective knowledge or the kind of knowledge that is acquired by means of demonstrations; still less does it require knowledge of reflective knowledge, i.e. knowing that we know. . . . It is quite sufficient that we should know it by that internal awareness which always precedes reflective knowledge" ("non quod ad hoc [the certainty of being following from thinking] requiratur scienda reflexa vel per demonstrationem acquisita, et multo minus scientia scientiae reflexae, per quam sciat se scire. . . . Sed omnino sufficit ut id sciat cogitadone ilia intema, quae reflexam semper antecedit"). Regarding this awareness, Jean-Marie Beyssade has very nicely shown that it "ought not to be understood here in the sense of reflexive awareness." *La philosophie première de Descartes* (Paris: Flammarion, 1979), 234. Otherwise *reflexio* and *reflectare* never appear in the text of the *Meditations*.

20. In this way, *repraesentare* in AT VII:8, 19, 23; 40, 11, 15; 43, 3, 30; 44, 7; CSM II:7, 28, 29, 30, etc.; these occurrences concern always a *res*, never an *ego* or the *cogitatio*. As for the substantive *repraesentatio*, it simply *never* appears in the *Meditations*. For this double factual motive, the representative interpretation of the *ego cogito, ergo sum* seems, at the very least, highly problematic.

21. Gueroult, *Descartes selon l'ordre des raisons*, 1:116, 95, 94, respectively (see, on reflection, 66, 68, 80, 81, 89, etc.)The reasons to avoid the exclusively reflexive and representative interpretation of the *ego cogito* have often been set out—by, among others, Ferdinand Alquié, *La découverte métaphysique de l'homme chez Descartes* (Paris: Presses Universitaires de France, 1950), chap. 9 (of which "a presence so intimate . . . that no reflection, no doubt . . . would know to prevail against it," 189); Michel Henry, *Généalogie de la psychanalyse* (Paris: Presses Universitaires de France, 1985), chap. 3 [trans. Douglas Brick, *The Genealogy of Psychoanalysis* (Stanford, Calif.: Stanford University Press, 1993)]; and Jean-Luc Marion, *Cartesian Questions*, chap. 5, etc.

22. "Entre ces idées, outre celle qui me représente a moi-même." *Meditationes de prima philosophia/Méditations Métaphysiques, texte latin et traduction du Duc de Luynes* (Paris: Vrin, 1960), 43. AT IXA:34, 3.

23. AT VII:42, 29. *Exhibere* implies in a way something already phenomenological in that he "does nothing at all to go beyond the limits of that which appears to me" and thus remains "in the thought of pure *appearing*" (Beyssade, *La philosophie première de Descartes*, 234–235; my emphasis).

24. "Réflexion enveloppée par le processus constitutif du cogito." Gueroult, *Descartes selon l'ordre des raisons*, 60.

25. The most remarkable analytic interpretations always lean on the canonical formulation, even when, in fact, they pass beyond it. In this way, for example, Jaako Hintikka introduces his so fecund and correct interpretation of the formula of the Second Meditation as performative, not only beginning from the canonical formula, which is precisely missing here, but also as a relation between *cogito* and *sum*: "Their relation is rather comparable to that of a process to its product." Jaako Hintikka, "*Cogito, ergo sum*: Inference or Performance?" *Philosophical Review* 71 (1962): 3–32. But is there such a "relation" between them? Similarly, Harry Frankfurt concentrates all his effort on the transition between *cogito* (of whom the truth would not be proven) and *sum*: see *Demons, Dreamers, and Madmen: The Defense of Reason in Descartes' Meditations* (Indianapolis: Bobbs-Merrill, 1970). But the question remains of knowing if these are the terms (and not only the modes of their articulation) that permit to hear what Descartes in fact gains as "first principle."

26. Edwin M. Curley, *Descartes Against the Skeptics* (Cambridge, Mass.: Harvard University Press, 1978), 72. The same thing is noted by Margaret Wilson: "This passage is widely known as an instance of the '*cogito* reasoning,' despite the fact that the famous formulation 'I think, therefore I

am' (*cogito ergo sum*) appears only in cognate passages in other works—not in the *Meditations* itself" (*Descartes* [London: Routledge, 1978], 52), going back to the *Discourse* and to the *Principia Philosophiae*; or also in Beyssade: "The proposition *I am, I exist*, seems indeed to have constituted, in the *Second Meditation*, the fixed and immovable point on which the whole edifice of the first philosophy is built." *La philosophie première de Descartes*, 217. But it is astonishing that on the same page the title of chap. 5 has another formulation, which still remains in accord with the canonical interpretation: "je pense, donc je suis." Also Etienne Balibar: "But the statement in the Meditations is different. It is simply *Ego sum, ego existo*. All immediate, internal reference to *cogitare* and to the *cogitatio* disappears." The designation of this statement as "*cogito*" is then, at best, an interpretation. "Ego sum, ego existo: Descartes au point d'hérésie," *Bulletin de la Société française de Philosophie* 86 (1992): 83.

27. "Denique statuendum sit hoc pronuntiatum, *Ego sum, ego existo* quoties a me profertur vel mente concipiatur, necessario esse verum"; "haec sola [cf. Cogitatio] a me divelli nequit. Ego sum, ego existo." Respectively AT VI:32, 19; CSM I:127 (see 33, 17; CSM I:127–28 and AT II:247, 2; not translated in CSMK); AT VII:140, 20–21; CSM II:100 (the addition of *sive existo* is security for the same addition in the French text of *D.M.* in the Latin translation of the *Specimina* by P. de Courcelles, AT VI:588, 25 as remarked by Étienne Gilson, *Descartes, Discours de la méthode, texte et commentaire* [Paris, 1925], 292); then AT VIIIA–:7, 7–8 (§7, see §10, 8, 9); AT V:147, 9, 15 (the only occurrence, and marginal at that, of the most habitually used formula which has then scarcely any legitimacy), AT X:368, 21–22; CSM I:14 (where the logical connective is missing); and, finally, AT VII:25, 11–13 and 27, 8–9; CSMK III:333.I omit here the two formulas that replace *cogito* by *dubito* (*Recherche de la vérité*, AT X:515, 5–6 and 525, 15–18, and *Notae in programma quoddam*, AT VIIIB–:354, 18–21; CSM I:301), or that use another antecedent (AT VII:352, 11–12; CSM II:244: *ambulo*; AT VII:37, 26, 38, 9–10; CSM II:26 [both]: *je respire*, etc.). On all these formulas, see Henri Gouhier, *Essais sur Descartes* (Paris: Vrin, 1949), 117–27, and Jean-Marie Beyssade, *Descartes: L'entretien avec Burman* (Paris: Presses Universitaires de France, 1981), 18–19.

28. Jaako Hintikka, "*Cogito, ergo sum*." It remains most astonishing nevertheless that here Hintikka still relies on the canonical formulation that, to be precise, *does not* allow to confirm his own, otherwise so remarkable, interpretation. (Although it does not think the ontological dimension to which it lays claim.) See my discussion in *Sur la théologie blanche de Descartes: Analogie, creation des vérités éternelles et fondement* (Paris: Presses Universitaires de France, first ed. 1981, second ed. 1991), §16, "La performance du *cogito*."

29. Husserl, *First Philosophy* 1, §10, *Husserliana* VII, ed. Ulrich Melle (Dordrecht: Kluwer Academic Publishers, 1988), 64.

30. "Nondum satis intelligo quisnam sim ego ille, qui jam necessario sum" ("mais je ne connais pas encore assez clairement ce que je suis, moi qui suis certain qui je suis"). AT VII:25, 14–15 = AT IXA:21, 39–40; CSM II:17, as commented upon by E. Balibar, "Descartes au point d'hérésie," 92–95. And one should cite a subsequent edition of the French translation, which is even clearer: "This me, that is to say my soul, by which *I am that which I am* is entirely distinct from the body." AT IXA:62, 20–21, my emphasis. See my remarks and criticism in the "Bulletin cartésien 23," *Archives de Philosophie* 57, no. 4 (1995).

31. AT VII:25, 15–18; CSM II:17: the ego finds itself for a time in an anonymous situation: I am, but I ignore what (or who) I am.

32. AT VII:24, 19–25, 24; AT IXA:19, 17–38; CSM II:16–17.

33. "Aliquis Deus, vel quocumque nomine illum vocem." AT VII:24, 21–22; CSM II:16.

34. On this necessary indeterminacy, see my remarks in *Prisme métaphysique de Descartes* (Paris: Presses Universitaires de France, 1986) §16, 223ff.; trans. Jeffrey L. Kosky, *On Descartes'*

Metaphysical Prism: The Constitution and the Limits of Onto-theo-logy in Cartesian Thought (Chicago: University of Chicago Press, 1999), §16, 212ff. [Throughout the rest of the book Marion's page references have been changed to refer to the English translation of this work. —Trans.]

35. "Me met en l'esprit [d]es pensées" IX A:19, 20.

36. Cf. AT VII:39, 10–14; 77, 23–27; 79, 10; CSM II:27, 54, 55. This hypothesis is enough to put up for discussion Descartes's supposed total ignorance of anything unconscious. Cf. Geneviève Rodis-Lewis, *Le problème de l'inconscient et le cartésianisme* (Paris: Presses Universitaires de France, 1950), chap. 1.

37. "Numquid ergo saltem ego aliquid sum?" AT VII:24, 24–25; CSM II:16. "Moi donc à tout le moins ne suis-je pas quelque chose?" IXA:19, 23.

38. AT VII:25, 2–4; CSM II:16 actually takes up VII:21, 3–7; CSM II:14. The addition of *mentes* (*any spirits*, confirming AT IXA:19, 27) matters more here than the omission of the technical list of the simple material (and common) natures. Is it a matter of a simple lapse, or rather of a sophisticated shift, extending the doubt concerning the principal intellectual nature, contrary to the stated doctrine of the *Meditations*? In this second case, must one attribute this shift to Descartes deceiving us (but why?) or, rather, can one attribute it to the ego as still uncertain and deceiving itself? On the major role of the simple natures (especially the material and the common ones) in the performance of doubt, see *Cartesian Questions*, chap. 3, §4 and §5.

39. "Imo certe ego eram, si quid mihi persuasi."

40. "Certe ego [sum], si quid mihi persuasi."

41. [The French can indicate both the passive "I am persuaded" and the reflexive "I have persuaded myself." Throughout this section Marion plays on the two meanings of the construction. —Trans.]

42. Foucault saw this perfectly: "It is true that the *cogito* is the absolute beginning; but one must not forget that the evil genius is anterior to it. . . . And that is not because the truth which takes its illumination in the *cogito* ends by masking the shadow of the evil genius entirely but because one must forget its perpetually menacing power." *Histoire de la folie à l'âge classique* (Paris: Plon, 1961), 196. Further occurrences reestablish, moreover, the real alterity of this persuasion: (a) "Yet when I turn to the things themselves which I think I perceive very clearly, I am so convinced by them that I spontaneously declare" ("quoties vero ad ipsas res, quas valde clare percipere arbitror, me converto, tam plane ab illis [rebus] persuadeor, ut sponte"; AT VII:36, 12–15; CSM II:25)—persuasion by the things themselves, conversion to the things as other than me, in short no solipsism at all; (b) "my intellect has not yet come upon any persuasive reason in favor of one alternative rather than the other" ("nullam adhuc intellectui meo rationem occurrere, quae mihi unum magis quam aliud persuadeat"; AT VII: 59, 10–12; CSM II:41)—the persuasion does not result from a self-conviction, but from the succession (*occurrere*) to the understanding of the ego of a constraining reason; through lack of this advent (hence of alterity), persuasion is not accomplished; (c) "I am always brought back to the fact that it is only what I clearly and distinctly perceive that completely convinces me" ("semper eo res redit, ut ea me sola plane persuadeant, quae clare et distincte percipio"; AT VII:68, 22–23; CSM II:47)—persuasion depends on evidence, hence on the immediate presence of the thing inasmuch as it is different from my thought, still of alterity. This is what Francis Jacques has seen perfectly: "One will ask: can anything preserve the privileged experience of the ego? I believe it, still and always the affirmation of an instance is not objectivable, not representable. The *I* does not posit itself without the *you, and in that the solipsism is finished* [my emphasis]. But in the final account, it is neither the ego nor the dyad formed by the *I* and the *you* that signifies, but the relation between them, which will engender them both." *L'espace logique de l'interlocution: Dialogues II* (Paris: Presses Universitaires de France, 1985), 505, see 550–557.

43. The irreducibility of this *quid* marks maybe one of the rare limits of the interpretation of the *cogito* as auto-affection by Michel Henry, *Généalogie de la psychanalyse*, chap. 3.

44. Must one understand "igitur ego etiam sum, si me fallit" (AT VII:25, 8; CSM II:17) as *I am, even if he is deceiving me* (concession, as if *etiam si* amounted to *etiamsi*), or as *if he deceive me, I too am*? The translation by De Luynes does not resolve it: "There is hence no doubt that I am, if he deceives me" (IXA:19, 28); I maintain the latter interpretation, because the other occurrences of *etiam* in the Second Meditation go in that direction—in particular several lines before: "Does it not follow that I too do not exist?"; "nonne igitur etiam me non esse?" (VII:25, 4–5 or 29, 1 and 29, 7; CSM VII:16 or 19).

45. AT VII, respectively 7, 20; 18, 1–2; 73, 15–16; CSM II:7, 12, 51.

46. In this way one could respond to the subtle objection of Margaret Wilson against the reading of the *ego sum* as a performative (Hintikka)—the performative supposes "the existence of an audience" ("Performance," 71), now the ego remains alone and pronounces its performative in a private language ("vel mente concipitur," VII:25, 14; CSM II:17). In effect, the ego indisputably has at its disposal an audience, and its performative remains public, because it *responds* to the one who deceives it (eventually in not deceiving it or in not being himself). The ego responds, hears itself *respond*, hears itself speak, hears itself spoken, discovers itself being inasmuch as spoken by or before an other: *cogito me cogitatum, ergo sum.*

47. "Je pris garde que, pendant que *je* voulais ainsi penser que tout était faux, il fallait nécessairement que *moi*, qui le pensais, fusse quelque chose. Et remarquant que cette vérité, *je pense, donc je suis* était si ferme et si assurée, que toutes les extravagantes suppositions des Sceptiques n'étaient pas capables de l'ébranler, *je* trouvais que *je* pouvais la recevoir, sans scrupule, pour le premier principe que *je* cherchais." AT VI:32, 15–23; CSM I:127; my emphasis.

48. "Repugnat enim [there is in effect a contradiction] ut putemus id quod cogitat eo tempore quo cogitat non existere. Atque haec cognitio *ego cogito, ergo sum*, est omnium prima et certissima, quae cuilibet ordine philosophanti occurrat." *Principles of Philosophy* 1 §7; AT VIIIA:7, 6–7; CSM I:194–95. The absence of an other then constrains Descartes at (badly) founding the existence of the ego on an uncertain universal principle (§10; AT VIIIA:8, 13), of which discussion is, in fact, lacking.

49. We suppose here, against the majority of critics, that the certitude of the first principle, which remains such even if it turns out to be the highest truth, is here not put into question by any doubt (*post festum*).

50. My emphasis. "Yet when I turn to the things themselves which I think I perceive very clearly, I am so convinced by them that I spontaneously declare: *let whoever can do so deceive me*, he will never bring it about that I am nothing, so long as I continue to think I am something"; "et au contraire, lorsque je me tourne vers les choses que je pense concevoir fort clairement, je suis tellement persuadé par elles, que moi-même je me laisse emporter a ces paroles: *Me trompe qui* pourra, si est-ce qu'*il* ne saurait jamais faire que je ne sois rien, tandis que je penserai être quelque chose"; "*fallat me quisquis* potest, numquam tamen *efficiet* ut nihil sim, quamdiu me aliquid esse cogitabo." AT VII:36, 15; AT IXA:28, 25–30; CSM II:25.

51. "Cogitabo me esse" / "je penserai être quelque chose."

52. "Me trompe qui pourra" / "fallat me quisquis potest."

53. "Je conçois cette ressemblance (dans laquelle l'idée de Dieu se trouve contenue) par la même faculté par laquelle je me conçois moi-même." AT IXA:41, 12–14; CSM II:35.

54. AT VII:51, 21–23: "and that I perceive that likeness . . . by the same faculty which enables me to perceive myself" (literally: "and that likeness to be perceived by me . . . through the same faculty by which I myself am perceived by myself"). CSM II:35.

55. "Je connais aussi en même temps, que celui duquel je depends possède en soi toutes ces grandes choses auxquelles j'aspire." AT IXA:41, 17–19; CSM II:35 (trans. mod.).

56. See AT VII:53, 9–1:2; CSM II:37: "And when I consider the fact that I have doubts, or that I am a thing that is incomplete and dependent, then there arises in me a clear and distinct idea of a being who is independent and complete, that is, an idea of God" ("Cumque attendo me dubitare, sive esse rem incompletam et dependentem, adeo clara et distincta idea entis independentis et completi, hoc est Dei, mihi occurrit"; 55, 19–21; CSM II:39); "For since I now know that my own nature is very weak and limited, whereas the nature of God is immense, incomprehensible and infinite" ("Cum enim; jam sciam naturam meam esse valde infirmam et limitatam, Dei autem naturam esse immensam, incomprehensibilem, infinitam"); and positively (AT VII:57, 12–15; CSM II:40): "It is only the will, or freedom of choice, which I experience within me to be so great that the idea of any greater faculty is beyond my grasp; so much so that it is above all in virtue of the will that I understand myself to bear in some way the image and likeness of God" ("Sola est voluntas, sive arbitrii libertas, quam tantam in me experior ut nullius majoris ideam apprehendam; adeo ut illa praecipue sit, ratione cujus imaginem quandam et similtudinem Dei in me referre intelligo"). See already AT VII:9, 15–18; CSM II:8. One could also suggest the hypothesis that the three dreams of *Olympica* (X:179–90) outline already such an original interlocution of a still undefined subjectivity. See Fernand Hallyn, "Une 'feintise,'" in *Les "Olympiques" de Descartes*, ed. Fernand Hallyn (Geneva: Libr. Droz, 1995).

57. "Je vous suis bien obligé de ce que vous m'apprenez les endroits de saint Augustin, qui peuvent servir pour autoriser mes opinions: quelques autres de mes amis avaient déjà fait le semblable; et j'ai très grande satisfaction de ce que mes pensées s'accordent avec celles d'un si saint et excellent personnage." *To Mesland*, 2 May 1644, AT IV:113, 12–17; CSMK III:232. See AT III:248, 4–7; CSMK III:159: "but I am very glad to find myself in agreement with St. Augustine, if only to hush the little minds who have tried to find fault with the principle" ("mais je ne laisse pas d'être bien aisé d'avoir rencontré avec saint Augustin, quand ce ne serait que pour fermer la bouche aux petits esprits qui ont tache de regabeler sur ce principe").

58. "Je ne m'arrêterai point ici à le [Arnauld] remercier du secours qu'il m'a donné en me fortifiant de l'autorité de saint Augustin, et de ce qu'il a proposé mes raisons de telle sorte qu'il semblait avoir peur que les autres ne les trouvassent pas assez fortes et convaincantes." Fourth Replies, AT IXA:170; AT VII:219, 7; CSM II:154: "for bringing in the authority of St. Augustine to support me" ("quod divi Augustini authoritate adjuvarit").

59. "[Un] passage de saint Augustin." *To Mersenne*, 25 May 1637, AT I:376, 20; not translated in CSMK. The identification rests on an allusion Descartes subsequently made to this comparison made by Mersenne (and forgotten by him): "Some time ago, you drew my attention to a passage from St Augustine concerning my *I am thinking therefore I exist*, and I think you have asked me about it again since then. It is in Book Eleven, chapter 26 of *De Civitate Dei*." December 1640, AT III:261, 9–13; CSMK III:161. It is confirmed by his letter of 15 November 1638: "I looked for the letter in which you quote the passage from Saint Augustine, but I have not yet been able to find it; nor have I managed to obtain the works of the Saint, so that I could look up what you told me, for which I am grateful." *To Mersenne*, AT II:435, 19–23; CSMK III:129. This conclusion is shared by Léon Blanchet, *Les antécédents historiques du Je pense, donc je suis* (1920; Paris: Presses Universitaires de France, 1985), 56.

60. "Nulla in his veris Academicorum argumenta fonnido dicentium: Quid si falleris? Si enim fallor, sum. Nam qui non est, utique nec falli potest: ac per hoc sum, si fallor. Quia ergo sum si tailor, quo modo esse me fallor, quando certum est me esse, si fallor?"; "En cette triple

assurance, je ne redoute aucun des arguments des Academiciens me disant: Quoi! et si tu trompais? Car si je me trompe, je suis. Qui n'est pas, certes ne peut pas non plus se tromper: par suite, si je me trompe, c'est que je suis. Du moment donc que je suis, si je me trompe, comment me tromper en croyant que je suis, quand il est certain que je suis si je me trompe?"

61. "[Le] passage de saint Augustin, parce qu'il ne semble pas s'en servir a même usage que je fais." *To Mersenne*, 25 May 1637; AT I:376, 20–21; not translated in CSMK.

62. "Vous m'avez obligé de m'avertir du passage de saint Augustin, auquel mon *je pense, donc je suis* a quelque rapport: je l'ai été lire aujourd'hui en la bibliothèque de cette ville [Leyde], et je trouve veritablement qu'il s'en sert pour prouver la certitude de notre être, et ensuite pour faire voir qu'il y a en nous quelque image de la Trinité, en ce que nous sommes, nous savons que nous sommes, et aimons cet être et cette science qui est en nous; au lieu que je m'en sers pour faire connaître que ce *moi*, qui pense, est une *substance immaterielle*, et qui n'a rien de corporel; qui sont deux choses fort differentes." *To X*, November 1640, AT III:247, 1–248, 1; to Colvius, 14 November 1640, CSMK III:159.

63. No occurrence of *immatériel* in 1647 (see André Robinet, *Cogito 75. René Descartes: Méditations métaphysiques* [Paris: Vrin, 1976]) or of *immaterialis* in 1641.

64. Augustine, *De libero arbitrio* 2.3: "Abs te quaero ut de manifestissimis capiamus exordium, utrum tu ipse sis, an tu forte metuis ne hac in interrogatione falleris, cum utique, si non esses, falli omnino non potes"; "Et, pour partir des choses les plus manifestes, je te demanderai d'abord si toi-même, tu existes. Maîs peut-être crains-tu de te tromper en cette question, alors que tu ne pourrais absolument pas te tromper, si tu n'étais pas du tout."

65. "Sed est deceptor nescio quis, summe potens, summe callidus, qui de industria me semper fallit. Haud dubie igitur ego etiam sum, si me fallit." AT VII:25, 5–8; CSM II:17. [Cottingham renders this passage as "But there is a deceiver of supreme power and cunning who is deliberately and constantly deceiving me." Haldane's translation reads: "But there is some deceiver or other, very powerful and very cunning, who. . . ."] Arnauld quotes this and the passage from Augustine above at AT VII:197, 24–198, 8; CSM II:139.

66. AT VII:219, 6–9; CSM II:154.

67. AT VII:198, 5; CSM II:139.

68. "[Que] c'est une chose qui de soi est si simple et naturelle à inferer, qu'on est, de ce qu'on doute, qu'elle aurait pu tomber sous la plume de qui que ce soit." *To X*, November 1640, AT III:248, 1–4; to Colvius, 14 November 1640, CSMK III:159. (The "any writer" happened to be St. Augustine! It is hard to imagine any greater insolence.) See also AT VII:551, 9; CSM II:376 (cf. AT VII:130, 20–23; CSM II:94).

69. Arnauld tries once again, several years later (letter to Descartes, 3 June 1648, AT V:186, 11–12), to inscribe Descartes within the Augustinian tradition by invoking this time *De Trinitate* X.14: "But no one can possibly doubt that he lives and remembers, understands, wills, thinks, knows, and judges. For even if he doubts, he lives: if he doubts what has made him doubt, he remembers; if he doubts, he understands that he is doubting; if he doubts, he wishes to be certain; if he doubts, he thinks; if he doubts, he knows that he is ignorant; if he doubts, he judges that he ought not to be hasty in assenting. A man may doubt everything else, but he should not doubt any of these facts; for if they were not so, he could doubt of nothing." Augustine, *Later Works*, ed. John Barnaby (Philadelphia: Westminster, 1955), 85–86.("Vivere se tamen et meminisse, et intelligere, et velle et cogitare, et scrire, et judicare, quis dubitet? Quandoquidem etiam si dubitat, vivit: si dubitat, unde dubitet, meminit; si dubitat, dubitare se intelligit; si dubitat, esse vult; si dubitat, cogitat; si dubitat, scit se nescire; si dubitat, judicat non se temere consentire oportere. Quisquis igitur aliunde dubitat, de his omnibus dubitare neon debet; quae si non essent de ulla

re dubitare non posset." Descartes, in his reply (30 June, AT IV:194ff.) passes over this suggestion in silence insofar as it rests on the development of a similar tautology and therefore contradicts the original formulation. Besides, we see no compelling reason to suppose that Descartes could have known this passage before the redaction of his *Meditations*, despite the authoritative opinions of Léon Blanchet ("the probability . . . very great," *Les antécédents historiques*, 59–61) and Henri Gouhier ("seems therefore," *Cartésianisme et augustinisme au XVIIe siècle* [Paris: Vrin, 1978], 175). See the evidence compiled by G. Rodis-Lewis, "Augustinisme et cartésianisme," *Augustinus Magister* 1 (1954): 1087ff. The work by Gareth B. Matthews, *Thought's Ego in Augustine and Descartes* (Ithaca, N.Y.: Cornell University Press, 1992), is, despite its title, thoroughly useless on account of its misunderstanding of the texts. That, at least, is not the case with Edwin Curley, *Descartes Against the Skeptics*, 173, or Stephen Menn, "Descartes and Augustine," (Ph.D. dissertation, University of Chicago, 1990).

70. Emmanuel Levinas, *Totalité et infini* (The Hague: Martinus Nijhoff, 1961), 66; trans. Alphonso Lingis as *Totality and Infinity: An Essay on Exteriority* (Pittsburgh: Duquesne University Press, 1969), 93. See the texts more specifically dedicated to an interpretation of Descartes: "L'idée d'infini en nous," in *La passion de la raison: Hommage à F. Alquié*, ed. Nicolas Grimaldi and Jean-Luc Marion (Paris: Presses Universitaires de France, 1988), reprinted in Emmanuel Levinas, *Entre nous: Essais sur le penser-à-l'autre* (Paris: Grasset, 1991); Trans. Michael B. Smith and Barbara Harshav as "The Idea of the Infinite in Us," in *Entre Nous: On Thinking-of-the-Other* (New York: Columbia University Press, 1998), 219–222. Gilles Deleuze opposes to the *I think* (in fact, to its canonical interpretation) that "the spontaneity of which I have consciousness . . . cannot be comprised by the attribute of a substantial and spontaneous being, but only by the affection of a passive me which feels that its own proper thought . . . that by which it says 'I,' is exercised in it and on it, not by it. . . . He sees it as an Other in him." *Différence et répétition*, 7th ed. (Paris: Presses Universitaires de France, 1993), 116ff. This objection even describes the *ego existo* according to its original alterity.

71. Following, for example, Natalie Depraz, *Transcendance et incarnation. Le statut de l'intersubjectivité comme altérité à soi chez Husserl* (Paris: Vrin, 1995).

Introduction to Part IV: Revelation and Apophasis

1. See J. G. Fichte, *Attempt at a Critique of All Revelation*, trans. and intro. Garrett Green (Cambridge: Cambridge University Press, 1978), Immanuel Kant, *Religion within the Limits of Reason Alone*, trans. Theodore M. Greene and Hoyt H. Hudson (New York: Harper & Row, 1960); Emmanuel Levinas, *Of God Who Comes to Mind*, trans. Bettina Bergo (Stanford, Calif.: Stanford University Press, 1998), xi. Note, though, that for Levinas the infinite is revealed "in the strong sense of this term"; *Totality and Infinity: An Essay on Exteriority*, trans. Alphonso Lingis (The Hague: Martinus Nijhoff, 1979), 62; see also 73.

2. See Manfred Schröter, ed., *Schellings Werke, Nach der Original in neuer Anordnung* (Munich: C. H. Beck'sche, 1927–1946/54), vols. 3, 4, 13, and 14.

3. See, in particular, Karl Barth, *Church Dogmatics*, I: *The Doctrine of the Word of God*, part 1, ed. G. W. Bromily and T. F. Torrance, trans. G. W. Bromily (Edinburgh: T. & T. Clark, 1936), chap. 2; and Hans Urs von Balthasar, "Word and Revelation," the first half of *Explorations in Theology*, I: *The Word Made Flesh*, trans. A. V. Littledale with Alexander Dru (San Francisco: Ignatius Press, 1989). Also see Larry Chapp, "Revelation," *The Cambridge Companion to Hans Urs von Balthasar*, ed. Edward T. Oakes and David Moss (Cambridge: Cambridge University Press, 2004), 11–23.

4. Considerable attention has been given to Marion's understanding of revelation. See, in particular, Shane Mackinlay, *Interpreting Excess: Jean-Luc Marion, Saturated Phenomena, and*

Hermeneutics (New York: Fordham University Press, 2010), chap. 8; Christina M. Gschwandt-ner, *Reading Jean-Luc Marion: Exceeding Metaphysics* (Bloomington: Indiana University Press, 2007), chap. 5; and Thomas A. Carlson, "Blindness and the Decision to See: On Revelation and Reception in Jean-Luc Marion," in *Counter-Experiences: Reading Jean-Luc Marion*, ed. Kevin Hart (Notre Dame, Ind.: Notre Dame University Press, 2007), 153–179.

5. For a detailed discussion of Marion and the Greek Fathers, especially Saint Gregory of Nyssa and Pseudo-Dionysius the Areopagite, see Tasmin Jones, *A Genealogy of Marion's Philosophy of Religion: Apparent Darkness* (Bloomington: Indiana University Press, 2011).

6. See David B. Burrell, "Reflections on 'Negative Theology' in the Light of a Recent Venture to Speak of 'God without Being,'" *Postmodernism and Christian Philosophy*, ed. Roman Theodore Ciapalo, intro. Jude P. Dougherty (Mishawaka, Ind.: American Maritain Association, 1997), 58–67. Also see Derek J. Morrow, "Aquinas, Marion, Analogy, and *Esse*: A Phenomenology of Divine Names?" *International Philosophical Quarterly* 46 (2006): 25–42.

7. See Martin Heidegger, "The Onto-Theological Constitution of Metaphysics," *Identity and Difference*, trans. Joan Stambaugh (Chicago: University of Chicago Press, 2002).

8. See Jean-Luc Marion, *The Erotic Phenomenon*, trans. Stephen E. Lewis (Chicago: University of Chicago Press, 2007), §28.

9. See Derrida, *Given Time*, I: *Counterfeit Money*, trans. Peggy Kamuf (Chicago: University of Chicago Press, 1992), 29; *Negotiations: Interventions and Interviews 1971–2001*, ed. Elizabeth Rottenberg (Stanford, Calif.: Stanford University Press, 2002), 349; *Mémoires: For Paul de Man*, trans. Cecile Lindsay et al. (New York: Columbia University Press, 1986), chap. 1.

The Prototype and the Image
Translated by James K. A. Smith. Reprinted from Jean-Luc Marion, *The Crossing of the Visible* (Stanford University Press, 2004), 66–87. Copyright © 2004 by the Board of Trustees of Leland Stanford Jr. University for the English Translation; © 1996 Presses Universitaires de France. All rights reserved. Used with the permission of Stanford University Press, www.sup.org.

1. [The qualifier *iconomaque* literally means "enemy of the icon"; below it will stand in contrast to *iconodoule*, meaning "servant of the icon." To avoid cumbersome locutions, I have generally translated the former simply as "iconoclastic." —Trans.]

2. [Given the intentionally phenomenological employment of the term in this context, here I follow Thomas A. Carlson's rendering of *donation* (following Jean-Luc Marion's wishes) as "givenness," in order to indicate its link with *Gegebenheit* in the Husserlian corpus. —Trans.]

3. Second Council of Nicaea, Actio VII, after Mansi XIII.378 s; also quoted in R. Denzinger, ed., *Enchiridion Symbolorum*, n. 302. [Marion essentially follows the translation given by C. Von Schönborn, *L'Icône du Christ* (Fribourg: 1976), p. 143. Square brackets are the author's.—Trans.]

4. [Marion regularly refers to this passage as "Canon 7" of the Second Council of Nicaea. However, the passage is located in Actio VII, and the canons are distinguished from the actios. When a direct citation is made, I correct the reference to "Actio"; otherwise, I have retained the author's use of "canon." —Trans.]

5. Denzinger, *Enchiridion Symbolorum*, nn. 302 and 304, which one should supplement with the Latin version (of Anastase) of the Council of Constantinople IV (869), Canon 3: "typus pretiosae crucis" (ibid., n. 337). See previously Justin, *First Apology*, 60.3.

6. Denzinger, *Enchiridion Symbolorum*, n. 392, citing Saint Basil, *De Spiritu Sancto*, XVIII.45. With this formula, it should be not a matter of a particular theological opinion, but a matter of the fundamental matrix of all doctrine in the service of the icon [*iconodoule*], before and after Nicaea II.

7. John of Damascus, *The Orthodox Faith* [cited hereafter as *Or.*], IV.16, in *PG*, vol. 94,1169a. Compare the similar formula: "the type and the icon of what was to come" (John of Damascus, *Against Those Who Refuse Icons, Or.*, III.26, in *PG*, vol. 94, 1345b).

8. John of Damascus, *Against Those Who Refuse Icons, Or.*, 10 and III.21, in *PG*, vol. 94, 1241a and 1341a.

9. John of Damascus, *The Orthodox Faith*, IV.16, in *PG*, vol. 94, 1172b. Note also the fine invective: "While you venerate the icon of the Cross, made from some material, you should not also venerate the icon of the Crucified and of that which bears the salvific cross!" (*Or.*, II.19, in *PG*, vol. 94, 130b).

10. *Or.*, II.11, in *PG*, vol. 94, 1296c (see also *Or.*, III.10, in *PG,* vol. 94, 1033a).

11. The episode in Matthew 13:53–58 indicates not only the distance between the knowledge [*la connaissance*] of Christ (according to the flesh) and the recognition [*reconnaissance*] of him (according to the Spirit), but above all that the invisible absolutely crosses the visible itself. In this sense the blinding of the disciples on the road to Emmaus (Luke 24:17, 25) depicts the hermeneutic situation of every unbelieving gaze before the icon. [For a further exploration of this; see Marion's more recent article "They Recognized Him, and He Became Invisible to Them," *Modern Theology* 18 (2002): 149ff. —Trans.] It would remain, evidently, to specify the difference between the misunderstanding [*la méconnaissance*] of the Eucharist (substantial presence) and that of the icon (intentional presence).

12. "One can rightly observe, for example, the effectiveness of inverted perspective in the alcove of Daphnée, where the Transfiguration is reproduced; it appears to push us toward our own encounter with the Christ of Glory, between the adoration of Moses and Elijah." L. Bouyer, *Vérité des icons. La tradition iconographique chrétienne et sa signification*, 2d ed. (Paris, 1990), p. 34.

13. The specification of Christ as the icon of the invisible God is directly admitted as being foundational to every doctrine that serves the icon [*iconodoule*]; for example, according to John of Damascus: "The first icon—according to nature and without any parallel—of the invisible God is the Son of the Father" (*Or.*, III.18, in *PG,* vol. 94, 1340a). From this perfect equivalence of form between the Father and the Son (see Saint Basil, *De Spiritu Sancto*, XVIII.45), it then becomes lawful to bring out, according to an increasingly typical parallel, other genres of icons: "those by which God is served" (by which is meant specifically "the wood of the cross" and "the nails"); the Gospels and cultural instruments; icons in the normal sense; and finally our next one, the civil authorities and private authorities. Thus, under the title of "living icon of the invisible God" (John of Damascus, *Or.*, II.15, in *PG*, vol. 94, 1301), of a "living icon, better a living being in itself [πντοοῦσα ζωή]" (Saint Basil, *Contra Eunome*, I.18, in *PG*, vol. 29, 552b), or of "physical icons" (Theodore Studite, *Antirrheticus*, in *PG*, vol. 99, 501a), Christ determines the rules of every icon and its conditions of validity. The only imitation that can be claimed by the common icon would thus be, contrary to any mimetic aesthetic, the *imitatio Christi*, such that it first rules the life of every believer.

14. Denzinger, *Enchiridion Symbolorum*, n. 302.

15. See, for example, Theodore Studite: "The prototype is in the icon not according to the modality of substance . . . but according to the resemblance of the hypostasis" (*Antirrheticus*, III.3, in *PG*, vol. 99, 420a). Or: "these are two different things, the icon and the prototype, and the difference does not reside in the hypostasis, but is made according to the definition of the substance" (Epistle 212, in *PG*, vol. 99, 1640a). It is necessary to underline that "the image is purely relational" and that its "presence is intentional, pneumatic" (Schönborn, *L'icône du Christ*, pp. 209 and 224). Just as the hypostasis is concretized in the face (πρoσώπoν) and the face itself is made to share the two natures by the union of the two wills, the icon, as long as it is

a type of the face, should be contemplated according to the union of wills: the one in prayer [*l'orant*] unites his will to theirs, unified by Christ in repeating the union of the human will and the divine will by Christ.

16. Saint Basil, *De Spiritu Sancto*, XVIII.45, which depends upon *Letter* XXXVIII.8 (pseudo-Basil? Gregory of Nyssa?), in *PG*, vol. 32, 240a–c, and, among others, Athanasius, *Against the Arians*, III.5, in *PG*, vol. 26, 332a–b.

17. [Friedrich Nietzsche, *Thus Spoke Zarathustra*, in *The Portable Nietzsche*, trans. Walter Kaufmann (New York, 1968), p. 171. —Trans.]

18. Ludwig A. Feuerbach, *The Essence of Christianity*, trans. George Eliot (New York, 1957). [The original is in Feuerbach, *Gesammelte Werke*, standard ed. (Berlin, 1968), vol. 5, p. 11. —Trans.]

19. "ἀγάπης εἰκόνα," Maximus the Confessor, *Letter* XLIV, in *PG*, vol. 91, 644b. If the Incarnation offers an icon of charity, it would also be necessary conversely to conclude that Christ, by being made charity for men, is given as an icon only by accomplishing charity. Thus charity alone would render the icon possible.

Thomas Aquinas and Onto-theo-logy

Reprinted from Michael Kessler and Christian Sheppard, eds., *Mystics: Presence and Aporia* (University of Chicago Press, 2007), 38–74. This chapter is a translation of "Saint Thomas d'Aquin et onto-theo-logie," first published in the *Revue Thomiste* 95 (1995) by B. Gendreau, R. Rally, and M. Sweeney, revised and completed by the author.

1. I have used the standard translations of Being/entity, but I want to make clear that by "Being" I exclusively mean "to be," *esse, Sein, être,* as opposed to *ens, Seiende, étant.*

2. On those two issues, I would like to take a more balanced position than that of my earlier study *Dieu sans l'être* (Paris: Fayard, 1982; reprint, Paris: Presses Universitaires de France, 1991). See, too, my acknowledgments in the preface to *God without Being: Hors-Texte*, trans. Thomas A. Carlson (Chicago: University of Chicago Press, 1991), xvii–xxv, and "Metaphysics and Phenomenology: A Relief for Theology," *Critical Inquiry* 20, no. 4 (1994).

3. Martin Heidegger, "Die onto-thelogische Verfassung der Metaphysik," in *Identität und Differenz* (Pfullingen: G. Neske, 1957), 63, translated as *Identity and Difference*, trans. J. Stambaugh (New York: Harper & Row, 1969), 71 (modified).

4. Given that, indeed, God should and could be said and thought as a being, even a supreme one. And this raises the question of whether we should doubt the accuracy of naming him according to being in general.

5. I refer, indeed, to George Berkeley, *Principles of Human Knowledge*, ed. Howard Robinson (Oxford: Oxford University Press, 1996), 1, secs. 2–3.

6. See a more detailed analysis in my study *On Descartes' Metaphysical Prism: The Constitution and the Limits of Onto-theo-logy in Cartesian Thought*, trans. Jeffrey L. Kosky (Paris: Presses Universitaires de France, 1986; reprint, Chicago: University of Chicago Press, 1999).

7. Heidegger, *Identität and Differenz*, 51 (*Identity and Difference*, 60).

8. Heidegger, *Identität and Differenz*, 61 and 64 (*Identity and Difference*, 69 and 72).

9. See the accurate definitions of "metaphysics" given in the forewords to the commentaries to Aristotle's *Physics, Metaphysics, On Generation and Corruption* (Pro. 2), and to *De Coelo* (Pro.1.1). But first of all, "Suprema veto inter eas [scientia philosophica], scilicet metaphysica, disputat contra negantem sua principia, si adversarius aliquid concedit; si autem nihii concedit, non potest cum eo disputare, potest tamen solvere rationes ipsius" (St. Thomas, *Summa Theologiae* Ia, q.1, a.8). Or, "Aliqua scientia acquisita est circa res divinas, sicut scientia metaphysicae"

(*Summa Theologiae* IIa–IIac, q.9, a.2, 0 bj.2). And, "Metaphysica, quac circa divina versatur" (Saint Thomas, *Summa contra Gentiles* 1,4). I want to emphasize that this connection between *metaphysica* and the divine does not fit the definition produced by the commentary on *Metaphysics* in *In duodecim libros Metaphysicorum Aristotelis expositio, Proemium*, ed. M. K Cathala (Turin: Marietti, 1964), 1.

10. *In duodecim libros Metaphysicorum*, ed. Cathala, 1 ff.

11. The first quote is from *Summa Theologiae* la, q.1, a.1, ad 2. The second quote is from St. Thomas, *Expositio super librunt. Boethii de Trinitate*, question 5, answer 4, ed. B. Decker (Leiden: Brill, 1959), 195, or *Opuscula omnia*, ed. P. Mandonnet (Paris: P. Lethielleux, 1929), 3:119–120. See "hoc modo [mainly *procedere ex principiis notis lumine superioris scientiae*] sacra doctrina est scientia, quia procedit ex principiis notis lumine superioris scientiae, quae scilicet est scientia Dei et beatorum" (*Summa Theologiae* Ia, q.1, a.2, c.). About this double status of theology, see also M. Corbin, *Le chemin de la théologie chez Thomas d'Aquin* (Paris: Beauchesne, 1974), chap. 2 (and in particular sec. 2), as well as G. Kalinowski, "Esquisse de révolution d'une conception de la métaphysique," *Saint Thomas d'Aquin aujourd'hui: Recherches de philosophie* 6 (1963).

12. "Res divinae non tractantur a philosophis, nisi prout sunt rerum minium principia. Et ideo pertractantur in illa doctrina, in qua ponuntur illa quae stint communia omnibus entibus, quae habet subjectum ens in quantum ens" (*Expositio super librum Boethhi de Trinitate*, ed. Decker, 194; in *Opuscula omnia*, ed. Mandonnet, 3:119).

13. "Theologia ergo philosophica determinat de separatis secundo modo sicut de subjectis, de separatis autem prima modo sicut de principiis subjectis. Theologia vero sacrae Scripturae tractat de separatis prima modo sicut de subjectis" (*Expositio super librum Boethhi de Trinitate*, ed. Decker, 195; in *Opuscula omnia*, ed. Mandonnet, 3:120).

14. "Subjectum in illa [mainly *scientia*] potest dici Deus, quia ratio entitate magis reservatur in Deo quam caeteris entibus. Et inde dicitur quod scientia metaphysicae esse divina et de Deo" (Giles de Rome, *Commentarium in primum librum Sententiarium*, Prologue, question 1, [Venice: heredum O. Scotus, 1521], fol. 2rb). See A. Zimmermann, *Ontologie oder Metaphysik? Die Discussion über den Gegenstand der Metaphysik ins 13. tend 14. Jahrhundert* (Leiden: Brill, 1965), 144–47.

15. "Cum dicis 'Deus effugiat rationem entis,' dico quad falsum et immo verisimile [Deus] ens est" (*Commentarium*, question 9, ad 1, fol. 4vb). See Zimmermann, *Ontologie oder Metaphysik?* and J.-F. Courtine, *Suárez et le système de la métaphysique* (Paris: Presses Universitaires de France, 1990), 114 ff. and 128 ff.

16. "Similter dico quad in metaphysicis ens in quantum ens est subjectum principaliter per se et primo. Ex quia ratio entis melius et verius salvatur in Deo quam in alio ente, propter hoc dico, quad Deus est subjectum principale illius scientiae, non per se et prima, sed ex consequenti" (Giles de Rome, *Quaestiones metaphysicales* q. 5 [Venice, n.d.; reprint, Frankfurt am Main: Minerva, 1966], fol. 3rb). What is assumed here is precisely what should have been demonstrated against the authority of Thomas Aquinas, i.e., that the *ratio entis* [*in quantum entis*] is better achieved by God than by any finite entity.

17. John Duns Scotus, *Ordinatio*, I, distinction 3, question 3, numbers 126 and 139, vol. 3 of Opera omnia, ed. Carolus Balic (Civitas Vaticana Typis Polyglottis Vaticanis, 1954), 79 and 87, and, in French, *Sur la connaissance de Dieu et l'univocité de l'étant*, ed. and trans. Olivier Boulnois (Paris: Presses Universitaires de France, 1988), 137 and 148. See also O. Boulnois, "Quand commence l'onto-theo-logie? Aristote, Thomas d'Aquin et Duns Scot," *Revue Thomiste* 95, no. 1 (1995): 85–108.

18. Francisco Suárez, *Disputationes metaphysicae* 1, s.1, n. 13 and n. 26, in *Opera omnia*, ed. Charles Berton et al. (Paris: apud Ludovicum Vivès, 1866), 25:6 and 11. See n. 19 ("absolute Deus cadit sub objectum hujus scientia") and n. 20 ("Nec D. Thomas unquam oppositer docuit [?], sed solum hanc scientiam [metaphysicam] pervenire ad cognitionem Dei sub ratione principii, non tamen negat eamdem scientiam tractare de Deo ut de praecipuo objecto") (p. 9), which seems obviously (and intentionally?) wrong. And II, s.2, n.11: "Ens, de quo nune loquimur, est commune enti creato et increato" (p. 73); such a community amounts, in a very consistent way, to destroy the analogy: "Si alterum negandum esset, potius analogia, quae incerta est, quam unitas conceptus, quae verb rationibus videatur demonstrari, esset neganda" (II, s.2, n. 36; p. 81). On this issue, see J.-L. Marion, *Sur la théologie blanche de Descartes* (Paris: Presses Universitaires de France, 1981; reprint, Paris: Presses Universitaires de France, 1992), 135 ff.

19. *Expositio in librum Dionysii de Divinis nominibus*, V, II (ed. Ceslas Pera [Turin: Marietti, 1950], par. 660; in *Opuscula omnia*, ed. Mandonnet, 2:499): "Primo quidem quantum ad hoc quad alia existentia dependent ab esse communi, non autem Deus, sed magis esse commune a Deo. . . . Secundo, quantum ad hoc quad omnia existentia continentur sub ipso esse communi, non autem Deus, sed magis esse commune confinetur sub ejus virtute, quia virtus divina plus extenditur quam ipsum esse creatum."

20. *Summa Theologiae* Ia, q.5, a.2, resp.: "Primum autem in conceptione intellectus cadit ens, quia secundum hoc unimquodque cognoscibile est, inquantum est actu . . . ; und ens est proprium objectum intellectus et sic est primum intelligibile." See *In Sententiarum Libros* I, distinction 38, question 1, answer 4, ad 4 (and distinction 8, question 1, answer 3), *De Veritate*, question 1, answer 1, c., and *De ente et essentia*, Proemium: "Ens autem et essentia sunt quae primo intellectu concipiuntur, ut dicit Avicenna in V Metaphysica" (in *Opuscula omnia*, ed. Mandonnet, 1:1.45); *In duodecim libros Metaphysicorum* I, question 2, n. 46: "Nam primo in intellectu cadit ens, ut Avicenna dicit" (ed. Cathala, 13). On this issue (and some others), see E. Gilson's "Elements d'une métaphysique thomiste de l'être," n. 1, in *Autour de saint Thomas* (Paris: J. Vrin, 1983), 97. Concerning Thomas Aquinas's relations to Avicenna, see G. C. Anawati, "Saint Thomas d'Aquin et al Métaphysique d'Avicenne," avec l'appendice sur "Les notions, définitions ou distinctions d'Avicenne approuvées par saint Thomas," in *Colloque commemoratif saint Thomas d'Aquin: Saint Thomas Aquinas commemorative colloquium (1274–1974)* (Ottawa: Université Saint-Paul, 1974).

21. *Summa Theologiae* Ia, q.3, a.4, ad 2.

22. *Summa Contra Gentiles* I, sec. 26, n.4 and ad 2m.: "Divinum autem esse est absque additione non solum in cogitatione, sed etiam in rerum natura, nec solum in additione, sed etiam absque receptibilitate additionis." See, too, *De Potentia* VII, answer 2, ad 4: "Esse divinum, quod est ejus substantia, non est esse commune, sed est esse distinctum a qualibet alio esse"; or *De Potentia* VII, answer 2, ad 6: "Divinum esse non est ens commune?' Or *De ente et essentia* VI: "Nec oportet, si dicamus quad Deus eat esse tantum, ut in errorem incidamus qui Deum dixerunt ease illud esse universale quo quaelibet res formaliter est. Hoc enim esse quod Deus est, hujus conditionis est ut nulla sibi additio fieri possit: unde per ipsam suam puritatem est esse distinctum ab omni esse" (in *Opuscula omnia*, ed. Mandonnet, 2:159).

23. *Contra Gentiles* I, sec. 12: "Nam hoc intelligitur de esse, quo Deus in se ipso subsistit, quod nobis quale sit, ignotum est, sicut ejus essentia."

24. See, on the history of the concept of *analogia entis*, J.-L. Marion, ed., "L'analogie," special issue of *Les Études Philosophiques*, nos. 3–4 (1989).

25. *Summa Theologiae* Ia, q.3, a.4, ad 2: "Ease dupliciter dicitur: uno modo significat actum essendi; alio modo significat compositionem propositionis quod anima adinvenit conjugens praedicatum subjecto."

26. Ibid., Is, q.3, a.4: "Deus non solum est sua essentia . . sed etiam suum esse."

27. Ibid., Ia, q.6, a.3; and q.12, a.4; and then q.45, a.5, ad 1m. Too many and too well known texts could be quoted here, which have no need of it.

28. Ibid., Ia, q.3, a.4 and, then q.45, a.6.

29. Ibid., Ia, q.13, a.5 and Ia–IIae, q.20, a.3, ad 3: "Analogiam et proportionem."

30. Ibid., Is, q.13, a.5. I rely, indeed, on the illuminating study by Bernard Montagnes, *La doctrine de l'analogie de l'être selon saint Thomas d'Aquin* (Paris: Librairie Lecottre, J. Gabalda, 1963), and I disagree with P. Aubenque, "Sur la naissance de la doctrine pseudo-aristotélicienne de l'analogie de l'être" (*Les Études Philosophiques*, nos. 3–4 [1989], 291 ff.), whose analysis fits better Cajetanus or Suárez than Thomas Aquinas.

31. *Summa Theologiae*, q.13, a.5, and *Contra Gentiles* I, sec. 34.

32. Ibid., Ia, q.2, a.3: "Ergo est necesse ponere aliquam causam efficientem primam, quam omnes Deum nominant."

33. *Contra Gentiles* I, sec. 31: "Deum non possumus cognoscere naturaliter nisi ex effectibus deveniendo in ipsum."

34. Ibid., I, sec. 34 and sec. 33.

35. In *Expositio super librum Boethii de Trinitate,* question 1, answer 2, ad 3m. (in *Opuscula omnia*, ed. Mandonnet, 3:33). Sec *Contra Gentiles* sec. 54: "Proportio ad Deum secundum quod proportio significat quamcumque habitudinem unius ad alterum, vet materiae ad formam, vel causae ad effectum"; as well as *Summa Theologiae* Ia, q.12, a.1, ad 4m ("proportio creaturae ad Deum being understood ut effectus ad causam"), etc.

36. René Descartes, letter to Mersenne, April 27, 1630 (in *Ouevres de Descartes*, ed. Charles Adam and Paul Tannery [Paris: J. Vrin, 1964–74], 1:151).

37. *In Dionysii De Divinis Nominibus,* IV, 2 (in *Opuscula omnia*, ed. Mandonnet, 2:452). Concerning the doctrine of Dionysius on αἰτία, see my analysis in *L'idole et la distance* (Paris: Bernard Grasset, 1977; reprint, Paris: Bernard Grasset, 1991), sec. 14, 196 ff. From time to time Thomas Aquinas (more often than does Albert the Great) writes *causatum* in the place of *effectum*, which obviously refers more to Dionysius than to Aristotle.

38. *Summa Theologiae* Ia, q.12, a.12.

39. Ibid., Ia, q.8, a.3. For *causa essendi*, see ibid., Ia, q.45; *De Potentia*, question 3, answer 6; and *Contra Gentiles* II, sec. 6: "Allis cams essendi existit."

40. *Summa Theologiae* I, q.65, a.5, ad 4. See Ix, q.45, a.6: "Create est proprie causare, sive producere esse rerum"; or q.105, a.5: "Ipse Deus est proprie causa ipsius esse universalis in rebus"; and *De Potentia*, question 3, answer 5, ad 1: "Licet causa prima, quae Deus est, non intret essentiam rerum creatarum; tamen esse, quod rebus creatis inest, non potest intelligi nisi ut deductum ab esse divino."

41. Dionysius, *On Divine Names,* V, 7 and V, 8 (Migne, *Patrologia graeca* 3, cols. 821B and 824A). Which is literally commented on by Thomas: "[Deus] non solum est causa quantum ad fieri rerum, sed quantum ad totum esse" (*Expositio in librum Dionysii de Divinis nominibus*, ed. Pera, 235, par. 631; in *Opuscula omnia*, ed. Mandonnet, 2:487).

42. The phrase *universalis provisor totius entis* is from *Summa Theologiae* Ia, q.22, a2, ad 2.

43. *Liber de causis,* XXI, sec. 166 et IV, sec. 37.

44. First *De causis et processu universitatis a prima causa*, ed. W. Fauser, vol. 17A of *Opera omnia* (Aschendorff: Monasterii Westfalorum, 1993), 18; then *Metaphysica*, ed. Bernard Geyer, vol. 16, pt. 2, of *Opera omnia* (Aschendorff: Monasterii Westfalorum, 1964), XI, 1, c.3, p.463 (see I, I, c.1 [16, pt. 1:3]; 1,4, c.8 [16, pt, 1:57];1(1,c.3 [16, pt. 1:163]). Classical commentary by A. de Libera, *Albert le Grand et la philosophie* (Paris: J. Vrin, 1990), 78 ff.

45. *Contra Gentiles* III, sec. 66. See: "Primus autem effectus est ipsum esse, quod omnibus aliis effectibus praesupponitur et ipsum non praesupponit aliquem aliud effectum; et ideo oportet quod dare esse inquantum hujusmodi sit effectus primus causae solius secundum propriam virtutem" (*De Potentia,* question 3, answer 4, reap.); and also: "Ostensum est antem supra, quod Deus est primum et perfectissimum ens, unde oportet quod sit causa essendi omnibus quae esse habent" (*Compendium neologiae* I, sec. 68, in *Opuscula omnia,* ed. Mandonnet, 2:37); so, it is only insofar as it is the effect in first place of creation that the *esse* cap be said to be "first."

46. *De Potentia*, question 3, answer 7: "Ipsum enim esse est communissimum effectus primus et intimior omnibus aliis effetus."

47. Respectively, *Summa Theologiae* Ia, q.2, a.3, *resp.*: "Nec est possibile quod aliquid sit causa efficiens sui ipsius, quia sic esset prius seipso, quod est impossibile"; and also *Contra Gentiles* I, sec. 18, n.4; or *Summa Theologiae* Ia, q.19, a.5, respectively. The denial of any possible *causa sui* was not restricted to Thomas Aquinas, but a unanimous statement from Anselm *(Monologion* VI) unto Suárez (*Disputationes metaphysicae* sec. I, n.27; XXIX, sec. I, n. 20, 25:11 and 26:27). See my studies on that issue in *Sur la théologie blanche de Descartes*, sec. 18, 427 ff, and "Entre analogie et principe de raison: la causa sui," in *Descartes: Objecter et répondre*, ed. J.-M. Beyssade and J.-L. Marion (Paris: Presses Universitaires de France, 1994), 308–314. One remains free indeed to build up a completely different concept of *causa sui* (as, for instance, S. Breton did in his "Réflexions sur la causa sui," *Revue des sciences philosophiques et théologiques* 70 [1986]), or even to claim that it would fit better the transcendence of the Christian God. Nevertheless, as Thomas Aquinas carefully shifted away from it, as did Christian theology, why take the risk of an unnecessary ambiguity? In that case, why should the so-called *bullitio* (the overwhelming essence of God according to Eckhart) be named *causa sui*?

48. See *Iae Responsiones*, in *Ouevres de Descartes*, ed. Adam and Tannery, 8:108, 7–18: Descartes did not take seriously the logical inconsistency of the *causa sui*, calling it "nugatoria quaestio," widely known ("*quis nescit . .?*"); but, if the difficulty was so superficial, why did he never answer it?

49. *Summa Theologiae* Ia, q.3, a.7: "Deus non habet causam, . . . cum sit prima causa efficiens"; or *Contra Gentiles* I, sec. 22: "Deus autem est prima causa, non habens causam."

50. *De ente et essentia* V: "Non autem potest esse quod ipsum esse sit causatum ab ipsa forma vel quidditate rei, dico sicut a causa efficiente; qui a sic aliqua res esset causa sui ipsius et aliqua res seipsam in esse produceret, quod est impossibile. Ergo oportet quod omnis talis res, cujus esse est aliud quam natura sua, habet esse ab alio" (in *Opuscula omnia*, ed. Mandonnet, 1:157; ed. Raimondo Spiazzi [Turin: Marietti, 1949], chap. 4, p.13, line 27).

51. Suárez, *Disputationes metaphysicae*, XII, Prologue, 25:372 if. In the opposite vein, Thomas Aquinas admitted a possible difference between the essence and the cause: "Essentia rei vel est res ipsa, vel se habet ad ipsam, aliquo modo, ut causa" (*Contra Gentiles* I, 21).

52. René Descartes, *Meditationes de prima philosophia, Secundae Responsiones*, in *Ouevres de Descartes*, ed. Adam and Tannery, 7:164 ff.: "Nulla res existit de qua non possit quaeri quaenam sit causa cur existit. Hoc enim de ipso Deo quaeri potest."

53. Benedict de Spinoza, *Korte Verhandeling*, I, sec. 10.

54. Along those lines, see Saint Bonaventura, *Itinerarium mentis in Deum*, VI, 1–2. On the history of that turn, see U. von Strasbourg, *De summo bono*, II, 1, 1–3 (ed. K. Flasch and L. Sturlese [Hamburg: F. Meiner, 1987], 27 ff.) following the commentary by A. de Libera, *Albert le Grand et la philosophie*, 80 ff. Along with my arguments in *God without Bring*, chap, 3, sec. 3, see the classical qudy by A. Feder, "Das Aquinate Kommentar zu Pseudo-Dionysius' *De Divinis Nominibus*: Ein Beitrag zur Arbeitsmethode des hlg. Thomas," *Scholastik* 1 (1926), reprinted in *Thomas von Aquin, Wege der Forschung*, vol. 188, pt. 1 (Darmstadt: Wissensthaftliche Buchgesellschaft, 1978),

50 ff.; and more recently, U. M. Lindblad, *L'intelligibilité de l'être selon saint Thomas d'Aquin et selon Martin Heidegger* (Berne and New York: Publications de l'Universite Européenne, 1987), sec. 3, p. 180. To be fair to Thomas Aquinas, it should be said that even his main argument to submit the name of "good" to the name of "being" remains very careful and balanced: *bonum* is still the first name, if we consider God as a cause (and the cause of the *esse*); but the fact is that Thomas himself is the first to emphasize that God plays the role of a cause, even regarding the *esse creatum*; so, to some extent, he sticks, too, to the traditional primacy of *bonum* over *esse*. One cannot refrain from mentioning the very original definition of "being" formulated by B. Lonergan: "Being is the objective of the pure desire to know" (*Insight* [London: Longmans, 1957], II, 12, p. 348). In that case, too, *esse* implicitly depends on *bonum* as the object of desire.

55. E. Gilson: "La métaphysique thomiste s'accorde mai du nom d'onto-logie, car elle est une considération de l'être plus encore qu'un discours sur l'étant; elle n'est même pas une onto-theologie, pour la simple raison qu'elle pose Dieu au-delà de l'étant, comme l'Etre même" ([*L'être et l'essence*, 2d ed. [Paris: J. Vrin, 19621, 372). But it is not enough to go beyond entity for God to avoid going into onto-theo-logy because any familiarity with being ascribes him to this metaphysical constitution. Onto-theology deals with being as well as entities, insofar as metaphysical being remains always oriented toward and questioned for the sake of entity. However, how could God amount to "to be" without assuming the figure of an entity whatsoever? Even if so, this paradox should be explained as such.

56. The quoted material is from Immanuel Kant, *Kritik der reinen Vernunft,* A632/B660. See my "Is the Ontological Argument Ontological?" *Journal of the History of Philosophy* 30, no. 2 (April 1992), reprinted in *Questions cartésiennes*, vol. 1, *Méthode et métaphysique* (Paris: Presses Universitaires de France, 1991) and in *Cartesian Questions: Method and Metaphysics* (Chicago: University of Chicago Press, 1998), chap. 7, secs. 1–2.

57. By the way, I directly oppose the tactics of Gilson: "L'être de Heidegger est le vrai, non parce qu'il se définit contre Dieu, mais parce se définit comme Dieu, n'étant qu'un autre nom du Dieu judeo-chrétien de l'Exode"; and, as a result, Heidegger should be granted among Christians with "des compagnons inconnus sur la voie on l'on dirait parfois qu'il se croit seul" (Gilson, "Dieu et l'être," *Revue Thomiste* [1962], reprinted in *Constantes philosophiques de la question de l'être* [Paris: J. Vrin, 1983], 211, 377). As if Christians were interested, in their quest for God, first and only by being! May not Revelation give us more than being, which, after all, remains still the issue of philosophy? Same diplomatic and at least inappropriate plot in J. B. Lotz, *Martin Heidegger und Thomas von Aquin: Mensch, Zeit, Sein* (Pfullingen: Neske, 1975), and *Martin Heidegger et Thomas d'Aquin: Homme, temps, être,* trans. Philibert Secretan (Paris: Presses Universitaires de France, 1988); or, with less accuracy, in K. Rahner (*Geist in der Welt: Zur Metaphysik der endlichen Erkenntnis bei Thomas von Aquin*, 2d ed. [Munich: Kösel, 1957]), II, 3, sec, 6. in any case, the point always amounts to imagining, as a good feature about him, that Thomas Aquinas would have foreseen what Heidegger was first able to express correctly. One may wonder whether this statement is more unfair to Thomas (portrayed as a mere forerunner rather than with achievements of his own) or to Heidegger (depicted as an unconscious Christian when he was consciously non-Christian).

58. *De Potentia,* question 7, answer 2, ad 4: "Esse divinum quod est ejus substantia non est esse commune, sed est esse distinctum a quolibet alio ente. Unde per ipsum suum esse Deus differt a quolibet alio ente."

59. C. Fabro, *Participation et causalité* (Louvain: Presses Universitaires de Louvain, 1961), 253.

60. *Contra Gentiles*, sec. 22: "Deus igitur non habet essentiam, quae non sit suum esse" (and I, sec. 25).

61. *Summa Theologiae* Ia, q.12, a.2: "Essentia Dei est ipsum esse ejus"; and 13,11: "Cum esse Dei sit ipsa essentia."

62. *De ente et essentia* VI: "Aliquid enim est, sicut Deus, cujus essentia est ipsum suum esse; et ideo inveniuntur philosophi dicentes quod Deus non habet quidditatem vel essentiam, quia essentia sua non est aliud quam esse suum" (ed. Spiazzi, p.14, line 30; in *Opuscula omnia*, ed. Mandonnet, 2:159). Gilson often quotes that text in *Constantes philosophiques*, 199 (without giving any reference), in "Eléments d'une métaphysique," 109 (with an inaccurate reference: *De ente et essentia* V, 30), in *Le Thomisme: Introduction a la philosophie de St. Thomas d'Aquin* (Paris: J. Vrin, 1965), 135, n. 3 (wrong reference), and finally in *L'être et l'essence* (115, correct reference).

63. *In Sententiarum Libros* 1, distinction 2, question 1, answer 3, solutio: "Quidam dicunt, ut Avicenna (*Liber de Intelligentiis* I) et Rabbi Moyses (I, c.57–58) quod res illa quae Deus est, en quoddam esse subsistens, nec aliquid nisi esse in Deo est: unde dicunt quod est sine essentia." This is quoted by Gilson in *L'être et l'essence* (199, without giving any reference) and in "Elements d'une métaphysique," where he seems to admit that Thomas has agreed with Avicenna and Maimonides (109). What we might wonder about, rather, is that (i) this thesis, so profoundly Christian according to Gilson, could owe so much to "'a la perspicacité de certains theologiens musulmans, puis à celle du philosophe Avicenne," more perhaps than to that of the "théologien Thomas d'Aquin"; and (ii) that this thesis—was rebuked by "la majorité des théologiens chrétiens, dont d'illustres thomistes" (*L'être et l'essence*, 200). Everything happens as if the Christian philosophy was ironically first worked out by Jews and Muslims. See Avicenna: "Primus igitur non habet quidditatem" (*Metaphysica* VIII, 4, in *Avicenna latinus*, ed. S. van Riet [Louvain: E. Peeters and Editions Orientalistes; Leiden: E. J. Brill, 1980], 4:400, 398 and 401). And "Le Premier n'a pas de quiddité autre que l'être (al-anniya)" (*Kitab alshifa* VIII, ed. Georges Anawati [Paris: P Guenther, 1927], 2:86). Commentary by A. Forest, *La structure métaphysique du concret selon saint Thomas d'Aquin* (Paris: J. Vrin, 1931), app. C, 331–60; and by A. Wohlman, *Thomas d'Aquin et Maimonide: Un dialogue exemplaire* (Paris, 1988), chap. 4, 105 ff., establishes close comparisons between Thomas Aquinas, Maimonides, and Avicenna; see also D. Burrell, *Knowing the Unknowable God: Ibn-Sina, Maimonides, Aquinas* (Notre Dame, Ind.: Notre Dame University Press, 1986), and "Aquinas and Islamic and Jewish Thinkers," in *The Cambridge Companion to Aquinas*, ed. N. Kretzmann and E. Stump (Cambridge: Cambridge University Press, 1993). Other sources, directly coming from Neoplatonism, may have also played an actual role (S. Pines, "Les textes arabes dits plotinienes et le courant 'porphyrien' dans le néo-platonisme grec," in *Studies in Arabic Versions of Greek Texts and Mediaeval Science*, The Collected Works of Shlomo Pines [Jerusalem: Magnes Press, Hebrew University, 1986]).

64. *Metaphysica* Z,1.1028b2–3. The same question would be without doubt also for *Metaphysica* 7.1072b26 ss. and above all τῇ οὐσίᾳ ὢν ἐνεργείᾳ (*On the Soul* III, 5,430 a 18).

65. *De Potentia,* question 7, answer 2, ad 1: "Sicut ejus [Dei] substantia ignota, ita et esse"; *In librum De divinis Nominibus* VII, 4: "Cognoscitur [Deus] per ignorantiam nostram, inquantum scilicet hoc ipsum Deum cognoscere, quod not scimus nos ignorare de Deo quid sit" (in *Opuscula omnia*, ed. Mandonnet, 2;534; in *Expositio in librum Dionysii de Divinis nominibus*, ed. Pera, line 731); *Contra Gentiles* III, see. 49: "Quid vero sit penitus manet incognitum" (see also I, secs. 11 and 12); *Summa Theologiae* Ia, q.12, a.13, ad 1: "Licet per revelationem gratiae in hac vita non cognoscimus de Deo quid est, et sic ei quasi ignoto conjungamur."

66. *Summa Theologiae* Ia, 1.3, a.4, ad 2.

67. Ibid., 1a, q.3, a.11: "Intellectus autem noster non potest ipsam Dei essentiam cognoscere in statu vitae secundum quod in se est, sed quemcumque modum determinat circa id quod de Deo intelligit, deficit a modo quo Deus in se sit" (resp.); "Adhuc magis proprium nomen est

Tetragrammaton, quod est impositum ad significandam ipsam substantiam incommunicabilem et, ut sic liceat loqui, singularem" (ad 2).

68. A perfect example of this new effort is P. W. Roseman, *Omne ens est illiquid: Introduction à la lecture du "système" philosophique de saint Thomas d'Aquin* (Louvain: Éditions Peeters, 1996), in particular chap. 2, "*Ipsum esse subsistens*: Dieu a-t-il à l'être?" [Should God have to be?].

The Possible and Revelation

Translated by Christina M. Gschwandtner. Reprinted from Jean-Luc Marion, *The Visible and the Revealed* (Fordham University Press, 2008), 1–17.

1. That is, the inclusion of the essay in *Religionsphilosophie Heute*, ed. A. Halder and K. Kienzler (Düsseldorf: Patmos, 1988).

2. Immanuel Kant, *Kritik der reinen Vernunft*, 2d ed., vol. 3 of *Kants Werke* (1787; Berlin: Walter de Gruyter, 1968); trans. Norman Kemp Smith under the title *Immanuel Kant's Critique of Pure Reason* (London: Macmillan, 1964), A85/B117. All references to this work will refer to pages in the first and second German editions, given in the margins of the Kemp Smith translation.

3. Immanuel Kant, *Die Religion innerhalb der Grenzen der blossen Vernunft*, bk. 3, div. 1, § 6, *Kants Gesammelte Schriften, Akademie Ausgabe* (Berlin: Königlich Preussische Akademie der Wissenschaften, 1902–1910), 6:110 G; trans. Theodore M. Greene and Hoyt H. Hudson under the title *Religion Within the Limits of Reason Alone* (New York: Harper & Row, 1960), 100–101.

4. G. W. F. Hegel, *Phänomenologie des Geistes*, ed. W. Bonsiepen and R. Heede, Gesammelte Werke (Hamburg: Felix Meiner, 1980), 11:313; trans. A. V. Miller under the title *Phenomenology of Spirit* (Oxford: Oxford University Press, 1977), 459.

5. Aristotle, *Metaphysics*, 8, 1049b5 (see 1051 a2–3).

6. Martin Heidegger, *Sein und Zeit*, 10th ed. (Tübingen: Max Niemeyer, 1963), §7, 38; trans. John Macquarrie and Edward Robinson under the title *Being and Time* (New York: Harper & Row, 1962), 62. Given that Heidegger pays homage to Husserl in this statement, one can suppose that in his eyes this reversal between actuality and possibility is due to Husserl.

7. Husserl, *Idee der Phänomenologie*, ed. W. Biemel, vol. 2 of *Husserliana: Edmund Husserl Gesammelte Werke* (The Hague: Martinus Nijhoff, 1950–), henceforth Hua, 74; trans. William P. Alston and George Nakhnikian under the title *The Idea of Phenomenology* (The Hague: Martinus Nijhoff, 1964), 59.

8. Husserl, *Ideen zu einer reinen Phänomenologie und phänomenologischen Philosophie: Erstes Buch, Allgemeine Einführung in die reine Phänomenologie*, §24, ed. W. Biemel (The Hague: Martinus Nijhoff, 1950), Hua, 3:74; trans. F. Kersten under the title *Ideas Pertaining to a Pure Phenomenology and to a Phenomenological Philosophy: First Book, General Introduction to a Pure Phenomenology* (The Hague: Martinus Nijhoff, 1982).

9. Respectively, Husserl, *Cartesian Meditations*, V, §46, Hua, 1:133, and Heidegger, *Being and Time*, §7, 36/60 (or *Prolegomena zur Geschichte des Zeitbegriffs*), §9, *Gesamtausgabe* (Frankfurt am Main: Vittorio Klostermann, 1976–), 20:119. Here and throughout, where dual page numbers are given, the page in the original language precedes the page in the English translation. The *Gesamtausgabe* will hereafter be cited as *GA*.

10. Heidegger, *Prolegomena*, §32, *GA*, 22: 423.

11. [Throughout, *l'être/Sein* is translated as "Being" and *l'étant/Seiendes* as "being." —Trans.]

12. Heidegger, Letter to R. Munier, 16 April 1973 (trans. R. Munier), in *M. Heidegger*, ed. M. Haar, Cahiers de l'Herne (Paris: L'Herne, 1983), 112.

13. Heidegger, *Being and Time*, §7, 36/60.

14. Ibid., §7, 35 (see 28 and 31)/59 (see 50 and 54).

15. See my study on this point in *Réduction et donation. Recherches sur Husserl, Heidegger et la phénoménologie* (Paris: Presses Universitaires de France, 1989); trans. Thomas A. Carlson under the title *Reduction and Givenness: Investigations of Husserl, Heidegger, and Phenomenology* (Evanston, Ill.: Northwestern University Press, 1998), chap. 1.

16. Rudolf Bultmann, "Der Begriff der Offenbarung im Neuen Testament" (1929), in his *Glauben und Verstehen*, vol. 3 (Tübingen: Mohr Siebeck, 1961), respectively 21 and 23. Or also, "There is no possibility for the reader to return behind the sermon, albeit to a "historical Jesus" (ibid., 21). On this text, see my essay "Remarques sur le concept de Révélation chez R. Bultmann," *Résurrection*, no. 27 (1968): 29–42. A deeper study of the relation of Barth to Husserl is H. J. Adriaanse, *Zur Sachen selbst. Versuch einer Konfrontation der Theologie Barths mit der phänomenologischen Philosophie Edmund Husserls* (The Hague: Mouton, 1974).

17. Heidegger, "Phänomenologie und Theologie" (1927), *Wegmarken, GA*, vol. 9, respectively 52 and 53, trans. James G. Hart and John C. Maraldo under the title "Phenomenology and Theology," in *Pathmarks*, ed. William McNeill (Cambridge: Cambridge University Press, 1998), 39–62. One must here remark a very Bultmannian formula: "faith is an appropriation of revelation that co-constitutes the Christian occurrence, that is, the mode of existence that specifies a factical Dasein's Christianness as a particular form of destiny" (ibid., 53f/45).

18. Heidegger, "Brief über den Humanismus," in *Wegmarken, GA*, 9:351 (see 326, 331, and 361); trans. Frank A. Capuzzi under the title "Letter on Humanism," in *Pathmarks*, ed. McNeill, 239–267.

19. Ibid., 338f./258. On the interpretation of these texts and, in general, the subordination of the Revelation of God by himself, see my discussion with Jean Beaufret (and F. Fédier), in Jean-Luc Marion, *Dieu sans l'être. Hors-texte* (Paris: Arthème Fayard, 1982); trans. Thomas A. Carlson under the title *God Without Being* (Chicago: University of Chicago Press, 1991), chapter 2, §4–5 and chapter 3, §2–4.

20. Heidegger, "Wozu Dichter?" *Holzwege, GA*, 5:270; trans. Julian Young and Kenneth Haynes as "Why Poets?" in *Off the Beaten Track* (Cambridge: Cambridge University Press, 2002), 200–241.

21. Karl Rahner, *Grundkurs des Glaubens: Einführung in den Begriff des Christentums* (Freiburg im Breisgau: Herder, 1976), 127.

22. Ibid., 44, 128, and 127.

23. Husserl, *Logische Untersuchungen: Prolegomena zur reinen Logik* §36 (Tübingen: Max Niemeyer, 1913), 1:117; trans. J. N. Findlay under the title *Logical Investigations: Prolegomena to a Pure Logic* (London: Routledge, 1970), 140; and *Ideen* I, §150, *Hua* 3: 371; trans. W. R. Boyce Gibson under the title *Ideas* I (New York: MacMillan, 1931), 418.

24. Husserl, *Ideas* I, §51, 122/157.

25. Heidegger, "Phenomenology and Theology," 66/53.

26. Michel Henry, *L'essence de la manifestation* (Paris: Presses Universitaires de France, 1963) and *Philosophie et phénoménologie du corps* (Paris: Presses Universitaires de France, 1965).

27. Didier Franck, *Chair et corps: Sur la phénoménologie de Husserl* (Paris: Minuit, 1981) and "La chair et le problème de la constitution temporelle" (1984; rpt. in *Dramatique des phénomènes* [Paris: Presses Universitaires de France, 2001]).

28. Emmanuel Levinas, *La théorie de l'intuition dans la phénoménologie de Husserl* (Paris: Alcan, 1930) and *En découvrant l'existence avec Husserl et Heidegger* (Paris: Vrin, 1949, 1974). See J. Colette's very good clarification, "Lévinas et la phénoménologie husserlienne," in Emmanuel Levinas, *Les cahiers de la nuit surveillée*, ed. Emmanuel Levinas and Jacques Rolland (Lagrasse: Verdier, 1984).

29. Martin Heidegger, *Metaphysische Anfangsgründe der Logik im Ausgang von Leibniz*, GA, 26:117 (see 211).

30. [Marion is here employing aesthetic imagery (especially from painting) for the possible experience of revelation and its transgression of the horizon. —Trans.]

31. Husserl, *Logical Investigations*, §39, 3:122/2:766.

32. Heidegger, *Being and Time*, §43 b, 209–211/193–195.

What Cannot Be Said: Apophasis and the Discourse of Love

Translated by Arianne Conty. Reprinted from Jean-Luc Marion, *The Visible and the Revealed* (Fordham University Press, 2008), 101–118.

1. 1 Corinthians 2:9, quoting Isaiah 64:4: "From ages past no one has heard, no ear has perceived, no eye has seen any God besides you, who works for those who wait for him."

2. Descartes, *Meditations*, Fifth Replies, *Oeuvres de Descartes*, ed. Charles Adams and Paul Tannery, 11 vols. (Paris: Vrin, CNRS, 1964–79], VII:368, 2–4.

3. John Chrysostom, *Peri akataleptou*, *Patrologia Graeca* 48, col. 720; trans. Paul W. Harkins under the title *On the Incomprehensible Nature of God* (Washington, D.C.: Catholic University of America Press, 1984).

4. Immanuel Kant, *Kritik der reinen Vernunft*, 2nd ed., vol. 3 of *Kants Werke* (1787; Berlin: Walter de Gruyter, 1968); trans. Norman Kemp Smith under the title *Immanuel Kant's Critique of Pure Reason* (London: Macmillan, 1964), A761/B789.

5. Ludwig Wittgenstein, *Tractatus Logico-philosophicus* (London: Routledge, 1922), 7.

6. Martin Heidegger, "Protocole à un séminaire sur la conférence *Zeit und Sein*," *Questions* IV, ed. Jean Beaufret (Paris: Gallimard, 1976), 83; the German version can be found in *Zur Sache des Denkens* (Tübingen: Max Niemeyer, 1969), 51. Compare with: "It must remain an open question whether the nature of Western languages is in itself marked with the exclusive brand of metaphysics . . . or whether these languages offer other possibilities of utterance—and that means at the same time of a *telling silence*" (Heidegger, *Identität und Differenz* [Pfullingen: G. Neske, 1957], 66, emphasis added; trans. Joan Stambaugh under the title *Identity and Difference* [New York: Harper & Row, 1969], 73).

7. Wittgenstein, *Tractatus Logico-philosophicus* 6.522 (see also 6.432 and 6.44).

8. Jacques Derrida, "Comment ne pas parler: *Dénégations*," in *Psyché: Inventions de l'autre* (Paris: Galilée, 1987), 535–595, trans. Ken Frieden under the title "How to Avoid Speaking," in *Languages of the Unsayable: The Play of Negativity in Literature and Literary Theory*, ed. Sanford Budick and Wolfgang Iser (New York: Columbia University Press, 1989), 3–70; and then *Donner le temps: I. La fausse monnaie* (Paris: Galilée, 1991), trans. Peggy Kamuf under the title *Given Time: I. Counterfeit Money* (Chicago: University of Chicago Press, 1991); and *Sauf le nom (Post Scriptum)* (Paris: Galilée, 1993), trans. John P. Leavey, Jr., under the same title in Derrida, *On the Name*, ed. Thomas Dutoit (Stanford: Stanford University Press, 1998), 35–85, in which he discusses my *L'idole et la distance* (Paris: Bernard Grasset, 1977), trans. Thomas A. Carlson under the title of *The Idol and Distance: Five Studies* (New York: Fordham University Press, 2001); *Dieu sans l'être* (Paris: Arthème Fayard, 1982), trans. Thomas A. Carlson under the title *God Without Being* (Chicago: University of Chicago Press, 1991), and *Réduction et donation: Recherches sur Husserl, Heidegger et la phénoménologie* (Paris: Presses Universitaires de France, 1989); trans. Thomas A. Carlson under the title *Reduction and Givenness: Investigations of Husserl, Heidegger, and Phenomenology* (Evanston, Ill.: Northwestern University Press, 1998).

9. Derrida, *Sauf le nom*, 70/63.

10. John Scotus Eriugena, *De Divisione Naturae*, I, 14, *Patrologia Latina* 122, col. 462.

11. Aristotle, *On Interpretation* 4, 17a4.

12. See my response to Derrida, "In the Name: How to Avoid Speaking of 'Negative Theology,'" in *God, the Gift, and Postmodernism*, ed. John D. Caputo and Michael Scanlon (Bloomington: Indiana University Press, 1999), 20–42, and then in *De surcroît: Études sur les phénomènes saturés* (Paris: Presses Universitaires de France, 2001), 162–71; trans. Robyn Horner and Vincent Berraud under the title *In Excess: Studies of Saturated Phenomena* (New York: Fordham University Press, 2002), chap. 6, "In the Name: How to Avoid Speaking of It," esp. section 2, 134–142.

13. Stendhal, *La chartreuse de Parme*, chap. 28.

14. Husserl, *Logische Untersuchungen*, 2 vols. (Halle: Max Niemeyer, 1922), 1:26, esp. 2:82ff.; trans. J. N. Findlay under the title *Logical Investigations*, 2 vols. (London: Routledge & Kegan Paul, 1970).

15. J. L. Austin, *How to Do Things with Words* (Cambridge, Mass.: Harvard University Press, 1962), 109.

16. "Thus we distinguish the locutionary act (and within it the phonetic, the phatic, and the rhetic acts) which has a *meaning* [from] the illocutionary act which has a certain *force* in saying something" (ibid., 121).

17. Montaigne, *Essais*, I, 28, ed. P. Villey (Paris: V. L. Saulnier, 1965), 1:189.

18. Austin, *How to Do Things with Words*, 15.

19. Stanley Cavell, "La passion," in the collective work modestly entitled *Quelle philosophie pour the XXIe siècle? L'organon du nouveau siècle* (Paris: Pompidou Center, 2001), 373; the English original can be found as "Performative and Passionate Utterance," in Cavell, *Philosophy the Day after Tomorrow* (Cambridge, Mass.: Harvard University Press, 2005), 181; further citations will be to the English version. Cavell's discussion of Austin's conditions has been helpful for my own analysis.

20. Austin and Searle should not be confused on this point. Austin classifies "to promise" among the commisives (*How to Do Things with Words*, 157), mentions insincerity (18, 40), and has not a single word to say about "to love." J. R. Searle, *Speech Acts: An Essay in the Philosophy of Language* (Cambridge: Cambridge University Press, 1969), 57–62, gives a thorough analysis of the illocutionary act "to promise" (including the promise without sincerity) but without making the slightest allusion to "I love you."

21. Austin, *How to Do Things with Words*, 109. In this sense, it remains a performative (110).

22. Searle, *Speech Acts*, 25.

23. Cavell, "Performative and Passionate Utterance," 173.

24. Roland Barthes hesitates on this point: sometimes, he is confused: "this word [I-love-you] is always *true* (it has no other referent than its offering of itself: it is a performative)"; sometimes, he sees things correctly, though not without imprecision: "The atopia of love, what is proper to it and allows it to escape from all theses, is that *in the last instance* we can speak of it only according to *a strict allocutionary determination*; in the discourse on love there is always a person to whom one speaks, even if this person takes the form of a ghost or a creature from the future. No one wants to talk about love, if it is not *for* someone" (*Fragments d'un discours amoureux* [Paris: Seuil, 1977], 176 and 88; trans. Richard Howard as *A Lover's Discourse: Fragments* (New York: Hill and Wang, 1978); translated modified for this context. Or rather, no one wants to speak *about* love, if not to someone who is *loved*, for one can very well speak *about* love without love, and without a loved one.

25. Austin, *How to Do Things with Words*, 101 (my emphasis).

26. Cavell, "Performative and Passionate Utterance," 180.

27. Austin, *How to Do Things with Words*, 122 and 119.

28. Cavell, "Performative and Passionate Utterance," 180; cf. Austin: "The 'I' that accomplishes the action does thus come essentially into the picture" (*How to Do Things with Words*, 61).

29. Austin, *How to Do Things with Words*, 119.

30. Cavell, "Performative and Passionate Utterance."

31. Descartes mentions this in *Passions de l'âme*, §82, *Oeuvres de Descartes*, ed. Charles Adams and Paul Tannery, 11 vols. (Paris: Vrin, CNRS, 1964–79), XI, 388–389.

32. Barthes's opinion could not be more misplaced: "Once the first avowal has been made, '*I love you*' has no meaning whatsoever; it merely repeats in an enigmatic mode—so blank does it appear—the old message (which may not have been transmitted in these words). I repeat it though it may no longer have any relevance; it leaves language behind, it rambles, where?" (*Fragments*, 175/147; trans. modified). It does not ramble, since it repeats, and it does not repeat in a void, since it thereby maintains the lover's discourse, despite the apophasis that apophasis inevitably provokes. It is only this repetition that gives time to the lover's discourse, its only possible time, possibly precisely despite the impossibility that the present inflicts upon it.

33. Alphonse de Lamartine, "Le poète mourant," *Les Nouvelles Méditations* (Paris: U. Canel, 1823), 125–126.

The Impossible for Man—God

Translated by Anne Davenport. Reprinted from Jean-Luc Marion, "The Impossible for Man—God," in *Transcendence and Beyond* (Indiana University Press, 2007), ed. John D. Caputo, 17–44. Copyright © 2007. Reprinted with permission of Indiana University Press.

1. Husserl, *Cartesianische Meditationen*, Hua I, p. 72.

2. Husserl: "*So heisst das Ding selbst mind schlechthin transzendent*" (*Mem* 1, *Hua* III, p. 96).

3. Heidegger, "*Sein ist das* transeendens *schlechthin*" (*Sein und Zeit*, sec. 7, p. 38).

4. [Respectively: "being insofar as it is indifferent to finite and infinite," and "transcendent and is outside of every genus." —Trans.]

5. ["They are such that they transcend being insofar as being is indifferent to finite and infinite." —Trans.] Duns Scotus, *Ordinatio 1*, d. 8, n. 113, in *Opera Omnia*, ed. C. Balk (Rome: Vatican Polyglot, 1956), vol. 4, p. 206.

6. ["The definition of transcendentals is that no predicate stands above them, except being." —Trans.] Ibid., p. 206.

7. ["God thus *does not* have an essence that is not his very being." —Trans.] Aquinas, *Summa contra Gentiles*, bk. 1, chap. 21. See J.-L. Marion, "Thomas Aquinas et onto-theologie," *Revue Thomiste* 95 (1995), which appears in translation in this collection.

8. The formula is mentioned by Pettus Fonseca, *Institutionum Dialecticarum libri octo* (Lyon, 1611), bk. 1, chap. 28; and is cited and discussed by Jean-Francois Courtine in *Suárez et le système de la métaphysique* (Paris: Presses Universitaires de France, 1990), p. 267. On the doctrine of transcendentals, see Courtine, *Suárez et le système*, p. 355ff; and L. Honnefelder, *Ens inquantum ens: Der Begriff des Seienden als Gegenstand der Metaphysik nach der Lehre von Johannes Duns Scotus*, Beitrage zur Geschichte der Philosophic mind Theologie des Mittelalters, ri.s. 16 (Münster: Aschendorff, 1979); as well as Theo Kobusch, "Das Seiende als transzendentaler oder supertranszendentaler Begriff," in *John Duns Scotus: Metaphysics and Ethics*, ed. L Honnefelder, R. Wood, and M. Dreyer (Leiden: Brill, 1996).

9. Francisco Suárez, *Disputationes metaphysicae*, disp. 1, sec. 1, ii. 19, in *Opera omnia*, ed. C. Berton (Paris: Vives, 1866), vol. 25, p. 8, my emphasis ["God in an absolute manner falls under the object of this science (metaphysics) because this science is the most perfect *natural*

wisdom; therefore it treats of all first and most universal things and causes, and of the most general first principles, which include God himself." —Trans.]. See my analysis in J.-L. Marion, *Sur la théologie blanche de Descartes: Analogie, creation des vérités éternelles et fondement*, 2nd ed. (Paris: Presses Universitaires de France, 1991), p. 11ff.

10. Heidegger, "Zur Seinsfrage," *Wegmarken*, Gesamtausgabe, vol. 9 (Frankfurt: Klostermann, 1967), p. 395.

11. Jules Renard, *Journal 1887–1910*, ed. L. Guiehard and L. Signaux (Paris: Pléiade, 1960), p. 227.

12. ["Incomprehensibility as such is contained in the definition of infinity." —Trans.] Descartes, *De Responsiones*, in *Oeuvres de Descartes*, ed. C. Adam and P. Tannery (Paris: Vrin, 1964–1976) (henceforth AR) vol. 7, pp. 368, 3–4.

13. Hobbes says it with great clarity: "Whatsoever we imagine is *Finite*. Therefore there is no idea or conception of anything we call *Infinite*. No man can have in his mind an image of infinite magnitude; nor conceive infinite swiftness, infinite time, or infinite force, or infinite power. When we say any thing is infinite, we signify only, that we are not able to conceive the ends, and bounds of the thing named; having no conception of the thing, but of our own inability. And therefore the Name of *God* is used, not to make us conceive him; (for he is *Incomprehensible*; and his greatness, and power are unconceivable;) but that we may honour him" (*Leviathan*, bk. 1, chap. 3).

14. Heidegger has established not only the finitude of *Dasein*: "*Urspranglicher als der mensch ist die Endlichkeit des Daseins in ihm*" (*Kant und das Problem der Metaphysik*).

15. See Jocelyn Benoist, in his critique of my first works: "Is it enough not to be in order to be a concept of God?" And: "It is hardly sufficient, either, to not be an object in order to be God" (*L'idée de la phénoménologie* [Paris: Beauchesne, 2001], pp. 86, 96). I am obviously arguing against my own thesis concerning the unavoidable necessity of the counter-experience as the only mode of experience appropriate to the phenomenality of saturated phenomena. See J.-L. Marion, *Etant donné: Essai d'une phénoménologie de la donation* (Paris: Presses Universitaires de France, 1997); in translation as *Being Given: Toward a Phenomenology of Givenness*, trans. Jeffrey L. Kosky (Stanford: Stanford University Press, 2002).

16. [In the legal sense of "rendered invalid by prescription." —Trans.]

17. Descartes: "*Qui autem negant se habere ideam Dei, sed vice illius efformant aliquod idolum etc.,? mineri negant et rem concedunt*" (*Secundae Responsiones*, AT 7, pp. 139, 5–7).

18. [The French here involves a play on words that cannot easily be rendered in English. —Trans.]

19. "There is nothing, they say, that god cannot effectuate." Cicero, *De Divinatione*, bk. 2, sec. 41; in *De senectute; De amicitia; De divinatione,* ed. and trans. W. A. Falconer (Cambridge, Mass.: Harvard University Press, 1923), p. 468.

20. Aquinas, *Summa Theologica*, bk. 1, q. 25, a. 3, resp.: "God is called omnipotent because he can do all things that are possible absolutely, which is the second way of saying that a thing is possible."

21. Descartes, *Meditationes*, med. 1, in AT 7, pp. 21, 1–2: "Infixed, so to speak, in my mind is an old Opinion, that there is a God who can do all things."

22. Hume, *An Essay Concerning Human Understanding*, bk. 4, sec. 10; ed. P. H. Niddich (Oxford: Oxford University Press, 975), p. 620. The emergence of modern "atheism" has naturally had to assume still a residual definition of the nonexisting or supposed nonexisting "God"; this was precisely the notion of "universal cause," as W. Schröder has established in *Ursprünge des Atheismus: Untersuchungen zur Metaphysik- und Religionskritik des 17. und 18. Jahrhunderts*

(Stuttgart, 1998), p. 209ff. On the privilege of causality (as the most abstract and empty of determinations), see also J.-L. Marion, "The Idea of God," in *The Cambridge History of Seventeenth-Century Philosophy*, ed. M. Ayers and D. Garber (Cambridge: Cambridge University Press, 1998), vol. 1, pp. 265–304; this article is reproduced as chap. 10 of J.-L. Marion, *Questions cartésiennes. L'égo et Dieu* (Paris: Presses Universitaires de France, 1996).

23. Kierkegaard, *Samlede Vaerker*, 2nd ed., ed. A. B. Drachmann, L. Heiberg, and H. O. Lange (Copenhagen: Nordisk Forlag, 1920–1936), vol. 9, p. 81; the French translation appears as *Les oeuvres de l'amour* in the *Oeuvres complètes*, ed. P-H. Tissean and E.-M. Tisseau (Paris, 1980), vol. 14, p. 62. Cf. Augustine: "*omnipotens, qui facis mirabilia solos*" (*Confessions*, bk. 4, chap. 15, par. 24).

24. The clearest indication of this conclusion is found in the recent work of John D. Caputo, for example: "It can be said in defense of the Kingdom of God that it is not simply impossible, but rather, let us say, *the* impossible." This is from "The Poetic of the Impossible and the Kingdom of God," in *The Blackwell Companion to Postmodern Theology* (Oxford: Oxford University Press, 2001); which is reprinted in *Rethinking Philosophy of Religion: Approaches from Continental Philosophy*, ed. Philip Goodchild (New York: Fordham University Press, 2002). See also *A Passion for the Impossible: John D. Caputo in Focus*, ed. M. Dooley (New York: SOW Press, 2003); and "Apostles of the Impossible: On God and the Gift in Derrida and Marion," in *God, the Gift, and Postmodernism*, ed. John D. Caputo and Michael J. Scanlon (Bloomington: Indiana University Press, 1999), which appeared also in *Philosophia* 78 (2003).

25. Cf. Georges Bataille, *Le petit*, in *Oeuvres complètes* (Paris: Gallimard, 1971), vol. 3., p. 47: "*A la place de Dieu . . . il n'y a que l'impossible et non Dieu.*" [Instead of God . . . there is only the impossible and not God." —Trans.]

26. Nicholas of Cusa, *Trialogus de possest*, in *Werke*, ed. Paul Wilpert (Berlin, 1967), vol. 2,. p. 66; or in the *Philosophische-theologische Schriften*, ed. L. Gabriel, D. Dupré, and W. Dupré (Vienna, 1966), vol. 2, p. 340; "Hence, as nothing is impossible with God, we must, by means of what is impossible in the world, raise ourselves to contemplate God, with whom impossibility is necessity."

27. Kant, *Critique of Pure Reason,* A590/13619, or A6021/B630.

28. One could indeed argue that Descartes and Hegel answer Kant correctly: the case of all other entities, we are right to distinguish concept and existence, but this "habit" no longer holds in God's case, who by definition constitutes an exception to the general rule governing common beingness. (For Descartes, cf. *Meditationes*, med. 5, in AT 7, pp. 66, 2–15; *De Responsiones*, in AT 7, pp. 116, 8–19; and *Principia philosophia* I, 16. For Hegel, cf. *Wissenschaft der Logik*, ed. G. Iasson, Hamburg: Meiner, 1934, vol. 1, p. 75.)

29. ["So that God alone is what he can be, which no creature can, since potency and act are not the same, except in the first principle." —Trans.] Nicholas of Cusa, *Trialogos de possest*, in Wilpert, p. 646; in Gabriel et al., p. 274. Also: "Deus *sit absoluta* potentia *et actus atque utriusque nexus et deo sit actu omne possibile esse.*"

30. "Uncreated possibility is his very possest." In other words, God is necessarily possible. —Trans.]

31. Nicholas of Cusa, *Trialogus de possest, in* Wilpert, p. 654; in Gabriel et al., pp. 300, 302. St. Nicholas of Cusa, *Trialogus de possest, in* Wilpert, p. 649; in Gabriel et al., p. 284. See also: "supra *mime nomen quo id, quod potest esse, est nominabile, immo supra ipsum esse et non esse omni modo quo illa intelligi possunt*" (Wilpert, p. 653). Possibility here is exactly equivalent to indifference with regard to the difference between being and nonbeing.

32. Kant, *Critique of Pure Reason*, A290/B346.

33. Aquinas, *Summa Theologica*, bk. l, q. 25, a. 3, resp.: God is called omnipotent because he can do all things that are possible absolutely; which is the second way of saying a thing is possible. For a thing is said to be possible or impossible according to the relation in which the very terms stand to one another. . . . Therefore, everything that does not imply a contradiction is numbered among those possible things, in respect of which God is omnipotent. (For Aquinas, see also the *Summa contra Gentiles*, bk. 1, chaps; 22, 25.) This limitation of divine omnipotence to what is logically possible remains Duns Scotus's position: "Alio modo omnipotens accipitur proprie theologice, prout omnipotens dicitur qui potest in mime effectum et quodcumque possibile (hoc est in quodcumque quod non est: ex se necessarium nec includit contradictionem)." (*Ordinatio* 1, d. 42, n. 9, in *Opera omnia*, vol. 6, p. 343; and even by way of *potentia absoluta:* see *Ordinatio 1,* d. 44, n. 7, p. 365ff); and even Ockham's position—see *Quodlibet* III q. 3; VI, q. 6, On Ockham, see also Philotheus Boehner, *Collected Articles* on *Ockham*, ed. E. M. Buytacrt (New York: Franciscan Institute, 1958), p. 151ff.; as well as the texts translated by Elizabeth Karger in her article "Causalité Divine et Tout-Puissance," in *La puissance et son ombre: de Pierre Lombard a Luther,* ed. O. Boulnois (Paris: Aubier, 1994), pp. 321–356.

34. Malebranche, *Traité de Morale*, bk. 2, pt. 9, chap. 12, in *Oeuvres complètes de Malebranche*, ed. A. Robinet (Paris: Vrin, 1958/1984), vol. 11 (ed. M. Adam, 1966), p. 226.

35. Christian Wolff, *Philosophia prima sive Ontologia* (Frankfurt and Leipzig, 1730), 79.

36. Descartes, letter to Arnauld of 29 July 1648, in AT 5, pp. 223, 229; see my clarification in *Sur la théologie blanche de Descartes*, pp. 296–303.

37. A. G. Baumgarten, *Metaphysica* (Halle, 1739), S 7; in the recent edition (Hildesheim and New York: Olms, 1982), see S. 8.

38. Heidegger, *Sein und Zeit*, sect. 7, p. 38.

39. On birth, see some clarifications in J.-L. Marion, *De Surcroît: Études sur les phénomènes saturés* (Paris: Presses Universitaires de France, 2001); in translation as *In Excess: Studies in Saturated Phenomena*, trans. Robyn Homer and Vincent Bertaud (New York: Fordham University Press, 2004), p. 49ff; or see "The Reason of the Gift" in this collection.

40. "*Para tou Theou*," following the Nestle-Aland text, in the genitive not the dative: Not only "for him" but "from his standpoint, his side" (*Novum Testamentum Graece et Latine*, 25th ed., ed. E. Nestle and K. Aland [Stuttgart: Wittembergische Bibelanstalt, 1967], ad loc.). See, at both extremes, Straek-Billerbeek, who translates "*von Gott her*" (*Kommentär zum Neueun Testament* [Munich, 1924], vol. 2, p. 100); and C. Tresmontant, who translates "coming on God's part" (*Evangile de Laic* [Paris, 1987], p, 10). [The Vulgate translates: "*quid non erit impossibile apud Deum omne verbum*"; and the Revised Standard Version gives: "For with God nothing will be impossible." —Trans.]

41. As at Luke 1:42 (cf. Acts 10:37); and see H. Scharmarm's remarks in *Das Lukasevangelium* (Freiburg and Vienna: Herder, 1969), p. 57. In contrast, Thomas Aquinas surprisingly reduces the Licari formula, "*non erit impossibile apud Denim mune verbum*" (Vulgate), to the possible as non-contradictory—"*id enim quod contradictionem implicat verbum esse non potest, quia? luaus intellectus potest illud concipere*" (*Summa Theologica*, bk. 1, q. 25, a. 3, resp.)—and therefore lowers divine transcendence to the level of metaphysics as simple omnipotence. He therefore limits it as well by what is possible: "*sub omnipotentia Dei non cadit aliquid quod contradictionem implicat*" (1A. 1, q. 25, a, 4).

42. As also in Mark 14:36: "Abba, O Father, all things are possible with thee."

43. This point is emphasized by J. Reding and J. L. Swellengrebel: "The future tense, however, is preferable because it shows that the reference is also to what will happen to Mary" (*A Translator's Handbook on the Gospel of Luke* [Leiden: Brill, 1971], p. 62ff.); and also by F. Bo-

von: "*die futurische Form steht ihn Rahmen einer Theologie der Hoffnung: Gott wind bald die mögliche Unmöglichkeit verwirklichen*" (*Das Evangelium nach Lukas* [Zurich: Neukirchener, 1989], p. 77ff.).

44. Origen, *Contra Celsum*, bk. 5, chaps. 14; 23; in the *Sources chrétiennes* edition as *Contre Celse*, ed. M. Borret (Paris: Cerf, 1967–1976), vol. 3, pp. 48, 70. A similar answer is given by Gregory of Nazianzius in sections 10 and 11 of his thirtieth theological discourse (*Sources chrétiennes* no. 250, ed. P. Gallay [Paris: Cerf, 1978], pp. 243ff).

45. Augustine, De *Symbolo*, 1, 2, PL 40, col. 627. See further, "sicut nec potestas ejus se, dei minuitur, cum dicitur mori fallique non posse. Sic enim hoc non potest, ut potius, si posset, minoris esset utique potestatis. Recte quippe omnipotens dicitur, qui tamen mori et falli non potest. Dicitur enim omnipotens faciendo quod vult, non patiendo quod non vult; quod ei si accideret, nequaquam esset omnipotens. Unde propterea quaedam non potest, quia omnipotens est" (*De Civitate Dei*, bk. 5, ch. 10, sec. 1; trans. and ed. G. Bardy and G. Combes [Paris: Cerf, 1959], vol. 1, p. 684); in the same vein, we may note Hugh of St. Victor's effort to redefine a possible of nonontic order: "Ergo summe potens est, quia potest omne quod possibile est, nec ideo minus potest, quia impossibilia non potest: impossibilia posse non esset posse, sed non posse. Itaque amnia potest Deus, quae posse potentia est; et ideo vere omnipotens est, quia impotens esse non potest" (*De Sacramentis christianae fidei*, II, 2, PL 176, col. 216). Or Aquinas's attempt: "peccare est deficere a prefecta actione; male posse peccare est posse deficere in agendo, quod repugnat omnipotentiae; et propter hoc Deus non potest peccare, quia est omnipotens" (*Summa Theologica*, bk. 1, q. 25, a. 3). In any event, we may well doubt whether even a critical redefinition of what in itself is possible would suffice to reach the [im-]possible on God's side.

46. I am following here Jean-Marie Lustiger's remarkable commentary in *La Promesse* (Paris: Parole et Silence, 2002), p. 24ff.

47. Similarly, for men it is more difficult that the heaven and earth pass away, whereas for God this remains "much easier (*eukopōteron*) than that a single dot of the law become void (Luke 16:17)—which is to say of that to which God has committed his Word—therefore concerning Christ and through him. In the law, God literally (practically to the dot) risks his word, and therefore his Word, Christ. He risks his head and his life—which he will in fact lose.

48. V. Jantelevitch, *L'imprescriptible: Pardonner? Dans l'honneur et la dignité*, 2nd ed. (Paris, 1966), p. 43; reprinted as *Pardonner?* (Paris: Le Pavillon, 1971); my italics.

49. Aristotle, *Nicomachean Ethics*, bk. 3, ch. 1, 1110a ff.

Introduction to Part V: On Love and Sacrifice

1. See Emmanuel Levinas, *Totality and Infinity: An Essay on Exteriority*, trans. Alphonso Lingis (The Hague: Martinus Nijhoff, 1979), 86.

2. See Emmanuel Levinas, "Enigma and Phenomena," in *Collected Philosophical Papers*, trans. Alphonso Lingis (The Hague: Martinus Nijhoff, 1987), chap. 5.

3. See Levinas, *Totality and Infinity*, 29, and *Of God Who Comes to Mind*, trans. Bettina Bergo (Stanford, Calif.: Stanford University Press, 1998), 166.

4. See Emmanuel Levinas, *Autrement que savoir, avec des études de Guy Petitdemange et Jacques Rolland* (Paris: Éditions Osiris, 1988), 74–75.

5. See Levinas's comments on this topic in his interview with Richard Kearney, "Ethics of the Infinite," in *Dialogues with Contemporary Continental Thinkers: The Phenomenological Heritage* (Manchester: Manchester University Press, 1984), 58.

6. Jean-Luc Marion, *The Erotic Phenomenon*, trans. Stephen E. Lewis (Chicago: University of Chicago Press, 2007), 37.

7. Augustine, *Confessions*, ed. James J. O'Donnell, 3 vols (Oxford: Clarendon Press, 1992), 3:4.

8. For more on this theme, see Marion, *Certitudes négatives* (Paris: Grasset, 2010), chap. 1.

9. See Jacques Derrida, *The Gift of Death*, bound with *Literature in Secret*, 2nd ed., trans. David Wills (Chicago: University of Chicago Press, 2007), chap. 3.

The Intentionality of Love

Translated by Stephen E. Lewis. Reprinted from Jean-Luc Marion, *Prolegomena to Charity* (Fordham University Press, 2002), 71–101.

1. Emmanuel Levinas, *Totalité et infini. Essai sur l'extériorité* (The Hague: Martinus Nijhoff, 1961), p. 232; *Totality and Infinity: An Essay on Exteriority*, trans. Alphonso Lingis (The Hague: Martinus Nijhoff, 1979), 254.

2. Edmund Husserl, *Ideen* I, 36, Husserliana III (The Hague: Martinus Nijhoff, 1950), 81; *Ideas: General Introduction to Pure Phenomenology,* trans. W. R. Boyce Gibson (London: George Allen & Unwin, 1931 [1967]), 120.

3. Racine, *Phèdre* I, 3, v. 273–277; *Phaedra and Figaro*, trans. Robert Lowell (New York: Farrar, Straus and Cudahy, 1961), 24–25.

4. Descartes, *Dioptrique* IV, in *Oeuvres philosophiques*, ed. Adam-Tannery (Paris: Vrin, 1906 [1966]) VI, 6–7; *The Philosophical Writings of Descartes*, trans. John Cottingham, Robert Stoothaff, and Dugald Murdoch (Cambridge: Cambridge University Press, 1985), 1:164.

5. *Pensées* 323/688.

6. Baudelaire, *Fusées* XI, in *Oeuvres complètes*, "Pléiade," ed. Y.-G. Le Dantec and Claude Pichois (Paris: Pléiade, 1966), 1256.

7. *Cartesianische Meditationen* §62, Husserliana 1, 175; *Cartesian Meditations: An Introduction to Phenomenology*, trans. Dorion Cairns (Dordecht: Kluwer, 1995), 148–149.

8. [The French *invisable* signifies "that at which one cannot aim" (*viser*, "to target," "to aim at"). —Trans.]

9. Un Dieu Homme?" In "Qui est Jesus-Christ?" *Recherches et Debats* 62 (1968): 186–492, reprinted in *Entre nous. Essais sur le penser-à-l'autre* (Paris: Editions Grasset & Fasquelle, 1991), 69–76. See "La trace de l'autre," in *Tijdschrift voor Filosofie* (1963, no. 3), reprinted in *En découvrant l'existence avec Husserl et Heidegger* (Paris: J. Vrin, 1988), 195: "Consciousness loses its primary place. The visitation consists in upsetting the very egoism of the I, the face unseats the intentionality that aims at it. At issue here is the putting into question of the consciousness, and not a consciousness of the putting into question."

10. [The French title of this section is "je n'est pas le premier venu." *Le premier venu* means, literally, "the first to arrive"; when used with a negative in a sentence like that of the title, however, it means "X is not just anybody." Both meanings are played upon here and throughout the section as a way to argue, against Levinas, that the other is always a particular other, "not just anybody" but always "Just such" a particular other (*un tel*). —Trans.]

11. Levinas, *Totalité et infini*, 189; trans. Lingis, 214.

12. Emmanuel Levinas, *De Dieu qui vient à l'idée* (Paris: J. Vrin, 1982), 250; *Of God Who Comes to Mind*, trans. Bettina Bergo (Stanford, Calif.: Stanford University Press, 1998), 166. It could even be that the other, neither known nor replaceable, belongs, more than to the past and the present, to the future—no matter what happens, the other will always be just such (*tel*).

13. Criticism (for example in *De Dieu qui vient à l'idée*, 81–83, 145–148) of Heidegger, *Sein und Zeit*, 9: "The Being of this entity is *in each case mine*. This entity, in its Being, comports itself toward its Being. As entity of this Being, it is delivered over to its own Being. Being is that which

is an issue for this entity each time." (*Being and Time*, trans. Macquarrie and Robinson [New York: Harper & Row, 1962], 67 [translation modified].) *Jemeinigkeit* compels *Dasein* to personalize with a pronoun the verb to be only on the basis of its radical claim (*Anspruch*) by Being. Whence Levinas's attempt to institute a claim prior to that of Being (*De Dieu*, 245, 265; see *Le temps et l'autre,* 2d ed. [Montpelier: Fata Morgana, 1979], 133 ff.).

14. "Because it is necessarily the case that in corporeal nature we find true unities, without which there would be absolutely no multitudes nor collection, it must be that that which makes corporeal substance would be something which responds to that which I call the self [*moy*] in us, which is indivisible and yet acting" (G. W. Leibniz, *Système nouveau pour expliquer la nature des substances*, in *Die philosophischen Schriften*, ed. Gerhardt, 4:473). As a result, on the basis of the I, and without ever contesting it, every other Other can, be reached: "The reflexive acts, which enable us to think of that which is called I . . . and it is thus that in thinking of ourselves we think of Being, of Substance, of the simple and compound, of the immaterial, and of God himself" (*Monadologie*, §30; *G. W. Leibniz's Monadology: An Edition for Students*, ed. Nicholas Rescher [Pittsburgh: University of Pittsburgh Press, 1991], 21). Whence the perfect diagnosis offered by Nietzsche (14:791): "We have borrowed the concept of unity from our 'I' concept—our oldest article of faith" (Nietzsche, *Werke*, ed. Colli and Montinari [Berlin: Walter de Gruyter, 1972], vol. 111/3, p. 50; *The Will to Power*, trans. Walter Kaufmann [New York: Viking Press, 1962], 338).

15. Levinas's critique of intentionality admits different degrees; sometimes it is only a question of freeing intentionality from the pair subject/object (*En découvrant l'existence*, 139) or from the couple noesis/noema (*Totalité et infini*, 271); other times, it is more radically a question of attaining "a non-intentional thought whose devotion can be translated by no preposition in our language—not even the *to* which we use" (*De Dieu*, 250; see also 184, 243, 261; *Of God Who Comes to Mind*, trans. Bergo [modified], 166). No doubt, today, its author would no longer subscribe completely to the thematization that he gave of love in terms of intentionality: "The act of love has a sense. . . . The characteristic of the loved object is precisely to be given in a *love intention*, an intention which is irreducible to a purely theoretical representation" (*La théorie de l'intuition dans la phénoménologie de Husserl* [Paris: Alean, 1930], p. 75; *The Theory of Intuition in Husserl's Phenomenology*, trans. André Orianne [Evanston, Ill.: Northwestern University Press, 1973], 44–45); the meaning of the act of love (if it is still a matter of an act) exempts love not only from "purely theoretical representation," but even more from every intention, because from all intentionality.

Concerning the Lover, and His Advance
Translated by Stephen E. Lewis. Reprinted from Jean-Luc Marion, *The Erotic Phenomenon* (University of Chicago Press, 2006), 67–105.

The Creation of the Self
Translated by Jeffrey R. Kosky. Reprinted from Jean-Luc Marion, *In the Self's Place: The Approach of Saint Augustine* (Stanford University Press, 2012), 230–287. Copyright © 2012 by the Board of Trustees of Leland Stanford Jr. University for the English translation; © 2008 Presses Universitaires de France. All rights reserved. Used with the permission of Stanford University Press, www.sup.org.

1. I should note that here it is not a matter of the moral defect of a place, my heart, not yet purified, denounced in other texts. "Invocas Deum, quando in te vocas Deum. Hoc est enim illum invocare, illum in te vocare, quodam modo eum in domum cordis tui invitare. Non autem auderes tantum patrem familias invitare, nisi noses ei habitaculum praeparare. Si enim tibi dicat Deus: Ecce invocasti me, venio ad te, quo intrabo, tantae sordes conscientiae tuae sustinebo? Si

servum meum in domum tuam invitares, nonne prius eam mundare curares? Invocas me in cor tuam, et plenum est rapinis." [You invoke God when you call him into yourself. For that is what it means to invoke him: to call him into yourself, to invite him in some fashion into the house of your heart. Now you would not dare to invite even the father of your family if you had not prepared a lodging for him. But if God says to you: 'Behold, you called me, I come unto you, where will I enter? If you invite my servant into your house, wouldn't you take care first to clean it? You called me to come into your body, and it is full of rapaciousness.] (*Commentary on Psalm* 30, 2, s. 3, 4 *PL* 36, 249).

2. See: "et exclamaverunt voce magna: "Ipse fecit nos . . . responsion[ibus] caeli et terrae et omnium . . . dicentium 'Non sumus Deus' et 'Ipse fecit nos.'" ['He, he alone made us' . . . the responses of heaven and earth and of all things . . . saying: 'We are not God' and 'He, he alone made us."] (X 6, 9, 14, 156). Or: "Ecce sunt caelum et terra, clamant, quod facta sint; mutantur enim atque variantur. Quidquid autem factum non est et tamen est, non est *in eo* quicquam, quod ante non erat: quod est mutari atque variari. Clamant etiam, quod se ipsa non fecerint." [Behold heaven and earth, which say that they were made; they change and vary. Everything that was not made but which nevertheless is does not give *place* for anything whatsoever that was not there beforehand: which is what is called changing and varying. They cry aloud, too, that they did not make themselves.] (XI, 4, 6, 14, 280).

3. When it takes on a positive sense, it is always a matter of the very *here* (*ibi*) of God or of a *here* seen from God's point of view, which becomes acceptable for us only eschatologically: "*Ibi* esse nostrum non habebit mortem, *ibi* nosse nostrum non habebit errorem, *ibi* amare nostrum non habebit offensionem." [*Here*, no more death for our being, *here* no more error for our knowledge, *here* no more offense done to our love.] (*City of God* XI, 28, 35, 122).

4. See *Vetus Latina. Die Reste der altlateinischen Bibel*, ed. P. Sabatier and E. Beuron (Freiburg, 1951), 2:2–6.

5. "Ève," in *Oeuvres poétiques completes*, ed. F. Porché, "La Pléiade" (Paris: Gallimard, 1967), 936.

6. De Natura boni XVIII 18, 1, 454. See: "materies informis corporalium formarum capax ab eis ὕλην appellaretur" (*Contra Faustum* XXI, 4, PL 42, 39).

7. See: "nec intelligis, cum Deus dicitur *de* nihilo fecisse quod fecit, non dixit aliud quia *de* seipso non fecit. . . . *De* nihilo est ergo, quod non est *de* aliquo." [You do not understand that when it is said that God made what he made *with* nothing, nothing other than this is being said: he did not make it *with* himself . . . . That is made *with* nothing which is not made *with* something.] (*Contre Julianum* V, 31, PL 45, 1470). In other words, God created starting from and with the stuff of the only imaginable contrary to him, nothingness: "Ei ergo qui summe est, non potest esse contrarium nisi quod non est." [Nothing can be contrary to him who exists supremely, except what is not.] (*De Natura boni*, XIX, 19, 1, 456.)

8. See the study by J. Pepin, "Recherches sur le sense et l'origine de l'expression caelum caeli dans le livre XII des Confessions de saint Augustin," *Archivium Latinitatis Medii Aevi* (*Bulletin du Cange*, 23–33, 1953, reprinted in *"Ex Platonicorum Persona." Etudes sur les lectures philosophiques de saint Augustin* [Amsterdam, 1997], as chapter VI, "Le platonisme judeo-chrétien de'Alexandrie et l'exegese augustinienne du 'ciel du ciel'"). He comes to several conclusions: (a) Other biblical bases (Deuteronomy 10, 14; Amos 9, 6; Psalm 113, 24, but also Psalm 67, 34 and 148, 4); (b) the origin of the theme in Philo, *De Opifice Mundi* §35 and especially Saint Ambrose, *Expositio Psalmi* 118, 8: "Unde et caelum purius et defaecatius ad omni labe peccati est, longeque remotius ab illo de quo scriptum est 'Sicut volatilia caeli' (Matthew 6, 26)" (CSEL 62, 127); (c) its posterity (Prosper of Aquitaine, *Expositio in Psalmos* 118, 16 PL 51, 329); (d) its plurivocity (formless matter of the intellectual creature, of the visible world, and the formed being

of the invisible creature by opposition to the physical sky); and above all, (d) its ambiguous status including both "intellectual creature near in dignity to the divine Word," but which also "inasmuch as it turns away from Wisdom . . . lives wretchedly in uniformity, but . . . receives counsel by turning toward it" (216). See also H. Armstrong, "Spiritual or Intelligible Matter in Plotinus and St. Augustine," *Augustinus Magister* I (1954), and A. Solignac, *BA* 14, 592ff.

9. See: "spiritualem vel intellectualem illam creaturam semper faciem Dei contemplantem" [this spiritual and intellectual creature who is always contemplating the face of God] (XII, 17, 24, 14, 380).

10. Or *casta civitas tua* (XII, 15, 20, 14, 372).

11. *Confessiones*, XII, 16, 23, 14, 378. This wonderful text melds Psalm 122 (the ascent to Jerusalem) and Philippians 3:13.

12. I am here taking up an illuminating hypothesis put forward by J. J. O'Donnell, ed., Augustine, *Confessions*, 3 vols. (Oxford: Clarendon Press, 1992).

13. I am following the reconstitution of the text attempted by J. J. O'Donnell (ibid., 3:344ff) on the basis of Beuron, *Vetus Latina*, 16–17 and 26.

14. The Vulgate says either *in species suas* (Genesis 1:21) or *secundum species suas* (Genesis 1:24) *or juxta species suas* (Genesis 1:25) as well as *secundum genus suum* (Genesis 1:21) or also *in genere suo* (Genesis 1:24, 25).

15. *De Genesi ad litteram* III, 12, 20, BA 48, 242ff. Farther along the same text observes that in order to create man, God does not say *fiat*, but passes into the plural: "Faciamus hominem ad imaginem et similitudinem nostram" (III, 19, 29, ibid., 258), indicating in this way not only the Trinity, but also the direct implication of God, which no longer harbors the neutrality of (efficient) causality and abstract omnipotence.

16. Certainly, in this same text, Saint Augustine hopes that we will not say "Hominem vero non imaginem, sed ad imaginem" (ibid.), arguing on the basis of the authority of 1 Corinthians 11:7: "Man should not cover his head, for he is the image and glory of God" (doubtless, for that matter, wrongly, because this is about ἀνήρ/*vir*, not *homo* and because our question concerns less the image's status than the likeness of this image). But he concedes at least that even if man is not always reducible to the *ad imaginem*, this restriction never applies to the Son, "imago aequalis Patri." Concerning the importance of this *ad*, see the note "L'homme à l'image," in *BA* 15, p. 589; H. Somers, "Image de Die. Les sources de l'exégèse de saint Augustin," *Revue des études augustiniennes*, 1961; P. Hadot, "L'image de la Trinité dans l'âme chez Victorinus et chez saint Augustin," *Studia Patristica* 6 (1962), and R. A. Markus, "*Imago* and *similitudo* in Augustine," *Revue des études augustiniennes* 1964.

17. *De Civitate Dei*, XI, 2, BA 35, 36. This is indeed a case of a reflection on *ad imaginem*: "Cum enim homo rectissime intellegatur, vel si hoc non potest, saltem credatur factus *ad* imaginem Dei" (ibid.).

18. "[I]n its proper sense, however, the distinction of being an image belongs only to man," says quite beautifully Etienne Gilson, *Introduction à la pensée de saint Augustin*, 288ff [English trans., 219]. But in a sense still more radical than he seems to suppose: not because man *is* the image, but because he appears *in, according to, by reference to* the unimagable and thus bears his image.

19. Commentary on Psalm 42:6, *PL* 36, 480.

20. Terms that are very nearly confirmed by the *Confessiones*: "Trinitatem omnipotentem quis intelliget? Et quis non loquitur earn si tamen earn? . . . Vellem ut haec tria cogitarent homines in se ipsis . . . sed dico autem haec tria: esse, nosse, velle. Sum enim et scio et volo: sum sciens et volens, et scio esse me et velle, et volo esse et scire." [Who understands the omnipotent Trinity and who can speak of it, if indeed it is it of which he speaks? . . . I would like for men to think

in themselves these three things. . . . I will say them, these three things: being, knowing, willing. For I am and know and will: I am knowing and willing, and I know myself being and willing, and I will being and knowing.] (XIII, 11, 12, 14, 442).

21. *De Trinitate*, XIV, 8, 11, 16, 374.

22. Ibid., XIV, 12, 18, 16, 386.

23. Ibid.

24. *De Monibus Ecclesiae Catholica contra Manicheos* I, 4, 6 *BA* 1, 144.

25. Levinas: "The face is signification, and signification without context . . . . In this sense one can say that the face is not 'seen.' It is what cannot become a content, which your thought would embrace, it is uncontainable, it leads you beyond" *Ethique et infini. Entretien avec Philippe Nemo* (Paris, 1982), 90–91 [English trans., 86–87].

26. Nietzsche, "als das 'abschatzende Tier an sich," *Zur Genealogie der Moral,* II, §8 [English trans., 70].

27. Heidegger, *Was ist Metaphysik?* in *Wegmarken, GA* 9, 118 [English trans., 108].

28. Heidegger, *Brief über den 'Humanismus',* 342 [English trans., 210].

29. Gregory of Nyssa, *On the Creation of Man* XI, 3, *PG* 44, col 156 b [English trans., 396–397 (modified)]. See also the same teaching in, among others, Basil of Casearea, *Against Eunomius* III, 6, *PG*, 29, col. 668 b ff., as well as John Chrysostom, *On the Incomprehensibility of God* V, 259ff.

30. *Confessiones*, X, 5, 7, 14, 150. This citation of 1 Corinthians 2:11ff, which we saw was diverted from its obvious sense in Saint Paul, returns to it again *in fine* within the frame of a complete response to the question of what we are: "Quomodo ergo scimus et nos 'quae a Deo donata sunt nobis'? Respondetur mihi, quoniam quae per ejus Spiritum scimus etiam sic 'nem scit nisi Spiritus Dei.'" [How then do we too know 'the things that God has given us'? The response given to me is this: the things that we know by the Spirit, even in this way, 'nobody knows them except the Spirit of God.'] (XIII 31, 46, 14, 512). What we know of ourselves, since that too, comes to us as a gift, we know only inasmuch as the Spirit knows it in us and for us. We are *ego*, but of a *cogito* that is displaced, by reference, *unto* the image and resemblance of the incomprehensible. I think myself in another thought besides my own, more mine than whatever I myself might think myself.

31. *Confessiones*, X, 5, 7, 14, 152, which cites at the end Psalm 89:8.

32. *Letter* 157, 2, 9: "Anima quippe velut pondere, amore fertur quocumque fertur. Jubemur itaque detrahere de pondere cupiditatis quod accedat ad pondus caritatis, donec illud consumatur, hoc perficiatur. [The soul, wherever it goes, is taken there by its love as by a weight. Let us strive then to shake off the weight of desire so as to add to the weight of charity, to the point that the first is consumed and the latter completed.]" (*PL* 33, 677).

33. *De Trinitate* XI, 11, 18, 16, 210.

34. Aristotle, *Physics* IV, 8, 214 b 12–16.

35. Iamblichus uses this distinction to explain that the νοῦς can descend if it goes toward the body, but ascend if it goes toward the intelligible (according to Simplicius, *Commentary of the Categories, Commentaries in Aristotelum Graeca,* ed. C. Kalbfleisch [Berlin, 2007], 8:128, 1, 32–35). See the evidence collected by D. O'Brien, "Pondus meum, amor meus' (Conf., XIII, 9, 10): Augustin et Iamblique," *Revue d'histoire des religions* 4 (1981), and *Studia Patristica* 16 (1985); R. J. O'Connell, *Imagination and Metaphysics in St. Augustine* [Milwaukee, 1968], 4–16ff., as well as J. J. O'Donnell, 3:356ff. This rapprochement (as also with Aristotle and Plotinus) still remains highly approximate, since it concerns neither love nor even weight, but quantities in the incorporeal (ἐν τοῖς ἀσωμάτοις).

36. "Terrena et humida [partes] suopte nutu et suopondere ad pares angulos in terram et in mare *ferantur,* reliquae duae partes, una ignea, altera animalis, ut illae superiores in medium locum mundi *gravitate ferantur et pondere,* sic hae rursus rectis lineis in coelestem locum *subvolent,* sive ipsa natura superiora appetente, sive quod a gravioribus leviora natura repellantur" (*Tusculanes,* I, 17, 40). See also: "Inde est indagationata initiorum et tanquam seminum . . . unde terra et quibus librata ponderibus, quibus cavemis maria sustineantur, qua omnia delata *gravitate* medium mundi locum semper *expetant,* qui idem infimus in rotundo" (*Tusculanes,* V, 24, 69, resp. 48 and 496).

37. *De Quantitate animae,* XXII, 37, *BA* 5, 302.

38. Commentary on Psalm 29:2, 10 *PL* 36, 222.

39. *De Civitate Dei,* XXII, 11, 1, 37, 602. Likewise: "Sed necesse est, *inquiunt,* ut terrena corpora naturalepondus vel in terra tenat, vel cogat ad terram et ideo in caelo esse non possint." [It is necessary, *they say,* that the natural *weight* of earthly bodies either maintains them on the earth or forces them toward the earth and that therefore they cannot be in the heavens.] (*De Civitate Dei,* XIII, 18, 35, 298.)

40. See a commentary on this verse in *De Genesi ad litteram,* IV, 3, 7–6, 14, *BA* 48, 288–298, and *De Genesi contra Manicheos,* I, 16, 25–26, *BA* 50, 212ff. (and the note on 515ff).

41. *Bucolics,* II, 65, ed. F. Plessi and P. Legay (Paris, 1903), 14.

42. Commentary on the Gospel of John, 26, 4, *PL* 35, 1608. See "amandi trahitur" (26, 5, ibid., 1609).

43. 2 Corinthians 4:17, on which Saint Augustine offered little commentary.

44. *De Musica* VI, 11, 29, *BA* 7, 424.

45. Letter 55, 10, 18 *PL* 33, 212ff. See also: "Et est pondus voluntatis et amoris, ubi apparet, quanti quidque in appetendo, fugiendo, praeponendo postponendoque pendatur." [And in the weight of the will and of the soul appears what is at issue in what one seeks, what one flees, what one prioritizes, and what one postpones, and its price.] (*De Genesi ad litteram* IV, 4, 8 *BA* 48, 290). Or: "Et ordinem aliquem petit aut tenet, *sicut* sunt pondera vel collocationes corporum, *atque* amores aut delectationes animarum." [And (every creation of God) asks for and possesses a certain order, the loves and pleasure of souls *as well* as the weight and placement of bodies.] (*De Trinitate,* VI, 10, 12, 15, 498.)

46. *De Civitate Dei,* XI, 28, 35, 122.

47. Ibid., 26, 35, 84.

48. *De Libero Arbitrio,* III, 1, 2, 6, 326.

49. *Sermon,* 344, 1, *PL,* 39, 1512. See "*pondere* superbiae meae in ima decidebam" [the *weight* of my pride makes me fall lower] (*Confessiones,* IV, 15, 27, 13, 454). And: "et non stabam frui Deo meo, sed rapiebar ad te decore tuo moxque deripebar abs te *pondere meo* et ruebam in ista cum gemitu; *et pondus* hoc consuetudo carnalis" [and I did not remain stable in the enjoyment of you, but I was ravished unto you by your beauty, then all at once I was hoisted away far from you [dragged] by my own *weight,* and I collapsed in grief among the things around me; and this *weight* was the habit of the flesh] (VII, 17, 23, 13, 626). This confirms: "*pondere* malae suae consuetudinis" [beneath the *weight* of bad habit] (*De Genesi contra Manicheos,* II, 22, 34, 50, 352). And one more time: "Amant enim requiem, sive piae animae, sive iniquae; sed qua perveniunt ad id quod amant, plurimae nesciunt. . . . Nam sicut corpus tam diu nititurpondere sive deorsum versus sive sursum versus, donec ad locum quo nititur veniens conquiescat . . . sic animae ad ea quae amant propterea nituntur ut perveniendo requiescant" (Letter 55, 10, 18ff., *PL* 33, 212ff.).

50. *De Trinitate,* VIII, 2, 3, 16, 32. See: "tanta vis amoris, ut ea quae cum amore diu cogitaverit, eisque curae glutino inhaeserit, attrahat secum etiam cum ad se cogitandum quodam

modo redit" [so great is the strength of love that what it (the spirit) has, for a long time, thought lovingly and that to which it is stuck in caring about it, it *draws it along* with it in some fashion [even] when it turns back toward itself in order to think itself] (*De Trinitate* X, 5, 7, 16, 134).

51. Commentary on the Gospel of John, VI, 20, *PL* 35, 1435.

52. *Confessiones*, X, 28, 39, 14, 208.

53. Commentary on Psalm 86:3, *PL* 37, 1 (respectively 1102 and 1103).

54. Commentary on Psalm 121, 1 *PL* 37, 1618.

Sketch of a Phenomenological Concept of Sacrifice

Translated by Stephen E. Lewis. Reprinted from Jean-Luc Marion, *The Reason of the Gift* (University Press of Virginia, 2011), 69–90. This essay responds in certain ways to my earlier "Esquisse d'un concept phénoménologique du don," which appeared in *Filosofia della rivelazione*, ed. M. M. Olivetti (Rome: Biblioteca dell' *Archivio di Filosofia*, 1994); "Sketch of a Phenomenological Concept of the Gift," trans. John Conley, SJ, and Danielle Poe, in *Postmodern Philosophy and Christian Thought*, ed. Merold Westphal (Bloomington: Indiana University Press, 1999), 122–143; also published in English in Jean-Luc Marion, *The Visible and the Revealed*, trans. Christina M. Gschwandtner (New York: Fordham University Press, 2008), 80–100.

1. The same goes for anyone who puts his life in danger, ultimately for nothing, or almost nothing (the "adventurer" or the so-called extreme athlete). The question arises, at what point does such a figure, mundane as it appears, correspond—as its modern heir—to the figure of the master in the dialectic of recognition (the slave remaining within the domain of the profane, where he does not destroy himself)?

2. This was moreover the classical argument (forged by the Reformation, then taken up by the Enlightenment) against a peaceful but also radical figure of sacrifice—monastic vows: to renounce power, riches, and reproduction amounts to destroying goods, which allow the world to live and to increase, and this renunciation even makes one enter into the field of the sacred, in this case into a life that, if it is not outside the world, is at least oriented eschatalogically toward the alteration of this world.

3. The attempts to define sacrifice made by Henri Hubert and Marcel Mauss in the famous *Essai stir la nature et la fonction du sacrifice* (published first in the *Année sociologique* in 1898, then in Marcel Mauss, *Oeuvres*, ed. Victor Karady, vol. 1: *Les fonctions sociales du sacré* [Paris: Minuit, 1968]; *Sacrifice: Its Nature and Function*, trans. W. D. Halls [Chicago: University of Chicago Press, 1964]) are characterized by their poverty and their silence on the central (in fact the only) problem of the function and the intrinsic logic of sacrifice (its signification, its intention, its mechanism of compensation, etc.), contrasting all the more with the wealth of details on the actual practice of sacrifice. So if we suppose that "[s]acrifice [. . .] was originally a gift made by the primitive [sic] to supernatural forces to which he must bind himself" (193; trans. Halls, 2, modified), it remains to be understood whether and how these "forces" tolerate being thus "bound." The same abstraction and the same insufficiency obtain in the definition that is ultimately adopted: "Thus we finally arrive at the following definition: *Sacrifice is a religious act which, through the consecration of a victim, modifies the condition of the moral person who accomplishes it or that of certain objects with which he is concerned*" (205; trans. Halls, 13): what does "consecration" here signify? How is the person in question "modified"? When is it a matter of "objects" more than of him, and which objects? And, indeed, in what sense can or must this act be called "religious"? Who or what allows the "modification" in question? No response is given, because the questions are not even raised. These extraordinary approximations lead back inevitably to the features, themselves already highly imprecise, of the Maussian concept of the gift.

(a) Sacrifice becomes a reciprocal gift that won't acknowledge itself as such: "If on the other hand, one seeks to bind the divinity by a contract, the sacrifice has rather the form of an attribution: *do ut des* is the principle" (272; trans. Halls, 65–66, modified); but what does it mean to bind "contractually" a "divinity" that has precisely the characteristic of being able to recuse itself from any contract and any reciprocity? (b) The destruction is assumed to be effective by itself and, without further consideration, it is assimilated to the accomplished sacrifice without recognizing that at best it fulfills only one of its conditions, but not the principle one (acceptance of the gift by the divinity): "*This procedure* [the sacrifice!] *consists in establishing a line of communication between the sacred and the profane worlds through the mediation of a victim, that is, of a thing that in the course of the ceremony is destroyed*"(302; trans. Halls, 97); but who cannot see that the difficulty of such a "line of communication" consists precisely in the fact that the "sacred world" has no reason to accept it unless one can explain how the contrary could be the case? (c) Thus one ends by granting that the sacrifice, in the end, isn't one: "The sacrificer gives up something of himself but he does not give himself. Prudently, he sets himself aside. This is because if he gives, it is partly in order to receive" (304; trans. Halls, 100). One can hardly avoid reading this conclusion as an admission of failure to supply a rigorous definition of sacrifice.

4. Jacques Derrida, *Donner le temps*, 1: *La fausse monnaie* (Paris: Galilée 1991), 42; *Given Time*, 1: *Counterfeit Money,* trans. Peggy Kamuf (Chicago: University of Chicago Press, 1992), 27.

5. See Jean-Luc Marion, *Étant donné: Essai d'une phénoménologie de la donation*, §§9–11 (Paris: Presses Universitaires de France, 1997, 1998), 124–61; *Being Given: Toward a Phenomenology of Givenness,* trans. Jeffrey L. Kosky (Stanford, Calif.: Stanford University Press, 2002), 85–113; and, to begin, Marion, "Esquisse d'un concept phénoménologique du don" (cited above, unnumbered note).

6. "Quemadmodum, fratres, si sponsus faceret sponsae suae annulum, et illa acceptum annulum plus diligeret quam sponsum qui illi fecit annulum, none in ipso dono sponsi adultera anima deprehenderetur, quamvis hoc amaret quod dedit sponsus? Certe hoc amaret quod dedit sponsus; tamen si diceret: Sufficit mihi annulus iste, iam illius faciem nolo videre, qualis esset? Quis non detestaretur hanc amentiam? Quis non adulterinum animum convinceret? Amas aurum pro viro, amas annulum pro sponso; si hoc est in te, ut ames annulum pro sponso tuo, et nolis videre sponsum tuum, ad hoc tibi arrham dedit, ut non te oppigneraret, sed averteret" (St. Augustine, *In Epistulam Primam Iohannis Tractatus*, 2.11; English translation available in *The Fathers of the Church: St. Augustine, Tractates on the Gospel of John* 112–24, *Tractates on the First Epistle of John*, trans. John W. Rettig [Washington, D.C.: Catholic University of America Press, 1995], 154).

7. Martin Heidegger, *Zeit und Sein*, in *Zur Sache des Denkens*, in *GA* 14 (Frankfurt a./M.: Vittorio Klostermann, 2007), 12; *On Time and Being*, trans. Joan Stambaugh (New York: Harper and Row, 1972), 8.

8. Martin Heidegger, *Die onto-theo-logische Verfassung der Metaphysik*, in *Identität und Differenz*, in *GA* 11 (Frankfurt a./M.: Vittorio Klostermann, 2006), 71; *The Onto-theological Constitution of Metaphysics*, in *Identity and Difference*, trans. Joan Stambaugh (Chicago: University of Chicago Press, 2002), 64–65 (trans. modified).

9. Let us recall that we are dealing here with the three marks of the phenomenon as given (see *Étant donné,* §13, 170–171; *Being Given*, 119–120).

10. See the analysis of Roland de Vaux, *Les sacrifices de l'Ancien Testament* (Paris: J. Gabalda, 1964). In another sense, if one grants Ishmael the status of true firstborn, though born of a slave, he too is found rendered unto God by the sending into the desert (Genesis 21:9 ff.).

11. I translate Genesis 18:14 following the version of the Septuagint (μή ἀδυνατῆσει παρὰ τῷ θεῷ ῥῆμα), in conformity with Luke 1:37, which quotes it οὐκ ἀδυνατῆσει παρὰ τῷ θεῷ πὰν ῥῆμα.

12. The death of the Christ accomplishes a sacrifice in *this* sense (more than in the common sense): by returning his spirit to the Father, who gives it to him, Jesus prompts the veil of the Temple (which separates God from men and makes him invisible to them) to be torn, and at once appears himself as "truly the son of God" (Matt. 27:51, 54), thus making appear not himself, but the invisible Father. The gift given thus allows both the giver and the process (here Trinitarian) of givenness to be seen. See my sketch in Jean-Luc Marion, "La reconnaissance du don," *Revue Catholique International Communio* 33/1, no. 195 (January–February 2008).

13. Georges Bataille, *Théorie de la religion,* in *Oeuvres completes,* vol. 7(Paris: Gallimard, 1976), 310; *Theory of Religion,* trans. Robert Hurley (New York: Zone Books, 1989), 48–49 (trans. modified). More explicitly, Josef Ratzinger writes: "Christian sacrifice does not consist in a giving of what God would not have without us but in our becoming totally receptive and letting ourselves be completely taken over by him. Letting God act on us—that is Christian sacrifice. . . . In this form of worship human achievements are not placed before God; on the contrary, it consists in man's letting himself be endowed with gifts" (*Introduction to Christianity*, trans. J. R. Foster [San Francisco: Ignatius Press, 1990, 2004], 283).

14. Emmanuel Levinas, "Enigme et phénomène," in *En découvrant l'existence avec Husserl et Heidegger* (Paris: Vrin, 1949, 1974), 215; "Enigma and Phenomenon," trans. Alphonso Lingis, in *Emmanuel Levinas: Basic Philosophical Writings,* ed. Adriaan T. Peperzak, Simon Critchley, and Robert Bernasconi (Bloomington: Indiana University Press, 1996), 77.

15. Jan Patočka, "The Dangers of Technicization in Science According to E. Husserl and the Essence of Technology as Danger According to M. Heidegger" (1973), in Erazim V. Kohák, *Jan Patočka: Philosophy and Selected Writings* (Chicago: University of Chicago Press, 1989), 332 (trans. modified in light of the French translation: Patočka, *Liberté et sacrifice: Écrits politiques,* trans. Erika Abrams [Grenoble: Jérôme Millon, 1990], 266). On this question, see the work of Emilie Tardivel, "Transcendance et liberté: Lévinas, Patočka et la question du mil," *Cahiers d'Études Lévinassiennes,* no. 7 (March 2008): 155–175.

16. Saint Augustine, *De civitate dei*, 10.6, Bibliothèque Augustinienne, vol. 34, 446; *The City of God Against the Pagans,* trans. R. W. Dyson (Cambridge: Cambridge University Press, 1998), 400. See St. Thomas Aquinas: "omne opus virtutis dicitur esse sacrificium, inquantum ordinatur ad Dei reverentiam" (*Summa theologicae Iia–IIae,* q.81, a.4, *ad* 1).

Name Index

Heidegger (*continued*)
467n23, 468n24; and metaphysics, 48–52;
on mood, 22; on nihilism, 66; on "new
beginning," 66, 103; on phenomenon, 10;
on plurality of phenomenologies, 1–2; on
technique, 2
Henry, Michel, 3, 4, 5, 9, 31–32, 185, 489n22
Hintikka, Jaakko, 256, 506n28, 508n46
Hölderlin, Friedrich, 40, 53–54
Husserl, Edmund: on crisis in science, 2–3; on *ego
cogito*, 254; on flesh, 132, 191; on God, 22;
on intersubjectivity, 247, 268, 367;
phenomenology, 8; on sedimentation, 3;
on technique, 2–3, 14; *Logical Investigations*,
79–107 *passim*, 254, 473n37

Janicaud, Dominique, 5, 40
John of Damascus, Saint, 21, 40, 275

Kant, Immanuel, 7, 11, 14, 18, 24, 25, 26, 47, 61,
85, 146, 252–53, 465n8

Lacoste, Jean-Yves, 3, 454n36
Lambert, Johnann Heinrich, 7
Leibniz, Gottfried Wilhelm, 24, 48–49, 178,
209, 247, 484n38, 488n13
Lessius, Leonardus, 227, 228, 230
Levinas, Emmanuel, 3, 5, 29, 32–34, 76, 191,
195, 268, 359, 376–77
Lipps, Theodor, 2

Malebranche, Nicolas, 19, 47–48, 240, 252
Marcel, Gabriel, 451n1
Marx, Karl, 60, 161, 487n11, 488n12
Meinong, Alexius, 4, 11
Merleau-Ponty, Maurice, 3, 9, 185, 247
Mersenne, Marin, 17, 217–18, 265
Montale, Eugenio, 12

Nicolas of Cusa, 349
Nietzsche, Friedrich, 19, 34, 40, 53–54, 57, 61, 89,
90, 253, 282–83

Origen, 29, 354

Pascal, Blaise, 19, 23, 234–36, 365, 457n97,
501n7
Patočka, Jan, 449, 458n124, 538n15
Paul the Apostle, Saint, 45, 51–56 *passim*, 74,
427
Pfänder, Alexander, 2
Plato, 6, 47, 50, 282, 416
Proclus, 6, 116
Plotinus, 26, 47, 50, 116, 416
Pseudo-Dionysius the Areopagite, 21, 54, 55,
56, 227, 299, 301, 308
Ptolemy, 6

Rahner, Karl, 320
Richard of Saint Victor, 22, 494n23
Romano, Claude, 460n161
Rorty, Richard, 19
Rothko, Mark, 142

Sartre, Jean-Paul, 3, 79, 371, 467n19
Scheler, Max, 1–2, 5
Schelling, F. J. W., 26, 61, 314
Scotus, Duns, 217, 296, 340
Simplicus, 6
Sophocles, 193
Spinoza, Baruch, 19, 48, 109, 116,
135, 252
Stendhal, 130, 328–30, 332
Suárez, Francisco, 18, 200–1, 204, 207, 217, 220,
232–33, 294–95, 341, 492n11

Teresa of Ávila, Saint, 29
Theodore the Studite, Saint, 21, 40, 513n13
Turner, J. M. W., 112–13
Twardowski, Kasimierz, 4

Vattimo, Gianni, 19

William of Ockham, 232
Wittgenstein, Ludwig, 46, 251, 326

General Index

l'adonné, 5, 25, 27, 29–30, 76, 138
amazement, 109, 477n4
Angst, 22, 33, 76
analogy, 295–98; analogia entis, 220, 288,
    296, 498n11; of experience, 113–14; loss of,
    216–24; ruin of, 48; without analogy,
    115–17
appresentation, 181–82, 321,374
atheism, 5, 30, 43–46, 48, 53, 60–62, 61, 68, 231,
    343, 467n19. See also God: death of
attunements, 22
auto-affection, 132, 134, 402, 404

bedazzlement, 106, 111–13, 117, 151, 477n16,
    485n44
body, 9, 181
boredom, 22–23, 76

call, the, 4, 76, 190, 334
confessio, 360, 411–12, 416–22
constitution, 183–84, 192
contemplation, 226, 419
creation, 411, 415–18
cross, the, 52–53, 56, 274–79

Dasein, 59, 68, 324
death, 10, 193–94
deconstruction, 27, 34–36, 448
distance, 46, 52–55

ego, 198, 234–49 passim, 250–69 passim
eidos, 13
epochē, 12–13, 231. See also reduction
eternal truths, 17, 197, 213–24 passim, 264
event, 27, 114, 130–31
Evidenz, 15–16, 95, 98–103
experience, 8, 24, 137–38, 147–49; analogies of,
    114–16; counter-experience, 77, 119, 120–21,
    146–47, 149–50, 344; Erlebnis, 318; and "I,"
    251; and impossible, 342–45; lived experiences,
    24, 364–65, 373–75; and love, 372–74;
    nonthetic, 12; unity of, 114

face, 27, 77, 133–34, 136, 151, 187–96 passim,
    360, 376–77, 404–6
fatherhood, 77, 167–71
flesh, 27, 32, 132–33, 143, 181, 186, 188, 191,
    337
forgiveness, 355–57, 445
Fourfold, 67, 73
friendship, 10

gaze, 4, 21, 57, 111, 119, 131–33, 238, 284,
    359–60, 379–80, 405; and boredom, 23;
    conversion of, 11–12; crossing of, 372–74;
    inversion of, 121–22; invisible, 368–69
gift, 21, 37–38, 156–80 passim, 439–49, 462n198;
    counter-gift, 439; givability, 175; givee,
    157–58; given gift, 158; giver, 157

13; erotic, 360, 381–82, 385, 388, 393, 395–99; and Fink, 30; first, second and third reductions, 76; third reduction, 4, 23. See also *epochē*

revelation, 5, 28–30, 34, 136–37, 272–72, 312–38 *passim*, 344; as *modus sine modo*, 29; and saturation, 323–24, 480n2

Rückfrage, 3

sacrifice, 359–61, 436–49 *passim*; and Abraham, 445–49

senses, 141–45; spiritual senses, 29

solipsism, 198, 268

soul, 10, 29, 365, 484n38

speech acts, 330–34

technique, 1–2

theology, 21, apophatic, 36–37, 271–72, 325–38; blank, 1, 17, 198, 203, 208–12; correlational, 21; and faith, 194; mystical, 326–28, 337; *theo*logy/theo*logy*, 21, 203

transcendence, 12, 18, 22, 45, 339–40; and immanence, 31–32; and infinity, 33; phenomenological / theological, 33, 339–40

truth, 151–52

visibility, 5, 46, 154, 99, 110, 119, 184–87

witness, 121–23, 153–55

Perspectives in Continental Philosophy
John D. Caputo, series editor

John D. Caputo, ed., *Deconstruction in a Nutshell: A Conversation with Jacques Derrida.*

Michael Strawser, *Both/And: Reading Kierkegaard—From Irony to Edification.*

Michael D. Barber, *Ethical Hermeneutics: Rationality in Enrique Dussel's Philosophy of Liberation.*

James H. Olthuis, ed., *Knowing* Other-*wise: Philosophy at the Threshold of Spirituality.*

James Swindal, *Reflection Revisited: Jürgen Habermas's Discursive Theory of Truth.*

Richard Kearney, *Poetics of Imagining: Modern and Postmodern.* Second edition.

Thomas W. Busch, *Circulating Being: From Embodiment to Incorporation—Essays on Late Existentialism.*

Edith Wyschogrod, *Emmanuel Levinas: The Problem of Ethical Metaphysics.* Second edition.

Francis J. Ambrosio, ed., *The Question of Christian Philosophy Today.*

Jeffrey Bloechl, ed., *The Face of the Other and the Trace of God: Essays on the Philosophy of Emmanuel Levinas.*

Ilse N. Bulhof and Laurens ten Kate, eds., *Flight of the Gods: Philosophical Perspectives on Negative Theology.*

Trish Glazebrook, *Heidegger's Philosophy of Science.*

Kevin Hart, *The Trespass of the Sign: Deconstruction, Theology, and Philosophy.*

Mark C. Taylor, *Journeys to Selfhood: Hegel and Kierkegaard.* Second edition.

Dominique Janicaud, Jean-François Courtine, Jean-Louis Chrétien, Michel Henry, Jean-Luc Marion, and Paul Ricoeur, *Phenomenology and the "Theological Turn": The French Debate.*

Karl Jaspers, *The Question of German Guilt.* Introduction by Joseph W. Koterski, S.J.

Jean-Luc Marion, *The Idol and Distance: Five Studies.* Translated with an introduction by Thomas A. Carlson.

Jeffrey Dudiak, *The Intrigue of Ethics: A Reading of the Idea of Discourse in the Thought of Emmanuel Levinas.*

Robyn Horner, *Rethinking God as Gift: Marion, Derrida, and the Limits of Phenomenology.*

Mark Dooley, *The Politics of Exodus: Søren Kierkegaard's Ethics of Responsibility.*

Merold Westphal, *Overcoming Onto-Theology: Toward a Postmodern Christian Faith.*

Edith Wyschogrod, Jean-Joseph Goux, and Eric Boynton, eds., *The Enigma of Gift and Sacrifice.*

Stanislas Breton, *The Word and the Cross.* Translated with an introduction by Jacquelyn Porter.

Jean-Luc Marion, *Prolegomena to Charity.* Translated by Stephen E. Lewis.

Peter H. Spader, *Scheler's Ethical Personalism: Its Logic, Development, and Promise.*

Jean-Louis Chrétien, *The Unforgettable and the Unhoped For.* Translated by Jeffrey Bloechl.

Don Cupitt, *Is Nothing Sacred? The Non-Realist Philosophy of Religion: Selected Essays.*

Jean-Luc Marion, *In Excess: Studies of Saturated Phenomena.* Translated by Robyn Horner and Vincent Berraud.

Phillip Goodchild, *Rethinking Philosophy of Religion: Approaches from Continental Philosophy.*

William J. Richardson, S.J., *Heidegger: Through Phenomenology to Thought.*

Jeffrey Andrew Barash, *Martin Heidegger and the Problem of Historical Meaning.*

Jean-Louis Chrétien, *Hand to Hand: Listening to the Work of Art.* Translated by Stephen E. Lewis.

Jean-Louis Chrétien, *The Call and the Response.* Translated with an introduction by Anne Davenport.

D. C. Schindler, *Han Urs von Balthasar and the Dramatic Structure of Truth: A Philosophical Investigation.*

Julian Wolfreys, ed., *Thinking Difference: Critics in Conversation.*

Allen Scult, *Being Jewish/Reading Heidegger: An Ontological Encounter.*

Richard Kearney, *Debates in Continental Philosophy: Conversations with Contemporary Thinkers.*

Jennifer Anna Gosetti-Ferencei, *Heidegger, Hölderlin, and the Subject of Poetic Language: Toward a New Poetics of Dasein.*

Jolita Pons, *Stealing a Gift: Kierkegaard's Pseudonyms and the Bible.*

Jean-Yves Lacoste, *Experience and the Absolute: Disputed Questions on the Humanity of Man.* Translated by Mark Raftery-Skehan.

Charles P. Bigger, *Between* Chora *and the Good: Metaphor's Metaphysical Neighborhood.*

Dominique Janicaud, *Phenomenology "Wide Open": After the French Debate.* Translated by Charles N. Cabral.

Ian Leask and Eoin Cassidy, eds., *Givenness and God: Questions of Jean-Luc Marion.*

Jacques Derrida, *Sovereignties in Question: The Poetics of Paul Celan.* Edited by Thomas Dutoit and Outi Pasanen.

William Desmond, *Is There a Sabbath for Thought? Between Religion and Philosophy.*

Bruce Ellis Benson and Norman Wirzba, eds., *The Phenomenology of Prayer.*

S. Clark Buckner and Matthew Statler, eds., *Styles of Piety: Practicing Philosophy after the Death of God.*

Kevin Hart and Barbara Wall, eds., *The Experience of God: A Postmodern Response.*

John Panteleimon Manoussakis, *After God: Richard Kearney and the Religious Turn in Continental Philosophy.*

John Martis, *Philippe Lacoue-Labarthe: Representation and the Loss of the Subject.*

Jean-Luc Nancy, *The Ground of the Image.*

Edith Wyschogrod, *Crossover Queries: Dwelling with Negatives, Embodying Philosophy's Others.*

Gerald Bruns, *On the Anarchy of Poetry and Philosophy: A Guide for the Unruly.*

Brian Treanor, *Aspects of Alterity: Levinas, Marcel, and the Contemporary Debate.*

Simon Morgan Wortham, *Counter-Institutions: Jacques Derrida and the Question of the University.*

Leonard Lawlor, *The Implications of Immanence: Toward a New Concept of Life.*

Clayton Crockett, *Interstices of the Sublime: Theology and Psychoanalytic Theory.*

Bettina Bergo, Joseph Cohen, and Raphael Zagury-Orly, eds., *Judeities: Questions for Jacques Derrida.* Translated by Bettina Bergo and Michael B. Smith.

Jean-Luc Marion, *On the Ego and on God: Further Cartesian Questions*. Translated by Christina M. Gschwandtner.

Jean-Luc Nancy, *Philosophical Chronicles*. Translated by Franson Manjali.

Jean-Luc Nancy, *Dis-Enclosure: The Deconstruction of Christianity*. Translated by Bettina Bergo, Gabriel Malenfant, and Michael B. Smith.

Andrea Hurst, *Derrida Vis-à-vis Lacan: Interweaving Deconstruction and Psychoanalysis*.

Jean-Luc Nancy, *Noli me tangere: On the Raising of the Body*. Translated by Sarah Clift, Pascale-Anne Brault, and Michael Naas.

Jacques Derrida, *The Animal That Therefore I Am*. Edited by Marie-Louise Mallet, translated by David Wills.

Jean-Luc Marion, *The Visible and the Revealed*. Translated by Christina M. Gschwandtner and others.

Michel Henry, *Material Phenomenology*. Translated by Scott Davidson.

Jean-Luc Nancy, *Corpus*. Translated by Richard A. Rand.

Joshua Kates, *Fielding Derrida*.

Michael Naas, *Derrida From Now On*.

Shannon Sullivan and Dennis J. Schmidt, eds., *Difficulties of Ethical Life*.

Catherine Malabou, *What Should We Do with Our Brain?* Translated by Sebastian Rand, Introduction by Marc Jeannerod.

Claude Romano, *Event and World*. Translated by Shane Mackinlay.

Vanessa Lemm, *Nietzsche's Animal Philosophy: Culture, Politics, and the Animality of the Human Being*.

B. Keith Putt, ed., *Gazing Through a Prism Darkly: Reflections on Merold Westphal's Hermeneutical Epistemology*.

Eric Boynton and Martin Kavka, eds., *Saintly Influence: Edith Wyschogrod and the Possibilities of Philosophy of Religion*.

Shane Mackinlay, *Interpreting Excess: Jean-Luc Marion, Saturated Phenomena, and Hermeneutics*.

Kevin Hart and Michael A. Signer, eds., *The Exorbitant: Emmanuel Levinas Between Jews and Christians*.

Bruce Ellis Benson and Norman Wirzba, eds., *Words of Life: New Theological Turns in French Phenomenology*.

William Robert, *Trials: Of Antigone and Jesus*.

Brian Treanor and Henry Isaac Venema, eds., *A Passion for the Possible: Thinking with Paul Ricoeur*.

Kas Saghafi, *Apparitions—Of Derrida's Other*.

Nick Mansfield, *The God Who Deconstructs Himself: Sovereignty and Subjectivity Between Freud, Bataille, and Derrida*.

Don Ihde, *Heidegger's Technologies: Postphenomenological Perspectives*.

Françoise Dastur, *Questioning Phenomenology*. Translated by Robert Vallier.

Suzi Adams, *Castoriadis's Ontology: Being and Creation*.

Richard Kearney and Kascha Semonovitch, eds., *Phenomenologies of the Stranger: Between Hostility and Hospitality*.

Michael Naas, *Miracle and Machine: Jacques Derrida and the Two Sources of Religion, Science, and the Media*.

Alena Alexandrova, Ignaas Devisch, Laurens ten Kate, and Aukje van Rooden, *Re-treating Religion: Deconstructing Christianity with Jean-Luc Nancy*. Preamble by Jean-Luc Nancy.

Emmanuel Falque, *The Metamorphosis of Finitude: An Essay on Birth and Resurrection*. Translated by George Hughes.

Scott M. Campbell, *The Early Heidegger's Philosophy of Life: Facticity, Being, and Language*.

Françoise Dastur, *How Are We to Confront Death? An Introduction to Philosophy*. Translated by Robert Vallier. Foreword by David Farrell Krell.

Christina M. Gschwandtner, *Postmodern Apologetics? Arguments for God in Contemporary Philosophy*.

Ben Morgan, *On Becoming God: Late Medieval Mysticism and the Modern Western Self*.

Neal DeRoo, *Futurity in Phenomenology: Promise and Method in Husserl, Levinas, and Derrida*.

Sarah LaChance Adams and Caroline R. Lundquist eds., *Coming to Life: Philosophies of Pregnancy, Childbirth, and Mothering*.

Thomas Claviez, ed., *The Conditions of Hospitality: Ethics, Politics, and Aesthetics on the Threshold of the Possible*.

Adam S. Miller, *Speculative Grace: Bruno Latour and Object-Oriented Theology*. Foreword by Levi R. Bryant

Jean-Luc Marion, *The Essential Writings*. Edited by Kevin Hart.

Roland Faber and Jeremy Fackenthal, eds., *Theopoetic Folds: Philosophizing Multifariousness*.

Jean-Luc Nancy, *Corpus II: Writings on Sexuality*.

David Nowell Smith, *Sounding/Silence: Martin Heidegger at the Limits of Poetics*.